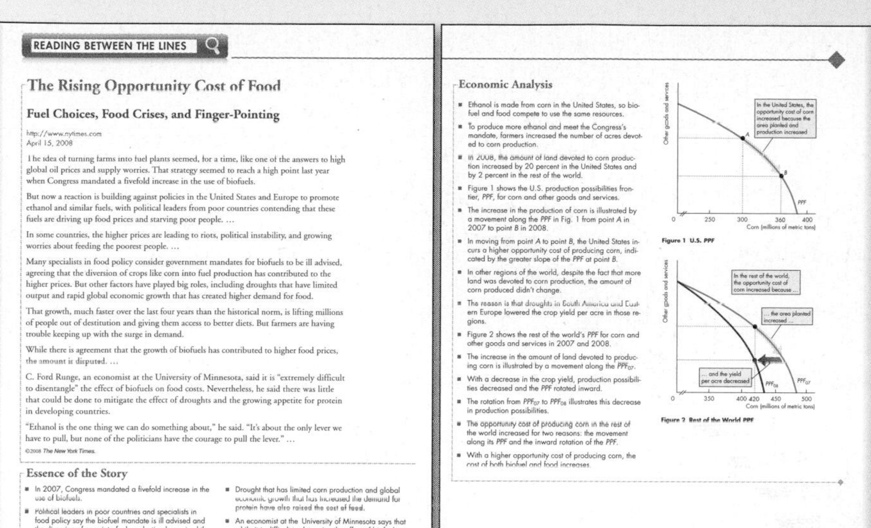

READING BETWEEN THE LINES

## The Rising Opportunity Cost of Food

### Fuel Choices, Food Crises, and Finger-Pointing

http://www.nytimes.com
April 15, 2008

The idea of turning farms into fuel plants seemed, for a time, like one of the answers to high global oil prices and supply worries. That strategy seemed to reach a high point last year when Congress mandated a fivefold increase in the use of biofuels.

But now a reaction is building against policies in the United States and Europe to promote ethanol and similar fuels, with political leaders from poor countries contending that these fuels are driving up food prices and starving poor people. …

In some countries, the higher prices are leading to riots, political instability, and growing worries about feeding the poorest people. …

Many specialists in food policy consider government mandates for biofuels to be ill advised, agreeing that the diversion of crops like corn into fuel production has contributed to the higher prices. But other factors have played big roles, including droughts that have limited output and rapid global economic growth that has created higher demand for food.

That growth, much faster over the last four years than the historical norm, is lifting millions of people out of destitution and giving them access to better diets. But farmers are having trouble keeping up with the surge in demand.

While there is agreement that the growth of biofuels has contributed to higher food prices, the amount is disputed. …

C. Ford Runge, an economist at the University of Minnesota, said it is "extremely difficult to disentangle" the effect of biofuels on food costs. Nevertheless, he said there was little that could be done to mitigate the effect of droughts and the growing appetite for protein in developing countries.

"Ethanol is the one thing we can do something about," he said. "It's about the only lever we have to pull, but none of the politicians have the courage to pull the lever." …

©2008 *The New York Times.*

### Essence of the Story

- In 2007, Congress mandated a fivefold increase in the use of biofuels.
- Political leaders in poor countries and specialists in food policy say the biofuel mandate is ill advised and the diversion of corn into fuel production has raised the cost of food.
- Drought that has limited corn production and global economic growth that has increased the demand for protein have also raised the cost of food.
- An economist at the University of Minnesota says that while it is difficult to determine the effect of biofuels on food costs, it is the only factor under our control.

46

### Economic Analysis

- Ethanol is made from corn in the United States, so biofuel and food compete to use the same resources.
- To produce more ethanol and meet the Congress's mandate, farmers increased the number of acres devoted to corn production.
- In 2008, the amount of land devoted to corn production increased by 20 percent in the United States and by 2 percent in the rest of the world.
- Figure 1 shows the U.S. production possibilities frontier, *PPF*, for corn and other goods and services.
- The increase in the production of corn is illustrated by a movement along the *PPF* in Fig. 1 from point *A* in 2007 to point *B* in 2008.
- In moving from point *A* to point *B*, the United States incurs a higher opportunity cost of producing corn, indicated by the greater slope of the *PPF* at point *B*.
- In other regions of the world, despite the fact that more land was devoted to corn production, the amount of corn produced didn't change.
- The reason is that droughts in South America and Eastern Europe lowered the crop yield per acre in those regions.
- Figure 2 shows the rest of the world's *PPF* for corn and other goods and services in 2007 and 2008.
- The increase in the amount of land devoted to producing corn is illustrated by a movement along the $PPF_{07}$.
- With a decrease in the crop yield, production possibilities decreased and the *PPF* rotated inward.
- The rotation from $PPF_{07}$ to $PPF_{08}$ illustrates this decrease in production possibilities.
- The opportunity cost of producing corn in the rest of the world increased for two reasons: the movement along its *PPF* and the inward rotation of the *PPF*.
- With a higher opportunity cost of producing corn, the cost of both biofuel and food increases.



**Figure 1 U.S. *PPF***



**Figure 2 Rest of the World *PPF***

47

## Reading Between the Lines

At the end of each chapter, *Reading Between the Lines* uses economic tools to critically evaluate a news article about the chapter-opening issue.

## News-based End-of-chapter Problems

New end-of-chapter problems based on current news stories are also available for practice in MyEconLab.

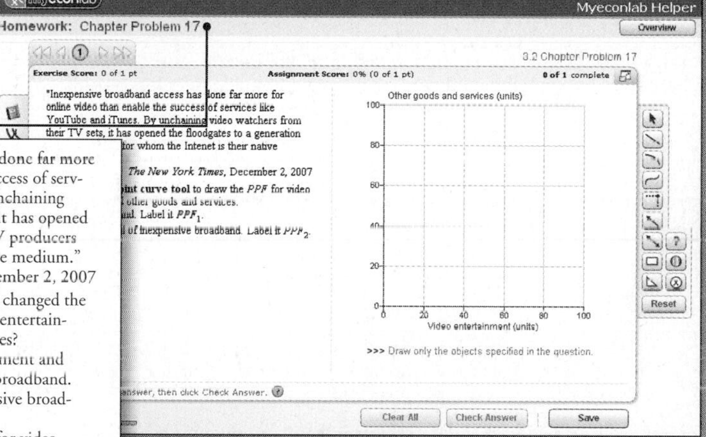



17. "Inexpensive broadband access has done far more for online video than enable the success of services like YouTube and iTunes. By unchaining video watchers from their TV sets, it has opened the floodgates to a generation of TV producers for whom the Internet is their native medium."

*The New York Times,* December 2, 2007

a. How has inexpensive broadband changed the production possibilities of video entertainment and other goods and services?
b. Sketch a *PPF* for video entertainment and other goods and services before broadband.
c. Show how the arrival of inexpensive broadband has changed the *PPF.*
d. Sketch a marginal benefit curve for video entertainment.
e. Show how opening the "floodgates to a generation of TV producers for whom the Internet is their native medium" might have changed the marginal benefit from video entertainment.
f. Explain how the quantity of video entertainment that achieves allocative efficiency has changed.

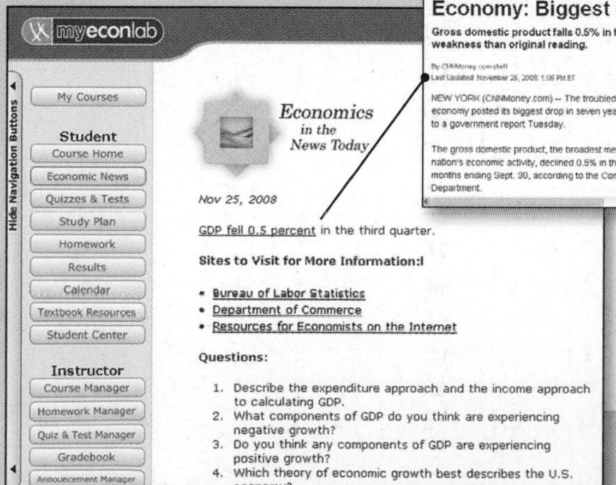



## Economics in the News myeconlab

To keep you informed about the latest economic news, Parkin uploads two relevant articles daily, one each covering microeconomic and macroeconomic topics. He also includes discussion questions, links to additional online resources, and references to related textbook chapters in the textbook.

# MACROECONOMICS

NINTH EDITION

MICHAEL PARKIN
University of Western Ontario

**Addison-Wesley**
Boston San Francisco New York
London Toronto Sydney Tokyo Singapore Madrid
Mexico City Munich Paris Cape Town Hong Kong Montreal

| | |
|---|---|
| **Publisher** | Denise Clinton |
| **Editor in Chief** | Donna Battista |
| **Senior Acquisitions Editor** | Adrienne D'Ambrosio |
| **Development Editor** | Deepa Chungi |
| **Managing Editor** | Nancy Fenton |
| **Photo Researcher** | Beth Anderson |
| **Production Coordinator** | Alison Eusden |
| **Director of Media** | Susan Schoenberg |
| **Content Lead for MyEconLab** | Douglas Ruby |
| **Senior Media Producer** | Melissa Honig |
| **Executive Marketing Manager** | Roxanne McCarley |
| **Rights and Permissions Advisor** | Shannon Barbe |
| **Senior Manufacturing Buyer** | Carol Melville |
| **Copyeditor** | Catherine Baum |
| **Cover Design** | Joyce Wells |
| **Technical Illustrator** | Richard Parkin |
| **Text Design, Project Management and Page Make-up** | Elm Street Publishing Services |

Origami cover art folded by Michael G. LaFosse from handmade paper made by Richard L. Alexander, Origamido, Inc.

Photo credits appear on page C-1, which constitutes a continuation of the copyright page.



**Library of Congress Cataloging-in-Publication Data**

Parkin, Michael, 1939–
Macroeconomics/Michael Parkin. — 9th ed.
p. cm.
Includes index.
ISBN 0-321-59288-3; 978-0-321-59288-0 (alk. paper)
1. Macroeconomics. I. Title.
HB171.5.P313 2008
330—dc22

1 2 3 4 5 6 7 8 10—CRK—12 11 10 09 08

**Addison-Wesley**
is an imprint of

www.pearsonhighered.com

ISBN 10: 0-321-59288-3
ISBN 13: 978-0-321-59288-0

TO

ROBIN

# ABOUT
# THE AUTHOR

**Michael Parkin** received his training as an economist at the Universities of Leicester and Essex in England. Currently in the Department of Economics at the University of Western Ontario, Canada, Professor Parkin has held faculty appointments at Brown University, the University of Manchester, the University of Essex, and Bond University. He is a past president of the Canadian Economics Association and has served on the editorial boards of the *American Economic Review* and the *Journal of Monetary Economics* and as managing editor of the *Canadian Journal of Economics*. Professor Parkin's research on macroeconomics, monetary economics, and international economics has resulted in over 160 publications in journals and edited volumes, including the *American Economic Review*, the *Journal of Political Economy*, the *Review of Economic Studies*, the *Journal of Monetary Economics*, and the *Journal of Money, Credit and Banking*. He became most visible to the public with his work on inflation that discredited the use of wage and price controls. Michael Parkin also spearheaded the movement toward European monetary union. Professor Parkin is an experienced and dedicated teacher of introductory economics.

# BRIEF CONTENTS

# PREFACE

**Historic is a big word.** Yet it accurately describes the economic events and policy responses that followed the subprime mortgage crisis of August 2007. Economics moved from the business report to the front page as fear gripped producers, consumers, financial institutions, and governments. The unimaginable repeat of a Great Depression gradually became imaginable as house prices plunged, credit markets froze, financial institutions failed, governments (both in the United States and around the world) mounted massive bailouts and rescues, the Fed made loans and bought debts of a quality that central banks don't normally touch, and the prices of items from gasoline and food to stocks and currencies fluctuated wildly.

Even the *idea* that the market is an efficient mechanism for allocating scarce resources came into question as some political leaders trumpeted the end of capitalism and the dawn of a new economic order in which tighter regulation reigned in unfettered greed.

Rarely do teachers of economics have such a rich feast on which to draw. And rarely are the principles of economics more surely needed to provide the solid foundation on which to think about economic events and navigate the turbulence of economic life.

Although thinking like an economist can bring a clearer perspective to and deeper understanding of today's events, students don't find the economic way of thinking easy or natural. *Macroeconomics* seeks to put clarity and understanding in the grasp of the student through its careful and vivid exploration of the tension between self interest and the social interest, the role and power of incentives—of opportunity cost and marginal benefit—and demonstrating the possibility that markets supplemented by other mechanisms, might allocate resources efficiently.

Parkin students begin to think about issues the way real economists do and learn how to explore difficult policy problems and make more informed decisions in their own economic lives.

## The Ninth Edition Revision

The ninth edition of *Macroeconomics* retains all of the improvements achieved from its predecessors, with its thorough and detailed presentation of the principles of economics, its emphasis on real-world examples and applications, its development of critical thinking skills, its diagrams renowned for pedagogy and precision, and its path-breaking technology.

This comprehensive revision also incorporates and responds to the suggestions for improvements made by reviewers and users, in both the broad architecture of the text and chapter-by-chapter.

**Current issues organize each chapter.** News stories about today's major economic events tie each chapter together, from new chapter-opening vignettes to end-of-chapter problems and online practice. Students learn to use economic tools to analyze their own daily decisions and recent real-world events and issues.

Each chapter includes a discussion of a critical issue of our time, to demonstrate how economic theory can be applied to explore a particular debate or question. Issues of central importance include:

- Gains and tensions from globalization, the rise of Asia, and the changing structure of the global economy in Chapters 2 and 6
- High and rising cost of food in Chapters 2 and 3
- Fluctuations in gas and oil prices and the effects of high gas prices on auto sales in Chapter 3
- Fed and government rescues and bailouts in Chapters 7 and 14
- Financial instability of 2008 in Chapters 7, 10, and 14
- Currency fluctuations in Chapters 8 and 9
- Recession of 2008–2009 in Chapters 10, 11, 12, and 13
- Real-world examples and applications appear in the body of each chapter and in the end-of-chapter problems and applications. Each chapter has approximately 10 new additional problems tied to current news and events. All of these problems have parallel questions in MyEconLab.

Questions that appear daily in MyEconLab in the *Economics in the News* are also available in MyEconLab for assignment as homework, quizzes, or tests.

## Highlights of the Macro Revision

The thoroughly updated coverage of macroeconomics is now organized in four parts: *monitoring the trends and fluctuations*, *understanding the trends*, *understanding the fluctuations*, and *macroeconomic policy*. The introductory chapter of previous editions is now redistributed across the other chapters as needed. The content of the previous edition's chapter on the classical model is distributed between the economic growth chapter and a new chapter on financial markets. In addition to these organizational changes, the macroeconomics chapters feature the following seven major revisions.

1. ***Measuring GDP and Economic Growth*** (Chapter 4): This chapter now includes a description and discussion of the recent history of real GDP growth and fluctuations found in the previous edition's introductory macro chapter. The explanation of the real GDP calculation has been simplified, and the current chain-dollar method of real GDP calculation is presented in a new Math Note at the end of the chapter.
2. ***Monitoring Jobs and Inflation*** (Chapter 5): This substantially revised chapter has a simplified coverage of the anatomy and types of unemployment but a more comprehensive explanation of the sources of unemployment. As today's unemployment is compared with that of the Great Depression, the empirical relationship between cyclical unemployment and the output gap is more clearly illustrated. The measurement of the price level and inflation is motivated with a discussion of inflation and why it is a problem. The chapter also includes new material on alternative price indexes including the personal consumption expenditure deflator as well as the concept of core inflation. The chapter now concludes with a brief section on the general use of real variables in macroeconomics.
3. ***Economic Growth*** (Chapter 6): The process of economic growth now begins with an explanation of what determines potential GDP (adapted from the previous edition's classical model chapter), which is followed by an explanation of what makes potential GDP grow. The sources of labor productivity growth are thoroughly explored.
4. ***Finance, Saving, and Investment*** (Chapter 7): New to the ninth edition, this chapter provides a thorough and extensive explanation of financial markets and institutions and their role in providing the funds for investment, an enginc of economic growth. The circular flow model of Chapter 4 is extended to include the flows in the market for loanable funds that finance investment. The chapter explains the role of government in the market for loanable funds and explains crowding out and the role of debt and the government budget deficit. The chapter also includes a discussion of borrowing and lending in the global loanable funds market. The credit crisis of 2008 is a central example used to illustrate the working of this vital macroeconomic market.
5. ***Money, the Price Level, and Inflation*** (Chapter 8): This chapter is heavily revised to simplify the explanation of the money creation process. A Math Note at the end of the chapter provides a more comprehensive analysis of this process. The explanation of the role and functions of the Federal Reserve includes coverage of the Fed's role in the 2008 credit crisis.
6. ***Aggregate Supply and Aggregate Demand*** (Chapter 10): This chapter is a streamlined version of the previous edition's content, but with a new and more detailed explanation and illustration of the U.S. business cycle. The added clarity and focus of this chapter reflects the tone and goals of the ninth edition.
7. ***Fiscal Policy*** (Chapter 13) and ***Monetary Policy*** (Chapter 14): These chapters are revised to incorporate the dramatic policy responses to the ongoing slowdown and increasingly likely recession of 2008–2009.
8. ***International Trade Policy*** (Chapter 15): This chapter provides an opportunity to teach the sources of the gains from international trade and the consequences of protection in the context of a macro course and without the need for a heavy investment in welfare economics concepts.

## Features to Enhance Teaching and Learning

### Chapter Openers

Each chapter opens with a student-friendly vignette that raises questions to motivate the student and focus the chapter. This chapter-opening story is woven into the main body of the chapter and is explored in the *Reading Between the Lines* feature that ends each chapter.

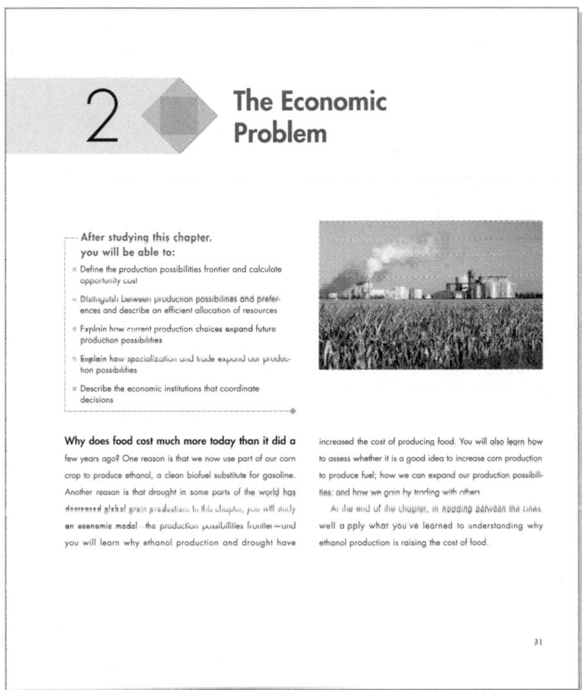

2 The Economic Problem

After studying this chapter, you will be able to:

- Define the production possibilities frontier and calculate opportunity cost
- Distinguish between production possibilities and preferences and describe an efficient allocation of resources
- Explain how current production choices expand future production possibilities
- Explain how specialization and trade expand our production possibilities
- Describe the economic institutions that coordinate decisions

**Why does food cost much more today than it did a** few years ago? One reason is that we now use part of our corn crop to produce ethanol, a clean biofuel substitute for gasoline. Another reason is that drought in some parts of the world has decreased global grain production. In this chapter, you will study an economic model—the production possibilities frontier—and you will learn why ethanol production and drought have increased the cost of producing food. You will also learn how to assess whether it is a good idea to increase corn production to produce fuel; how we can expand our production possibilities; and how we gain by trading with others.

At the end of the chapter, in *Reading Between the Lines*, we'll apply what you've learned to understanding why ethanol production is raising the cost of food.

31

### Chapter Objectives

A list of learning objectives enables students to see exactly where the chapter is going and to set their goals before they begin the chapter.

### Key Terms

Highlighted terms simplify the student's task of learning the vocabulary of economics. Each highlighted term appears in an end-of-chapter list with page numbers, in an end-of-book glossary with page numbers, boldfaced in the index, in the Web glossary, and in the Web Flash Cards.

### Diagrams That Show the Action

Through the past eight editions, this book has set new standards of clarity in its diagrams; the ninth edition continues to uphold this tradition. My goal has always been to show "where the economic action is." The diagrams in this book continue to generate an enormously positive response, which confirms my view that graphical analysis is the most powerful tool available for teaching and learning economics.

Because many students find graphs hard to work with, I have developed the entire art program with the study and review needs of the student in mind.

The diagrams feature:

- Original curves consistently shown in blue
- Shifted curves, equilibrium points, and other important features highlighted in red
- Color-blended arrows to suggest movement
- Graphs paired with data tables
- Diagrams labeled with boxed notes
- Extended captions that make each diagram and its caption a self-contained object for study and review.

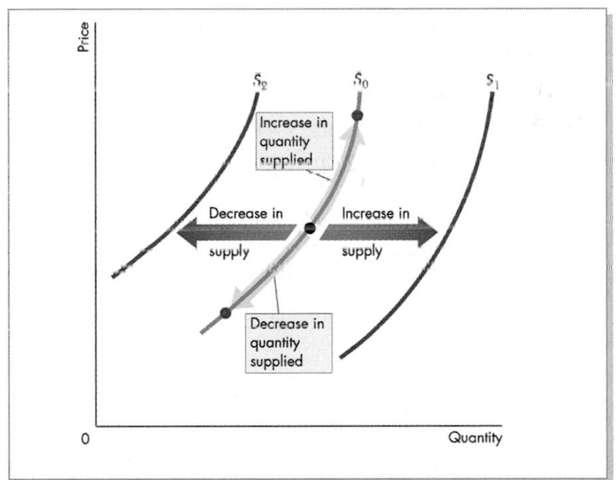


### In-Text Review Quizzes

A review quiz at the end of most major sections enables students to determine whether a topic needs further study before moving on. This feature includes a reference to the appropriate MyEconLab study plan to help students further test their understanding.

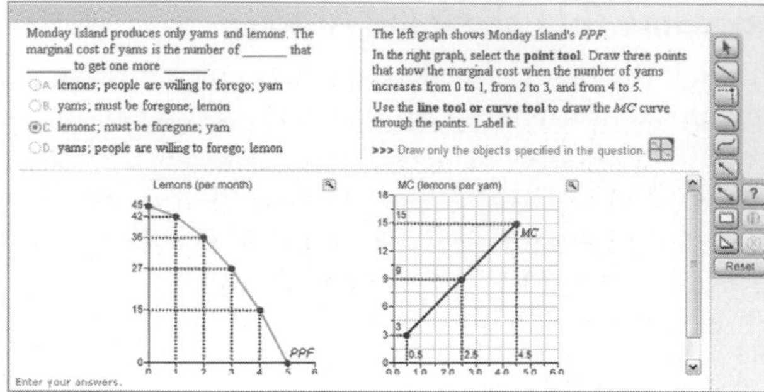


## Reading Between the Lines

In *Reading Between the Lines*, which appears at the end of each chapter, students apply the tools they have just learned by analyzing an article from a newspaper or news Web site. Each article sheds additional light on the questions first raised in the Chapter Opener.

Questions about the article also appear with the end-of-chapter problems and applications.

## End-of-Chapter Study Material

Each chapter closes with a concise summary organized by major topics, lists of key terms, figures and tables (all with page references), problems and applications. These learning tools provide students with a summary for review and exam preparation.

## News-Based End-of-Chapter Questions

Each chapter's problems and applications section now includes an additional set of news-based real-world problems that are new to the ninth edition. All of the problems and applications are also available for self-assessment or assignment as a homework, quiz, or test in MyEconLab.

## Interviews with Economists

Each major part of the text closes with a summary feature that includes an interview with a leading economist whose research and expertise correlates to what the student has just learned. These interviews explore the background, education, and research these prominent economics have conducted, as well as advice for those who want to continue the study of economics. New interviewees in this ninth edition are Stephanie Schmitt-Grohé and Richard Clarida, both of Columbia University.

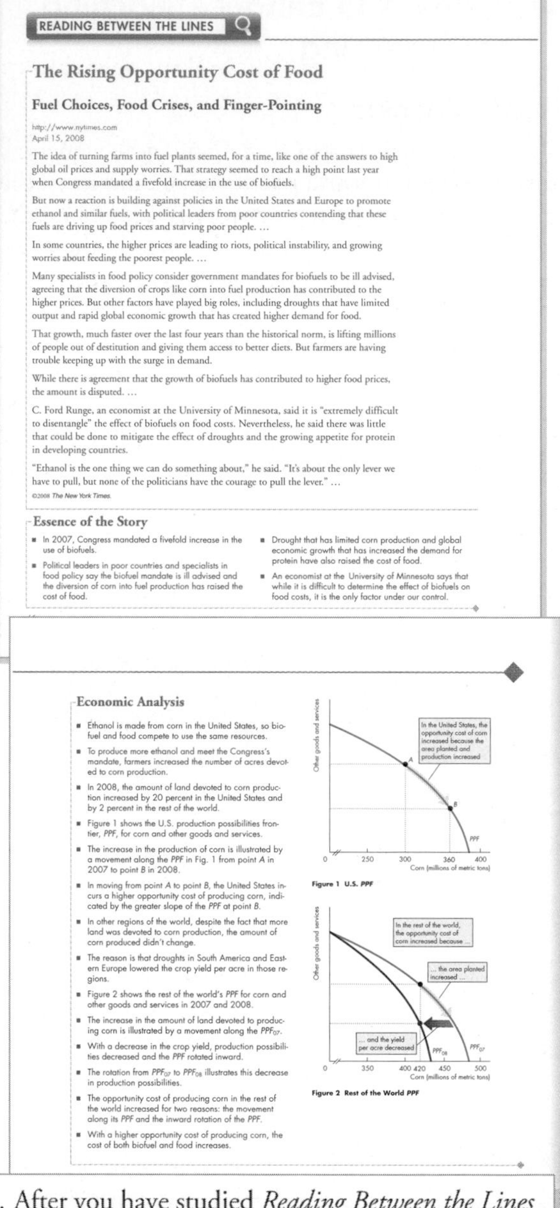

READING BETWEEN THE LINES

### The Rising Opportunity Cost of Food

**Fuel Choices, Food Crises, and Finger-Pointing**

http://www.nytimes.com
April 15, 2008

The idea of turning farms into fuel plants seemed, for a time, like one of the answers to high global oil prices and supply worries. That strategy seemed to reach a high point last year when Congress mandated a fivefold increase in the use of biofuels.

But now a reaction is building against policies in the United States and Europe to promote ethanol and similar fuels, with political leaders from poor countries contending that these fuels are driving up food prices and starving poor people. …

In some countries, the higher prices are leading to riots, political instability, and growing worries about feeding the poorest people. …

Many specialists in food policy consider government mandates for biofuels to be ill advised, agreeing that the diversion of crops like corn into fuel production has contributed to the higher prices. But other factors have played big roles, including droughts that have limited output and rapid global economic growth that has created higher demand for food.

That growth, much faster over the last four years than the historical norm, is lifting millions of people out of destitution and giving them access to better diets. But farmers are having trouble keeping up with the surge in demand.

While there is agreement that the growth of biofuels has contributed to higher food prices, the amount is disputed. …

C. Ford Runge, an economist at the University of Minnesota, said it is "extremely difficult to disentangle" the effect of biofuels on food costs. Nevertheless, he said there was little that could be done to mitigate the effect of droughts and the growing appetite for protein in developing countries.

"Ethanol is the one thing we can do something about," he said. "It's about the only lever we have to pull, but none of the politicians have the courage to pull the lever." …

©2008 *The New York Times*

**Essence of the Story**

- In 2007, Congress mandated a fivefold increase in the use of biofuels.
- Political leaders in poor countries and specialists in food policy say the biofuel mandate is ill advised and the diversion of corn into fuel production has raised the cost of food.
- Drought that has limited corn production and global economic growth that has increased the demand for protein have also raised the cost of food.
- An economist at the University of Minnesota says that while it is difficult to determine the effect of biofuels on food costs, it is the only factor under our control.

**Economic Analysis**

- Ethanol is made from corn in the United States, so biofuel and food compete to use the same resources.
- To produce more ethanol and meet the Congress's mandate, farmers increased the number of acres devoted to corn production.
- In 2008, the amount of land devoted to corn production increased by 20 percent in the United States and by 2 percent in the rest of the world.
- Figure 1 shows the U.S. production possibilities frontier, *PPF*, for corn and other goods and services.
- The increase in the production of corn is illustrated by a movement along the *PPF* in Fig. 1 from point *A* in 2007 to point *B* in 2008.
- In moving from point *A* to point *B*, the United States incurs a higher opportunity cost of producing corn, indicated by the greater slope of the *PPF* at point *B*.
- In other regions of the world, despite the fact that more land was devoted to corn production, the amount of corn produced didn't change.
- The reason is that droughts in South America and Eastern Europe lowered the crop yield per acre in those regions.
- Figure 2 shows the rest of the world's *PPF* for corn and other goods and services in 2007 and 2008.
- The increase in the amount of land devoted to producing corn is illustrated by a movement along the $PPF_{07}$.
- With a decrease in the crop yield, production possibilities decreased and the *PPF* rotated inward.
- The rotation from $PPF_{07}$ to $PPF_{08}$ illustrates this decrease in production possibilities.
- The opportunity cost of producing corn in the rest of the world increased for two reasons: the movement along its *PPF* and the inward rotation of the *PPF*.
- With a higher opportunity cost of producing corn, the cost of both biofuel and food increases.



**Figure 1 U.S. PPF**



**Figure 2 Rest of the World PPF**

21. After you have studied *Reading Between the Lines* on pp. 46–47, answer the following questions:
    a. How has an Act of the United States Congress increased U.S. production of corn?
    b. Why would you expect an increase in the quantity of corn produced to raise the opportunity cost of corn?
    c. Why did the cost of producing corn increase in the rest of the world?
    d. Is it possible that the increased quantity of corn produced, despite the higher cost of production, moves the United States closer to allocative efficiency?

## For the Instructor

This book enables you to achieve three objectives in your principles course:

- Focus on the economic way of thinking
- Explain the issues and problems of our time
- Choose your own course structure

### Focus on the Economic Way of Thinking

As an instructor, you know how hard it is to encourage a student to think like an economist. But that is your goal. Consistent with this goal, the text focuses on and repeatedly uses the central ideas: choice; tradeoff; opportunity cost; the margin; incentives; the gains from voluntary exchange; the forces of demand, supply, and equilibrium; the pursuit of economic rent; the tension between self-interest and the social interest; and the scope and limitations of government actions.

### Explain the Issues of Our Global Economy

Students must *use* the central ideas and tools if they are to begin to *understand* them. There is no better way to motivate students than by using the tools of economics to explain the issues that confront today's world. Issues such as globalization and the emergence of China and India as major economic forces; the mortgage crisis, the recent bankruptcy, absorption or federally funded bailout of American banks, stock market fluctuations, the new economy with new near-monopolies such as eBay and Google; the widening income gap between rich and poor; the reallocation of resources toward counterterrorism; the disappearing tropical rain forests and the challenge that this tragedy of the commons creates; the challenge of managing the world's water resources; the looming debt that arises from our newly emerged federal budget deficit; our vast and rising international deficit and debt; and the tumbling value of the dollar on the foreign exchange market.

### Flexible Structure

You have preferences for how you want to teach your course. I have organized this book to enable you to do so. The flexibility chart and alternative sequences table that appear on pages xxiii–xxiv demonstrate this book's flexibility. Whether you want to teach a traditional course that blends theory and policy or focuses on current policy issues, *Macroeconomics* gives you the choice.

### Supplemental Resources

**Instructor's Manuals** We have streamlined and reorganized the Instructor's Manual to reflect the focus and intuition of the ninth edition. The Instructor's Manual, written by Jeffrey Reynolds of Northern Illinois University, integrates the teaching and learning package and serves as a guide to all the supplements.

Each chapter contains:

- A chapter overview.
- A list of what's new in the ninth edition.
- ***Lecture Notes*** Ready-to-use lecture notes from each chapter enable a new user of Parkin to walk into a classroom armed to deliver a polished lecture. The lecture notes provide an outline of the chapter; concise statements of key material; alternate tables and figures, key terms, definitions, and boxes that highlight key concepts, provide an interesting anecdote, or suggest how to handle a difficult idea; additional discussion questions; additional problems; and the solutions to these problems. The chapter outline and teaching suggestions sections are keyed to the PowerPoint® lecture notes.
- ***Worksheets*** Another innovative feature of the Instructor's Manual is a set of Worksheets prepared by Patricia Kuzyk of Washington State University. These Worksheets ask students to contemplate real-world problems that illustrate economic principles. An example includes showing the effect of the catastrophic events of 9/11 using a marginal cost/marginal benefit diagram, and calculating the effects of funding Social Security for the huge number of baby boomer retirees. Instructors can assign these as in-class group projects or as homework. There is a Worksheet for every chapter of the book.

**Solutions Manual** For ease of use and instructor reference, a comprehensive solutions manual provides instructors with solutions to the Review Quizzes and the end-of-chapter problems. The Solutions Manual is available in hard copy and electronically on the Instructor's Resource Center CD-ROM, and in the instructor's resources section of MyEconLab, and on the Instructor's Resource Center.

**Test Banks** Three separate Test Banks provide multiple-choice, true-false, numerical, fill-in-the-blank, short-answer, and essay questions.

Mark Rush of the University of Florida reviewed and edited all existing questions to ensure their clarity and consistency with the ninth edition and incorporated new questions into the thousands of existing Test Bank questions. Written by Jeffrey Reynolds, these problems follow the style and format of the end-of chapter text problems and provide the instructor with a whole new set of testing opportunities and/or homework assignments. Additionally, end-of-part tests contain questions that cover all the chapters in the part and feature integrative questions that span more than one chapter.

***New News-based Problems*** The ninth edition includes a set of problems in each chapter that are based directly on current events, newspaper stories or magazine articles. Written by Carol Dole of Jacksonville University, these questions link the real world to concepts students have learned in class. With these news-based questions, instructors will be able to showcase how economics exists in the world outside the classroom.

The Test Banks are available in hard copy and electronically on the Instructor's Resource Center CD-ROM, in the instructor's resources section of MyEconLab, and on the Instructor's Resource Center.

**PowerPoint® Resources** Robin Bade and I have developed a full-color Microsoft® PowerPoint Lecture Presentation for each chapter that includes all the figures and tables from the text, animated graphs, and speaking notes. The lecture notes in the Instructor's Manual and the slide outlines are correlated, and the speaking notes are based on the Instructor's Manual teaching suggestions. A separate set of PowerPoint files containing large-scale versions of all the text's figures (most of them animated) and tables (some of which are animated) are also available. The presentations can be used electronically in the classroom or can be printed to create hard copy transparency masters. This item is available for Macintosh® and Windows®.

**Clicker-Ready PowerPoint Resources** This edition features the addition of clicker-ready PowerPoint slides for the Personal Response System you use. Each chapter of the text includes ten multiple-choice questions that test important concepts. Instructors can assign these as in-class assignments or review quizzes.

**Instructor's Resource Center CD-ROM** Fully compatible with Windows® and Macintosh®, this CD-ROM contains electronic files of every instructor supplement for the ninth edition. Files included are: Microsoft® Word and Adobe® PDF files of the Instructor's Manual, Test Bank and Solutions Manual; complete PowerPoint slides; and the Computerized TestGen® Test Bank. Add this useful resource to your exam copy bookbag, or locate your local Pearson Education sales representative at **www.pearsonhighered.educator** to request a copy.

***Computerized Testbank Component*** Fully networkable, it is available for Windows and Macintosh. TestGen's graphical interface enables instructors to view, edit, and add questions; transfer questions to tests; and print different forms of tests. Tests can be formatted with varying fonts and styles, margins, and headers and footers, as in any word-processing document. Search and sort features let the instructor quickly locate questions and arrange them in a preferred order. QuizMaster, working with your school's computer network, automatically grades the exams, stores the results on disk, and allows the instructor to view or print a variety of reports.

Instructors can download supplements from a secure, instructor-only source via the Pearson Higher Education Instructor Resource Center Web page (www.pearsonhighered.com/irc).

**Study Guide** The ninth edition Study Guide by Mark Rush is carefully coordinated with the text, MyEconLab, and the Test Banks. Each chapter of the Study Guide contains:

- Key concepts
- Helpful hints
- True/false/uncertain questions
- Multiple-choice questions
- Short-answer questions
- Common questions or misconceptions that the student explains as if he or she were the teacher
- Each part allows students to test their cumulative understanding with questions that go across chapters and work a sample midterm examination.

**MyEconLab** MyEconLab creates a perfect pedagogical loop that provides not only text-specific assessment and practice problems, but also tutorial support to make sure students learn from their mistakes.

At the core of MyEconLab are the following features:

***Auto-graded Tests and Assignments*** MyEconLab comes with two preloaded Sample tests for each chapter so students can self-assess their understanding of the material. Instructors can assign these Sample Tests or create assignments using end-of-chapter problems and applications, Test Bank questions, or their own custom exercises.

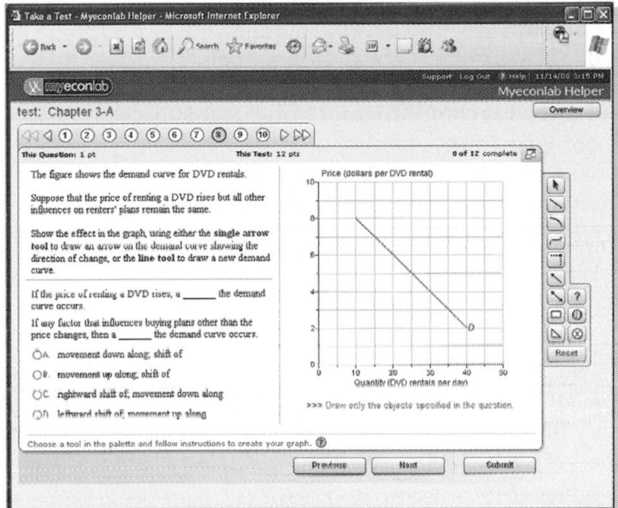


***Study Plan*** A Study Plan is generated from each student's results on Sample Tests and instructor assignments. Students can clearly see which topics they have mastered—and, more importantly, which they need to work on. The Study Plan consists of material from the in-text Review Quizzes and end-of-chapter Problems and Applications. The Study Plan links to additional practice problems and tutorial help on those topics.

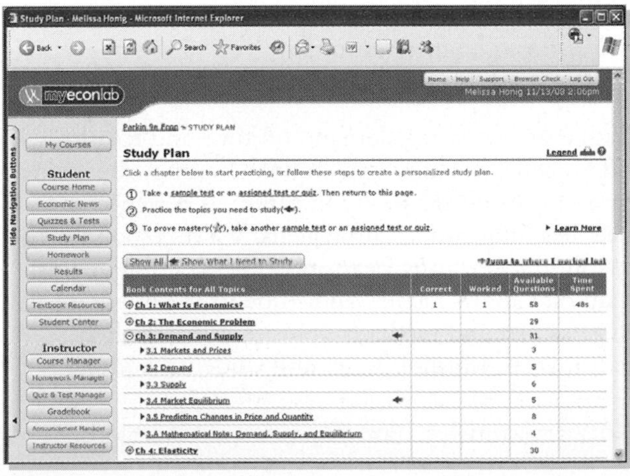


***Unlimited Practice*** Many Study Plan and instructor-assigned exercises contain algorithmically generated values to ensure that students get as much practice as they need. Every problem links students to learning resources that further reinforce concepts they need to master.

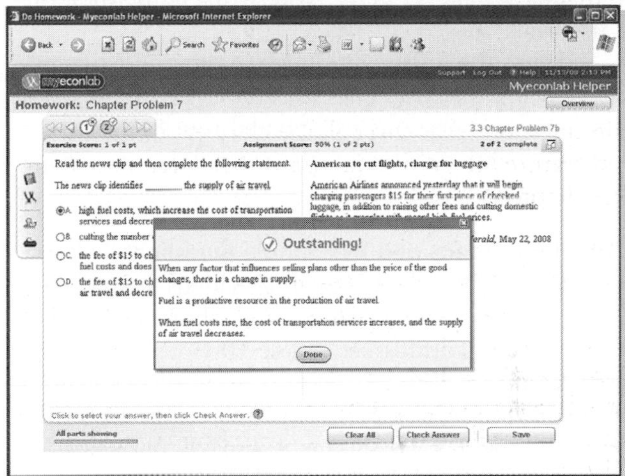


***Learning Resources*** Each practice problem contains a link to the eText page that discusses the concept being applied. Students also have access to guided solutions, animated graphs, audio narrative, flashcards, and live tutoring.

***Economics in the News*** Daily news updates during the school year are available in MyEconLab. Most days the author posts two links to relevant news articles from

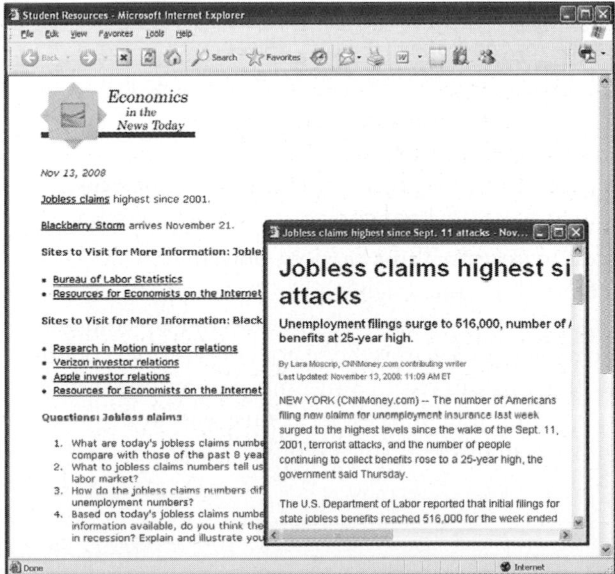

the day's headlines. One link directs students to a microeconomics article, and the other directs students to a macroeconomics article. Each article is accompanied by additional links, discussion questions, and a reference to relevant chapters in the textbook. An archive of *Economics in the News* articles and questions is also available.

New to the ninth edition are instructor-assignable *Economics in the News* questions in MyEconLab. These news analysis questions are updated routinely to ensure the latest news and news analysis problems are available for assignment.

**Economics Videos and Assignable Questions Featuring abc NEWS** Economics videos featuring ABC news enliven your course with short news clips featuring real-world issues. These 10 videos, available in MyEconLab, feature news footage and commentary by economists. Questions and problems for each video clip are available for assignment in MyEconLab.

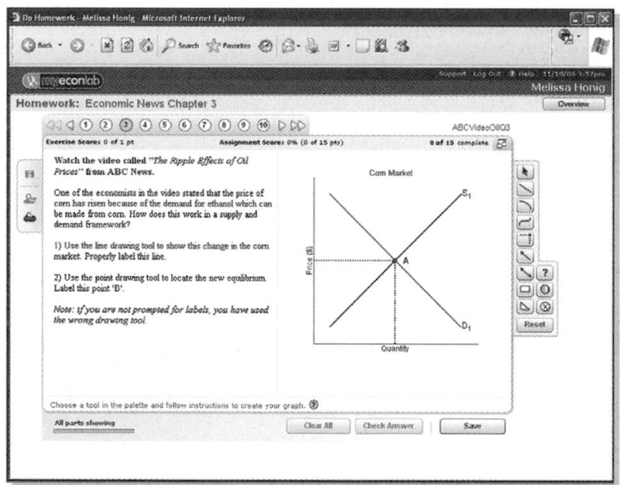


**Pearson Tutoring Services powered by SMARTHINKING** A subscription to MyEconLab includes complimentary access to Pearson Tutor Services, powered by SMARTHINKING Inc. Highly qualified tutors use whiteboard technology and feedback tools to help students understand and master the major concepts of economics. Students can receive real-time, one-on-one instruction, submit questions for a response within 24 hours, and view archives of past sessions.

## Special Editions

**Economist.com Edition** The premier online source of economic news analysis, Economist.com provides your students with insight and opinion on current economic events. Through an agreement between Addison-Wesley and *The Economist*, your students can receive a low-cost subscription to this premium Web site for 12 weeks, including the complete text of the current issue of *The Economist* and access to *The Economist's* searchable archives. Other features include Web-only weekly articles, news feeds with current world and business news, and stock market and currency data. Professors who adopt this special edition will receive a complimentary one-year subscription to Economist.com.

**The Wall Street Journal Edition** Addison-Wesley is also pleased to provide your students with access to *The Wall Street Journal*, the most respected and trusted daily source for information on business and economics. For a small additional charge, Addison-Wesley offers your students a subscription to *The Wall Street Journal* and WSJ.com. A 15-week subscription is available. Adopting professors will receive a complimentary one-year subscription to *The Wall Street Journal* as well as access to WSJ.com.

**Financial Times Edition** Featuring international news and analysis from FT journalists in more than 50 countries, the *Financial Times* will provide your students with insights and perspectives on economic developments around the world. The Financial Times Edition provides your students with a 15-week subscription to one of the world's leading business publications. Adopting professors will receive a complimentary one-year subscription to the *Financial Times* as well as access to FT.com.

## Pearson Choices

With ever-increasing demand on time and resources, today's college faculty and students want greater value, innovation, and flexibility in products designed to meet teaching and learning goals. We've responded to that need by creating Pearson Choices, a unique program that allows faculty and students to choose from a range of text and media formats that match their teaching and learning styles and students' budgets.

**Books à la Carte Plus Edition** For the student who wants a more flexible portable text, there is a three-hole punched version of *Economics*. Students who use this version can take only what they need to class, incorporate their own notes, and save money. This version is packaged with a laminated study card and comes with access to MyEconLab.

**CourseSmart** CourseSmart's mission is to improve teaching and learning through the availability of a lower-cost alternative to the traditional textbook, in a reliable Web application. For additional information, log onto www.coursesmart.com

**Standalone Access to MyEconLab and the Complete eText** Students may purchase access to MyEconLab, which includes online access to the complete, searchable eText, online at www.myeconlab.com or through the campus bookstore.

**MyEconLab** Students may purchase access to MyEconLab's assessment and learning resources. Partial access to the eText is included, which links practice problems to relevant sections of the text. Go to www.myeconlab.com for more information.

**Print Upgrade to the à la Carte Edition from within MyEconLab** Students may purchase an upgrade to the à la carte edition of *Economics* at any point following their online purchase of MyEconLab.

**Pearson Custom Business Resources** The Pearson Custom Database offers instructors the option of building their own book by selecting just the chapters they want and ordering them to fit their syllabus. Professors can also select chapters of the accompanying Study Guide as well as readings from Miller/Benjamin/North's *The Economics of Public Issues* and Miller/Benjamin's *The Economics of Macro Issues*. For additional information contact your Pearson representative.

## Acknowledgments

I thank my current and former colleagues and friends at the University of Western Ontario who have taught me so much. They are Jim Davies, Jeremy Greenwood, Ig Horstmann, Peter Howitt, Greg Huffman, David Laidler, Phil Reny, Chris Robinson, John Whalley, and Ron Wonnacott. I also thank Doug McTaggart and Christopher Findlay, co-authors of the Australian edition, and Melanie Powell and Kent Matthews, co-authors of the European edition. Suggestions arising from their adaptations of earlier editions have been helpful to me in preparing this edition.

I thank the several thousand students whom I have been privileged to teach. The instant response that comes from the look of puzzlement or enlightenment has taught me how to teach economics.

It is a special joy to thank the many outstanding editors, media specialists, and others at Addison-Wesley who contributed to the concerted publishing effort that brought this edition to completion. Denise Clinton, Publisher, has played a major role in the evolution of this text since its third edition, and her insights and ideas can still be found in this new edition. Donna Battista, Editor-in-Chief for Economics and Finance, is hugely inspiring and has provided overall direction to the project. As ever, Adrienne D'Ambrosio, Senior Acquisitions Editor for Economics and my sponsoring editor, played a major role in shaping this revision and the many outstanding supplements that accompany it. Adrienne brings intelligence and insight to her work and is the unchallengeable pre-eminent economics editor. Deepa Chungi, Development Editor, brought a fresh eye to the development process, obtained outstanding reviews from equally outstanding reviewers, digested and summarized the reviews, and made many solid suggestions as she diligently worked through the drafts of this edition. Nancy Fenton, Managing Editor, managed the entire production and design effort with her usual skill, played a major role in envisioning and implementing the cover design, and coped fearlessly with a tight production schedule. Susan Schoenberg, Director of Media, directed the development of MyEconLab; Doug Ruby, Content Lead for MyEconLab, managed a complex and thorough reviewing process for the content of MyEconLab; and Melissa Honig, Senior Media Producer, ensured that all our media assets were correctly assembled. Roxanne McCarley, Executive Marketing Manager, provided inspired marketing strategy and direction. Catherine Baum provided a careful, consistent, and intelligent copy edit and accuracy check. Joyce Wells designed the cover and package and yet again surpassed the challenge of ensuring that we meet the highest design standards. Joe Vetere provided endless technical help with the text and art files. And Heather Johnson with the other members of an outstanding editorial and production team at Elm Street including Debbie Kubiak kept the project on track on an impossibly tight schedule. I thank all of these wonderful people. It has been inspiring to work with them and to share in creating what I believe is a truly outstanding educational tool.

I thank Luke Armstrong of Lee College for providing the news-based applications that appear at the end of each chapter. Luke has been using this type of material with his students and has now shared his talent with a wider audience.

I thank our talented ninth edition supplements authors—Jeff Reynolds, Pat Kuzyk, and Carol Dole.

I especially thank Mark Rush, who yet again played a crucial role in creating another edition of this text and package. Mark has been a constant source of good advice and good humor.

I thank the many exceptional reviewers who have shared their insights through the various editions of this book. Their contribution has been invaluable.

I thank the people who work directly with me. Jeannie Gillmore provided outstanding research assistance on many topics, including the *Reading Between the Lines* news articles. Richard Parkin created the electronic art files and offered many ideas that improved the figures in this book. And Laurel Davies managed an ever-growing and ever more complex MyEconLab database.

As with the previous editions, this one owes an enormous debt to Robin Bade. I dedicate this book to her and again thank her for her work. I could not have written this book without the tireless and unselfish help she has given me. My thanks to her are unbounded.

Classroom experience will test the value of this book. I would appreciate hearing from instructors and students about how I can continue to improve it in future editions.

*Michael Parkin*
London, Ontario, Canada
michael.parkin@uwo.ca

## Reviewers

**Eric Abrams**, Hawaii Pacific University
**Christopher Adams**, Federal Trade Commission
**Tajudeen Adenekan**, Bronx Community College
**Syed Ahmed**, Cameron University
**Frank Albritton**, Seminole Community College
**Milton Alderfer**, Miami-Dade Community College
**William Aldridge**, Shelton State Community College
**Donald L. Alexander**, Western Michigan University
**Terence Alexander**, Iowa State University
**Stuart Allen**, University of North Carolina, Greensboro
**Sam Allgood**, University of Nebraska, Lincoln
**Neil Alper**, Northeastern University
**Alan Anderson**, Fordham University
**Lisa R. Anderson**, College of William and Mary
**Jeff Ankrom**, Wittenberg University
**Fatma Antar**, Manchester Community Technical College
**Kofi Apraku**, University of North Carolina, Asheville
**Moshen Bahmani-Oskooee**, University of Wisconsin, Milwaukee
**Donald Balch**, University of South Carolina
**Mehmet Balcilar**, Wayne State University
**Paul Ballantyne**, University of Colorado
**Sue Bartlett**, University of South Florida
**Jose Juan Bautista**, Xavier University of Louisiana
**Valerie R. Bencivenga**, University of Texas, Austin
**Ben Bernanke**, Chairman of Federal Reserve
**Radha Bhattacharya**, California State University, Fullerton
**Margot Biery**, Tarrant County College, South
**John Bittorowitz**, Ball State University
**David Black**, University of Toledo
**Kelly Blanchard**, Purdue University
**S. Brock Blomberg**, Claremont McKenna College
**William T. Bogart**, Case Western Reserve University
**Giacomo Bonanno**, University of California, Davis
**Tan Khay Boon**, Nanyard Technological University
**Sunne Brandmeyer**, University of South Florida
**Audie Brewton**, Northeastern Illinois University
**Baird Brock**, Central Missouri State University
**Byron Brown**, Michigan State University
**Jeffrey Buser**, Columbus State Community College
**Alison Butler**, Florida International University
**Tania Carbiener**, Southern Methodist University
**Kevin Carey**, American University
**Kathleen A. Carroll**, University of Maryland, Baltimore County
**Michael Carter**, University of Massachusetts, Lowell
**Edward Castronova**, California State University, Fullerton
**Francis Chan**, Fullerton College
**Ming Chang**, Dartmouth College
**Subir Chakrabarti**, Indiana University-Purdue University
**Joni Charles**, Texas State University
**Adhip Chaudhuri**, Georgetown University
**Gopal Chengalath**, Texas Tech University
**Daniel Christiansen**, Albion College
**Kenneth Christianson**, Binghamton University
**John J. Clark**, Community College of Allegheny County, Allegheny Campus
**Cindy Clement**, University of Maryland
**Meredith Clement**, Dartmouth College
**Michael B. Cohn**, U. S. Merchant Marine Academy
**Robert Collinge**, University of Texas, San Antonio
**Carol Condon**, Kean University
**Doug Conway**, Mesa Community College
**Larry Cook**, University of Toledo
**Bobby Corcoran**, retired, Middle Tennessee State University
**Kevin Cotter**, Wayne State University
**James Peery Cover**, University of Alabama, Tuscaloosa
**Erik Craft**, University of Richmond
**Eleanor D. Craig**, University of Delaware
**Jim Craven**, Clark College
**Jeremy Cripps**, American University of Kuwait
**Elizabeth Crowell,** University of Michigan, Dearborn
**Stephen Cullenberg**, University of California, Riverside
**David Culp**, Slippery Rock University
**Norman V. Cure**, Macomb Community College
**Dan Dabney**, University of Texas, Austin
**Andrew Dane**, Angelo State University
**Joseph Daniels**, Marquette University
**Gregory DeFreitas**, Hofstra University
**David Denslow**, University of Florida
**Mark Dickie**, University of Central Florida
**James Dietz**, California State University, Fullerton
**Carol Dole**, State University of West Georgia
**Ronald Dorf**, Inver Hills Community College
**John Dorsey**, University of Maryland, College Park
**Eric Drabkin**, Hawaii Pacific University
**Amrik Singh Dua**, Mt. San Antonio College
**Thomas Duchesneau**, University of Maine, Orono
**Lucia Dunn**, Ohio State University
**Donald Dutkowsky**, Syracuse University
**John Edgren**, Eastern Michigan University
**David J. Eger**, Alpena Community College
**Harry Ellis, Jr.**, University of North Texas
**Ibrahim Elsaify**, Goldey-Beacom College
**Kenneth G. Elzinga**, University of Virginia
**Patrick Emerson**, Oregon State University
**Tisha Emerson**, Baylor University
**Monica Escaleras**, Florida Atlantic University
**Antonina Espiritu**, Hawaii Pacific University

**Gwen Eudey**, University of Pennsylvania
**Barry Falk**, Iowa State University
**M. Fazeli**, Hofstra University
**Philip Fincher**, Louisiana Tech University
**F. Firoozi**, University of Texas, San Antonio
**Nancy Folbre**, University of Massachusetts, Amherst
**Kenneth Fong**, Temasek Polytechnic (Singapore)
**Steven Francis**, Holy Cross College
**David Franck**, University of North Carolina, Charlotte
**Mark Frank**, Sam Houston State University
**Roger Frantz**, San Diego State University
**Mark Frascatore**, Clarkson University
**Alwyn Fraser**, Atlantic Union College
**Marc Fusaro**, East Carolina University
**James Gale**, Michigan Technological University
**Susan Gale**, New York University
**Roy Gardner**, Indiana University
**Eugene Gentzel**, Pensacola Junior College
**Kirk Gifford**, Brigham Young University, Idaho
**Scott Gilbert**, Southern Illinois University, Carbondale
**Andrew Gill**, California State University, Fullerton
**Robert Giller**, Virginia Polytechnic Institute and State University
**Robert Gillette**, University of Kentucky
**James N. Giordano**, Villanova University
**Maria Giuili**, Diablo College
**Susan Glanz**, St. John's University
**Robert Gordon**, San Diego State University
**Richard Gosselin**, Houston Community College
**John Graham**, Rutgers University
**John Griffen**, Worcester Polytechnic Institute
**Wayne Grove**, Syracuse University
**Robert Guell**, Indiana State University
**Jamie Haag**, Pacific University, Oregon
**Gail Heyne Hafer**, Lindenwood University
**Rik W. Hafer**, Southern Illinois University, Edwardsville
**Daniel Hagen**, Western Washington University
**David R. Hakes**, University of Northern Iowa
**Craig Hakkio**, Federal Reserve Bank, Kansas City
**Bridget Gleeson Hanna**, Rochester Institute of Technology
**Ann Hansen**, Westminster College
**Seid Hassan**, Murray State University
**Jonathan Haughton**, Suffolk University
**Randall Haydon**, Wichita State University
**Denise Hazlett**, Whitman College
**Julia Heath**, University of Memphis
**Jac Heckelman**, Wake Forest University
**Jolien A. Helsel**, Kent State University
**James Henderson**, Baylor University
**Doug Herman**, Georgetown University
**Jill Boylston Herndon**, University of Florida
**Gus Herring**, Brookhaven College
**John Herrmann**, Rutgers University
**John M. Hill**, Delgado Community College
**Jonathan Hill**, Florida International University
**Lewis Hill**, Texas Tech University
**Steve Hoagland**, University of Akron
**Tom Hoerger**, Fellow, Research Triangle Institute
**Calvin Hoerneman**, Delta College
**George Hoffer**, Virginia Commonwealth University
**Dennis L. Hoffman**, Arizona State University
**Paul Hohenberg**, Rensselaer Polytechnic Institute
**Jim H. Holcomb**, University of Texas, El Paso
**Harry Holzer**, Georgetown University
**Linda Hooks**, Washington and Lee University
**Jim Horner**, Cameron University
**Djehane Hosni**, University of Central Florida
**Harold Hotelling, Jr.**, Lawrence Technical University
**Calvin Hoy**, County College of Morris
**Ing-Wei Huang**, Assumption University, Thailand
**Julie Hunsaker**, Wayne State University
**Beth Ingram**, University of Iowa
**Jayvanth Ishwaran**, Stephen F. Austin State University
**Michael Jacobs**, Lehman College
**S. Hussain Ali Jafri**, Tarleton State University
**Dennis Jansen**, Texas A&M University
**Barbara John**, University of Dayton
**Barry Jones**, Binghamton University
**Garrett Jones**, Southern Florida University
**Frederick Jungman**, Northwestern Oklahoma State University
**Paul Junk**, University of Minnesota, Duluth
**Leo Kahane**, California State University, Hayward
**Veronica Kalich**, Baldwin-Wallace College
**John Kane**, State University of New York, Oswego
**Eungmin Kang**, St. Cloud State University
**Arthur Kartman**, San Diego State University
**Gurmit Kaur**, Universiti Teknologi (Malaysia)
**Louise Keely**, University of Wisconsin, Madison
**Manfred W. Keil**, Claremont McKenna College
**Elizabeth Sawyer Kelly**, University of Wisconsin, Madison
**Rose Kilburn**, Modesto Junior College
**Robert Kirk**, Indiana University-Purdue University, Indianapolis
**Norman Kleinberg**, City University of New York, Baruch College
**Robert Kleinhenz**, California State University, Fullerton
**John Krantz**, University of Utah
**Joseph Kreitzer**, University of St. Thomas
**Patricia Kuzyk**, Washington State University
**David Lages**, Southwest Missouri State University
**W. J. Lane**, University of New Orleans
**Leonard Lardaro**, University of Rhode Island
**Kathryn Larson**, Elon College
**Luther D. Lawson**, University of North Carolina, Wilmington
**Elroy M. Leach**, Chicago State University

**Jim Lee**, Texas A & M, Corpus Christi
**Sang Lee**, Southeastern Louisiana University
**Robert Lemke**, Florida International University
**Mary Lesser**, Iona College
**Jay Levin**, Wayne State University
**Arik Levinson**, University of Wisconsin, Madison
**Tony Lima**, California State University, Hayward
**William Lord**, University of Maryland, Baltimore County
**Nancy Lutz**, Virginia Polytechnic Institute and State University
**Brian Lynch**, Lakeland Community College
**Murugappa Madhavan**, San Diego State University
**K. T. Magnusson**, Salt Lake Community College
**Svitlana Maksymenko**, University of Pittsburgh
**Mark Maier**, Glendale Community College
**Jean Mangan**, Staffordshire University Business School
**Denton Marks**, University of Wisconsin, Whitewater
**Michael Marlow**, California Polytechnic State University
**Akbar Marvasti**, University of Houston
**Wolfgang Mayer**, University of Cincinnati
**John McArthur**, Wofford College
**Amy McCormick**, Mary Baldwin College
**Russel McCullough**, Iowa State University
**Gerald McDougall**, Wichita State University
**Stephen McGary**, Brigham Young University-Idaho
**Richard D. McGrath**, Armstrong Atlantic State University
**Richard McIntyre**, University of Rhode Island
**John McLeod**, Georgia Institute of Technology
**Mark McLeod**, Virginia Polytechnic Institute and State University
**B. Starr McMullen**, Oregon State University
**Mary Ruth McRae**, Appalachian State University
**Kimberly Merritt**, Cameron University
**Charles Meyer**, Iowa State University
**Peter Mieszkowski**, Rice University
**John Mijares**, University of North Carolina, Asheville
**Richard A. Miller**, Wesleyan University
**Judith W. Mills**, Southern Connecticut State University
**Glen Mitchell**, Nassau Community College
**Jeannette C. Mitchell**, Rochester Institute of Technology
**Khan Mohabbat**, Northern Illinois University
**Bagher Modjtahedi**, University of California, Davis
**W. Douglas Morgan**, University of California, Santa Barbara
**William Morgan**, University of Wyoming
**James Morley**, Washington University in St. Louis
**William Mosher**, Clark University
**Joanne Moss**, San Francisco State University
**Nivedita Mukherji**, Oakland University
**Francis Mummery**, Fullerton College
**Edward Murphy**, Southwest Texas State University
**Kevin J. Murphy**, Oakland University
**Kathryn Nantz**, Fairfield University
**William S. Neilson**, Texas A&M University
**Bart C. Nemmers**, University of Nebraska, Lincoln
**Melinda Nish**, Orange Coast College
**Anthony O'Brien**, Lehigh University
**Norman Obst**, Michigan State University
**Constantin Ogloblin**, Georgia Southern University
**Mary Olson**, Tulane University
**Terry Olson**, Truman State University
**James B. O'Neill**, University of Delaware
**Farley Ordovensky**, University of the Pacific
**Z. Edward O'Relley**, North Dakota State University
**Donald Oswald**, California State University, Bakersfield
**Jan Palmer**, Ohio University
**Michael Palumbo**, Chief, Federal Reserve Board
**Chris Papageorgiou**, Louisiana State University
**G. Hossein Parandvash**, Western Oregon State College
**Randall Parker**, East Carolina University
**Robert Parks**, Washington University
**David Pate**, St. John Fisher College
**James E. Payne**, Illinois State University
**Donald Pearson**, Eastern Michigan University
**Steven Peterson**, University of Idaho
**Mary Anne Pettit**, Southern Illinois University, Edwardsville
**William A. Phillips**, University of Southern Maine
**Dennis Placone**, Clemson University
**Charles Plot**, California Institute of Technology, Pasadena
**Mannie Poen**, Houston Community College
**Kathleen Possai**, Wayne State University
**Ulrika Praski-Stahlgren**, University College in Gavle-Sandviken, Sweden
**Edward Price**, Oklahoma State University
**Rula Qalyoubi**, University of Wisconsin, Eau Claire
**K. A. Quartey**, Talladega College
**Herman Quirmbach**, Iowa State University
**Jeffrey R. Racine**, University of South Florida
**Peter Rangazas**, Indiana University-Purdue University, Indianapolis
**Vaman Rao**, Western Illinois University
**Laura Razzolini**, University of Mississippi
**Rob Rebelein**, University of Cincinnati
**J. David Reed**, Bowling Green State University
**Robert H. Renshaw**, Northern Illinois University
**Javier Reyes**, University of Arkansas
**Jeff Reynolds**, Northern Illinois University
**Rupert Rhodd**, Florida Atlantic University
**W. Gregory Rhodus**, Bentley College
**Jennifer Rice**, Indiana University, Bloomington
**John Robertson**, Paducah Community College
**Malcolm Robinson**, University of North Carolina, Greensboro
**Richard Roehl**, University of Michigan, Dearborn
**Carol Rogers**, Georgetown University
**William Rogers**, University of Northern Colorado

**Thomas Romans**, State University of New York, Buffalo
**David R. Ross**, Bryn Mawr College
**Thomas Ross**, Baldwin Wallace College
**Robert J. Rossana**, Wayne State University
**Jeffrey Rous**, University of North Texas
**Rochelle Ruffer**, Youngstown State University
**Mark Rush**, University of Florida
**Allen R. Sanderson**, University of Chicago
**Gary Santoni**, Ball State University
**John Saussy**, Harrisburg Area Community College
**Don Schlagenhauf**, Florida State University
**David Schlow**, Pennsylvania State University
**Paul Schmitt**, St. Clair County Community College
**Jeremy Schwartz**, Hampden-Sydney College
**Martin Sefton**, University of Nottingham
**James Self**, Indiana University
**Esther-Mirjam Sent**, University of Notre Dame
**Rod Shadbegian**, University of Massachusetts, Dartmouth
**Gerald Shilling**, Eastfield College
**Dorothy R. Siden**, Salem State College
**Mark Siegler**, California State University at Sacramento
**Scott Simkins**, North Carolina Agricultural and Technical State University
**Chuck Skoro**, Boise State University
**Phil Smith**, DeKalb College
**William Doyle Smith**, University of Texas, El Paso
**Sarah Stafford**, College of William and Mary
**Rebecca Stein**, University of Pennsylvania
**Frank Steindl**, Oklahoma State University
**Jeffrey Stewart**, New York University
**Allan Stone**, Southwest Missouri State University
**Courtenay Stone**, Ball State University
**Paul Storer**, Western Washington University
**Richard W. Stratton**, University of Akron
**Mark Strazicich**, Ohio State University, Newark
**Michael Stroup**, Stephen F. Austin State University
**Robert Stuart**, Rutgers University
**Della Lee Sue**, Marist College
**Abdulhamid Sukar**, Cameron University
**Terry Sutton**, Southeast Missouri State University
**Gilbert Suzawa**, University of Rhode Island
**David Swaine**, Andrews University
**Jason Taylor**, Central Michigan University
**Mark Thoma**, University of Oregon
**Janet Thomas**, Bentley College
**Kiril Tochkov**, SUNY at Binghamton
**Kay Unger**, University of Montana
**Anthony Uremovic**, Joliet Junior College
**David Vaughn**, City University, Washington
**Don Waldman**, Colgate University
**Francis Wambalaba**, Portland State University
**Rob Wassmer**, California State University, Sacramento
**Paul A. Weinstein**, University of Maryland, College Park
**Lee Weissert**, St. Vincent College
**Robert Whaples**, Wake Forest University
**David Wharton**, Washington College
**Mark Wheeler**, Western Michigan University
**Charles H. Whiteman**, University of Iowa
**Sandra Williamson**, University of Pittsburgh
**Brenda Wilson**, Brookhaven Community College
**Larry Wimmer**, Brigham Young University
**Mark Witte**, Northwestern University
**Willard E. Witte**, Indiana University
**Mark Wohar**, University of Nebraska, Omaha
**Laura Wolff**, Southern Illinois University, Edwardsville
**Cheonsik Woo**, Vice President, Korea Development Institute
**Douglas Wooley**, Radford University
**Arthur G. Woolf**, University of Vermont
**John T. Young**, Riverside Community College
**Michael Youngblood**, Rock Valley College
**Peter Zaleski**, Villanova University
**Jason Zimmerman**, South Dakota State University
**David Zucker**, Martha Stewart Living Omnimedia

## Supplements Authors

**Sue Bartlett**, University of South Florida
**Kelly Blanchard**, Purdue University
**James Cobbe**, Florida State University
**Carol Dole**, Jacksonville University
**Karen Gebhardt**, Colorado State University
**John Graham**, Rutgers University
**Jill Herndon**, University of Florida
**Patricia Kuzyk**, Washington State University
**Sang Lee**, Southeastern Louisiana University
**James Morley**, Washington University in St. Louis
**William Mosher**, Clark University
**Constantin Ogloblin**, Georgia Southern University
**Edward Price**, Oklahoma State University
**Jeff Reynolds**, Northern Illinois University
**Mark Rush**, University of Florida
**Michael Stroup**, Stephen F. Austin State University
**Della Lee Sue**, Marist College
**Nora Underwood**, University of Central Florida

# FLEXIBILITY
## BY CHAPTER

| Core | Policy | Optional |
|---|---|---|
| 1 What is Economics? | | 1 Appendix: Graphs in Economics |
| 2 The Economic Problem | | |
| 3 Demand and Supply | | |
| 4 Measuring GDP and Economic Growth | | |
| 5 Monitoring Jobs and the Price Level | | |
| 6 Economic Growth | | |
| 7 Finance, Saving, and Investment | | |
| 8 Money, the Price Level, and Inflation | | 9 The Exchange Rate and the Balance of Payments |
| 10 Aggregate Supply and Aggregate Demand | | 11 Expenditure Multipliers: The Keynesian Model |
| | | 12 U.S. Inflation, Unemployment, and Business Cycle |
| | 13 Fiscal Policy | |
| | 14 Monetary Policy | 15 International Trade Policy |

# THREE ALTERNATIVE **MACRO SEQUENCES**

| Classical Perspective | Keynesian Perspective | Monetarist Perspective |
|---|---|---|
| **1** What Is Economics? | **1** What Is Economics? | **1** What Is Economics? |
| **2** The Economic Problem | **2** The Economic Problem | **2** The Economic Problem |
| **3** Demand and Supply | **3** Demand and Supply | **3** Demand and Supply |
| **4** Measuring GDP and Economic Growth | **4** Measuring GDP and Economic Growth | **4** Measuring GDP and Economic Growth |
| **5** Monitoring Jobs and Inflation | **5** Monitoring Jobs and Inflation | **5** Monitoring Jobs and Inflation |
| **6** Economic Growth | **11** Expenditure Multipliers: The Keynesian Model | **7** Finance, Saving, and Investment |
| **7** Finance, Saving, and Investment | **10** Aggregate Supply and Aggregate Demand | **8** Money, the Price Level, and Inflation |
| **8** Money, the Price Level, and Inflation | **12** U.S. Inflation, Unemployment, and Business Cycle (omit real business cycles) | **9** The Exchange Rate and the Balance of Payments |
| **9** The Exchange Rate and the Balance of Payments | **13** Fiscal Policy (omit supply-side sections) | **10** Aggregate Supply and Aggregate Demand |
| **10** Aggregate Supply and Aggregate Demand | **8** Money, the Price Level, and Inflation | **12** U.S. Inflation, Unemployment, and Business Cycle (omit the real business cycle section) |
| **12** U.S. Inflation, Unemployment, and Business Cycle | **14** Monetary Policy | **14** Monetary Policy |
| **13** Fiscal Policy | **6** Economic Growth | **13** Fiscal Policy |
| **14** Monetary Policy | **7** Finance, Saving, and Investment | **6** Economic Growth |
| **15** International Trade Policy | **9** Money and Exchange Rates | **15** International Trade Policy |
| | **15** International Trade Policy | |

# TABLE OF CONTENTS

## PART ONE INTRODUCTION 1

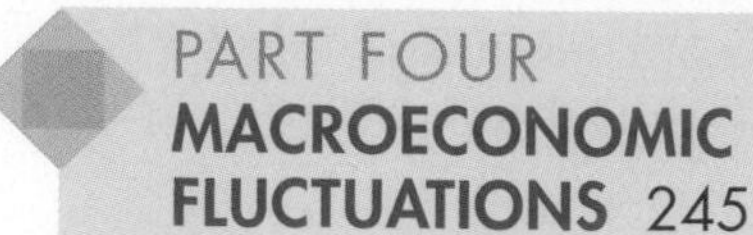

# What Is Economics?

**After studying this chapter, you will be able to:**

- Define economics and distinguish between microeconomics and macroeconomics
- Explain the two big questions of economics
- Explain the key ideas that define the economic way of thinking
- Explain how economists go about their work as social scientists

**You are studying economics at a time of extra**ordinary change. The United States is the world's most powerful nation, but China, India, Brazil, and Russia, nations with a combined population that dwarfs our own, are emerging to play ever greater roles in an expanding global economy. The technological change that is driving this expansion has brought us the laptops, wireless broadband, iPods, DVDs, cell phones, and video games that have transformed the way we work and play. But this expanding global economy has also brought us skyrocketing food and fuel prices and is contributing to global warming and climate change.

Your life will be shaped by the challenges you face and the opportunities that you create. But to face those challenges and seize the opportunities they present, you must understand the powerful forces at play. The economics that you're about to learn will become your most reliable guide. This chapter gets you started. It describes the questions that economists try to answer and the ways in which they search for the answers.

## Definition of Economics

All economic questions arise because we want more than we can get. We want a peaceful and secure world. We want clean air, lakes, and rivers. We want long and healthy lives. We want good schools, colleges, and universities. We want spacious and comfortable homes. We want an enormous range of sports and recreational gear from running shoes to jet skis. We want the time to enjoy sports, games, novels, movies, music, travel, and hanging out with our friends.

What each one of us can get is limited by time, by the incomes we earn, and by the prices we must pay. Everyone ends up with some unsatisfied wants. What we can get as a society is limited by our productive resources. These resources include the gifts of nature, human labor and ingenuity, and tools and equipment that we have produced.

Our inability to satisfy all our wants is called **scarcity**. The poor and the rich alike face scarcity. A child wants a $1.00 can of soda and two 50¢ packs of gum but has only $1.00 in his pocket. He faces scarcity. A millionaire wants to spend the weekend playing golf *and* spend the same weekend attending a business strategy meeting. She faces scarcity. A society wants to provide improved health care, install a computer in every classroom, explore space, clean polluted lakes and rivers, and so on. Society faces scarcity. Even parrots face scarcity!

Faced with scarcity, we must *choose* among the available alternatives. The child must *choose* the soda *or* the gum. The millionaire must *choose* the golf game *or* the meeting. As a society, we must *choose* among health care, national defense, and education.

The choices that we make depend on the incentives that we face. An **incentive** is a reward that encourages an action or a penalty that discourages one. If the price of soda falls, the child has an *incentive* to choose more soda. If a profit of $10 million is at stake, the millionaire has an *incentive* to skip the golf game. As computer prices tumble, school boards have an *incentive* to connect more classrooms to the Internet.

**Economics** is the social science that studies the *choices* that individuals, businesses, governments, and entire societies make as they cope with *scarcity* and the *incentives* that influence and reconcile those choices. The subject divides into two main parts:

- Microeconomics
- Macroeconomics

### Microeconomics

**Microeconomics** is the study of the choices that individuals and businesses make, the way these choices interact in markets, and the influence of governments. Some examples of microeconomic questions are: Why are people buying more DVDs and fewer movie tickets? How would a tax on e-commerce affect eBay?

### Macroeconomics

**Macroeconomics** is the study of the performance of the national economy and the global economy. Some examples of macroeconomic questions are: Why did income growth slow in the United States in 2008? Can the Federal Reserve keep our economy expanding by cutting interest rates?

*Not only do I want a cracker—we all want a cracker!*



### Review Quiz

1. List some examples of scarcity in the United States today.
2. Use the headlines in today's news to provide some examples of scarcity around the world.
3. Use today's news to illustrate the distinction between microeconomics and macroeconomics.

Work Study Plan 1.1 and get instant feedback.

## Two Big Economic Questions

Two big questions summarize the scope of economics:

- How do choices end up determining *what, how,* and *for whom* goods and services are produced?
- How can choices made in the pursuit of *self-interest* also promote the *social interest*?

### What, How, and For Whom?

**Goods and services** are the objects that people value and produce to satisfy human wants. *Goods* are physical objects such as cell phones and automobiles. *Services* are tasks performed for people such as cell-phone service and auto-repair service.

**What?** What we produce varies across countries and changes over time. In the United States today, agriculture accounts for less than 1 percent of total production, manufactured goods for 20 percent, and services (retail and wholesale trade, health care, and education are the biggest ones) for 80 percent. In contrast, in China today, agriculture accounts for more than 10 percent of total production, manufactured goods for 50 percent, and services for 40 percent. Figure 1.1 shows these numbers and also the percentages for Brazil, which fall between those for the United States and China.

What determines these patterns of production? How do choices end up determining the quantities of cell phones, automobiles, cell-phone service, auto-repair service, and the millions of other items that are produced in the United States and around the world?

**FIGURE 1.1** What Three Countries Produce

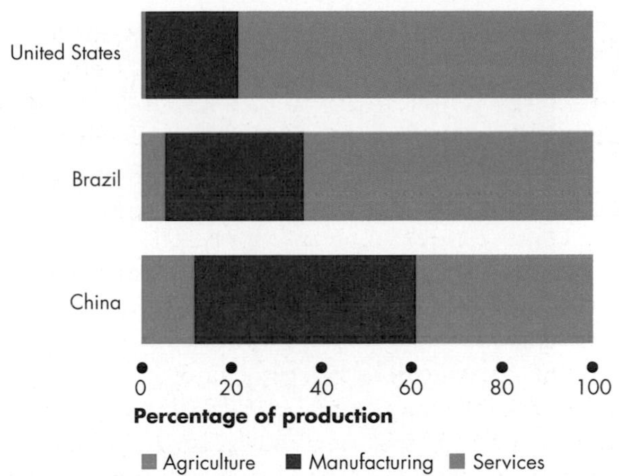


The richer the country, the more of its production is services and the less is food and manufactured goods.

*Source of data*: CIA Factbook 2008, Central Intelligence Agency.

**How?** Goods and services are produced by using productive resources that economists call **factors of production**. Factors of production are grouped into four categories:

- Land
- Labor
- Capital
- Entrepreneurship

***Land*** The "gifts of nature" that we use to produce goods and services are called **land**. In economics, land is what in everyday language we call *natural resources*. It includes land in the everyday sense together with minerals, oil, gas, coal, water, air, forests, and fish.

Our land surface and water resources are renewable and some of our mineral resources can be recycled. But the resources that we use to create energy are nonrenewable—they can be used only once.

***Labor*** The work time and work effort that people devote to producing goods and services is called **labor**. Labor includes the physical and mental efforts of all the people who work on farms and construction sites and in factories, shops, and offices.

The *quality* of labor depends on **human capital**, which is the knowledge and skill that people obtain from education, on-the-job training, and work experience. You are building your own human capital right now as you work on your economics course, and your human capital will continue to grow as you gain work experience.

Human capital expands over time. Today, 86 percent of the population of the United States have completed high school and 28 percent have a college or university degree. Figure 1.2 shows these measures of the growth of human capital in the United States over the past century.

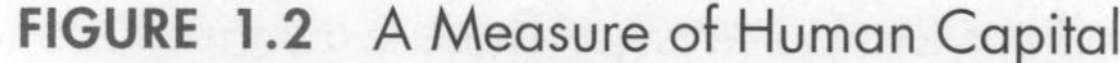

**FIGURE 1.2** A Measure of Human Capital

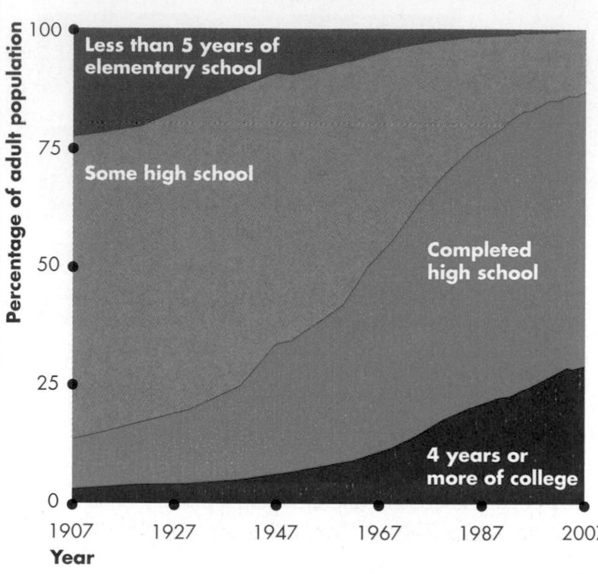


Today, 28 percent of the population have 4 years or more of college, up from 2 percent in 1905. A further 58 percent have completed high school, up from 10 percent in 1905.

*Source of data:* U.S. Census Bureau, *Statistical Abstract of the United States.*

myeconlab animation

***Capital*** The tools, instruments, machines, buildings, and other constructions that businesses use to produce goods and services are called **capital**.

In everyday language, we talk about money, stocks, and bonds as being "capital." These items are *financial* capital. Financial capital plays an important role in enabling businesses to borrow the funds that they use to buy physical capital. But because financial capital is not used to produce goods and services, it is not a productive resource.

***Entrepreneurship*** The human resource that organizes labor, land, and capital is called **entrepreneurship**. Entrepreneurs come up with new ideas about what and how to produce, make business decisions, and bear the risks that arise from these decisions.

What determines the quantities of factors of production that are used to produce goods and services?

**For Whom?** Who consumes the goods and services that are produced depends on the incomes that people earn. A large income enables a person to buy large quantities of goods and services. A small income leaves a person with few options and small quantities of goods and services.

People earn their incomes by selling the services of the factors of production they own:

- Land earns **rent**.
- Labor earns **wages**.
- Capital earns **interest**.
- Entrepreneurship earns **profit**.

Which factor of production earns the most income? The answer is labor. Wages and fringe benefits are around 70 percent of total income. Land, capital, and entrepreneurship share the rest. These percentages have been remarkably constant over time.

Knowing how income is shared among the factors of production doesn't tell us how it is shared among individuals. And the distribution of income among individuals is extremely unequal. You know of some people who earn very large incomes: Oprah Winfrey made $260 million in 2007; and Bill Gates' wealth increased by $2 billion in 2008.

You know of even more people who earn very small incomes. Servers at McDonald's average around $6.35 an hour; checkout clerks, cleaners, and textile and leather workers all earn less than $10 an hour.

You probably know about other persistent differences in incomes. Men, on the average, earn more than women; whites earn more than minorities; college graduates earn more than high-school graduates.

We can get a good sense of who consumes the goods and services produced by looking at the percentages of total income earned by different groups of people. The 20 percent of people with the lowest incomes earn about 5 percent of total income, while the richest 20 percent earn close to 50 percent of total income. So on average, people in the richest 20 percent earn more than 10 times the incomes of those in the poorest 20 percent.

Why is the distribution of income so unequal? Why do women and minorities earn less than white males?

Economics provides some answers to all these questions about what, how, and for whom goods and services are produced and much of the rest of this book will help you to understand those answers.

We're now going to look at the second big question of economics: When does the pursuit of self-interest promote the social interest? This question is a difficult one both to appreciate and to answer.

## How Can the Pursuit of Self-Interest Promote the Social Interest?

Every day, you and 304 million other Americans, along with 6.7 billion people in the rest of the world, make economic choices that result in *what*, *how*, and *for whom* goods and services are produced.

**Self-Interest** A choice is in your **self-interest** if you think that choice is the best one available for you. You make most of your choices in your self-interest. You use your time and other resources in the ways that make the most sense to you, and you don't think too much about how your choices affect other people. You order a home delivery pizza because you're hungry and want to eat. You don't order it thinking that the delivery person needs an income.

When you act on your self-interested economic choices, you come into contact with thousands of other people who produce and deliver the goods and services that you decide to buy or who buy the things that you sell. These people have made their own choices—what to produce and how to produce it, whom to hire or to work for, and so on—in their self-interest. When the pizza delivery person shows up at your door, he's not doing you a favor. He's earning his income and hoping for a good tip.

**Social Interest** Self-interested choices promote the **social interest** if they lead to an outcome that is the best for society as a whole—an outcome that uses resources efficiently and distributes goods and services equitably (or fairly) among individuals.

Resources are used efficiently when goods and services are produced

1. At the lowest possible cost, and
2. In the quantities that give the greatest possible benefit.

**The Big Question** How can we organize our economic lives so that when each one of us makes choices that are in our self-interest, it turns out that these choices also promote the social interest? Does voluntary trading in free markets achieve the social interest? Do we need government action to guide our choices to achieve the social interest? Do we need international cooperation and treaties to achieve the global social interest?

Let's put flesh on these broad questions with some examples.

## Self-Interest and the Social Interest

To get started thinking about the tension between self-interest and the social interest, we'll consider five topics that generate discussion in today's world. Here, we will briefly introduce the topics and identify some of the economic questions that they pose. We'll return to each one of them as you learn more of the economic ideas and tools that can be used to understand these issues. The topics are

- Globalization
- The information-age economy
- Global warming
- Natural resource depletion
- Economic instability

**Globalization** The term *globalization* means the expansion of international trade, borrowing and lending, and investment.

Whose self-interest does globalization serve? Is it only in the self-interest of the multinational firms that produce in low-cost regions and sell in high-price regions? Is globalization in the interest of consumers who buy lower-cost goods? Is globalization in the interest of the worker in Malaysia who sews your new running shoes? Is globalization in your self-interest and in the social interest? Or should we limit globalization and restrict imports of cheap foreign-produced goods and services?

### Globalization Today

#### Life in a Small and Ever Shrinking World

Every day, 40,000 people travel by air between the United States and Asia and Europe. A phone call or a video-conference with people who live 10,000 miles apart is a common and easily affordable event.

When Nike produces sports shoes, people in China, Indonesia, or Malaysia get work. When Apple designs a new generation iPod, electronics factories in China, Japan, Korea, and Taiwan produce and assemble the parts. When Nintendo creates a new game for the Wii, programmers in India write the code. And when China Airlines buys new airplanes, Americans who work at Boeing build them.

While globalization brings expanded production and job opportunities for Asian workers, it destroys many American jobs. Workers across the manufacturing industries must learn new skills, or take lower-paid service jobs, or retire earlier than planned.

**The Information-Age Economy** The technological change of the 1990s and 2000s has been called the *Information Revolution.*

During the information revolution were scarce resources used in the best possible way? Who benefitted from Bill Gates' decision to quit Harvard and create Microsoft? Did Microsoft produce operating systems for the personal computer that served the social interest? Did it sell its programs for prices that served the social interest? Did Bill Gates have to be paid what has now grown to $55 billion to produce the successive generations of Windows, Microsoft Office, and other programs? Did Intel make the right quality of chips and sell them in the right quantities for the right prices? Or was the quality too low and the price too high? Would the social interest have been better served if Microsoft and Intel had faced competition from other firms?

**Global Warming** Global warming and its effect on climate change is a huge political issue today. Every serious political leader is acutely aware of the problem and of the popularity of having proposals that might lower carbon emissions.

Every day, when you make self-interested choices to use electricity and gasoline, you contribute to carbon emissions; you leave your carbon footprint. You can lessen your carbon footprint by walking, riding a bike, taking a cold shower, or planting a tree.

But can each one of us be relied upon to make decisions that affect the Earth's carbon-dioxide concentration in the social interest? Must governments change the incentives we face so that our self-interested choices advance the social interest? How can governments change incentives? How can we encourage the use of wind and solar power to replace the burning of fossil fuels that bring climate change?

## The Source of the Information-Age

### So Much from One Tiny Chip

The microprocessor or computer chip created the information age. Gordon Moore of Intel predicted in 1965 that the number of transistors that could be placed on one chip would double every 18 months (Moore's law). This prediction turned out to be remarkably accurate. In 1980, an Intel chip had 60,000 transistors. In 2008, Intel's Core 2 Duo processor that you might be using on your personal computer has 291 million transistors.

The spinoffs from faster and cheaper computing were widespread. Telecommunications became clearer and faster; music and movie recording became more realistic; routine tasks that previously required human decision and action were automated.

All the new products and processes, and the low-cost computing power that made them possible, were produced by people who made choices in their own self-interest. They did not result from any grand design or government economic plan.

When Gordon Moore set up Intel and started making chips, no one had told him to do so, and he wasn't thinking how much easier it would be for you to turn in your essay on time if you had a faster laptop. When Bill Gates quit Harvard to set up Microsoft, he wasn't thinking about making it easier to use a computer. Moore, Gates, and thousands of other entrepreneurs were in hot pursuit of the big prizes that many of them succeeded in winning.

## A Hotter Planet

### Melting Ice and the Changing Climate

Retreating polar icecaps are a vivid illustration of a warming planet. Over the past 100 years, the Earth's surface air temperature is estimated to have risen by about three quarters of a degree Celsius. Uncertainty surrounds the causes, likely future amount, and effects of this temperature increase.

The consensus is that the temperature is rising because the amount of carbon dioxide in the Earth's atmosphere is increasing, and that human economic activity is a source of the increased carbon concentration.

Forests convert carbon dioxide to oxygen and so act as carbon sinks, but they are shrinking.

Two thirds of the world's carbon emissions come from the United States, China, the European Union, Russia, and India. The fastest growing emissions are coming from India and China.

Burning fossil fuels—coal and oil—to generate electricity and to power airplanes, automobiles, and trucks pours a staggering 28 billions tons—4 tons per person—of carbon dioxide into the atmosphere each year.

The amount of future global warming and its effects are uncertain. If the temperature rise continues, the Earth's climate will change, ocean levels will rise, and low-lying coastal areas will need to be protected against the rising tides by expensive barriers.

**Natural Resource Depletion** Tropical rainforests and ocean fish stocks are disappearing quickly. No one owns these resources and everyone is free to take what they want. When Japanese, Spanish, and Russian trawlers scoop up fish in international waters, no one keeps track of the quantities of fish they catch and no one makes them pay. The fish are free.

Each one of us makes self-interested economic choices to buy products that destroy natural resources and kill wild fish stocks. When you buy soap or shampoo or eat fish and contribute to the depletion of natural resources, are your self-interested choices damaging the social interest? If they are, what can be done to change your choices so that they serve the social interest?

**Economic Instability** The past 20 years have been ones of remarkable economic stability, so much so that they've been called the *Great Moderation*. Even the economic shockwaves of 9/11 brought only a small dip in the strong pace of U.S. and global economic expansion. But in August 2007, a period of financial stress began.

Banks' choices to lend and people's choices to borrow were made in self-interest. But did this lending and borrowing serve the social interest? Did the Fed's bail out of troubled banks serve the social interest? Or might the Fed's rescue action encourage banks to repeat their dangerous lending in the future?

## Running Out of Natural Resources
### Disappearing Forests and Fish

Tropical rainforests in South America, Africa, and Asia support the lives of 30 million species of plants, animals, and insects—approaching 50 percent of all the species on the planet. These rainforests provide us with the ingredients for many goods, including soaps, mouthwashes, shampoos, food preservatives, rubber, nuts, and fruits. The Amazon rainforest alone converts about 1 trillion pounds of carbon dioxide into oxygen each year.

Yet tropical rainforests cover less than 2 percent of the earth's surface and are heading for extinction. Logging, cattle ranching, mining, oil extraction, hydroelectric dams, and subsistence farming destroy an area the size of two football fields every second, or an area larger than New York City every day. At the current rate of destruction, almost all the tropical rainforest ecosystems will be gone by 2030.

What is happening to the tropical rainforests is also happening to ocean fish stocks. Overfishing has almost eliminated cod from the Atlantic Ocean and the southern bluefin tuna from the South Pacific Ocean. Many other species of fish are on the edge of extinction in the wild and are now available only from fish farms.

## The End of the Great Moderation
### A Credit Crunch

Flush with funds, and offering record low interest rates, banks went on a lending spree to home buyers. Rapidly rising home prices made home owners feel well off and they were happy to borrow and spend. Home loans were bundled into securities that were sold and resold to banks around the world.

In 2006, interest rates began to rise, the rate of rise in home prices slowed, and borrowers defaulted on their loans. What started as a trickle became a flood. By mid-2007, banks took losses that totaled billions of dollars as more people defaulted.

Global credit markets stopped working, and people began to fear a prolonged slowdown in economic activity. Some even feared the return of the economic trauma of the *Great Depression* of the 1930s when more than 20 percent of the U.S. labor force was unemployed. The Federal Reserve, determined to avoid a catastrophe, started lending on a very large scale to the troubled banks.

## Review Quiz

1 Describe the broad facts about *what*, *how*, and *for whom* goods and services are produced.
2 Use headlines from the recent news to illustrate the potential for conflict between self-interest and the social interest.

Work Study Plan 1.2 and get instant feedback.

We've looked at five topics that illustrate the big question: How can choices made in the pursuit of self-interest also promote the social interest? While working through this book, you will encounter the principles that help economists figure out when the social interest is being served, when it is not, and what might be done when the social interest is not being served?

## The Economic Way of Thinking

The questions that economics tries to answer tell us about the *scope of economics.* But they don't tell us how economists *think* about these questions and go about seeking answers to them.

You're now going to begin to see how economists approach economic questions. We'll look at the ideas that define the *economic way of thinking.* This way of thinking needs practice, but it is powerful, and as you become more familiar with it, you'll begin to see the world around you with a new and sharper focus.

### Choices and Tradeoffs

Because we face scarcity, we must make choices. And when we make a choice, we select from the available alternatives. For example, you can spend Saturday night studying for your next economics test and having fun with your friends, but you can't do both of these activities at the same time. You must choose how much time to devote to each. Whatever choice you make, you could have chosen something else.

You can think about your choice as a tradeoff. A **tradeoff** is an exchange—giving up one thing to get something else. When you choose how to spend your Saturday night, you face a tradeoff between studying and hanging out with your friends.

**Guns Versus Butter** The classic tradeoff is between guns and butter. "Guns" and "butter" stand for any pair of goods. They might actually be guns and butter. Or they might be broader categories such as national defense and food. Or they might be any pair of specific goods or services such as cola and pizza, baseball bats and tennis rackets, colleges and hospitals, realtor services and career counseling.

Regardless of the specific objects that guns and butter represent, the guns-versus-butter tradeoff captures a hard fact of life: If we want more of one thing, we must give up something else to get it. To get more "guns" we must give up some "butter."

The idea of a tradeoff is central to economics. We'll look at some examples, beginning with the big questions: What, How, and For Whom goods and services are produced? We can view each of these questions in terms of tradeoffs.

### *What, How,* and *For Whom* Tradeoffs

The questions what, how, and for whom goods and services are produced all involve tradeoffs that are similar to that between guns and butter.

***What* Tradeoffs** What goods and services are produced depends on choices made by each one of us, by our government, and by the businesses that produce the things we buy. Each of these choices involves a tradeoff.

Each one of us faces a tradeoff when we choose how to spend our income. You go to the movies this week, but you forgo a few cups of coffee to buy the ticket. You trade off coffee for a movie.

The federal government faces a tradeoff when it chooses how to spend our tax dollars. Congress votes for more national defense but cuts back on educational programs. Congress trades off education for national defense.

Businesses face a tradeoff when they decide what to produce. Nike hires Tiger Woods and allocates resources to designing and marketing a new golf ball but cuts back on its development of a new running shoe. Nike trades off running shoes for golf balls.

***How* Tradeoffs** How businesses produce the goods and services we buy depends on their choices. These choices involve tradeoffs. For example, when Krispy Kreme opens a new store with an automated production line and closes one with a traditional kitchen, it trades off labor for capital. When American Airlines replaces check-in agents with self check-in kiosks, it also trades off labor for capital.

***For Whom* Tradeoffs** For whom goods and services are produced depends on the distribution of buying power. Buying power can be redistributed—transferred from one person to another—in three ways: by voluntary payments, by theft, or through taxes and benefits organized by government. Redistribution brings tradeoffs.

Each of us faces a tradeoff when we choose how much to contribute to the United Nations' famine relief fund. You donate $50 and cut your spending. You trade off your own spending for a small increase in economic equality. We also face a tradeoff when we vote to increase the resources for catching thieves and enforcing the law. We trade off goods and services for an increase in the security of our property.

We also face a *for whom* tradeoff when we vote for taxes and social programs that redistribute buying power from the rich to the poor. These redistribution programs confront society with what has been called the **big tradeoff**—the tradeoff between equality and efficiency. Taxing the rich and making transfers to the poor bring greater economic equality. But taxing productive activities such as running a business, working hard, and developing a more productive technology discourages these activities. So taxing productive activities means producing less. A more equal distribution means there is less to share.

Think of the problem of how to share a pie that everyone contributes to baking. If each person receives a share of the pie that is proportional to her or his effort, everyone will work hard and the pie will be as large as possible. But if the pie is shared equally, regardless of contribution, some talented bakers will slack off and the pie will shrink. The big tradeoff is one between the size of the pie and how equally it is shared. We trade off some pie for increased equality.

## Choices Bring Change

What, how, and for whom goods and services are produced changes over time. The quantity and range of goods and services available today is much greater than it was a generation ago. But the quality of economic life (and its rate of improvement) doesn't depend purely on nature and on luck. It depends on many of the choices made by each one of us, by governments, and by businesses. These choices also involve tradeoffs.

One choice is that of how much of our income to consume and how much to save. Our saving can be channeled through the financial system to finance businesses and to pay for new capital that increases production. The more we save, the more financial capital is available for businesses to use to buy physical capital, so the more goods and services we can produce in the future. When you decide to save an extra $1,000 and forgo a vacation, you trade off the vacation for a higher future income. If everyone saves an extra $1,000 and businesses buy more equipment that increases production, future consumption per person rises. As a society, we trade off current consumption for economic growth and higher future consumption.

A second choice is how much effort to devote to education and training. By becoming better educated and more highly skilled, we become more productive and are able to produce more goods and services. When you decide to remain in school for another two years to complete a professional degree and forgo a huge chunk of leisure time, you trade off leisure today for a higher future income. If everyone becomes better educated, production increases and income per person rises. As a society, we trade off current consumption and leisure time for economic growth and higher future consumption.

A third choice is how much effort to devote to research and the development of new products and production methods. Ford Motor Company can hire people either to design a new robotic assembly line or to operate the existing plant and produce cars. The robotic plant brings greater productivity in the future but means smaller current production—a tradeoff of current production for greater future production.

Seeing choices as tradeoffs emphasizes the idea that to get something, we must give up something. What we give up is the cost of what we get. Economists call this cost the *opportunity cost.*

## Opportunity Cost

"There's no such thing as a free lunch" expresses the central idea of economics: Every choice has a cost. The **opportunity cost** of something is the highest-valued alternative that we must give up to get it.

For example, you face an opportunity cost of being in school. That opportunity cost is the highest-valued alternative that you would do if you were not in school. If you quit school and take a job at McDonald's, you earn enough to go to ball games and movies and spend lots of free time with your friends. If you remain in school, you can't afford these things. You will be able to buy these things when you graduate and get a job, and that is one of the payoffs from being in school. But for now, when you've bought your books, you have nothing left for games and movies. Working on assignments leaves even less time for hanging out with your friends. Giving up games, movies, and free time is part of the opportunity cost of being in school.

All the *what, how,* and *for whom* tradeoffs involve opportunity cost. The opportunity cost of some guns is the butter forgone; the opportunity cost of a movie ticket is the number of cups of coffee forgone.

And the choices that bring change also involve opportunity cost. The opportunity cost of more goods and services in the future is less consumption today.

## Choosing at the Margin

You can allocate the next hour between studying and instant messaging your friends. But the choice is not all or nothing. You must decide how many minutes to allocate to each activity. To make this decision, you compare the benefit of a little bit more study time with its cost—you make your choice at the **margin**.

The benefit that arises from an increase in an activity is called **marginal benefit**. For example, suppose that you're spending four nights a week studying and your grade point average (GPA) is 3.0. You decide that you want a higher GPA and decide to study an extra night each week. Your GPA rises to 3.5. The marginal benefit from studying for one extra night a week is the 0.5 increase in your GPA. It is *not* the 3.5. You already have a 3.0 from studying for four nights a week, so we don't count this benefit as resulting from the decision you are now making.

The cost of an increase in an activity is called **marginal cost**. For you, the marginal cost of increasing your study time by one night a week is the cost of the additional night not spent with your friends (if that is your best alternative use of the time). It does not include the cost of the four nights you are already studying.

To make your decision, you compare the marginal benefit from an extra night of studying with its marginal cost. If the marginal benefit exceeds the marginal cost, you study the extra night. If the marginal cost exceeds the marginal benefit, you do not study the extra night.

By evaluating marginal benefits and marginal costs and choosing only those actions that bring greater benefit than cost, we use our scarce resources in the way that makes us as well off as possible.

## Responding to Incentives

When we make choices we respond to incentives. A change in marginal cost or a change in marginal benefit changes the incentives that we face and leads us to change our choice.

For example, suppose your economics instructor gives you a set of problems and tells you that all the problems will be on the next test. The marginal benefit from working these problems is large, so you diligently work them all. In contrast, if your math instructor gives you a set of problems and tells you that none of the problems will be on the next test, the marginal benefit from working these problems is lower, so you skip most of them.

The central idea of economics is that we can predict how choices will change by looking at changes in incentives. More of an activity is undertaken when its marginal cost falls or its marginal benefit rises; less of an activity is undertaken when its marginal cost rises or its marginal benefit falls.

Incentives are also the key to reconciling self-interest and social interest. When our choices are *not* in the social interest, it is because of the incentives we face. One of the challenges for economists is to figure out the incentive systems that result in self-interested choices also being in the social interest.

## Human Nature, Incentives, and Institutions

Economists take human nature as given and view people as acting in their self-interest. All people—consumers, producers, politicians, and public servants—pursue their self-interest.

Self-interested actions are not necessarily *selfish* actions. You might decide to use your resources in ways that bring pleasure to others as well as to yourself. But a self-interested act gets the most value for *you* based on *your* view about value.

If human nature is given and if people act in their self-interest, how can we take care of the social interest? Economists answer this question by emphasizing the crucial role that institutions play in influencing the incentives that people face as they pursue their self-interest.

A system of laws that protect private property and markets that enable voluntary exchange are the fundamental institutions. You will learn as you progress with your study of economics that where these institutions exist, self-interest can indeed promote the social interest.

### Review Quiz

1. Provide three everyday examples of tradeoffs and describe the opportunity cost involved in each.
2. Provide three everyday examples to illustrate what we mean by choosing at the margin.
3. How do economists predict changes in choices?
4. What do economists say about the role of institutions in promoting the social interest?

Work Study Plan 1.3 and get instant feedback.

## Economics as Social Science and Policy Tool

Economics is both a science and a set of tools that can be used to make policy decisions.

### Economics as Social Science

As social scientists, economists seek to discover how the economic world works. In pursuit of this goal, like all scientists, they distinguish between two types of statements: positive and normative.

**Positive Statements** *Positive* statements are about what is. They say what is currently believed about the way the world operates. A positive statement might be right or wrong, but we can test a positive statement by checking it against the facts. "Our planet is warming because of the amount of coal that we're burning" is a positive statement. "A rise in the minimum wage will bring more teenage unemployment" is another positive statement. Each statement might be right or wrong, and it can be tested.

A central task of economists is to test positive statements about how the economic world works and to weed out those that are wrong. Economics first got off the ground in the late 1700s, so economics is a young subject compared with, for example, math and physics, and much remains to be discovered.

**Normative Statements** *Normative* statements are statements about what ought to be. These statements depend on values and cannot be tested. The statement "We ought to cut back on our use of coal" is a normative statement. "The minimum wage should not be increased" is another normative statement. You may agree or disagree with either of these statements, but you can't test them. They express an opinion, but they don't assert a fact that can be checked. They are not economics.

**Unscrambling Cause and Effect** Economists are especially interested in positive statements about cause and effect. Are computers getting cheaper because people are buying them in greater quantities? Or are people buying computers in greater quantities because they are getting cheaper? Or is some third factor causing both the price of a computer to fall and the quantity of computers to increase?

To answer questions such as these, economists create and test economic models. An **economic model** is a description of some aspect of the economic world that includes only those features that are needed for the purpose at hand. For example, an economic model of a cell-phone network might include features such as the prices of calls, the number of cell-phone users, and the volume of calls. But the model would ignore such details as cell-phone colors and ringtones.

A model is tested by comparing its predictions with the facts. But testing an economic model is difficult because we observe the outcomes of the simultaneous operation of many factors. To cope with this problem, economists use natural experiments, statistical investigations, and economic experiments.

**Natural Experiment** A natural experiment is a situation that arises in the ordinary course of economic life in which the one factor of interest is different and other things are equal (or similar). For example, Canada has higher unemployment benefits than the United States, but the people in the two nations are similar. So to study the effect of unemployment benefits on the unemployment rate, economists might compare the United States with Canada.

**Statistical Investigation** A statistical investigation looks for correlation—a tendency for the values of two variables to move together (either in the same direction or in opposite directions) in a predictable and related way. For example, cigarette smoking and lung cancer are correlated. Sometimes a correlation shows a causal influence of one variable on the other. For example, smoking causes lung cancer. But sometimes the direction of causation is hard to determine.

Steven Levitt, the author of *Freakonomics,* whom you can meet on pp. 224–226, is a master in the use of a combination of the natural experiment and statistical investigation to unscramble cause and effect. He has used the tools of economics to investigate the effects of good parenting on education (not very strong), to explain why drug dealers live with their mothers (because they don't earn enough to live independently), and (controversially) the effects of abortion law on crime.

**Economic Experiment** An economic experiment puts people in a decision-making situation and varies the influence of one factor at a time to discover how they respond.

## Economics as Policy Tool

Economics is useful. It is a toolkit for making decisions. And you don't need to be a fully-fledged economist to think like one and to use the insights of economics as a policy tool.

Economics provides a way of approaching problems in all aspects of our lives. Here, we'll focus on the three broad areas of:

- Personal economic policy
- Business economic policy
- Government economic policy

**Personal Economic Policy** Should you take out a student loan? Should you get a weekend job? Should you buy a used car or a new one? Should you rent an apartment or take out a loan and buy a condominium? Should you pay off your credit card balance or make just the minimum payment? How should you allocate your time between study, working for a wage, caring for family members, and having fun? How should you allocate your time between studying economics and your other subjects? Should you quit school after getting a bachelor's degree or should you go for a master's or a professional qualification?

All these questions involve a marginal benefit and a marginal cost. And although some of the numbers might be hard to pin down, you will make more solid decisions if you approach these questions with the tools of economics.

**Business Economic Policy** Should Sony make only flat panel televisions and stop making conventional ones? Should Texaco get more oil and gas from the Gulf of Mexico or from Alaska? Should Palm outsource its online customer services to India or run the operation from California? Should Marvel Studios produce Spider-Man 4, a sequel to Spider-Man 3? Can Microsoft compete with Google in the search engine business? Can eBay compete with the surge of new Internet auction services? Is Jason Giambi really worth $23,400,000 to the New York Yankees?

Like personal economic questions, these business questions involve the evaluation of a marginal benefit and a marginal cost. Some of the questions require a broader investigation of the interactions of individuals and firms. But again, by approaching these questions with the tools of economics and by hiring economists as advisers, businesses can make better decisions.

**Government Economic Policy** How can California balance its budget? Should the federal government cut taxes or raise them? How can the tax system be simplified? Should people be permitted to invest their Social Security money in stocks that they pick themselves? Should Medicaid and Medicare be extended to the entire population? Should there be a special tax to penalize corporations that send jobs overseas? Should cheap foreign imports of furniture and textiles be limited? Should the farms that grow tomatoes and sugar beets receive a subsidy? Should water be transported from Washington and Oregon to California?

These government policy questions call for decisions that involve the evaluation of a marginal benefit and a marginal cost and an investigation of the interactions of individuals and businesses. Yet again, by approaching these questions with the tools of economics, governments make better decisions.

Notice that all the policy questions we've just posed involve a blend of the positive and the normative. Economics can't help with the normative part—the objective. But for a given objective, economics provides a method of evaluating alternative solutions. That method is to evaluate the marginal benefits and marginal costs and to find the solution that brings the greatest available gain.

### Review Quiz

1. What is the distinction between a positive statement and a normative statement? Provide an example (different from those in the chapter) of each type of statement.
2. What is a model? Can you think of a model that you might use (probably without thinking of it as a model) in your everyday life?
3. What are the three ways in which economists try to disentangle cause and effect?
4. How is economics used as a policy tool?
5. What is the role of marginal analysis in the use of economics as a policy tool?

Work Study Plan 1.4 and get instant feedback.

# SUMMARY

## Key Points

### Definition of Economics (p. 2)

- All economic questions arise from scarcity—from the fact that wants exceed the resources available to satisfy them.
- Economics is the social science that studies the choices that people make as they cope with scarcity.
- The subject divides into microeconomics and macroeconomics.

### Two Big Economic Questions (pp. 3–7)

- Two big questions summarize the scope of economics:
  1. How do choices end up determining *what*, *how*, and *for whom* goods and services are produced?
  2. When do choices made in the pursuit of *self-interest* also promote the *social interest*?

### The Economic Way of Thinking (pp. 8–10)

- Every choice is a tradeoff—exchanging more of something for less of something else.
- The classic guns-versus-butter tradeoff represents all tradeoffs.
- All economic questions involve tradeoffs.
- The big social tradeoff is that between equality and efficiency.
- The highest-valued alternative forgone is the opportunity cost of what is chosen.
- Choices are made at the margin and respond to incentives.

### Economics as Social Science and Policy Tool (pp. 11–12)

- Economists distinguish between positive statements—what is—and normative statements—what ought to be.
- To explain the economic world, economists create and test economic models.
- Economics is used in personal, business, and government economic policy decisions.
- The main policy tool is the evaluation and comparison of marginal cost and marginal benefit.

## Key Terms

Big tradeoff, 9
Capital, 4
Economic model, 11
Economics, 2
Entrepreneurship, 4
Factors of production, 3
Goods and services, 3
Human capital, 3
Incentive, 2
Interest, 4
Labor, 3
Land, 3
Macroeconomics, 2
Margin, 10
Marginal benefit, 10
Marginal cost, 10
Microeconomics, 2
Opportunity cost, 9
Profit, 4
Rent, 4
Scarcity, 2
Self-interest, 5
Social interest, 5
Tradeoff, 8
Wages, 4

## PROBLEMS and APPLICATIONS

myeconlab Work problems 1–6 in Chapter 1 Study Plan and get instant feedback.
Work problems 7–12 as Homework, a Quiz, or a Test if assigned by your instructor.

1. Apple Computer Inc. decides to make iTunes freely available in unlimited quantities.
   a. How does Apple's decision change the opportunity cost of a download?
   b. Does Apple's decision change the incentives that people face?
   c. Is Apple's decision an example of a microeconomic or a macroeconomic issue?
2. Which of the following pairs does not match:
   a. Labor and wages?
   b. Land and rent?
   c. Entrepreneurship and profit?
   d. Capital and profit?
3. Explain how the following news headlines concern self-interest and the social interest:
   a. Wal-Mart Expands in Europe
   b. McDonald's Moves into Salads
   c. Food Must Be Labeled with Nutrition Information
4. The night before an economics test, you decide to go to the movies instead of staying home and working your MyEconLab Study Plan. You get 50 percent on your test compared with the 70 percent that you normally score.
   a. Did you face a tradeoff?
   b. What was the opportunity cost of your evening at the movies?
5. Which of the following statements is positive, which is normative, and which can be tested?
   a. The U.S. government should cut its imports.
   b. China is the United States' largest trading partner.
   c. If the price of antiretroviral drugs increases, HIV/AIDS sufferers will decrease their consumption of the drugs.
6. As London prepares to host the 2012 Olympic Games, concern about the cost of the event increases. An example:

   **Costs Soar for London Olympics**

   The regeneration of East London is set to add extra £1.5 billion to taxpayers' bill.

   *The Times*, London, July 6, 2006

   Is the cost of regenerating East London an opportunity cost of hosting the 2012 Olympic Games? Explain why or why not.
7. Before starring as Tony Stark in *Iron Man*, Robert Downey Jr. had played in 45 movies that had average first-weekend box office revenues of a bit less than $5 million. *Iron Man* grossed $102 million on its opening weekend.
   a. How do you expect the success of *Iron Man* to influence the opportunity cost of hiring Robert Downey Jr.?
   b. How have the incentives for a movie producer to hire Robert Downey Jr. changed?
8. How would you classify a movie star as a factor of production?
9. How does the creation of a successful movie influence what, how, and for whom goods and services are produced?
10. How does the creation of a successful movie illustrate self-interested choices that are also in the social interest?
11. Look at today's *Wall Street Journal.*
    a. What is the top economic news story? With which of the big questions does it deal? (It must deal with at least one of them and might deal with more than one.)
    b. What tradeoffs does the news item discuss or imply?
    c. Write a brief summary of the news item using the economic vocabulary that you have learned in this chapter and as many as possible of the key terms listed on p. 13.
12. Use the link in MyEconLab (Textbook Resources, Chapter 1) to visit *Resources for Economists on the Internet.* This Web site is a good place from which to search for economic information on the Internet.

    Click on "Blogs, Commentaries, and Podcasts," and then click on the Becker-Posner Blog.
    a. Read the latest blog by these two outstanding economists.
    b. As you read this blog, think about what it is saying about the "what," "how," and "for whom" questions.
    c. As you read this blog, think about what it is saying about self-interest and the social interest.

# Graphs in Economics

**After studying this appendix, you will be able to:**

- Make and interpret a time-series graph, a cross-section graph, and a scatter diagram
- Distinguish between linear and nonlinear relationships and between relationships that have a maximum and a minimum
- Define and calculate the slope of a line
- Graph relationships among more than two variables

## Graphing Data

A graph represents a quantity as a distance on a line. In Fig. A1.1, a distance on the horizontal line represents temperature, measured in degrees Fahrenheit. A movement from left to right shows an increase in temperature. The point 0 represents zero degrees Fahrenheit. To the right of 0, the temperature is positive. To the left of 0 (as indicated by the minus sign), the temperature is negative. A distance on the vertical line represents height, measured in thousands of feet. The point 0 represents sea level. Points above 0 represent feet above sea level. Points below 0 (indicated by a minus sign) represent feet below sea level.

By setting two scales perpendicular to each other, as in Fig. A1.1, we can visualize the relationship between two variables. The scale lines are called *axes*. The vertical line is the *y*-axis, and the horizontal line is the *x*-axis. Each axis has a zero point, which is shared by the two axes and called the *origin*.

We need two bits of information to make a two-variable graph: the value of the *x* variable and the value of the *y* variable. For example, off the coast of Alaska, the temperature is 32 degrees—the value of *x*. A fishing boat is located at 0 feet above sea level—the value of *y*. These two bits of information appear as point *A* in Fig. A1.1. A climber at the top of Mount McKinley on a cold day is 20,320 feet above sea level in a zero-degree gale. These two pieces of information appear as point *B*. On a warmer day, a climber might be at the peak of Mt. McKinley when the temperature is 32 degrees, at point *C*.

**FIGURE A1.1** Making a Graph

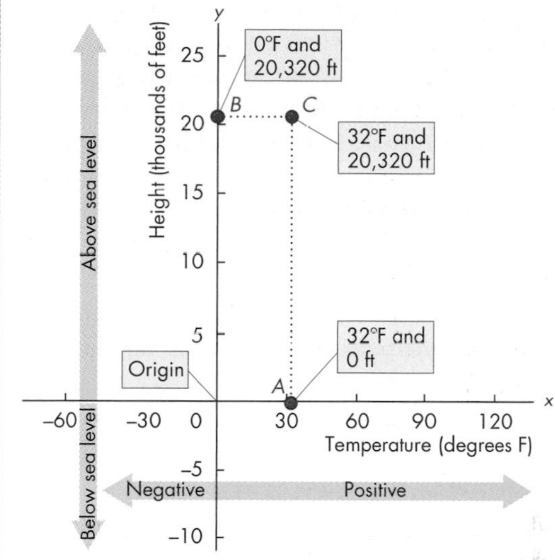


Graphs have axes that measure quantities as distances. Here, the horizontal axis (*x*-axis) measures temperature, and the vertical axis (*y*-axis) measures height. Point *A* represents a fishing boat at sea level (0 on the *y*-axis) on a day when the temperature is 32°F. Point *B* represents a climber at the top of Mt. McKinley, 20,320 feet above sea level at a temperature of 0°F. Point *C* represents a climber at the top of Mt. McKinley, 20,320 feet above sea level at a temperature of 32°F.

myeconlab animation

We can draw two lines, called *coordinates*, from point *C*. One, called the *y*-coordinate, runs from *C* to the horizontal axis. Its length is the same as the value marked off on the *y*-axis. The other, called the *x*-coordinate, runs from *C* to the vertical axis. Its length is the same as the value marked off on the *x*-axis. We describe a point on a graph by the values of its *x*-coordinate and its *y*-coordinate.

Graphs like that in Fig. A1.1 can show any type of quantitative data on two variables. Economists use three types of graphs based on the principles in Fig. A1.1 to reveal and describe the relationships among variables. They are

- Time-series graphs
- Cross-section graphs
- Scatter diagrams

## Time-Series Graphs

A **time-series graph** measures time (for example, months or years) on the *x*-axis and the variable or variables in which we are interested on the *y*-axis. Figure A1.2 is an example of a time-series graph. It provides some information about the price of gasoline. In this figure, we measure time in years starting in 1973. We measure the price of gasoline (the variable that we are interested in) on the *y*-axis.

The point of a time-series graph is to enable us to visualize how a variable has changed over time and how its value in one period relates to its value in another period.

A time-series graph conveys an enormous amount of information quickly and easily, as this example illustrates. It shows

- The *level* of the price of gasoline—when it is *high* and *low*. When the line is a long way from the *x*-axis, the price is high, as it was, for example, in 1981. When the line is close to the *x*-axis, the price is low, as it was, for example, in 1998.
- How the price *changes*—whether it *rises* or *falls*. When the line slopes upward, as in 1979, the price is rising. When the line slopes downward, as in 1986, the price is falling.
- The *speed* with which the price changes—whether it rises or falls *quickly* or *slowly*. If the line is very steep, then the price rises or falls quickly. If the line is not steep, the price rises or falls slowly. For example, the price rose quickly between 1978 and 1980 and slowly between 1994 and 1996. The price fell quickly between 1985 and 1986 and slowly between 1990 and 1994.

A time-series graph also reveals whether there is a **trend**—a general tendency for a variable to move in one direction. A trend might be upward or downward. In Fig. A1.2, the price of gasoline had a general tendency to fall during the 1980s and 1990s. That is, although the price rose and fell, the general tendency was for it to fall—the price had a downward trend. During the 2000s, the trend has been upward.

A time-series graph also helps us to detect fluctuations in a variable around its trend. You can see some peaks and troughs in the price of gasoline in Fig. A1.2.

Finally, a time-series graph also lets us quickly compare the variable in different periods. Figure A1.2 shows that the 1970s and 1980s were different from

**FIGURE A1.2** A Time-Series Graph

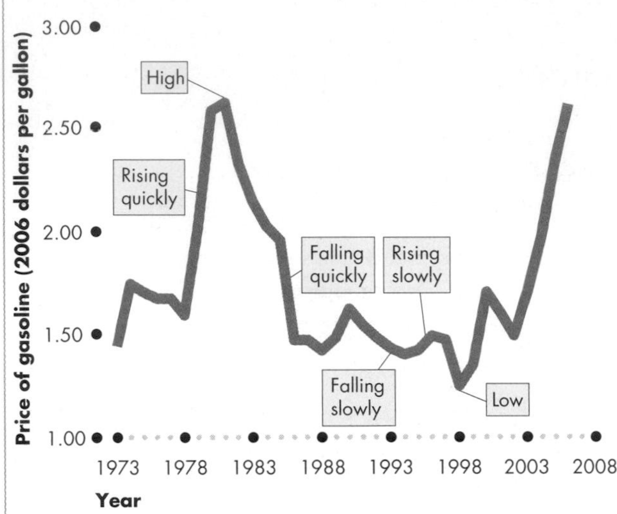


A time-series graph plots the level of a variable on the *y*-axis against time (day, week, month, or year) on the *x*-axis. This graph shows the price of gasoline (in 2006 dollars per gallon) each year from 1973 to 2006. It shows us when the price of gasoline was *high* and when it was *low*, when the price *increased* and when it *decreased*, and when the price changed *quickly* and when it changed *slowly*.

myeconlab animation

the 1990s. The price of gasoline fluctuated more during the 1970s and 1980s than it did in the 1990s.

You can see that a time-series graph conveys a wealth of information, and it does so in much less space than we have used to describe only some of its features. But you do have to "read" the graph to obtain all this information.

## Cross-Section Graphs

A **cross-section graph** shows the values of an economic variable for different groups or categories at a point in time. Figure A1.3, called a *bar chart*, is an example of a cross-section graph.

The bar chart in Fig. A1.3 shows 10 leisure pursuits and the percentage of the U. S. population that participated in them during 2005. The length of each bar indicates the percentage of the population. This figure enables you to compare the popularity of these 10 activities. And you can do so much more quickly and clearly than by looking at a list of numbers.

**FIGURE A1.3** A Cross-Section Graph

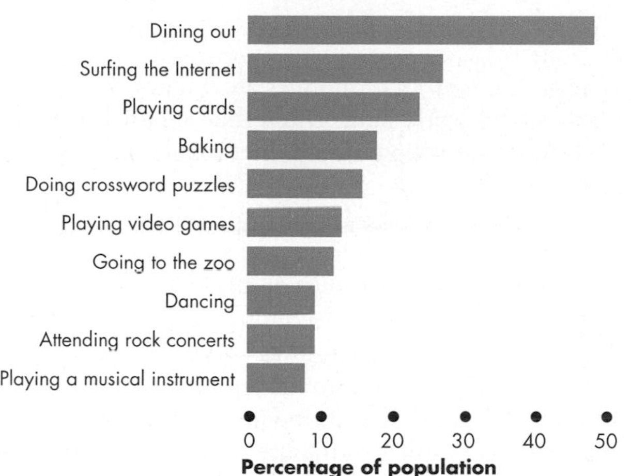


A cross-section graph shows the level of a variable across categories or groups. This bar chart shows 10 popular leisure activities and the percentage of the U.S. population that engages in each of them.

## Scatter Diagrams

A **scatter diagram** plots the value of one variable against the value of another variable. Such a graph reveals whether a relationship exists between two variables and describes their relationship. Figure A1.4(a) shows the relationship between expenditure and income. Each point shows expenditure per person and income per person in a given year from 1997 to 2007. The points are "scattered" within the graph. The point labeled *A* tells us that in 2000, income per person was $25,472 and expenditure per person was $23,862. The dots in this graph form a pattern, which reveals that as income increases, expenditure increases.

Figure A1.4(b) shows the relationship between the number of computers sold and the price of a computer. This graph shows that as the price of a computer falls, the number of computers sold increases.

Figure A1.4(c) shows a scatter diagram of inflation and unemployment in the United States. Here, the dots show no clear relationship between these two variables.

**FIGURE A1.4** Scatter Diagrams

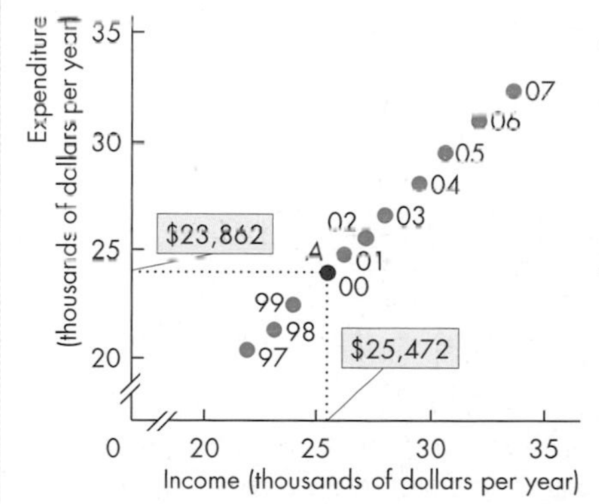


**(a) Expenditure and income**

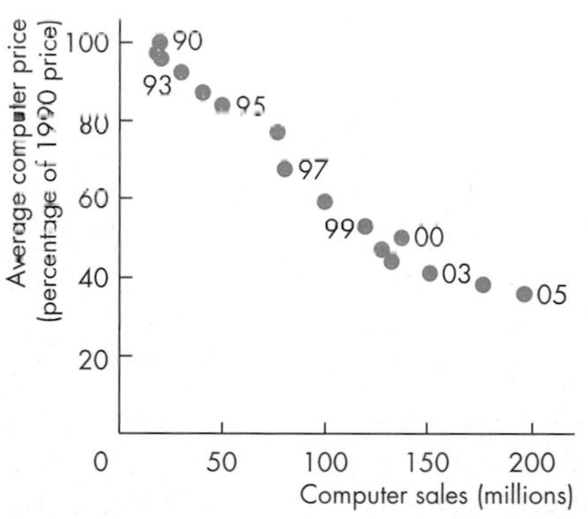


**(b) Computer sales and prices**

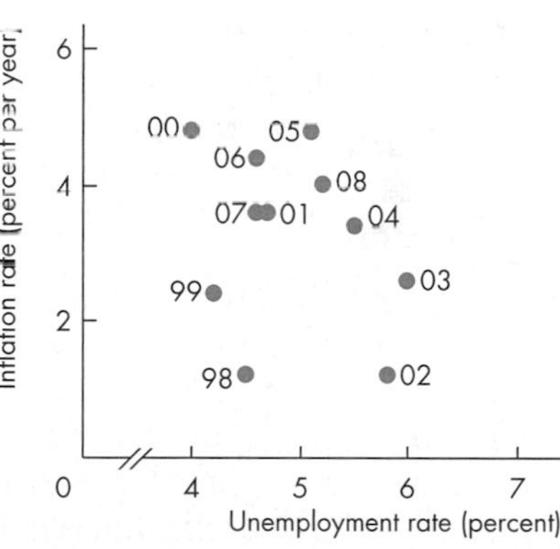


**(c) Unemployment and inflation**

A scatter diagram reveals the relationship between two variables. Part (a) shows the relationship between expenditure and income. Each point shows the values of the two variables in a specific year. For example, point *A* shows that in 2000, average income was $25,472 and average expenditure was $23,862. The pattern formed by the points shows that as income increases, expenditure increases.

Part (b) shows the relationship between the price of a computer and the number of computers sold from 1990 to 2005. This graph shows that as the price of a computer falls, the number of computers sold increases.

Part (c) shows a scatter diagram of the U.S. inflation rate and the unemployment rate from 1998 to 2008. This graph shows that inflation and unemployment are not closely related.

myeconlab animation

**Breaks in the Axes** Two of the graphs you've just looked at, Fig. A1.4(a) and Fig. A1.4(c), have breaks in their axes, as shown by the small gaps. The breaks indicate that there are jumps from the origin, 0, to the first values recorded.

In Fig. A1.4(a), the breaks are used because the lowest value of expenditure exceeds $20,000 and the lowest value of income exceeds $20,000. With no breaks in the axes, there would be a lot of empty space, all the points would be crowded into the top right corner, and we would not be able to see whether a relationship exists between these two variables. By breaking the axes, we are able to bring the relationship into view.

Putting a break in one or both axes is like using a zoom lens to bring the relationship into the center of the graph and magnify it so that the relationship fills the graph.

**Misleading Graphs** Breaks can be used to highlight a relationship, but they can also be used to mislead—to make a graph that lies. The most common way of making a graph lie is to use axis breaks and to either stretch or compress a scale. For example, suppose that in Fig. A1.4(a), the *y*-axis that measures expenditure ran from zero to $35,000 while the *x*-axis was the same as the one shown. The graph would now create the impression that despite a huge increase in income, expenditure had barely changed.

To avoid being misled, it is a good idea to get into the habit of always looking closely at the values and the labels on the axes of a graph before you start to interpret it.

**Correlation and Causation** A scatter diagram that shows a clear relationship between two variables, such as Fig. A1.4(a) or Fig. A1.4(b), tells us that the two variables have a high correlation. When a high correlation is present, we can predict the value of one variable from the value of the other variable. But correlation does not imply causation.

Sometimes a high correlation is a coincidence, but sometimes it does arise from a causal relationship. It is likely, for example, that rising income causes rising expenditure (Fig. A1.4a) and that the falling price of a computer causes more computers to be sold (Fig. A1.4b).

You've now seen how we can use graphs in economics to show economic data and to reveal relationships. Next, we'll learn how economists use graphs to construct and display economic models.

## Graphs Used in Economic Models

The graphs used in economics are not always designed to show real-world data. Often they are used to show general relationships among the variables in an economic model.

An *economic model* is a stripped-down, simplified description of an economy or of a component of an economy such as a business or a household. It consists of statements about economic behavior that can be expressed as equations or as curves in a graph. Economists use models to explore the effects of different policies or other influences on the economy in ways that are similar to the use of model airplanes in wind tunnels and models of the climate.

You will encounter many different kinds of graphs in economic models, but there are some repeating patterns. Once you've learned to recognize these patterns, you will instantly understand the meaning of a graph. Here, we'll look at the different types of curves that are used in economic models, and we'll see some everyday examples of each type of curve. The patterns to look for in graphs are the four cases in which

- Variables move in the same direction.
- Variables move in opposite directions.
- Variables have a maximum or a minimum.
- Variables are unrelated.

Let's look at these four cases.

### Variables That Move in the Same Direction

Figure A1.5 shows graphs of the relationships between two variables that move up and down together. A relationship between two variables that move in the same direction is called a **positive relationship** or a **direct relationship**. A line that slopes upward shows such a relationship.

Figure A1.5 shows three types of relationships, one that has a straight line and two that have curved lines. But all the lines in these three graphs are called curves. Any line on a graph—no matter whether it is straight or curved—is called a *curve*.

A relationship shown by a straight line is called a **linear relationship**. Figure A1.5(a) shows a linear relationship between the number of miles traveled in

**FIGURE A1.5** Positive (Direct) Relationships

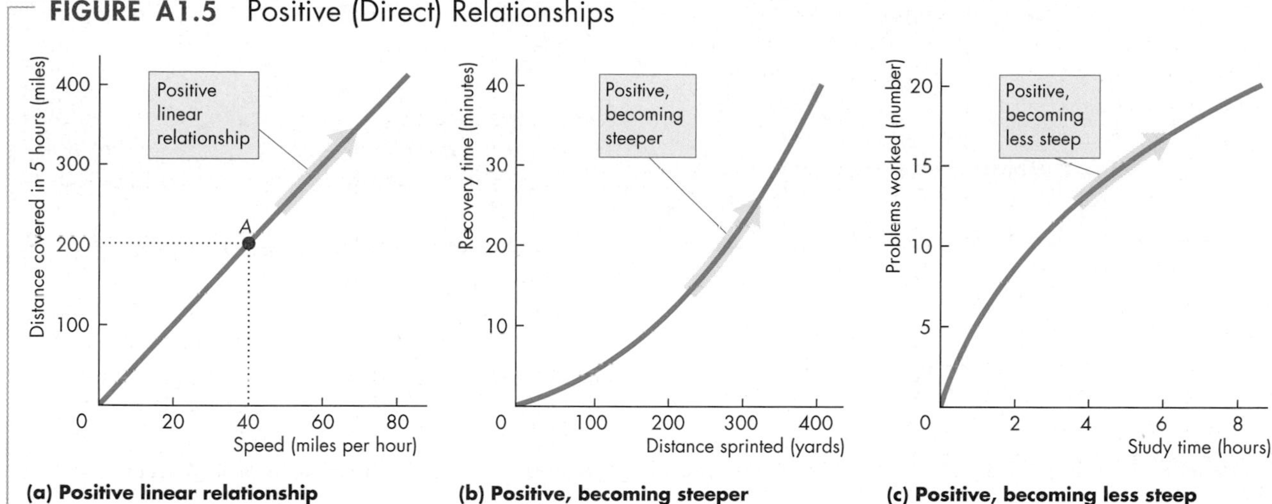


**(a) Positive linear relationship** **(b) Positive, becoming steeper** **(c) Positive, becoming less steep**

Each part of this figure shows a positive (direct) relationship between two variables. That is, as the value of the variable measured on the *x*-axis increases, so does the value of the variable measured on the *y*-axis. Part (a) shows a linear relationship—as the two variables increase together, we move along a straight line. Part (b) shows a positive relationship such that as the two variables increase together, we move along a curve that becomes steeper. Part (c) shows a positive relationship such that as the two variables increase together, we move along a curve that becomes flatter.

myeconlab animation

5 hours and speed. For example, point *A* shows that we will travel 200 miles in 5 hours if our speed is 40 miles an hour. If we double our speed to 80 miles an hour, we will travel 400 miles in 5 hours.

Figure A1.5(b) shows the relationship between distance sprinted and recovery time (the time it takes the heart rate to return to its normal resting rate). This relationship is an upward-sloping one that starts out quite flat but then becomes steeper as we move along the curve away from the origin. The reason this curve slopes upward and becomes steeper is because the additional recovery time needed from sprinting an additional 100 yards increases. It takes less than 5 minutes to recover from sprinting 100 yards but more than 10 minutes to recover from sprinting 200 yards.

Figure A1.5(c) shows the relationship between the number of problems worked by a student and the amount of study time. This relationship is an upward-sloping one that starts out quite steep and becomes flatter as we move along the curve away from the origin. Study time becomes less productive as the student spends more hours studying and becomes more tired.

## Variables That Move in Opposite Directions

Figure A1.6 shows relationships between things that move in opposite directions. A relationship between variables that move in opposite directions is called a **negative relationship** or an **inverse relationship.**

Figure A1.6(a) shows the relationship between the hours spent playing squash and the hours spent playing tennis when the total number of hours available is 5. One extra hour spent playing tennis means one hour less playing squash and vice versa. This relationship is negative and linear.

Figure A1.6(b) shows the relationship between the cost per mile traveled and the length of a journey. The longer the journey, the lower is the cost per mile. But as the journey length increases, even though the cost per mile decreases, the fall in the cost is smaller the longer the journey. This feature of the relationship is shown by the fact that the curve slopes downward, starting out steep at a short journey length and then becoming flatter as the journey length increases. This relationship arises because some of the costs are fixed, such as auto insurance, and the fixed costs are spread over a longer journey.

**FIGURE A1.6** Negative (Inverse) Relationships

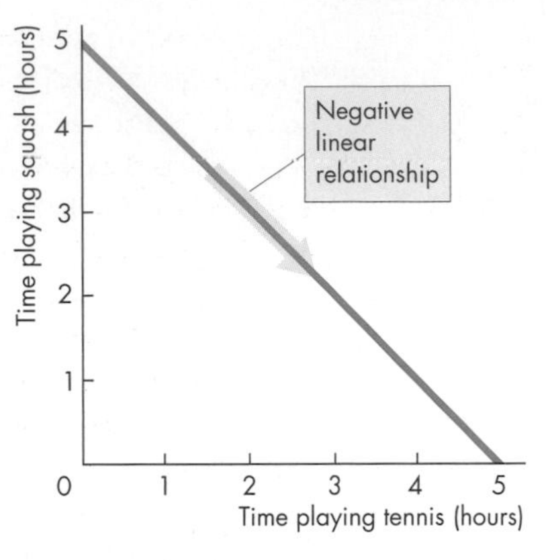


**(a) Negative linear relationship**

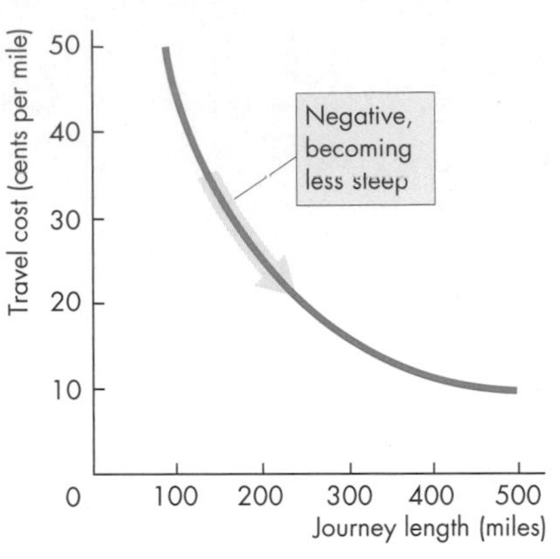


**(b) Negative, becoming less steep**

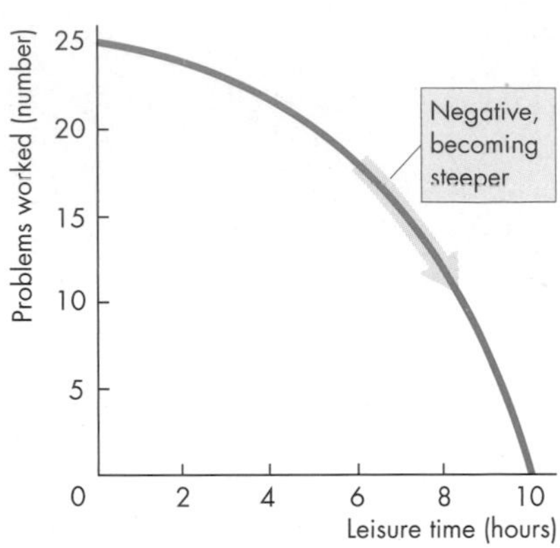


**(c) Negative, becoming steeper**

Each part of this figure shows a negative (inverse) relationship between two variables. That is, as the value of the variable measured on the *x*-axis increases, the value of the variable measured on the *y*-axis decreases. Part (a) shows a linear relationship. The total time spent playing tennis and squash is 5 hours. As the time spent playing tennis increases, the time spent playing squash decreases, and we move along a straight line. Part (b) shows a negative relationship such that as the journey length increases, the travel cost decreases as we move along a curve that becomes less steep. Part (c) shows a negative relationship such that as leisure time increases, the number of problems worked decreases as we move along a curve that becomes steeper.

Figure A1.6(c) shows the relationship between the amount of leisure time and the number of problems worked by a student. Increasing leisure time produces an increasingly large reduction in the number of problems worked. This relationship is a negative one that starts out with a gentle slope at a small number of leisure hours and becomes steeper as the number of leisure hours increases. This relationship is a different view of the idea shown in Fig. A1.5(c).

## Variables That Have a Maximum or a Minimum

Many relationships in economic models have a maximum or a minimum. For example, firms try to make the maximum possible profit and to produce at the lowest possible cost. Figure A1.7 shows relationships that have a maximum or a minimum.

Figure A1.7(a) shows the relationship between rainfall and wheat yield. When there is no rainfall, wheat will not grow, so the yield is zero. As the rainfall increases up to 10 days a month, the wheat yield increases. With 10 rainy days each month, the wheat yield reaches its maximum at 40 bushels an acre (point *A*). Rain in excess of 10 days a month starts to lower the yield of wheat. If every day is rainy, the wheat suffers from a lack of sunshine and the yield decreases to zero. This relationship is one that starts out sloping upward, reaches a maximum, and then slopes downward.

Figure A1.7(b) shows the reverse case—a relationship that begins sloping downward, falls to a minimum, and then slopes upward. Most economic costs are like this relationship. An example is the relationship between the cost per mile and speed for a car trip. At low speeds, the car is creeping in a traffic snarl-up. The number of miles per gallon is low, so the cost per mile is high. At high speeds, the car is traveling faster than its efficient speed, using a large quantity of gasoline, and again the number of miles per gallon is low and the cost per mile is high. At a speed of 55 miles an hour, the cost per mile is at its minimum (point *B*). This relationship is one that starts out sloping downward, reaches a minimum, and then slopes upward.

FIGURE A1.7 Maximum and Minimum Points

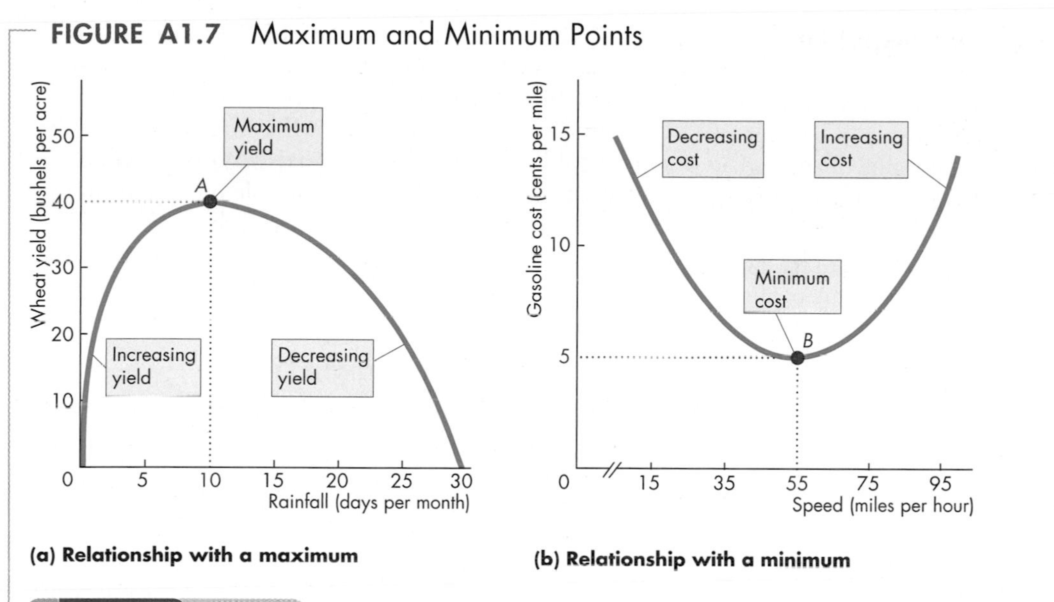

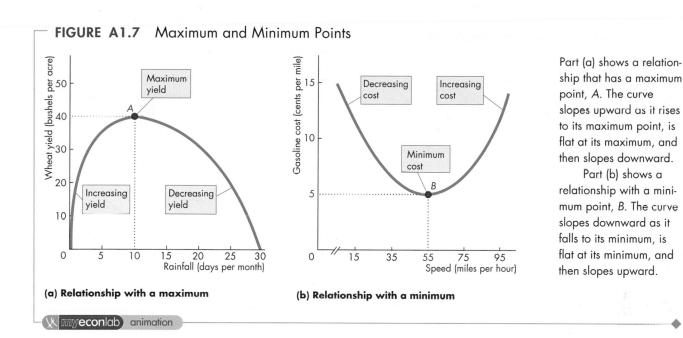

(a) Relationship with a maximum

(b) Relationship with a minimum

Part (a) shows a relationship that has a maximum point, *A*. The curve slopes upward as it rises to its maximum point, is flat at its maximum, and then slopes downward.

Part (b) shows a relationship with a minimum point, *B*. The curve slopes downward as it falls to its minimum, is flat at its minimum, and then slopes upward.

myeconlab animation

## Variables That Are Unrelated

There are many situations in which no matter what happens to the value of one variable, the other variable remains constant. Sometimes we want to show the independence between two variables in a graph, and Fig. A1.8 shows two ways of achieving this.

In describing the graphs in Fig. A1.5 through A1.7, we have talked about curves that slope upward or slope downward, and curves that become less steep or steeper. Let's spend a little time discussing exactly what we mean by slope and how we measure the slope of a curve.

FIGURE A1.8 Variables That Are Unrelated

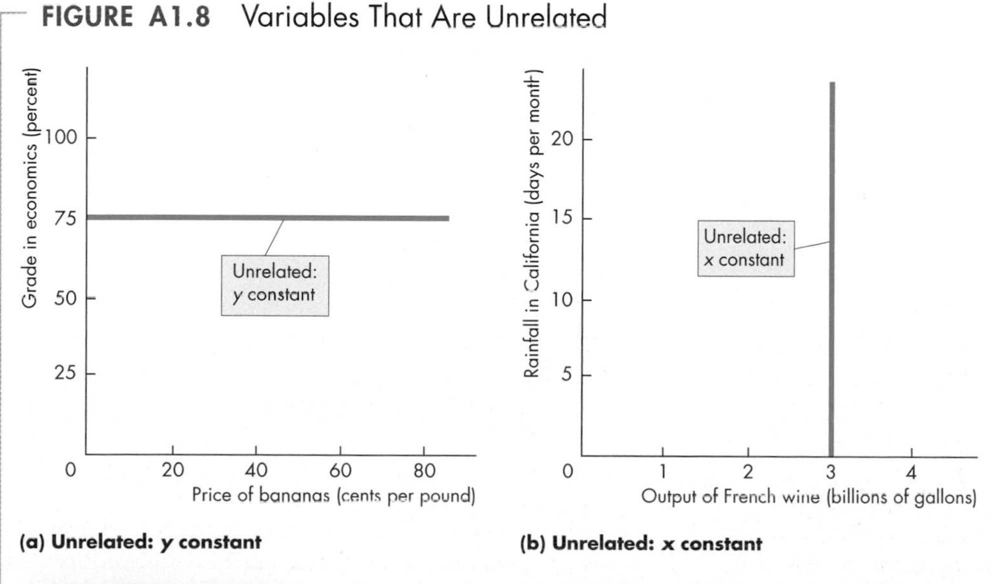


(a) Unrelated: *y* constant

(b) Unrelated: *x* constant

This figure shows how we can graph two variables that are unrelated. In part (a), a student's grade in economics is plotted at 75 percent on the *y*-axis regardless of the price of bananas on the *x*-axis. The curve is horizontal.

In part (b), the output of the vineyards of France on the *x*-axis does not vary with the rainfall in California on the *y*-axis. The curve is vertical.

myeconlab animation

## The Slope of a Relationship

We can measure the influence of one variable on another by the slope of the relationship. The **slope** of a relationship is the change in the value of the variable measured on the *y*-axis divided by the change in the value of the variable measured on the *x*-axis. We use the Greek letter Δ (*delta*) to represent "change in." Thus $\Delta y$ means the change in the value of the variable measured on the *y*-axis, and $\Delta x$ means the change in the value of the variable measured on the *x*-axis. Therefore the slope of the relationship is

$$\Delta y / \Delta x.$$

If a large change in the variable measured on the *y*-axis ($\Delta y$) is associated with a small change in the variable measured on the *x*-axis ($\Delta x$), the slope is large and the curve is steep. If a small change in the variable measured on the *y*-axis ($\Delta y$) is associated with a large change in the variable measured on the *x*-axis ($\Delta x$), the slope is small and the curve is flat.

We can make the idea of slope clearer by doing some calculations.

### The Slope of a Straight Line

The slope of a straight line is the same regardless of where on the line you calculate it. The slope of a straight line is constant. Let's calculate the slopes of the lines in Fig. A1.9. In part (a), when *x* increases

**FIGURE A1.9** The Slope of a Straight Line

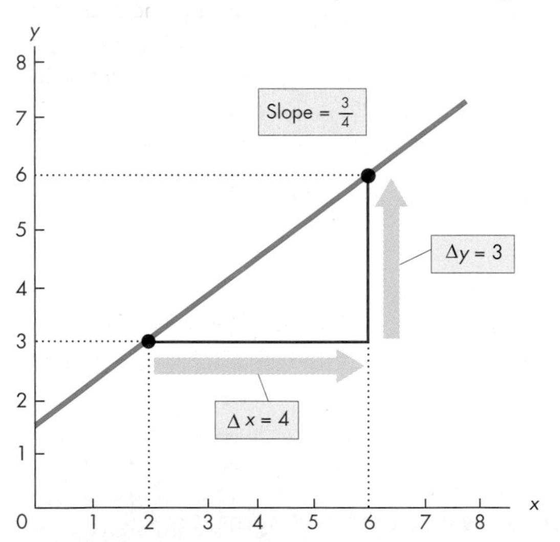


**(a) Positive slope**

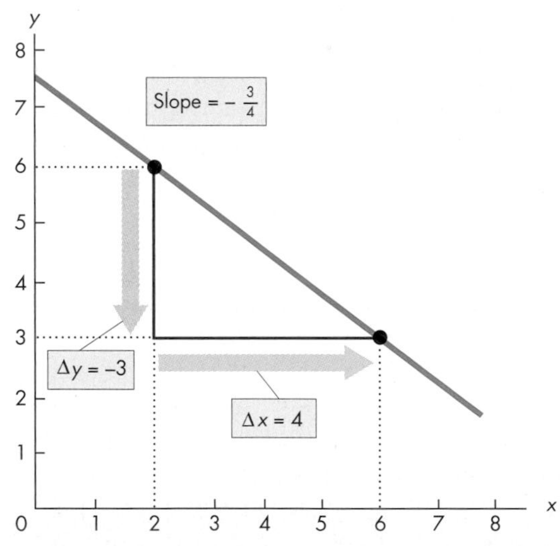


**(b) Negative slope**

To calculate the slope of a straight line, we divide the change in the value of the variable measured on the *y*-axis ($\Delta y$) by the change in the value of the variable measured on the *x*-axis ($\Delta x$) as we move along the curve.

Part (a) shows the calculation of a positive slope. When *x* increases from 2 to 6, $\Delta x$ equals 4. That change in *x* brings about an increase in *y* from 3 to 6, so $\Delta y$ equals 3. The slope ($\Delta y/\Delta x$) equals 3/4.

Part (b) shows the calculation of a negative slope. When *x* increases from 2 to 6, $\Delta x$ equals 4. That increase in *x* brings about a decrease in *y* from 6 to 3, so $\Delta y$ equals –3. The slope ($\Delta y/\Delta x$) equals –3/4.

myeconlab animation

from 2 to 6, $y$ increases from 3 to 6. The change in $x$ is +4—that is, $\Delta x$ is 4. The change in $y$ is +3—that is, $\Delta y$ is 3. The slope of that line is

$$\frac{\Delta y}{\Delta x} = \frac{3}{4}.$$

In part (b), when $x$ increases from 2 to 6, $y$ decreases from 6 to 3. The change in $y$ is *minus* 3—that is, $\Delta y$ is −3. The change in $x$ is *plus* 4—that is, $\Delta x$ is 4. The slope of the curve is

$$\frac{\Delta y}{\Delta x} = \frac{-3}{4}.$$

Notice that the two slopes have the same magnitude (3/4), but the slope of the line in part (a) is positive (+3/+4 = 3/4) while that in part (b) is negative (−3/+4 = −3/4). The slope of a positive relationship is positive; the slope of a negative relationship is negative.

## The Slope of a Curved Line

The slope of a curved line is trickier. The slope of a curved line is not constant, so the slope depends on where on the curved line we calculate it. There are two ways to calculate the slope of a curved line: You can calculate the slope at a point, or you can calculate the slope across an arc of the curve. Let's look at the two alternatives.

**Slope at a Point** To calculate the slope at a point on a curve, you need to construct a straight line that has the same slope as the curve at the point in question. Figure A1.10 shows how this is done. Suppose you want to calculate the slope of the curve at point *A*. Place a ruler on the graph so that it touches point *A* and no other point on the curve, then draw a straight line along the edge of the ruler. The straight red line is this line, and it is the tangent to the curve at point *A*. If the ruler touches the curve only at point *A*, then the slope of the curve at point *A* must be the same as the slope of the edge of the ruler. If the curve and the ruler do not have the same slope, the line along the edge of the ruler will cut the curve instead of just touching it.

Now that you have found a straight line with the same slope as the curve at point *A*, you can calculate the slope of the curve at point *A* by calculating the slope of the straight line. Along the straight line, as $x$

**FIGURE A1.10** Slope at a Point

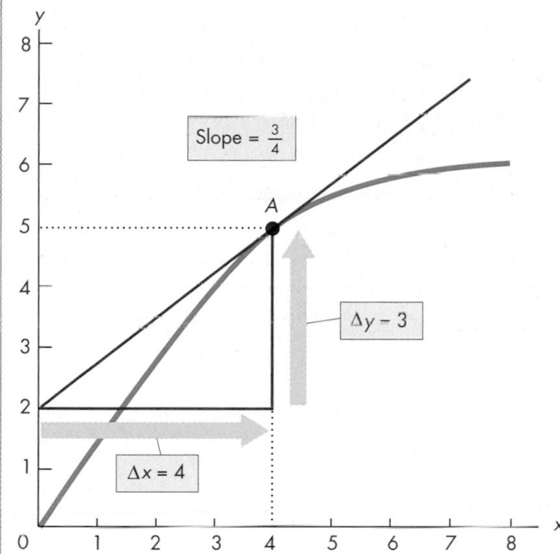


To calculate the slope of the curve at point *A*, draw the red line that just touches the curve at *A*—the tangent. The slope of this straight line is calculated by dividing the change in *y* by the change in *x* along the line. When *x* increases from 0 to 4, $\Delta x$ equals 4. That change in x is associated with an increase in *y* from 2 to 5, so $\Delta y$ equals 3. The slope of the red line is 3/4. So the slope of the curve at point *A* is 3/4.

increases from 0 to 4 ($\Delta x = 4$) $y$ increases from 2 to 5 ($\Delta y = 3$). Therefore the slope of the straight line is

$$\frac{\Delta y}{\Delta x} = \frac{3}{4}.$$

So the slope of the curve at point *A* is 3/4.

**Slope Across an Arc** An arc of a curve is a piece of a curve. In Fig. A1.11, you are looking at the same curve as in Fig. A1.10. But instead of calculating the slope at point *A*, we are going to calculate the slope across the arc from *B* to *C*. You can see that the slope at *B* is greater than at *C*. When we calculate the slope across an arc, we are calculating the average slope between two points. As we move along the arc from *B* to *C*, $x$ increases from 3 to 5 and $y$ increases from 4 to 5.5. The change in $x$ is 2 ($\Delta x = 2$), and the change

**FIGURE A1.11** Slope Across an Arc

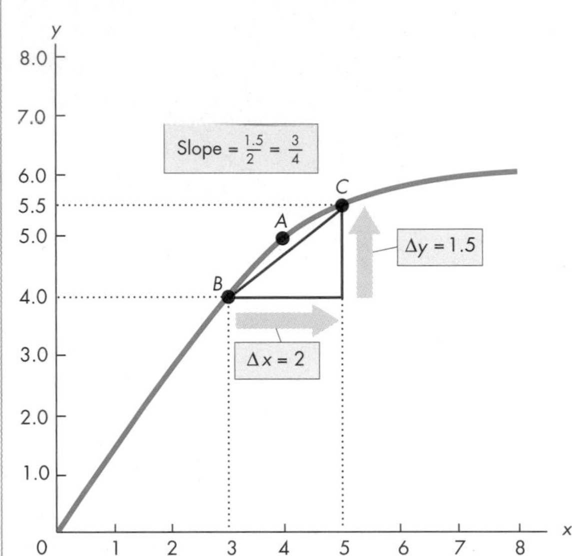


To calculate the average slope of the curve along the arc *BC*, draw a straight line from *B* to *C*. The slope of the line *BC* is calculated by dividing the change in *y* by the change in *x*. In moving from *B* to *C*, $\Delta x$ equals 2 and $\Delta y$ equals 1.5. The slope of the line *BC* is 1.5 divided by 2, or 3/4. So the slope of the curve across the arc *BC* is 3/4.

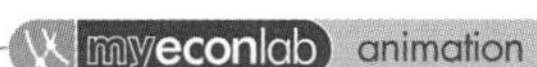


in *y* is 1.5 ($\Delta y = 1.5$). Therefore the slope is

$$\frac{\Delta y}{\Delta x} = \frac{1.5}{2} = \frac{3}{4}.$$

So the slope of the curve across the arc *BC* is 3/4.

This calculation gives us the slope of the curve between points *B* and *C*. The actual slope calculated is the slope of the straight line from *B* to *C*. This slope approximates the average slope of the curve along the arc *BC*. In this particular example, the slope across the arc *BC* is identical to the slope of the curve at point *A*. But the calculation of the slope of a curve does not always work out so neatly. You might have fun constructing some more examples and a few counterexamples.

You now know how to make and interpret a graph. But so far, we've limited our attention to graphs of two variables. We're now going to learn how to graph more than two variables.

## Graphing Relationships Among More Than Two Variables

We have seen that we can graph the relationship between two variables as a point formed by the *x*- and *y*-coordinates in a two-dimensional graph. You might be thinking that although a two-dimensional graph is informative, most of the things in which you are likely to be interested involve relationships among many variables, not just two. For example, the amount of ice cream consumed depends on the price of ice cream and the temperature. If ice cream is expensive and the temperature is low, people eat much less ice cream than when ice cream is inexpensive and the temperature is high. For any given price of ice cream, the quantity consumed varies with the temperature; and for any given temperature, the quantity of ice cream consumed varies with its price.

Figure A1.12 shows a relationship among three variables. The table shows the number of gallons of ice cream consumed each day at various temperatures and ice cream prices. How can we graph these numbers?

To graph a relationship that involves more than two variables, we use the *ceteris paribus* assumption.

***Ceteris Paribus*** ***Ceteris paribus*** means "if all other relevant things remain the same." To isolate the relationship of interest in a laboratory experiment, we hold other things constant. We use the same method to graph a relationship with more than two variables.

Figure A1.12(a) shows an example. There, you can see what happens to the quantity of ice cream consumed when the price of ice cream varies and the temperature is held constant. The line labeled 70°F shows the relationship between ice cream consumption and the price of ice cream if the temperature remains at 70°F. The numbers used to plot that line are those in the third column of the table in Fig. A1.12. For example, if the temperature is 70°F, 10 gallons are consumed when the price is 60¢ a scoop, and 18 gallons are consumed when the price is 30¢ a scoop. The curve labeled 90°F shows consumption as the price varies if the temperature remains at 90°F.

We can also show the relationship between ice cream consumption and temperature when the price of ice cream remains constant, as shown in Fig. A1.12(b). The curve labeled 60¢ shows how the consumption of ice cream varies with the tempera-

**FIGURE A1.12** Graphing a Relationship Among Three Variables

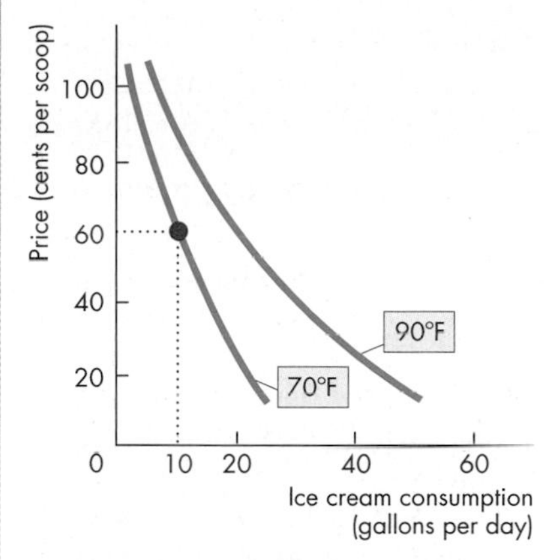


**(a) Price and consumption at a given temperature**

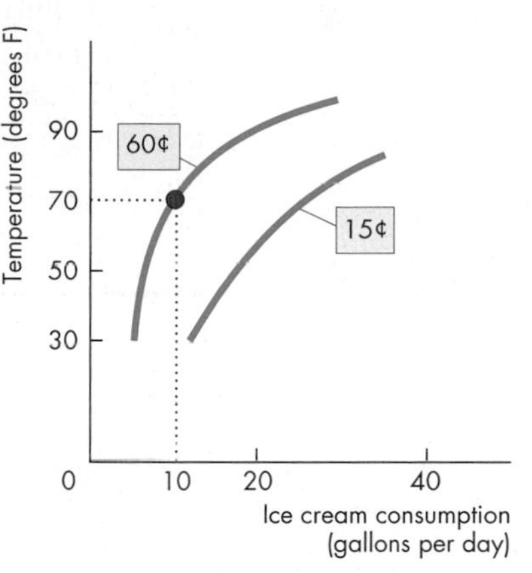


**(b) Temperature and consumption at a given price**

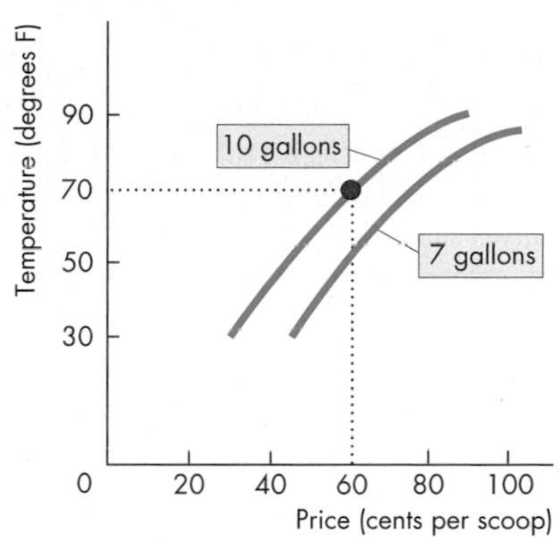


**(c) Temperature and price at a given consumption**

| Price (cents per scoop) | Ice cream consumption (gallons per day) | | | |
|---|---|---|---|---|
| | 30°F | 50°F | 70°F | 90°F |
| 15 | 12 | 18 | 25 | 50 |
| 30 | 10 | 12 | 18 | 37 |
| 45 | 7 | 10 | 13 | 27 |
| **60** | 5 | 7 | **10** | 20 |
| 75 | 3 | 5 | 7 | 14 |
| 90 | 2 | 3 | 5 | 10 |
| 105 | 1 | 2 | 3 | 6 |

Ice cream consumption depends on its price and the temperature. The table tell us how many gallons of ice cream are consumed each day at different prices and different temperatures. For example, if the price is 60¢ a scoop and the temperature is 70°F, 10 gallons of ice cream are consumed. This set of values is highlighted in the table and each part of the figure.

To graph a relationship among three variables, the value of one variable is held constant. Part (a) shows the relationship between price and consumption when temperature is held constant. One curve holds temperature at 90°F and the other holds it at 70°F. Part (b) shows the relationship between temperature and consumption when price is held constant. One curve holds the price at 60¢ a scoop and the other holds it at 15¢ a scoop. Part (c) shows the relationship between temperature and price when consumption is held constant. One curve holds consumption at 10 gallons and the other holds it at 7 gallons.

myeconlab animation

ture when the price of ice cream is 60¢ a scoop, and a second curve shows the relationship when the price is 15¢ a scoop. For example, at 60¢ a scoop, 10 gallons are consumed when the temperature is 70°F and 20 gallons are consumed when the temperature is 90°F.

Figure A1.12(c) shows the combinations of temperature and price that result in a constant consumption of ice cream. One curve shows the combinations that result in 10 gallons a day being consumed, and the other shows the combinations that result in 7 gallons a day being consumed. A high price and a high temperature lead to the same consumption as a lower price and a lower temperature. For example, 10 gallons of ice cream are consumed at 70°F and 60¢ a scoop, at 90°F and 90¢ a scoop, and at 50°F and 45¢ a scoop.

With what you have learned about graphs, you can move forward with your study of economics. There are no graphs in this book that are more complicated than those that have been explained in this appendix.

# MATHEMATICAL NOTE

## Equations of Straight Lines

If a straight line in a graph describes the relationship between two variables, we call it a linear relationship. Figure 1 shows the *linear relationship* between a person's expenditure and income. This person spends $100 a week (by borrowing or spending previous savings) when income is zero. And out of each dollar earned, this person spends 50 cents (and saves 50 cents).

All linear relationships are described by the same general equation. We call the quantity that is measured on the horizontal axis (or $x$-axis) $x$, and we call the quantity that is measured on the vertical axis (or $y$-axis) $y$. In the case of Fig. 1, $x$ is income and $y$ is expenditure.

### A Linear Equation

The equation that describes a straight-line relationship between $x$ and $y$ is

$$y = a + bx.$$

In this equation, $a$ and $b$ are fixed numbers and they are called constants. The values of $x$ and $y$ vary, so these numbers are called variables. Because the equation describes a straight line, the equation is called a *linear equation.*

The equation tells us that when the value of $x$ is zero, the value of $y$ is $a$. We call the constant $a$ the $y$-axis intercept. The reason is that on the graph the straight line hits the $y$-axis at a value equal to $a$. Figure 1 illustrates the $y$-axis intercept.

For positive values of $x$, the value of $y$ exceeds $a$. The constant $b$ tells us by how much $y$ increases above $a$ as $x$ increases. The constant $b$ is the slope of the line.

### Slope of Line

As we explain in the chapter, the *slope* of a relationship is the change in the value of $y$ divided by the change in the value of $x$. We use the Greek letter $\Delta$ (delta) to represent "change in." So $\Delta y$ means the change in the value of the variable measured on the $y$-axis, and $\Delta x$ means the change in the value of the variable measured on the $x$-axis. Therefore the slope of the relationship is

$$\Delta y / \Delta x.$$

To see why the slope is $b$, suppose that initially the value of $x$ is $x_1$, or $200 in Fig. 2. The corresponding value of $y$ is $y_1$, also $200 in Fig. 2. The equation of the line tells us that

$$y_1 = a + bx_1. \quad (1)$$

Now the value of $x$ increases by $\Delta x$ to $x_1 + \Delta x$ (or $400 in Fig. 2). And the value of $y$ increases by $\Delta y$ to $y_1 + \Delta y$ (or $300 in Fig. 2).

The equation of the line now tells us that

$$y_1 + \Delta y = a + b(x_1 + \Delta x) \quad (2)$$

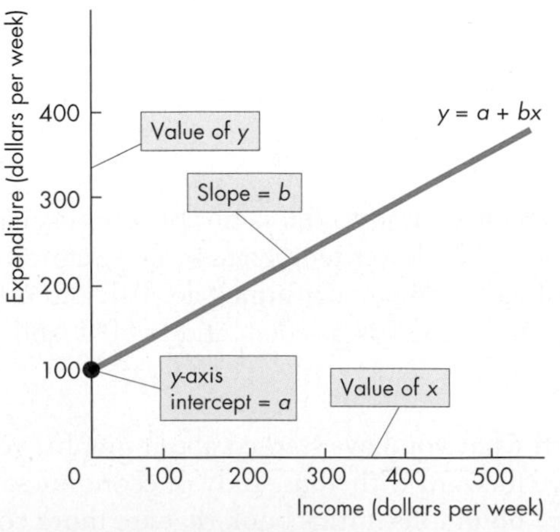


**Figure 1 Linear relationship**

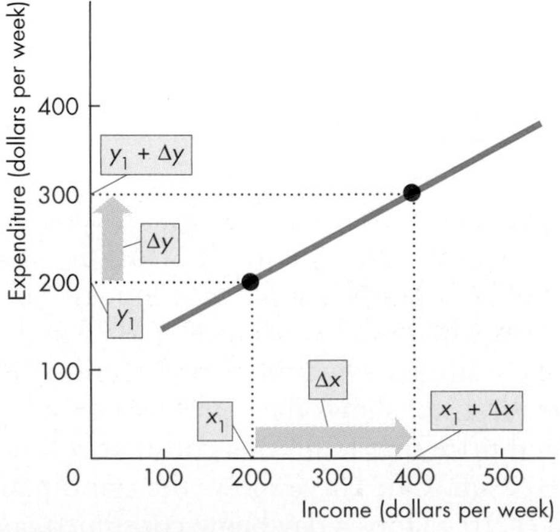


**Figure 2 Calculating slope**

To calculate the slope of the line, subtract equation (1) from equation (2) to obtain

$$\Delta y = b\Delta x \qquad (3)$$

and now divide equation (3) by $\Delta x$ to obtain

$$\Delta y/\Delta x = b.$$

So the slope of the line is $b$.

## Position of Line

The $y$-axis intercept determines the position of the line on the graph. Figure 3 illustrates the relationship between the $y$-axis intercept and the position of the line. In this graph, the $y$-axis measures saving and the $x$-axis measures income.

When the $y$-axis intercept, $a$, is positive, the line hits the $y$-axis at a positive value of $y$—as the blue line does. Its $y$-axis intercept is 100. When the $y$-axis intercept, $a$, is zero, the line hits the $y$-axis at the origin—as the purple line does. Its $y$-axis intercept is 0. When the $y$-axis intercept, $a$, is negative, the line hits the $y$-axis at a negative value of $y$—as the red line does. Its $y$-axis intercept is –100.

As the equations of the three lines show, the value of the $y$-axis intercept does not influence the slope of the line. All three lines have a slope equal to 0.5.

## Positive Relationships

Figure 1 shows a positive relationship—the two variables $x$ and $y$ move in the same direction. All positive relationships have a slope that is positive. In the equation of the line, the constant $b$ is positive. In this example, the $y$-axis intercept, $a$, is 100. The slope $b$ equals $\Delta y/\Delta x$, which in Fig. 2 is 100/200 or 0.5. The equation of the line is

$$y = 100 + 0.5x.$$

## Negative Relationships

Figure 4 shows a negative relationship—the two variables $x$ and $y$ move in the opposite direction. All negative relationships have a slope that is negative. In the equation of the line, the constant $b$ is negative. In the example in Fig. 4, the $y$-axis intercept, $a$, is 30. The slope, $b$, equals $\Delta y/\Delta x$, which is –20/2 or –10. The equation of the line is

$$y = 30 + (-10)x$$

or

$$y = 30 - 10x.$$

## Example

A straight line has a $y$-axis intercept of 50 and a slope of 2. What is the equation of this line?
The equation of a straight line is

$$y = a + bx$$

where $a$ is the $y$-axis intercept and $b$ is the slope.
So the equation is

$$y = 50 + 2x.$$

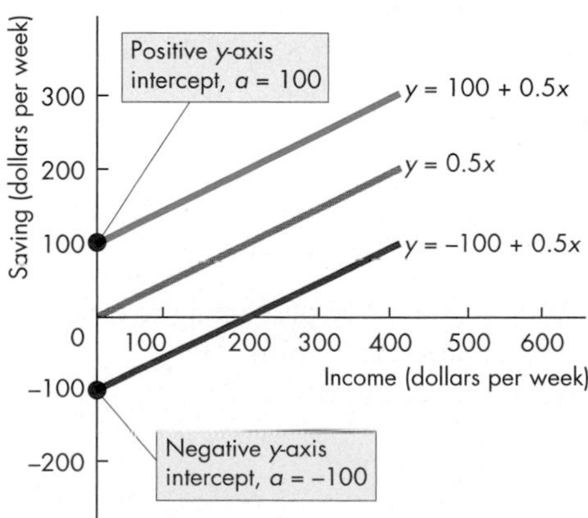


**Figure 3 The *y*-axis intercept**

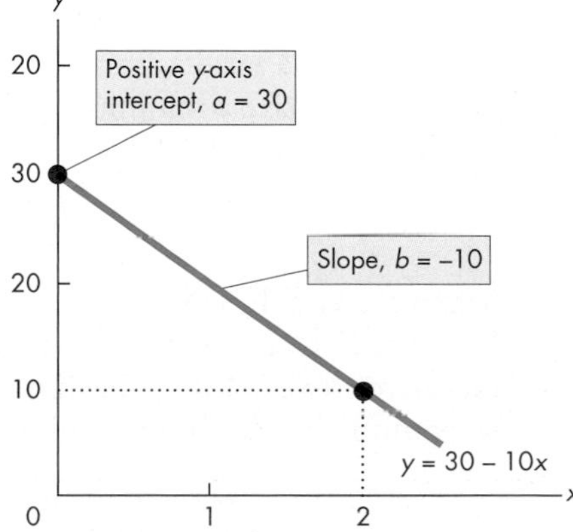


**Figure 4 Negative relationship**

## Review Quiz

1 What are the three types of graphs used to show economic data?
2 Give an example of a time-series graph.
3 List three things that a time-series graph shows quickly and easily.
4 Give three examples, different from those in the chapter, of scatter diagrams that show a positive relationship, a negative relationship, and no relationship.
5 Draw some graphs to show the relationships between two variables
   a. That move in the same direction.
   b. That move in opposite directions.
   c. That have a maximum.
   d. That have a minimum.
6 Which of the relationships in question 5 is a positive relationship and which is a negative relationship?
7 What are the two ways of calculating the slope of a curved line?
8 How do we graph a relationship among more than two variables?

Work Study Plan 1A and get instant feedback.

## SUMMARY

### Key Points

**Graphing Data** (pp. 15–18)

- A time-series graph shows the trend and fluctuations in a variable over time.
- A cross-section graph shows how the value of a variable changes across the members of a population.
- A scatter diagram shows the relationship between two variables. It shows whether two variables are positively related, negatively related, or unrelated.

**Graphs Used in Economic Models** (pp. 18–21)

- Graphs are used to show relationships among variables in economic models.
- Relationships can be positive (an upward-sloping curve), negative (a downward-sloping curve), positive and then negative (have a maximum point), negative and then positive (have a minimum point), or unrelated (a horizontal or vertical curve).

**The Slope of a Relationship** (pp. 22–24)

- The slope of a relationship is calculated as the change in the value of the variable measured on the $y$-axis divided by the change in the value of the variable measured on the $x$-axis—that is, $\Delta y/\Delta x$.
- A straight line has a constant slope.
- A curved line has a varying slope. To calculate the slope of a curved line, we calculate the slope at a point or across an arc.

**Graphing Relationships Among More Than Two Variables** (pp. 24–25)

- To graph a relationship among more than two variables, we hold constant the values of all the variables except two.
- We then plot the value of one of the variables against the value of another.

### Key Figures



### Key Terms

*Ceteris paribus*, 24
Cross-section graph, 16
Direct relationship, 18
Inverse relationship, 19
Linear relationship, 18
Negative relationship, 19
Positive relationship, 18
Scatter diagram, 17
Slope, 22
Time-series graph, 16
Trend, 16

## PROBLEMS and APPLICATIONS

myeconlab Work problems 1–5 in Chapter 1A Study Plan and get instant feedback.
Work problems 6–10 as Homework, a Quiz, or a Test if assigned by your instructor.

1. The spreadsheet provides data on the U.S. economy: Column A is the year, column B is the inflation rate, column C is the interest rate, column D is the growth rate, and column E is the unemployment rate.

| | A | B | C | D | E |
|---|---|---|---|---|---|
| 1 | 1997 | 2.8 | 7.6 | 2.5 | 5.6 |
| 2 | 1998 | 2.9 | 7.4 | 3.7 | 5.4 |
| 3 | 1999 | 2.3 | 7.3 | 4.5 | 4.9 |
| 4 | 2000 | 1.6 | 6.5 | 4.2 | 4.5 |
| 5 | 2001 | 2.2 | 7.0 | 4.4 | 4.2 |
| 6 | 2002 | 3.4 | 7.6 | 3.7 | 4.0 |
| 7 | 2003 | 2.8 | 7.1 | 0.8 | 4.7 |
| 8 | 2004 | 1.6 | 6.5 | 3.6 | 5.8 |
| 9 | 2005 | 2.3 | 5.7 | 3.1 | 6.0 |
| 10 | 2006 | 2.5 | 5.6 | 2.9 | 4.6 |
| 11 | 2007 | 4.1 | 5.6 | 2.2 | 4.6 |

a. Draw a time-series graph of the inflation rate.
b. In which year(s) (i) was inflation highest, (ii) was inflation lowest, (iii) did it increase, (iv) did it decrease, (v) did it increase most, and (vi) did it decrease most?
c. What was the main trend in inflation?
d. Draw a scatter diagram of the inflation rate and the interest rate. Describe the relationship.
e. Draw a scatter diagram of the growth rate and the unemployment rate. Describe the relationship.

2. **'Hulk' Tops Box Office With Sales of $54.5 Million:**

| Movie | Theaters (number) | Revenue (dollars per theater) |
|---|---|---|
| Hulk | 3,505 | 15,560 |
| The Happening | 2,986 | 10,214 |
| Zohan | 3,462 | 4,737 |
| Crystal Skull | 3,804 | 3,561 |

Bloomberg.com, June 15, 2008

a. Draw a graph to show the relationship between the revenue per theater on the *y*-axis and the number of theaters on the *x*-axis. Describe the relationship.
b. Calculate the slope of the relationship between 3,462 and 3,804 theaters.

3. Calculate the slope of the following relationship.

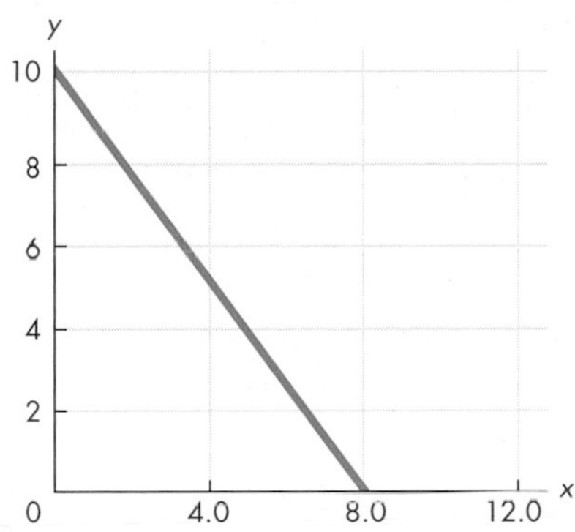


4. Calculate the slope of the following relationship:
a. At point *A* and at point *B*.
b. Across the arc *AB*.

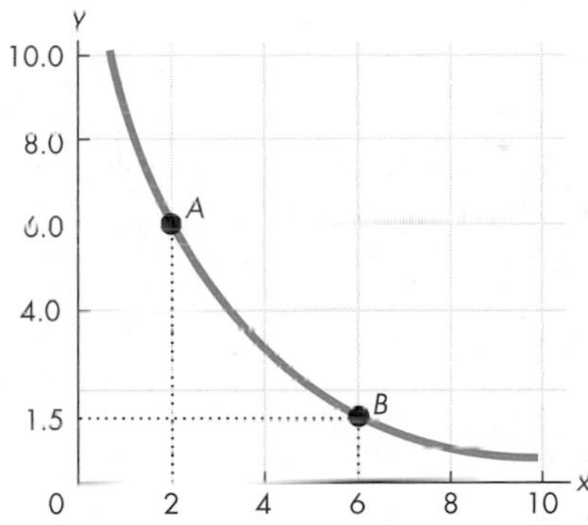


5. The table gives the price of a balloon ride, the temperature, and the number of rides a day.

| Price (dollars per ride) | Balloon rides (number per day) | | |
|---|---|---|---|
| | 50°F | 70°F | 90°F |
| 5 | 32 | 40 | 50 |
| 10 | 27 | 32 | 40 |
| 15 | 18 | 27 | 32 |

Draw graphs to show the relationship between
a. The price and the number of rides, holding the temperature constant. Describe this relationship.
b. The number of rides and temperature, holding the price constant.

6. The spreadsheet provides data on oil and gasoline: Column A is the year, column B is the price of oil (dollars per barrel), column C is the price of gasoline (cents per gallon), column D is U.S. oil production, and column E is the U.S. quantity of gasoline refined (both in millions of barrels per day).

| | A | B | C | D | E |
|---|---|---|---|---|---|
| 1 | 1997 | 16 | 117 | 2.35 | 8.3 |
| 2 | 1998 | 9 | 98 | 2.28 | 8.3 |
| 3 | 1999 | 24 | 131 | 2.15 | 8.3 |
| 4 | 2000 | 22 | 145 | 2.13 | 8.0 |
| 5 | 2001 | 18 | 111 | 2.12 | 8.3 |
| 6 | 2002 | 30 | 144 | 2.10 | 8.8 |
| 7 | 2003 | 28 | 153 | 2.07 | 8.7 |
| 8 | 2004 | 36 | 184 | 1.98 | 9.2 |
| 9 | 2005 | 52 | 224 | 1.89 | 8.9 |
| 10 | 2006 | 57 | 239 | 1.86 | 9.4 |
| 11 | 2007 | 90 | 303 | 1.86 | 9.1 |

a. Draw a time-series graph of the quantity of gasoline refined.
b. In which year(s) (i) was the quantity of gasoline refined highest, (ii) was it lowest, (iii) did it increase, (iv) did it decrease, (v) did it increase most, and (vi) did it decrease most?
c. What was the main trend in this quantity?
d. Draw a scatter diagram of the price of oil and the quantity of oil. Describe the relationship.
e. Draw a scatter diagram of the price of gasoline and the quantity of gasoline. Describe the relationship.

7. Draw a graph that shows the relationship between the two variables $x$ and $y$:

| $x$ | 0 | 1 | 2 | 3 | 4 | 5 |
|---|---|---|---|---|---|---|
| $y$ | 25 | 24 | 22 | 18 | 12 | 0 |

a. Is the relationship positive or negative?
b. Does the slope of the relationship increase or decrease as the value of $x$ increases?
c. Think of some economic relationships that might be similar to this one.
d. Calculate the slope of the relationship between $x$ and $y$ when $x$ equals 3.
e. Calculate the slope of the relationship across the arc as $x$ increases from 4 to 5.

8. Calculate the slope of the following relationship at point $A$.

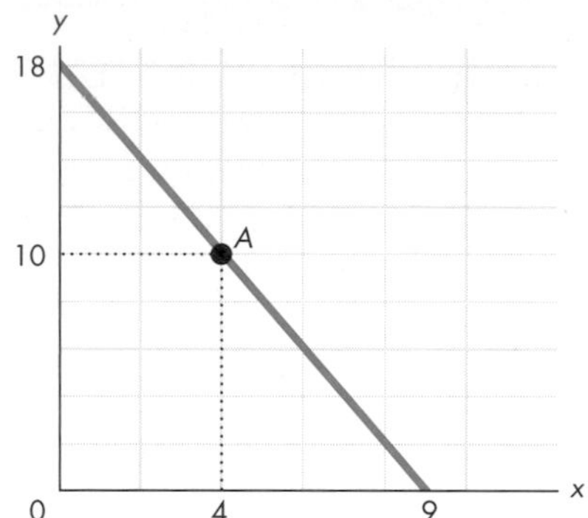


9. Calculate the slope of the following relationship:
a. At point $A$ and at point $B$.
b. Across the arc $AB$.

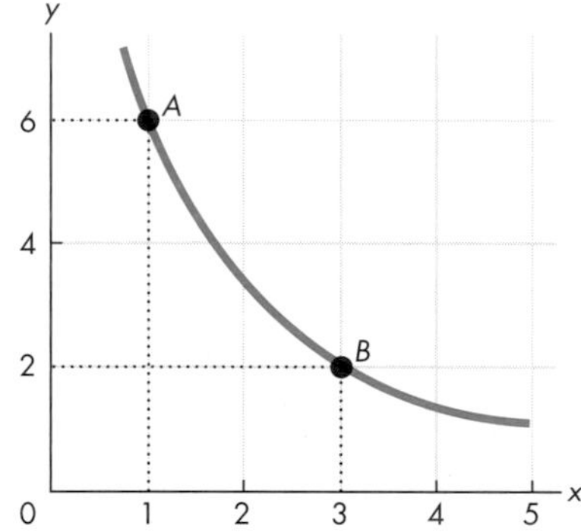


10. The table gives information about umbrellas: price, the number purchased, and rainfall.

| Price (dollars per umbrella) | Umbrellas (number per day) | | |
|---|---|---|---|
| | 0 | 1 | 2 |
| | (inches of rainfall) | | |
| 20 | 4 | 7 | 8 |
| 30 | 2 | 4 | 7 |
| 40 | 1 | 2 | 4 |

Draw graphs to show the relationship between
a. Price and the number of umbrellas purchased, holding the amount of rainfall constant. Describe this relationship.
b. The number of umbrellas purchased and the amount of rainfall, holding the price constant. Describe this relationship.

# 2 The Economic Problem

**After studying this chapter, you will be able to:**

- Define the production possibilities frontier and calculate opportunity cost
- Distinguish between production possibilities and preferences and describe an efficient allocation of resources
- Explain how current production choices expand future production possibilities
- Explain how specialization and trade expand our production possibilities
- Describe the economic institutions that coordinate decisions

**Why does food cost much more today than it did a** few years ago? One reason is that we now use part of our corn crop to produce ethanol, a clean biofuel substitute for gasoline. Another reason is that drought in some parts of the world has decreased global grain production. In this chapter, you will study an economic model—the production possibilities frontier—and you will learn why ethanol production and drought have increased the cost of producing food. You will also learn how to assess whether it is a good idea to increase corn production to produce fuel; how we can expand our production possibilities; and how we gain by trading with others.

At the end of the chapter, in *Reading Between the Lines*, we'll apply what you've learned to understanding why ethanol production is raising the cost of food.

# Production Possibilities and Opportunity Cost

Every working day, in mines, factories, shops, and offices and on farms and construction sites across the United States, 138 million people produce a vast variety of goods and services valued at $50 billion. But the quantities of goods and services that we can produce are limited both by our available resources and by technology. And if we want to increase our production of one good, we must decrease our production of something else—we face a tradeoff. You are going to learn about the production possibilities frontier, which describes the limit to what we can produce and provides a neat way of thinking about and illustrating the idea of a tradeoff.

The **production possibilities frontier** (*PPF*) is the boundary between those combinations of goods and services that can be produced and those that cannot. To illustrate the *PPF*, we focus on two goods at a time and hold the quantities produced of all the other goods and services constant. That is, we look at a *model* economy in which everything remains the same except for the production of the two goods we are considering.

Let's look at the production possibilities frontier for cola and pizza, which stand for *any* pair of goods or services.

## Production Possibilities Frontier

The *production possibilities frontier* for cola and pizza shows the limits to the production of these two goods, given the total resources and technology available to produce them. Figure 2.1 shows this production possibilities frontier. The table lists some combinations of the quantities of pizza and cola that can be produced in a month given the resources available. The figure graphs these combinations. The *x*-axis shows the quantity of pizzas produced, and the *y*-axis shows the quantity of cola produced.

The *PPF* illustrates *scarcity* because we cannot attain the points outside the frontier. These points describe wants that can't be satisfied. We can produce at any point *inside* the *PPF* or *on* the *PPF*. These points are attainable. Suppose that in a typical month, we produce 4 million pizzas and 5 million cans of cola. Figure 2.1 shows this combination as point *E* and as possibility *E* in the table. The figure

**FIGURE 2.1** Production Possibilities Frontier

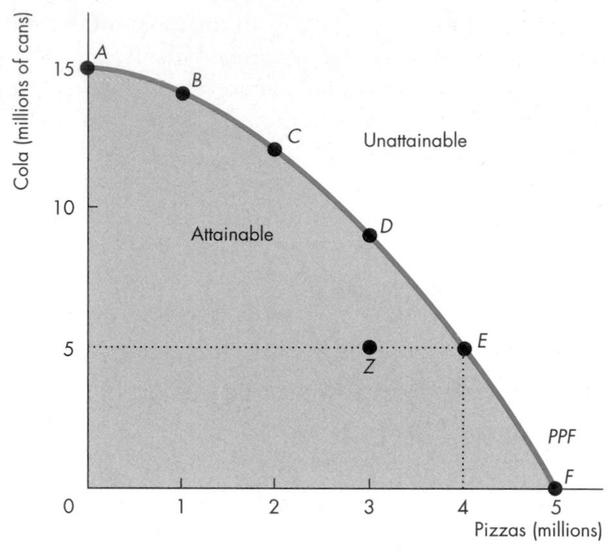


| Possibility | Pizzas (millions) | | Cola (millions of cans) |
|---|---|---|---|
| *A* | 0 | and | 15 |
| *B* | 1 | and | 14 |
| *C* | 2 | and | 12 |
| *D* | 3 | and | 9 |
| *E* | 4 | and | 5 |
| *F* | 5 | and | 0 |

The table lists six production possibilities for cola and pizzas. Row *A* tells us that if we produce no pizza, the maximum quantity of cola we can produce is 15 million cans. Points *A*, *B*, *C*, *D*, *E*, and *F* in the figure represent the rows of the table. The curve passing through these points is the production possibilities frontier (*PPF* ).

The *PPF* separates the attainable from the unattainable. Production is possible at any point *inside* the orange area or *on* the frontier. Points outside the frontier are unattainable. Points inside the frontier, such as point *Z*, are inefficient because resources are wasted or misallocated. At such points, it is possible to use the available resources to produce more of either or both goods.

also shows other production possibilities. For example, we might stop producing pizza and move all the people who produce it into producing cola. Point *A* in the figure and possibility *A* in the table show this case. The quantity of cola produced increases to 15 million cans, and pizza production dries up. Alternatively, we might close the cola factories and switch all the resources into producing pizza. In this situation, we produce 5 million pizzas. Point *F* in the figure and possibility *F* in the table show this case.

## Production Efficiency

We achieve **production efficiency** if we produce goods and services at the lowest possible cost. This outcome occurs at all the points *on* the *PPF.* At points *inside* the *PPF*, production is inefficient because we are giving up more than necessary of one good to produce a given quantity of the other good.

For example, at point *Z* in Fig. 2.1, we produce 3 million pizzas and 5 million cans of cola. But we could produce 3 million pizzas and 9 million cans of cola. Our pizzas cost more cola than necessary. We can get them for a lower cost. Only when we produce *on* the *PPF* do we incur the lowest possible cost of production.

Production is *inefficient* inside the *PPF* because resources are either *unused* or *misallocated* or both.

Resources are *unused* when they are idle but could be working. For example, we might leave some of the factories idle or some workers unemployed.

Resources are *misallocated* when they are assigned to tasks for which they are not the best match. For example, we might assign skilled pizza chefs to work in a cola factory and skilled cola producers to work in a pizza shop. We could get more pizzas *and* more cola from these same workers if we reassigned them to the tasks that more closely match their skills.

## Tradeoff Along the *PPF*

Every choice *along* the *PPF* involves a *tradeoff.* On the *PPF* in Fig. 2.1, we trade off cola for pizzas.

Tradeoffs arise in every imaginable real-world situation, and you reviewed several of them in Chapter 1. At any given point in time, we have a fixed amount of labor, land, capital, and entrepreneurship. By using our available technologies, we can employ these resources to produce goods and services, but we are limited in what we can produce. This limit defines a boundary between what we can attain and what we cannot attain. This boundary is the real-world's production possibilities frontier, and it defines the tradeoffs that we must make. On our real-world *PPF*, we can produce more of any one good or service only if we produce less of some other goods or services.

When doctors want to spend more on AIDS and cancer research, they face a tradeoff: more medical research for less of some other things. When Congress wants to spend more on education and health care, it faces a tradeoff: more education and health care for less national defense or less private spending (because of higher taxes). When an environmental group argues for less logging, it is suggesting a tradeoff: greater conservation of endangered wildlife for less paper. When you want to study more, you face a tradeoff: more study time for less leisure or sleep.

All tradeoffs involve a cost—an opportunity cost.

## Opportunity Cost

The **opportunity cost** of an action is the highest-valued alternative forgone. The *PPF* makes this idea precise and enables us to calculate opportunity cost. Along the *PPF*, there are only two goods, so there is only one alternative forgone: some quantity of the other good. Given our current resources and technology, we can produce more pizzas only if we produce less cola. The opportunity cost of producing an additional pizza is the cola we *must* forgo. Similarly, the opportunity cost of producing an additional can of cola is the quantity of pizza we must forgo.

In Fig. 2.1, if we move from point *C* to point *D*, we get 1 million more pizzas but 3 million fewer cans of cola. The additional 1 million pizzas *cost* 3 million cans of cola. One pizza costs 3 cans of cola.

We can also work out the opportunity cost of moving in the opposite direction. In Fig. 2.1, if we move from point *D* to point *C*, the quantity of cola produced increases by 3 million cans and the quantity of pizzas produced decreases by 1 million. So if we choose point *C* over point *D*, the additional 3 million cans of cola *cost* 1 million pizzas. One can of cola costs 1/3 of a pizza.

**Opportunity Cost Is a Ratio** Opportunity cost is a ratio. It is the decrease in the quantity produced of one good divided by the increase in the quantity produced of another good as we move along the production possibilities frontier.

Because opportunity cost is a ratio, the opportunity cost of producing an additional can of cola is equal to the *inverse* of the opportunity cost of producing an additional pizza. Check this proposition by returning to the calculations we've just worked through. When we move along the *PPF* from *C* to *D*, the opportunity cost of a pizza is 3 cans of cola. The inverse of 3 is 1/3. If we decrease the production of pizza and increase the production of cola by moving from *D* to *C*, the opportunity cost of a can of cola must be 1/3 of a pizza. That is exactly the number that we calculated for the move from *D* to *C*.

**Increasing Opportunity Cost** The opportunity cost of a pizza increases as the quantity of pizzas produced increases. The outward-bowed shape of the *PPF* reflects increasing opportunity cost. When we produce a large quantity of cola and a small quantity of pizza—between points *A* and *B* in Fig. 2.1—the frontier has a gentle slope. An increase in the quantity of pizzas costs a small decrease in the quantity of cola—the opportunity cost of a pizza is a small quantity of cola.

When we produce a large quantity of pizza and a small quantity of cola—between points *E* and *F* in Fig. 2.1—the frontier is steep. A given increase in the quantity of pizzas *costs* a large decrease in the quantity of cola, so the opportunity cost of a pizza is a large quantity of cola.

The *PPF* is bowed outward because resources are not all equally productive in all activities. People with many years of experience working for PepsiCo are good at producing cola but not very good at making pizzas. So if we move some of these people from PepsiCo to Domino's, we get a small increase in the quantity of pizzas but a large decrease in the quantity of cola.

Similarly, people who have spent years working at Domino's are good at producing pizzas, but they have no idea how to produce cola. So if we move some of these people from Domino's to PepsiCo, we get a small increase in the quantity of cola but a large decrease in the quantity of pizzas. The more of either good we try to produce, the less productive are the additional resources we use to produce that good and the larger is the opportunity cost of a unit of that good.

## Increasing Opportunity Cost

### Opportunity Cost on the Farm

Sanders Wright, a homesick Mississippi native, is growing cotton in Iowa. But the growing season is short and commercial success unlikely. Cotton does not grow well in Iowa, but corn does. A farm with irrigation can produce 300 bushels of corn per acre—twice the U.S. average.

Ronnie Gerik, a Texas cotton farmer, has started to grow corn. But Ronnie doesn't have irrigation and instead relies on rainfall. That's not a problem for cotton, which just needs a few soakings a season. But it's a big problem for corn, which needs an inch of water a week. Also, corn can't take the heat like cotton, and if the temperature rises too much, Ronnie will be lucky to get 100 bushels an acre.

An Iowa corn farmer gives up almost no cotton to produce his 300 bushels of corn per acre—corn has a low opportunity cost. But Ronnie Gerick gives up a huge amount of cotton to produce his 100 bushels of corn per acre. By switching some land from cotton to corn, Ronnie has increased the production of corn, but the additional corn has a high opportunity cost.

"Deere worker makes 'cotton pickin' miracle happen," WCFCourier.com; and "Farmers stampede to corn," *USA Today.*

## Review Quiz

1 How does the production possibilities frontier illustrate scarcity?
2 How does the production possibilities frontier illustrate production efficiency?
3 How does the production possibilities frontier show that every choice involves a tradeoff?
4 How does the production possibilities frontier illustrate opportunity cost?
5 Why is opportunity cost a ratio?
6 Why does the *PPF* for most goods bow outward so that opportunity cost increases as the quantity produced of a good increases?

Work Study Plan 2.1 and get instant feedback.

We've seen that what we can produce is limited by the production possibilities frontier. We've also seen that production on the *PPF* is efficient. But we can produce many different quantities on the *PPF*. How do we choose among them? How do we know which point on the *PPF* is the best one?

## Using Resources Efficiently

We achieve *production efficiency* at every point on the *PPF*. But which point is best? The answer is the point on the *PPF* at which goods and services are produced in the quantities that provide the greatest possible benefit. When goods and services are produced at the lowest possible cost and in the quantities that provide the greatest possible benefit, we have achieved **allocative efficiency.**

The questions that we raised when we reviewed the five big issues in Chapter 1 are questions about allocative efficiency. To answer such questions, we must measure and compare costs and benefits.

### The *PPF* and Marginal Cost

The **marginal cost** of a good is the opportunity cost of producing one more unit of it. We calculate marginal cost from the slope of the *PPF*. As the quantity of pizzas produced increases, the *PPF* gets steeper and the marginal cost of a pizza increases. Figure 2.2 illustrates the calculation of the marginal cost of a pizza.

Begin by finding the opportunity cost of pizza in blocks of 1 million pizzas. The cost of the first million pizzas is 1 million cans of cola; the cost of the second million pizzas is 2 million cans of cola; the cost of the third million pizzas is 3 million cans of cola, and so on. The bars in part (a) illustrate these calculations.

The bars in part (b) show the cost of an average pizza in each of the 1 million pizza blocks. Focus on the third million pizzas—the move from *C* to *D* in part (a). Over this range, because 1 million pizzas cost 3 million cans of cola, one of these pizzas, on average, costs 3 cans of cola—the height of the bar in part (b).

Next, find the opportunity cost of each additional pizza—the marginal cost of a pizza. The marginal cost of a pizza increases as the quantity of pizzas produced increases. The marginal cost at point *C* is less than it is at point *D*. On the average over the range from *C* to *D*, the marginal cost of a pizza is 3 cans of cola. But it exactly equals 3 cans of cola only in the middle of the range between *C* and *D*.

The red dot in part (b) indicates that the marginal cost of a pizza is 3 cans of cola when 2.5 million pizzas are produced. Each black dot in part (b) is interpreted in the same way. The red curve that passes through these dots, labeled *MC*, is the marginal cost curve. It shows the marginal cost of a pizza at each quantity of pizzas as we move along the *PPF*.

**FIGURE 2.2** The *PPF* and Marginal Cost

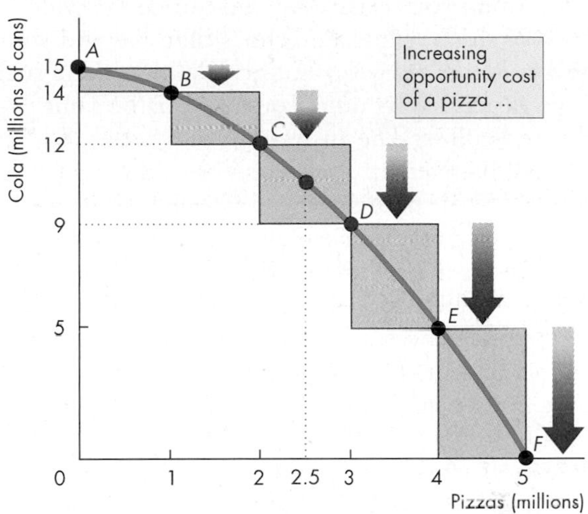


**(a) *PPF* and opportunity cost**

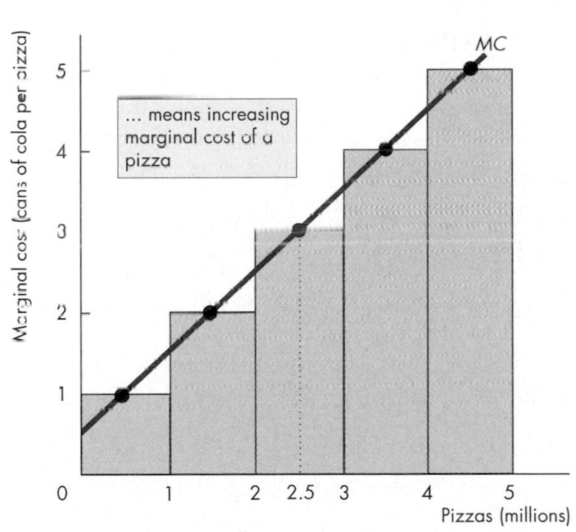


**(b) Marginal cost**

Marginal cost is calculated from the slope of the *PPF*. As the quantity of pizzas produced increases, the *PPF* gets steeper and the marginal cost of a pizza increases. The bars in part (a) show the opportunity cost of pizza in blocks of 1 million pizzas. The bars in part (b) show the cost of an average pizza in each of these 1 million blocks. The red curve, *MC*, shows the marginal cost of a pizza at each point along the *PPF*. This curve passes through the center of each of the bars in part (b).

animation

## Preferences and Marginal Benefit

Look around your classroom and notice the wide variety of shirts, pants, and shoes that you and your fellow students are wearing today. Why is there such a huge variety? Why don't you all wear the same styles and colors? The answer lies in what economists call preferences. **Preferences** are a description of a person's likes and dislikes.

You've seen that we have a concrete way of describing the limits to production: the *PPF*. We need a similarly concrete way of describing preferences. To describe preferences, economists use the concept of marginal benefit. The **marginal benefit** from a good or service is the benefit received from consuming one more unit of it.

We measure the marginal benefit from a good or service by the most that people are *willing to pay* for an additional unit of it. The idea is that you are willing to pay less for a good than it is worth to you but you are not willing to pay more than it is worth. So the most you are willing to pay for something measures its marginal benefit.

Economists illustrate preferences using the **marginal benefit curve**, which is a curve that shows the relationship between the marginal benefit from a good and the quantity consumed of that good. It is a general principle that the more we have of any good or service, the smaller is its marginal benefit and the less we are willing to pay for an additional unit of it. This tendency is so widespread and strong that we call it a principle—the *principle of decreasing marginal benefit.*

The basic reason why marginal benefit from a good or service decreases as we consume more of it is that we like variety. The more we consume of any one good or service, the more we tire of it and would prefer to switch to something else.

Think about your willingness to pay for a pizza. If pizza is hard to come by and you can buy only a few slices a year, you might be willing to pay a high price to get an additional slice. But if pizza is all you've eaten for the past few days, you are willing to pay almost nothing for another slice.

You've learned to think about cost as opportunity cost, not as a dollar cost. You can think about marginal benefit and willingness to pay in the same way. The marginal benefit, measured by what you are willing to pay for something, is the quantity of other goods and services that you are willing to forgo. Let's continue with the example of cola and pizza and illustrate preferences this way.

**FIGURE 2.3** Preferences and the Marginal Benefit Curve

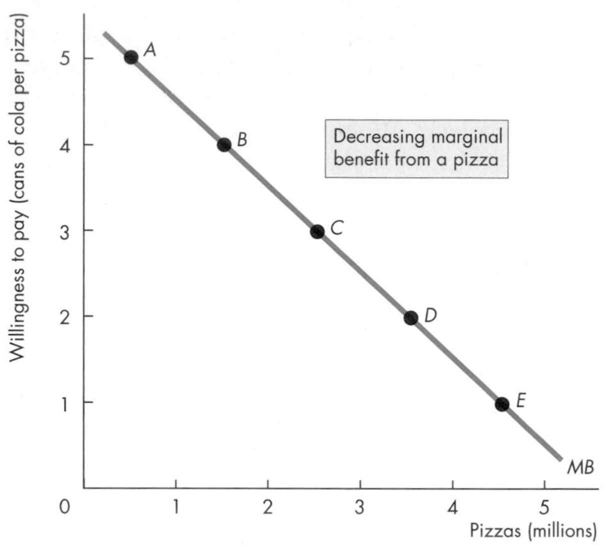


| Possibility | Pizzas (millions) | Willingness to pay (cans of cola per pizza) |
|---|---|---|
| *A* | 0.5 | 5 |
| *B* | 1.5 | 4 |
| *C* | 2.5 | 3 |
| *D* | 3.5 | 2 |
| *E* | 4.5 | 1 |

The smaller the quantity of pizzas produced, the more cola people are willing to give up for an additional pizza. If pizza production is 0.5 million, people are willing to pay 5 cans of cola per pizza. But if pizza production is 4.5 million, people are willing to pay only 1 can of cola per pizza. Willingness to pay measures marginal benefit. A universal feature of people's preferences is that marginal benefit decreases.

Figure 2.3 illustrates preferences as the willingness to pay for pizza in terms of cola. In row *A*, pizza production is 0.5 million, and at that quantity, people are willing to pay 5 cans of cola per pizza. As the quantity of pizzas produced increases, the amount that people are willing to pay for a pizza falls. When pizza production is 4.5 million, people are willing to pay only 1 can of cola per pizza.

Let's now use the concepts of marginal cost and marginal benefit to describe allocative efficiency.

**FIGURE 2.4** Efficient Use of Resources

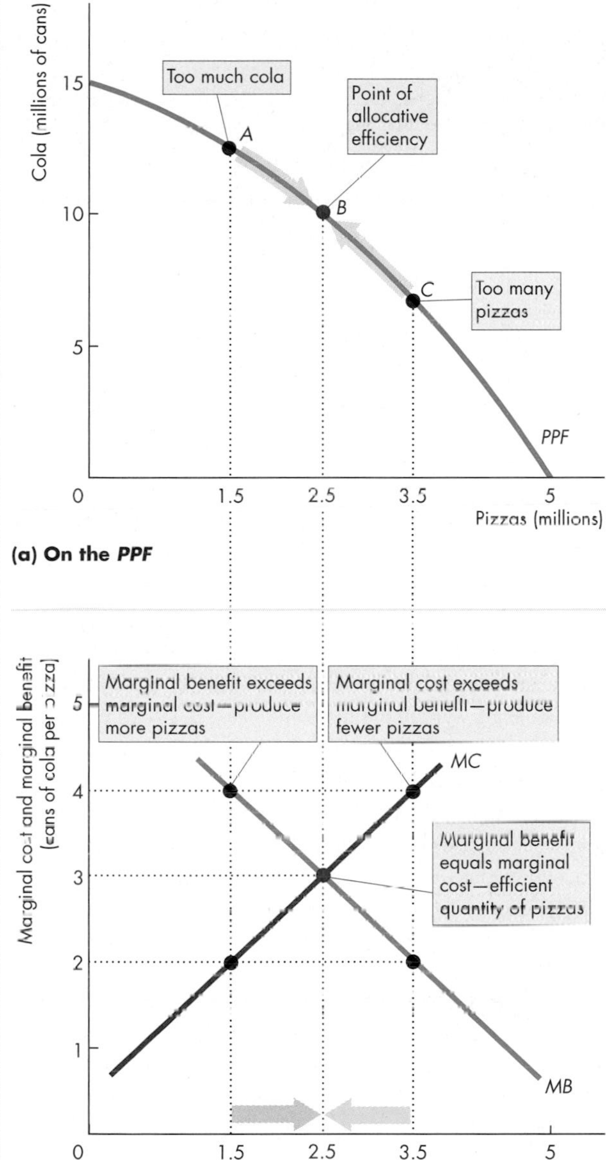


The greater the quantity of pizzas produced, the smaller is the marginal benefit (*MB*) from pizza—the less cola people are willing to give up to get an additional pizza. But the greater the quantity of pizzas produced, the greater is the marginal cost (*MC*) of a pizza—the more cola people must give up to get an additional pizza. When marginal benefit equals marginal cost, resources are being used efficiently.

myeconlab animation

## Allocative Efficiency

At *any* point on the *PPF*, we cannot produce more of one good without giving up some other good. At the *best* point on the *PPF,* we cannot produce more of one good without giving up some other good that provides greater benefit. We are producing at the point of allocative efficiency—the point on the *PPF* that we prefer above all other points.

Suppose in Fig. 2.4, we produce 1.5 million pizzas. The marginal cost of a pizza is 2 cans of cola, and the marginal benefit from a pizza is 4 cans of cola. Because someone values an additional pizza more highly than it costs to produce, we can get more value from our resources by moving some of them out of producing cola and into producing pizza.

Now suppose we produce 3.5 million pizzas. The marginal cost of a pizza is now 4 cans of cola, but the marginal benefit from a pizza is only 2 cans of cola. Because the additional pizza costs more to produce than anyone thinks it is worth, we can get more value from our resources by moving some of them away from producing pizza and into producing cola.

Suppose we produce 2.5 million pizzas. Marginal cost and marginal benefit are now equal at 3 cans of cola. This allocation of resources between pizza and cola is efficient. If more pizzas are produced, the forgone cola is worth more than the additional pizzas. If fewer pizzas are produced, the forgone pizzas are worth more than the additional cola.

## Review Quiz

1. What is marginal cost? How is it measured?
2. What is marginal benefit? How is it measured?
3. How does the marginal benefit from a good change as the quantity produced of that good increases?
4. What is allocative efficiency and how does it relate to the production possibilities frontier?
5. What conditions must be satisfied if resources are used efficiently?

Work Study Plan 2.2 and get instant feedback.

You now understand the limits to production and the conditions under which resources are used efficiently. Your next task is to study the expansion of production possibilities.

# Economic Growth

During the past 30 years, production per person in the United States has doubled. Such an expansion of production is called **economic growth**. Economic growth increases our *standard of living,* but it doesn't overcome scarcity and avoid opportunity cost. To make our economy grow, we face a tradeoff—the faster we make production grow, the greater is the opportunity cost of economic growth.

## The Cost of Economic Growth

Economic growth comes from technological change and capital accumulation. **Technological change** is the development of new goods and of better ways of producing goods and services. **Capital accumulation** is the growth of capital resources, including *human capital.*

Because of technological change and capital accumulation, we have an enormous quantity of cars that provide us with more transportation than was available when we had only horses and carriages; we have satellites that provide global communications on a much larger scale than that available with the earlier cable technology. But if we use our resources to develop new technologies and produce capital, we must decrease our production of consumption goods and services. New technologies and new capital have an opportunity cost. Let's look at this opportunity cost.

Instead of studying the *PPF* of pizza and cola, we'll hold the quantity of cola produced constant and examine the *PPF* for pizzas and pizza ovens. Figure 2.5 shows this *PPF* as the blue curve *ABC*. If we devote no resources to producing pizza ovens, we produce at point *A*. If we produce 3 million pizzas, we can produce 6 pizza ovens at point *B*. If we produce no pizza, we can produce 10 ovens at point *C*.

The amount by which our production possibilities expand depends on the resources we devote to technological change and capital accumulation. If we devote no resources to this activity (point *A*), our *PPF* remains at *ABC*—the blue curve in Fig. 2.5. If we cut the current production of pizza and produce 6 ovens (point *B*), then in the future, we'll have more capital and our *PPF* will rotate outward to the position shown by the red curve. The fewer resources we use for producing pizza and the more resources we use for producing ovens, the greater is the future expansion of our production possibilities.

**FIGURE 2.5** Economic Growth

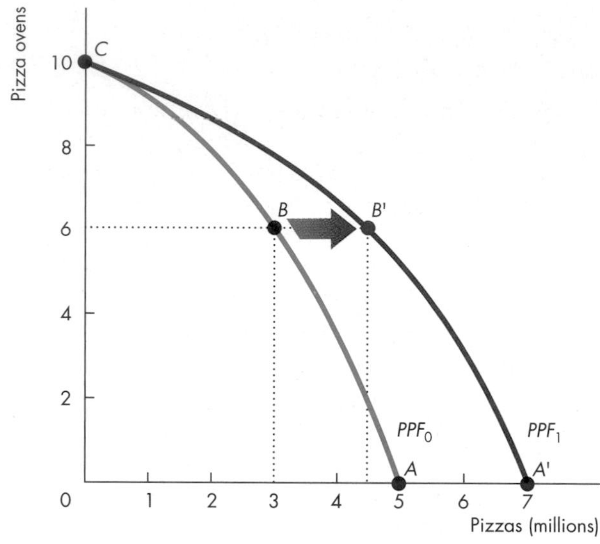


$PPF_0$ shows the limits to the production of pizza and pizza ovens, with the production of all other goods and services remaining the same. If we devote no resources to producing pizza ovens and produce 5 million pizzas, our production possibilities will remain the same $PPF_0$. But if we decrease pizza production to 3 million and produce 6 ovens, at point *B*, our production possibilities expand. After one period, the *PPF* rotates outward to $PPF_1$ and we can produce at point *B*', a point outside the original $PPF_0$. We can rotate the *PPF* outward, but we cannot avoid opportunity cost. The opportunity cost of producing more pizzas in the future is fewer pizzas today.

Economic growth is not free. To make it happen, we use more resources to produce new ovens and fewer resources to produce pizzas. In Fig. 2.5, we move from *A* to *B*. There is no free lunch. The opportunity cost of more pizzas in the future is fewer pizzas today. Also, economic growth is no magic formula for abolishing scarcity. On the new production possibilities frontier, we continue to face a tradeoff and opportunity cost.

The ideas about economic growth that we have explored in the setting of the pizza industry also apply to nations. Hong Kong and the United States provide an interesting case study.

## Economic Growth

### Hong Kong Catching Up to the United States

In 1968, the production possibilities per person in the United States were more than four times those in Hong Kong (see the figure). The United States devotes one fifth of its resources to accumulating capital and in 1968 was at point *A* on its *PPF*. Hong Kong devotes one third of its resources to accumulating capital and in 1968, Hong Kong was at point *A* on its *PPF*.

Since 1968, both countries have experienced economic growth, but because Hong Kong devotes a bigger fraction of its resources to accumulating capital, its production possibilities have expanded more quickly.

By 2008, production possibilities per person in Hong Kong had reached 94 percent of those in the United States. If Hong Kong continues to devote more resources to accumulating capital than we do (at point *B* on its 2008 *PPF*), it will continue to grow more rapidly. But if Hong Kong decreases capital accumulation (moving to point *D* on its 2008 *PPF*), then its rate of economic growth will slow.

Hong Kong is typical of the fast-growing Asian economies, which include Taiwan, Thailand, South Korea, and China. Production possibilities expand in these countries by between 5 and almost 10 percent a year.

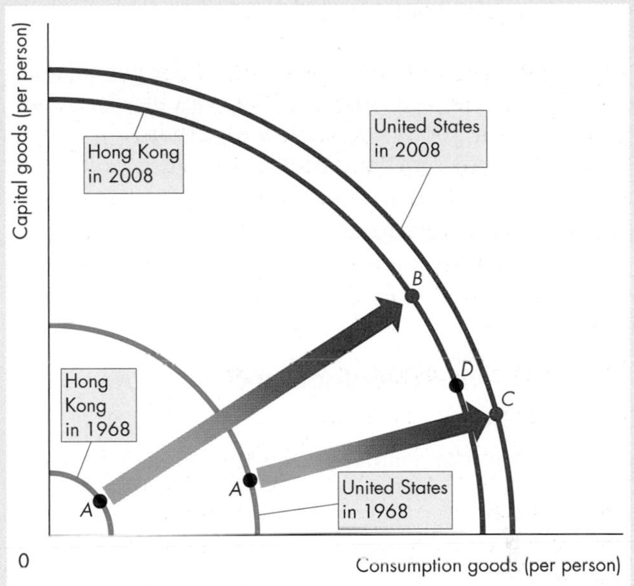


**Economic Growth in the United States and Hong Kong**

If such high economic growth rates are maintained, these other Asian countries will continue to close the gap between themselves and the United States, as Hong Kong is doing.

### A Nation's Economic Growth

The experiences of the United States and Hong Kong make a striking example of the effects of our choices about consumption and capital goods on the rate of economic growth.

If a nation devotes all its factors of production to producing consumption goods and services and none to advancing technology and accumulating capital, its production possibilities in the future will be the same as they are today.

To expand production possibilities in the future, a nation must devote fewer resources to producing consumption goods and services and some resources to accumulating capital and developing new technologies. As production possibilities expand, consumption in the future can increase. The decrease in today's consumption is the opportunity cost of tomorrow's increase in consumption.

## Review Quiz

1 What generates economic growth?
2 How does economic growth influence the production possibilities frontier?
3 What is the opportunity cost of economic growth?
4 Why has Hong Kong experienced faster economic growth than the United States?
5 Does economic growth overcome scarcity?

Work Study Plan 2.3 and get instant feedback.

Next, we're going to study another way in which we expand our production possibilities—the amazing fact that *both* buyers and sellers gain from specialization and trade.

## Gains from Trade

People can produce for themselves all the goods and services that they consume, or they can produce one good or a few goods and trade with others. Producing only one good or a few goods is called *specialization.* We are going to learn how people gain by specializing in the production of the good in which they have a *comparative advantage* and trading with others.

### Comparative Advantage and Absolute Advantage

A person has a **comparative advantage** in an activity if that person can perform the activity at a lower opportunity cost than anyone else. Differences in opportunity costs arise from differences in individual abilities and from differences in the characteristics of other resources.

No one excels at everything. One person is an outstanding pitcher but a poor catcher; another person is a brilliant lawyer but a poor teacher. In almost all human endeavors, what one person does easily, someone else finds difficult. The same applies to land and capital. One plot of land is fertile but has no mineral deposits; another plot of land has outstanding views but is infertile. One machine has great precision but is difficult to operate; another is fast but often breaks down.

Although no one excels at everything, some people excel and can outperform others in a large number of activities—perhaps even in all activities. A person who is more productive than others has an **absolute advantage**.

Absolute advantage involves comparing productivities—production per hour—whereas comparative advantage involves comparing opportunity costs.

Notice that a person who has an absolute advantage does not have a *comparative* advantage in every activity. John Grisham is a better lawyer and a better author of fast-paced thrillers than most people. He has an absolute advantage in these two activities. But compared to others, he is a better writer than lawyer, so his *comparative* advantage is in writing.

Because ability and resources vary from one person to another, people have different opportunity costs of producing various goods. These differences in opportunity cost are the source of comparative advantage.

Let's explore the idea of comparative advantage by looking at two smoothie bars: one operated by Liz and the other operated by Joe.

**Liz's Smoothie Bar** Liz produces smoothies and salads. In Liz's high-tech bar, she can turn out either a smoothie or a salad every 2 minutes—see Table 2.1. If Liz spends all her time making smoothies, she can produce 30 an hour. And if she spends all her time making salads, she can also produce 30 an hour. If she splits her time equally between the two, she can produce 15 smoothies and 15 salads an hour. For each additional smoothie Liz produces, she must decrease her production of salads by one, and for each additional salad she produces, she must decrease her production of smoothies by one. So

> Liz's opportunity cost of producing 1 smoothie is 1 salad,

and

> Liz's opportunity cost of producing 1 salad is 1 smoothie.

Liz's customers buy smoothies and salads in equal quantities, so she splits her time equally between the two items and produces 15 smoothies and 15 salads an hour.

**Joe's Smoothie Bar** Joe also produces smoothies and salads, but his bar is smaller than Liz's. Also, Joe has only one blender, and it's a slow, old machine. Even if Joe uses all his resources to produce smoothies, he can produce only 6 an hour—see Table 2.2. But Joe is good at making salads, so if he uses all his resources to make salads, he can produce 30 an hour.

Joe's ability to make smoothies and salads is the same regardless of how he splits an hour between the two tasks. He can make a salad in 2 minutes or a smoothie in 10 minutes. For each additional smoothie

**TABLE 2.1** Liz's Production Possibilities

| Item | Minutes to produce 1 | Quantity per hour |
|---|---|---|
| Smoothies | 2 | 30 |
| Salads | 2 | 30 |

**TABLE 2.2** Joe's Production Possibilities

| Item | Minutes to produce 1 | Quantity per hour |
|---|---|---|
| Smoothies | 10 | 6 |
| Salads | 2 | 30 |

Joe produces, he must decrease his production of salads by 5. And for each additional salad he produces, he must decrease his production of smoothies by 1/5 of a smoothie. So

> Joe's opportunity cost of producing 1 smoothie is 5 salads,

and

> Joe's opportunity cost of producing 1 salad is 1/5 of a smoothie.

Joe's customers, like Liz's, buy smoothies and salads in equal quantities. So Joe spends 50 minutes of each hour making smoothies and 10 minutes of each hour making salads. With this division of his time, Joe produces 5 smoothies and 5 salads an hour.

**Liz's Absolute Advantage** Table 2.3(a) summarizes the production of Liz and Joe. You can see that Liz is three times as productive as Joe—her 15 smoothies and salads an hour are three times Joe's 5. Liz has an absolute advantage over Joe in producing both smoothies and salads. But Liz has a comparative advantage in only one of the activities.

**Liz's Comparative Advantage** In which of the two activities does Liz have a comparative advantage? Recall that comparative advantage is a situation in which one person's opportunity cost of producing a good is lower than another person's opportunity cost of producing that same good. Liz has a comparative advantage in producing smoothies. Her opportunity cost of a smoothie is 1 salad, whereas Joe's opportunity cost of a smoothie is 5 salads.

**Joe's Comparative Advantage** If Liz has a comparative advantage in producing smoothies, Joe must have a comparative advantage in producing salads. Joe's opportunity cost of a salad is 1/5 of a smoothie, whereas Liz's opportunity cost of a salad is 1 smoothie.

## Achieving the Gains from Trade

Liz and Joe run into each other one evening in a singles bar. After a few minutes of getting acquainted, Liz tells Joe about her amazing smoothie business. Her only problem, she tells Joe, is that she would like to produce more because potential customers leave when her lines get too long.

Joe isn't sure whether to risk spoiling his chances by telling Liz about his own struggling business. But he takes the risk. When he explains to Liz that he spends 50 minutes of every hour making 5 smoothies and 10 minutes making 5 salads, Liz's eyes pop. "Have I got a deal for you!" she exclaims.

Here's the deal that Liz sketches on a table napkin. Joe stops making smoothies and allocates all his time to producing salads. And Liz stops making salads and allocates all her time to producing smoothies. That is, they both specialize in producing the good in which they have a comparative advantage. Together they produce 30 smoothies and 30 salads—see Table 2.3(b).

**TABLE 2.3** Liz and Joe Gain from Trade

| **(a) Before trade** | **Liz** | **Joe** |
|---|---|---|
| Smoothies | 15 | 5 |
| Salads | 15 | 5 |
| **(b) Specialization** | **Liz** | **Joe** |
| Smoothies | 30 | 0 |
| Salads | 0 | 30 |
| **(c) Trade** | **Liz** | **Joe** |
| Smoothies | sell 10 | buy 10 |
| Salads | buy 20 | sell 20 |
| **(d) After trade** | **Liz** | **Joe** |
| Smoothies | 20 | 10 |
| Salads | 20 | 10 |
| **(e) Gains from trade** | **Liz** | **Joe** |
| Smoothies | +5 | +5 |
| Salads | +5 | +5 |

They then trade. Liz sells Joe 10 smoothies and Joe sells Liz 20 salads—the price of a smoothie is 2 salads—see Table 2.3(c).

After the trade, Joe has 10 salads—the 30 he produces minus the 20 he sells to Liz. He also has the 10 smoothies that he buys from Liz. So Joe now has increased the quantities of smoothies and salads that he can sell—see Table 2.3(d).

Liz has 20 smoothies—the 30 she produces minus the 10 she sells to Joe. She also has the 20 salads that she buys from Joe. Liz has increased the quantities of smoothies and salads that she can sell—see Table 2.3(d). Liz and Joe both gain 5 smoothies and 5 salads an hour—see Table 2.3(e).

To illustrate her idea, Liz grabs a fresh napkin and draws the graphs in Fig. 2.6. The blue *PPF* in part (a) shows Joe's production possibilities. Before trade, he is producing 5 smoothies and 5 salads an hour at point *A*.

The blue *PPF* in part (b) shows Liz's production possibilities. Before trade, she is producing 15 smoothies and 15 salads an hour at point *A*.

Liz's proposal is that they each specialize in producing the good in which they have a comparative advantage. Joe produces 30 salads and no smoothies at point *B* on his *PPF*. Liz produces 30 smoothies and no salads at point *B* on her *PPF*.

Liz and Joe then trade smoothies and salads at a price of 2 salads per smoothie or 1/2 a smoothie per salad. Joe gets smoothies for 2 salads each, which is less than the 5 salads it costs him to produce a smoothie. Liz gets salads for 1/2 a smoothie each, which is less than the 1 smoothie that it costs her to produce a salad.

With trade, Joe has 10 smoothies and 10 salads at point *C*—a gain of 5 smoothies and 5 salads. Joe moves to a point *outside* his *PPF*.

**FIGURE 2.6** The Gains from Trade

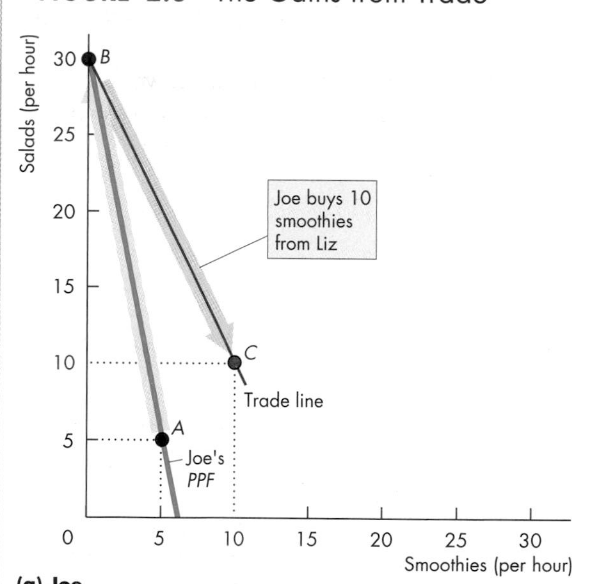


**(a) Joe**

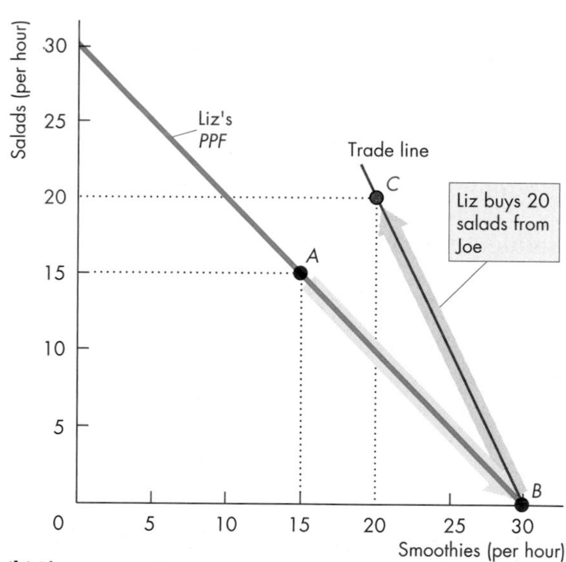


**(b) Liz**

Joe initially produces at point *A* on his *PPF* in part (a), and Liz initially produces at point *A* on her *PPF* in part (b). Joe's opportunity cost of producing a salad is less than Liz's, so Joe has a comparative advantage in producing salads. Liz's opportunity cost of producing a smoothie is less than Joe's, so Liz has a comparative advantage in producing smoothies. If Joe specializes in making salads, he produces 30 salads and no smoothies at point *B* on his *PPF*. If Liz specializes in making smoothies, she produces 30 smoothies and no salads at point *B* on her *PPF*. They exchange salads for smoothies along the red "Trade line." Liz buys salads from Joe for less than her opportunity cost of producing them. Joe buys smoothies from Liz for less than his opportunity cost of producing them. Each goes to point *C*—a point outside his or her *PPF*. Both Joe and Liz increase production by 5 smoothies and 5 salads with no change in resources.

myeconlab animation

With trade, Liz has 20 smoothies and 20 salads at point *C*—a gain of 5 smoothies and 5 salads. Liz moves to a point *outside* her *PPF*.

Despite Liz's absolute advantage in producing smoothies and salads, both Liz and Joe gain from specializing—producing the good in which they have a comparative advantage—and trading.

The gains that we achieve from international trade are similar to those achieved by Joe and Liz in this example. When Americans buy T-shirts from China and when China buys Boeing aircraft from the United States, both countries gain. We get our shirts at a lower cost than that at which we can produce them, and China gets its aircraft at a lower cost than that at which it can produce them.

### Dynamic Comparative Advantage

At any given point in time, the resources and technologies available determine the comparative advantages that individuals and nations have. But just by repeatedly producing a particular good or service, people become more productive in that activity, a phenomenon called **learning-by-doing.** Learning-by-doing is the basis of *dynamic* comparative advantage. **Dynamic comparative advantage** is a comparative advantage that a person (or country) has acquired by specializing in an activity and becoming the lowest-cost producer as a result of learning-by-doing.

Singapore, for example, pursued dynamic comparative advantage when it decided to begin a bio technology industry in which it initially didn't have a comparative advantage.

### Review Quiz

1 What gives a person a comparative advantage?
2 Distinguish between comparative advantage and absolute advantage.
3 Why do people specialize and trade?
4 What are the gains from specialization and trade?
5 What is the source of the gains from trade?
6 How does dynamic comparative advantage arise?

Work Study Plan 2.4 and get instant feedback.

## Economic Coordination

People gain by specializing in the production of those goods and services in which they have a comparative advantage and then trading with each other. Liz and Joe, whose production of salads and smoothies we studied earlier in this chapter, can get together and make a deal that enables them to enjoy the gains from specialization and trade. But for billions of individuals to specialize and produce millions of different goods and services, their choices must somehow be coordinated.

Two competing economic coordination systems have been used: central economic planning and decentralized markets.

Central economic planning might appear to be the best system because it can express national priorities. But when this system was tried, as it was for 60 years in Russia and for 30 years in China, it was a miserable failure. Today, these and most other previously planned economies are adopting a decentralized market system.

To make decentralized coordination work, four complementary social institutions that have evolved over many centuries are needed. They are

- Firms
- Markets
- Property rights
- Money

### Firms

A **firm** is an economic unit that hires factors of production and organizes those factors to produce and sell goods and services. Examples of firms are your local gas station, Wal-Mart, and General Motors.

Firms coordinate a huge amount of economic activity. For example, Wal-Mart buys or rents large buildings, equips them with storage shelves and checkout lanes, and hires labor. Wal-Mart directs the labor and decides what goods to buy and sell.

But Wal-Mart doesn't produce the goods that it sells. It could do so. Wal-Mart could own and coordinate the production of all the things that it sells in its stores. It could also produce all the raw materials that are used to produce the things that it sells. But Sam Walton would not have become one of the wealthiest people in the world if he had followed that path. The reason is that if a firm gets too big, it can't keep track of all the information that is needed to coordinate its activities. It is more efficient for firms to specialize (just as Liz and Joe did) and trade with each other. This trade between firms takes place in markets.

## Markets

In ordinary speech, the word *market* means a place where people buy and sell goods such as fish, meat, fruits, and vegetables. In economics, a *market* has a more general meaning. A **market** is any arrangement that enables buyers and sellers to get information and to do business with each other. An example is the market in which oil is bought and sold—the world oil market. The world oil market is not a place. It is the network of oil producers, oil users, wholesalers, and brokers who buy and sell oil. In the world oil market, decision makers do not meet physically. They make deals by telephone, fax, and direct computer link.

Markets have evolved because they facilitate trade. Without organized markets, we would miss out on a substantial part of the potential gains from trade. Enterprising individuals and firms, each pursuing their own self-interest, have profited from making markets—standing ready to buy or sell the items in which they specialize. But markets can work only when property rights exist.

## Property Rights

The social arrangements that govern the ownership, use, and disposal of anything that people value are called **property rights**. *Real property* includes land and buildings—the things we call property in ordinary speech—and durable goods such as plant and equipment. *Financial property* includes stocks and bonds and money in the bank. *Intellectual property* is the intangible product of creative effort. This type of property includes books, music, computer programs, and inventions of all kinds and is protected by copyrights and patents.

Where property rights are enforced, people have the incentive to specialize and produce the goods in which they have a comparative advantage. Where people can steal the production of others, resources are devoted not to production but to protecting possessions. Without property rights, we would still be hunting and gathering like our Stone Age ancestors.

## Money

**Money** is any commodity or token that is generally acceptable as a means of payment. Liz and Joe didn't use money in the example above. They exchanged salads and smoothies. In principle, trade in markets can exchange any item for any other item. But you can perhaps imagine how complicated life would be if we exchanged goods for other goods. The "invention" of money makes trading in markets much more efficient.

## Circular Flows Through Markets

Figure 2.7 shows the flows that result from the choices that households and firms make. Households specialize and choose the quantities of labor, land, capital, and entrepreneurial services to sell or rent to firms. Firms choose the quantities of factors of production to hire. These (red) flows go through the *factor markets*. Households choose the quantities of goods and services to buy, and firms choose the quantities to produce. These (red) flows go through the *goods markets*. Households receive incomes and make expenditures on goods and services (the green flows).

How do markets coordinate all these decisions?

## Coordinating Decisions

Markets coordinate decisions through price adjustments. To see how, think about your local market for hamburgers. Suppose that too few hamburgers are available and some people who want to buy hamburgers are not able to do so. To make buying and selling plans the same, either more hamburgers must be offered for sale or buyers must scale down their appetites (or both). A rise in the price of a hamburger produces this outcome. A higher price encourages producers to offer more hamburgers for sale. It also encourages some people to change their lunch plans. Fewer people buy hamburgers, and more buy hot dogs. More hamburgers (and more hot dogs) are offered for sale.

Alternatively, suppose that more hamburgers are available than people want to buy. In this case, to make the choices of buyers and sellers compatible, more hamburgers must be bought or fewer hamburgers must be offered for sale (or both). A fall in the price of a hamburger achieves this outcome. A lower price encourages firms to produce a smaller quantity of hamburgers. It also encourages people to buy more hamburgers.

**FIGURE 2.7** Circular Flows in the Market Economy

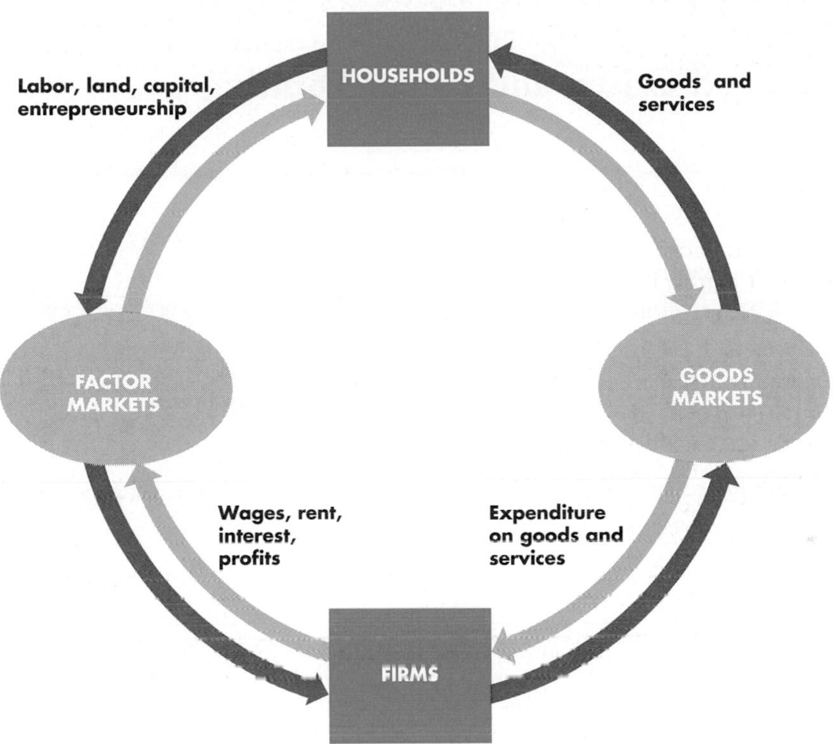


Households and firms make economic choices and markets coordinate these choices.

Households choose the quantities of labor, land, capital, and entrepreneurial services to sell or rent to firms in exchange for wages, rent, interest, and profit. Households also choose how to spend their incomes on the various types of goods and services available.

Firms choose the quantities of factors of production to hire and the quantities of goods and services to produce.

Goods markets and factor markets coordinate these choices of households and firms.

The counterclockwise red flows are real flows—the flow of factors of production from households to firms and the flow of goods and services from firms to households.

The clockwise green flows are the payments for the red flows. They are the flow of incomes from firms to households and the flow of expenditure on goods and services from households to firms.

myeconlab animation

## Review Quiz

1. Why are social institutions such as firms, markets, property rights, and money necessary?
2. What are the main functions of markets?
3. What are the flows in the market economy that go from firms to households and the flows from households to firms?

myeconlab Work Study Plan 2.5 and get instant feedback.

◆ You have now begun to see how economists approach economic questions. Scarcity, choice, and divergent opportunity costs explain why we specialize and trade and why firms, markets, property rights, and money have developed. You can see all around you the lessons you've learned in this chapter. *Reading Between the Lines* on pp. 46–47 provides an opportunity to apply the *PPF* model to deepen your understanding of the reasons for the increase in the cost of food associated with the increase in corn production.

READING BETWEEN THE LINES 

# The Rising Opportunity Cost of Food

## Fuel Choices, Food Crises, and Finger-Pointing

http://www.nytimes.com
April 15, 2008

The idea of turning farms into fuel plants seemed, for a time, like one of the answers to high global oil prices and supply worries. That strategy seemed to reach a high point last year when Congress mandated a fivefold increase in the use of biofuels.

But now a reaction is building against policies in the United States and Europe to promote ethanol and similar fuels, with political leaders from poor countries contending that these fuels are driving up food prices and starving poor people. …

In some countries, the higher prices are leading to riots, political instability, and growing worries about feeding the poorest people. …

Many specialists in food policy consider government mandates for biofuels to be ill advised, agreeing that the diversion of crops like corn into fuel production has contributed to the higher prices. But other factors have played big roles, including droughts that have limited output and rapid global economic growth that has created higher demand for food.

That growth, much faster over the last four years than the historical norm, is lifting millions of people out of destitution and giving them access to better diets. But farmers are having trouble keeping up with the surge in demand.

While there is agreement that the growth of biofuels has contributed to higher food prices, the amount is disputed. …

C. Ford Runge, an economist at the University of Minnesota, said it is "extremely difficult to disentangle" the effect of biofuels on food costs. Nevertheless, he said there was little that could be done to mitigate the effect of droughts and the growing appetite for protein in developing countries.

"Ethanol is the one thing we can do something about," he said. "It's about the only lever we have to pull, but none of the politicians have the courage to pull the lever." …



## Essence of the Story

- In 2007, Congress mandated a fivefold increase in the use of biofuels.
- Political leaders in poor countries and specialists in food policy say the biofuel mandate is ill advised and the diversion of corn into fuel production has raised the cost of food.
- Drought that has limited corn production and global economic growth that has increased the demand for protein have also raised the cost of food.
- An economist at the University of Minnesota says that while it is difficult to determine the effect of biofuels on food costs, it is the only factor under our control.

## Economic Analysis

- Ethanol is made from corn in the United States, so biofuel and food compete to use the same resources.
- To produce more ethanol and meet the Congress's mandate, farmers increased the number of acres devoted to corn production.
- In 2008, the amount of land devoted to corn production increased by 20 percent in the United States and by 2 percent in the rest of the world.
- Figure 1 shows the U.S. production possibilities frontier, *PPF*, for corn and other goods and services.
- The increase in the production of corn is illustrated by a movement along the *PPF* in Fig. 1 from point *A* in 2007 to point *B* in 2008.
- In moving from point *A* to point *B*, the United States incurs a higher opportunity cost of producing corn, indicated by the greater slope of the *PPF* at point *B*.
- In other regions of the world, despite the fact that more land was devoted to corn production, the amount of corn produced didn't change.
- The reason is that droughts in South America and Eastern Europe lowered the crop yield per acre in those regions.
- Figure 2 shows the rest of the world's *PPF* for corn and other goods and services in 2007 and 2008.
- The increase in the amount of land devoted to producing corn is illustrated by a movement along the $PPF_{07}$.
- With a decrease in the crop yield, production possibilities decreased and the *PPF* rotated inward.
- The rotation from $PPF_{07}$ to $PPF_{08}$ illustrates this decrease in production possibilities.
- The opportunity cost of producing corn in the rest of the world increased for two reasons: the movement along its *PPF* and the inward rotation of the *PPF*.
- With a higher opportunity cost of producing corn, the cost of both biofuel and food increases.

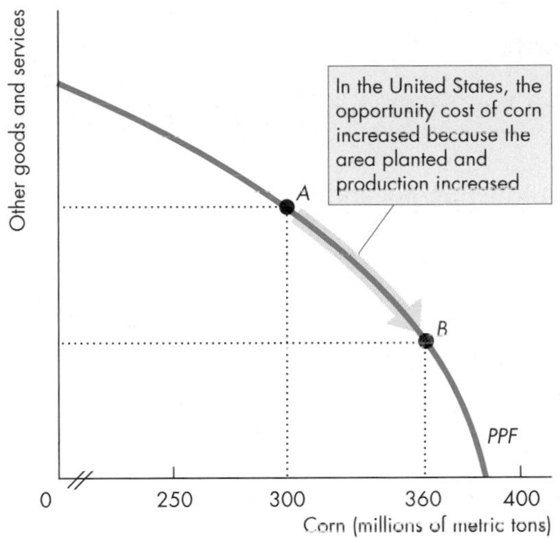


**Figure 1 U.S. *PPF***

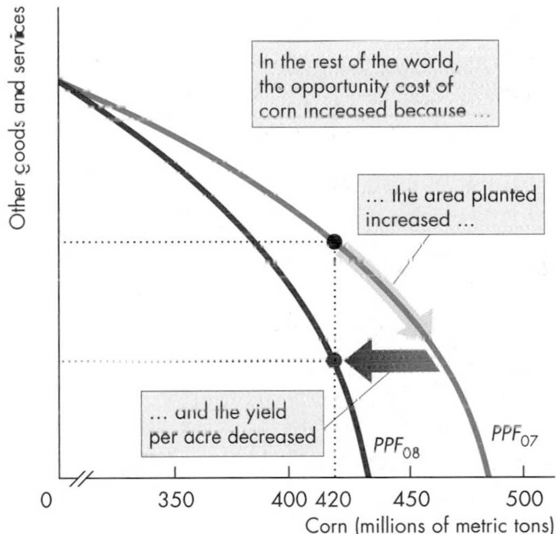


**Figure 2 Rest of the World *PPF***

## SUMMARY

### Key Points

#### Production Possibilities and Opportunity Cost (pp. 32–34)

- The production possibilities frontier, *PPF*, is the boundary between production levels that are attainable and those that are not attainable when all the available resources are used to their limit.
- Production efficiency occurs at points on the *PPF*.
- Along the *PPF*, the opportunity cost of producing more of one good is the amount of the other good that must be given up.
- The opportunity cost of all goods increases as the production of the good increases.

#### Using Resources Efficiently (pp. 35–37)

- Allocative efficiency occurs when goods and services are produced at the least possible cost and in the quantities that bring the greatest possible benefit.
- The marginal cost of a good is the opportunity cost of producing one more unit of it.
- The marginal benefit from a good is the benefit received from consuming one more unit of it, measured by the willingness to pay for it.
- The marginal benefit of a good decreases as the amount of the good available increases.
- Resources are used efficiently when the marginal cost of each good is equal to its marginal benefit.

#### Economic Growth (pp. 38–39)

- Economic growth, which is the expansion of production possibilities, results from capital accumulation and technological change.
- The opportunity cost of economic growth is forgone current consumption.

#### Gains from Trade (pp. 40–43)

- A person has a comparative advantage in producing a good if that person can produce the good at a lower opportunity cost than everyone else.
- People gain by specializing in the activity in which they have a comparative advantage and trading with others.
- Dynamic comparative advantage arises from learning-by-doing.

#### Economic Coordination (pp. 43–45)

- Firms coordinate a large amount of economic activity, but there is a limit to the efficient size of a firm.
- Markets coordinate the economic choices of people and firms.
- Markets can work efficiently only when property rights exist.
- Money makes trading in markets more efficient.

### Key Figures



### Key Terms

## PROBLEMS and APPLICATIONS

myeconlab Work problems 1–11 in Chapter 2 Study Plan and get instant feedback.
Work problems 12–21 as Homework, a Quiz, or a Test if assigned by your instructor.

1. Brazil produces ethanol from sugar, and the land used to grow sugar can be used to grow food crops. Suppose that Brazil's production possibilities for ethanol and food crops are as follows

| Ethanol (barrels per day) | | Food crops (tons per day) |
|---|---|---|
| 70 | and | 0 |
| 64 | and | 1 |
| 54 | and | 2 |
| 40 | and | 3 |
| 22 | and | 4 |
| 0 | and | 5 |

   a. Draw a graph of Brazil's *PPF* and explain how your graph illustrates scarcity.
   b. If Brazil produces 40 barrels of ethanol a day, how much food must it produce if it achieves production efficiency?
   c. Why does Brazil face a tradeoff on its *PPF*?
   d. If Brazil increases its production of ethanol from 40 barrels per day to 54 barrels per day, what is the opportunity cost of the additional ethanol?
   e. If Brazil increases its production of food crops from 2 tons per day to 3 tons per day, what is the opportunity cost of the additional food?
   f. What is the relationship between your answers to d and e?
   g. Does Brazil face an increasing opportunity cost of ethanol? What feature of the *PPF* that you've drawn illustrates increasing opportunity cost?
2. Define marginal cost and use the information provided in the table in problem 1 to calculate the marginal cost of producing a ton of food when the quantity produced is 2.5 tons per day.
3. Define marginal benefit, explain how it is measured, and explain why the information provided in the table in problem 1 does not enable you to calculate the marginal benefit of food.
4. Distinguish between *production efficiency* and *allocative efficiency*. Explain why many production possibilities achieve production efficiency but only one achieves allocative efficiency.
5. Harry enjoys tennis but wants a high grade in his economics course. The figure shows the limits to what he can achieve: It is Harry's *PPF* for these two "goods."

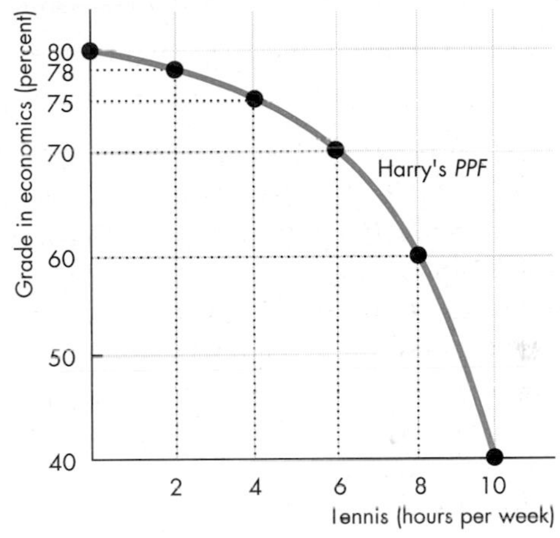


The following figure shows Harry's *MB* curve for tennis.

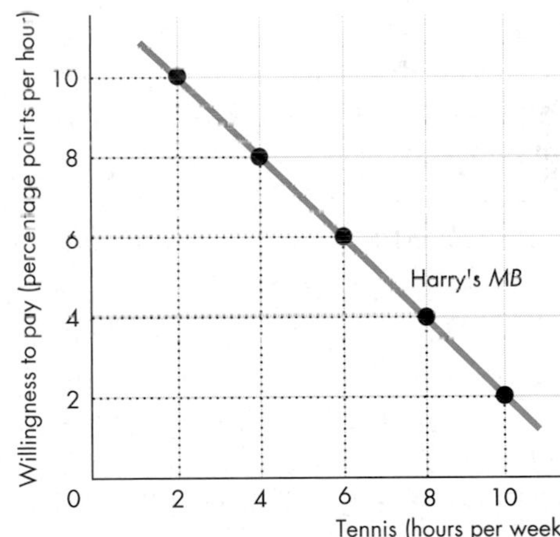


   a. What is Harry's marginal cost of tennis if he plays for (i) 3 hours a week; (ii) 5 hours a week; and (iii) 7 hours a week?
   b. If Harry uses his time to achieve allocative efficiency, what is his economics grade and how many hours of tennis does he play?
   c. Explain why Harry would be worse off getting a grade higher than your answer to b.
   d. If Harry becomes a tennis superstar with big earnings from tennis, what happens to his *PPF*, *MB* curve, and efficient time allocation?

e. If Harry suddenly finds high grades in economics easier to attain, what happens to his *PPF*, *MB* curve, and efficient time allocation?

6. A farm grows wheat and produces pork. The marginal cost of producing each of these products increases as more of it is produced.
   a. Make a graph that illustrates the farm's *PPF*.
   b. The farm adopts a new technology that allows it to use fewer resources to fatten pigs. Use your graph to illustrate the impact of the new technology on the farm's *PPF*.
   c. With the farm using the new technology described in b, has the opportunity cost of producing a ton of wheat increased, decreased, or remained the same? Explain and illustrate your answer.
   d. Is the farm more efficient with the new technology than it was with the old one? Why?

7. In an hour, Sue can produce 40 caps or 4 jackets and Tessa can produce 80 caps or 4 jackets.
   a. Calculate Sue's opportunity cost of producing a cap.
   b. Calculate Tessa's opportunity cost of producing a cap.
   c. Who has a comparative advantage in producing caps?
   d. If Sue and Tessa specialize in producing the good in which each of them has a comparative advantage, and they trade 1 jacket for 15 caps, who gains from the specialization and trade?

8. Suppose that Tessa buys a new machine for making jackets that enables her to make 20 jackets an hour. (She can still make only 80 caps per hour.)
   a. Who now has a comparative advantage in producing jackets?
   b. Can Sue and Tessa still gain from trade?
   c. Would Sue and Tessa still be willing to trade 1 jacket for 15 caps? Explain your answer.

9. "America's baby-boomers are embracing tea for its health benefits," said *The Economist* (July 8, 2005, p. 65). The article went on to say: "Even though the climate is suitable, tea-growing [in the United States] is simply too costly, since the process is labor-intensive and resists automation." Using this information:
   a. Sketch a *PPF* for the production of tea and other goods and services in India.
   b. Sketch a *PPF* for the production of tea and other goods and services in the United States.
   c. Sketch a marginal cost curve for the production of tea in India.
   d. Sketch a marginal cost curve for the production of tea in the United States.
   e. Sketch the marginal benefit curve for tea in the United States before and after the baby-boomers began to appreciate the health benefits of tea.
   f. Explain why the United States does not produce tea and instead imports it from India.
   g. Explain how the quantity of tea that achieves allocative efficiency has changed.
   h. Does the change in preferences toward tea affect the opportunity cost of producing tea?

10. Brazil produces ethanol from sugar at a cost of 83 cents per gallon. The United States produces ethanol from corn at a cost of $1.14 per gallon. Sugar grown on one acre of land produces twice the quantity of ethanol as the corn grown on an acre. The United States imports 5 percent of its ethanol consumption and produces the rest itself. Since 2003, U.S. ethanol production has more than doubled and U.S. corn production has increased by 45 percent.
    a. Does Brazil or the United States have a comparative advantage in producing ethanol?
    b. Do you expect the opportunity cost of producing ethanol in the United States to have increased since 2003? Explain why.
    c. Sketch the *PPF* for ethanol and other goods and services for the United States.
    d. Sketch the *PPF* for ethanol and other goods and services for Brazil.
    e. Sketch a figure similar to Fig. 2.6 on p. 42 to show how both the United States and Brazil can gain from specialization and trade.
    f. Do you think the United States has achieved production efficiency in its manufacture of ethanol? Explain why or why not.
    g. Do you think the United States has achieved allocative efficiency in its manufacture of ethanol? Explain why or why not.

11. For 50 years, Cuba has had a centrally planned economy in which the government makes the big decisions on how resources will be allocated. Why would you expect Cuba's production possibilities (per person) to be smaller than those of the United States? What are the social institutions that help the U.S. economy achieve allocative efficiency that Cuba might lack?

12. Suppose that Yucatan's production possibilities are

| Food (pounds per month) | | Sunscreen (gallons per month) |
|---|---|---|
| 300 | and | 0 |
| 200 | and | 50 |
| 100 | and | 100 |
| 0 | and | 150 |

a. Draw a graph of Yucatan's *PPF* and explain how your graph illustrates a tradeoff.
b. If Yucatan produces 150 pounds of food per month, how much sunscreen must it produce if it achieves production efficiency?
c. What is Yucatan's opportunity cost of producing 1 pound of food?
d. What is Yucatan's opportunity cost of producing 1 gallon of sunscreen?
e. What is the relationship between your answers to c and d?
f. Does Yucatan face an increasing opportunity cost of food? What feature of a *PPF* illustrates increasing opportunity cost and why does the *PPF* that you have drawn not have this feature?

13. What is the marginal cost of a pound of food in Yucatan in problem 12 when the quantity produced is 150 pounds per day? What is special about the marginal cost of food in Yucatan?

14. In Yucatan, which has the production possibilities shown in the table in problem 12, preferences are described by the following table.

| Sunscreen (gallons per month) | Willingness to pay (pounds of food per gallon) |
|---|---|
| 25 | 3 |
| 75 | 2 |
| 125 | 1 |

a. What is the marginal benefit from sunscreen and how it is measured?
b. What information provided in the table above and the table in problem 12 do we need to be able to calculate the marginal benefit from sunscreen in Yucatan?
c. Draw a graph of Yucatan's marginal benefit from sunscreen.

15. "Dr. Arata Kochi, the World Health Organization malaria chief, ... [says that] eradication is counterproductive. With enough money, he said, current tools like nets, medicines and DDT could drive down malaria cases 90 percent. 'But eliminating the last 10 percent is a tremendous task and very expensive,' Dr. Kochi said. 'Even places like South Africa should think twice before taking this path.'"

*The New York Times*, March 4, 2008

a. Is Dr. Kochi talking about *production efficiency* or *allocative efficiency* or both?
b. Make a graph with the percentage of malaria cases eliminated on the $x$-axis and the marginal cost and marginal benefit of driving down malaria cases on the $y$-axis. On your graph:
(i) Draw a marginal cost curve that is consistent with Dr. Kochi's opinion reported in the news article.
(ii) Draw a marginal benefit curve that is consistent with Dr. Kochi's opinion reported in the news article.
(iii) Identify the quantity of malaria eradicated that achieves allocative efficiency.

16. Capital accumulation and technological change bring economic growth, which means that the *PPF* keeps shifting outward: Production that was unattainable yesterday becomes attainable today; and production that is unattainable today will become attainable tomorrow. Why doesn't this process of economic growth mean that scarcity is being defeated and will one day be gone?

17. "Inexpensive broadband access has done far more for online video than enable the success of services like YouTube and iTunes. By unchaining video watchers from their TV sets, it has opened the floodgates to a generation of TV producers for whom the Internet is their native medium."

*The New York Times,* December 2, 2007

a. How has inexpensive broadband changed the production possibilities of video entertainment and other goods and services?
b. Sketch a *PPF* for video entertainment and other goods and services before broadband.
c. Show how the arrival of inexpensive broadband has changed the *PPF*.
d. Sketch a marginal benefit curve for video entertainment.
e. Show how opening the "floodgates to a generation of TV producers for whom the Internet is their native medium" might have changed the marginal benefit from video entertainment.
f. Explain how the quantity of video entertainment that achieves allocative efficiency has changed.

18. Kim can produce 40 pies an hour or 400 cookies an hour. Liam can produce 100 pies an hour or 200 cookies an hour.
    a. Calculate Kim's opportunity cost of producing a pie.
    b. Calculate Liam's opportunity cost of producing a pie.
    c. Who has a comparative advantage in producing pies?
    d. If Kim and Liam spend 30 minutes of each hour producing pies and 30 minutes producing cookies, how many pies and cookies does each of them produce?
    e. Suppose that Kim and Liam increase the time they spend producing the good in which they have a comparative advantage by 15 minutes. What will be the increase in the total number of pies and cookies they produce?
    f. What is the highest price of a pie at which Kim and Liam would agree to trade pies and cookies?
    g. If Kim and Liam specialize and trade, what are the gains from trade?
19. Before the Civil War, the South traded with the North and with England. The South sold cotton and bought manufactured goods and food. During the war, one of President Lincoln's first actions was to blockade the ports, which prevented this trade. The South had to increase its production of munitions and food.
    a. In what did the South have a comparative advantage?
    b. Draw a graph to illustrate production, consumption, and trade in the South before the Civil War.
    c. Was the South consuming inside, on, or outside its *PPF*? Explain your answer.
    d. Draw a graph to show the effects of the Civil War on consumption and production in the South.
    e. Did the Civil War change any opportunity costs in the South? Did the opportunity cost of everything rise? Did any items cost less?
    f. Illustrate your answer to e with appropriate graphs.
20. "A two-time N.B.A. All-Star, Barron Davis has quietly been moonlighting as a [movie] producer since 2005, when he and a high school buddy, Cash Warren, formed a production company called Verso Entertainment.

    In January, Verso's first feature-length effort, "Made in America," a gang-life documentary directed by Stacy Peralta, had its premiere to good reviews at Sundance Film Festival and is being courted by distributors."

    *The New York Times,* February 24, 2008

    a. Does Barron Davis have an *absolute* advantage in basketball and movie directing and is this the reason for his success in both activities?
    b. Does Barron Davis have a comparative advantage in basketball or movie directing or both and is this the reason for his success in both activities?
    c. Sketch a *PPF* between playing basketball and producing other goods and services for Barron Davis and for yourself.
    d. How do you (and people like you) and Barron Davis (and people like him) gain from specialization and trade?
21. After you have studied *Reading Between the Lines* on pp. 46–47, answer the following questions:
    a. How has an Act of the United States Congress increased U.S. production of corn?
    b. Why would you expect an increase in the quantity of corn produced to raise the opportunity cost of corn?
    c. Why did the cost of producing corn increase in the rest of the world?
    d. Is it possible that the increased quantity of corn produced, despite the higher cost of production, moves the United States closer to allocative efficiency?
22. Use the links on MyEconLab (Textbook Resources, Chapter 2, Weblinks) to obtain data on the tuition and other costs of enrolling in the MBA program at a school that interests you.
    a. Draw a *PPF* that shows the tradeoff that you would face if you decided to enroll in the MBA program.
    b. Do you think your marginal benefit of an MBA exceeds your marginal cost?
    c. Based on your answer to b, do you plan to enroll in an MBA program? Is your answer to this question consistent with using your time to achieve your self-interest?

# 3 Demand and Supply

**After studying this chapter, you will be able to:**

- Describe a competitive market and think about a price as an opportunity cost
- Explain the influences on demand
- Explain the influences on supply
- Explain how demand and supply determine prices and quantities bought and sold
- Use the demand and supply model to make predictions about changes in prices and quantities

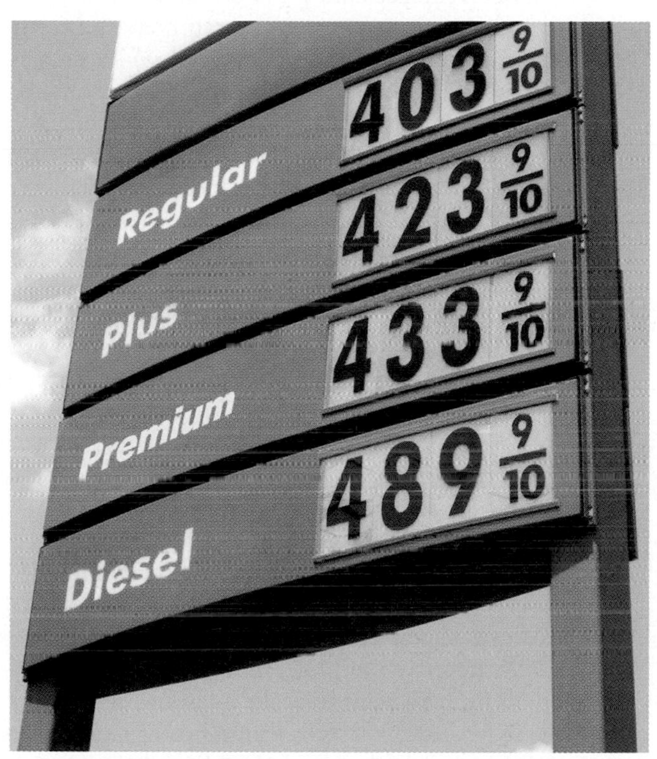


**What makes the prices of oil and gasoline double in** just one year? Will these prices keep on rising? Are the oil companies taking advantage of people? This chapter enables you to answer these and similar questions about prices—prices that rise, prices that fall, and prices that fluctuate.

You already know that economics is about the choices people make to cope with scarcity and how those choices respond to incentives. Prices act as incentives. You're going to see how people respond to prices and how prices get determined by demand and supply. The demand and supply model that you study in this chapter is the main tool of economics. It helps us to answer the big economic question: What, how, and for whom goods and services are produced?

At the end of the chapter, in *Reading Between the Lines*, we'll apply the model to market for gasoline and explain why the price increased so sharply in 2008.

## Markets and Prices

When you need a new pair of running shoes, want a bagel and a latte, plan to upgrade your cell phone, or need to fly home for Thanksgiving, you must find a place where people sell those items or offer those services. The place in which you find them is a *market.* You learned in Chapter 2 (p. 44) that a market is any arrangement that enables buyers and sellers to get information and to do business with each other.

A market has two sides: buyers and sellers. There are markets for *goods* such as apples and hiking boots, for *services* such as haircuts and tennis lessons, for *resources* such as computer programmers and earthmovers, and for other manufactured *inputs* such as memory chips and auto parts. There are also markets for money such as Japanese yen and for financial securities such as Yahoo! stock. Only our imagination limits what can be traded in markets.

Some markets are physical places where buyers and sellers meet and where an auctioneer or a broker helps to determine the prices. Examples of this type of market are the New York Stock Exchange and the wholesale fish, meat, and produce markets.

Some markets are groups of people spread around the world who never meet and know little about each other but are connected through the Internet or by telephone and fax. Examples are the e-commerce markets and the currency markets.

But most markets are unorganized collections of buyers and sellers. You do most of your trading in this type of market. An example is the market for basketball shoes. The buyers in this $3 billion-a-year market are the 45 million Americans who play basketball (or who want to make a fashion statement). The sellers are the tens of thousands of retail sports equipment and footwear stores. Each buyer can visit several different stores, and each seller knows that the buyer has a choice of stores.

Markets vary in the intensity of competition that buyers and sellers face. In this chapter, we're going to study a **competitive market**—a market that has many buyers and many sellers, so no single buyer or seller can influence the price.

Producers offer items for sale only if the price is high enough to cover their opportunity cost. And consumers respond to changing opportunity cost by seeking cheaper alternatives to expensive items.

We are going to study how people respond to *prices* and the forces that determine prices. But to pursue these tasks, we need to understand the relationship between a price and an opportunity cost.

In everyday life, the *price* of an object is the number of dollars that must be given up in exchange for it. Economists refer to this price as the **money price**.

The *opportunity cost* of an action is the highest-valued alternative forgone. If, when you buy a cup of coffee, the highest-valued thing you forgo is some gum, then the opportunity cost of the coffee is the *quantity* of gum forgone. We can calculate the quantity of gum forgone from the money prices of the coffee and the gum.

If the money price of coffee is $1 a cup and the money price of gum is 50¢ a pack, then the opportunity cost of one cup of coffee is two packs of gum. To calculate this opportunity cost, we divide the price of a cup of coffee by the price of a pack of gum and find the *ratio* of one price to the other. The ratio of one price to another is called a **relative price**, and a *relative price is an opportunity cost.*

We can express the relative price of coffee in terms of gum or any other good. The normal way of expressing a relative price is in terms of a "basket" of all goods and services. To calculate this relative price, we divide the money price of a good by the money price of a "basket" of all goods (called a *price index*). The resulting relative price tells us the opportunity cost of the good in terms of how much of the "basket" we must give up to buy it.

The demand and supply model that we are about to study determines *relative prices,* and the word "price" means *relative* price. When we predict that a price will fall, we do not mean that its *money* price will fall—although it might. We mean that its *relative* price will fall. That is, its price will fall *relative* to the average price of other goods and services.

### Review Quiz

1. What is the distinction between a money price and a relative price?
2. Explain why a relative price is an opportunity cost.
3. Think of examples of goods whose relative price has risen or fallen by a large amount.

Work Study Plan 3.1 and get instant feedback.

Let's begin our study of demand and supply, starting with demand.

## Demand

If you demand something, then you

1. Want it,
2. Can afford it, and
3. Plan to buy it.

*Wants* are the unlimited desires or wishes that people have for goods and services. How many times have you thought that you would like something "if only you could afford it" or "if it weren't so expensive"? Scarcity guarantees that many—perhaps most—of our wants will never be satisfied. Demand reflects a decision about which wants to satisfy.

The **quantity demanded** of a good or service is the amount that consumers plan to buy during a given time period at a particular price. The quantity demanded is not necessarily the same as the quantity actually bought. Sometimes the quantity demanded exceeds the amount of goods available, so the quantity bought is less than the quantity demanded.

The quantity demanded is measured as an amount per unit of time. For example, suppose that you buy one cup of coffee a day. The quantity of coffee that you demand can be expressed as 1 cup per day, 7 cups per week, or 365 cups per year.

Many factors influence buying plans, and one of them is the price. We look first at the relationship between the quantity demanded of a good and its price. To study this relationship, we keep all other influences on buying plans the same and we ask: How, other things remaining the same, does the quantity demanded of a good change as its price changes?

The law of demand provides the answer.

### The Law of Demand

The **law of demand** states

> Other things remaining the same, the higher the price of a good, the smaller is the quantity demanded; and the lower the price of a good, the greater is the quantity demanded.

Why does a higher price reduce the quantity demanded? For two reasons:

- Substitution effect
- Income effect

**Substitution Effect** When the price of a good rises, other things remaining the same, its *relative* price—its opportunity cost—rises. Although each good is unique, it has *substitutes*—other goods that can be used in its place. As the opportunity cost of a good rises, the incentive to economize on its use and switch to a substitute becomes stronger.

**Income Effect** When a price rises, other things remaining the same, the price rises *relative* to income. Faced with a higher price and an unchanged income, people cannot afford to buy all the things they previously bought. They must decrease the quantities demanded of at least some goods and services. Normally, the good whose price has increased will be one of the goods that people buy less of.

To see the substitution effect and the income effect at work, think about the effects of a change in the price of an energy bar. Several different goods are substitutes for an energy bar. For example, an energy drink could be consumed instead of an energy bar.

Suppose that an energy bar initially sells for $3 and then its price falls to $1.50. People now substitute energy bars for energy drinks—the substitution effect. And with a budget that now has some slack from the lower price of an energy bar, people buy even more energy bars—the income effect. The quantity of energy bars demanded increases for these two reasons.

Now suppose that an energy bar initially sells for $3 and then the price doubles to $6. People now buy fewer energy bars and more energy drinks—the substitution effect. And faced with a tighter budget, people buy even fewer energy bars—the income effect. The quantity of energy bars demanded decreases for these two reasons.

### Demand Curve and Demand Schedule

You are now about to study one of the two most used curves in economics: the demand curve. And you are going to encounter one of the most critical distinctions: the distinction between *demand* and *quantity demanded.*

The term **demand** refers to the entire relationship between the price of a good and the quantity demanded of that good. Demand is illustrated by the demand curve and the demand schedule. The term *quantity demanded* refers to a point on a demand curve—the quantity demanded at a particular price.

Figure 3.1 shows the demand curve for energy bars. A **demand curve** shows the relationship between the quantity demanded of a good and its price when all other influences on consumers' planned purchases remain the same.

The table in Fig. 3.1 is the demand schedule for energy bars. A *demand schedule* lists the quantities demanded at each price when all the other influences on consumers' planned purchases remain the same. For example, if the price of a bar is 50¢, the quantity demanded is 22 million a week. If the price is $2.50, the quantity demanded is 5 million a week. The other rows of the table show the quantities demanded at prices of $1.00, $1.50, and $2.00.

We graph the demand schedule as a demand curve with the quantity demanded on the *x*-axis and the price on the *y*-axis. The points on the demand curve labeled *A* through *E* correspond to the rows of the demand schedule. For example, point *A* on the graph shows a quantity demanded of 22 million energy bars a week at a price of 50¢ a bar.

**Willingness and Ability to Pay** Another way of looking at the demand curve is as a willingness-and-ability-to-pay curve. The willingness and ability to pay is a measure of *marginal benefit.*

If a small quantity is available, the highest price that someone is willing and able to pay for one more unit is high. But as the quantity available increases, the marginal benefit of each additional unit falls and the highest price that someone is willing and able to pay also falls along the demand curve.

In Fig. 3.1, if only 5 million energy bars are available each week, the highest price that someone is willing to pay for the 5 millionth bar is $2.50. But if 22 million energy bars are available each week, someone is willing to pay 50¢ for the last bar bought.

## A Change in Demand

When any factor that influences buying plans other than the price of the good changes, there is a **change in demand.** Figure 3.2 illustrates an increase in demand. When demand increases, the demand curve shifts rightward and the quantity demanded at each price is greater. For example, at $2.50 a bar, the quantity demanded on the original (blue) demand curve is 5 million energy bars a week. On the new (red) demand curve, at $2.50 a bar, the quantity demanded is 15 million bars a week. Look closely at the numbers in the table and check that the quantity demanded at each price is greater.

**FIGURE 3.1** The Demand Curve

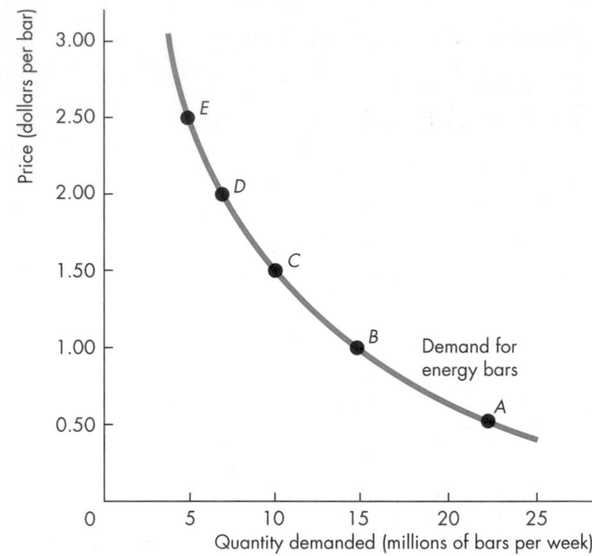


| | Price (dollars per bar) | Quantity demanded (millions of bars per week) |
|---|---|---|
| *A* | 0.50 | 22 |
| *B* | 1.00 | 15 |
| *C* | 1.50 | 10 |
| *D* | 2.00 | 7 |
| *E* | 2.50 | 5 |

The table shows a demand schedule for energy bars. At a price of 50¢ a bar, 22 million bars a week are demanded; at a price of $1.50 a bar, 10 million bars a week are demanded. The demand curve shows the relationship between quantity demanded and price, other things remaining the same. The demand curve slopes downward: As the price decreases, the quantity demanded increases.

The demand curve can be read in two ways. For a given price, the demand curve tells us the quantity that people plan to buy. For example, at a price of $1.50 a bar, people plan to buy 10 million bars a week. For a given quantity, the demand curve tells us the maximum price that consumers are willing and able to pay for the last bar available. For example, the maximum price that consumers will pay for the 15 millionth bar is $1.00.

**FIGURE 3.2** An Increase in Demand

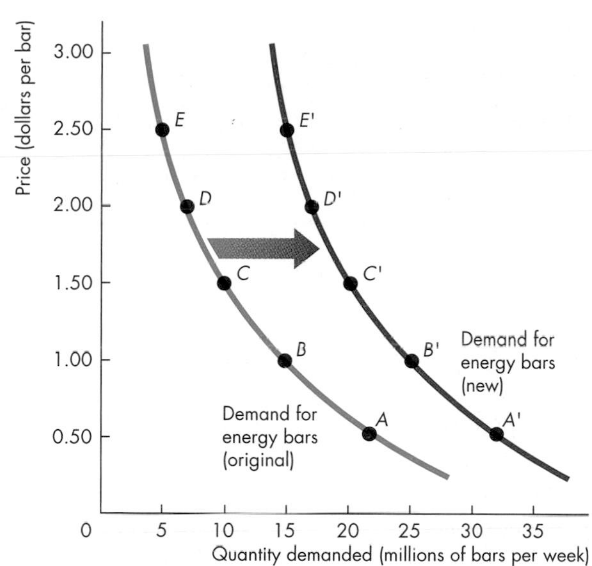


| | Original demand schedule Original income | | | New demand schedule New higher income | |
|---|---|---|---|---|---|
| | Price (dollars per bar) | Quantity demanded (millions of bars per week) | | Price (dollars per bar) | Quantity demanded (millions of bars per week) |
| A | 0.50 | 22 | A' | 0.50 | 32 |
| B | 1.00 | 15 | B' | 1.00 | 25 |
| C | 1.50 | 10 | C' | 1.50 | 20 |
| D | 2.00 | 7 | D' | 2.00 | 17 |
| E | 2.50 | 5 | E' | 2.50 | 15 |

A change in any influence on buyers' plans other than the price of the good itself results in a new demand schedule and a shift of the demand curve. A change in income changes the demand for energy bars. At a price of $1.50 a bar, 10 million bars a week are demanded at the original income (row C of the table) and 20 million bars a week are demanded at the new higher income (row C'). A rise in income increases the demand for energy bars. The demand curve shifts *rightward*, as shown by the shift arrow and the resulting red curve.

myeconlab animation

Six main factors bring changes in demand. They are changes in

- The prices of related goods
- Expected future prices
- Income
- Expected future income and credit
- Population
- Preferences

**Prices of Related Goods** The quantity of energy bars that consumers plan to buy depends in part on the prices of substitutes for energy bars. A **substitute** is a good that can be used in place of another good. For example, a bus ride is a substitute for a train ride; a hamburger is a substitute for a hot dog; and an energy drink is a substitute for an energy bar. If the price of a substitute for an energy bar rises, people buy less of the substitute and more energy bars. For example, if the price of an energy drink rises, people buy fewer energy drinks and more energy bars. The demand for energy bars increases.

The quantity of energy bars that people plan to buy also depends on the prices of complements with energy bars. A **complement** is a good that is used in conjunction with another good. Hamburgers and fries are complements, and so are energy bars and exercise. If the price of an hour at the gym falls, people buy more gym time *and more* energy bars.

**Expected Future Prices** If the price of a good is expected to rise in the future and if the good can be stored, the opportunity cost of obtaining the good for future use is lower today than it will be when the price has increased. So people retime their purchases—they substitute over time. They buy more of the good now before its price is expected to rise (and less afterward), so the demand for the good today increases.

For example, suppose that a Florida frost damages the season's orange crop. You expect the price of orange juice to rise, so you fill your freezer with enough frozen juice to get you through the next six months. Your current demand for frozen orange juice has increased, and your future demand has decreased.

Similarly, if the price of a good is expected to fall in the future, the opportunity cost of buying the good today is high relative to what it is expected to be in the future. So again, people retime their purchases. They buy less of the good now before its price falls, so the demand for the good decreases today and increases in the future.

Computer prices are constantly falling, and this fact poses a dilemma. Will you buy a new computer now, in time for the start of the school year, or will you wait until the price has fallen some more? Because people expect computer prices to keep falling, the current demand for computers is less (and the future demand is greater) than it otherwise would be.

**Income** Consumers' income influences demand. When income increases, consumers buy more of most goods; and when income decreases, consumers buy less of most goods. Although an increase in income leads to an increase in the demand for *most* goods, it does not lead to an increase in the demand for *all* goods. A **normal good** is one for which demand increases as income increases. An **inferior good** is one for which demand decreases as income increases. As incomes increase, the demand for air travel (a normal good) increases and the demand for long-distance bus trips (an inferior good) decreases.

**Expected Future Income and Credit** When income is expected to increase in the future, or when credit is easy to obtain, demand might increase now. For example, a salesperson gets the news that she will receive a big bonus at the end of the year, so she goes into debt and buys a new car right now.

**Population** Demand also depends on the size and the age structure of the population. The larger the population, the greater is the demand for all goods and services; the smaller the population, the smaller is the demand for all goods and services.

For example, the demand for parking spaces or movies or just about anything that you can imagine is much greater in New York City (population 7.5 million) than it is in Boise, Idaho (population 150,000).

Also, the larger the proportion of the population in a given age group, the greater is the demand for the goods and services used by that age group.

For example, during the 1990s, a decrease in the college-age population decreased the demand for college places. During those same years, the number of Americans aged 85 years and over increased by more than 1 million. As a result, the demand for nursing home services increased.

**TABLE 3.1** The Demand for Energy Bars

**The Law of Demand**

*The quantity of energy bars demanded*

| *Decreases if:* | *Increases if:* |
|---|---|
| ■ The price of an energy bar rises | ■ The price of an energy bar falls |

**Changes in Demand**

*The demand for energy bars*

| *Decreases if:* | *Increases if:* |
|---|---|
| ■ The price of a substitute falls | ■ The price of a substitute rises |
| ■ The price of a complement rises | ■ The price of a complement falls |
| ■ The price of an energy bar is expected to fall | ■ The price of an energy bar is expected to rise |
| ■ Income falls* | ■ Income rises* |
| ■ Expected future income falls or credit becomes harder to get | ■ Expected future income rises or credit becomes easier to get |
| ■ The population decreases | ■ The population increases |

*An energy bar is a normal good.

**Preferences** Demand depends on preferences. *Preferences* determine the value that people place on each good and service. Preferences depend on such things as the weather, information, and fashion. For example, greater health and fitness awareness has shifted preferences in favor of energy bars, so the demand for energy bars has increased.

Table 3.1 summarizes the influences on demand and the direction of those influences.

## A Change in the Quantity Demanded Versus a Change in Demand

Changes in the influences on buyers' plans bring either a change in the quantity demanded or a change in demand. Equivalently, they bring either a movement along the demand curve or a shift of the demand curve. The distinction between a change in the quantity demanded and a change in demand is the same as that between a movement along the demand curve and a shift of the demand curve.

A point on the demand curve shows the quantity demanded at a given price. So a movement along the demand curve shows a **change in the quantity demanded**. The entire demand curve shows demand. So a shift of the demand curve shows a *change in demand*. Figure 3.3 illustrates these distinctions.

**Movement Along the Demand Curve** If the price of the good changes but no other influence on buying plans changes, we illustrate the effect as a movement along the demand curve.

A fall in the price of a good increases the quantity demanded of it. In Fig. 3.3, we illustrate the effect of a fall in price as a movement down along the demand curve $D_0$.

A rise in the price of a good decreases the quantity demanded of it. In Fig. 3.3, we illustrate the effect of a rise in price as a movement up along the demand curve $D_0$.

**A Shift of the Demand Curve** If the price of a good remains constant but some other influence on buyers' plans changes, there is a change in demand for that good. We illustrate a change in demand as a shift of the demand curve. For example, if more people work out at the gym, consumers buy more energy bars regardless of the price of a bar. That is what a rightward shift of the demand curve shows—more energy bars are demanded at each price.

In Fig. 3.3, there is a *change in demand* and the demand curve shifts when any influence on buyers' plans changes, other than the price of the good. Demand *increases* and the demand curve *shifts rightward* (to the red demand curve $D_1$) if the price of a substitute rises, the price of a complement falls, the expected future price of the good rises, income increases (for a normal good), expected future income or credit increases, or the population increases. Demand *decreases* and the demand curve *shifts leftward* (to the red demand curve $D_2$) if the price of a substitute falls, the price of a complement rises, the expected future price of the good falls, income decreases (for a normal good), expected future income or credit decreases, or the population decreases. (For an inferior good, the effects of changes in income are in the opposite direction to those described above.)

**FIGURE 3.3** A Change in the Quantity Demanded Versus a Change in Demand

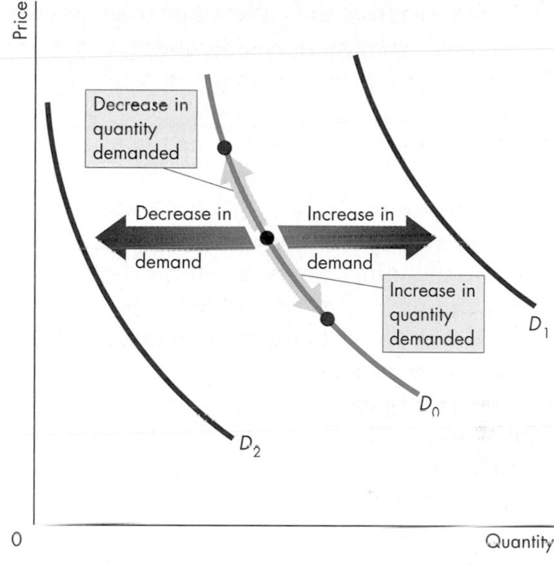


When the price of the good changes, there is a movement along the demand curve and *a change in the quantity demanded,* shown by the blue arrows on demand curve $D_0$. When any other influence on buyers' plans changes, there is a shift of the demand curve and *a change in demand.* An increase in demand shifts the demand curve rightward (from $D_0$ to $D_1$). A decrease in demand shifts the demand curve leftward (from $D_0$ to $D_2$)

## Review Quiz

1. Define the quantity demanded of a good or service.
2. What is the law of demand and how do we illustrate it?
3. What does the demand curve tell us about the price that consumers are willing to pay?
4. List all the influences on buying plans that change demand, and for each influence, say whether it increases or decreases demand.
5. Why does demand not change when the price of a good changes with no change in the other influences on buying plans?

myeconlab Work Study Plan 3.2 and get instant feedback.

## Supply

If a firm supplies a good or service, the firm

1. Has the resources and technology to produce it,
2. Can profit from producing it, and
3. Plans to produce it and sell it.

A supply is more than just having the *resources* and the *technology* to produce something. *Resources and technology* are the constraints that limit what is possible.

Many useful things can be produced, but they are not produced unless it is profitable to do so. Supply reflects a decision about which technologically feasible items to produce.

The **quantity supplied** of a good or service is the amount that producers plan to sell during a given time period at a particular price. The quantity supplied is not necessarily the same amount as the quantity actually sold. Sometimes the quantity supplied is greater than the quantity demanded, so the quantity sold is less than the quantity supplied.

Like the quantity demanded, the quantity supplied is measured as an amount per unit of time. For example, suppose that GM produces 1,000 cars a day. The quantity of cars supplied by GM can be expressed as 1,000 a day, 7,000 a week, or 365,000 a year. Without the time dimension, we cannot tell whether a particular quantity is large or small.

Many factors influence selling plans, and again one of them is the price of the good. We look first at the relationship between the quantity supplied of a good and its price. Just as we did when we studied demand, to isolate the relationship between the quantity supplied of a good and its price, we keep all other influences on selling plans the same and ask: How does the quantity supplied of a good change as its price changes when other things remain the same?

The law of supply provides the answer.

### The Law of Supply

The **law of supply** states:

> Other things remaining the same, the higher the price of a good, the greater is the quantity supplied; and the lower the price of a good, the smaller is the quantity supplied.

Why does a higher price increase the quantity supplied? It is because *marginal cost increases.* As the quantity produced of any good increases, the marginal cost of producing the good increases. (You can refresh your memory of increasing marginal cost in Chapter 2, p. 35.)

It is never worth producing a good if the price received for the good does not at least cover the marginal cost of producing it. When the price of a good rises, other things remaining the same, producers are willing to incur a higher marginal cost, so they increase production. The higher price brings forth an increase in the quantity supplied.

Let's now illustrate the law of supply with a supply curve and a supply schedule.

### Supply Curve and Supply Schedule

You are now going to study the second of the two most used curves in economics: the supply curve. And you're going to learn about the critical distinction between *supply* and *quantity supplied.*

The term **supply** refers to the entire relationship between the price of a good and the quantity supplied of it. Supply is illustrated by the supply curve and the supply schedule. The term *quantity supplied* refers to a point on a supply curve—the quantity supplied at a particular price.

Figure 3.4 shows the supply curve of energy bars. A **supply curve** shows the relationship between the quantity supplied of a good and its price when all other influences on producers' planned sales remain the same. The supply curve is a graph of a supply schedule.

The table in Fig. 3.4 sets out the supply schedule for energy bars. A *supply schedule* lists the quantities supplied at each price when all the other influences on producers' planned sales remain the same. For example, if the price of a bar is 50¢, the quantity supplied is zero—in row *A* of the table. If the price of a bar is \$1.00, the quantity supplied is 6 million energy bars a week—in row *B*. The other rows of the table show the quantities supplied at prices of \$1.50, \$2.00, and \$2.50.

To make a supply curve, we graph the quantity supplied on the *x*-axis and the price on the *y*-axis, just as in the case of the demand curve. The points on the supply curve labeled *A* through *E* correspond to the rows of the supply schedule. For example, point *A* on the graph shows a quantity supplied of zero at a price of 50¢ an energy bar.

**FIGURE 3.4** The Supply Curve

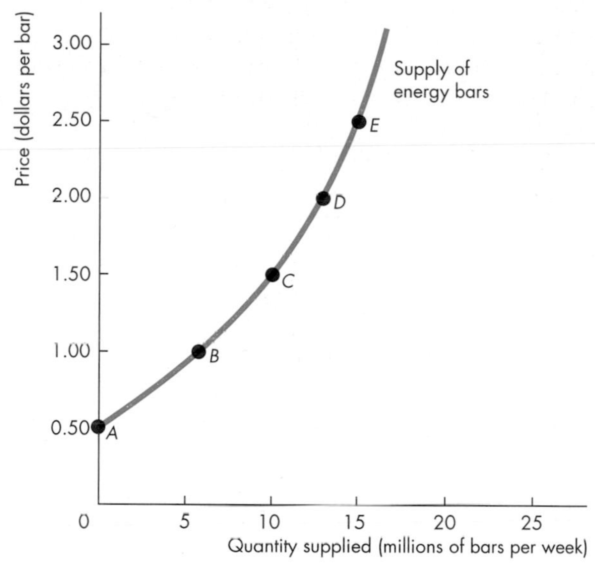


| | Price (dollars per bar) | Quantity supplied (millions of bars per week) |
|---|---|---|
| *A* | 0.50 | 0 |
| *B* | 1.00 | 6 |
| *C* | 1.50 | 10 |
| *D* | 2.00 | 13 |
| *E* | 2.50 | 15 |

The table shows the supply schedule of energy bars. For example, at a price of $1.00, 6 million bars a week are supplied; at a price of $2.50, 15 million bars a week are supplied. The supply curve shows the relationship between the quantity supplied and the price, other things remaining the same. The supply curve slopes upward: As the price of a good increases, the quantity supplied increases.

A supply curve can be read in two ways. For a given price, the supply curve tells us the quantity that producers plan to sell at that price. For example, at a price of $1.50 a bar, producers are willing to sell 10 million bars a week. For a given quantity, the supply curve tells us the minimum price at which producers are willing to sell one more bar. For example, if 15 million bars are produced each week, the lowest price at which a producer is willing to sell the 15 millionth bar is $2.50.

myeconlab animation

**Minimum Supply Price** The supply curve can be interpreted as a minimum-supply-price curve—a curve that shows the lowest price at which someone is willing to sell. This lowest price is the *marginal cost.*

If a small quantity is produced, the lowest price at which someone is willing to sell one more unit is low. But as the quantity produced increases, the marginal cost of each additional unit rises, so the lowest price at which someone is willing to sell rises along the supply curve.

In Fig. 3.4, if 15 million bars are produced each week, the lowest price at which someone is willing to sell the 15 millionth bar is $2.50. But if 10 million bars are produced each week, someone is willing to accept $1.50 for the last bar produced.

## A Change in Supply

When any factor that influences selling plans other than the price of the good changes, there is a **change in supply**. Six main factors bring changes in supply. They are changes in

- The prices of factors of production
- The prices of related goods produced
- Expected future prices
- The number of suppliers
- Technology
- The state of nature

**Prices of Factors of Production** The prices of the factors of production used to produce a good influence its supply. To see this influence, think about the supply curve as a minimum-supply-price curve. If the price of a factor of production rises, the lowest price that a producer is willing to accept for that good rises, so supply decreases. For example, during 2008, as the price of jet fuel increased, the supply of air travel decreased. Similarly, a rise in the minimum wage decreases the supply of hamburgers.

**Prices of Related Goods Produced** The prices of related goods that firms produce influence supply. For example, if the price of energy gel rises, firms switch production from bars to gel. The supply of energy bars decreases. Energy bars and energy gel are *substitutes in production*—goods that can be produced by using the same resources. If the price of beef rises, the supply of cowhide increases. Beef and cowhide are *complements in production*—goods that must be produced together.

**Expected Future Prices** If the price of a good is expected to rise, the return from selling the good in the future is higher than it is today. So supply decreases today and increases in the future.

**The Number of Suppliers** The larger the number of firms that produce a good, the greater is the supply of the good. And as firms enter an industry, the supply in that industry increases. As firms leave an industry, the supply in that industry decreases.

**Technology** The term "technology" is used broadly to mean the way that factors of production are used to produce a good. A technology change occurs when a new method is discovered that lowers the cost of producing a good. For example, new methods used in the factories that produce computer chips have lowered the cost and increased the supply of chips.

**The State of Nature** The state of nature includes all the natural forces that influence production. It includes the state of the weather and, more broadly, the natural environment. Good weather can increase the supply of many agricultural products and bad weather can decrease their supply. Extreme natural events such as earthquakes, tornadoes, and hurricanes can also influence supply.

Figure 3.5 illustrates an increase in supply. When supply increases, the supply curve shifts rightward and the quantity supplied at each price is larger. For example, at $1.00 per bar, on the original (blue) supply curve, the quantity supplied is 6 million bars a week. On the new (red) supply curve, the quantity supplied is 15 million bars a week. Look closely at the numbers in the table in Fig. 3.5 and check that the quantity supplied is larger at each price.

Table 3.2 summarizes the influences on supply and the directions of those influences.

**FIGURE 3.5** An Increase in Supply

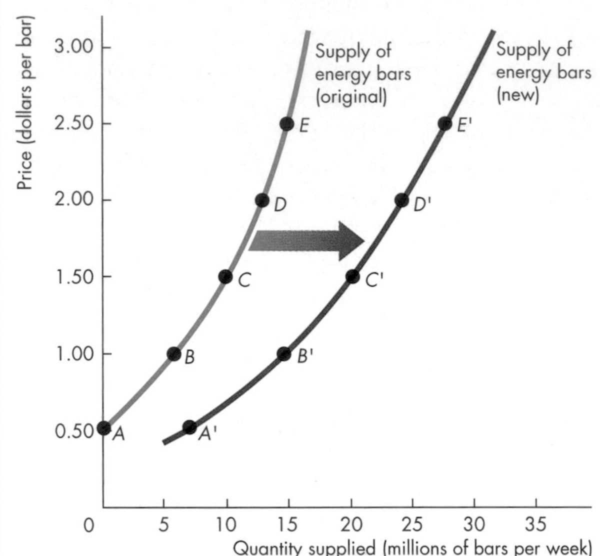


| Original supply schedule Old technology | | | New supply schedule New technology | | |
|---|---|---|---|---|---|
| | Price (dollars per bar) | Quantity supplied (millions of bars per week) | | Price (dollars per bar) | Quantity supplied (millions of bars per week) |
| A | 0.50 | 0 | A' | 0.50 | 7 |
| B | 1.00 | 6 | B' | 1.00 | 15 |
| C | 1.50 | 10 | C' | 1.50 | 20 |
| D | 2.00 | 13 | D' | 2.00 | 25 |
| E | 2.50 | 15 | E' | 2.50 | 27 |

A change in any influence on sellers' plans other than the price of the good itself results in a new supply schedule and a shift of the supply curve. For example, a new, cost-saving technology for producing energy bars changes the supply of energy bars. At a price of $1.50 a bar, 10 million bars a week are supplied when producers use the old technology (row C of the table) and 20 million energy bars a week are supplied when producers use the new technology (row C'). An advance in technology *increases* the supply of energy bars. The supply curve shifts *rightward*, as shown by the shift arrow and the resulting red curve.

## A Change in the Quantity Supplied Versus a Change in Supply

Changes in the influences on producers' planned sales bring either a change in the quantity supplied or a change in supply. Equivalently, they bring either a movement along the supply curve or a shift of the supply curve.

A point on the supply curve shows the quantity supplied at a given price. A movement along the supply curve shows a **change in the quantity supplied.** The entire supply curve shows supply. A shift of the supply curve shows a *change in supply*.

Figure 3.6 illustrates and summarizes these distinctions. If the price of the good falls and other things remain the same, the quantity supplied of that good decreases and there is a movement down along the supply curve $S_0$. If the price of the good rises and other things remain the same, the quantity supplied increases and there is a movement up along the supply curve $S_0$. When any other influence on selling plans changes, the supply curve shifts and there is a *change in supply*. If supply increases, the supply curve shifts rightward to $S_1$. If supply decreases, the supply curve shifts leftward to $S_2$.

**TABLE 3.2** The Supply of Energy Bars

**The Law of Supply**

*The quantity of energy bars supplied*

| *Decreases if:* | *Increases if:* |
|---|---|
| ■ The price of an energy bar falls | ■ The price of an energy bar rises |

**Changes in Supply**

*The supply of energy bars*

| *Decreases if:* | *Increases if:* |
|---|---|
| ■ The price of a factor of production used to produce energy bars rises | ■ The price of a factor of production used to produce energy bars falls |
| ■ The price of a substitute in production rises | ■ The price of a substitute in production falls |
| ■ The price of a complement in production falls | ■ The price of a complement in production rises |
| ■ The price of an energy bar is expected to rise | ■ The price of an energy bar is expected to fall |
| ■ The number of suppliers of bars decreases | ■ The number of suppliers of bars increases |
| ■ A technology change decreases energy bar production | ■ A technology change increases energy bar production |
| ■ A natural event decreases energy bar production | ■ A natural event increases energy bar production |

**FIGURE 3.6** A Change in the Quantity Supplied Versus a Change in Supply

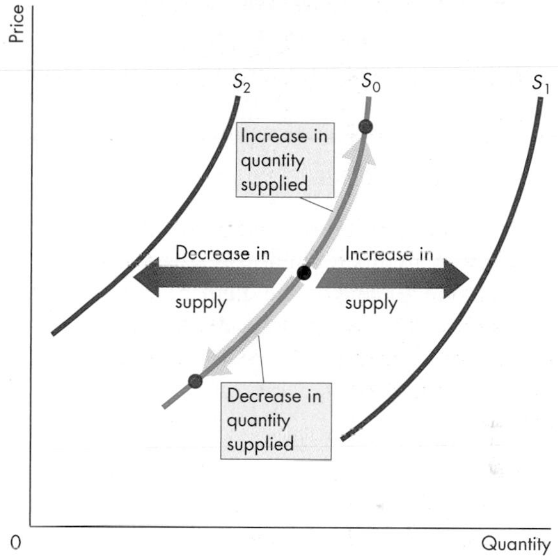


When the price of the good changes, there is a movement along the supply curve and *a change in the quantity supplied*, shown by the blue arrows on supply curve $S_0$. When any other influence on selling plans changes, there is a shift of the supply curve and a *change in supply*. An increase in supply shifts the supply curve rightward (from $S_0$ to $S_1$), and a decrease in supply shifts the supply curve leftward (from $S_0$ to $S_2$).

myeconlab animation

## Review Quiz

1 Define the quantity supplied of a good or service.
2 What is the law of supply and how do we illustrate it?
3 What does the supply curve tell us about the producer's minimum supply price?
4 List all the influences on selling plans, and for each influence, say whether it changes supply.
5 What happens to the quantity of cell phones supplied and the supply of cell phones if the price of a cell phone falls?

myeconlab Work Study Plan 3.3 and get instant feedback.

Now we're going to combine demand and supply and see how prices and quantities are determined.

## Market Equilibrium

We have seen that when the price of a good rises, the quantity demanded *decreases* and the quantity supplied *increases.* We are now going to see how the price adjusts to coordinate the plans of buyers and sellers and achieve an equilibrium in the market.

An *equilibrium* is a situation in which opposing forces balance each other. Equilibrium in a market occurs when the price balances the plans of buyers and sellers. The **equilibrium price** is the price at which the quantity demanded equals the quantity supplied. The **equilibrium quantity** is the quantity bought and sold at the equilibrium price. A market moves toward its equilibrium because

- Price regulates buying and selling plans.
- Price adjusts when plans don't match.

### Price as a Regulator

The price of a good regulates the quantities demanded and supplied. If the price is too high, the quantity supplied exceeds the quantity demanded. If the price is too low, the quantity demanded exceeds the quantity supplied. There is one price at which the quantity demanded equals the quantity supplied. Let's work out what that price is.

Figure 3.7 shows the market for energy bars. The table shows the demand schedule (from Fig. 3.1) and the supply schedule (from Fig. 3.4). If the price of a bar is 50¢, the quantity demanded is 22 million bars a week but no bars are supplied. There is a shortage of 22 million bars a week. This shortage is shown in the final column of the table. At a price of $1.00 a bar, there is still a shortage but only of 9 million bars a week. If the price of a bar is $2.50, the quantity supplied is 15 million bars a week but the quantity demanded is only 5 million. There is a surplus of 10 million bars a week. The one price at which there is neither a shortage nor a surplus is $1.50 a bar. At that price, the quantity demanded is equal to the quantity supplied: 10 million bars a week. The equilibrium price is $1.50 a bar, and the equilibrium quantity is 10 million bars a week.

Figure 3.7 shows that the demand curve and the supply curve intersect at the equilibrium price of $1.50 a bar. At each price *above* $1.50 a bar, there is a surplus of bars. For example, at $2.00 a bar, the surplus is 6

**FIGURE 3.7** Equilibrium

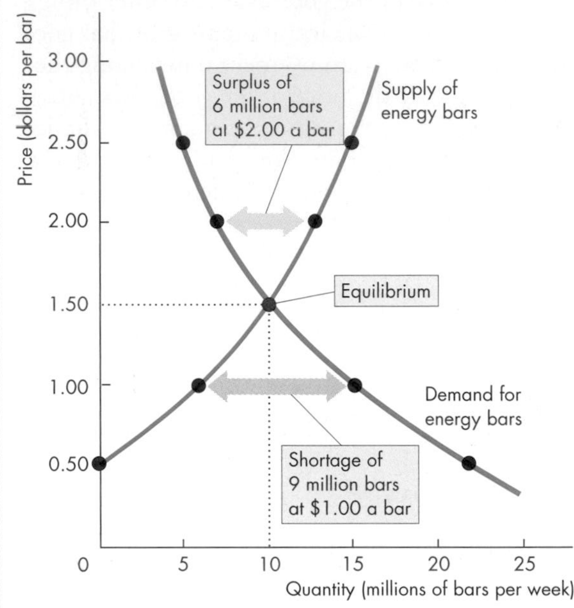


| Price (dollars per bar) | Quantity demanded | Quantity supplied | Shortage (–) or surplus (+) |
|---|---|---|---|
| | (millions of bars per week) | | |
| 0.50 | 22 | 0 | –22 |
| 1.00 | 15 | 6 | –9 |
| **1.50** | **10** | **10** | **0** |
| 2.00 | 7 | 13 | +6 |
| 2.50 | 5 | 15 | +10 |

The table lists the quantity demanded and the quantity supplied as well as the shortage or surplus of bars at each price. If the price is $1.00 a bar, 15 million bars a week are demanded and 6 million are supplied. There is a shortage of 9 million bars a week, and the price rises.

If the price is $2.00 a bar, 7 million bars a week are demanded and 13 million are supplied. There is a surplus of 6 million bars a week, and the price falls.

If the price is $1.50 a bar, 10 million bars a week are demanded and 10 million bars are supplied. There is neither a shortage nor a surplus. Neither buyers nor sellers have an incentive to change the price. The price at which the quantity demanded equals the quantity supplied is the equilibrium price. And 10 million bars a week is the equilibrium quantity.

million bars a week, as shown by the blue arrow. At each price *below* $1.50 a bar, there is a shortage of bars. For example, at $1.00 a bar, the shortage is 9 million bars a week, as shown by the red arrow.

## Price Adjustments

You've seen that if the price is below equilibrium, there is a shortage and that if the price is above equilibrium, there is a surplus. But can we count on the price to change and eliminate a shortage or a surplus? We can, because such price changes are beneficial to both buyers and sellers. Let's see why the price changes when there is a shortage or a surplus.

**A Shortage Forces the Price Up** Suppose the price of an energy bar is $1. Consumers plan to buy 15 million bars a week, and producers plan to sell 6 million bars a week. Consumers can't force producers to sell more than they plan, so the quantity that is actually offered for sale is 6 million bars a week. In this situation, powerful forces operate to increase the price and move it toward the equilibrium price. Some producers, noticing lines of unsatisfied consumers, raise the price. Some producers increase their output. As producers push the price up, the price rises toward its equilibrium. The rising price reduces the shortage because it decreases the quantity demanded and increases the quantity supplied. When the price has increased to the point at which there is no longer a shortage, the forces moving the price stop operating and the price comes to rest at its equilibrium.

**A Surplus Forces the Price Down** Suppose the price of a bar is $2. Producers plan to sell 13 million bars a week, and consumers plan to buy 7 million bars a week. Producers cannot force consumers to buy more than they plan, so the quantity that is actually bought is 7 million bars a week. In this situation, powerful forces operate to lower the price and move it toward the equilibrium price. Some producers, unable to sell the quantities of energy bars they planned to sell, cut their prices. In addition, some producers scale back production. As producers cut the price, the price falls toward its equilibrium. The falling price decreases the surplus because it increases the quantity demanded and decreases the quantity supplied. When the price has fallen to the point at which there is no longer a surplus, the forces moving the price stop operating and the price comes to rest at its equilibrium.

### The Best Deal Available for Buyers and Sellers

When the price is below equilibrium, it is forced upward. Why don't buyers resist the increase and refuse to buy at the higher price? Because they value the good more highly than the current price and they can't satisfy their demand at the current price. In some markets—for example, the markets that operate on eBay—the buyers might even be the ones who force the price up by offering to pay a higher price.

When the price is above equilibrium, it is bid downward. Why don't sellers resist this decrease and refuse to sell at the lower price? Because their minimum supply price is below the current price and they cannot sell all they would like to at the current price. Normally, it is the sellers who force the price down by offering lower prices to gain market share.

At the price at which the quantity demanded and the quantity supplied are equal, neither buyers nor sellers can do business at a better price. Buyers pay the highest price they are willing to pay for the last unit bought, and sellers receive the lowest price at which they are willing to supply the last unit sold.

When people freely make offers to buy and sell and when demanders try to buy at the lowest possible price and suppliers try to sell at the highest possible price, the price at which trade takes place is the equilibrium price—the price at which the quantity demanded equals the quantity supplied. The price coordinates the plans of buyers and sellers, and no one has an incentive to change it.

### Review Quiz

1. What is the equilibrium price of a good or service?
2. Over what range of prices does a shortage arise?
3. Over what range of prices does a surplus arise?
4. What happens to the price when there is a shortage?
5. What happens to the price when there is a surplus?
6. Why is the price at which the quantity demanded equals the quantity supplied the equilibrium price?
7. Why is the equilibrium price the best deal available for both buyers and sellers?

myeconlab Work Study Plan 3.4 and get instant feedback.

## Predicting Changes in Price and Quantity

The demand and supply model that we have just studied provides us with a powerful way of analyzing influences on prices and the quantities bought and sold. According to the model, a change in price stems from a change in demand, a change in supply, or a change in both demand and supply. Let's look first at the effects of a change in demand.

### An Increase in Demand

When more and more people join health clubs, the demand for energy bars increases. The table in Fig. 3.8 shows the original and new demand schedules for energy bars (the same as those in Fig. 3.2) as well as the supply schedule of energy bars.

When demand increases, there is a shortage at the original equilibrium price of $1.50 a bar. To eliminate the shortage, the price must rise. The price that makes the quantity demanded and quantity supplied equal again is $2.50 a bar. At this price, 15 million bars are bought and sold each week. When demand increases, both the price and the quantity increase.

Figure 3.8 shows these changes. The figure shows the original demand for and supply of energy bars. The original equilibrium price is $1.50 an energy bar, and the quantity is 10 million energy bars a week. When demand increases, the demand curve shifts rightward. The equilibrium price rises to $2.50 an energy bar, and the quantity supplied increases to 15 million energy bars a week, as highlighted in the figure. There is an *increase in the quantity supplied* but *no change in supply*—a movement along, but no shift of, the supply curve.

### A Decrease in Demand

We can reverse this change in demand. Start at a price of $2.50 a bar with 15 million energy bars a week being bought and sold, and then work out what happens if demand decreases to its original level. Such a decrease in demand might arise if people switch to energy gel (a substitute for energy bars). The decrease in demand shifts the demand curve leftward. The equilibrium price falls to $1.50 a bar, and the equilibrium quantity decreases to 10 million bars a week.

**FIGURE 3.8** The Effects of a Change in Demand

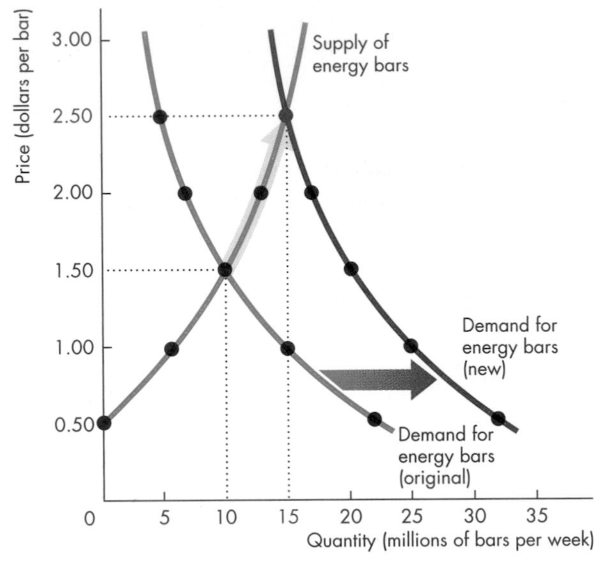


| Price (dollars per bar) | Quantity demanded (millions of bars per week) Original | New | Quantity supplied (millions of bars per week) |
|---|---|---|---|
| 0.50 | 22 | 32 | 0 |
| 1.00 | 15 | 25 | 6 |
| **1.50** | **10** | 20 | **10** |
| 2.00 | 7 | 17 | 13 |
| **2.50** | 5 | **15** | **15** |

Initially, the demand for energy bars is the blue demand curve. The equilibrium price is $1.50 a bar, and the equilibrium quantity is 10 million bars a week. When more health-conscious people do more exercise, the demand for energy bars increases and the demand curve shifts rightward to become the red curve.

At $1.50 a bar, there is now a shortage of 10 million bars a week. The price of a bar rises to a new equilibrium of $2.50. As the price rises to $2.50, the quantity supplied increases—shown by the blue arrow on the supply curve—to the new equilibrium quantity of 15 million bars a week. Following an increase in demand, the quantity supplied increases but supply does not change—the supply curve does not shift.

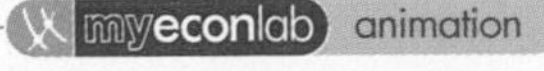

animation

We can now make our first two predictions:

1. When demand increases, both the price and the quantity increase.
2. When demand decreases, both the price and the quantity decrease.

## An Increase in Supply

When Nestlé (the producer of PowerBar) and other energy bar producers switch to a new cost-saving technology, the supply of energy bars increases. Figure 3.9 shows the new supply schedule (the same one that was shown in Fig. 3.5). What are the new equilibrium price and quantity? The price falls to $1.00 a bar, and the quantity increases to 15 million bars a week. You can see why by looking at the quantities demanded and supplied at the old price of $1.50 a bar. The quantity supplied at that price is 20 million bars a week, and there is a surplus of bars. The price falls. Only when the price is $1.00 a bar does the quantity supplied equal the quantity demanded.

Figure 3.9 illustrates the effect of an increase in supply. It shows the demand curve for energy bars and the original and new supply curves. The initial equilibrium price is $1.50 a bar, and the quantity is 10 million bars a week. When supply increases, the supply curve shifts rightward. The equilibrium price falls to $1.00 a bar, and the quantity demanded increases to 15 million bars a week, highlighted in the figure. There is an *increase in the quantity demanded* but *no change in demand*—a movement along, but no shift of, the demand curve.

## A Decrease in Supply

Start out at a price of $1.00 a bar with 15 million bars a week being bought and sold. Then suppose that the cost of labor or raw materials rises and the supply of energy bars decreases. The decrease in supply shifts the supply curve leftward. The equilibrium price rises to $1.50 a bar, and the equilibrium quantity decreases to 10 million bars a week.

We can now make two more predictions:

1. When supply increases, the quantity increases and the price falls.
2. When supply decreases, the quantity decreases and the price rises.

**FIGURE 3.9** The Effects of a Change in Supply

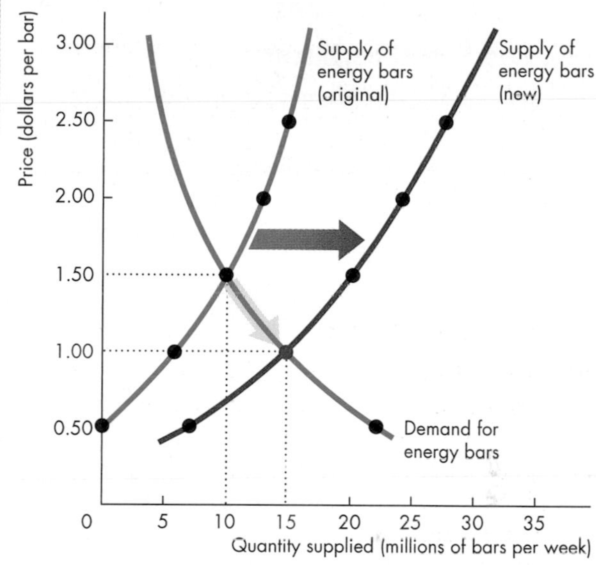


| Price (dollars per bar) | Quantity demanded (millions of bars per week) | Quantity supplied (millions of bars per week) | |
|---|---|---|---|
| | | Original | New |
| 0.50 | 22 | 0 | 7 |
| **1.00** | **15** | 6 | **15** |
| **1.50** | **10** | **10** | 20 |
| 2.00 | 7 | 13 | 25 |
| 2.50 | 5 | 15 | 27 |

Initially, the supply of energy bars is shown by the blue supply curve. The equilibrium price is $1.50 a bar, and the equilibrium quantity is 10 million bars a week. When the new cost-saving technology is adopted, the supply of energy bars increases and the supply curve shifts rightward to become the red curve.

At $1.50 a bar, there is now a surplus of 10 million bars a week. The price of an energy bar falls to a new equilibrium of $1.00 a bar. As the price falls to $1.00, the quantity demanded increases—shown by the blue arrow on the demand curve—to the new equilibrium quantity of 15 million bars a week. Following an increase in supply, the quantity demanded increases but demand does not change—the demand curve does not shift.

## How Markets Interact to Reallocate Resources

### Fuel, Food, and Fertilizer

The demand and supply model provides insights into all competitive markets. Here, we'll apply what you've learned to the markets for

- Crude oil
- Corn
- Fertilizers

### Crude Oil

Crude oil is like the life-blood of the global economy. It is used to fuel our cars, airplanes, trains, and buses, to generate electricity, and to produce a wide range of plastics. When the price of crude oil rises, the cost of transportation, power, and materials all increase.

In 2006, the price of a barrel of oil was $50. In 2008, the price had reached $135. While the price of oil has been rising, the quantity of oil produced and consumed has barely changed. Since 2006, the world has produced a steady 85 million barrels of oil a day.

Who or what has been raising the price of oil? Is it the fault of greedy oil producers?

Oil producers might be greedy, and some of them might be big enough to withhold supply and raise the price, but it wouldn't be in their self-interest to do so. The higher price would bring forth a greater quantity supplied from other producers and the profit of the one limiting supply would fall.

Producers could try to cooperate and jointly withhold supply. The Organization of Petroleum Exporting Countries, OPEC, is such a group of suppliers. But OPEC doesn't control the world supply and its members self-interests are to produce the quantities that give them the maximum attainable profit.

So even though the global oil market has some big players, they don't fix the price. Instead, the actions of thousands of buyers and sellers and the forces of demand and supply determine the price of oil. So how have demand and supply changed?

Because the price has increased with an unchanged quantity, demand must have increased and supply must have decreased.

Demand has increased for two reasons. First, world production, particularly in China and India, is expanding at a rapid rate. The increased production of electricity, gasoline, plastics, and other oil-using goods has increased the demand for oil.

Second, the rapid expansion of production in China, India, and other developing economies is expected to continue. So the demand for oil is expected to keep increasing at a rapid rate. As the demand for oil keeps increasing, the price of oil will keep rising *and be expected* to keep rising.

A higher expected future price increases demand yet further. It also decreases supply because producers know they can get a greater return from their oil by leaving it in the ground and selling it in a later year.

So an *expected* rise in price brings both an increase in demand and a decrease in supply, which in turn brings an *actual* rise in price.

Because an expected price rise brings an actual price rise, it is possible for expectations to create a process called a **speculative bubble**. In a speculative bubble, the price rises purely because it is expected to rise and events reinforce the expectation. No one knows whether the world oil market was in a bubble in 2008, but bubbles always burst, so we will eventually know.

Figure 1 illustrates the events that we've just described and summarizes the forces at work on demand and supply in the world market for oil.

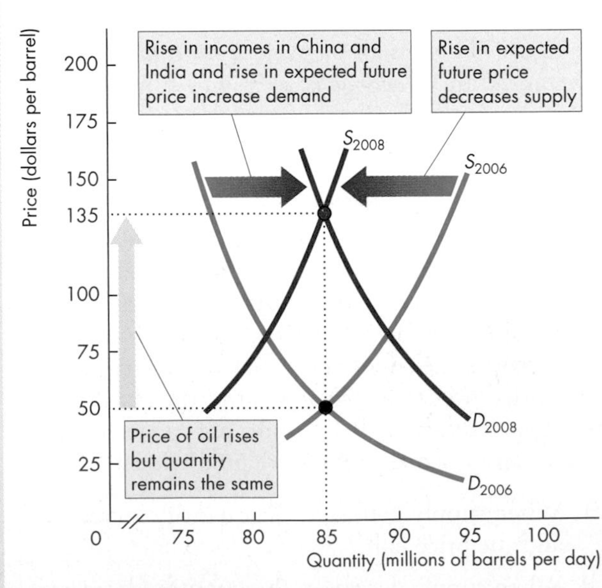


**Figure 1 The Market for Crude Oil**

## Corn

Corn is used as food, animal feed, and a source of ethanol. Global corn production increased during the past few years, but the price also increased.

The story of the production and price of corn, like the story of the price of oil, begins in China and India. Greater production and higher incomes in these countries have increased the demand for corn.

Some of the increase in demand is for corn as food. But more of the increase is for corn as cattle feed, driven by an increased demand for beef—it takes 7 pounds of corn to produce 1 pound of beef.

In addition, mandated targets for ethanol production (see Chapter 2, pp. 34 and 46–47) have increased the demand for corn as a source of biofuel.

While the demand for corn has increased, the supply has decreased. Drought in several parts of the world cut production and decreased supply. Higher fertilizer prices increased the cost of growing corn, which also decreased supply.

So the demand for corn increased and the supply of corn decreased. This combination of changes in demand and supply raised the price of corn. Also, the increase in demand was greater than the decrease in supply, so the quantity of corn increased.

Figure 2 provides a summary of the events that we've just described in the market for corn.

## Fertilizers

Nitrogen, potassium, and potash are not on your daily shopping list, but you consume them many times each day. They are the reason why our farms are so productive. And like the prices of oil and corn, the prices of fertilizers have gone skyward.

The increase in the global production of corn and other grains as food and sources of biofuels has increased the demand for fertilizers.

All fertilizers are costly to produce and use energy-intensive processes. Nitrogen is particularly energy intensive and uses natural gas. Potash is made from deposits of chloride and sodium chloride that are found 900 meters or deeper underground, and energy is required to bring the material to the surface and more energy is used to separate the chemicals and turn them into fertilizer.

All energy sources are substitutes, so the rise in the price of oil has increased the prices of all other energy sources. Consequently, the energy cost of producing fertilizers has risen. This higher cost of production has decreased the supply of fertilizers.

The increase in demand and the decrease in supply combine to raise the price. The increase in demand has been greater than the decrease in supply, so the quantity of fertilizer has increased. Figure 3 illustrates the market for fertilizers.

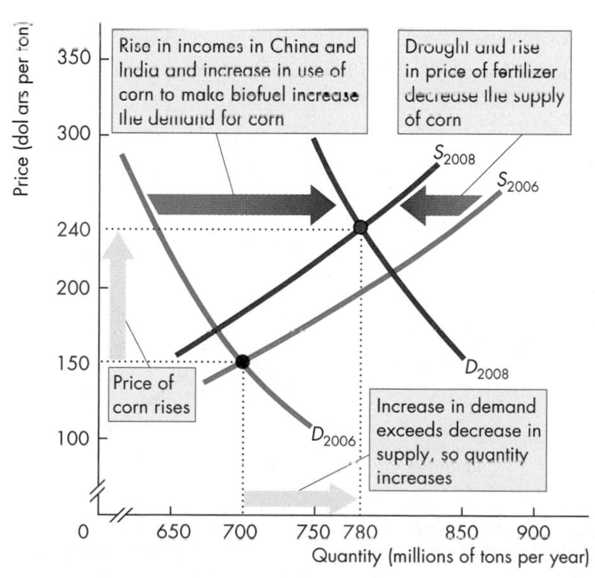


**Figure 2 The Market for Corn**

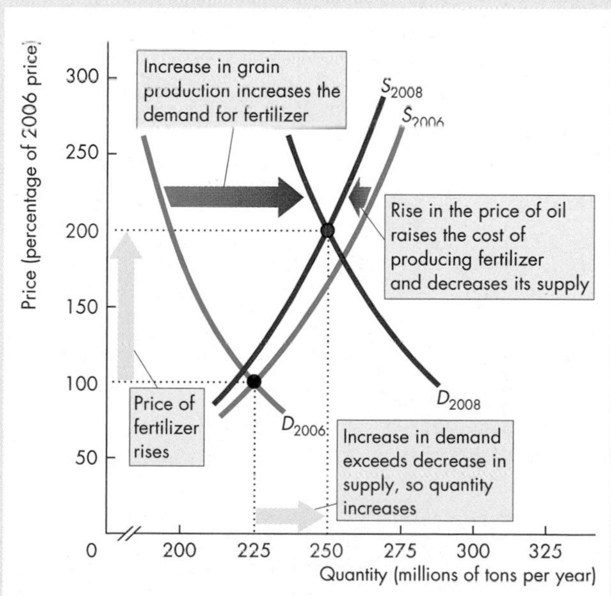


**Figure 3 The Market for Fertilizer**

**FIGURE 3.10** The Effects of All the Possible Changes in Demand and Supply

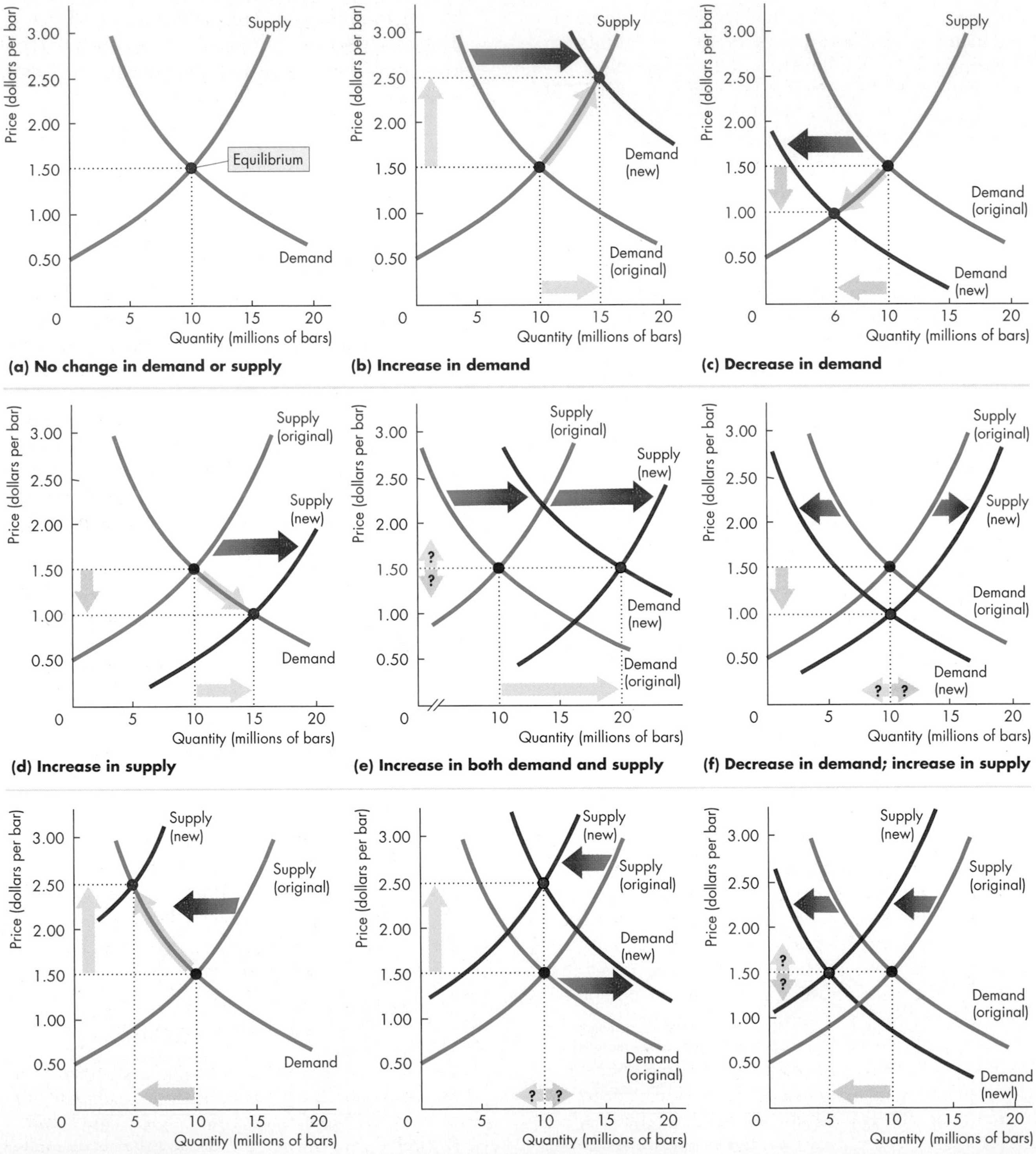

**(a) No change in demand or supply**

**(b) Increase in demand**

**(c) Decrease in demand**

**(d) Increase in supply**

**(e) Increase in both demand and supply**

**(f) Decrease in demand; increase in supply**

**(g) Decrease in supply**

**(h) Increase in demand; decrease in supply**

**(i) Decrease in both demand and supply**

myeconlab animation

## All the Possible Changes in Demand and Supply

Figure 3.10 brings together and summarizes the effects of all the possible changes in demand and supply. With what you've learned about the effects of a change in *either* demand or supply, you can predict what happens if *both* demand and supply change together. Let's begin by reviewing what you already know.

**Change in Demand with No Change in Supply** The first row of Fig. 3.10, parts (a), (b), and (c), summarizes the effects of a change in demand with no change in supply. In part (a), with no change in either demand or supply, neither the price nor the quantity changes. With an *increase* in demand and no change in supply in part (b), both the price and quantity increase. And with a *decrease* in demand and no change in supply in part (c), both the price and the quantity decrease.

**Change in Supply with No Change in Demand** The first column of Fig. 3.10, parts (a), (d), and (g), summarizes the effects of a change in supply with no change in demand. With an *increase* in supply and no change in demand in part (d), the price falls and quantity increases. And with a *decrease* in supply and no change in demand in part (g), the price rises and the quantity decreases.

**Increase in Both Demand and Supply** You've seen that an increase in demand raises the price and increases the quantity. And you've seen that an increase in supply lowers the price and increases the quantity. Fig. 3.10(e) combines these two changes. Because either an increase in demand or an increase in supply increases the quantity, the quantity also increases when both demand and supply increase. But the effect on the price is uncertain. An increase in demand raises the price and an increase in supply lowers the price, so we can't say whether the price will rise or fall when both demand and supply increase. We need to know the magnitudes of the changes in demand and supply to predict the effects on price. In the example in Fig. 3.10(e), the price does not change. But notice that if demand increases by slightly more than the amount shown in the figure, the price will rise. And if supply increases by slightly more than the amount shown in the figure, the price will fall.

**Decrease in Both Demand and Supply** Figure 3.10(i) shows the case in which demand and supply *both decrease*. For the same reasons as those we've just reviewed, when both demand and supply decrease, the quantity decreases, and again the direction of the price change is uncertain.

**Decrease in Demand and Increase in Supply** You've seen that a decrease in demand lowers the price and decreases the quantity. And you've seen that an increase in supply lowers the price and increases the quantity. Fig. 3.10(f) combines these two changes. Both the decrease in demand and the increase in supply lower the price, so the price falls. But a decrease in demand decreases the quantity and an increase in supply increases the quantity, so we can't predict the direction in which the quantity will change unless we know the magnitudes of the changes in demand and supply. In the example in Fig. 3.10(f), the quantity does not change. But notice that if demand decreases by slightly more than the amount shown in the figure, the quantity will decrease. And if supply increases by slightly more than the amount shown in the figure, the quantity will increase.

**Increase in Demand and Decrease in Supply** Figure 3.10(h) shows the case in which demand increases and supply decreases. Now, the price rises, and again the direction of the quantity change is uncertain.

### Review Quiz

What is the effect on the price of an MP3 player (such as an iPod) and the quantity of MP3 players if

1. The price of a PC falls or the price of an MP3 download rises? (Draw the diagrams!)
2. More firms produce MP3 players or electronics workers' wages rise? (Draw the diagrams!)
3. Any two of the events in questions 1 and 2 occur together? (Draw the diagrams!)

myeconlab Work Study Plan 3.5 and get instant feedback.

Now that you understand the demand and supply model and the predictions that it makes, try to get into the habit of using the model in your everyday life. To see how you might use the model, take a look at *Reading Between the Lines* on pp. 72–73, which uses the tools of demand and supply to explain the rising price of gasoline in 2008.

# Demand and Supply: The Price of Gasoline

## Record Gas Prices Squeeze Drivers

Americans feel the pinch as retail gasoline hits all-time high of $3.51 a gallon

CNN Money
April 22, 2008

NEW YORK (AP)—Cabbies here complain their take-home pay is thinner than it used to be. Trucking companies across the country are making drivers slow down to conserve fuel. Filling station owners plead that really, really, the skyrocketing prices aren't their fault. …

With gas prices now averaging $3.51 a gallon nationwide, … more and more Americans who have to drive are weighing the need for each and every trip. … Some would-be drivers are considering less energy-dependent alternatives simply for money's sake.

In Los Angeles, for example, fiction writer Brian Edwards sold his gas-guzzling Ford truck and now relies on his skateboard or the bus to get around. Sharon Cooper of Chicago, meanwhile, said she is planning to buy a bicycle to use on her 2 1/2-mile commute to work. …

"It's hell," said legal aide Zebib Yemane, … "When going downhill, I used to step on the gas. Now I don't." …

"Bottom line, we can't afford it no more, man. It's too much," Bak Zoumane said as he filled up his yellow cab at a BP station in midtown New York. The West African immigrant said his next car will likely be a hybrid so he won't have to pay so much at the pump.

Gasoline prices typically rise in the spring as stations switch over to pricier summer-grade fuel and demand picks up as more travelers take to the road.

But this year prices are rising even faster than normal, experts say, because of the massive jump in benchmark crude prices, which spiked to a record $117.76 a barrel Monday. …



## Essence of the Story

- The retail price of gasoline hit a record high of $3.51 a gallon in April 2008.
- Gas station owners said the high prices weren't their fault.
- Drivers weighed the need for each trip and conserved energy by slowing down, easing off the gas when going down hill, or switching to hybrid vehicles.
- Some people found alternative means of transportation that include the bus, a bicycle, or even a skateboard.
- The switch to summer-grade fuel and a seasonal increase in travel normally raise the price of gasoline in the spring.
- In 2008, gas prices rose faster than normal because of a large rise in the price of crude oil, which reached $118 a barrel.

## Economic Analysis

- In April 2007, the average price of gasoline was \$2.75 a gallon and 9.3 million barrels of gasoline were consumed on average each day.
- Figure 1 shows the market for gasoline in April 2007. The demand curve is *D*, the supply curve is $S_{2007}$, and the market equilibrium is at 9.3 million barrels a day and \$2.75 a gallon.
- Two main factors influenced the demand for gasoline in the year to April 2008.
- Slightly higher incomes increased demand and the gradual move toward hybrid vehicles and the increased use of ethanol decreased demand.
- The combined effects of these two factors left the demand for gasoline the same in 2008 as it had been in 2007.
- The price of crude oil was the biggest influence on the market for gasoline during 2007 and 2008.
- Between April 2007 and April 2008, the price of crude oil increased from \$65 a barrel to \$118 a barrel.
- The rise in the price of crude oil raised the cost of producing gasoline and decreased the supply of gasoline.
- Figure 2 shows what had happened in the market for gasoline by April 2008.
- Demand remained unchanged, but supply decreased from $S_{2007}$ to $S_{2008}$.
- Because demand was unchanged and supply decreased, the price increased and the quantity decreased.
- The equilibrium price increased from \$2.75 a gallon to \$3.51 a gallon and the equilibrium quantity decreased from 9.3 million barrels a day to 9.2 million barrels a day.
- You can see the effects of drivers conserving gasoline, switching to hybrid vehicles, and finding alternative means of transportation that include the bus, a bicycle, or even a skateboard.
- This analysis of the market for gasoline emphasizes the distinction between a change in demand and a *change in the quantity demanded* and a change in supply and a *change in the quantity supplied.*
- In this example, there is a change in supply, no change in demand, and a change in the quantity demanded.
- Supply decreases—the supply curve shifts leftward.
- The demand curve does not shift, but as the price of gasoline rises, the quantity of gasoline demanded decreases in a movement along the demand curve *D*.

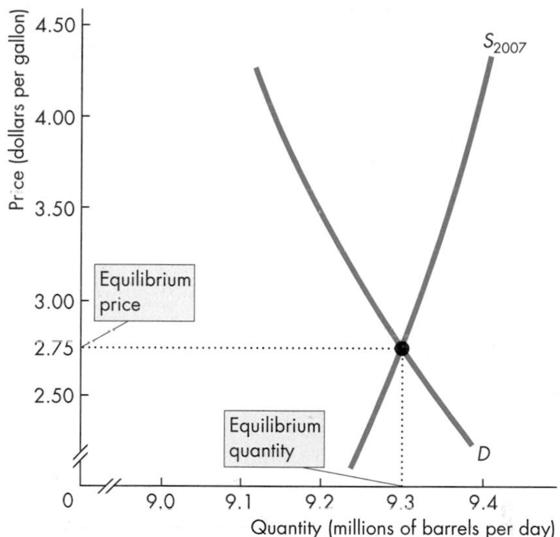


**Figure 1 The gasoline market in 2007**

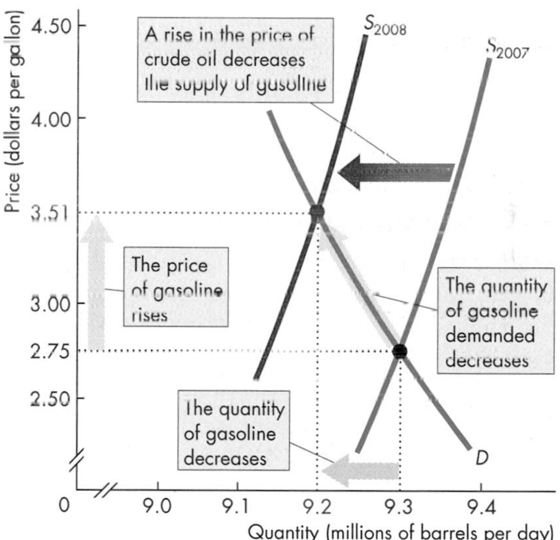


**Figure 2 The gasoline market in 2008**

# MATHEMATICAL NOTE

## Demand, Supply, and Equilibrium

### Demand Curve

The law of demand says that as the price of a good or service falls, the quantity demanded of that good or service increases. We can illustrate the law of demand by drawing a graph of the demand curve or writing down an equation. When the demand curve is a straight line, the following equation describes it:

$$P = a - bQ_D,$$

where $P$ is the price and $Q_D$ is the quantity demanded. The $a$ and $b$ are positive constants.

The demand equation tells us three things:

1. The price at which no one is willing to buy the good ($Q_D$ is zero). That is, if the price is $a$, then the quantity demanded is zero. You can see the price $a$ in Figure 1. It is the price at which the demand curve hits the $y$-axis—what we call the demand curve's "intercept on the $y$-axis."
2. As the price falls, the quantity demanded increases. If $Q_D$ is a positive number, then the price $P$ must be less than $a$. And as $Q_D$ gets larger, the price $P$ becomes smaller. That is, as the quantity increases, the maximum price that buyers are willing to pay for the last unit of the good falls.
3. The constant $b$ tells us how fast the maximum price that someone is willing to pay for the good falls as the quantity increases. That is, the constant $b$ tells us about the steepness of the demand curve. The equation tells us that the slope of the demand curve is $-b$.

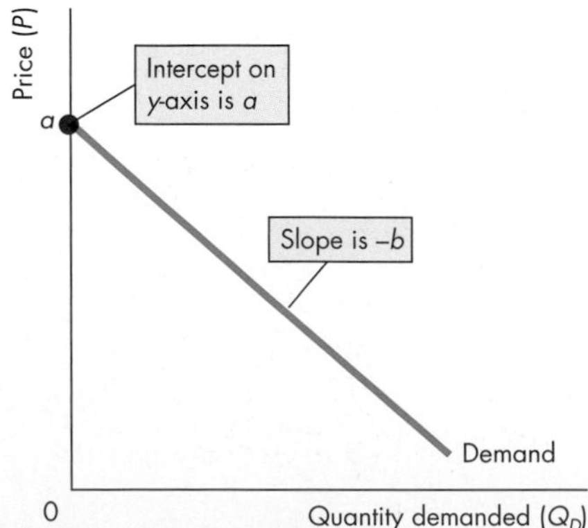


**Figure 1 Demand curve**

### Supply Curve

The law of supply says that as the price of a good or service rises, the quantity supplied of that good or service increases. We can illustrate the law of supply by drawing a graph of the supply curve or writing down an equation. When the supply curve is a straight line, the following equation describes it:

$$P = c + dQ_S,$$

where $P$ is the price and $Q_S$ is the quantity supplied. The $c$ and $d$ are positive constants.

The supply equation tells us three things:

1. The price at which sellers are not willing to supply the good ($Q_S$ is zero). That is, if the price is $c$, then no one is willing to sell the good. You can see the price $c$ in Figure 2. It is the price at which the supply curve hits the $y$-axis—what we call the supply curve's "intercept on the $y$-axis."
2. As the price rises, the quantity supplied increases. If $Q_S$ is a positive number, then the price $P$ must be greater than $c$. And as $Q_S$ increases, the price $P$ becomes larger. That is, as the quantity increases, the minimum price that sellers are willing to accept for the last unit rises.
3. The constant $d$ tells us how fast the minimum price at which someone is willing to sell the good rises as the quantity increases. That is, the constant $d$ tells us about the steepness of the supply curve. The equation tells us that the slope of the supply curve is $d$.

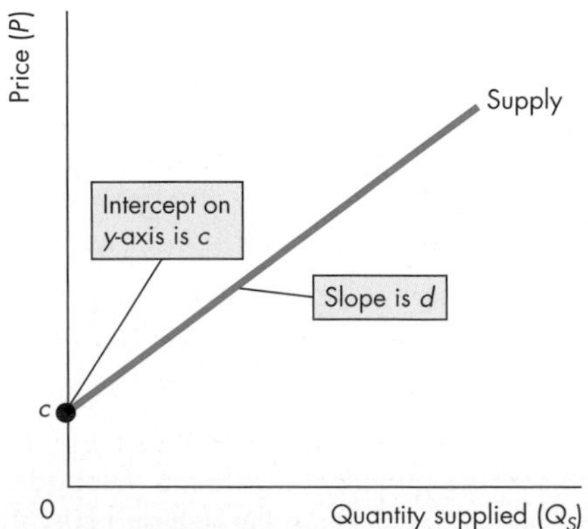


**Figure 2 Supply curve**

## Market Equilibrium

Demand and supply determine market equilibrium. Figure 3 shows the equilibrium price ($P^*$) and equilibrium quantity ($Q^*$) at the intersection of the demand curve and the supply curve.

We can use the equations to find the equilibrium price and equilibrium quantity. The price of a good adjusts until the quantity demanded $Q_D$ equals the quantity supplied $Q_S$. So at the equilibrium price ($P^*$) and equilibrium quantity ($Q^*$),

$$Q_D = Q_S = Q^*.$$

To find the equilibrium price and equilibrium quantity, substitute $Q^*$ for $Q_D$ in the demand equation and $Q^*$ for $Q_S$ in the supply equation. Then the price is the equilibrium price ($P^*$), which gives

$$P^* = a - bQ^*$$
$$P^* = c + dQ^*.$$

Notice that

$$a - bQ^* = c + dQ^*.$$

Now solve for $Q^*$:

$$a - c = bQ^* + dQ^*$$
$$a - c = (b + d)Q^*$$
$$Q^* = \frac{a - c}{b + d}.$$

To find the equilibrium price, ($P^*$), substitute for $Q^*$ in either the demand equation or the supply equation.

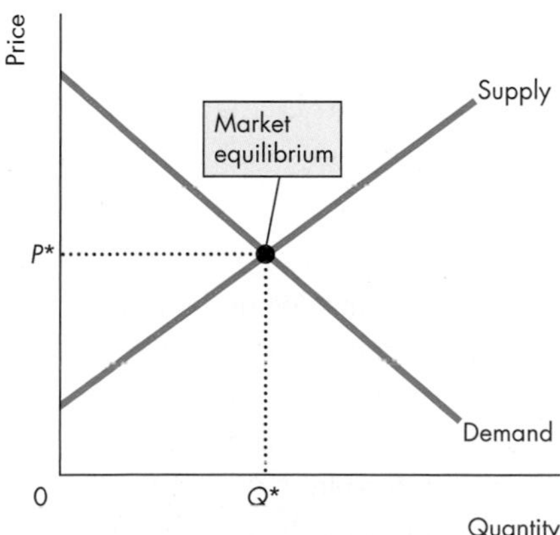


**Figure 3 Market equilibrium**

Using the demand equation, we have

$$P^* = a - b\left(\frac{a - c}{b + d}\right)$$
$$P^* = \frac{a(b + d) - b(a - c)}{b + d}$$
$$P^* = \frac{ad + bc}{b + d}.$$

Alternatively, using the supply equation, we have

$$P^* = c + d\left(\frac{a - c}{b + d}\right)$$
$$P^* = \frac{c(b + d) + d(a - c)}{b + d}$$
$$P^* = \frac{ad + bc}{b + d}.$$

## An Example

The demand for ice-cream cones is

$$P = 800 - 2Q_D.$$

The supply of ice-cream cones is

$$P = 200 + 1Q_S.$$

The price of a cone is expressed in cents, and the quantities are expressed in cones per day.

To find the equilibrium price ($P^*$) and equilibrium quantity ($Q^*$), substitute $Q^*$ for $Q_D$ and $Q_S$ and $P^*$ for $P$. That is,

$$P^* = 800 - 2Q^*$$
$$P^* = 200 + 1Q^*.$$

Now solve for $Q^*$:

$$800 - 2Q^* = 200 + 1Q^*$$
$$600 = 3Q^*$$
$$Q^* = 200.$$

And

$$P^* = 800 - 2(200)$$
$$= 400.$$

The equilibrium price is $4 a cone, and the equilibrium quantity is 200 cones per day.

## SUMMARY

### Key Points

**Markets and Prices** (p. 54)

- A competitive market is one that has so many buyers and sellers that no single buyer or seller can influence the price.
- Opportunity cost is a relative price.
- Demand and supply determine relative prices.

**Demand** (pp. 55–59)

- Demand is the relationship between the quantity demanded of a good and its price when all other influences on buying plans remain the same.
- The higher the price of a good, other things remaining the same, the smaller is the quantity demanded—the law of demand.
- Demand depends on the prices of related goods (substitutes and complements), expected future prices, income, expected future income and credit, population, and preferences.

**Supply** (pp. 60–63)

- Supply is the relationship between the quantity supplied of a good and its price when all other influences on selling plans remain the same.
- The higher the price of a good, other things remaining the same, the greater is the quantity supplied—the law of supply.
- Supply depends on the prices of resources used to produce a good, the prices of related goods produced, expected future prices, the number of suppliers, technology, and the state of nature.

**Market Equilibrium** (pp. 64–65)

- At the equilibrium price, the quantity demanded equals the quantity supplied.
- At any price above equilibrium, there is a surplus and the price falls.
- At any price below equilibrium, there is a shortage and the price rises.

**Predicting Changes in Price and Quantity** (pp. 66–71)

- An increase in demand brings a rise in the price and an increase in the quantity supplied. A decrease in demand brings a fall in the price and a decrease in the quantity supplied.
- An increase in supply brings a fall in the price and an increase in the quantity demanded. A decrease in supply brings a rise in the price and a decrease in the quantity demanded.
- An increase in demand and an increase in supply bring an increased quantity but an uncertain price change. An increase in demand and a decrease in supply bring a higher price but an uncertain change in quantity.

### Key Figures



### Key Terms

## PROBLEMS and APPLICATIONS

Work problems 1–13 in Chapter 3 Study Plan and get instant feedback.
Work problems 16–28 as Homework, a Quiz, or a Test if assigned by your instructor.

1. William Gregg owned a mill in South Carolina. In December 1862, he placed a notice in the *Edgehill Advertiser* announcing his willingness to exchange cloth for food and other items. Here is an extract:

   1 yard of cloth for 1 pound of bacon
   2 yards of cloth for 1 pound of butter
   4 yards of cloth for 1 pound of wool
   8 yards of cloth for 1 bushel of salt

   a. What is the relative price of butter in terms of wool?
   b. If the money price of bacon was 20¢ a pound, what do you predict was the money price of butter?
   c. If the money price of bacon was 20¢ a pound and the money price of salt was $2.00 a bushel, do you think anyone would accept Mr. Gregg's offer of cloth for salt?
2. The price of food increased during the past year.
   a. Explain why the law of demand applies to food just as it does to all other goods and services.
   b. Explain how the substitution effect influences food purchases and provide some examples of substitutions that people might make when the price of food rises and other things remain the same.
   c. Explain how the income effect influences food purchases and provide some examples of the income effect that might occur when the price of food rises and other things remain the same.
3. Place the following goods and services into pairs of likely substitutes and into pairs of likely complements. (You may use an item in more than one pair.) The goods and services are

   coal, oil, natural gas, wheat, corn, rye, pasta, pizza, sausage, skateboard, roller blades, video game, laptop, iPod, cell phone, text message, email, phone call, voice mail
4. During 2008, the average income in China increased by 10 percent. Compared to 2007, how do you expect the following would change:
   a. The demand for beef? Explain your answer.
   b. The demand for rice? Explain your answer.
5. In January 2007, the price of gasoline was $2.38 a gallon. By May 2008, the price had increased to $3.84 a gallon. Assume that there were no changes in average income, population, or any other influence on buying plans. How would you expect the rise in the price of gasoline to affect
   a. The demand for gasoline? Explain your answer.
   b. The quantity of gasoline demanded? Explain your answer.
6. In 2008, the price of corn increased by 35 percent and some cotton farmers in Texas stopped growing cotton and started to grow corn.
   a. Does this fact illustrate the law of demand or the law of supply? Explain your answer.
   b. Why would a cotton farmer grow corn?
7. **American to Cut Flights, Charge for Luggage**

   American Airlines announced yesterday that it will begin charging passengers $15 for their first piece of checked luggage, in addition to raising other fees and cutting domestic flights as it grapples with record-high fuel prices.

   *Boston Herald*, May 22, 2008

   a. How does this news clip illustrate a change in supply? Explain your answer.
   b What is the influence on supply identified in the news clip? Explain your answer.
   c. Explain how supply changes.
8. **Oil Soars to New Record Over $135**

   The price of oil hit a record high above $135 a barrel on Thursday—more than twice what it cost a year ago ... OPEC has so far blamed price rises on speculators and says there is no shortage of oil.

   BBC News, May 22, 2008

   a. Explain how the price of oil can rise even though there is no shortage of oil.
   b If a shortage of oil does occur, what does that imply about price adjustments and the role of price as a regulator in the market for oil?
   c If OPEC is correct, what factors might have

changed demand and/or supply and shifted the demand curve and/or the supply curve to cause the price to rise?

9. "As more people buy computers, the demand for Internet service increases and the price of Internet service decreases. The fall in the price of Internet service decreases the supply of Internet service." Is this statement true or false? Explain.

10. The following events occur one at a time:
    (i) The price of crude oil rises.
    (ii) The price of a car rises.
    (iii) All speed limits on highways are abolished.
    (iv) Robots cut car production costs.

    Which of these events will increase or decrease (state which occurs)
    a. The demand for gasoline?
    b. The supply of gasoline?
    c. The quantity of gasoline demanded?
    d. The quantity of gasoline supplied?

11. The demand and supply schedules for gum are

| Price (cents per pack) | Quantity demanded (millions of packs a week) | Quantity supplied (millions of packs a week) |
|---|---|---|
| 20 | 180 | 60 |
| 40 | 140 | 100 |
| 60 | 100 | 140 |
| 80 | 60 | 180 |
| 100 | 20 | 220 |

    a. Draw a graph of the gum market, label the axes and the curves, and mark in the equilibrium price and quantity.
    b. Suppose that the price of gum is 70¢ a pack. Describe the situation in the gum market and explain how the price adjusts.
    c. Suppose that the price of gum is 30¢ a pack. Describe the situation in the gum market and explain how the price adjusts.
    d. A fire destroys some factories that produce gum and the quantity of gum supplied decreases by 40 million packs a week at each price. Explain what happens in the market for gum and illustrate the changes on your graph.
    e. If at the time the fire occurs in d, there is an increase in the teenage population, which increases the quantity of gum demanded by 40 million packs a week at each price, what are the new equilibrium price and quantity of gum? Illustrate these changes in your graph.

12. **Eurostar Boosted by Da Vinci Code**

    Eurostar, the train service linking London to Paris … , said on Wednesday first-half sales rose 6 per cent, boosted by devotees of the blockbuster Da Vinci movie.

    CNN, July 26, 2006

    a. Explain how Da Vinci Code fans helped to raise Eurostar's sales.
    b. CNN commented on the "fierce competition from budget airlines." Explain the effect of this competition on Eurostar's sales.
    c. What markets in Paris do you think these fans influenced? Explain the influence on three markets.

13. **Of Gambling, Grannies, and Good Sense**

    Nevada has the fastest growing elderly population of any state. … Las Vegas has … plenty of jobs for the over 50s.

    *The Economist*, July 26, 2006

    Explain how grannies have influenced the
    a. Demand side of some Las Vegas markets.
    b. Supply side of other Las Vegas markets.

14. Use the link on MyEconLab (Textbook Resources, Chapter 3, Web Links) to obtain data on the prices and quantities of bananas in 1985 and 2002.
    a. Make a graph to illustrate the market for bananas in 1985 and 2002.
    b. On the graph, show the changes in demand and supply and the changes in the quantity demanded and the quantity supplied that are consistent with the price and quantity data.
    c. Why do you think the demand for and supply of bananas changed?

15. Use the link on MyEconLab (Textbook Resources, Chapter 3, Web Links) to obtain data on the price of oil since 2000.
    a. Describe how the price of oil changed.
    b. Use a demand-supply graph to explain what happens to the price when supply increases or decreases and demand is unchanged.
    c. What do you predict would happen to the price of oil if a new drilling technology permitted deeper ocean sources to be used?
    d. What do you predict would happen to the price of oil if a clean and safe nuclear technology were developed?
    e. How does a higher price of oil influence the market for ethanol?
    f. How does an increase in the supply of ethanol influence the market for oil?

16. What features of the world market for crude oil make it a competitive market?
17. The money price of a textbook is $90 and the money price of the Wii game *Super Mario Galaxy* is $45.
    a. What is the opportunity cost of a textbook in terms of the Wii game?
    b. What is the relative price of the Wii game in terms of textbooks?
18. The price of gasoline has increased during the past year.
    a. Explain why the law of demand applies to gasoline just as it does to all other goods and services.
    b. Explain how the substitution effect influences gasoline purchases and provide some examples of substitutions that people might make when the price of gasoline rises and other things remain the same.
    c. Explain how the income effect influences gasoline purchases and provide some examples of the income effects that might occur when the price of gasoline rises and other things remain the same.
19. Classify the following pairs of goods and services as substitutes, complements, substitutes in production, or complements in production.
    a. Bottled water and health club memberships
    b. French fries and baked potatoes
    c. Leather purses and leather shoes
    d. SUVs and pickup trucks
    e. Diet coke and regular coke
    f. Low-fat milk and cream
20. Think about the demand for the three popular game consoles: XBox, PS3, and Wii. Explain the effect the following event on the demand for XBox games and the quantity of XBox games demanded, other things remaining the same.
    a. The price of an XBox falls.
    b. The prices of a PS3 and a Wii fall.
    c. The number of people writing and producing XBox games increases.
    d. Consumers' incomes increase.
    e. Programmers who write code for XBox games become more costly to hire.
    f. The price of an XBox game is expected to fall.
    g. A new game console comes onto the market, which is a close substitute for XBox.
21. In 2008, as the prices of homes fell across the United States, the number of homes offered for sale decreased.
    a. Does this fact illustrate the law of demand or the law of supply? Explain your answer.
    b. Why would home owners hold off trying to sell?
22. **G.M. Cuts Production for Quarter**

    General Motors cut its fourth-quarter production schedule by 10 percent on Tuesday as a tightening credit market caused sales at the Ford Motor Company, Chrysler and even Toyota to decline in August. … Bob Carter, group vice president for Toyota Motor Sales USA, said … dealerships were still seeing fewer potential customers browsing the lots.

    *The New York Times*, September 5, 2007

    Explain whether this news clip illustrates
    a. A change in supply
    b. A change in the quantity supplied
    c. A change in demand
    d. A change in the quantity demanded
23. The figure illustrates the market for pizza.

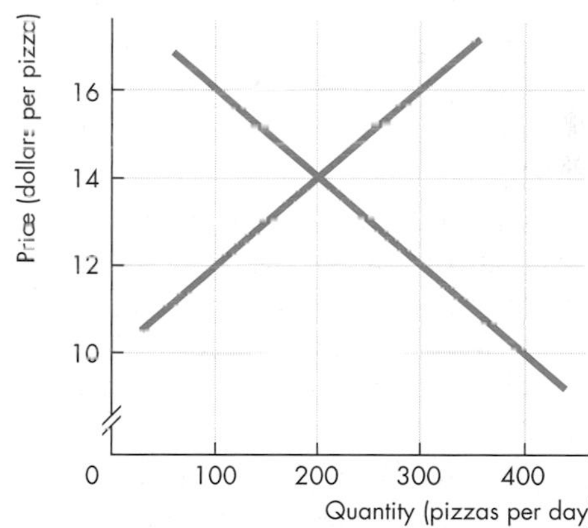


    a. Label the curves. Which curve shows the willingness to pay for a pizza?
    b. If the price of a pizza is $16, is there a shortage or a surplus and does the price rise or fall?
    c. Sellers want to receive the highest possible price, so why would they be willing to accept less than $16 a pizza?
    d. If the price of a pizza is $12, is there a shortage or a surplus and does the price rise or fall?
    e. Buyers want to pay the lowest possible price, so why would they be willing to pay more than $12 for a pizza?

24. **Plenty of "For Sale" Signs but Actual Sales Lagging**

Like spring flowers, the "For Sale" signs are sprouting in front yards all over the country. But anxious sellers are facing the most brutal environment in decades, with a slumping economy, falling home prices, and rising mortgage foreclosures.

*The New York Times*, May 26, 2008

a. Describe the changes in demand and supply in the market for homes in the United States.
b. Is there a surplus of homes?
c. What does the information in the news clip imply about price adjustments and the role of price as a regulator in the market for homes?

25. **'Popcorn Movie' Experience Gets Pricier**

... cinemas are raising ... prices. ... Demand for field corn, used for animal feed, ... corn syrup and ... ethanol, has caused its price to explode. That's caused some farmers to shift from popcorn to easier-to-grow field corn, cutting supply and pushing its price higher, too. ...

*USA Today*, May 24, 2008

Explain and illustrate graphically the events described in the news clip in the markets for

a. Popcorn.
b. Viewing movies in the theater.

26. The table sets out the demand and supply schedules for potato chips.

| Price (cents per bag) | Quantity demanded (millions of bags per week) | Quantity supplied (millions of bags per week) |
|---|---|---|
| 50 | 160 | 130 |
| 60 | 150 | 140 |
| 70 | 140 | 150 |
| 80 | 130 | 160 |
| 90 | 120 | 170 |
| 100 | 110 | 180 |

a. Draw a graph of the potato chip market and mark in the equilibrium price and quantity.
b. If the price is 60¢ a bag, is there a shortage or a surplus, and how does the price adjust?
c. If a new dip increases the quantity of potato chips that people want to buy by 30 million bags per week at each price, how does the demand and/or supply of chips change?
d. If a new dip has the effect described in c, how does the price and quantity of chips change?
e. If a virus destroys potato crops and the quantity of potato chips produced decreases by 40 million bags a week at each price, how does the supply of chips change?
f. If the virus that destroys the potato crops in e hits just as the new dip in c comes onto the market, how does the price and quantity of chips change?

27. **Sony's Blu-Ray Wins High-Definition War**

Toshiba Corp. yesterday raised the white flag in the war over the next-generation home movie format, announcing the end of its HD DVD business in a victory for Sony Corp.'s Blu-ray technology. The move could finally jump-start a high-definition home DVD market that has been hamstrung as consumers waited on the sidelines for the battle to play out in a fight reminiscent of the VHS-Betamax videotape war of the 1980s.

*The Washington Times*, February 20, 2008

How would you expect the end of Toshiba's HD DVD format to influence

a. The price of a used Toshiba player on eBay? Would the outcome that you predict result from a change in demand or a change in supply or both, and in which directions?
b. The price of a Blu-ray player?
c. The demand for Blu-ray format movies?
d. The supply of Blu-ray format movies?
e. The price of Blu-ray format movies?
f. The quantity of Blu-ray format movies?

28. After you have studied *Reading Between the Lines* on pp. 76–77, answer the following questions:

a. How high did the retail price of gasoline go in April 2008?
b. What substitutions did drivers make to decrease the quantity of gasoline demanded?
c. Why would the switch to summer-grade fuel and the seasonal increase in travel normally raise the price of gasoline in the spring?
d. What were the two main factors that influenced the demand for gasoline in 2008 and how did they change demand?
e. What was the main influence on the supply of gasoline during 2007 and 2008 and how did supply change?
f. How did the combination of the factors you have noted in d and e influence the price and quantity of gasoline?
g. Was the change in quantity a change in the quantity demanded or a change in the quantity supplied?

PART ONE

**UNDERSTANDING** THE SCOPE OF ECONOMICS

# Your Economic Revolution

Three periods in human history stand out as ones of economic revolution. The first, the *Agricultural Revolution,* occurred 10,000 years ago. In what is today Iraq, people learned to domesticate animals and plant crops. People stopped roaming in search of food and settled in villages, towns, and cities where they specialized in the activities in which they had a comparative advantage and developed markets in which to exchange their products. Wealth increased enormously.

You are studying economics at a time that future historians will call the *Information Revolution.* Over the entire world, people are embracing new information technologies and prospering on an unprecedented scale.

Economics was born during the *Industrial Revolution,* which began in England during the 1760s. For the first time, people began to apply science and create new technologies for the manufacture of textiles and iron, to create steam engines, and to boost the output of farms.

During all three economic revolutions, many have prospered but many have been left behind. It is the range of human progress that poses the greatest question for economics and the one that Adam Smith addressed in the first work of economic science: What causes the differences in wealth among nations?

*Many people had written about economics before* **Adam Smith**, *but he made economics a science. Born in 1723 in Kirkcaldy, a small fishing town near Edinburgh, Scotland, Smith was the only child of the town's customs officer. Lured from his professorship (he was a full professor at 28) by a wealthy Scottish duke who gave him a pension of £300 a year—ten times the average income at that time—Smith devoted ten years to writing his masterpiece:* An Inquiry into the Nature and Causes of the **Wealth of Nations**, *published in 1776.*

*Why, Adam Smith asked, are some nations wealthy while others are poor? He was pondering these questions at the height of the Industrial Revolution, and he answered by emphasizing the role of the division of labor and free markets.*

*To illustrate his argument, Adam Smith described two pin factories. In the first, one person, using the hand tools available in the 1770s, could make 20 pins a day. In the other, by using those same hand tools but breaking the process into a number of individually small operations in which people specialize—by the* division of labor*—ten people could make a staggering 48,000 pins a day. One draws out the wire, another straightens it, a third cuts it, a fourth points it, a fifth grinds it. Three specialists make the head, and a fourth attaches it. Finally, the pin is polished and packaged.*

"It is not from the benevolence of the butcher, the brewer, or the baker that we expect our dinner, but from their regard to their own interest."

**ADAM SMITH**
*The Wealth of Nations*

*But a large market is needed to support the division of labor: One factory employing ten workers would need to sell more than 15 million pins a year to stay in business!*

# TALKING WITH

# Jagdish Bhagwati

**Jagdish Bhagwati** is University Professor at Columbia University. Born in India in 1934, he studied at Cambridge University in England, MIT, and Oxford University before returning to India. He returned to teach at MIT in 1968 and moved to Columbia in 1980. A prolific scholar, Professor Bhagwati also writes in leading newspapers and magazines throughout the world. He has been much honored for both his scientific work and his impact on public policy. His greatest contributions are in international trade but extend also to developmental problems and the study of political economy.

Michael Parkin talked with Jagdish Bhagwati about his work and the progress that economists have made in understanding the benefits of economic growth and international trade since the pioneering work of Adam Smith.

*Professor Bhagwati, what attracted you to economics?*

When you come from India, where poverty hits the eye, it is easy to be attracted to economics, which can be used to bring prosperity and create jobs to pull up the poor into gainful employment.

I learned later that there are two broad types of economist: those who treat the subject as an arid mathematical toy and those who see it as a serious social science.

If Cambridge, where I went as an undergraduate, had been interested in esoteric mathematical economics, I would have opted for something else. But the Cambridge economists from whom I learned—many among the greatest figures in the discipline—saw economics as a social science. I therefore saw the power of economics as a tool to address India's poverty and was immediately hooked.

*Who had the greatest impact on you at Cambridge?*

Most of all, it was Harry Johnson, a young Canadian of immense energy and profound analytical gifts. Quite unlike the shy and reserved British dons, Johnson was friendly, effusive, and supportive of students who flocked around him. He would later move to Chicago, where he became one of the most influential members of the market-oriented Chicago school. Another was Joan Robinson, arguably the world's most impressive female economist.

When I left Cambridge for MIT, going from one Cambridge to the other, I was lucky to transition from one phenomenal set of economists to another. At MIT, I learned much from future Nobel laureates Paul Samuelson and Robert Solow. Both would later become great friends and colleagues when I joined the MIT faculty in 1968.

*After Cambridge and MIT, you went to Oxford and then back to India. What did you do in India?*

I joined the Planning Commission in New Delhi, where my first big job was to find ways of raising the bottom 30 percent of India's population out of poverty to a "minimum income" level.

*And what did you prescribe?*

My main prescription was to "grow the pie." My research suggested that the share of the bottom 30 percent of the pie did not seem to vary dramatically with differences in economic and political systems. So growth in the pie seemed to be the principal (but not the only) component of an anti-poverty strategy. To supplement growth's good effects on the poor, the Indian planners were also dedicated to education, health, social reforms, and land reforms. Also, the access of the lowest-income and socially disadvantaged groups to the growth process and its benefits was to be improved in many ways, such as extension of credit without collateral.

Today, this strategy has no rivals. Much empirical work shows that where growth has occurred, poverty has lessened. It is nice to know that one's basic take on an issue of such central importance to humanity's well-being has been borne out by experience!

> My main prescription was to "grow the pie" ... Today, this strategy has no rivals. Much empirical work shows that where growth has occurred, poverty has lessened.

*You left India in 1968 to come to the United States and an academic job at MIT. Why?*

While the decision to emigrate often reflects personal factors—and they were present in my case—the offer of a professorship from MIT certainly helped me make up my mind. At the time, it was easily the world's most celebrated department. Serendipitously, the highest-ranked departments at MIT were not in engineering and the sciences but in linguistics (which had Noam Chomsky) and economics (which had Paul Samuelson). Joining the MIT faculty was a dramatic breakthrough: I felt stimulated each year by several fantastic students and by several of the world's most creative economists.

*We hear a lot in the popular press about fair trade and level playing fields. What's the distinction between free trade and fair trade? How can the playing field be unlevel?*

Free trade simply means allowing no trade barriers such as tariffs, subsidies, and quotas. Trade barriers make domestic prices different from world prices for traded goods. When this happens, resources are not being used efficiently. Basic economics from the time of Adam Smith tells us why free trade is good for us and why barriers to trade harm us, though our understanding of this doctrine today is far more nuanced and profound than it was at its creation.

Fair trade, on the other hand, is almost always a sneaky way of objecting to free trade. If your rivals are hard to compete with, you are not likely to get protection simply by saying that you cannot hack it. But if you say that your rival is an "unfair" trader, that is an easier sell! As international competition has grown fiercer, cries of "unfair trade" have therefore multiplied. The lesser rogues among the protectionists ask for "free and fair trade," whereas the worst ones ask for "fair, not free, trade."

> Fair trade ... is almost always a sneaky way of objecting to free trade.

*At the end of World War II, the General Agreement of Tariffs and Trade (GATT) was established and there followed several rounds of multilateral trade negotiations and reductions in barriers to trade. How do you assess the contribution of GATT and its successor, the World Trade Organization (WTO)?*

The GATT has made a huge contribution by overseeing massive trade liberalization in industrial goods among the developed countries. GATT rules, which "bind" tariffs to negotiated ceilings, prevent the raising of tariffs and have prevented tariff wars like those of the 1930s in which mutual and retaliatory tariff barriers were raised, to the detriment of everyone.

The GATT was folded into the WTO at the end of the Uruguay Round of trade negotiations, and the WTO is institutionally stronger. For instance, it has a binding dispute settlement mechanism, whereas the GATT had no such teeth. It is also more ambitious in its scope, extending to new areas such as the environment, intellectual property protection, and investment rules.

We now have a world of uncoordinated and inefficient trade policies.

*Running alongside the pursuit of multilateral free trade has been the emergence of bilateral trade agreements such as NAFTA and the European Union (EU). How do you view the bilateral free trade areas in today's world?*

Unfortunately, there has been an explosion of bilateral free trade areas today. By some estimates, the ones in place and others being plotted approach 400! Each bilateral agreement gives preferential treatment to its trading partner over others. Because there are now so many bilateral agreements, such as those between the United States and Israel and between the United States and Jordan, the result is a chaotic pattern of different tariffs depending on where a product comes from. Also, "rules of origin" must be agreed upon to determine whether a product is, say, Jordanian or Taiwanese if Jordan qualifies for a preferential tariff but Taiwan does not and Taiwanese inputs enter the Jordanian manufacture of the product.

I have called the resulting crisscrossing of preferences and rules of origin the "spaghetti bowl" problem. The world trading system is choking under these proliferating bilateral deals. Contrast this complexity with the simplicity of a multilateral system with common tariffs for all WTO members.

We now have a world of uncoordinated and inefficient trade policies. The EU makes bilateral free trade agreements with different non-EU countries, so the United States follows with its own bilateral agreements; and with Europe and the United States doing it, the Asian countries, long wedded to multilateralism, have now succumbed to the mania.

Instead, if the United States had provided leadership by rewriting rules to make the signing of such bilateral agreements extremely difficult, this plague on the trading system today might well have been averted.

*Despite the benefits that economics points to from multilateral free trade, the main organization that pursues this goal, the WTO, is having a very hard time with the anti-globalization movement. What can we say about globalization that puts the WTO and its work in proper perspective?*

The anti-globalization movement contains a diverse set of activists. Essentially, they all claim to be stakeholders in the globalization phenomenon. But there are those who want to drive a stake through the system, as in Dracula films, and there are those who want to exercise their stake in the system. The former want to be heard; the latter, to be listened to. For a while, the two disparate sets of critics were milling around together, seeking targets of opportunity at international conferences such as WTO's November 2000 meeting in Seattle, where the riots broke out. Now things have settled down, and the groups that want to work systematically and seriously at improving the global economy's functioning are much more in play.

But the WTO is also seen, inaccurately for the most part, as imposing trade sanctions that override concerns such as environmental protection. For example, U.S. legislation bans the importing of shrimp that is harvested without the use of turtle-excluding devices. India and others complained, but the WTO upheld the U.S. legislation. Ignorant of the facts, demonstrators took to the streets dressed as turtles protesting the WTO decision!

*What advice do you have for a student who is just starting to study economics? Is economics a good subject in which to major?*

I would say: enormously so. In particular, we economists bring three unique insights to good policy making.

First, economists look for second- and subsequent-round effects of actions.

Second, we correctly emphasize that a policy cannot be judged without using a counterfactual. It is a witticism that an economist, when asked how her husband was, said, "compared to what?"

Third, we uniquely and systematically bring the principle of social cost and social benefit to our policy analysis.

PART TWO **Monitoring Macroeconomic Trends and Fluctuations**

# 4 Measuring GDP and Economic Growth

**After studying this chapter, you will be able to:**

- Define GDP and use the circular flow model to explain why GDP equals aggregate expenditure and aggregate income
- Explain how the Bureau of Economic Analysis measures U.S. GDP and real GDP
- Describe how real GDP is used to measure economic growth and fluctuations and explain the limitations of real GDP as a measure of economic well-being

**Will our economy remain weak through 2009 or will** it begin to expand more rapidly? Will it sink into recession, or worse, depression? Many U.S. corporations wanted to know the answers to these questions at the beginning of 2009. Google wanted to know whether to expand its server network and introduce new services or hold off on any new launches. Amazon.com wanted to know whether to increase its warehousing facilities. To assess the state of the economy and to make big decisions about business expansion, firms such as Google and Amazon use forecasts of GDP. What exactly is GDP and what does it tell us about the state of the economy?

To reveal the rate of growth or shrinkage of production, we must remove the effects of inflation and assess how production is *really* changing. How do we remove the effects of inflation to reveal *real* production?

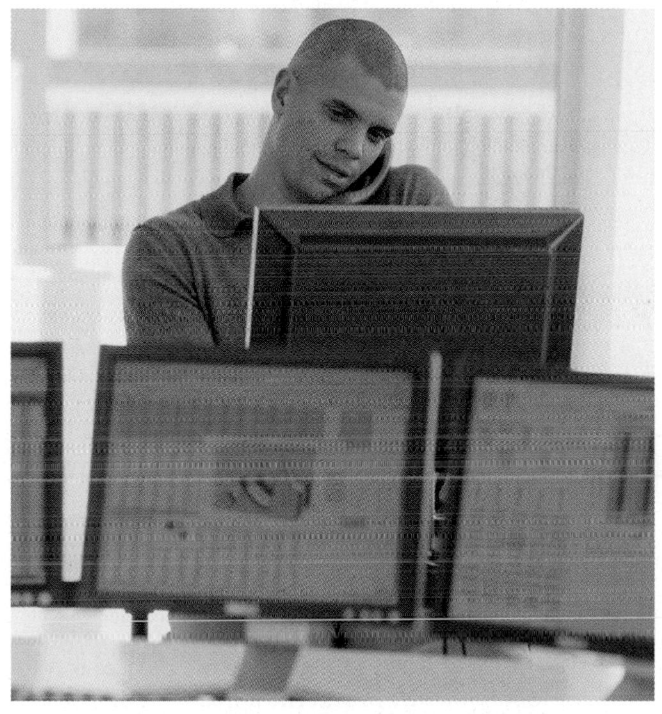

Some countries are rich while others are poor. How do we compare economic well-being in one country with that in another? How can we make international comparisons of production?

In this chapter, you will find out how economic statisticians at the Bureau of Economic Analysis measure GDP and the economic growth rate. You will also learn about the uses and the limitations of these measures. In *Reading Between the Lines* at the end of the chapter, we'll look at the U.S. economy during the slowdown that began in 2008.

## Gross Domestic Product

What exactly is GDP, how is it calculated, what does it mean, and why do we care about it? You are going to discover the answers to these questions in this chapter. First, what *is* GDP?

### GDP Defined

**GDP**, or **gross domestic product**, is the market value of the final goods and services produced within a country in a given time period. This definition has four parts:

- Market value
- Final goods and services
- Produced within a country
- In a given time period

We'll examine each in turn.

**Market Value** To measure total production, we must add together the production of apples and oranges, computers and popcorn. Just counting the items doesn't get us very far. For example, which is the greater total production: 100 apples and 50 oranges or 50 apples and 100 oranges?

GDP answers this question by valuing items at their *market values*—the prices at which items are traded in markets. If the price of an apple is 10 cents, then the market value of 50 apples is $5. If the price of an orange is 20 cents, then the market value of 100 oranges is $20. By using market prices to value production, we can add the apples and oranges together. The market value of 50 apples and 100 oranges is $5 plus $20, or $25.

**Final Goods and Services** To calculate GDP, we value the *final goods and services* produced. A **final good** (or service) is an item that is bought by its final user during a specified time period. It contrasts with an **intermediate good** (or service), which is an item that is produced by one firm, bought by another firm, and used as a component of a final good or service.

For example, a Ford truck is a final good, but a Firestone tire on the truck is an intermediate good. A Dell computer is a final good, but an Intel Pentium chip inside it is an intermediate good.

If we were to add the value of intermediate goods and services produced to the value of final goods and services, we would count the same thing many times—a problem called *double counting*. The value of a truck already includes the value of the tires, and the value of a Dell PC already includes the value of the Pentium chip inside it.

Some goods can be an intermediate good in some situations and a final good in other situations. For example, the ice cream that you buy on a hot summer day is a final good, but the ice cream that a restaurant buys and uses to make sundaes is an intermediate good. The sundae is the final good. So whether a good is an intermediate good or a final good depends on what it is used for, not what it is.

Some items that people buy are neither final goods nor intermediate goods and they are not part of GDP. Examples of such items include financial assets—stocks and bonds—and secondhand goods—used cars or existing homes. A secondhand good was part of GDP in the year in which it was produced, but not in GDP this year.

**Produced Within a Country** Only goods and services that are produced *within a country* count as part of that country's GDP. Nike Corporation, a U.S. firm, produces sneakers in Vietnam, and the market value of those shoes is part of Vietnam's GDP, not part of U.S. GDP. Toyota, a Japanese firm, produces automobiles in Georgetown, Kentucky, and the value of this production is part of U.S. GDP, not part of Japan's GDP.

**In a Given Time Period** GDP measures the value of production *in a given time period*—normally either a quarter of a year—called the quarterly GDP data—or a year—called the annual GDP data.

GDP measures not only the value of total production but also total income and total expenditure. The equality between the value of total production and total income is important because it shows the direct link between productivity and living standards. Our standard of living rises when our incomes rise and we can afford to buy more goods and services. But we must produce more goods and services if we are to be able to buy more goods and services.

Rising incomes and a rising value of production go together. They are two aspects of the same phenomenon: increasing productivity. To see why, we study the circular flow of expenditure and income.

## GDP and the Circular Flow of Expenditure and Income

Figure 4.1 illustrates the circular flow of expenditure and income. The economy consists of households, firms, governments, and the rest of the world (the rectangles), which trade in factor markets and goods (and services) markets. We focus first on households and firms.

**Households and Firms** Households sell and firms buy the services of labor, capital, and land in factor markets. For these factor services, firms pay income to households: wages for labor services, interest for the use of capital, and rent for the use of land. A fourth factor of production, entrepreneurship, receives profit.

Firms' retained earnings—profits that are not distributed to households—are part of the household sector's income. You can think of retained earnings as being income that households save and lend back to firms. Figure 4.1 shows the total income—*aggregate income*—received by households, including retained earnings, by the blue flow labeled *Y*.

Firms sell and households buy consumer goods and services—such as inline skates and haircuts—in the goods market. The total payment for these goods and services is **consumption expenditure**, shown by the red flow labeled *C*.

Firms buy and sell new capital equipment—such as computer systems, airplanes, trucks, and assembly line equipment—in the goods market. Some of what firms produce is not sold but is added to inventory. For example, if GM produces 1,000 cars and sells 950 of them, the other 50 cars remain in GM's inventory of unsold cars, which increases by 50 cars. When a firm adds unsold output to inventory, we can think of the firm as buying goods from itself. The

**FIGURE 4.1** The Circular Flow of Expenditure and Income

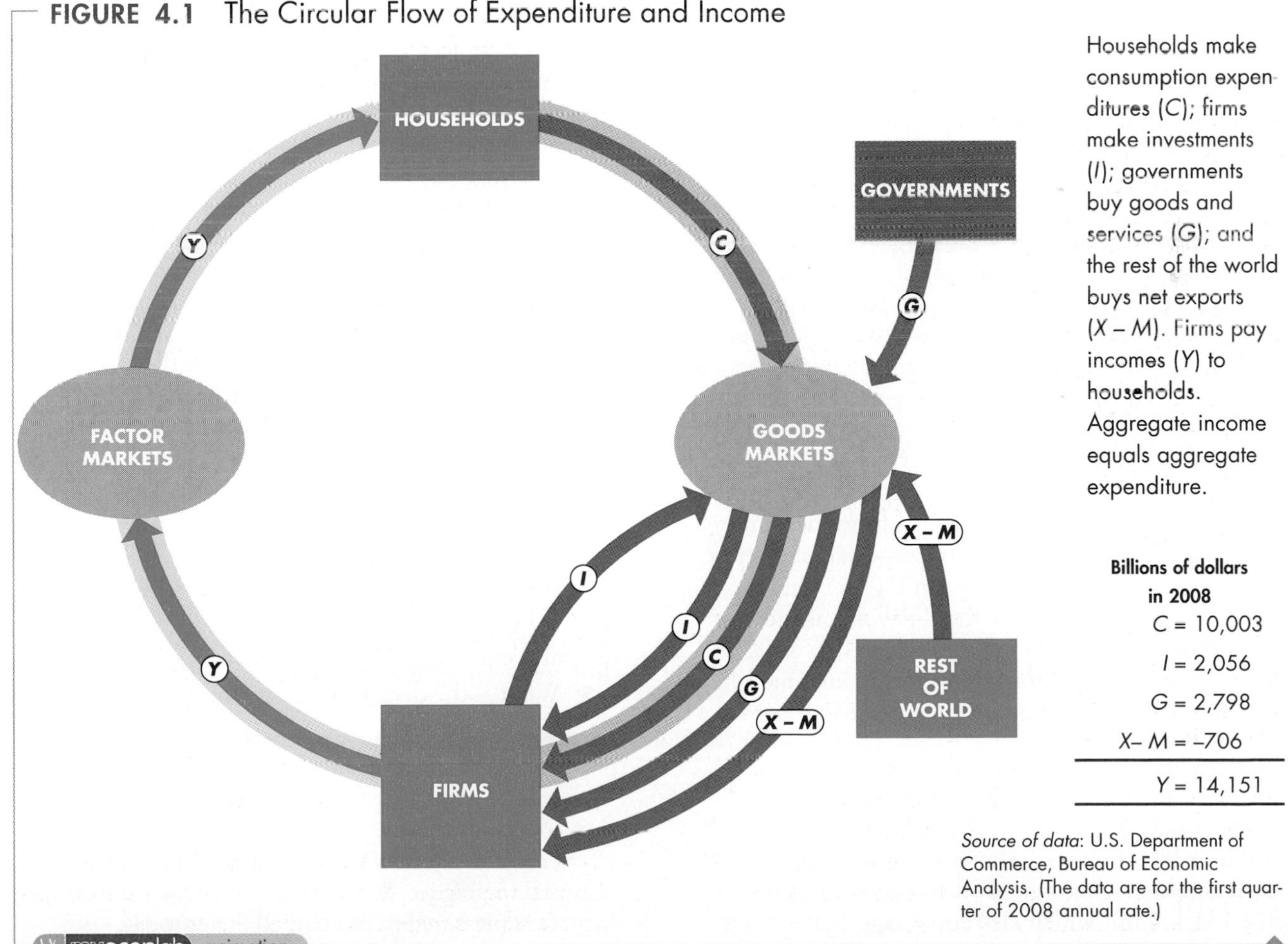


Households make consumption expenditures (*C*); firms make investments (*I*); governments buy goods and services (*G*); and the rest of the world buys net exports (*X* – *M*). Firms pay incomes (*Y*) to households. Aggregate income equals aggregate expenditure.

**Billions of dollars in 2008**

*C* = 10,003
*I* = 2,056
*G* = 2,798
*X* – *M* = –706
*Y* = 14,151

*Source of data*: U.S. Department of Commerce, Bureau of Economic Analysis. (The data are for the first quarter of 2008 annual rate.)

myeconlab animation

purchase of new plant, equipment, and buildings and the additions to inventories are **investment**, shown by the red flow labeled *I*.

**Governments** Governments buy goods and services from firms and their expenditure on goods and services is called **government expenditure**. In Fig. 4.1, government expenditure is shown as the red flow *G*.

Governments finance their expenditure with taxes. But taxes are not part of the circular flow of expenditure and income. Governments also make financial transfers to households, such as Social Security benefits and unemployment benefits, and pay subsidies to firms. These financial transfers, like taxes, are not part of the circular flow of expenditure and income.

**Rest of the World** Firms in the United States sell goods and services to the rest of the world—**exports**—and buy goods and services from the rest of the world—**imports**. The value of exports ($X$) minus the value of imports ($M$) is called **net exports**, the red flow $X - M$ in Fig 4.1. If net exports are positive, the net flow of goods and services is from U.S. firms to the rest of the world. If net exports are negative, the net flow of goods and services is from the rest of the world to U.S. firms.

**GDP Equals Expenditure Equals Income** Gross domestic product can be measured in two ways: By the total expenditure on goods and services or by the total income earned producing goods and services.

The total expenditure—*aggregate expenditure*—is the sum of the red flows in Fig. 4.1. Aggregate expenditure equals consumption expenditure plus investment plus government expenditure plus net exports.

Aggregate income is equal to the total amount paid for the services of the factors of production used to produce final goods and services—wages, interest, rent, and profit. The blue flow in Fig. 4.1 shows aggregate income. Because firms pay out as incomes (including retained profits) everything they receive from the sale of their output, aggregate income (the blue flow) equals aggregate expenditure (the sum of the red flows). That is,

$$Y = C + I + G + X - M.$$

The table in Fig. 4.1 shows the numbers for 2008. You can see that the sum of the expenditures is $14,151 billion, which also equals aggregate income.

Because aggregate expenditure equals aggregate income, the two methods of measuring GDP give the same answer. So

GDP equals aggregate expenditure and equals aggregate income.

The circular flow model is the foundation on which the national economic accounts are built.

## Why Is Domestic Product "Gross"?

"Gross" means before subtracting the depreciation of capital. The opposite of "gross" is "net," which means after subtracting the depreciation of capital.

**Depreciation** is the decrease in the value of a firm's capital that results from wear and tear and obsolescence. The total amount spent both buying new capital and replacing depreciated capital is called **gross investment**. The amount by which the value of capital increases is called **net investment**. Net investment equals gross investment minus depreciation.

For example if an airline buys 5 new airplanes and retires 2 old airplanes from service, its gross investment is the value of the 5 new airplanes, depreciation is the value of the 2 old airplanes retired, and net investment is the value of 3 new airplanes.

*Gross investment* is one of the expenditures included in the expenditure approach to measuring GDP. So the resulting value of total product is a gross measure.

*Gross profit*, which is a firm's profit before subtracting depreciation, is one of the incomes included in the income approach to measuring GDP. So again, the resulting value of total product is a gross measure.

## Review Quiz

1 Define GDP and distinguish between a final good and an intermediate good. Provide examples.
2 Why does GDP equal aggregate income and also equal aggregate expenditure?
3 What is the distinction between gross and net?

Work Study Plan 4.1 and get instant feedback.

Let's now see how the ideas that you've just studied are used in practice. We'll see how GDP and its components are measured in the United States today.

## Measuring U.S. GDP

The Bureau of Economic Analysis (BEA) uses the concepts in the circular flow model to measure GDP and its components in the *National Income and Product Accounts.* Because the value of aggregate production equals aggregate expenditure and aggregate income, there are two approaches available for measuring GDP, and both are used. They are

- The expenditure approach
- The income approach

### The Expenditure Approach

The *expenditure approach* measures GDP as the sum of consumption expenditure ($C$), investment ($I$), government expenditure on goods and services ($G$), and net exports of goods and services ($X - M$), corresponding to the red flows in the circular flow model in Fig. 4.1. Table 4.1 shows the result of this approach for 2008. The table uses the terms in the *National Income and Product Accounts.*

*Personal consumption expenditures* are the expenditures by U.S. households on goods and services produced in the United States and in the rest of the world. They include goods such as soda and books and services such as banking and legal advice. They also include the purchase of consumer durable goods, such as TVs and microwave ovens. But they do *not* include the purchase of new homes, which the BEA counts as part of investment.

*Gross private domestic investment* is expenditure on capital equipment and buildings by firms and the additions to business inventories. It also includes expenditure on new homes by households.

*Government expenditure on goods and services* is the expenditure by all levels of government on goods and services, such as national defense and garbage collection. It does *not* include *transfer payments,* such as unemployment benefits, because they are not expenditures on goods and services.

*Net exports of goods and services* are the value of exports minus the value of imports. This item includes airplanes that Boeing sells to British Airways (a U.S. export), and Japanese DVD players that Circuit City buys from Sony (a U.S. import).

Table 4.1 shows the relative magnitudes of the four items of aggregate expenditure.

**TABLE 4.1** GDP: The Expenditure Approach

| Item | Symbol | Amount in 2008 (billions of dollars) | Percentage of GDP |
|---|---|---|---|
| Personal consumption expenditures | $C$ | 10,003 | 70.7 |
| Gross private domestic investment | $I$ | 2,056 | 14.5 |
| Government expenditure on goods and services | $G$ | 2,798 | 19.8 |
| Net exports of goods and services | $X - M$ | –706 | –5.0 |
| **Gross domestic product** | **$Y$** | **14,151** | **100.0** |

The expenditure approach measures GDP as the sum of personal consumption expenditures ($C$), gross private domestic investment ($I$), government expenditure on goods and services ($G$), and net exports ($X - M$). In 2008, GDP measured by the expenditure approach was $14,151 billion. More than two thirds of aggregate expenditure is on personal consumption goods and services.

*Source of data:* U.S. Department of Commerce, Bureau of Economic Analysis.

### The Income Approach

The *income approach* measures GDP by summing the incomes that firms pay households for the factors of production they hire—wages for labor, interest for capital, rent for land, and profit for entrepreneurship. The *National Income and Product Accounts* divide incomes into five categories:

1. Compensation of employees
2. Net interest
3. Rental income
4. Corporate profits
5. Proprietors' income

*Compensation of employees* is the payment for labor services. It includes net wages and salaries (called "take-home pay") that workers receive plus taxes withheld on earnings plus fringe benefits such as Social Security and pension fund contributions.

*Net interest* is the interest households receive on loans they make minus the interest households pay on their own borrowing.

*Rental income* is the payment for the use of land and other rented resources.

*Corporate profits* are the profits of corporations, some of which are paid to households in the form of dividends and some of which are retained by corporations as undistributed profits. They are all income.

*Proprietors' income* is the income earned by the owner-operator of a business, which includes compensation for the owner's labor, the use of the owner's capital, and profit.

Table 4.2 shows these five incomes and their relative magnitudes. They sum to *net domestic income at factor cost*. The term "factor cost" is used because it is the cost of the factors of production used to produce final goods. When we sum the expenditures on final goods, we arrive at a total called *domestic product at market prices*. Market prices and factor cost diverge because of indirect taxes and subsidies.

An *indirect tax* is a tax paid by consumers when they buy goods and services. (In contrast, a *direct tax* is a tax on income.) State sales taxes and taxes on alcohol, gasoline, and tobacco products are indirect taxes. Because of indirect taxes, consumers pay more for some goods and services than producers receive. Market price exceeds factor cost. For example, if the sales tax is 7 percent, you pay $1.07 when you buy a $1 chocolate bar. The factor cost of the chocolate bar including profit is $1. The market price is $1.07.

A *subsidy* is a payment by the government to a producer. Payments made to grain growers and dairy farmers are subsidies. Because of subsidies, consumers pay less for some goods and services than producers receive. Factor cost exceeds market price.

To get from factor cost to market price, we add indirect taxes and subtract subsidies. Making this adjustment brings us to *net domestic income at market prices*. We still must get from a *net* to a *gross* measure.

Total expenditure is a *gross* number because it includes *gross* investment. Net domestic income at market prices is a net income measure because corporate profits are measured *after deducting depreciation*. They are a *net* income measure. To get from net income to gross income, we must *add depreciation*.

We've now arrived at GDP using the income approach. This number is not exactly the same as GDP using the expenditure approach. If a waiter doesn't report all his tips when he fills out his income tax return, they get missed in the income approach but they show up in the expenditure approach when he spends his income. So the sum of expenditures might exceed the sum of incomes. The sum of expenditures might exceed the sum of incomes because some expenditure items are estimated rather than directly measured.

The gap between the expenditure approach and the income approach is called the **statistical discrepancy** and it is calculated as the GDP expenditure total minus the GDP income total. The discrepancy is never large. In 2008, it was 0.3 percent of GDP.

**TABLE 4.2** GDP: The Income Approach

| Item | Amount in 2008 (billions of dollars) | Percentage of GDP |
|---|---|---|
| Compensation of employees | 8,037 | 56.8 |
| Net interest | 915 | 6.5 |
| Rental income | 39 | 0.3 |
| Corporate profits | 1,195 | 8.4 |
| Proprietors' income | 1,072 | 7.6 |
| *Net domestic income at factor cost* | 11,258 | 79.6 |
| Indirect taxes *less* subsidies | 1,071 | 7.6 |
| *Net domestic income at market prices* | 12,329 | 87.2 |
| Depreciation | 1,778 | 12.6 |
| **GDP (income approach)** | **14,107** | **99.7** |
| Statistical discrepancy | 44 | 0.3 |
| **GDP (expenditure approach)** | **14,151** | **100.0** |

The sum of all incomes equals *net domestic income at factor cost*. GDP equals net domestic income at factor cost plus indirect taxes less subsidies plus depreciation. In 2008, GDP measured by the income approach was $14,107 billion. This amount is $44 billion less than GDP measured by the expenditure approach—a statistical discrepancy of $44 billion or 0.3 percent of GDP. Compensation of employees—labor income—is by far the largest part of aggregate income.

*Source of data:* U.S. Department of Commerce, Bureau of Economic Analysis.

## Nominal GDP and Real GDP

Often, we want to *compare* GDP in two periods, say 2000 and 2008. In 2000, GDP was $9,817 billion and in 2008, it was $14,151 billion—44 percent higher than in 2000. This increase in GDP is a combination of an increase in production and a rise in prices. To isolate the increase in production from the rise in prices, we distinguish between *real* GDP and *nominal* GDP.

**Real GDP** is the value of final goods and services produced in a given year when *valued at the prices of a reference base year*. By comparing the value of production in the two years at the same prices, we reveal the change in production.

Currently, the reference base year is 2000 and we describe real GDP as measured in 2000 dollars—in terms of what the dollar would by in 2000.

**Nominal GDP** is the value of final goods and services produced in a given year valued at the prices of that year. Nominal GDP is just a more precise name for GDP.

Economists at the Bureau of Economic Analysis calculate real GDP using the method described in the Mathematical Note on pp. 100–101. Here, we'll explain the basic idea but not the technical details.

## Calculating Real GDP

We'll calculate real GDP for an economy that produces one consumption good, one capital good, and one government service. Net exports are zero.

Table 4.3 shows the quantities produced and the prices in 2000 (the base year) and in 2009. In part (a), we calculate nominal GDP in 2000. For each item, we multiply the quantity produced by its price to find the total expenditure on the item. We then sum the expenditures to find nominal GDP, which in 2000 is $100 million. Because 2000 is the base year, real GDP and nominal GDP both equal $100 million.

In Table 4.3(b), we calculate nominal GDP in 2009, which is $300 million. Nominal GDP in 2009 is three times its value in 2000. But by how much has production increased? Real GDP will tell us.

In Table 4.3(c), we calculate real GDP in 2009. The quantities of the goods and services produced are those of 2009, as in part (b). The prices are those in the reference base year—2000, as in part (a).

For each item, we multiply the quantity produced in 2009 by its price in 2000. We then sum these expenditures to find real GDP in 2009, which is $160 million. This number is what total expenditure would have been in 2009 if prices had remained the same as they were in 2000.

Nominal GDP in 2009 is three times its value in 2000, but real GDP in 2009 is only 1.6 times its 2000 value—a 60 percent increase in production.

**TABLE 4.3** Calculating Nominal GDP and Real GDP

| | Item | Quantity (millions) | Price (dollars) | Expenditure (millions of dollars) |
|---|---|---|---|---|
| **(a) In 2000** | | | | |
| *C* | T-shirts | 10 | 5 | 50 |
| *I* | Computer chips | 3 | 10 | 30 |
| *G* | Security services | 1 | 20 | 20 |
| *Y* | Real and Nominal GDP in 2000 | | | 100 |
| **(b) In 2009** | | | | |
| *C* | T-shirts | 4 | 5 | 20 |
| *I* | Computer chips | 2 | 20 | 40 |
| *G* | Security services | 6 | 40 | 240 |
| *Y* | Nominal GDP in 2009 | | | 300 |
| **(c) Quantities of 2009 valued at prices of 2000** | | | | |
| *C* | T-shirts | 4 | 5 | 20 |
| *I* | Computer chips | 2 | 10 | 20 |
| *G* | Security services | 6 | 20 | 120 |
| *Y* | Real GDP in 2009 | | | 160 |

In 2000, the reference base year, real GDP equals nominal GDP and was $100 million. In 2009, nominal GDP increased to $300 million. But real GDP in 2009 in part (c), which is calculated by using the quantities of 2009 in part (b) and the prices of 2000 in part (a) was only $160 million—a 60 percent increase from 2000.

## Review Quiz

1 What is the expenditure approach to measuring GDP?
2 What is the income approach to measuring GDP?
3 What adjustments must be made to total income to make it equal GDP?
4 What is the distinction between nominal GDP and real GDP?
5 How is real GDP calculated?

Work Study Plan 4.2 and get instant feedback.

## The Uses and Limitations of Real GDP

Economists use estimates of real GDP for two main purposes:

- To compare the standard of living over time
- To compare the standard of living across countries

### The Standard of Living Over Time

One method of comparing the standard of living over time is to calculate real GDP per person in different years. **Real GDP per person** is real GDP divided by the population. Real GDP per person tells us the value of goods and services that the average person can enjoy. By using *real* GDP, we remove any influence that rising prices and a rising cost of living might have had on our comparison.

We're interested in both the long-term trends and the shorter-term cycles in the standard of living.

**Long-Term Trend** A handy way of comparing real GDP per person over time is to express it as a ratio of some reference year. For example, in 1958, real GDP per person was $12,883 and in 2008, it was $38,422. So real GDP per person in 2008 was 3 times its 1958 level—that is, $38,422 ÷ $12,883 = 3. To the extent that real GDP per person measures the standard of living, people were three times as well off in 2008 as their grandparents had been in 1958.

Figure 4.2 shows the path of U.S. real GDP per person for the 50 years from 1958 to 2008 and highlights two features of our expanding living standard:

- The growth of potential GDP per person
- Fluctuations of real GDP per person

***The Growth of Potential GDP*** When all the economy's labor, capital, land, and entrepreneurial ability are fully employed, the value of real GDP is called **potential GDP**. Potential GDP per person, the smoother black line in Fig. 4.2, grows at a steady pace because the quantities of the factors of production and their productivity grow at a steady pace.

But potential GDP per person doesn't grow at a *constant* pace. During the 1960s, it grew at 2.7 percent per year, but then its growth rate slowed and growth after 1970 averaged only 2 percent per year. This slowdown might seem small, but it had big consequences, as you'll soon see.

**FIGURE 4.2** Rising Standard of Living in the United States

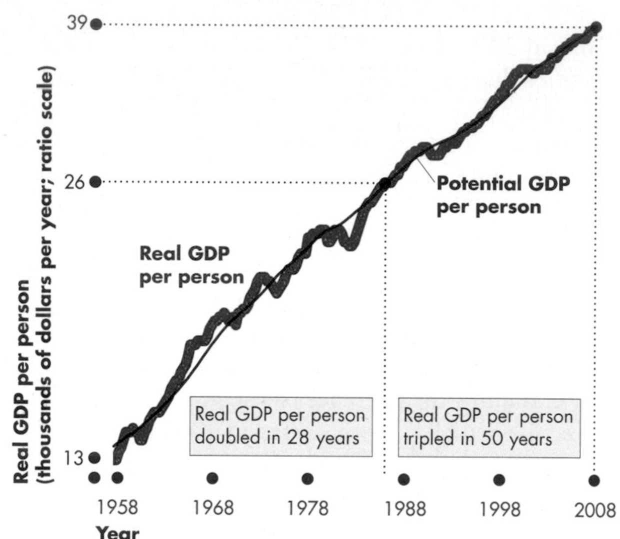


Real GDP per person in the United States doubled between 1958 and 1986 and tripled between 1958 and 2008. Real GDP per person, the red line, fluctuates around potential GDP per person, the black line.

*Sources of data*: Bureau of Economic Analysis and Congressional Budget Office.

myeconlab animation

***Fluctuations of Real GDP*** You can see that real GDP shown by the red line in Fig. 4.2 fluctuates around potential GDP. Sometimes, real GDP is above potential; sometimes, it is below potential; and sometimes, real GDP shrinks.

Let's take a closer look at the two features of our expanding living standard that we've just outlined.

**Productivity Growth Slowdown** You've just seen that the growth rate of real GDP per person slowed after 1970. How costly was that slowdown? The answer is provided by a number that we'll call the **Lucas wedge**, which is the dollar value of the accumulated gap between what real GDP per person would have been if the 1960s growth rate had persisted and what real GDP per person turned out to be.

University of Chicago economist and Nobel Laureate Robert E. Lucas Jr., who drew attention to this measure, remarked that once he began to think about the benefits of faster economic growth, he found it hard to think about anything else.

Figure 4.3 illustrates the Lucas wedge. The red line is actual real GDP per person and the thin black line is the trend that real GDP per person would have followed if the 1960s growth rate of potential GDP had persisted through the years to 2008.

You can see in the figure that the gap—the wedge—had accumulated to an astonishing $153,000 per person by 2008. The gap started out small during the 1970s but in 2008, real GDP per person was $12,400 per year lower than it would have been with no growth slowdown.

**Real GDP Fluctuations** We call the fluctuations in the pace of expansion of real GDP the business cycle. A **business cycle** is a periodic but irregular up-and-down movement of total production and other measures of economic activity. The business cycle isn't a regular, predictable, and repeating cycle like the phases of the moon. The timing and the intensity of the business cycle vary a lot, but every cycle has two phases:

1. Expansion
2. Recession

and two turning points:

1. Peak
2. Trough

Figure 4.4 shows these features of the most recent U.S. business cycle.

An **expansion** is a period during which real GDP increases. In the early stage of an expansion real GDP returns to potential GDP and as the expansion progresses, potential GDP grows and real GDP eventually exceeds potential GDP.

A common definition of **recession** is a period during which real GDP decreases—its growth rate is negative—for at least two successive quarters. But the National Bureau of Economic Research, which dates the U.S. business cycle phases and turning points, defines a recession more broadly as "a period of significant decline in total output, income, employment, and trade, usually lasting from six months to a

**FIGURE 4.3** The Cost of Slower Growth: The Lucas Wedge

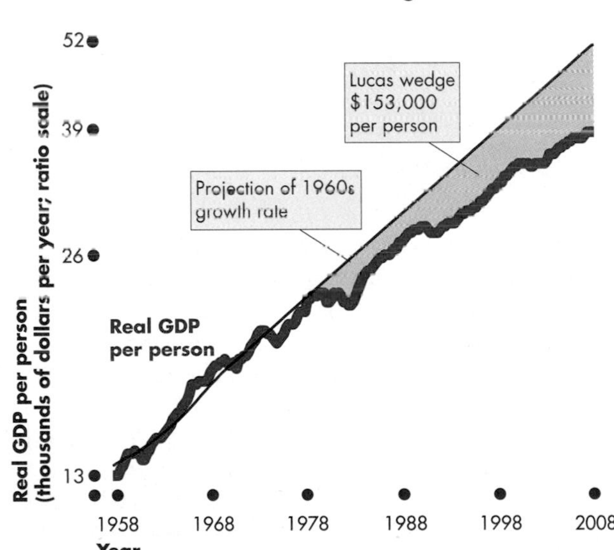


The black line projects the 1960s growth rate of real GDP per person to 2008. The Lucas wedge arises from the slowdown of productivity growth that began during the 1970s. The cost of the slowdown is $153,000 per person.

*Sources of data*: Bureau of Economic Analysis, Congressional Budget Office, and author's calculations.

myeconlab animation

**FIGURE 4.4** The Most Recent U.S. Business Cycle

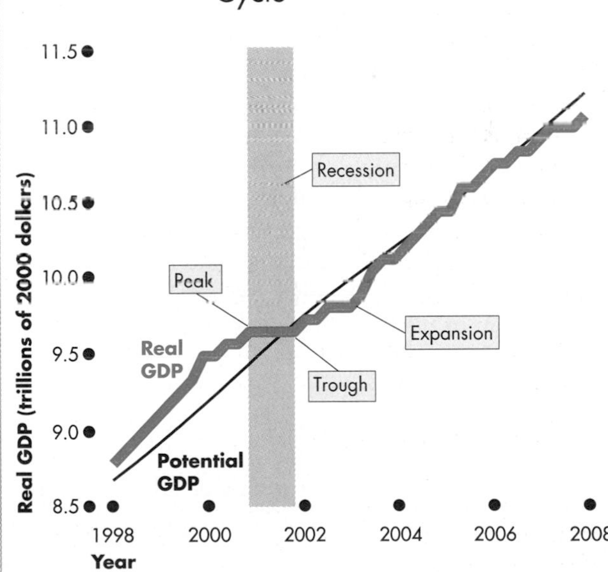


The most recent business cycle peak was in the fourth quarter of 2000. A recession ran from the first quarter through the third quarter of 2001. An expansion began in the fourth quarter of 2001.

*Sources of data*: Bureau of Economic Analysis, Congressional Budget Office, and National Bureau of Economic Research.

myeconlab animation

year, and marked by contractions in many sectors of the economy." This definition means that sometimes a recession is declared even though real GDP has not decreased for two successive quarters. The most recent recession, in 2001, was such a recession.

An expansion ends and recession begins at a business cycle peak. A *peak* is the highest level of real GDP that has been attained up to that time.

A recession ends at a *trough*, when real GDP reaches a temporary low point and from which the next expansion begins.

Let's now leave comparisons of the standard of living over time and look at those across countries.

## The Standard of Living Across Countries

Two problems arise in using real GDP to compare living standards across countries. First, the real GDP of one country must be converted into the same currency units as the real GDP of the other country. Second, the goods and services in both countries must be valued at the same prices. We'll look at these two problems by using a striking example: a comparison of the United States and China.

**China and the United States Compared** In 2008, real GDP per person in the United States was $38,422. The official Chinese statistics published in the International Monetary Fund's *World Economic Outlook* says that real GDP per person in China in 2008 was 16,400 yuan. (The yuan is the currency of China.) On average, during 2008, $1 U.S. was worth 8.3 yuan. If we use this exchange rate to convert 16,400 yuan into U.S. dollars, we get $1,976. This comparison of real GDP per person in China and the United States makes China look extremely poor. In 2008, real GDP per person in the United States was 19 times that in China, or real GDP person in China was less than 4 percent of that in the United States.

The red line in Fig. 4.5 shows real GDP per person in China from 1980 to 2008 when the market exchange rate is used to convert yuan to U.S. dollars.

**Purchasing Power Parity Comparison** Figure 4.5 shows a second estimate of China's real GDP per person that is much larger than the one we've just calculated. Let's see how this alternative measurement is made.

U.S. real GDP is measured by using prices that prevail in the United States. China's real GDP is measured by using prices that prevail in China. But the *relative prices* in these countries are very different.

**FIGURE 4.5** Two Views of Real GDP in China

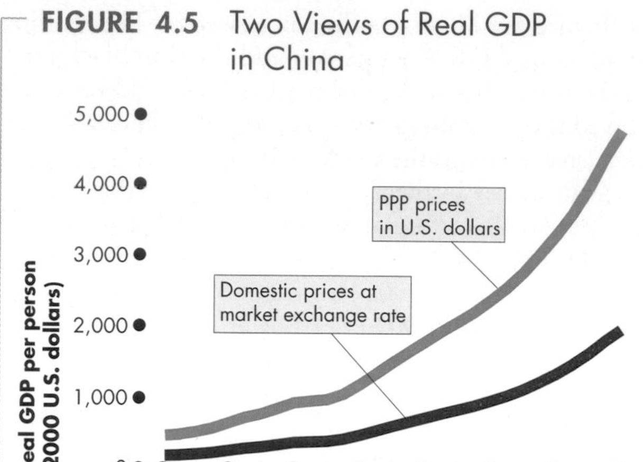


Real GDP per person in China has grown rapidly. But how rapidly it has grown and to what level depends on how real GDP is valued. When GDP is valued at the market exchange rate, China is a poor developing country in which income per person in 2008 is 5 percent of the U.S. level. But when GDP is valued at purchasing power parity prices, China seems to be much less poor with real GDP per person in 2008 at 12.5 percent of the U.S. level.

*Sources of data*: International Monetary Fund, *World Economic Outlook database*, April 2008 and Alan Heston, Robert Summers, and Bettina Aten, Penn World Table Version 6.1 Center for International Comparisons at the University of Pennsylvania (CICUP), October 2002.

myeconlab animation

The prices of some goods are higher in the United States than in China, so these items get a smaller weight in China's real GDP than they get in U.S. real GDP. For example, a Big Mac that costs $3.57 in Chicago costs 12.5 yuan, which is the equivalent of $1.83, in Shanghai. So in China's real GDP, a Big Mac gets about half the weight that it gets in U.S. real GDP.

At the same time, the prices of some goods are higher in China than in the United States, so these items get a bigger weight in China's real GDP than they get in U.S. real GDP. For example, a Buick LaCrosse that costs $25,000 in Chicago costs 239,800 yuan, which is the equivalent of $35,000, in Shanghai. So a Buick LaCrosse made in China gets about 40 percent more weight than the same car made in Detroit gets in U.S. real GDP.

More prices are lower in China than in the United States, so Chinese prices put a lower value on China's production than do U.S. prices.

To avoid putting a lower value on China's production, we use **purchasing power parity** or **PPP** prices, which are the same for both countries when converted at the market exchange rate. By using PPP prices, we make a more valid comparison of real GDP in China and the United States.

Alan Heston, Robert Summers, and Bettina Aten, economists in the Center for International Comparisons at the University of Pennsylvania, have used PPP prices to construct real GDP data for more than 100 countries. The IMF now uses a method similar to that of Heston, Summers, and Aten to calculate PPP estimates of real GDP in all countries. The PPP comparisons tell a remarkable story.

Figure 4.5 shows the PPP view of China's real GDP, the green line. According to the PPP comparisons, real GDP per person in the United States in 2008 was 8 times that of China, or real GDP per person in China was 12.5 percent of that in the United States.

You've seen how real GDP is used to make standard of living comparisons over time and across countries. But real GDP isn't a perfect measure of the standard of living and we'll now examine its limitations.

## Limitations of Real GDP

Real GDP measures the value of goods and services that are bought in markets. Some of the factors that influence the standard of living and that are not part of GDP are

- Household production
- Underground economic activity
- Health and life expectancy
- Leisure time
- Environmental quality
- Political freedom and social justice

**Household Production** An enormous amount of production takes place every day in our homes. Preparing meals, cleaning the kitchen, changing a light bulb, cutting the grass, washing the car, and caring for a child are all examples of household production. Because these productive activities are not traded in markets, they are not included in GDP.

The omission of household production from GDP means that GDP *underestimates* total production. But it also means that the growth rate of GDP *overestimates* the growth rate of total production. The reason is that some of the growth rate of market production (included in GDP) is a replacement for home production. So part of the increase in GDP arises from a decrease in home production.

Two trends point in this direction. One is the number of women who have jobs, which has increased from 54 percent in 1970 to 62 percent in 2008. The other is the trend in the market purchase of traditionally home-produced goods and services. For example, more and more families now eat in fast-food restaurants—one of the fastest-growing industries in the United States—and use day-care services. This trend means that an increasing proportion of food preparation and child care that were part of household production are now measured as part of GDP. So real GDP grows more rapidly than does real GDP plus home production.

**Underground Economic Activity** The *underground economy* is the part of the economy that is purposely hidden from the view of the government to avoid taxes and regulations or because the goods and services being produced are illegal. Because underground economic activity is unreported, it is omitted from GDP.

The underground economy is easy to describe, even if it is hard to measure. It includes the production and distribution of illegal drugs, production that uses illegal labor that is paid less than the minimum wage, and jobs done for cash to avoid paying income taxes. This last category might be quite large and includes tips earned by cab drivers, hairdressers, and hotel and restaurant workers.

Estimates of the scale of the underground economy in the United States range between 9 and 30 percent of GDP ($1,200 billion to almost $4,000 billion). Provided that the underground economy is a reasonably stable proportion of the total economy, the growth rate of real GDP still gives a useful estimate of changes in economic well-being and the standard of living. But sometimes production shifts from the underground economy to the rest of the economy, and sometimes it shifts the other way. The underground economy expands relative to the rest of the economy if taxes become especially high or if regulations become especially restrictive. And the underground economy shrinks relative to the rest of the economy if the burdens of taxes and regulations are eased. During the 1980s, when tax rates were cut, there was an increase in the reporting of previously hidden income and tax revenues increased. So some part (but probably a very small part) of the expansion of real GDP during the 1980s represented a shift from the underground economy rather than an increase in production.

**Health and Life Expectancy** Good health and a long life—the hopes of everyone—do not show up in real GDP, at least not directly. A higher real GDP enables us to spend more on medical research, health care, a good diet, and exercise equipment. And as real GDP has increased, our life expectancy has lengthened—from 70 years at the end of World War II to approaching 80 years today. Infant deaths and death in childbirth, two fearful scourges of the nineteenth century, have been greatly reduced.

But we face new health and life expectancy problems every year. AIDS and drug abuse are taking young lives at a rate that causes serious concern. When we take these negative influences into account, we see that real GDP growth overstates the improvements in the standard of living.

**Leisure Time** Leisure time is an economic good that adds to our economic well-being and the standard of living. Other things remaining the same, the more leisure we have, the better off we are. Our working time is valued as part of GDP, but our leisure time is not. Yet that leisure time must be at least as valuable to us as the wage that we earn for the last hour worked. If it were not, we would work instead of taking leisure. Over the years, leisure time has steadily increased. The workweek has become shorter, more people take early retirement, and the number of vacation days has increased. These improvements in economic well-being are not reflected in real GDP.

**Environmental Quality** Economic activity directly influences the quality of the environment. The burning of hydrocarbon fuels is the most visible activity that damages our environment. But it is not the only example. The depletion of nonrenewable natural resources, the mass clearing of forests, and the pollution of lakes and rivers are other major environmental consequences of industrial production.

Resources that are used to protect the environment are valued as part of GDP. For example, the value of catalytic converters that help to protect the atmosphere from automobile emissions is part of GDP. But if we did not use such pieces of equipment and instead polluted the atmosphere, we would not count the deteriorating air that we were breathing as a negative part of GDP.

An industrial society possibly produces more atmospheric pollution than an agricultural society does. But pollution does not always increase as we become wealthier. Wealthy people value a clean environment and are willing to pay for one. Compare the pollution in China today with pollution in the United States. China, a poor country, pollutes its rivers, lakes, and atmosphere in a way that is unimaginable in the United States.

**Political Freedom and Social Justice** Most people in the Western world value political freedoms such as those provided by the U.S. Constitution. And they value social justice—equality of opportunity and of access to social security safety nets that protect people from the extremes of misfortune.

A country might have a very large real GDP per person but have limited political freedom and social justice. For example, a small elite might enjoy political liberty and extreme wealth while the vast majority are effectively enslaved and live in abject poverty. Such an economy would generally be regarded as having a lower standard of living than one that had the same amount of real GDP but in which political freedoms were enjoyed by everyone. Today, China has rapid real GDP growth but limited political freedoms, while Poland and Ukraine have moderate real GDP growth but democratic political systems. Economists have no easy way to determine which of these countries is better off.

**The Bottom Line** Do we get the wrong message about the growth in economic well-being and the standard of living by looking at the growth of real GDP? The influences that are omitted from real GDP are probably important and could be large. Developing countries have a larger underground economy and a larger amount of household production than do developed countries. So as an economy develops and grows, part of the apparent growth of real GDP might reflect a switch from underground to regular production and from home production to market production. This measurement error overstates the growth in economic well-being and the improvement in the standard of living.

## A Broader Indicator of Economic Well-Being

### The Human Development Index

The limitations of real GDP reviewed in this chapter affects the standard of living and general well-being of every country. So to make international comparisons of the general state of economic well-being, we must look at real GDP and other indicators.

The United Nations has constructed a broader measure called the Human Development Index (HDI), which combines real GDP, life expectancy and health, and education. Real GDP per person (measured on the PPP basis) is a major component of the HDI

The dots in the figure show the relationship between real GDP per person and the HDI. The United States has the highest real GDP per person (with Norway and Luxembourg) but the twelfth highest HDI. (The countries with higher HDIs are named in the figure).

The HDI of the United States is lower than that of the 11 countries because the people of those countries live longer and have better access to health care and education than do Americans.

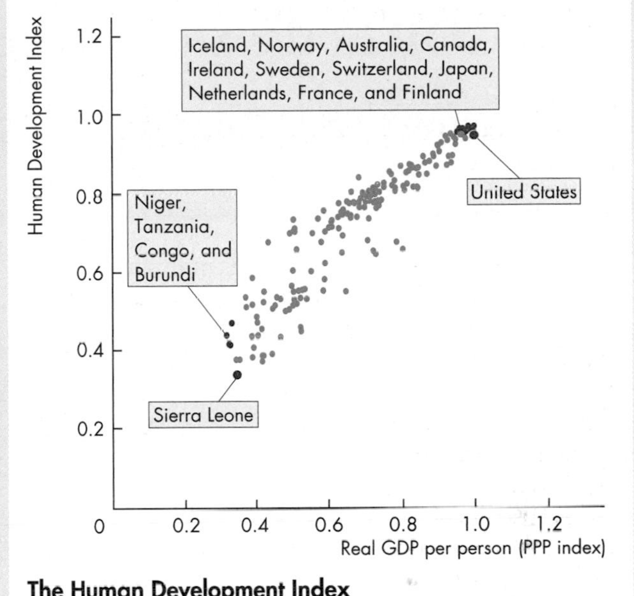


**The Human Development Index**

*Source of data:* United nations hdr.undp.org/en/statistics/data

Five African nations have the lowest real GDP per person and Sierra Leone has the lowest HDI.

Other influences on the standard of living include the amount of leisure time available, the quality of the environment, the security of jobs and homes, and the safety of city streets.

It is possible to construct broader measures that combine the many influences that contribute to human happiness. Real GDP will be one element in those broader measures, but it will by no means be the whole of those measures.

The United Nations Development Index (HDI) is one example of attempts to provide broader measures of economic well-being and the standard of living. But this measure places a good deal of weight on real GDP.

Dozens of other measures have been proposed. One includes resource depletion and emissions in a Green GDP measure. Another emphasizes the enjoyment of life rather than the production of goods in a "genuine progress index" or GPI.

Despite all the alternatives, real GDP per person remains the most widely used indicator of economic well-being.

## Review Quiz

1. Distinguish between real GDP and potential GDP and describe how each grows over time.
2. How does the growth rate of real GDP contribute to an improved standard of living?
3. What is a business cycle and what are its phases and turning points?
4. What is PPP and how does it help us to make valid international comparisons of real GDP?
5. Explain why real GDP might be an unreliable indicator of the standard of living?

myeconlab Work Study Plan 4.3 and get instant feedback.

You've now studied the methods used to measure GDP and real GDP. *Reading Between the Lines* on pp. 98–99 looks at U.S. real GDP in 2008.

Your next task is to learn how we measure employment and unemployment and the CPI.

READING BETWEEN THE LINES

# Real GDP in the Slowing Economy of 2008

## More Arrows Seen Pointing to a Recession

http://www.nytimes.com
August 1, 2008

The American economy expanded more slowly than expected from April to June, the government reported Thursday, while numbers for the last three months of 2007 were revised downward to show a contraction—the first official slide backward since the last recession in 2001.

Economists construed the tepid growth in the second quarter, combined with a surge in claims for unemployment benefits, as a clear indication that the economy remains mired in the weeds of a downturn. Many said the data increased the likelihood that a recession began late last year. …

President Bush zeroed in on the positive growth in the second quarter—a 1.9 percent annual rate of expansion, compared with an anticipated 2.3 percent rate. That follows growth of 0.9 percent in the first quarter. He claimed success for the $100 billion in tax rebates sent out by the government this year in a bid to spur spending, along with $52 billion in tax cuts for businesses. …

That the economy grew at all this spring is a testament to two bright spots—increased consumer spending fueled by the tax rebates, and the continuing expansion of American exports.

Consumer spending, which amounts to 70 percent of the economy, grew at a 1.5 percent annual rate between April and June, after growing at a meager 0.9 percent clip in the previous quarter. …

Exports expanded at a 9.2 percent annual pace in the second quarter, up from 5.1 percent in the first three months of the year. Foreign sales have been lubricated by the weak dollar, which makes American-made goods cheaper on world markets.

Adding to the improving trade picture, imports dropped by 6.6 percent, as Americans tightened their spending. Imports are subtracted from economic growth, so the effect was positive.

Over all, trade added 2.42 percentage points to the growth rate from April to June. Without that contribution, the economy would have contracted. …



## Essence of the Story

- Real GDP grew at an annual rate of 1.9 percent from April through June 2008.
- This growth was slower than anticipated but faster than the previous quarter.
- Economists feared that the slow growth might mean that the economy entered a recession in late 2007.
- Consumer spending, fueled by tax rebates, grew at an annual rate of 1.5 percent.
- Net exports, helped by a weak dollar, added 2.42 percentage points to the growth rate.

## Economic Analysis

- This news article reports real GDP numbers for the second quarter of 2008.
- The data for this quarter show slower than average growth but not the negative growth that signals recession.
- Figure 1 shows the real GDP growth rate (annualized) quarter to quarter from the first quarter of 2000 to the second quarter of 2008.
- The quarter to quarter growth rate fluctuated between a high of 7.3 percent in 2003 and a low of –1.4 percent in 2001.
- You can see slow growth in 2001, 2002, and into 2003 then more rapid growth in 2004 through 2006.
- The slow growth rate in 2007 started out at zero in the first quarter, jumped to 4.7 percent in the two middle quarters, and then fell back to being slightly negative in the final quarter.
- The 2008 growth rates increased each quarter but are well below the average since 2000, shown by the red line at 2.3 percent per year.
- Figure 2 shows the growth rates of the components of real GDP. The green bars are average growth rates from 2000 through 2007 and the orange bars are the growth rates for the second quarter of 2008.
- You can see that in the second quarter of 2008, as reported in the news article, consumption expenditure (*C*) grew at 1.5 percent. You can also see that net exports (*X* – *M*) made the main contribution to the growth of real GDP.
- Figure 2 shows that government expenditure increased and also contributed to the real GDP growth rate.
- Figure 2 shows a sign of possible recession: the large 15.7 percent decrease in investment (*I*).
- If exports stop growing, the decrease in investment and the slow growth of consumption expenditure will push real GDP growth negative, and a recession will occur.

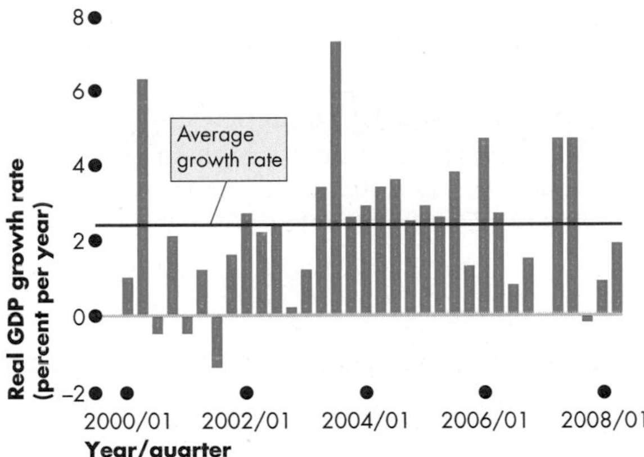


**Figure 1 Real GDP growth rates: 2000–2006**

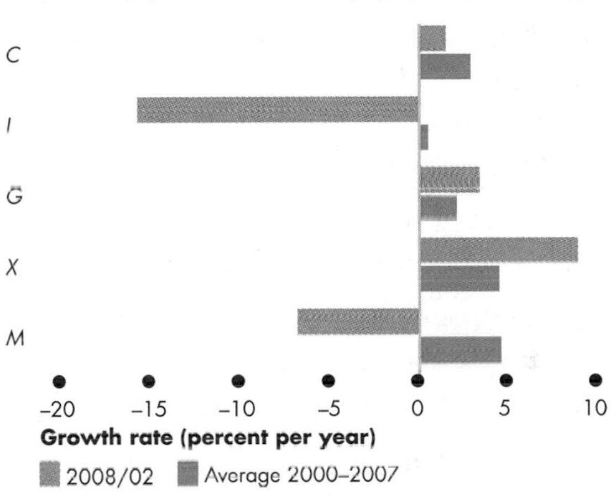


**Figure 2 Growth rates of real GDP components**

# MATHEMATICAL NOTE

## Chained-Dollar Real GDP

In the real GDP calculation on pp. 91–92, real GDP in 2009 is three times its value in 2000. But suppose that we use 2009 as the reference base year and value real GDP in 2000 at 2009 prices. If you do the math, you will see that real GDP in 2000 is $150 million at 2009 prices. GDP in 2009 is $300 million (in 2009 prices), so now the numbers say that real GDP has doubled. Which is correct: did real GDP double or triple? Should we use the prices of 2000 or 2009? The answer is that we need to use *both* sets of prices.

The Bureau of Economic Analysis uses a measure of real GDP called **chained-dollar real GDP**. Three steps are needed to calculate this measure:

- Value production in the prices of adjacent years
- Find the average of two percentage changes
- Link (chain) back to the reference base year

### Value Production in Prices of Adjacent Years

The first step is to value production in *adjacent* years at the prices of *both* years. We'll make these calculations for 2009 and its preceding year, 2008.

Table 1 shows the quantities produced and prices in the two years. Part (a) shows the nominal GDP calculation for 2008—the quantities produced in 2008 valued at the prices of 2008. Nominal GDP in 2008 is $145 million. Part (b) shows the nominal GDP calculation for 2009—the quantities produced in 2009 valued at the prices of 2009. Nominal GDP in 2009 is $172 million. Part (c) shows the value of the quantities produced in 2009 at the prices of 2008. This total is $160 million. Finally, part (d) shows the value of the quantities produced in 2008 at the prices of 2009. This total is $158 million.

**TABLE 1** Real GDP Calculation Step 1: Value Production in Adjacent Years at Prices of Both Years

| | Item | Quantity (millions) | Price (dollars) | Expenditure (millions of dollars) |
|---|---|---|---|---|
| **(a) In 2008** | | | | |
| C | T-shirts | 3 | 5 | 15 |
| I | Computer chips | 3 | 10 | 30 |
| G | Security services | 5 | 20 | 100 |
| Y | Real and Nominal GDP in 2008 | | | **145** |
| **(b) In 2009** | | | | |
| C | T-shirts | 4 | 4 | 16 |
| I | Computer chips | 2 | 12 | 24 |
| G | Security services | 6 | 22 | 132 |
| Y | Nominal GDP in 2009 | | | **172** |
| **(c) Quantities of 2009 valued at prices of 2008** | | | | |
| C | T-shirts | 4 | 5 | 20 |
| I | Computer chips | 2 | 10 | 20 |
| G | Security services | 6 | 20 | 120 |
| Y | 2009 production at 2008 prices | | | **160** |
| **(d) Quantities of 2008 valued at prices of 2009** | | | | |
| C | T-shirts | 3 | 4 | 12 |
| I | Computer chips | 3 | 12 | 36 |
| G | Security services | 5 | 22 | 110 |
| Y | 2008 production at 2009 prices | | | **158** |

Step 1 is to value the production of adjacent years at the prices of both years. Here, we value the production of 2008 and 2009 at the prices of both 2008 and 2009. The value of 2008 production at 2008 prices, in part (a), is nominal GDP in 2008. The value of 2009 production at 2009 prices, in part (b), is nominal GDP in 2009. Part (c) calculates the value of 2009 production at 2008 prices, and part (d) calculates the value of 2008 production at 2009 prices. We use these numbers in Step 2.

### Find the Average of Two Percentage Changes

The second step is to find the percentage change in the value of production based on the prices in the two adjacent years. Table 2 summarizes these calculations.

Part (a) shows that, valued at the prices of 2008, production increased from $145 million in 2008 to $160 million in 2009, an increase of 10.3 percent. Part (b) shows that, valued at the prices of 2009, production increased from $158 million in 2008 to $172 million in 2009, an increase of 8.9 percent. Part (c) shows that the average of these two percentage changes in the value of production is 9.6. That is, (10.3 + 8.9) ÷ 2 = 9.6.

By applying this average percentage change to real GDP, we can find the value of real GDP in 2009. Real GDP in 2008 is $145 million, so a 9.6 percent increase is $14 million, so real GDP in 2009 is $145

**TABLE 2** Real GDP Calculation Step 2: Find Average of Two Percentage Changes

| Value of Production | Millions of dollars | |
|---|---|---|
| **(a) At 2008 prices** | | |
| Nominal GDP in 2008 | 145 | |
| 2009 production at 2008 prices | 160 | |
| Percentage change in production at 2008 prices | | 10.3 |
| **(b) At 2009 prices** | | |
| 2008 production at 2009 prices | 158 | |
| Nominal GDP in 2009 | 172 | |
| Percentage change in production at 2009 prices | | 8.9 |
| **(c) Average of percentage change** | | **9.6** |

Using the numbers calculated in Step 1, the percentage change in production from 2008 to 2009 valued at 2008 prices is 10.3 percent, in part (a). The percentage change in production from 2008 to 2009 valued at 2009 prices is 8.9 percent, in part (b). The average of these two percentage changes is 9.6 percent, in part (c).

million plus $14 million, which equals $159 million. Because real GDP in 2008 is in 2008 dollars, real GDP in 2009 is also in 2008 dollars.

Although the real GDP of $159 million is expressed in 2008 dollars, the calculation uses the average of the prices of the final goods and services that make up GDP in 2008 and 2009.

## Link (Chain) Back to the Base Year

Today, the BEA uses 2000 as the reference base year. The third step in calculating real GDP is to express it in the prices of the reference base year. To do this, the BEA performs calculations like the ones that you've just worked through to find the percentage change in real GDP in each pair of years going back to 2000.

We start with nominal GDP in 2000, which equals real GDP in 2000. We then use the calculated percentage change for 2001 to find real GDP in 2001 expressed in the prices of 2000. We repeat this calculation for each year. In this way, real GDP in 2009 is linked (chained) to the base-year real GDP.

Figure 1 shows an example. Starting with real GDP in 2000 (assumed to be $100 million), we apply the calculated percentage changes to obtain

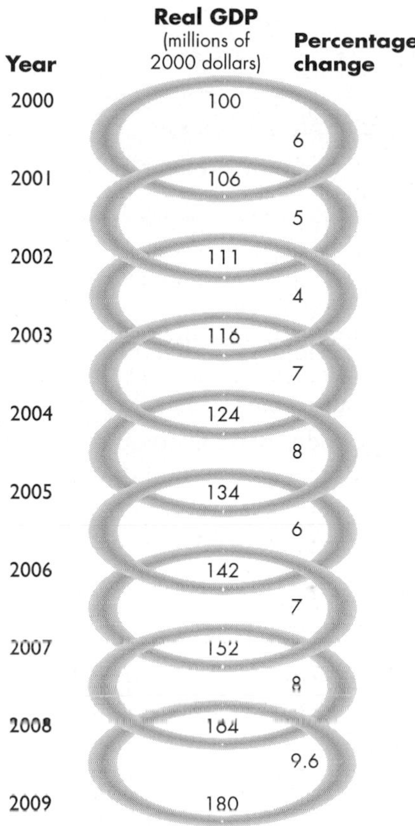


**Figure 1 Real GDP calculation step 3: link (chain) back to base year**

*chained-dollar real GDP* in 2000 dollars. By 2008, real GDP was $164 million (in 2000 dollars). In 2009, real GDP grew by 9.6 percent of $164 million, which is $16 million, so real GDP in 2009 was $180 million (in 2000 dollars).

## Exercise

The table provides data on the economy of Tropical Republic that produces only bananas and coconuts.

| **Quantities** | **2008** | **2009** |
|---|---|---|
| Bananas | 1,000 bunches | 1,100 bunches |
| Coconuts | 500 bunches | 525 bunches |
| **Prices** | | |
| Bananas | $2 a bunch | $3 a bunch |
| Coconuts | $10 a bunch | $8 a bunch |

Calculate Tropical Republic's nominal GDP in 2008 and 2009 and its chained-dollar real GDP in 2009 expressed in 2008 dollars.

## SUMMARY

### Key Points

**Gross Domestic Product** (pp. 86–88)

- GDP, or gross domestic product, is the market value of all the final goods and services produced in a country during a given period.
- A final good is an item that is bought by its final user, and it contrasts with an intermediate good, which is a component of a final good.
- GDP is calculated by using either the expenditure or income totals in the circular flow model.
- Aggregate expenditure on goods and services equals aggregate income and GDP.

**Measuring U.S. GDP** (pp. 89–91)

- Because aggregate expenditure, aggregate income, and the value of aggregate production are equal, we can measure GDP by using the expenditure approach or the income approach.
- The expenditure approach sums consumption expenditure, investment, government expenditure on goods and services, and net exports.
- The income approach sums wages, interest, rent, and profit (and indirect taxes less subsidies and depreciation).
- Real GDP is measured using a common set of prices to remove the effects of inflation from GDP.

**The Uses and Limitations of Real GDP** (pp. 92–97)

- Real GDP is used to compare the standard of living over time and across countries.
- Real GDP per person grows and fluctuates around the more smoothly growing potential GDP.
- A slowing of the growth rate of real GDP per person during the 1970s has lowered incomes by a large amount.
- International real GDP comparisons use PPP prices.
- Real GDP is not a perfect measure of the standard of living because it excludes household production, the underground economy, health and life expectancy, leisure time, environmental quality, and political freedom and social justice.

### Key Figures and Tables



### Key Terms

## PROBLEMS and APPLICATIONS

Work problems 1–11 in Chapter 4 Study Plan and get instant feedback.
Work problems 12–18 as Homework, a Quiz, or a Test if assigned by your instructor.

1. The figure below shows the flows of expenditure and income in the United States. During the second quarter of 2007, *B* was \$9,658 billion, *C* was \$2,147 billion, *D* was \$2,656 billion, and *E* was –\$723 billion. Name the flows and then calculate
   a. Aggregate expenditure.
   b. Aggregate income.
   c. GDP.
2. In the figure below, during the second quarter of 2008, *B* was \$10,144 billion, *C* was \$1,980 billion, *D* was \$2,869 billion, and *E* was –\$737 billion.

   Calculate the quantities in problem 1 during the second quarter of 2008.
3. In figure below, during the second quarter of 2006, *A* was \$13,134 billion, *B* was \$9,162 billion, *D* was \$3,340 billion, and *E* was –\$777 billion. Calculate
   a. Aggregate expenditure.
   b. Aggregate income.
   c. GDP.
   d. Government expenditure.
4. The firm that printed this textbook bought the paper from XYZ Paper Mills. Was this purchase of paper part of GDP? If not, how does the value of the paper get counted in GDP?
5. In the United Kingdom in 2005,

| Item | Billions of pounds |
|---|---|
| Wages paid to labor | 685 |
| Consumption expenditure | 791 |
| Taxes | 394 |
| Transfer payments | 267 |
| Profits | 273 |
| Investment | 209 |
| Government expenditure | 267 |
| Exports | 322 |
| Saving | 38 |
| Imports | 366 |

   a. Calculate GDP in the United Kingdom.
   b. Explain the approach (expenditure or income) that you used to calculate GDP.
6. Tropical Republic produces only bananas and coconuts. The base year is 2008, and the tables give the quantities produced and the prices.

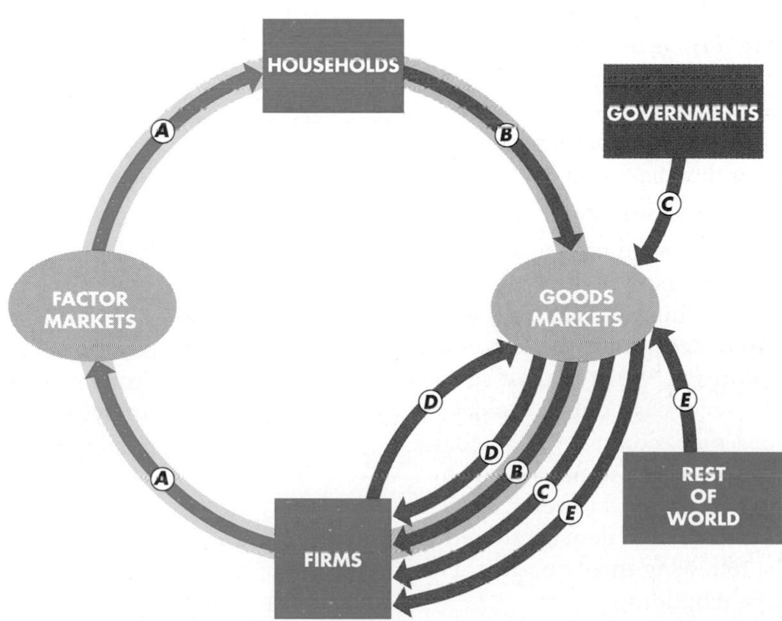

| **Quantities** | **2008** | **2009** |
|---|---|---|
| Bananas | 800 bunches | 900 bunches |
| Coconuts | 400 bunches | 500 bunches |
| **Prices** | | |
| Bananas | $2 a bunch | $4 a bunch |
| Coconuts | $10 a bunch | $5 a bunch |

a. Calculate Tropical Republic's nominal GDP in 2008 and 2009.
b. Calculate real GDP in 2009 in terms of the base-year prices.

7. Use the Data Grapher in MyEconLab to answer the following questions. In which country, in 2007 was
   a. The growth rate of real GDP highest: Canada, Japan, or the United States?
   b. The growth rate of real GDP lowest: France, China, or the United States?

8. **Toyota to Shift U.S. Manufacturing Efforts**

   Toyota Motor Corp. will start producing the hybrid Prius in the U.S. for the first time as the Japanese automaker adjusts its U.S. manufacturing operations to meet customer demands for smaller, more fuel-efficient vehicles. The company said Thursday it will start producing the Prius in 2010 at a plant it is building in Blue Springs, Mississippi. … This will be the first time the Prius, which has been on sale for more than a decade, will be built outside of Asia. …

   *CNN*, July 10, 2008

   a. Explain how this change by Toyota will influence U.S. GDP and the components of aggregate expenditure.
   b. Explain how this change by Toyota will influence the factor incomes that make up U.S. GDP.

9. **Toting Katrina's Severe Distortions**

   Hurricane Katrina could wind up being the most devastating storm to hit the U.S. Early forecasts of insured losses run as much as $26 billion. … As far as damage to the economy, the storm is likely to drop third-quarter gross domestic product (GDP) growth by 50 basis points, figures Beth Ann Bovino, senior economist at Standard & Poor's. She also expects consumer sentiment and production to be hurt. … However, likely repairs from hurricane-related damage should boost GDP in the following three quarters. This is largely because of rebuilding. …

   *BusinessWeek*, August 31, 2005

   a. Explain how a devastating storm can initially decrease GDP.
   b. How can a devastating storm then contribute to an increase in GDP?
   c. Does the increase in GDP indicate a rise in the standard of living as a result of the storm?

10. **Poor India makes millionaires at fastest pace**

    India, with the world's largest population of poor people living on less than a dollar a day, also paradoxically created millionaires at the fastest pace in the world in 2007. … Growing them at a blistering pace of 22.7 per cent, India added another 23,000 more millionaires in 2007 to its 2006 tally of 100,000 millionaires measured in dollars. … In contrast, developmental agencies put the number of subsistence level Indians living on less than a dollar a day at 350 million and those living on less than $2 a day at 700 million. In other words, for every millionaire, India has about 7,000 impoverished people. …

    *The Times of India*, June 25, 2008

    a. Why might a measurement of real GDP per person misrepresent the standard of living of the average Indian?
    b. Why might $1 a day and $2 a day under estimate the standard of living of the poorest Indians?

11. **Canada Agency Says 2nd Quarter GDP Dip Won't Prove Recession**

    Statistics Canada may not conclude the economy is in a recession even if gross domestic product contracts for a second straight quarter, according to one of the agency's top economists. … Defining a recession as two consecutive quarterly drops in GDP "is a silly, simplistic, simplification," Cross said by telephone. … The National Bureau of Economic Research, which chronicles business cycles in the U.S., defines a recession as "a significant decline in economic activity spread across the economy, lasting more than a few months, normally visible in real GDP, real income, employment, industrial production, and wholesale-retail sales."

    *Bloomberg*, June 18, 2008

    a. Why might defining a recession as "two consecutive quarterly drops in GDP" be too "simplistic"?
    b. Why might people still be feeling the pain of recession after an expansion begins?

12. **GDP Expands 11.4 Percent, Fastest in 13 Years**

China's economy expanded at its fastest pace in 13 years in 2007. … The country's Gross Domestic Product (GDP) grew 11.4 percent last year from 2006, to 24.66 trillion yuan ($3.42 trillion). … That marked a fifth year of double-digit growth for the world's fourth largest economy after the U.S., Japan, and Germany. The increase was especially remarkable given the fact that the United States is experiencing a slowdown due to the sub-prime crisis and housing slump. … According to Citigroup estimates, each one percent drop in the U.S. economy will shave 1.3 percent off China's growth, as Americans are heavy users of Chinese products. In spite of the uncertainties, the country's economy is widely expected to post its sixth year of double-digit growth in 2008 on investment and exports.

*The China Daily*, January 24, 2008

a. Use the expenditure approach for calculating China's GDP to explain why "each one percent drop in the U.S. economy will shave 1.3 percent off China's growth."
b. Why might China's recent double-digit GDP growth rates overstate the actual increase in the level of production taking place in China?
c. Explain the complications involved with attempting to compare the economic welfare in China and the United States by using the GDP for each country.

13. **Consumers Can't Save the Economy**

Consumers are too tapped out to lead the economy out of its troubles, according to a report on household credit released Wednesday. And even after things turn around, consumers weighed down by debt won't be able to spend as they did in the past.

Americans have little money on hand and banks aren't eager to lend anymore, said Scott Hoyt, senior director of consumer economics at Moody's Economy.com. … Sluggish consumer spending power means that the recovery may be a little slower and less vigorous, leaving it to corporations to spur the economy. It will also take years for consumers to straighten out their household budgets since their debt burdens are near record highs. Americans put 14.3 percent of their disposable income toward debt in the first quarter, near the record 14.5 percent reached at the end of 2006. By comparison, the rate was 12.3 percent in 2000. … Before the 1980s, consumer spending made up about 63 percent of the nation's gross domestic product, a key measure of the economy. Since then, it has grown to about 70 percent as Americans took on more debt to fuel their buying habits. Going forward, consumer spending will likely drift back to about 67 percent of GDP, Hoyt said. Americans simply can't sustain a near-zero savings rate and an ever-growing debt load.

*CNN*, May 22, 2008

a. How has the influence of consumer spending on GDP changed over the past three decades in the United States? What has allowed this change to take place?
b. Why does Hoyt predict that consumer spending will shrink as a percentage of GDP?

14. **Consumer Spending a Big Factor: NBS**

When the [Chinese] National Bureau of Statistics (NBS) in October released its consumption figures for the first three quarters, people were surprised to discover that consumers are playing an ever-important role in the growth of the economy. … Consumption contributed 37 percent of gross domestic product while foreign demand, or net exports, accounted for 21.4 percent. … The remaining 41.6 percent was made by investment. …

While exports are growing, imports are increasing at a faster pace, narrowing the gap and leading to shrinking net exports. … But challenges lie ahead. Consumption will continue to grow, but only slowly, analysts said, because the public are still bothered by spending pressures like Social Security, health, education and housing. With those uncertainties, they prefer to save rather than spend.

China remains a developing country with a relatively low level of income, which cannot provide a strong back-up for consumption. … The government has yet to provide adequate public services, such as education and health, and people prefer to save more in anticipation of rising future expenditure. … In 2006, rural residents earned about one third of the income earned by urban residents.

*The China Daily*, December 11, 2007

a. Compare the relative magnitudes of consumption expenditure, net exports, and investment in China with those in the United States.
b. Why is consumption expenditure in China so low?

15. **Totally Gross**

… Over the years, GNP and GDP have proved spectacularly useful in tracking economic change—both short-term fluctuations and long-run growth. Which isn't to say GDP doesn't miss some things. … [Amartya] Sen, a development economist at Harvard, has long argued that health is a big part of living standards—and in 1990 he helped create the United Nations' Human Development Index, which combines health and education data with per capita GDP to give a more complete view of the wealth of nations (the United States currently comes in 12th, while on per capita GDP alone, it ranks second). [Joseph] Stiglitz, a Columbia professor and former World Bank chief economist, advocates a "green net national product" that takes into account the depletion of natural resources. Also sure to come up … is the currently fashionable idea of trying to include happiness in the equation. The issue with these alternative benchmarks is not whether they have merit (most do) but whether they can be measured with anything like the frequency, reliability and impartiality of GDP. …

*Time*, April 21, 2008

a. Explain the factors identified here that limit the usefulness of using GDP to measure economic welfare.
b. What are the challenges involved in trying to incorporate measurements of those factors in an effort to better measure economic welfare?
c. What does the ranking of the United States in the Human Development Index (12th) imply about the levels of health and education relative to other nations?

16. **Boeing Bets the House**

Boeing plans to produce some components of its new 787 Dreamliner in Japan. The aircraft will be assembled in the United States, and much of the first year's production will be sold to ANA (All Nippon Airways), a Japanese airline.

*The New York Times*, May 7, 2006

a. Explain how Boeing's activities and its transactions affect U.S. and Japanese GDP.
b. Explain how ANA's activities and its transactions affect U.S. and Japanese GDP.
c. Use a circular flow diagram to illustrate your answers to a and b.

17. The United Nations' Human Development Index (HDI) is based on real GDP per person, life expectancy at birth, and indicators of the quality and quantity of education.
    a. Explain why the HDI might be better than real GDP as a measure of economic welfare.
    b. Which items in the HDI are part of real GDP and which items are not in real GDP?
    c. Do you think the HDI should be expanded to include items such as pollution, resource depletion, and political freedom? Explain.
    d. What other influences on economic welfare should be included in a comprehensive measure?
18. Study *Reading Between the Lines* on pp. 98–99 and then answer the following questions:
    a. Which components of aggregate expenditure increased at the fastest rate in the second quarter of 2008?
    b. Which components of aggregate expenditure increased at the slowest rate (or decreased at the fastest rate) in the second quarter of 2008?
    c. For how long has the U.S. economy been expanding since the last business cycle trough?
    d. Argue the case that the economy was in recession in 2007 and 2008.
    e. Argue the case that the economy was not in recession in 2007 and 2008.
19. Use the link on MyEconLab (Chapter Resources, Chapter 4, Web links) to find the available data from the BEA on GDP and the components of aggregate expenditure and aggregate income. The data are in current prices (nominal GDP) and constant prices (real GDP).
    a. What are the levels of nominal GDP and real (chained-dollar) GDP in the current quarter?
    b. What was the level of real GDP in the same quarter of the previous year?
    c. By what percentage has real GDP changed over the past year?

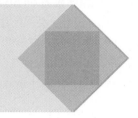

# 5 Monitoring Jobs and Inflation

## After studying this chapter, you will be able to:

- Explain why unemployment is a problem, define the unemployment rate, the employment-to-population ratio, and the labor force participation rate, and describe the trends and cycles in these labor market indicators
- Explain why unemployment is an imperfect measure of underutilized labor, why it is present even at full employment, and how unemployment and real GDP fluctuate together over a business cycle
- Explain why inflation is a problem, how we measure the price level and the inflation rate, and why the CPI measure of inflation might be biased

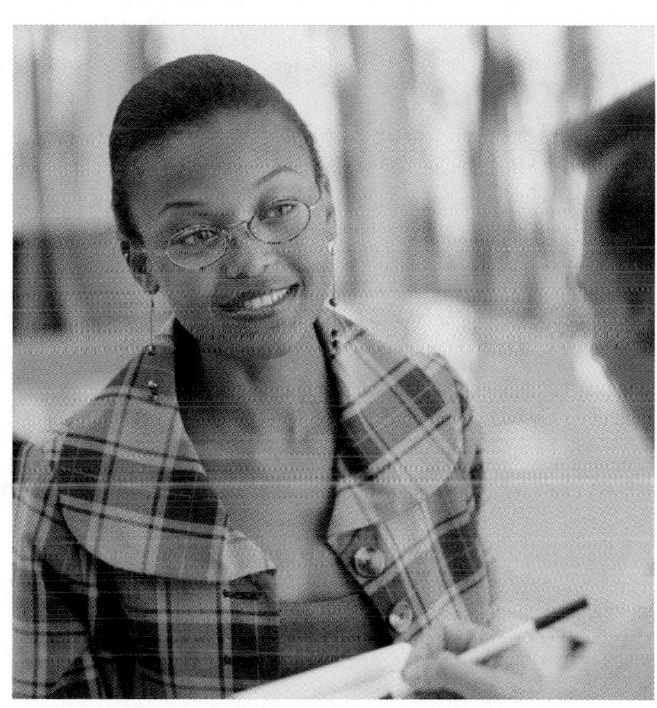

**Each month, we chart the course of employment** and unemployment as measures of U.S. economic health. How do we count the number of people working and the number unemployed? What do the level of employment and the unemployment rate tell us? Are they reliable vital signs for the economy?

We always have some unemployment—we never get to a point at which no one is unemployed. So what is full employment? How many people are unemployed when there is full employment?

Having a good job that pays a decent wage is only half of the equation that translates into a good standard of living. The other half is the cost of living. We track the cost of the items that we buy with another number that is published every month, the Consumer Price Index, or CPI. What is the CPI? How is it calculated? And does it provide a reliable guide to the changes in our cost of living?

As the U.S. economy expanded after a recession in 2001, job growth was weak and questions about the health of the labor market became of vital importance to millions of American families. *Reading Between the Lines*, at the end of this chapter, puts the spotlight on the labor market during the expansion of the past few years and the slowdown of 2008.

We begin by looking at unemployment: what it is, why it matters, and how we measure it.

## Employment and Unemployment

What kind of job market will you enter when you graduate? Will there be plenty of good jobs to choose among, or will jobs be so hard to find that you end up taking one that doesn't use your education and pays a low wage? The answer depends, to a large degree, on the total number of jobs available and on the number of people competing for them.

The U.S. economy is an incredible job-creating machine. In 2008, 146 million people had jobs, which was 15 million more than in 1998 and 31 million more than in 1988. But not everyone who wants a job can find one. On a typical day, 7 million people are unemployed. That's equivalent to the population of Los Angeles. During a recession, this number rises and during a boom year it falls. At its worst, during the Great Depression, one in every four workers was unemployed.

### Why Unemployment Is a Problem

Unemployment is a serious personal and social economic problem for two main reasons. It results in

- Lost production and incomes
- Lost human capital

**Lost Production and Incomes** The loss of a job brings a loss of income for the unemployed worker and a loss of production. The loss of income is devastating for the people who bear it and makes unemployment a frightening prospect for everyone. Today, employment benefits create a safety net, but they don't fully replace lost earnings and not every person who becomes unemployed receives benefits.

**Lost Human Capital** Prolonged unemployment permanently damages a person's job prospects by destroying human capital.

## The Great Depression

### What Keeps Ben Bernanke Awake at Night

The Great Depression began in October 1929, when the U.S. stock market crashed. It reached it deepest point in 1933, when 25 percent of the labor force was unemployed, and lasted until 1941, when the United States entered World War II. It was a depression that quickly spread globally to envelop most nations.

The 1930s were and remain the longest and worst period of high unemployment in history. Failed banks, shops, farms, and factories left millions of Americans without jobs, homes, and food. Without the support of government and charities, millions would have starved.

The Great Depression was an enormous political event: It fostered the rise of the German and Japanese militarism that were to bring the most devastating war humans have ever fought. It also led to President Franklin D. Roosevelt's "New Deal" which enhanced the role of government in economic life and made government intervention in markets popular and the market economy unpopular.

The Great Depression also brought a revolution in economics. British economist John Maynard Keynes published his *General Theory of Employment, Interest, and Money*, that created what we now call macroeconomics.

Many economists have studied the Great Depression and tried to determine why what started out as an ordinary recession became so devastating. Among them are Ben Bernanke, the Chairman of the Federal Reserve.

One of the reasons why the Fed has been so aggressive in cutting interest rates, saving Bear Sterns, and propping up Fannie Mae and Freddie Mac is because Ben Bernanke is so vividly aware of the horrors of total economic collapse and determined to avoid any risk of a repeat of the Great Depression.

Think about a manager who loses his job when his employer downsizes. The only work he can find is driving a taxi. After a year in this work, he discovers that he can't compete with new MBA graduates. Eventually, he gets hired as a manager but in a small firm and at a lower wage than before. He has lost some of his human capital.

The cost of unemployment is spread unequally, which makes it a highly charged political problem as well as a serious economic problem.

Governments make strenuous efforts to measure unemployment accurately and to adopt policies to moderate its level and ease its pain. Here, we'll learn how the U.S. government monitors unemployment.

## Current Population Survey

Every month, the U.S. Census Bureau surveys 60,000 households and asks a series of questions about the age and job market status of the members of each household. This survey is called the Current Population Survey. The Census Bureau uses the answers to describe the anatomy of the labor force.

Figure 5.1 shows the population categories used by the Census Bureau and the relationships among the categories.

The population divides into two broad groups: the working-age population and others who are too young to work or who live in institutions and are unable to work. The **working-age population** is the total number of people aged 16 years and over who are not in jail, hospital, or some other form of institutional care.

The Census Bureau divides the working-age population into two groups: those in the labor force and those not in the labor force. It also divides the labor force into two groups: the employed and the unemployed. So the **labor force** is the sum of the employed and the unemployed.

To be counted as employed in the Current Population Survey, a person must have either a full-time job or a part-time job. To be counted as *un*employed, a person must be available for work and must be in one of three categories:

1. Without work but has made specific efforts to find a job within the previous four weeks
2. Waiting to be called back to a job from which he or she has been laid off
3. Waiting to start a new job within 30 days

**FIGURE 5.1** Population Labor Force Categories

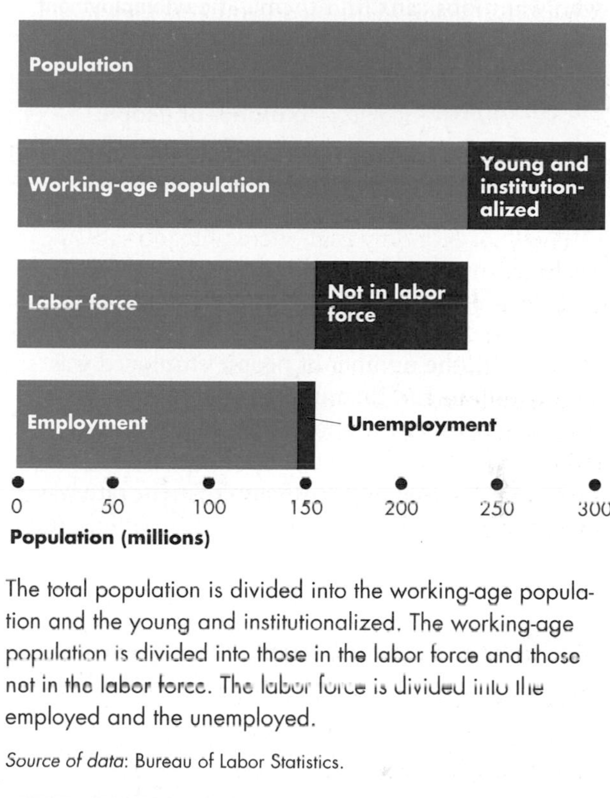


The total population is divided into the working-age population and the young and institutionalized. The working-age population is divided into those in the labor force and those not in the labor force. The labor force is divided into the employed and the unemployed.

*Source of data*: Bureau of Labor Statistics.

myeconlab animation

Anyone surveyed who satisfies one of these three criteria is counted as unemployed. People in the working-age population who are neither employed nor unemployed are classified as not in the labor force.

In 2008, the population of the United States was 304.5 million; the working-age population was 233.8 million. Of this number, 79.2 million were not in the labor force. Most of these people were in school full time or had retired from work. The remaining 154.6 million people made up the U.S. labor force. Of these, 145.8 million were employed and 8.8 million were unemployed.

## Three Labor Market Indicators

The Census Bureau calculates three indicators of the state of the labor market. They are

- The unemployment rate
- The employment-to-population ratio
- The labor force participation rate

**The Unemployment Rate** The amount of unemployment is an indicator of the extent to which people who want jobs can't find them. The **unemployment rate** is the percentage of the people in the labor force who are unemployed. That is,

$$\text{Unemployment rate} = \frac{\text{Number of people unemployed}}{\text{Labor force}} \times 100$$

and

$$\text{Labor force} = \begin{array}{l}\text{Number of people employed} + \\ \text{Number of people unemployed.}\end{array}$$

In 2008, the number of people employed was 145.8 million and the number unemployed was 8.8 million. By using the above equations, you can verify that the labor force was 154.6 million (145.8 million plus 8.8 million) and the unemployment rate was 5.7 percent (8.8 million divided by 154.6 million, multiplied by 100).

Figure 5.2 shows the unemployment rate from 1961 to 2008. The average unemployment rate during this period was 5.8 percent. As a percentage of the labor force in 2008, that represents 9 million people.

The unemployment rate fluctuates over the business cycle and reached a peak value after the recession ends.

The unemployment rate was lower during the 1960s than the 1970s and 1980s. The average rate fell during the 1990s and remained low during the 2000s, but not as low as it had been during the 1960s.

**The Employment-to-Population Ratio** The number of people of working age who have jobs is an indicator of both the availability of jobs and the degree of match between people's skills and jobs. The **employment-to-population ratio** is the percentage of people of working age who have jobs. That is,

$$\text{Employment-to-population ratio} = \frac{\text{Number of people employed}}{\text{Working-age population}} \times 100.$$

In 2008, the number of people employed was 145.8 million and the working-age population was 233.8 million. By using the above equation, you can calculate the employment-to-population ratio. It was 62.4 percent (145.8 million divided by 233.8 million, multiplied by 100).

Figure 5.3 shows the employment-to-population ratio. This indicator follows an upward trend before 2000 and then flattens off after 2000. The increase before 2000 means that the U.S. economy created

**FIGURE 5.2** The Unemployment Rate: 1960–2008

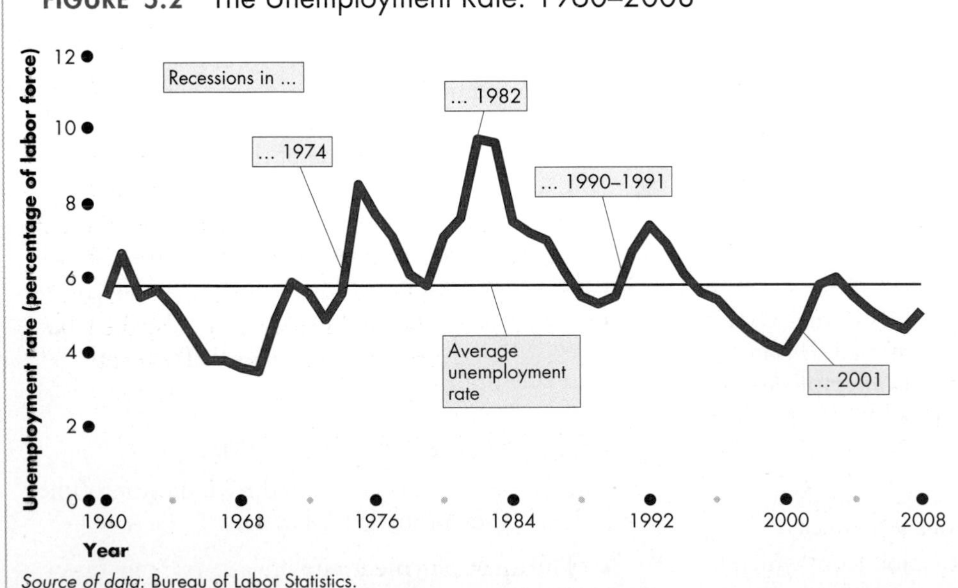


*Source of data*: Bureau of Labor Statistics.

The average unemployment rate from 1960 to 2008 was 5.8 percent. The unemployment rate increases in a recession, peaks after the recession ends, and decreases in an expansion. The unemployment rate fell to an unusually low point during the expansion of the 1990s and increased during the 2001 recession. As the economy expanded in 2003 through 2007, the unemployment rate fell below the average. It remained below the average in 2008 in spite of a slowing economy.

myeconlab animation

**FIGURE 5.3** Labor Force Participation and Employment: 1960–2008

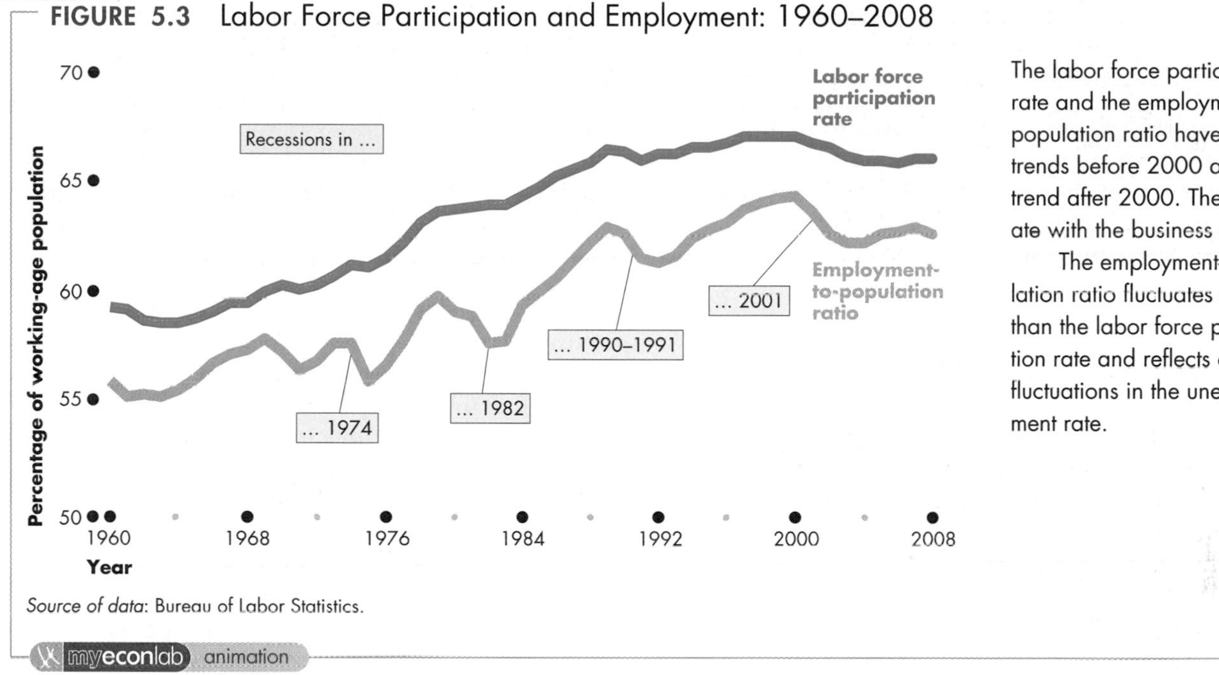


The labor force participation rate and the employment-to-population ratio have upward trends before 2000 and no trend after 2000. They fluctuate with the business cycle.

The employment-to-population ratio fluctuates more than the labor force participation rate and reflects cyclical fluctuations in the unemployment rate.

*Source of data*: Bureau of Labor Statistics.

jobs at a faster rate than the working-age population grew. This indicator also fluctuates: It falls during a recession and increases during an expansion.

**The Labor Force Participation Rate** The number of people in the labor force is an indicator of the willingness of people of working age to take jobs. The **labor force participation rate** is the percentage of the working-age population who are members of the labor force. That is,

$$\text{Labor force participation rate} = \frac{\text{Labor force}}{\text{Working-age population}} \times 100.$$

In 2008, the labor force was 154.6 million and the working-age population was 233.8 million. By using the above equation, you can calculate the labor force participation rate. It was 66.1 percent (154.6 million divided by 233.8 million, multiplied by 100).

Figure 5.3 shows the labor force participation rate. Like the employment-to-population ratio, this indicator has an upward trend before 2000 and then flattens off. It also has mild fluctuations around the trend. These fluctuations result from unsuccessful job seekers who are available and willing to work but have not made specific efforts to find a job within the previous four weeks. These workers temporarily leave the labor force during a recession and reenter during an expansion and become active job seekers.

## Review Quiz

1. What determines whether a person is in the labor force?
2. What distinguishes an unemployed person from a person who is not in the labor force?
3. Describe the trends and fluctuations in the U.S. unemployment rate between 1960 and 2008.
4. Describe the trends and fluctuations in the U.S. employment-to-population ratio and the labor force participation rate between 1960 and 2008.

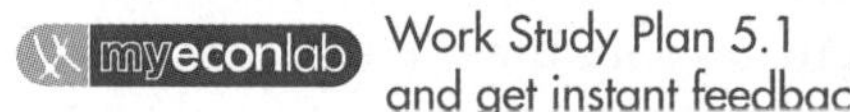

Work Study Plan 5.1 and get instant feedback.

You've seen how we measure employment and unemployment. Your next task is to see what the unemployment numbers tell us and what we mean by full employment.

## Unemployment and Full Employment

What does the unemployment rate seek to measure and does it provide an accurate measure?

The purpose of the unemployment rate is to measure the underutilization of labor resources, but it is an imperfect measure for two sets of reasons.

- It excludes some underutilized labor
- Some unemployment is unavoidable—is "natural."

### Underutilized Labor Excluded

Two types of underutilized labor are excluded from the official unemployment measure. They are

- Marginally attached workers
- Part-time workers who want full-time jobs

**Marginally attached workers** A **marginally attached worker** is a person who currently is neither working nor looking for work but has indicated that he or she wants and is available for a job and has looked for work sometime in the recent past. A subset of marginally attached workers is a group called discouraged workers.

A **discouraged worker** is a marginally attached worker who has stopped looking for a job because of repeated failure to find one. The numbers of marginally attached and discouraged workers is small. In August 2008, when the official unemployment rate was 6.1 percent, adding the marginally attached raised the rate to 7.0 percent of the labor force.

**Part-Time Workers Who Want Full-Time Jobs** Many part-time workers want to work part time. This arrangement fits in with the other demands on their time. But some part-time workers would like full-time jobs and can't find them. In the official statistics, these workers are called *economic part-time workers* and they are partly unemployed.

A large number of workers fall into this group, and the rate fluctuates with the overall unemployment rate. In August 2008, when the official unemployment rate was 6.1 percent, the economic part-time unemployment rate was 3.7 percent, which means that the overall unemployment rate including marginally attached workers was 10.7 percent of the labor force.

### "Natural" Unemployment

Unemployment arises from job search activity. There is always someone without a job who is searching for one, so there is always some unemployment. The key reason why there is always someone who is searching for a job is that the economy is a complex mechanism that is always changing—it is a churning economy.

**The Churning Economy** Some of the change in the churning economy comes from the transitions that people make through the stages of life—from being in school to finding a job, to working, perhaps to becoming unhappy with a job and looking for a new one, and finally, to retiring from full-time work.

In the United States in 2008, more than 3 million new workers entered the labor force and more than 2.5 million workers retired.

Other change comes from the transitions that businesses make. Every day, new firms are born, existing firms grow or shrink, and firms fail and go out of business. This process of business creation, expansion, contraction, and failure creates and destroys jobs.

Both of these transition processes—of people and businesses—create frictions and dislocations that make unemployment unavoidable.

**The Sources of Unemployment** In the churning economy that we've just described, people become unemployed if they

1. Lose their jobs and search for another job.
2. Leave their jobs and search for another job.
3. Enter or reenter the labor force to search for a job.

And people end a spell of unemployment if they

1. Are hired or recalled.
2. Withdraw from the labor force.

People who are laid off, either permanently or temporarily, from their jobs are called *job losers*. Some job losers become unemployed, but some immediately withdraw from the labor force. People who voluntarily quit their jobs are called *job leavers*. Like job losers, some job leavers become unemployed and search for a better job while others either withdraw from the labor force temporarily or permanently retire from work. People who enter or reenter the labor force are called *entrants* and *reentrants*. Entrants are mainly people who have just left school. Some entrants get a job right away and are never unemployed, but many spend time searching for their first job, and during this period, they are unemployed. Reentrants are people who have previously withdrawn from the labor force. Most of these people are formerly discouraged workers.

Figure 5.4 shows unemployment by reason for becoming unemployed. Job losers are the biggest source of unemployment. On the average, they account for around half of total unemployment. Also, their number fluctuates a great deal. At the trough of the recession of 1990–1991, on any given day, more than 5 million of the 9.4 million unemployed were job losers. In contrast, at the business cycle peak in March 2001, only 3.3 million of the 6 million unemployed were job losers.

**FIGURE 5.4** Unemployment by Reason

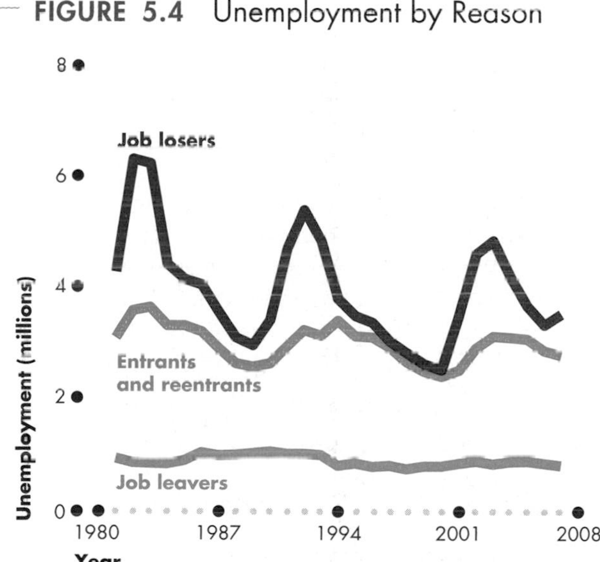


Everyone who is unemployed is a job loser, a job leaver, or an entrant or reentrant into the labor force. Most unemployment results from job loss. The number of job losers fluctuates more closely with the business cycle than do the numbers of job leavers and entrants and reentrants. Entrants and reentrants are the second most common type of unemployed people. Their number fluctuates with the business cycle because of discouraged workers. Job leavers are the least common type of unemployed people.

*Source of data:* Bureau of Labor Statistics.

myeconlab animation

Entrants and reentrants also make up a large component of the unemployed. Their number fluctuates but more mildly than the fluctuations in the number of job losers.

Job leavers are the smallest and most stable source of unemployment. On any given day, fewer than 1 million people are unemployed because they are job leavers. The number of job leavers is remarkably constant. To the extent that this number fluctuates, it does so in line with the business cycle: A slightly larger number of people leave their jobs in good times than in bad times.

**Frictions, Structural Change, and Cycles** The unemployment that arises from normal labor turnover—from people entering and leaving the labor force and from the ongoing creation and destruction of jobs—is **frictional unemployment.** Frictional unemployment is a permanent and healthy phenomenon in a dynamic, growing economy.

The unending flow of people into and out of the labor force and the processes of job creation and job destruction create the need for people to search for jobs and for businesses to search for workers. There are always businesses with unfilled jobs and people seeking jobs. Businesses don't usually hire the first person who applies for a job, and unemployed people don't usually take the first job that comes their way. Instead, both firms and workers spend time searching out what they believe will be the best match available. By this process of search, people can match their own skills and interests with the available jobs and find a satisfying job and a good income. While these unemployed people are searching, they are frictionally unemployed.

The unemployment that arises when changes in technology or international competition change the skills needed to perform jobs or change the locations of jobs is called **structural unemployment.** Structural unemployment usually lasts longer than frictional unemployment because workers must usually retrain and possibly relocate to find a job. When a steel plant in Gary, Indiana, is automated, some jobs in that city disappear. Meanwhile, new jobs for security guards, retail clerks, and life-insurance salespeople are created in Chicago, Indianapolis, and other cities. The unemployed former steelworkers remain unemployed for several months until they move, retrain, and get one of these jobs. Structural unemployment is painful, especially for older workers for whom the best available option might be to retire early or take a lower-skilled, lower-paying job. At some times, the amount of structural unemployment is modest. At other times, it is large, and at such times, structural unemployment can become a serious long-term problem. It was especially large during the late 1970s and early 1980s. During those years, oil price hikes and an increasingly competitive international environment destroyed jobs in traditional U.S. industries, such as auto and steel, and created jobs in new industries, such as electronics and bioengineering, as well as in banking and insurance. Structural unemployment was also present during the early 1990s as many businesses and governments "downsized."

Two other structural sources of higher unemployment are a **minimum wage**—a wage set by law above the equilibrium level—and an **efficiency wage**—a wage set by employers above the equilibrium level. A wage set above the equilibrium lowers the quantity of labor demanded, increases the quantity of labor supplied, and creates unemployment.

A firm might choose to pay an efficiency wage for four reasons. First, it enables the firm to face a steady stream of available new workers. Second, it attracts the most productive workers. Third, the fear of losing a well-paid job stimulates greater work effort. Fourth, workers are less likely to quit their jobs, so the firm has a lower rate of labor turnover and lower recruiting and training costs.

The firm balances these benefits against the cost of a higher wage and offers the wage rate that maximizes its profit.

The higher than normal unemployment that arises at a business cycle trough and the unusually low unemployment that exists at a business cycle peak is called **cyclical unemployment**. A worker who is laid off because the economy is in a recession and who gets rehired some months later when the expansion begins has experienced cyclical unemployment.

**What is "Natural" Unemployment?** Natural unemployment is the unemployment that arises from normal frictions and structural change when there is no cyclical unemployment—when all the unemployment is frictional and structural. Natural unemployment as a percentage of the labor force is called the **natural unemployment rate.**

**Full employment** is defined as a situation in which the unemployment rate equals the natural unemployment rate.

There can be a lot of unemployment at full employment, and the term "full employment" is an example of a technical economic term that does not correspond with everyday language. The term "natural unemployment rate" is another technical economic term whose meaning does not correspond with everyday language. For most people—especially for unemployed workers—there is nothing natural about unemployment. But if you think for a moment, you will come up with many other natural phenomena that are unpleasant. Floods, hurricanes, and the feeding frenzy of sharks are just three examples.

So when economists call a situation with a lot of unemployment one of "full employment" and describe the unemployment rate at full employment as the "natural rate," they are talking about the unemployment that results from natural physical constraints on the ease with which the labor market can match workers with jobs.

There is not much controversy about the existence of a natural unemployment rate. Nor is there much disagreement that it changes. The natural unemployment rate arises from the existence of labor market frictions and structural change, and it fluctuates because the frictions and the amount of structural change fluctuate. But economists don't agree about the size of the natural unemployment rate and the extent to which it fluctuates. Some economists believe that the natural unemployment rate fluctuates frequently and that at times of rapid demographic and technological change, the natural unemployment rate can be high. Others think that the natural unemployment rate changes slowly.

## Real GDP and Unemployment Over the Cycle

The quantity of real GDP at full employment is *potential GDP* (p. 494). Over the business cycle, real GDP fluctuates around potential GDP. The gap between real GDP and potential GDP is called the **output gap**. As the output gap fluctuates over the business cycle, the unemployment rate fluctuates around the natural unemployment rate.

Figure 5.5 illustrates these fluctuations in the United States between 1981 and 2008—the output gap in part (a) and the unemployment rate and natural unemployment rate in part (b).

When the economy is at full employment, the unemployment rate equals the natural unemploy-

**FIGURE 5.5** The Output Gap and the Unemployment Rate

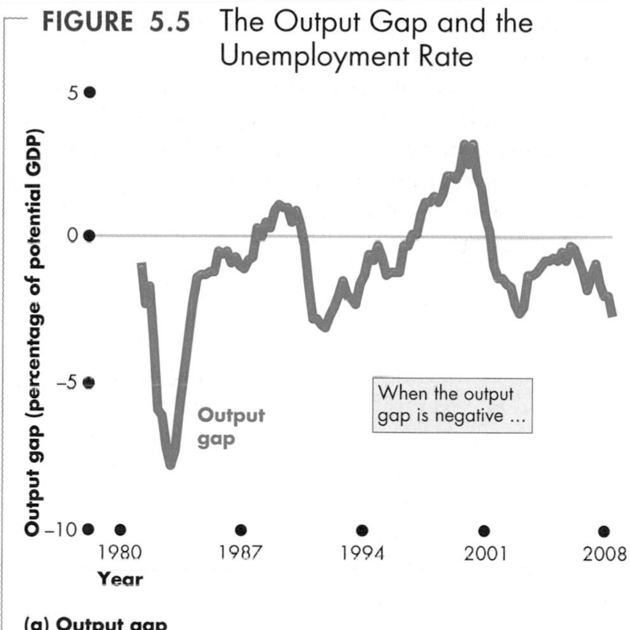


**(a) Output gap**

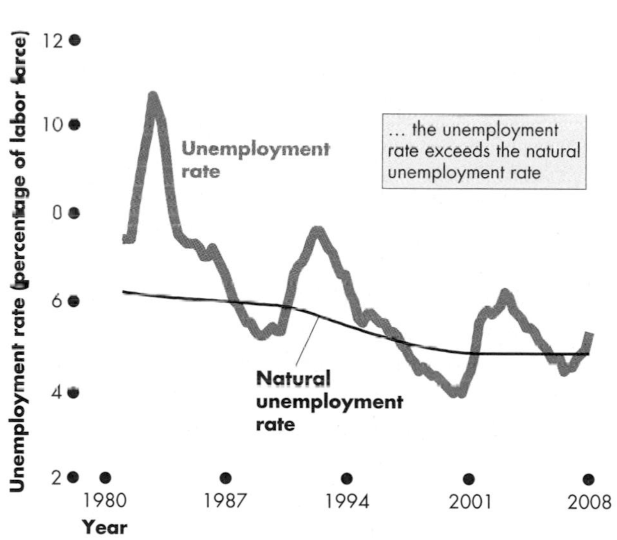


**(b) Unemployment rate**

As real GDP fluctuates around potential GDP in part (a), the unemployment rate fluctuates around the natural unemployment rate in part (b). At the end of the deep 1982 recession, the unemployment rate reached almost 11 percent. At the end of the milder 1990–1991 and 2001 recessions, unemployment peaked at lower rates. The natural unemployment rate decreased somewhat during the 1980s and 1990s.

*Sources of data*: Bureau of Economic Analysis, Bureau of Labor Statistics, and Congressional Budget Office.

myeconlab animation

ment rate and real GDP equals potential GDP so the output gap is zero. When the unemployment rate is less than the natural unemployment rate, real GDP is greater than potential GDP and the output gap is positive. And when the unemployment rate is greater than the natural unemployment rate, real GDP is less than potential GDP and the output gap is negative.

Figure 5.5(b) shows one view of the natural unemployment rate—the view of the Congressional Budget Office. Economists do not know the magnitude of the natural unemployment rate and that shown in the figure is only one estimate. It shows that the natural unemployment rate was 6.2 percent in 1981 and that it fell steadily through the 1980s and 1990s to 4.8 percent by 2000. This estimate of the natural unemployment rate in the United States is one that many, but not all, economists agree with.

## Review Quiz

1 What is the unemployment rate supposed to measure and why is it an imperfect measure?
2 Why might the official unemployment rate underestimate the underutilization of labor resources?
3 Why does unemployment arise and what makes some unemployment unavoidable?
4 Define frictional unemployment, structural unemployment, and cyclical unemployment. Give examples of each type of unemployment.
5 What is the natural unemployment rate?
6 How does the natural unemployment rate change and what factors might make it change?
7 How does the unemployment rate fluctuate over the business cycle?

Work Study Plan 5.2 and get instant feedback.

Your next task in this chapter is to see how we monitor the price level and the inflation rate. You will learn about the Consumer Price Index (CPI), which is monitored every month. You will also learn about other measures of the price level and the inflation rate.

## The Price Level and Inflation

What will it *really* cost you to pay off your student loan? What will your parent's life savings buy when they retire? The answers depend on what happens to the **price level**, the average level of prices, and the value of money.

We are interested in the price level for two main reasons. First, we want to measure the **inflation rate**, which is the annual percentage change of the price level. Second, we want to distinguish between the money values and real values of economic variables such as your student loan and your parent's savings.

We will begin by explaining why we're interested in the inflation rate—why inflation is a problem. We'll then look at the ways in which we measure the price level and the inflation rate. Finally, we'll return to the task of separating real values from money values of economic variables.

### Why Inflation Is a Problem

Inflation is a problem for several reasons, but the main one is that once it takes hold, its rate is unpredictable. Unpredictable inflation brings serious social and personal problems because it

- Redistributes income and wealth
- Diverts resources from production

**Redistributes Income and Wealth** Inflation makes the economy behave like a casino in which some people gain and some lose and no one can predict where the gains and losses will fall. Gains and losses occur because of unpredictable changes in the value of money. Money is used as a measuring rod of value in the transactions that we undertake. Borrowers and lenders, workers and employers, all make contracts in terms of money. If the value of money varies unpredictably over time, then the amounts *really* paid and received—the quantities of goods that the money will buy—also fluctuate unpredictably. Measuring value with a measuring rod whose units vary is a bit like trying to measure a piece of cloth with an elastic tape measure. The size of the cloth depends on how tightly the elastic is stretched.

**Diverts Resources from Production** In a period of rapid, unpredictable inflation, resources get diverted from productive activities to forecasting inflation. It can even become more profitable to forecast the inflation rate correctly than to invent a new product. Doctors, lawyers, accountants, farmers—just about everyone—can make themselves better off, not by specializing in the profession for which they have been trained but by spending more of their time dabbling as amateur economists and inflation forecasters and managing their investments.

From a social perspective, the diversion of talent that results from rapid inflation is like throwing scarce resources onto the garbage heap. This waste of resources is a cost of inflation.

At its worst, inflation becomes **hyperinflation**, an inflation rate so rapid that workers are paid twice a day because money loses its value so quickly. As soon as workers are paid, they rush out to spend their wages before the money loses too much value. In this situation, the economy grinds to a halt and society collapses. Hyperinflation is rare, but Zimbabwe has it today and several European and Latin American countries have experienced it.

It is to avoid the consequences of inflation that we pay close attention to it, even when its rate is low. We monitor inflation every month and devote considerable resources to measuring it accurately. You're now going to see how we do this.

### The Consumer Price Index

Every month, the Bureau of Labor Statistics (BLS) measures the price level by calculating the **Consumer Price Index (CPI)**, which is a measure of the average of the prices paid by urban consumers for a fixed basket of consumer goods and services. What you learn here will help you to make sense of the CPI and relate it to your own economic life. The CPI tells you what has happened to the value of the money in your pocket.

### Reading the CPI Numbers

The CPI is defined to equal 100 for a period called the **reference base period**. Currently, the reference base period is 1982–1984. That is, for the average of the 36 months from January 1982 through December 1984, the CPI equals 100.

In July 2008, the CPI was 220. This number tells us that the average of the prices paid by urban consumers for a fixed market basket of consumer goods and services was 120 percent higher in 2008 than it was on the average during 1982–1984.

## Constructing the CPI

Constructing the CPI is a huge operation that involves three stages:

- Selecting the CPI basket
- Conducting the monthly price survey
- Calculating the CPI

**The CPI Basket** The first stage in constructing the CPI is to select what is called the *CPI basket*. This basket contains the goods and services represented in the index and the relative importance attached to each of them. The idea is to make the relative importance of the items in the CPI basket the same as that in the budget of an average urban household. For example, because people spend more on housing than on bus rides, the CPI places more weight on the price of housing than on the price of a bus ride.

To determine the CPI basket, the BLS conducts a Consumer Expenditure Survey. Today's CPI basket is based on data gathered in the Consumer Expenditure Survey of 2004.

Figure 5.6 shows the CPI basket at the end of 2007. The basket contains around 80,000 goods and services arranged in the eight large groups shown in the figure. The most important item in a household's budget is housing, which accounts for 42 percent of total expenditure. Transportation comes next at 18 percent. Third in relative importance are food and beverages at 15 percent. These three groups account for three quarters of the average household budget. Medical care, recreation, and education and communication take 6 percent each. Another 4 percent is spent on apparel (clothing and footwear) and 3 percent is spent on other goods and services.

The BLS breaks down each of these categories into smaller ones. For example, the education and communication category breaks down into textbooks and supplies, tuition, telephone services, and personal computer services.

As you look at the relative importance of the items in the CPI basket, remember that they apply to the *average* household. *Individual* households are spread around the average. Think about your own expenditure and compare the basket of goods and services you buy with the CPI basket.

**The Monthly Price Survey** Each month, BLS employees check the prices of the 80,000 goods and services in the CPI basket in 30 metropolitan areas. Because the CPI aims to measure price *changes*, it is important that the prices recorded each month refer to exactly the same item. For example, suppose the price of a box of jelly beans has increased but a box now contains more beans. Has the price of jelly beans increased? The BLS employee must record the details of changes in quality or packaging so that price changes can be isolated from other changes.

**FIGURE 5.6** The CPI Basket

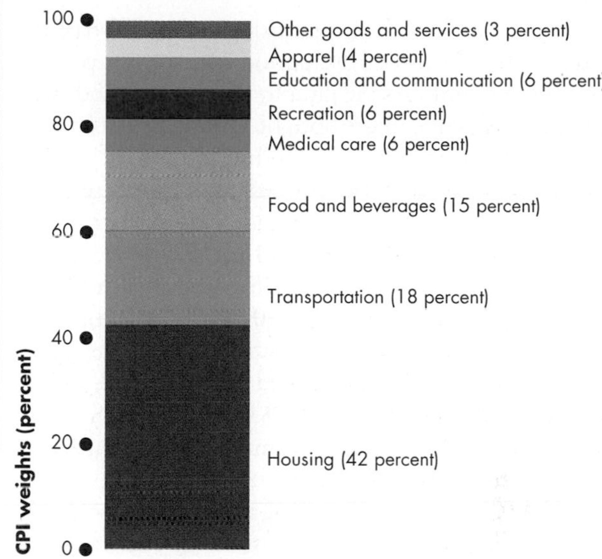


The CPI basket consists of the items that an average urban household buys. It consists mainly of housing (42 percent), transportation (18 percent), and food and beverages (15 percent). All other items add up to 25 percent of the total.

*Sources of data*: United States Census Bureau and Bureau of Labor Statistics.

myeconlab animation

Once the raw price data are in hand, the next task is to calculate the CPI.

**Calculating the CPI** To calculate the CPI, we

1. Find the cost of the CPI basket at base-period prices.
2. Find the cost of the CPI basket at current-period prices.
3. Calculate the CPI for the base period and the current period.

We'll work through these three steps for a simple example. Suppose the CPI basket contains only two goods and services: oranges and haircuts. We'll construct an annual CPI rather than a monthly CPI with the reference base period 2008 and the current period 2009.

Table 5.1 shows the quantities in the CPI basket and the prices in the base period and current period.

Part (a) contains the data for the base period. In that period, consumers bought 10 oranges at \$1 each and 5 haircuts at \$8 each. To find the cost of the CPI basket in the base-period prices, multiply the quantities in the CPI basket by the base-period prices. The cost of oranges is \$10 (10 at \$1 each), and the cost of haircuts is \$40 (5 at \$8 each). So total cost in the base period of the CPI basket is \$50 (\$10 + \$40).

Part (b) contains the price data for the current period. The price of an orange increased from \$1 to \$2, which is a 100 percent increase—(\$1 ÷ \$1) × 100 = 100. The price of a haircut increased from \$8 to \$10, which is a 25 percent increase—(\$2 ÷ \$8) × 100 = 25.

The CPI provides a way of averaging these price increases by comparing the cost of the basket rather than the price of each item. To find the cost of the CPI basket in the current period, 2009, multiply the quantities in the basket by their 2009 prices. The cost of oranges is \$20 (10 at \$2 each), and the cost of haircuts is \$50 (5 at \$10 each). So total cost of the fixed CPI basket at current-period prices is \$70 (\$20 + \$50).

You've now taken the first two steps toward calculating the CPI: calculating the cost of the CPI basket in the base period and the current period. The third step uses the numbers you've just calculated to find the CPI for 2008 and 2009.

The formula for the CPI is

$$\text{CPI} = \frac{\text{Cost of CPI basket at current prices}}{\text{Cost of CPI basket at base-period prices}} \times 100.$$

In Table 5.1, you established that in 2008 (the base period), the cost of the CPI basket was \$50 and in 2009, it was \$70. If we use these numbers in the CPI formula, we can find the CPI for 2008 and 2009. For 2008, the CPI is

$$\text{CPI in 2008} = \frac{\$50}{\$50} \times 100 = 100.$$

For 2009, the CPI is

$$\text{CPI in 2009} = \frac{\$70}{\$50} \times 100 = 140.$$

The principles that you've applied in this simplified CPI calculation apply to the more complex calculations performed every month by the BLS.

**TABLE 5.1** The CPI: A Simplified Calculation

**(a) The cost of the CPI basket at base-period prices: 2008**

| CPI basket | | | |
|---|---|---|---|
| **Item** | **Quantity** | **Price** | **Cost of CPI Basket** |
| Oranges | 10 | \$1.00 | \$10 |
| Haircuts | 5 | \$8.00 | \$40 |
| Cost of CPI basket at base-period prices | | | \$50 |

**(b) The cost of the CPI basket at current-period prices: 2009**

| CPI basket | | | |
|---|---|---|---|
| **Item** | **Quantity** | **Price** | **Cost of CPI Basket** |
| Oranges | 10 | \$2.00 | \$20 |
| Haircuts | 5 | \$10.00 | \$50 |
| Cost of CPI basket at current-period prices | | | \$70 |

## Measuring the Inflation Rate

A major purpose of the CPI is to measure changes in the cost of living and in the value of money. To measure these changes, we calculate the *inflation rate* as the annual percentage change in the CPI. To calculate the inflation rate, we use the formula:

$$\text{Inflation rate} = \frac{\text{CPI this year} - \text{CPI last year}}{\text{CPI last year}} \times 100.$$

We can use this formula to calculate the inflation rate in 2008. The CPI in July 2008 was 220, and the CPI in July 2007 was 208.3. So the inflation rate during the twelve months to July 2008 was

$$\text{Inflation rate} = \frac{(220 - 208.3)}{208.3} \times 100 = 5.6\%.$$

## Distinguishing High Inflation from a High Price Level

Figure 5.7 shows the CPI and the inflation rate in the United States during the 37 years between 1971 and 2008. The two parts of the figure are related and emphasize the distinction between high inflation and high prices.

Figure 5.7 shows that when the price level in part (a) *rises rapidly*, as it did during the 1970s and through 1982, the inflation rate in part (b) is *high*. When the price level in part (a) *rises slowly*, as it did after 1982, the inflation rate in part (b) is *low*.

A high inflation rate means that the price level is rising rapidly. A high price level means that there has been a sustained period of rising prices like that shown in Fig 5.7(a).

The CPI is not a perfect measure of the price level and changes in the CPI probably overstate the inflation rate. Let's look at the sources of bias.

## The Biased CPI

The main sources of bias in the CPI are

- New goods bias
- Quality change bias
- Commodity substitution bias
- Outlet substitution bias

**New Goods Bias** If you want to compare the price level in 2009 with that in 1969, you must somchow compare the price of a computer today with that of a typewriter in 1969. Because a PC is more expensive than a typewriter was, the arrival of the PC puts an upward bias into the CPI and its inflation rate.

**Quality Change Bias** Cars, CD players, and many other items get better every year. Part of the rise in the prices of these items is a payment for improved quality and is not inflation. But the CPI counts the entire price rise as inflation and so overstates inflation.

**Commodity Substitution Bias** Changes in relative prices lead consumers to change the items they buy. For example, if the price of beef rises and the price of chicken remains unchanged, people buy more chicken and less beef. This switch from beef to chicken might provides the same amount of protein and the same enjoyment as before and expenditure is the same as before. The price of protein has not changed. But because the CPI ignores the substitution of chicken for beef, it says the price of protein has increased.

**FIGURE 5.7** The CPI and the Inflation Rate

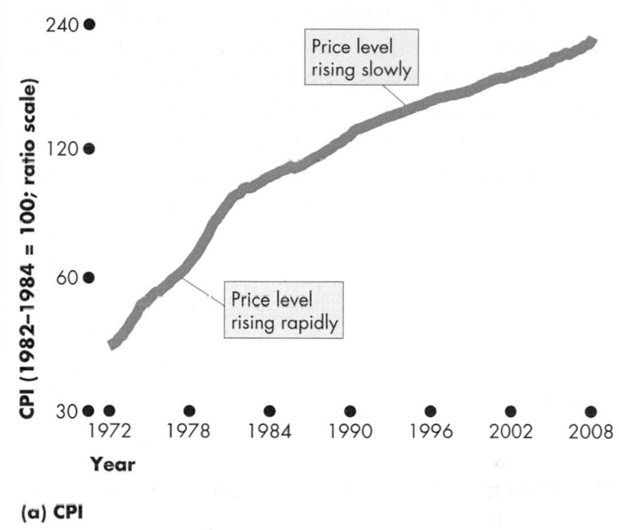


**(a) CPI**

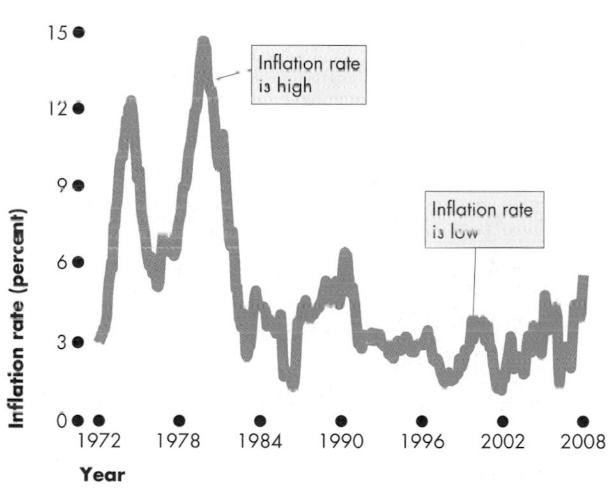


**(b) Inflation rate**

When the price level rises rapidly, the inflation rate is high, and when the price level rises slowly, the inflation rate is low. During the 1970s and through 1982, the price level increased rapidly in part (a) and the inflation rate was high in part (b). The inflation rate averaged 8 percent a year and sometimes exceeded 14 percent a year.

After 1982, the price level rose slowly in part (a) and the inflation rate was low in part (b). The inflation rate averaged 3.2 percent a year.

*Source of data*: Bureau of Labor Statistics.

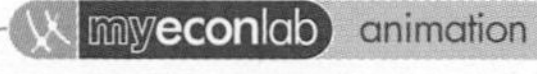

**Outlet Substitution Bias** When confronted with higher prices, people use discount stores more frequently and convenience stores less frequently. This phenomenon is called *outlet substitution.* The CPI surveys do not monitor outlet substitutions.

## The Magnitude of the Bias

You've reviewed the sources of bias in the CPI. But how big is the bias? This question was tackled in 1996 by a Congressional Advisory Commission on the Consumer Price Index chaired by Michael Boskin, an economics professor at Stanford University. This commission said that the CPI overstates inflation by 1.1 percentage points a year. That is, if the CPI reports that inflation is 3.1 percent a year, most likely inflation is actually 2 percent a year.

## Some Consequences of the Bias

The bias in the CPI distorts private contracts and increases government outlays. Many private agreements, such as wage contracts, are linked to the CPI. For example, a firm and its workers might agree to a three-year wage deal that increases the wage rate by 2 percent a year *plus* the percentage increase in the CPI. Such a deal ends up giving the workers more real income than the firm intended.

Close to a third of federal government outlays, including Social Security checks, are linked directly to the CPI. And while a bias of 1 percent a year seems small, accumulated over a decade it adds up to almost a trillion dollars of additional expenditures.

## Alternative Price Indexes

The CPI is just one of many alternative price level index numbers and because of the bias in the CPI, other measures are used for some purposes. We'll describe three alternatives to the CPI and explain when and why they might be preferred to the CPI. The alternatives are

- Chained CPI
- Personal consumption expenditure deflator
- GDP deflator

**Chained CPI** The *chained CPI* is a price index that is calculated using a similar method to that used to calculate *chained-dollar real GDP* described in Chapter 4 (see pp. 100–101).

The *chained* CPI overcomes the sources of bias in the CPI. It incorporates substitutions and new goods bias by using current and previous period quantities rather than fixed quantities from an earlier period.

The practical difference made by the chained CPI is small. This index has been calculated since 2000 and the average inflation rate since then as measured by the chained CPI is only 0.3 percentage points lower than the standard CPI—2.5 percent versus 2.8 percent per year.

**Personal Consumption Expenditure Deflator** The *personal consumption expenditure deflator* (or *PCE deflator*) is calculated from data in the national income accounts that you studied in Chapter 21. When the Bureau of Economic Analysis calculates *real GDP*, it also calculates the real values of its expenditure components: real consumption expenditure, real investment, real government expenditure, and real net exports. These calculations are done in the same way as that for real GDP described in simplified terms on p. 91 and more technically on pp. 100–101.

To calculate the PCE deflator, we use the formula:

$$\text{PCE deflator} = (\text{Nominal } C \div \text{Real } C) \times 100,$$

where $C$ is personal consumption expenditure.

The basket of goods and services included in the PCE deflator is broader than that in the CPI because it includes all consumption expenditure, not only the items bought by a typical urban family.

Again, the difference between the PCE deflator and the CPI is small. Since 2000, the inflation rate measured by the PCE deflator is 2.4 percent per year, 0.4 percentage points lower than the CPI inflation rate.

**GDP Deflator** The *GDP deflator* is a bit like the PCE deflator except that it includes all the goods and services that are counted as part of GDP. So it is an index of the prices of the items in consumption, investment, government expenditure, and net exports.

This broader price index is appropriate for macroeconomics because, like GDP itself, it is a comprehensive measure of the cost of the real GDP basket of goods and services.

Since 2000, the GDP deflator has increased at an average rate of 2.6 percent per year, only 0.2 percentage points below the CPI inflation rate.

**Core CPI Inflation** No matter whether we calculate the inflation rate using the CPI, the chained CPI, the personal consumption expenditure deflator, or the GDP deflator, the number bounces around a good deal from month to month or quarter to quarter. To determine whether the inflation rate is trending upward or downward, we need to strip the raw numbers of their volatility. The **core CPI inflation rate**, which is the CPI inflation rate excluding volatile elements, attempts to do just that and reveal the underlying inflation trend.

As a practical matter, the core CPI inflation rate is calculated as the percentage change in the CPI (or other price index) excluding food and fuel. The prices of these two items are among the most volatile.

While the core CPI inflation rate removes the volatile elements in inflation, it can give a misleading view of the true underlying inflation rate. If the relative prices of the excluded items are changing, the core CPI inflation rate will give a biased measure of the true underlying inflation rate.

Such a misleading account was given during the years between 2003 and 2008 when the relative prices of food and fuel were rising. The result was a core CPI inflation rate that was systematically below the CPI inflation rate. Figure 5.8 shows the two series since 2001. More refined measures of core inflation have been suggested that eliminate the bias.

## The Real Variables in Macroeconomics

You saw in Chapter 4 how we measure real GDP. And you've seen in this chapter how we can use nominal GDP and real GDP to provide another measure of the price level—the GDP deflator. But viewing real GDP as nominal GDP deflated, opens up the idea of other real variables. By using the GDP deflator, we can deflate other nominal variables to find their real values. For example, the *real wage rate* is the nominal wage rate divided by the GDP deflator.

We can adjust any nominal quantity or price variable for inflation by deflating it—by dividing it by the price level.

There is one variable that is a bit different—an interest rate. A real interest rate is *not* a nominal interest rate divided by the price level. You'll learn how to adjust the nominal interest rate for inflation to find the real interest rate in Chapter 7. But all the other real variables of macroeconomics are calculated by dividing a nominal variable by the price level.

**FIGURE 5.8** Core Inflation

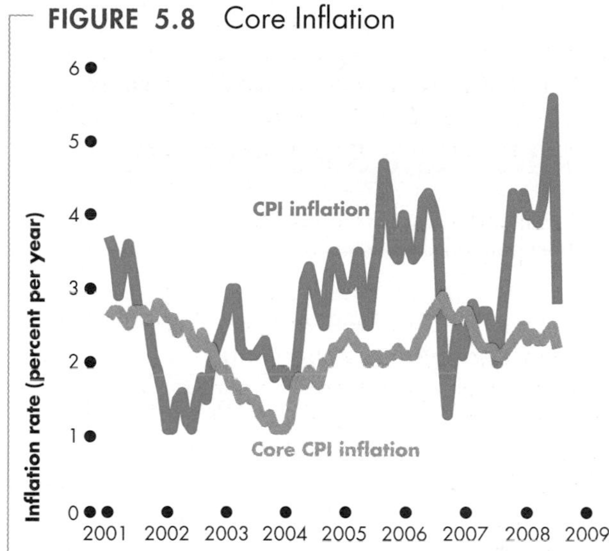


The core CPI inflation rate excludes volatile price changes of food and fuel. Since 2003, the core CPI inflation rate has mostly been below the CPI inflation rate because the relative prices of food and fuel have been rising.

*Source of data:* Bureau of Labor Statistics.

myeconlab animation

## Review Quiz

1. What is the price level?
2. What is the CPI and how is it calculated?
3. How do we calculate the inflation rate and what is the relationship between the CPI and the inflation rate?
4. What are the four main ways in which the CPI is an upward-biased measure of the price level?
5. What problems arise from the CPI bias?
6. What are the alternative measures of the price level and how do they address the problem of bias in the CPI?

myeconlab Work Study Plan 5.3 and get instant feedback.

You've now completed your study of the measurement of macroeconomic performance. Your task in the following chapters is to learn what determines that performance and how policy actions might improve it. But first, take a close-up look at the labor market in the slowdown of 2008 in *Reading Between the Lines* on pp. 122–123.

READING BETWEEN THE LINES

# Jobs in the Slowdown of 2008

## Jobless Rate Soars to 6.1%

http://money.cnn.com
September 5, 2008

The unemployment rate soared to a nearly five-year high in August as employers trimmed jobs for the eighth straight month, the government reported Friday.

The unemployment rate rose to 6.1%, the highest level since September 2003. That's up from 5.7% in July and 4.7% a year ago.

In addition, the economy suffered a net loss of 84,000 jobs in August, according to the U.S. Department of Labor, compared to a revised reading of a 60,000 job loss in July.

The U.S. economy has lost 605,000 jobs so far this year.

The jobs report immediately drew comment from the presidential candidates as well as the Bush administration.

The White House pointed to other economic readings, including last week's gross domestic product report. It showed second quarter growth jumping to a 3.3% annual rate, helped by economic stimulus checks and strong exports.

"While these (jobs) numbers are disappointing, what is most important is the overall direction the economy is headed," said the White House statement.

But the campaign of Democratic presidential candidate Barack Obama said the report points out the failure of Republican policies.

...

The unemployment rate doesn't tell the whole picture about how difficult the job market has become. It only counts those who looked for work during the month; it excludes the unemployed who want jobs but have stopped looking for work. And it also doesn't count those who want full-time jobs but can only find part-time positions.

The so-called underemployment rate, which includes those two other groups, rose to 10.7% —the highest reading since 1994.



## Essence of the Story

- The unemployment rate increased to 6.1 percent in August 2008, the highest level since September 2003.
- The unemployment rate was 5.7 percent in July and 4.7 percent in August 2007.
- Employment decreased by 84,000 in August and by 605,000 since January 2008.
- In contrast, second quarter real GDP increased at a 3.3 percent annual rate.
- The broader underemployment rate, which includes those who stopped looking for work and part-time workers who want full-time work increased to 10.7 percent, its highest rate since 1994.

## Economic Analysis

- This news article reports some labor market data for August 2008: the rise in the unemployment rate and the number of jobs lost.
- This weak labor market performance comes at the end of an unusually weak expansion from a recession in 2001.
- The figures show the job creation performance of the U.S. economy during the expansion that began in 2002 and place that expansion in a longer-term historical perspective.
- In Fig. 1, the *y*-axis shows the level of employment as a percentage of its level at the business cycle trough and the *x*-axis shows the number of months since the business cycle trough.
- By August 2008, the expansion had been running for 79 months (6 years and 7 months).
- The blue line in the figure shows the growth of employment during the 2002–2008 expansion.
- Employment peaked at the beginning of 2008 and then flattened off.
- The shaded area in the graph enables you to compare the 2002–2008 expansion with the previous U.S. business cycle expansions. That shaded area shows the range of employment over the first 54 months (4½ years) of those previous expansions.
- You can see that the current expansion runs along the bottom of the range of previous experience.
- Figure 2 shows a similar comparison for the unemployment rate.
- In an average expansion, the unemployment rate falls after 54 months to 70 percent of its trough level.
- In the current expansion, the unemployment rate actually increased and after 18 months stood at 10 percent above its trough level.
- As measured by the unemployment rate, the current expansion was similar to the weakest of the previous ones.
- The unemployment rate began to rise at the beginning of 2007, when the pace of job growth came to a standstill.

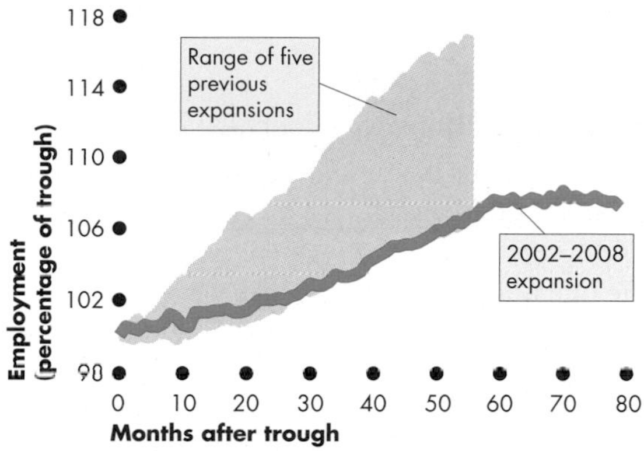


**Figure 1 Employment during the 2002–2008 expansion**

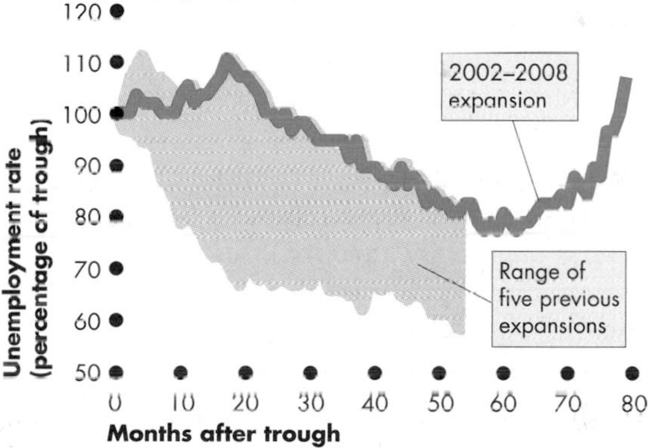


**Figure 2 The unemployment rate during the 2002–2008 expansion**

## SUMMARY

### Key Points

**Employment and Unemployment** (pp. 108–111)

- Unemployment is a serious personal, social, and economic problem because it results in lost output and income and a loss of human capital.
- The unemployment rate averaged 5.8 percent between 1961 and 2008. It increases in recessions and decreases in expansions.
- The labor force participation rate and the employment-to-population ratio have an upward trend and fluctuate with the business cycle.

**Unemployment and Full Employment** (pp. 112–115)

- The unemployment rate is an imperfect measure of the underutilization of labor resources because it excludes some underutilized labor and some unemployment is unavoidable.
- The unemployment rate underestimates the underutilization of labor resources because it excludes marginally attached workers and part-time workers who want full-time jobs.
- Some unemployment is unavoidable because people are constantly entering and leaving the labor force and losing or quitting jobs; also firms that create jobs are constantly being borne, expanding, contracting, and dying.
- Unemployment can be frictional, structural, or cyclical.
- When all unemployment is frictional and structural, the unemployment rate equals the natural unemployment rate, the economy is at full employment, and real GDP equals potential GDP.
- Over the business cycle, real GDP fluctuates around potential GDP and the unemployment rate fluctuates around the natural unemployment rate.

**The Price Level and Inflation** (pp. 116–121)

- Inflation is a problem because it redistributes income and wealth and diverts resources from production.
- The Consumer Price Index (CPI) is a measure of the average of the prices paid by urban consumers for a fixed basket of consumer goods and services.
- The CPI is defined to equal 100 for a reference base period—currently 1982–1984.
- The inflation rate is the percentage change in the CPI from one period to the next.
- Changes in the CPI probably overstate the inflation rate because of the bias that arises from new goods, quality changes, commodity substitution, and outlet substitution.
- The bias in the CPI distorts private contracts and increases government outlays.
- Alternative price level measures avoid the bias of the CPI but do not make a large difference to the measured inflation rate.
- Real economic variables are calculated by dividing nominal variables by the price level.

### Key Figures



### Key Terms

## PROBLEMS and APPLICATIONS

Work problems 1–9 in Chapter 5 Study Plan and get instant feedback.
Work problems 10–18 as Homework, a Quiz, or a Test if assigned by your instructor.

1. The Bureau of Labor Statistics reported the following data for the second quarter of 2008:
   Labor force: 154,294,000
   Employment: 146,089,000
   Working-age population: 233,410,000
   Calculate for that quarter the
   a. Unemployment rate.
   b. Labor force participation rate.
   c. Employment-to-population ratio.
2. In March 2007, the U.S. unemployment rate was 4.4 percent. In August 2008, the unemployment rate was 6.1 percent. Use this information to predict what happened between March 2007 and August 2008 to the numbers of
   a. Job losers and job leavers.
   b. Entrants and reentrants into the labor force.
3. In July 2009, in the economy of Sandy Island, 10,000 people were employed, 1,000 were unemployed, and 5,000 were not in the labor force. During August 2009, 80 people lost their jobs and didn't look for new ones, 20 people quit their jobs and retired, 150 people were hired or recalled, 50 people withdrew from the labor force, and 40 people entered or reentered the labor force to look for work. Calculate for July 2009
   a. The unemployment rate.
   b. The employment-to-population ratio.

   And calculate for the end of August 2009
   c. The number of people unemployed.
   d. The number of people employed.
   e. The unemployment rate.
4. The Bureau of Labor Statistics reported the following CPI data:

   | | |
   |---|---|
   | June 2006 | 201.9 |
   | June 2007 | 207.2 |
   | June 2008 | 217.4 |

   a. What do these numbers tell you about the price level in these three years?
   b. Calculate the inflation rates for the years ended June 2007 and June 2008.
   c. How did the inflation rate change in 2008?
   d. Why might these CPI numbers be biased?
   e. How do alternative price indexes help to avoid the bias in the CPI numbers?
5. The IMF *World Economic Outlook* reports the following price level data (2000 = 100):

   | Region | 2006 | 2007 | 2008 |
   |---|---|---|---|
   | United States | 117.1 | 120.4 | 124.0 |
   | Euro area | 113.6 | 117.1 | 119.6 |
   | Japan | 98.1 | 98.1 | 98.8 |

   a. Which region had the highest inflation rate in 2007 and which had the highest inflation rate in 2008?
   b. Describe the path of the price level in Japan.
6. **Nation's Economic Pain Deepens**

   A spike in the unemployment rate—the biggest in more than two decades—raised new concerns Friday that a weak labor outlook, high oil prices and continuing woes in the housing and credit markets are leading the U.S. economy into a painful recession. The government said Friday that the unemployment rate soared to 5.5% in May from 5% in April much higher than economists had forecast. The surge marked the biggest one-month jump in unemployment since February 1986, and the 5.5% rate is the highest level seen since October 2004. Unemployment is now a full percentage point higher than it was a year ago. …

   *CNN*, June 6, 2008

   a. How does the unemployment rate in May compare to the unemployment rate during the past few recessions?
   b. Why might the unemployment rate tend to actually underestimate the unemployment problem, especially during a recession?
   c. How does the unemployment rate in May compare to the estimated natural unemployment rate? What does this imply about the relationship between real GDP and potential GDP at this time?
7. **Michigan: Epicenter of Unemployment**

   Michigan, once the center of America's industrial heartland, now holds a more dubious distinction: It leads the U.S. in joblessness. The state's unemployment rate hit 8.5% in May … and compares with a figure of 5.5% for the whole U.S. in May. There's little mystery as to the cause. Detroit's bet on big trucks and sport-utility vehicles has turned snake-eyes. … Overall U.S. vehicle sales are expected to drop below 15 million this year. Three years ago, the industry sold 17 million cars and trucks. But bad as those unemployment figures look, the reality is actually worse. The official number is arrived at by surveying households and learning how many family members are unemployed but seeking work. So it does not reflect those who have given up finding a job, or those who are not yet looking but soon will be. … One of the bright spots, if you can call it that, for Michigan is the health-care industry. With baby boomers aging and their parents living longer, hospitals, nursing homes, clinics, and medical laboratories have the most jobs to offer in Michigan today. But the cruel irony is that there is a shortage of trained professionals. … Registered nurses and lab technicians are in big demand, with not enough applicants.

*BusinessWeek*, June 24, 2008

a. Why is the reality of the unemployment problem in Michigan actually worse than the 8.5% unemployment rate statistic?
b. Is this higher unemployment rate in Michigan frictional, structural, or cyclical? Explain.

8. **Inflation Getting "Uglier and Uglier"**

The Consumer Price Index, a key inflation reading, rose 4.2% through the 12 months ending in May, according to the Labor Department. … For the month of May, overall CPI rose 0.6% … the biggest increase since last November, when the overall CPI surged 0.9%. … The dramatic increases in energy costs were largely responsible for the overall inflation. Energy costs rose 4.4% in May, and surged 17.4% over the 12 months ending in May … transportation costs increased 2% in May, and jumped 8.1% over the 12 months ending in May. The index for household energy costs climbed 2.8% in May, its fourth consecutive jump, the Labor Department said. The price of food also pushed up overall costs. Food costs increased 0.3% in May, and jumped 5.1% during the 12 months ending in May. The price of milk was a big influence on the overall price, increasing 10.2% over the 12 months. … The cost of clothing was the one area where consumers got some relief. Apparel costs deflated 0.2% in May, and decreased 0.4% over the 12 months. The core CPI, which excludes the cost of food and energy, rose 0.2% in May. … The core CPI rose 2.3% during the 12 months ending in May.

*CNN*, June 13, 2008

a. How do the inflation rates described in this article compare to average inflation since 1983? How do they compare to average inflation during the 1970s and early 1980s?
b. Which components of the CPI basket are experiencing price increases faster than the average and which have price increases below the average?
c. What is the difference between the CPI and the core CPI? Why might the core CPI be a useful measurement and why might it be misleading?

9. **Dress for Less**

Since 1998, the price of a "Speedy" handbag — the entry-level style at Louis Vuitton—has more than doubled, to $685, indicative of a precipitous price increase throughout the luxury goods market. The price of Joe Boxer's "licky face" underwear, meanwhile, has dropped by nearly half, to $8.99, representing just as seismic a shift at the other end of the fashion continuum, where the majority of American consumers do their shopping.

As luxury fashion has become more expensive, mainstream apparel has become markedly less so. … Clothing is one of the few categories in the federal Consumer Price Index in which overall prices have declined—about 10 percent—since 1998 (the cost of communication is another). That news may be of solace to anyone whose budget has been stretched just to drive to work or to stop at the supermarket; in fashion, at least, there are still deals to be had. …

*The New York Times*, May 29, 2008

a. What percentage of the CPI basket does apparel comprise?
b. If luxury clothing prices have increased dramatically since the late 1990s, why has the clothing category of the CPI actually declined by about 10 percent?

10. In the New Orleans metropolitan area in August 2005, the labor force was 634,512 and 35,222 people were unemployed. In September 2005 following Hurricane Katrina, the labor force fell by 156,518 and the number employed fell by 206,024. Calculate the unemployment rate in August 2005 and in September 2005.
11. The IMF *World Economic Outlook* reports the following unemployment rates:

| Region | 2007 | 2008 |
|---|---|---|
| United States | 4.6 | 5.4 |
| Euro area | 7.4 | 7.3 |
| Japan | 3.9 | 3.9 |

    a. What do these numbers tell you about the phase of the business cycle in the United States, Euro area, and Japan in 2008?
    b. What do you think these numbers tell us about the relative size of the natural unemployment rates in the United States, the Euro area, and Japan?
    c. Do these numbers tell us anything about the relative size of the labor force participation rates and employment-to-population ratios in the three regions?
    d. Why might these unemployment numbers understate or overstate the true amount of unemployment?
12. A typical family on Sandy Island consumes only juice and cloth. Last year, which was the base year, the family spent $40 on juice and $25 on cloth. In the base year, juice was $4 a bottle and cloth was $5 a length. This year, juice is $4 a bottle and cloth is $6 a length. Calculate
    a. The CPI basket.
    b. The CPI in the current year.
    c. The inflation rate in the current year.
13. **A Half-Year of Job Losses**

    Employers trimmed jobs from their payrolls in June for the sixth straight month, as the government's closely watched report Thursday showed continued weakness in the labor market. … The June number brought to 438,000 the number of jobs lost by the U.S. economy so far this year. … The job losses in the monthly report were concentrated in manufacturing and construction, two sectors that have been badly battered in the current economic downturn. …

    *CNN*, July 3, 2008

    a. How do the job losses for the first half of 2008 compare to the total number of people employed?
    b. Based on the news clip, what might be the main source of increased unemployment?
    c. Based on the news clip, what might be the main type of increased unemployment?
14. **Out of a Job and Out of Luck at 54**

    Too young to retire, too old to get a new job. That's how many older workers are feeling these days. … Older job seekers are discovering the search is even rougher as many employers shy away from hiring those closer to retirement than to the start of their careers. … After they get the pink slip, older workers spend more time on the unemployment line. Many lack the skills to search for jobs in today's online world and to craft resumes and cover letters, experts say. … It took those age 55 and older an average of 21.1 weeks to land a new job in 2007, about five weeks longer than their younger counterparts, according to AARP. "Clearly older workers will be more adversely affected because of the time it takes to transition into another job," said Deborah Russell, AARP's director of workforce issues.

    *CNN*, May 21, 2008

    a. What type of unemployment might older workers be more prone to experience?
    b. Explain how the unemployment rate of older workers would be influenced by the business cycle.
    c. Why might older unemployed workers become marginally attached or discouraged workers during a recession?
15. **Governor Plans to Boost Economy with Eco-friendly Jobs**

    Oregon's 5.6 percent unemployment rate hovers close to the national average of 5.5 percent. … Less than four years ago, the state had one of the highest unemployment rates in the nation. [Oregon Governor] Kulongoski hopes to avoid a repeat of those days. When the 2009 Legislature meets, he'll present a package of proposals he thinks will keep the jobs picture bright, despite what may be going on elsewhere. The cornerstone, he says, is making sure public schools and universities get enough state dollars to meet growing demand for skilled workers. Those range from high school seniors looking to go straight into a vocation, such as welding or electrical wiring, to college grads armed with advanced marketing or engineering degrees. Beyond that, Kulongoski wants to … use state and federal money for bridges, roads and buildings to stimulate more construction jobs.

*The Oregonian*, July 8, 2008

a. What is the main type of unemployment that Governor Kulongoski is using policies to avoid? Explain.
b. How might these policies impact Oregon's natural unemployment rate? Explain.

16. **Economic "Misery" More Widespread**

Unemployment and inflation are typically added together to come up with a so-called "Misery Index." The "Misery Index" was often cited during periods of high unemployment and inflation, such as the mid 1970s and late 1970s to early 1980s.

And some fear the economy may be approaching those levels again. The official numbers produce a current Misery Index of only 8.9—inflation of 3.9% plus unemployment of 5%. That's not far from the Misery Index's low of 6.1 seen in 1998. … Some worry it could even approach the post-World War II record of 20.6 in 1980. …

*CNN*, May 13, 2008

a. Explain how the "Misery Index" might serve as a gauge of how the economy is performing.
b. How does the most current "Misery Index" compare to the high and low given in this article? (You may find it useful to use the link of MyEconLab—Chapter Resources, Chapter 5, Web links—to visit the Bureau of Labor Statistics Website for the current unemployment rate and the most recent 12-month change in the CPI.)

17. **The Great Inflation Cover-Up**

The 1996 Boskin Commission … was established to determine the accuracy of the CPI. The commission concluded that the CPI overstated inflation by 1.1%, and methodologies were adjusted to reflect that. Critics of the Boskin Commission suggest that the basis upon which the CPI was revised doesn't account for the way people actually purchase and consume products. The commission pointed to four biases inherent in the way the CPI was determined that supposedly contribute to overstatement. … But the Boskin critics note several reasonable exceptions to those biases. The Boskin Commission suggests that when customers substitute one good for another, the CPI should treat those goods equally. If [someone] orders a hanger steak instead of his beloved filet mignon because the hanger steak is cheaper, Boskin argues that the hanger steak prices should be compared with previous filet mignon prices. It's all beef, right? But critics of the Boskin report point to areas where substitution is so price-driven that consumers are pushed out of the category altogether. What happens when the consumer gives up steak entirely and switches to chicken? (Or to use a scarier example, goes from some health insurance to no health insurance?) Boskin also says that whatever you're paying in price increases is offset by the additional pleasure you get from better goods. To put it another way, you adjust for improvement in quality over time. … So, for example, energy price increases due to federally mandated environmental measures are offset by how much we all sit around enjoying the cleaner environment.

*Fortune*, April 3, 2008

a. What are the main sources of bias that are generally believed to make the CPI overstate the inflation rate? By how much did Boskin estimate the CPI overstates the inflation rate?
b. Do the substitutions among different kinds of meat make the CPI biased up or down?
c. Why does it matter if the CPI overstates or understates the inflation rate?

18. Study *Reading Between the Lines* on pp. 122–123 and then answer the following questions:
a. When did the unemployment rate peak after the 2001 recession?
b. When did the unemployment rate reach its lowest point in the 2002–2008 expansion?
c. Did the expansion of 2002–2008 create jobs at an unusually fast rate, an unusually slow rate, or an average rate?
d. Provide reasons why the first two years of the expansion didn't create many jobs.
e. Is the slow job growth and rise in unemployment after mid-2007 most likely cyclical, structural, or frictional? Explain.
f. Suggest some actions that the U.S. government might take if it wants to create more jobs.

# PART TWO

## UNDERSTANDING MACROECONOMIC TRENDS AND FLUCTUATIONS

# The Big Picture

Macroeconomics is a large and controversial subject that is interlaced with political ideological disputes. And it is a field in which charlatans as well as serious thinkers have much to say.

You have just learned in Chapters 4 and 5 how we monitor and measure the main macroeconomic variables. We use real GDP to calculate the rate of economic growth and business cycle fluctuations. And we use the CPI and other measures of the price level to calculate the inflation rate and to "deflate" nominal values to find *real* values.

In the chapters that lie ahead, you will learn the theories that economists have developed to explain economic growth, fluctuations, and inflation.

First, in Chapters 6 through 9, you will study the long-term trends. This material is central to the oldest question in macroeconomics that Adam Smith tried to answer: What are the causes of the wealth of nations? You will also study three other old questions that Adam Smith's contemporary and friend David Hume first addressed: What causes inflation? What causes international deficits and surpluses? And why do exchange rates fluctuate?

In Chapters 10 through 12, you will study macroeconomic fluctuations.

Finally, in Chapters 13, 14, and 15, you will study the policies that the federal government and Federal Reserve might adopt to make the economy perform well.

**David Hume**, *a Scot who lived from 1711 to 1776, did not call himself as an economist. "Philosophy and general learning" is how he described the subject of his life's work. Hume was an extraordinary thinker and writer. Published in 1742, his* Essays, Moral and Political, *range across economics, political science, moral philosophy, history, literature, ethics, and religion and explore such topics as love, marriage, divorce, suicide, death, and the immortality of the soul!*

*His economic essays provide astonishing insights into the forces that cause inflation, business cycle fluctuations, balance of payments deficits, and interest rate fluctuations; and they explain the effects of taxes and government deficits and debts.*

*Data were scarce in Hume's day, so he was not able to draw on detailed evidence to support his analysis. But he was empirical. He repeatedly appealed to experience and evidence as the ultimate judge of the validity of an argument. Hume's fundamentally empirical approach dominates macroeconomics today.*

"... in every kingdom into which money begins to flow in greater abundance than formerly, everything takes a new face: labor and industry gain life; the merchant becomes more enterprising, the manufacturer more diligent and skillful, and even the farmer follows his plow with greater alacrity and attention."

**DAVID HUME**
*Essays, Moral and Political*

# TALKING WITH

# Rich Clarida

**Richard H. Clarida** is the C. Lowell Harriss Professor of Economics at Columbia University, where he has taught since 1988. He graduated with highest honors from the University of Illinois at Urbana in 1979 and received his masters and Ph.D. in Economics from Harvard University in 1983, writing his dissertation under the supervision of Benjamin Friedman.

Professor Clarida has taught at Yale University and held public service positions as Senior Staff Economist with the President's Council of Economic Advisers in President Ronald Reagan's Administration and most recently as Assistant Secretary of the Treasury for Economic Policy in the Administration of President George W. Bush.

Professor Clarida has published a large number of articles in leading academic journals on monetary policy, exchange rates, interest rates, and international capital flows and is a frequent visitor at central banks around the world, including the Federal Reserve, the European Central Bank, and the Bank of England.

Michael Parkin talked with Richard Clarida about his research and some of the macroeconomic policy challenges facing the United States and the world today.

*Professor Clarida, why did you decide to become an economist and what drew you to macroeconomics?*

I had the great fortune to have some excellent, inspiring economics professors in college (Fred Gotheil and Matt Canzoneri) and decided by my sophomore year to put myself on a path that would take me to Ph.D. work in economics. To me, there was (and still is!) enormous appeal and satisfaction from being able to distill the complexities of the economy, really the global economy, into the major fundamental forces that are driving the interactions that are of interest to people. I'm by nature a 'big picture' guy but require and respect rigor and robustness of analysis. In college and grad school, the rational expectations revolution was just emerging and so it was quite an exciting time to be jumping into macro.

*When you consider the United States and global economies today, there are many topics that have made headlines, most notably, the state of our economy, the housing market, and the rise in power of developing countries. Let's start with the state of the U.S. economy. Are we in a recession? If we are, how long will it last and how severe do you think it will be?*

The U.S. economy appears to be in a recession in the summer of 2008. Unemployment is rising, the leading indicators are turning south, and sentiment is very negative. The U.S. economy has been hit by four significant, negative shocks: The bursting of the housing bubble, a major global dislocation in financial markets, record oil and gasoline prices, and the credit crunch as banks suffer losses and tighten lending standards.

The collapse of the housing market is a significant shock to aggregate demand. The dislocation in financial markets and the credit crunch is also a negative shock to aggregate demand. This is because tighter lending standards and higher credit spreads make it more expensive for firms and households to borrow for any given level of the interest rate set by the Fed, and thus have the effect of shifting the aggregate demand curve to the left. Higher oil and commodity prices are a negative supply shock, and shift the aggregate supply curve to the left. The

National Bureau of Economic Research (with whom I am affiliated as a Research Associate) is the arbiter of when a recession begins and ends. The Bureau looks at a wide range of macro indicators, not just GDP growth. It is often said that a recession requires two consecutive quarters of negative GDP growth, but this is not the definition used by the NBER. For example in 2001, the NBER declared the recession began in March and ended in November and yet there were not two consecutive quarters of negative GDP growth.

[The] United States is now lagging, not leading global growth, and the share of dollars in global portfolios will continue to trend down.

*As the recession gains momentum, do you think inflation will die out, or are we heading for stagflation like the 1970s?*

Headline inflation in the United States and elsewhere is well above the desired level of two percent that most central banks strive for. This is mostly due to oil and food prices, but inflation expectations are starting to drift up, and this makes central banks most uncomfortable. The Fed in 2008 is focused on easing interest rates to prevent a deep slump. However, I am confident that the Fed will eventually do what it takes to bring inflation back down to two percent.

The Fed has an implicit inflation target for headline inflation over a horizon of three years. It realizes that monetary policy operates with long lags, so it seeks to set a path for policy that it expects will bring inflation to two percent over several years.

*Is the current account deficit sustainable? Do you see it correcting?*

U.S. current account deficit has been shrinking as a share of GDP for almost two years. In a growing global economy, with the dollar as reserve currency, the U.S. can run a sustainable current account deficit of two to three percent of GDP forever. Most of the current deficit in excess of this level is due to the surge in oil prices to record levels. If oil stays here, saving will rise and investment will fall to narrow the current account deficit.

*In the past, the dollar has been relatively strong when compared to the euro, the pound and the yen, but now we are experiencing a weaker dollar with drastically unfavorable exchange rates. Is the dollar going to continue to go down? Does it matter?*

The dollar has been trending down for some time and I expect this to continue. The United States is now lagging, not leading global growth, and the share of dollars in global portfolios will continue to trend down. I don't see a free fall or crash landing in the dollar, if only because the euro, at this time, is not a viable alternative.

*Why isn't the euro a viable alternative to the dollar?*

At this time there is not an integrated financial market in Europe. There is a collection of a dozen markets. Also, with the privileges of being a global reserve currency come obligations. Global growth drives growing global demand for currency of the reserve country and this implies that the reserve currency country on average, runs a balance of payments deficit as Britain did until World War One and as the United States has since the 1960s.

*With regards to monetary policy, should the Fed target inflation like many other central banks do?*

The Fed has a dual mandate to keep prices stable and the economy at full employment. I do not foresee the Fed changing this mandate. Through their communication strategy, the Fed has moved pretty close to an inflation forecast target.

*With the tumultuous housing market and rise in foreclosures and bank failures, has the credit crisis reinstated fiscal policy as a stabilization tool?*

Given the huge impact that falling house prices have on wealth and the balance sheets of financial institutions, fiscal policy is proving to be a necessary tool in the cycle as it was in 1990-1992 with the S and L crisis.

As house prices fall, banks and financial institutions who made loans to finance these houses suffer

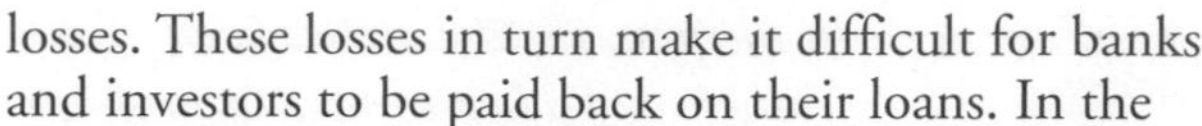

losses. These losses in turn make it difficult for banks and investors to be paid back on their loans. In the early 1990s, the government stepped in to insure that depositors in S&Ls got paid back in full. It shut down hundreds of financial institutions and made up the difference between the value of foreclosed property and deposits by increasing the budget deficit and issuing government bonds.

China ... seen a sharp rise in inflation and a surge in capital inflows in anticipation that its currency will strengthen.

*The world economy has been getting much attention in the press, as many Asian countries are growing in global market share in emerging and established industries. Are China and India going to keep nudging double digit growth rates for the foreseeable future?*

I am bullish on global growth prospects for the next five years for China, India, and the many other 'emerging' economies that are benefiting from a combination of favorable fundamentals and globalization.

*Is China's exchange rate policy a problem for the United States?*

China is allowing its currency to appreciate versus the dollar and will continue to do so. This is in China's interest as much as it is in the United States' interest.

China in recent years has seen a sharp rise in inflation and a surge in capital inflows in anticipation that its currency will strengthen. China has and will continue to allow its currency to strengthen in order to reduce inflation and short term capital inflows.

*What is your advice to a student who is just starting to study economics? Is it a good subject in which to major? What other subjects work well with it?*

It won't surprise you to learn that I think economics is an excellent subject in which to major. In many colleges, including Columbia, it is among the most popular majors. My advice would be to take a broad range of electives and to avoid the temptation to specialize in one narrow area of economics. Also, do as much data, statistics, and presentation work as you can. You will learn the most when you have to explain yourself to others.

# 6 Economic Growth

**After studying this chapter, you will be able to:**

- Define and calculate the economic growth rate and explain the implications of sustained growth
- Describe the economic growth trends in the United States and other countries and regions
- Explain how population growth and labor productivity growth make potential GDP grow
- Explain and measure the sources of labor productivity growth
- Explain the theories of economic growth and policies designed to increase the growth rate

**Real GDP *per person* in the United States** tripled between 1958 and 2008. If you live in a dorm that was built during the 1960s, it is likely to have just two power outlets: one for a desk lamp and one for a bedside lamp. Today, with the help of a power bar (or two), your room bulges with a personal computer, television and DVD player, microwave, refrigerator, coffeemaker, and toaster—and the list goes on. What has brought about this growth in production, incomes, and living standards?

We see even greater economic growth in modern Asia. At the mouth of the Yangtze River in one of the worlds great cities, Shanghai, people are creating businesses, investing in new technologies, developing local and global markets, and transforming their lives. Incomes have tripled in the short 13 years since 1995. Why are incomes in China growing so rapidly?

In this chapter, we study the forces that make real GDP grow, that make some countries grow faster than others, and that make growth rates sometimes slow down and sometimes speed up.

In *Reading Between the Lines* at the end of the chapter, we return to the economic growth of China and see how it compares with that of the United States.

## The Basics of Economic Growth

Economic growth is a sustained expansion of production possibilities measured as the increase in real GDP over a given period. Rapid economic growth maintained over a number of years can transform a poor nation into a rich one. Such have been the stories of Hong Kong, South Korea, Taiwan, and some other Asian economies. Slow economic growth or the absence of growth can condemn a nation to devastating poverty. Such has been the fate of Sierra Leone, Somalia, Zambia, and much of the rest of Africa.

The goal of this chapter is to help you to understand why some economies expand rapidly and others stagnate. We'll begin by learning how to calculate the economic growth rate and by discovering the magic of sustained growth.

### Calculating Growth Rates

We express the **economic growth rate** as the annual percentage change of real GDP. To calculate this growth rate, we use the formula:

$$\text{Real GDP growth rate} = \frac{\text{Real GDP in current year} - \text{Real GDP in previous year}}{\text{Real GDP in previous year}} \times 100.$$

For example, if real GDP in the current year is $11 trillion and if real GDP in the previous year was $10 trillion, then the economic growth rate is 10 percent.

The growth rate of real GDP tells us how rapidly the *total* economy is expanding. This measure is useful for telling us about potential changes in the balance of economic power among nations. But it does not tell us about changes in the standard of living.

The standard of living depends on **real GDP per person** (also called *per capita* real GDP), which is real GDP divided by the population. So the contribution of real GDP growth to the change in the standard of living depends on the growth rate of real GDP per person. We use the above formula to calculate this growth rate, replacing real GDP with real GDP per person.

Suppose, for example, that in the current year, when real GDP is $11 trillion, the population is 202 million. Then real GDP per person is $11 trillion divided by 202 million, which equals $54,455. And suppose that in the previous year, when real GDP was $10 trillion, the population was 200 million. Then real GDP per person in that year was $10 trillion divided by 200 million, which equals $50,000.

Use these two values of real GDP per person with the growth formula above to calculate the growth rate of real GDP per person. That is,

$$\text{Real GDP per person growth rate} = \frac{\$54,455 - \$50,000}{\$50,000} \times 100 = 8.9 \text{ percent.}$$

The growth rate of real GDP per person can also be calculated (approximately) by subtracting the population growth rate from the real GDP growth rate. In the example you've just worked through, the growth rate of real GDP is 10 percent. The population changes from 200 million to 202 million, so the population growth rate is 1 percent. The growth rate of real GDP per person is approximately equal to 10 percent minus 1 percent, which equals 9 percent.

Real GDP per person grows only if real GDP grows faster than the population grows. If the growth rate of the population exceeds the growth of real GDP, then real GDP per person falls.

### The Magic of Sustained Growth

Sustained growth of real GDP per person can transform a poor society into a wealthy one. The reason is that economic growth is like compound interest.

**Compound Interest** Suppose that you put $100 in the bank and earn 5 percent a year interest on it. After one year, you have $105. If you leave that $105 in the bank for another year, you earn 5 percent interest on the original $100 *and on the $5 interest that you earned last year*. You are now earning interest on interest! The next year, things get even better. Then you earn 5 percent on the original $100 and on the interest earned in the first year and the second year. You are even earning interest on the interest that you earned on the interest of the first year.

Your money in the bank is growing at a rate of 5 percent a year. Before too many years have passed, your initial deposit of $100 will have grown to $200. But after how many years?

The answer is provided by a formula called the **Rule of 70**, which states that the number of years it

**FIGURE 6.1** The Rule of 70

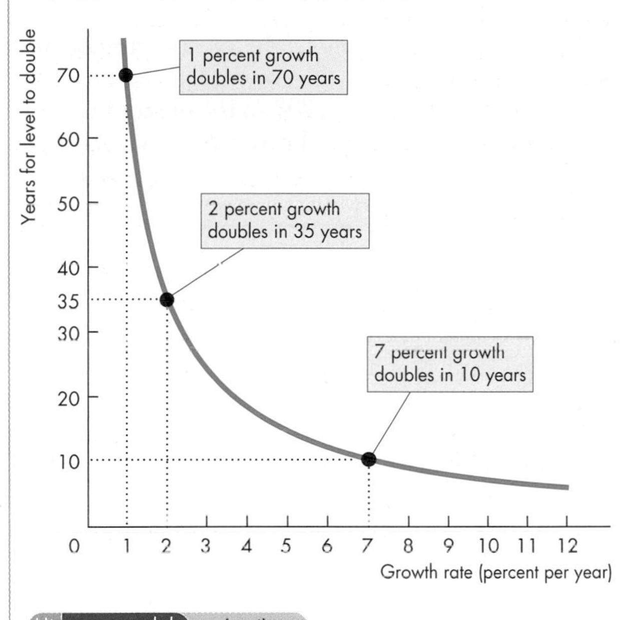


| Growth rate (percent per year) | Years for level to double |
|---|---|
| 1 | 70.0 |
| 2 | 35.0 |
| 3 | 23.3 |
| 4 | 17.5 |
| 5 | 14.0 |
| 6 | 11.7 |
| 7 | 10.0 |
| 8 | 8.8 |
| 9 | 7.8 |
| 10 | 7.0 |
| 11 | 6.4 |
| 12 | 5.8 |

The number of years it takes for the level of a variable to double is approximately 70 divided by the annual percentage growth rate of the variable.

myeconlab animation

takes for the level of any variable to double is approximately 70 divided by the annual percentage growth rate of the variable. Using the Rule of 70, you can now calculate how many years it takes your $100 to become $200. It is 70 divided by 5, which is 14 years.

## Applying the Rule of 70

The Rule of 70 applies to any variable, so it applies to real GDP per person. Figure 6.1 shows the doubling time for growth rates of 1 percent per year to 12 percent per year.

You can see that real GDP per person doubles in 70 years (70 divided by 1)—an average human life span—if the growth rate is 1 percent a year. It doubles in 35 years if the growth rate is 2 percent a year and in just 10 years if the growth rate is 7 percent a year.

We can use the Rule of 70 to answer other questions about economic growth. For example, in 2000, U.S. real GDP per person was approximately 8 times that of China. China's recent growth rate of real GDP per person was 7 percent a year. If this growth rate were maintained, how long would it take China's real GDP per person to reach that of the United States in 2000? The answer, provided by the Rule of 70, is 30 years. China's real GDP per person doubles in 10 years (70 divided by 7). It doubles again to 4 times its current level in another 10 years. And it doubles yet again to 8 times its current level in another 10 years. So after 30 years of growth at 7 percent a year, China's real GDP per person is 8 times its current level and equals that of the United States in 2000. Of course, after 30 years, U.S. real GDP per person would have increased, so China would still not have caught up to the United States.

## Review Quiz

1. What is economic growth and how do we calculate its rate?
2. What is the relationship between the growth rate of real GDP and the growth rate of real GDP per person?
3. Use the Rule of 70 to calculate the growth rate that leads to a doubling of real GDP per person in 20 years.

myeconlab Work Study Plan 6.1 and get instant feedback.

## Economic Growth Trends

You have just seen the power of economic growth to increase incomes. At a 1 percent growth rate, it takes a human life span to double the standard of living. But at a 7 percent growth rate, the standard of living doubles every decade. How fast is our economy growing? How fast are other economies growing? Are poor countries catching up to rich ones, or do the gaps between the rich and poor persist or even widen? Let's answer these questions.

### Growth in the U.S. Economy

Figure 6.2 shows real GDP per person in the United States for the hundred years from 1908 to 2008. The red line is actual real GDP and the black line is the trend in potential GDP. It is the trend that tells us about economic growth. The fluctuations around the trend tell us about the business cycle.

Two extraordinary events dominate the graph: the Great Depression of the 1930s, when growth stopped for a decade, and World War II of the 1940s when growth briefly exploded.

For the century as a whole, the average growth rate was 2 percent a year. But the growth rate has not remained constant. From 1908 to the onset of the Great Depression in 1929, the average growth rate was a bit lower than the century average at 1.6 percent a year. Between 1930 and 1950, averaging out the Great Depression and World War II, the growth rate was 2.2 percent a year. After World War II, the growth rate started out at 2 percent a year. It then increased and growth averaged 3 percent a year during the 1960s. In 1973, and lasting for a decade, the growth rate slowed. Growth picked up somewhat during the 1980s and even more during the 1990s dot-com expansion. But the growth rate never returned to the pace achieved during the fast-growing 1960s.

A major goal of this chapter is to explain why our economy grows and why the growth rate changes. Another goal is to explain variations in the economic growth rate across countries. Let's now look at some of these growth rates.

**FIGURE 6.2** A Hundred Years of Economic Growth in the United States

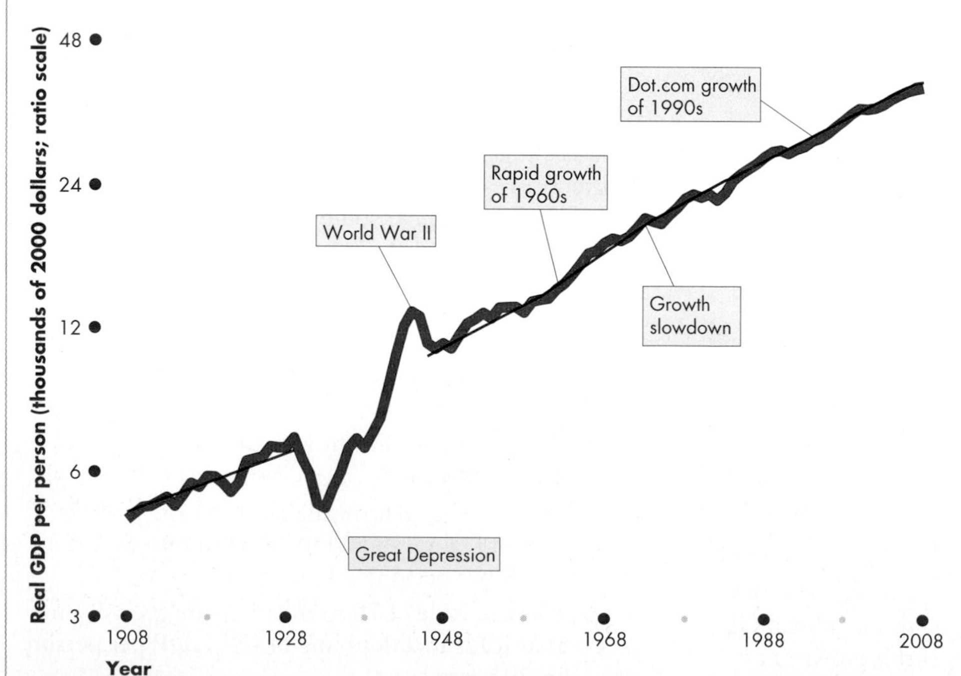


During the 100 years from 1908 to 2008, real GDP per person in the United States grew by 2 percent a year, on average. The growth rate was greater after World War II than it was before the Great Depression. Growth was most rapid during the 1960s. It slowed during the 1970s and speeded up again during the 1980s and 1990s, but it never returned to its 1960s' rate.

*Sources of data*: GDP (GNP) 1908–1928, Christina D. Romer, "World War I and the Postwar Depression: A Reinterpretation Based on Alternative Estimates of GNP," *Journal of Monetary Economics*, 22, 1988; 1929–2008, Bureau of Economic Analysis. Population, Census Bureau.

myeconlab animation

## Real GDP Growth in the World Economy

Figure 6.3 shows real GDP per person in the United States and in other countries between 1960 and 2008. Part (a) looks at the seven richest countries—known as the G7 nations. Among these nations, the United States has the highest real GDP per person. In 2008, Canada had the second-highest real GDP per person, ahead of Japan and France, Germany, Italy, and the United Kingdom (collectively the Europe Big 4).

During the forty-eight years shown here, the gaps between the United States, Canada, and the Europe Big 4 have been almost constant. But starting from a long way below, Japan grew fastest. It caught up to Europe in 1982 and to Canada in 1990. But during the 1990s, Japan's economy stagnated.

Many other countries are growing more slowly than, and falling farther behind, the United States. Figure 6.3(b) looks at some of these countries.

Real GDP per person in Central and South America was 29 percent of the U.S. level in 1960. It grew more quickly than the United States and reached 33 percent of the U.S. level by 1975, but then growth slowed and by 2008, real GDP per person in these countries was 29 percent of the U.S. level again.

In Central and Eastern Europe (former Communist countries), real GDP per person has grown more slowly than anywhere except Africa, and has fallen from 29 percent of the U.S. level in 1980 to 22 percent in 2008.

Real GDP per person in Africa, the world's poorest continent, has fallen from 10 percent of the U.S. level in 1960 to 5 percent in 2008.

**FIGURE 6.3** Economic Growth Around the World: Catch-Up or Not?

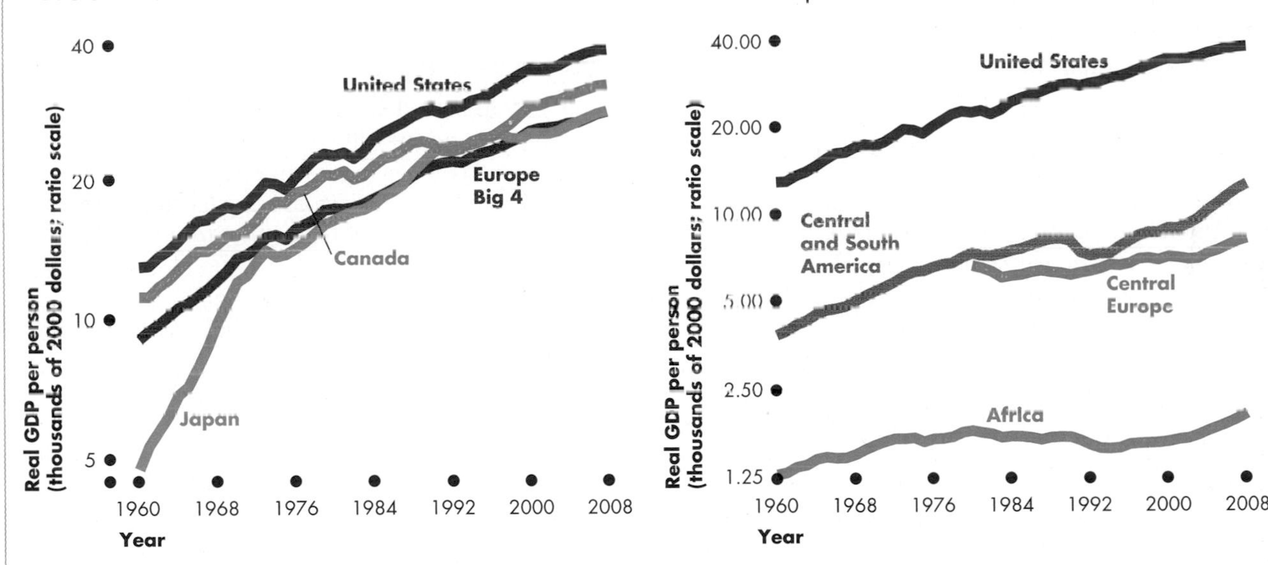


**(a) Catch-up?**

Real GDP per person has grown throughout the world. Among the rich industrial countries in part (a), real GDP per person has grown slightly faster in the United States than in Canada and the four big countries of Europe (France, Germany, Italy, and the United Kingdom). Japan had the fastest growth rate before 1973 but then growth slowed and Japan's economy stagnated during the 1990s.

**(b) No catch-up?**

Among a wider range of countries shown in part (b), growth rates have been lower than that of the United States. The gaps between the real GDP per person in the United States and in these countries have widened. The gap between the real GDP per person in the United States and Africa has widened by a large amount.

*Sources of data*: (1960–2004) Alan Heston, Robert Summers, and Bettina Aten, Penn World Table Version 6.2, Center for International Comparisons at the University of Pennsylvania (CICUP), September 2006; and (2005–2008) International Monetary Fund, *World Economic Outlook*, April 2008.

myeconlab animation

## Catch-Up in Asia

### Fast Trains on the Same Track

Five Asian economies, Hong Kong, Korea, Singapore, Taiwan, and China, have experienced spectacular growth, which you can see in the figure. During the 1960s, real GDP per person in these economies ranged from 2 to 22 percent of that in the United States. But by 2008, real GDP per person in Singapore surpassed that of the United States and that of Hong Kong was only a short distance behind.

The figure also shows that China is catching up but from a long way behind. China's real GDP per person increased from 2 percent of the U.S. level in 1960 to 12.5 percent in 2008.

The Asian economies shown here are like fast trains running on the same track at similar speeds and with a roughly constant gap between them. Singapore and Hong Kong are hooked together as the lead train, which runs about 15 years in front of Taiwan and Korea and about 40 years in front of the rest of China, which is the last train.

Real GDP per person in Korea in 2008 was similar to that in Hong Kong in 1988, and real GDP in China in 2008 was similar to that of Hong Kong in 1968. Between 1968 and 2008, Hong Kong transformed itself from a poor developing economy into one of the richest economies in the world.

The rest of China is now doing what Hong Kong has done. China has a population 200 times that of Hong Kong and more than 4 times that of the United States. So if China continues its rapid growth, the world economy will change dramatically.

As these fast-growing Asian economies catch up with the United States, we can expect their growth rates to slow. But it will be surprising if China's growth rate slows much before it has closed the gap on the United States.

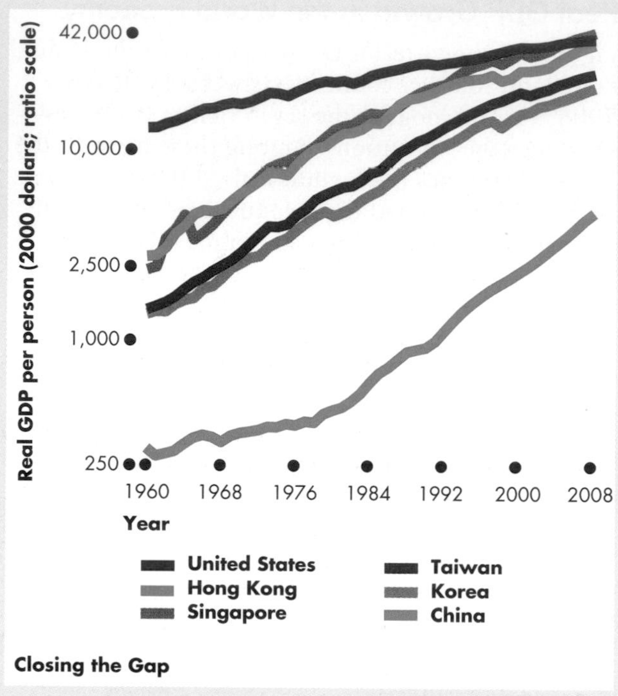


**Closing the Gap**

Even modest differences in economic growth rates sustained over a number of years bring enormous differences in the standard of living. And some of the differences that you've just seen are enormous. So the facts about economic growth in the United States and around the world raise some big questions.

What are the preconditions for economic growth? What sustains economic growth once it gets going? How can we identify the sources of economic growth and measure the contribution that each source makes? What can we do to increase the sustainable rate of economic growth?

We're now going to address these questions and discover the causes of economic growth. We start by seeing how potential GDP is determined and what makes it grow. We'll discover that labor productivity growth is the key to rising living standards and go on to explore the sources of this growth.

## Review Quiz

1. What has been the average growth rate of U.S. real GDP per person over the past 100 years? In which periods was growth the most rapid and in which periods was it the slowest?
2. Describe the gaps between real GDP per person in the United States and in other countries. For which countries is the gap narrowing? For which is it widening? And for which is it remaining the same?
3. Compare the growth rates and levels of real GDP per person in Hong Kong, Korea, Singapore, Taiwan, China, and the United States. How far is China's real GDP per person behind that of the other Asian economies?

myeconlab Work Study Plan 6.2 and get instant feedback.

## How Potential GDP Grows

Economic growth occurs when real GDP increases. But a one-shot rise in real GDP or a recovery from recession isn't economic growth. Economic growth is a sustained, year-after-year increase in *potential GDP*.

We'll begin our study of the process of economic growth by looking at potential GDP. We'll see how it is determined and what forces make it grow.

### How Potential GDP is Determined

Labor, capital, land, and entrepreneurship produce real GDP, and the productivity of the factors of production determines the quantity of real GDP that can be produced.

The quantity of land is fixed and on any given day, the quantities of entrepreneurial ability and capital are also fixed and their productivities are given. The quantity of labor employed is the only *variable* factor of production. Potential GDP is the level of real GDP when the quantity of labor employed is the full-employment quantity.

To determine potential GDP, we use a model with two components:

- The aggregate production function
- The aggregate labor market

**The Aggregate Production Function** When you studied the limits to production in Chapter 2 (see p. 32), you learned that the *production possibilities frontier* is the boundary between the combinations of goods and services that can be produced and those that cannot. Let's think about the production possibilities frontier for two "goods": real GDP and the quantity of leisure time.

Think of real GDP as a number of big shopping carts. Each cart contains some of each kind of different goods and services produced, and one cartload of items costs $1 trillion. To say that real GDP is $12 trillion means that you can think of real GDP as 12 very big shopping carts of goods and services.

The quantity of leisure time is the number of hours spent not working. Each leisure hour could have been spent working. If we spent all our time taking leisure, we would do no work and produce nothing. Real GDP would be zero. The more leisure we forgo, the greater is the quantity of labor and the greater is the quantity of real GDP produced.

But labor hours are not all equally productive. We use our most productive hours first and as more hours are worked less and less productive hours are used. So for each additional hour of leisure forgone (each additional hour of labor), real GDP increases but by successively smaller amounts.

The **aggregate production function** is the relationship that tell us how real GDP changes as the quantity of labor changes when all other influences on production remain the same. Figure 6.4 shows this relationship—the curve labeled *PF*. An increase in the quantity of labor (and a corresponding decrease in leisure hours) brings a movement along the production function and an increase in real GDP.

**The Aggregate Labor Market** The aggregate labor market determines the quantity of labor hours employed and the quantity of real GDP supplied. To see how the labor market works, we need to study the demand for labor, the supply of labor, and labor market equilibrium.

***The Demand for Labor*** The *demand for labor* is the relationship between the quantity of labor demanded and the real wage rate. The quantity of labor demanded is the number of labor hours hired by all the firms in the economy during a given period. This

**FIGURE 6.4** The Aggregate Production Function

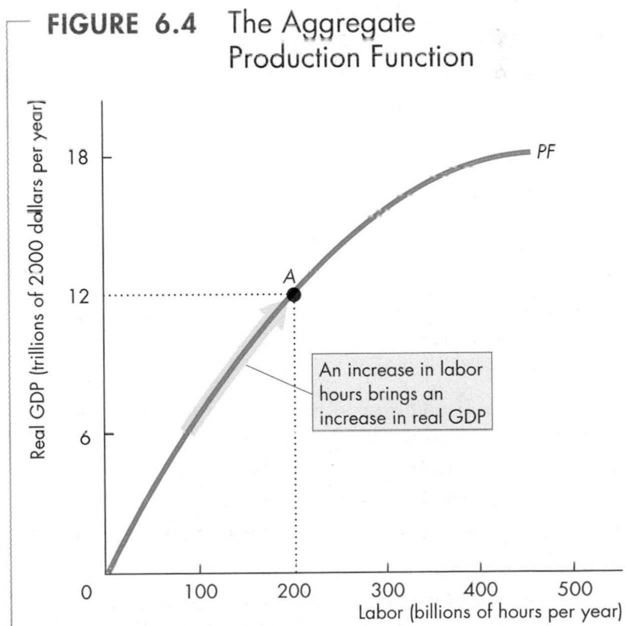


At point *A* on the aggregate production function *PF*, 200 billion hours of labor produce $12 trillion of real GDP.

myeconlab animation

quantity depends on the price of labor, which is the real wage rate.

The **real wage rate** is the money wage rate divided by the price level. The real wage rate is the quantity of goods and services that an hour of labor earns. It contrasts with the money wage rate, which is the number of dollars that an hour of labor earns.

The *real* wage rate influences the quantity of labor demanded because what matters to firms is not the number of dollars they pay (money wage rate) but how much output they must sell to earn those dollars.

The quantity of labor demanded *increases* as the real wage rate *decreases*—the demand for labor curve slopes downward. Why? The answer lies in the shape of the production function.

You've seen that along the production function, each additional hour of labor increases real GDP by successively smaller amounts. This tendency has a name: the *law of diminishing returns.* Because of diminishing returns, firms will hire more labor only if the real wage rate falls to match the fall in the extra output produced by that labor.

***The Supply of Labor*** The *supply of labor* is the relationship between the quantity of labor supplied and the real wage rate. The quantity of labor supplied is the number of labor hours that all the households in the economy plan to work during a given period. This quantity depends on the real wage rate.

The *real* wage rate influences the quantity of labor supplied because what matters to households is not the number of dollars they earn (money wage rate) but what they can buy with those dollars.

The quantity of labor supplied *increases* as the real wage rate *increases*—the supply of labor curve slopes upward. At a higher real wage rate, more people choose to work and more people choose to work longer hours if they can earn more per hour.

***Labor Market Equilibrium*** The price of labor is the real wage rate. The forces of supply and demand operate in labor markets just as they do in the markets for goods and services to eliminate a shortage or a surplus. But a shortage or a surplus of labor brings only a gradual change in the real wage rate. If there is a shortage of labor, the real wage rate rises to eliminate it; and if there is a surplus of labor, the real wage rate eventually falls to eliminate it. When there is neither a shortage nor a surplus, the labor market is in equilibrium—a full-employment equilibrium.

**FIGURE 6.5** Labor Market Equilibrium

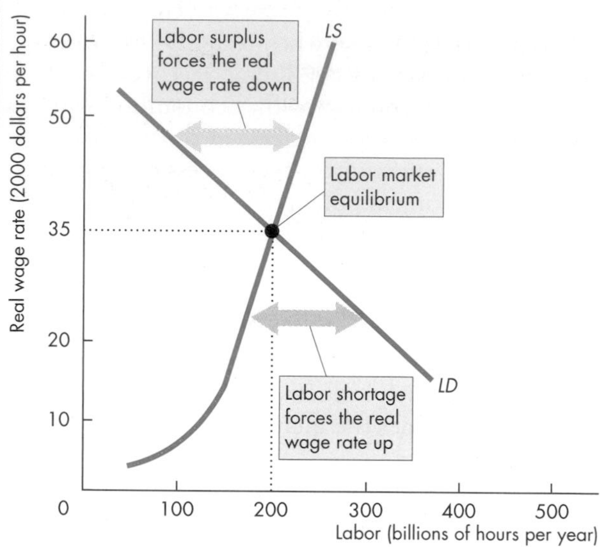


Labor market equilibrium occurs when the quantity of labor demanded equals the quantity of labor supplied. The equilibrium real wage rate is $35 an hour, and equilibrium employment is 200 billion hours per year.

At a wage rate above $35 an hour, there is a surplus of labor and the real wage rate falls to eliminate the surplus. At a wage rate below $35 an hour, there is a shortage of labor and the real wage rate rises to eliminate the shortage.

Figure 6.5 illustrates labor market equilibrium. The demand for labor curve is *LD* and the supply of labor curve *LS*. This labor market is in equilibrium at a real wage rate of $35 an hour and 200 billion hours a year are employed.

If the real wage rate exceeds $35 an hour, the quantity of labor supplied exceeds the quantity demanded and there is a surplus of labor. When there is a surplus of labor, the real wage rate falls toward the equilibrium real wage rate where the surplus is eliminated.

If the real wage rate is less than $35 an hour, the quantity of labor demanded exceeds the quantity supplied and there is a shortage of labor. When there is a shortage of labor, the real wage rate rises toward the equilibrium real wage rate where the shortage is eliminated.

If the real wage rate is $35 an hour, the quantity of labor demanded equals the quantity supplied and there is neither a shortage nor a surplus of labor. In this situation, there is no pressure in either direction on the real wage rate. So the real wage rate remains constant and the market is in equilibrium. At this equilibrium real wage rate and level of employment, the economy is at *full employment.*

**Potential GDP** You've seen that the production function tells us the quantity of real GDP that a given amount of labor can produce—see Fig. 6.4. The quantity of real GDP produced increases as the quantity of labor increases. At the equilibrium quantity of labor, the economy is at full employment, and the quantity of real GDP at full employment is potential GDP. So the full-employment quantity of labor produces potential GDP.

Figure 6.6 illustrates the determination of potential GDP. Part (a) shows labor market equilibrium. At the equilibrium real wage rate, equilibrium employment is 200 billion hours. Part(b) shows the production function. With 200 billion hours of labor, the economy can produce a real GDP of $12 trillion. The amount is potential GDP.

## What Makes Potential GDP Grow?

We can divide all the forces that make potential GDP grow into two categories:

- Growth of the supply of labor
- Growth of labor productivity

**Growth of the Supply of Labor** When the supply of labor grows, the supply of labor curve shifts rightward. The quantity of labor at a given real wage rate increases.

The quantity of labor is the number of workers employed multiplied by average hours per worker; and the number employed equals the employment-to-population ratio multiplied by the working-age population (see Chapter 5, p. 110). So the quantity of labor changes as a result of changes in

1. Average hours per worker
2. The employment-to-population ratio
3. The working-age population

Average hours per worker have decreased as the workweek has become shorter and the employment-to-population ratio has increased as more women have entered the labor force. The combined effects of

**FIGURE 6.6** The Labor Market and Potential GDP

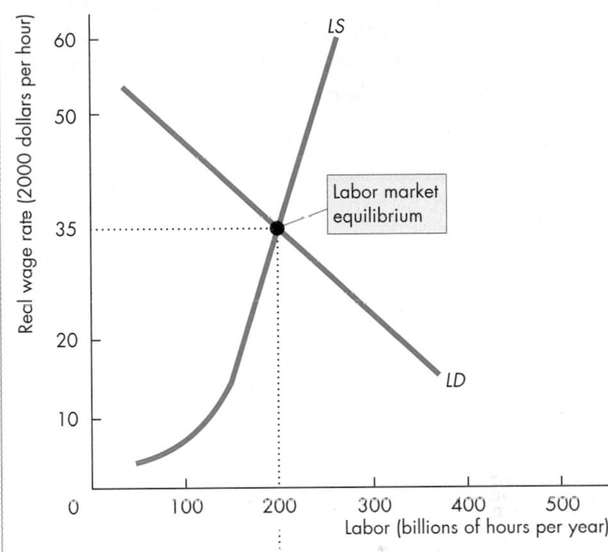


**(a) The labor market**

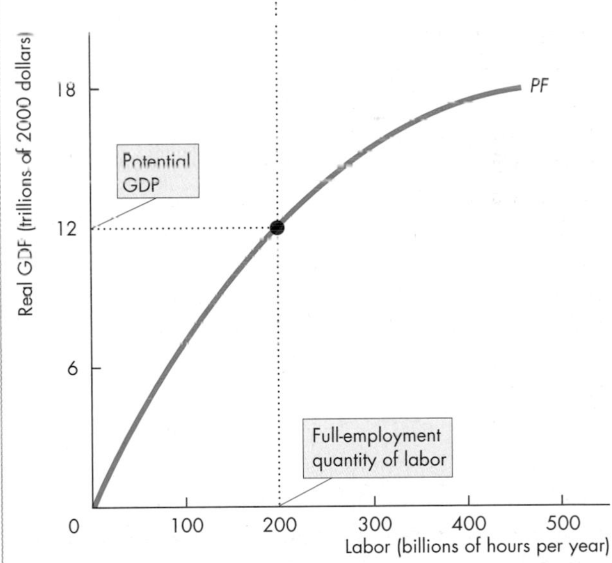


**(b) Potential GDP**

The economy is at full employment when the quantity of labor demanded equals the quantity of labor supplied, in part (a). The real wage rate is $35 an hour, and employment is 200 billion hours a year. Part (b) shows potential GDP. It is the quantity of real GDP determined by the production function at the full-employment quantity of labor.

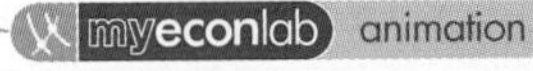

of these two factors have kept average hours per working-age person (approximately) constant.

Growth in the supply of labor has come from growth in the working-age population. In the long run, the working-age population grows at the same rate as the total population.

***The Effects of Population Growth*** Population growth brings growth in the supply of labor, but it does not change the demand for labor or the production function. The economy can produce more output by using more labor, but there is no change in the quantity of real GDP that a given quantity of labor can produce.

With an increase in the supply of labor and no change in the demand for labor, the real wage rate falls and the equilibrium quantity of labor increases. The increased quantity of labor produces more output and potential GDP increases.

***Illustrating the Effects of Population Growth*** Figure 6.7 illustrates the effects of an increase in the population. In Fig. 6.7(a), the demand for labor curve is $LD$ and initially the supply of labor curve is $LS_0$. The equilibrium real wage rate is \$35 an hour and the quantity of labor is 200 billion hours a year. In Fig. 6.7(b), the production function ($PF$) shows that with 200 billion hours of labor employed, potential GDP is \$12 trillion at point $A$.

An increase in the population increases the supply of labor and the supply of labor curve shifts rightward to $LS_1$. At a real wage rate of \$35 an hour, there is now a surplus of labor. So the real wage rate falls. In this example, the real wage rate will fall until it reaches \$25 an hour. At \$25 an hour, the quantity of labor demanded equals the quantity of labor supplied. The equilibrium quantity of labor increases to 300 billion a year.

Figure 6.7(b) shows the effect on real GDP. As the equilibrium quantity of labor increases from 200 billion to 300 billion hours, potential GDP increases along the production function from \$12 trillion to \$15 trillion at point $B$.

So an increase in the population increases the full-employment quantity of labor, increases potential GDP, and lowers the real wage rate. But the population increase *decreases* potential GDP per hour of labor. Initially, it was \$60 (\$12 trillion divided by 200 billion). With the population increase, potential GDP per hour of labor is \$50 (\$15 trillion divided by 300 billion). Diminishing returns are the source of the decrease in potential GDP per hour of labor.

**FIGURE 6.7** The Effects of an Increase in Population

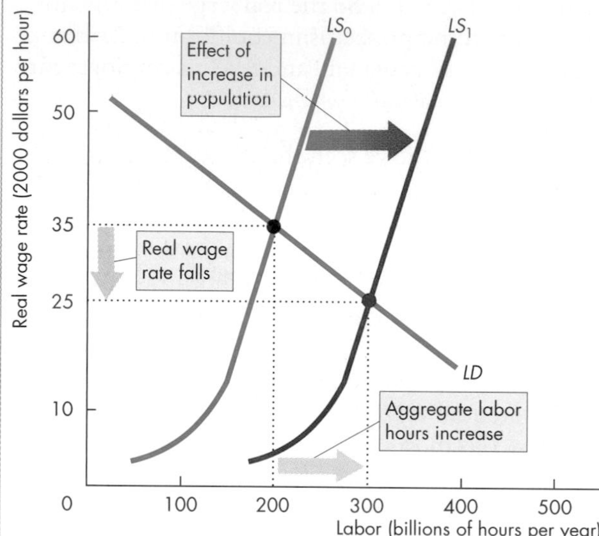


**(a) The labor market**

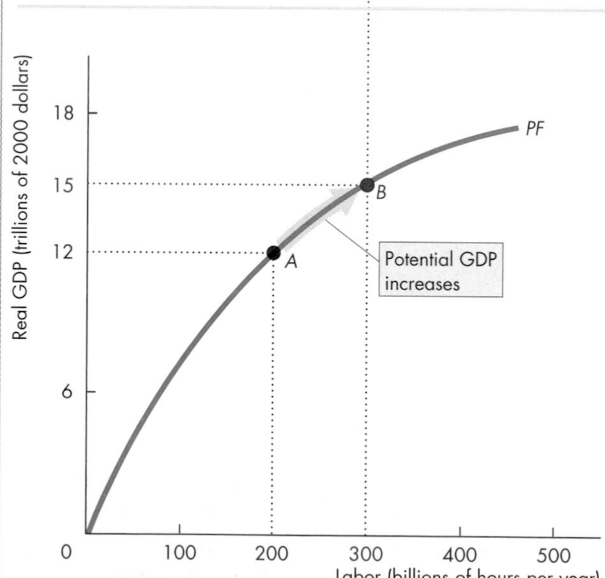


**(b) Potential GDP**

An increase in the population increases the supply of labor. In part (a), the supply of labor curve shifts rightward. The real wage rate falls and aggregate labor hours increase. In part (b), the increase in aggregate labor hours brings an increase in potential GDP. But diminishing returns bring a decrease in potential GDP per hour of labor.

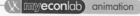

**Growth of Labor Productivity** **Labor productivity** is the quantity of real GDP produced by an hour of labor. It is calculated by dividing real GDP by aggregate labor hours. For example, if real GDP is \$12 trillion and aggregate hours are 200 billion, labor productivity is \$60 per hour.

When labor productivity grows, real GDP per person grows and brings a rising standard of living. Let's see how an increase in labor productivity changes potential GDP.

***Effects of an Increase in Labor Productivity*** If labor productivity increases, production possibilities expand. The quantity of real GDP that any given quantity of labor can produce increases. If labor is more productive, firms are willing to pay more for a given number of hours of labor so the demand for labor also increases.

With an increase in the demand for labor and *no change in the supply of labor*, the real wage rate rises and the quantity of labor supplied increases. The equilibrium quantity of labor also increases.

So an increase in labor productivity increases potential GDP for two reasons: Labor is more productive and more labor is employed.

***Illustrating the Effects of an Increase in Labor Productivity*** Figure 6.8 illustrates the effects of an increase in labor productivity.

In part (a), the production function initially is $PF_0$. With 200 billion hours of labor employed, potential GDP is \$12 trillion at point *A*.

In part (b), the demand for labor curve is $LD_0$ and the supply of labor curve is *LS*. The real wage rate is \$35 an hour, and the equilibrium quantity of labor is 200 billion hours a year.

Now labor productivity increases. In Fig. 6.8(a), the increase in labor productivity shifts the production function upward to $PF_1$. At each quantity of labor, more real GDP can be produced. For example, at 200 billion hours, the economy can now produce \$17 trillion of real GDP at point *B*.

In Fig. 6.8(b), the increase in labor productivity increases the demand for labor and the demand for labor curve shifts rightward to $LD_1$. At the initial real wage rate of \$35 an hour, there is now a shortage of labor. The real wage rate rises. In this example, the real wage rate will rise until it reaches \$45 an hour. At \$45 an hour, the quantity of labor demanded equals the quantity of labor supplied and the equilibrium quantity of labor is 225 billion a year.

**FIGURE 6.8** The Effects of an Increase in Labor Productivity

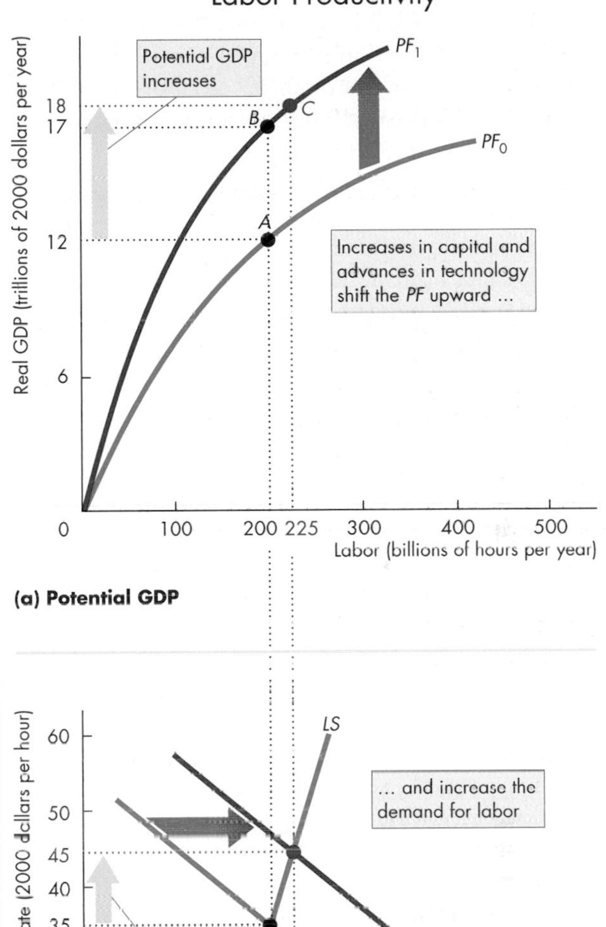


**(a) Potential GDP**

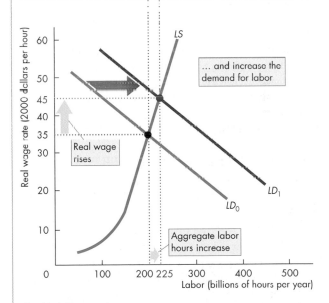

**(b) The labor market**

An increase in labor productivity shifts the production function upward from $PF_0$ to $PF_1$ in part (a) and shifts the demand for labor curve rightward from $LD_0$ to $LD_1$ in part (b). The real wage rate rises to \$45 an hour, and aggregate labor hours increase from 200 billion to 225 billion. Potential GDP increases from \$12 trillion to \$18 trillion.

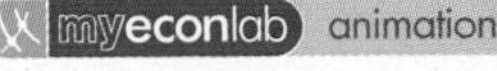

Figure 6.8(a) shows the effects of the increase in labor productivity on potential GDP. There are two effects. At the initial quantity of labor, real GDP increases to point *B* on the new production function. But as the equilibrium quantity of labor increases from 200 billion to 225 billion hours, potential GDP increases to $18 trillion at point *C*.

Potential GDP per hour of labor also increases. Initially, it was $60 ($12 trillion divided by 200 billion). With the increase in labor productivity, potential GDP per hour of labor is $80 ($18 trillion divided by 225 billion).

The increase in aggregate labor hours that you have just seen is a consequence of an increase in labor productivity. This increase in aggregate labor hours and labor productivity is an example of the interaction effects that economists seek to identify in their search for the ultimate *causes* of economic growth. In the case that we've just studied, aggregate labor hours increase but that increase is a *consequence*, not a cause, of the growth of potential GDP. The source of the increase in potential GDP is an increase in labor productivity.

Labor productivity is the key to increasing output per hour of labor and rising living standards. But what brings an increase in labor productivity? The next section answers this question.

## Review Quiz

1 What is the aggregate production function?
2 What determines the demand for labor, the supply of labor, and labor market equilibrium?
3 What determines potential GDP?
4 What are the two broad sources of potential GDP growth?
5 What are the effects of an increase in the population on potential GDP, the quantity of labor, the real wage rate, and potential GDP per hour of labor?
6 What are the effects of an increase in labor productivity on potential GDP, the quantity of labor, the real wage rate, and potential GDP per hour of labor?

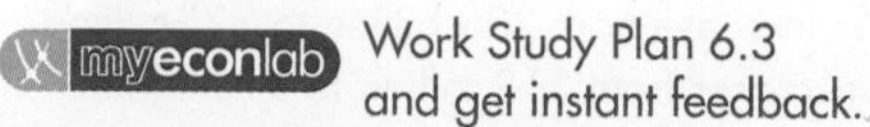

Work Study Plan 6.3 and get instant feedback.

## Why Labor Productivity Grows

You've seen that labor productivity growth makes potential GDP grow; and you've seen that labor productivity growth is essential if real GDP per person and the standard of living are to grow. But *why* does labor productivity grow? What are the preconditions that make labor productivity growth possible and what are the forces that make it grow? Why does labor productivity grow faster at some times and in some places than others?

### Preconditions for Labor Productivity Growth

The fundamental precondition for labor productivity growth is the *incentive* system created by firms, markets, property rights, and money. These four social institutions are the same as those described in Chapter 2 (see pp. 43–44) that enable people to gain by specializing and trading.

It was the presence of secure property rights in Britain in the middle 1700s that got the Industrial Revolution going. and it is their absence in some parts of Africa today that is keeping labor productivity stagnant.

With the preconditions for labor productivity growth in place, three things influence its pace:

- Physical capital growth
- Human capital growth
- Technological advances

### Physical Capital Growth

As the amount of capital per worker increases, labor productivity also increases. Production processes that use hand tools can create beautiful objects, but production methods that use large amounts of capital per worker are much more productive. The accumulation of capital on farms, in textile factories, in iron foundries and steel mills, in coal mines, on building sites, in chemical plants, in auto plants, in banks and insurance companies, and in shopping malls has added incredibly to labor productivity of our economy. The next time you see a movie that is set in the Old West or colonial times, look carefully at the small amount of capital around. Try to imagine how productive you would be in such circumstances compared with your productivity today.

## Human Capital Growth

Human capital—the accumulated skill and knowledge of human beings—is the most fundamental source of labor productivity growth. Human capital grows when a new discovery is made and it grows when more and more people learn how to use past discoveries.

The development of one of the most basic human skills—writing—was the source of some of the earliest major gains in productivity. The ability to keep written records made it possible to reap ever-larger gains from specialization and trade. Imagine how hard it would be to do any kind of business if all the accounts, invoices, and agreements existed only in people's memories.

Later, the development of mathematics laid the foundation for the eventual extension of knowledge about physical forces and chemical and biological processes. This base of scientific knowledge was the foundation for the technological advances of the Industrial Revolution and of today's information revolution.

But a lot of human capital that is extremely productive is much more humble. It takes the form of millions of individuals learning and becoming remarkably more productive by repetitively doing simple production tasks. One much-studied example of this type of human capital growth occurred in World War II. With no change in physical capital, thousands of workers and managers in U.S. shipyards learned from experience and accumulated human capital that more than doubled their productivity in less than two years.

## Technological Advances

The accumulation of physical capital and human capital have made a large contribution to labor productivity growth. But technological change—the discovery and the application of new technologies—has made an even greater contribution.

Labor is many times more productive today than it was a hundred years ago but not because we have more steam engines and more horse-drawn carriages per person. Rather, it is because we have transportation equipment that uses technologies that were unknown a hundred years ago and that are more productive than the old technologies were.

Technological advance arises from formal research and development programs and from informal trial and error, and it involves discovering new ways of getting more out of our resources.

To reap the benefits of technological change, capital must increase. Some of the most powerful and far-reaching fundamental technologies are embodied in human capital—for example, language, writing, and mathematics. But most technologies are embodied in physical capital. For example, to reap the benefits of the internal combustion engine, millions of horse-drawn carriages had to be replaced with automobiles; and to reap the benefits of digital music, millions of Discmans had to be replaced by iPods.

Figure 6.9 summarizes the sources of labor productivity growth and more broadly of real GDP growth. The figure also emphasizes that for real GDP per person to grow, real GDP growth must exceed the population growth rate.

**FIGURE 6.9** The Sources of Economic Growth

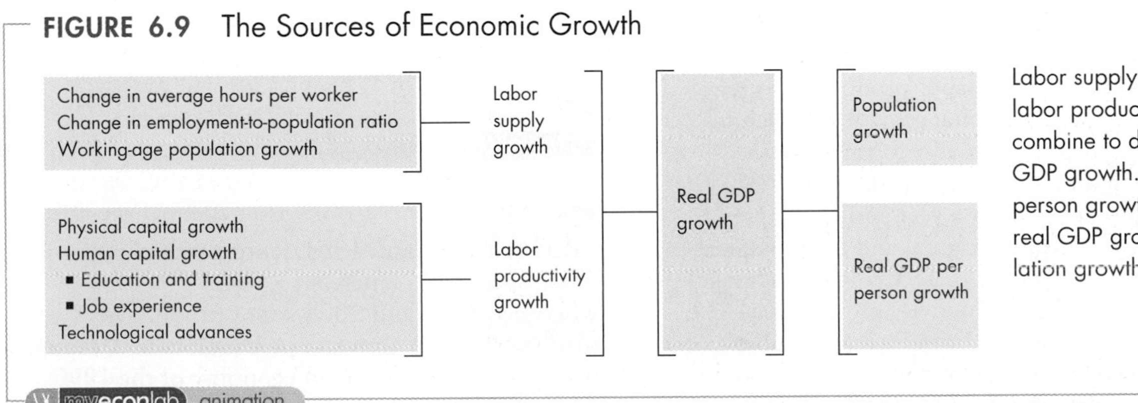


Labor supply growth and labor productivity growth combine to determine real GDP growth. Real GDP per person growth depends on real GDP growth and population growth.

## Growth Accounting

The accumulation of physical capital and human capital and the discovery of new technologies bring increased labor productivity. But how much does each source of labor productivity growth contribute? Edward F. Denison, an economist at the Brookings Institution, provided the answer by developing **growth accounting**, a tool that calculates the quantitative contribution to labor productivity growth of each of its sources. To make these calculations, we use the *one third rule*.

**The One Third Rule** Using data on capital, labor hours, and real GDP in the U.S. economy, Robert Solow of MIT estimated the effect of capital on labor productivity. In doing so, he discovered the **one third rule**, that on average, with no change in technology, a 1 percent increase in capital per hour of labor brings a 1/3 percent increase in labor productivity. We can use the one third rule to calculate the contributions of capital growth and technological change to the growth of labor productivity.

Suppose that capital per hour of labor grows by 3 percent a year and labor productivity grows by 2.5 percent a year. The one third rule tells us that capital growth contributed one third of 3 percent, which is 1 percent, to the growth of labor productivity. The rest of the 2.5 percent growth of labor productivity comes from technological change. That is, technological change contributed 1.5 percent, which is the 2.5 percent growth of labor productivity minus the estimated 1 percent contribution of capital growth.

**Accounting for the Productivity Growth Slowdown and Speedup** We can use the one third rule to measure the contributions to U.S. productivity growth. Figure 6.10 shows the results for the years 1960 through 2008.

Between 1960 and 1973, labor productivity grew by 3.7 percent a year and capital growth and technological change contributed equally to this growth.

Between 1973 and 1983, labor productivity growth slowed to 1.7 percent a year and a collapse of the contributions of human capital and technological change brought this slowdown. Technological change did not stop during the productivity growth slowdown. But its focus changed from increasing labor productivity to coping with energy price shocks and environmental protection. Real GDP per unit of energy used to produce it increased and slower labor productivity growth was its opportunity cost.

**FIGURE 6.10** Labor Productivity Growth

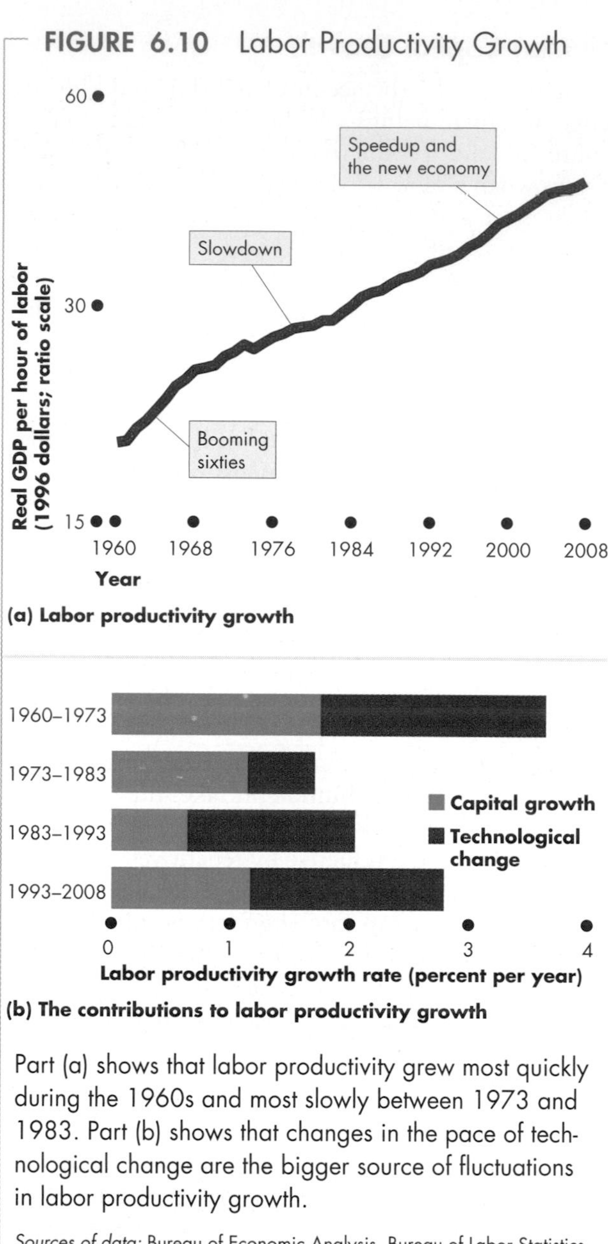


**(a) Labor productivity growth**

**(b) The contributions to labor productivity growth**

Part (a) shows that labor productivity grew most quickly during the 1960s and most slowly between 1973 and 1983. Part (b) shows that changes in the pace of technological change are the bigger source of fluctuations in labor productivity growth.

*Sources of data:* Bureau of Economic Analysis, Bureau of Labor Statistics, and author's calculations.

myeconlab animation

Between 1983 and 1993, labor productivity growth speeded to 2 percent a year.

Between 1993 and 2008, labor productivity growth speeded to almost 3 percent a year. Although growth in the new dot-com economy of the 1990s and 2000s was stronger than that of the 1970s, growth lagged a long way behind that of the booming sixties.

**Accounting for Faster Growth in Asia** You saw earlier in this chapter that some Asian economies are growing at much faster rates than the United States and other rich economies. Growth accounting can be used to quantify the sources of this more rapid growth. We don't have enough data to replicate the calculations that we have made for the United States, but we can use the general idea to see why these economies grow so fast.

Most fast-growing economies are starting from a long way behind the United States. In many industries in these economies, the technologies in use are not the latest and most productive. As a result, just by adopting more productive technologies that have already been developed elsewhere, these economies can grow faster than the rich economies.

In some cases, a developing economy can leapfrog over technologies still in use in developed economies. Telecommunication is a striking example. Developing economies are bypassing old technology land lines and installing cell phone networks.

To benefit from new technologies, developing economies must invest in new capital. The scale of investment influences how fast the new technologies spread. Table 6.1 shows some numbers. Most of the developing economies invest a larger percentage of their incomes in new capital than the United States invests. Because they invest such a large percentage of income, capital per hour of labor increases more rapidly, and so does labor productivity.

**TABLE 6.1** Investments in Six Economies

| Economy | Investment (percentage of GDP) |
|---|---|
| China | 28 |
| Hong Kong | 26 |
| Korea | 36 |
| Singapore | 44 |
| Taiwan | 19 |
| United States | 21 |

*Source of data*: (1960–2004) Alan Heston, Robert Summers, and Bettina Aten, Penn World Table Version 6.2, Center for International Comparisons at the University of Pennsylvania (CICUP), September 2006.

## Microloans Boost Growth

### Women Are the Better Borrowers

Microloans are very small loans made to poor, unemployed, potential entrepreneurs, who are often women. These people have no credit history that enables them to borrow from a bank.

Microloans originated in Bangladesh but have now spread throughout the developing world. They have become so successful that some regular banks are beginning to get into the business. These loans enable poor people to start a small business, employ a few people, and start to earn an income. As their incomes grow, they can pay off their microloan, and begin to save and accumulate more capital.

Kiva.org and MicroPlace.com (owned by eBay) are Web sites that enable people to lend money that is used to make microloans in developing economies.

Throughout the developing world, microloans are helping women to feed and clothe their families and to grow their small businesses, often in agriculture.

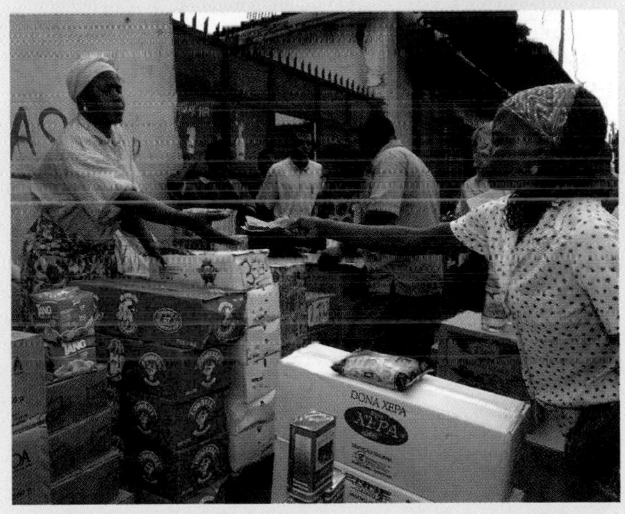

## Review Quiz

1. What are the preconditions for and sources of labor productivity growth?
2. What is the one third rule and how is it used?
3. What brought about the slower labor productivity growth between 1973 and 1983?

Work Study Plan 6.4 and get instant feedback.

## U.S. Economic Growth Since 1990

### Productivity Growth Outpaces Population Growth

We're going to look at the process that made U.S. real GDP grow between 1990 and 2008.

In 1990, employment was 210 billion labor hours, the real wage rate was $22 an hour, and real GDP and potential GDP were $7 trillion. (We are measuring in 2000 dollars.)

By 2008, labor hours had increased to 260 billion, the real wage rate had risen to $31 an hour, and real GDP and potential GDP had increased to $12 trillion (in 2000 dollars).

You can use the model that you've just studied to understand the process of growth that increased employment, the real wage rate, and potential GDP.

First, advances in technology and the investment in capital that brought us the Internet, the cell phone, MP3 audio, and MP4 video also brought us robots in factories and warehouses and more productive equipment in offices, shops, farms, and mines. As a result, labor productivity increased. And the increase in labor productivity was large—almost 50 percent. These same advances in technology and growth of capital increased the demand for labor.

Second, the population grew. In 1990, the working-age population was 190 million. By 2008, that number was 234 million—a 23 percent increase. This increase in the working-age population increased the supply of labor.

Because the percentage increase in labor productivity was much larger than the percentage increase in population, the combined effects of these changes increased employment, the real wage rate, and potential GDP.

The figures illustrate these outcomes. Figure 1 shows the U.S. production function in 1990 as $PF_{1990}$. Figure 2 shows the demand for labor in 1990 as $LD_{1990}$ and the supply of labor as $LS_{1990}$. In 1990, the equilibrium real wage rate was $22 an hour, and 210 billion hours of labor were employed. On the production function $PF_{1990}$, this equilibrium quantity of labor produced a potential GDP of $7 trillion.

By 2008, advances in technology and capital accumulation had increased labor productivity, which shifted the production function upward to $PF_{2008}$ and shifted the demand for labor curve to $LD_{2008}$. The increase in the working-age population had increased the supply of labor and shifted the supply of labor curve to $LS_{2008}$.

Because the percentage increase in labor productivity was much larger than the percentage increase in the working-age population, the demand for labor increased by more than the supply of labor. At the 2008 full-employment equilibrium, the real wage rate had increased to $31 an hour, employment had increased to 260 billion hours, and potential GDP had increased to $12 trillion.

The process described here is the source of rising living standards in the United States.

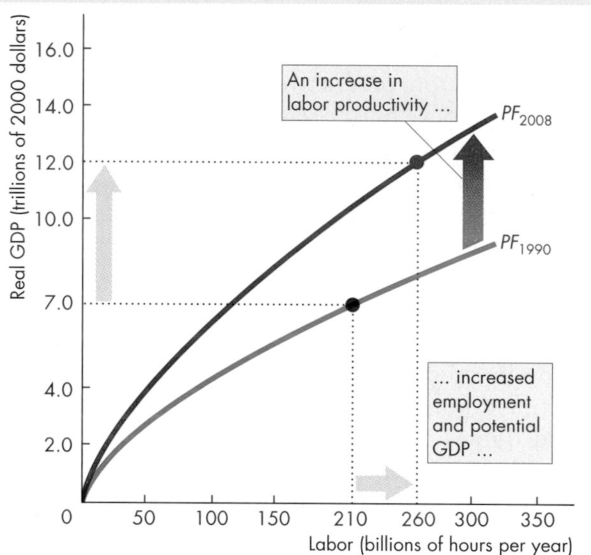


**Figure 1 U.S. Production Function**

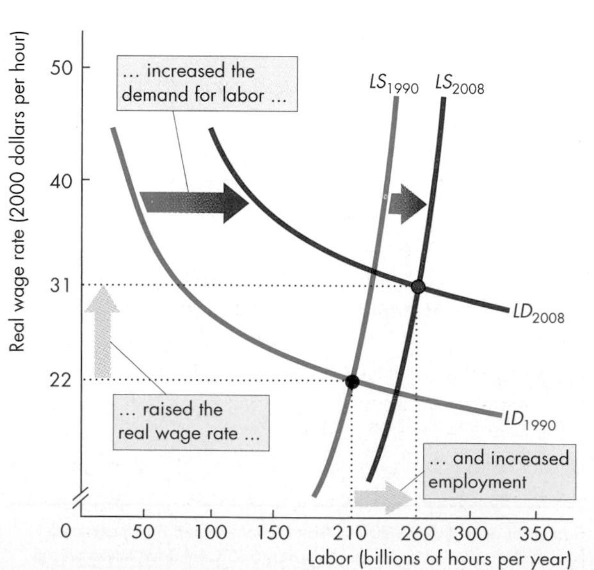


**Figure 2 U.S. Labor Market**

## Growth Theories and Policies

You've seen how population growth and labor productivity growth make potential GDP grow. You've also seen that the growth of physical capital and human capital and technological advances make labor productivity grow. How do all these factors interact? Growth theory addresses this question.

You're going to study three theories of economic growth, each of which gives some insights into the process of economic growth. But none provides a complete and definite answer to the basic questions: What causes economic growth and why do growth rates vary? Economics has some way to go before it can provide a definite answer to these questions. We study the three theories of growth:

- Classical growth theory
- Neoclassical growth theory
- New growth theory

### Classical Growth Theory

**Classical growth theory** is the view that the growth of real GDP per person is temporary and that when it rises above the subsistence level, a population explosion eventually brings it back to the subsistence level. Adam Smith, Thomas Robert Malthus, and David Ricardo—the leading economists of the late eighteenth century and early nineteenth century—proposed this theory, but the view is most closely associated with the name of Malthus and is sometimes called the *Malthusian theory*.

**Modern-Day Malthusians** Many people today are Malthusians. They say that if today's global population of 6.7 billion explodes to 11 billion by 2050 and perhaps 35 billion by 2300, we will run out of resources, real GDP per person will decline, and we will return to a primitive standard of living. We must act, say the Malthusians, to contain the population growth.

Modern-day Malthusians also point to global warming and climate change as reasons to believe that eventually, real GDP per person will decrease. Doomsday conditions, they believe, will arise as a direct consequence of today's economic growth and the vast and growing amounts of activity that are increasing the amount of carbon dioxide in Earth's atmosphere.

**Classical Theory of Population Growth** When the classical economists were developing their ideas about population growth, an unprecedented population explosion was under way. In Britain and other Western European countries, improvements in diet and hygiene had lowered the death rate while the birth rate remained high. For several decades, population growth was extremely rapid. After being stable for several centuries, the population of Britain increased by 40 percent between 1750 and 1800 and by a further 50 percent between 1800 and 1830. Meanwhile, an estimated 1 million people (about 20 percent of the 1750 population) left Britain for America and Australia before 1800, and outward migration continued on a similar scale through the nineteenth century. These facts are the empirical basis for the classical theory of population growth.

To explain the high rate of population growth, the classical economists used the idea of a **subsistence real wage rate**, which is the minimum real wage rate needed to maintain life. If the actual real wage rate is less than the subsistence real wage rate, some people cannot survive and the population decreases. In classical theory, when the real wage rate exceeds the subsistence real wage rate, the population grows. But an increasing population brings diminishing returns to labor, so labor productivity eventually decreases. This dismal implication led to economics being called the *dismal science*. The dismal implication is that no matter how much technological change occurs, the real wage rate is always pushed back toward the subsistence level.

The dismal conclusion of classical growth theory is a direct consequence of the assumption that the population explodes if real GDP per hour of labor exceeds the subsistence real wage rate. To avoid this conclusion, we need a different view of population growth. Neoclassical growth theory provides a different view.

### Neoclassical Growth Theory

**Neoclassical growth theory** is the proposition that real GDP per person grows because technological change induces an amount of saving and investment that makes capital per hour of labor grow. Growth ends only if technological change stops. Robert Solow of MIT suggested the most popular version of neoclassical growth theory in the 1950s.

Neoclassical growth theory's big break with its classical predecessor is its view about population growth.

**The Neoclassical Economics of Population Growth** The population explosion of eighteenth century Europe that created the classical theory of population eventually ended. The birth rate fell, and while the population continued to increase, its rate of increase became moderate. This slowdown in population growth seemed to make the classical theory less relevant. It also eventually led to the development of a modern economic theory of population growth.

The modern view is that although the population growth rate is influenced by economic factors, the influence is not a simple and mechanical one like that proposed by the classical economists. Key among the economic influences on population growth is the opportunity cost of a woman's time. As women's wage rates increase and their job opportunities expand, the opportunity cost of having children increases. Faced with a higher opportunity cost, families choose to have fewer children and the birth rate falls.

A second economic influence works on the death rate. The technological advance that brings increased labor productivity and increased incomes brings advances in health care that extends lives.

These two opposing economic forces influence the population growth rate. As incomes increase, both the birth rate and the death rate decrease. It turns out that these opposing forces almost offset each other, so the rate of population growth is independent of the economic growth rate.

This modern view of population growth and the historical trends that support it contradict the views of the classical economists. They also call into question the modern doomsday conclusion that the planet will one day be swamped with more people than it can support. Neoclassical growth theory adopts this modern view of population growth. Forces other than real GDP and its growth rate determine population growth.

**Technological Change** In neoclassical growth theory, the pace of technological change influences the economic growth rate but economic growth does not influence the pace of technological change. It is assumed that technological change results from chance. When we're lucky, we have rapid technological change, and when bad luck strikes, the pace of technological advance slows.

**The Basic Neoclassical Idea** To understand neoclassical growth theory, imagine the world of the mid-1950s, when Robert Solow is explaining his idea. Americans are enjoying post–World War II prosperity. Income per person is around $12,000 a year in today's money. The population is growing at about 1 percent a year. Saving and investment are about 18 percent of GDP, enough to keep the quantity of capital per hour of labor constant. Income per person is growing but not by much.

Then technology begins to advance at a more rapid pace across a range of activities. The transistor revolutionizes an emerging electronics industry. New plastics revolutionize the manufacture of household appliances. The interstate highway system revolutionizes road transportation. Jet airliners start to replace piston-engine airplanes and speed air transportation.

These technological advances bring new profit opportunities. Businesses expand, and new businesses are created to exploit the newly available profitable technologies. Investment and saving increase. The economy enjoys new levels of prosperity and growth. But will the prosperity last? And will the growth last? Neoclassical growth theory says that the *prosperity* will last but the *growth* will not last unless technology keeps advancing.

According to neoclassical growth theory, the prosperity will persist because there is no classical population growth to induce the wage rate to fall.

But growth will eventually stop if technology stops advancing, for two related reasons. First, the high profit rates that result from technological change bring increased saving and capital accumulation. But second, as more capital is accumulated, more and more projects are undertaken that have lower rates of return. The return on capital falls and the incentive to keep investing weakens. With weaker incentives to save and invest, saving decreases and the rate of capital accumulation slows.

**A Problem with Neoclassical Growth Theory** All economies have access to the same technologies, and capital is free to roam the globe, seeking the highest available real interest rate. Given these facts, neoclassical growth theory implies that growth rates and income levels per person around the world will converge. While there is some sign of convergence among the rich countries, as Fig. 6.3(a) shows, convergence is slow, and it does not appear to be imminent for all countries, as Fig. 6.3(b) shows.

New growth theory overcomes this shortcoming of neoclassical growth theory. It also explains what determines the pace of technological change.

## New Growth Theory

**New growth theory** holds that real GDP per person grows because of the choices people make in the pursuit of profit and that growth will persist indefinitely. Paul Romer of Stanford University developed this theory during the 1980s based on ideas of Joseph Schumpeter during the 1930s and 1940s.

The theory begins with two facts about market economies:

- Discoveries result from choices.
- Discoveries bring profit, and competition destroys profit.

**Discoveries and Choices** When people discover a new product or technique, they think of themselves as being lucky. They are right. But the pace at which new discoveries are made—and at which technology advances—is not determined by chance. It depends on how many people are looking for a new technology and how intensively they are looking.

**Discoveries and Profits** Profit is the spur to technological change. The forces of competition squeeze profits, so to increase profit, people constantly seek either lower-cost methods of production or new and better products for which people are willing to pay a higher price. Inventors can maintain a profit for several years by taking out a patent or a copyright, but eventually, a new discovery is copied, and profits disappear.

Two further facts play a key role in the new growth theory:

- Discoveries are a public capital good.
- Knowledge is capital that is not subject to the law of diminishing returns.

**Discoveries Are a Public Capital Good** Economists call a good a *public good* when no one can be excluded from using it and when one person's use does not prevent others from using it. National defense is one example of a public good. Knowledge is another.

In 1992, Marc Andreesen and his friend Eric Bina developed a browser they called Mosaic. This browser laid the foundation for today's Web browsers that have increased productivity by an unimaginably large amount.

While patents and copyrights protect the inventors or creators of new products and production processes and enable them to profit from their innovative ideas, once a new discovery has been made, everyone can benefit from its use. And one person's use of a new discovery does not prevent others from using it. Your use of a Web browser doesn't prevent someone else from using that same code simultaneously.

Because knowledge is a public good, as the benefits of a new discovery spread, free resources become available. These resources are free because nothing is given up when they are used. They have a zero opportunity cost. Knowledge is even more special because it is not subject to diminishing returns.

**Knowledge Capital Is Not Subject to Diminishing Returns** Production is subject to diminishing returns when one resource is fixed and the quantity of another resource changes. Adding labor to a fixed amount of capital or adding capital to a fixed amount of labor both bring diminishing marginal product—diminishing returns.

But increasing the stock of knowledge makes both labor and machines more productive. Knowledge capital does not bring diminishing returns.

The fact that knowledge capital does *not* experience diminishing returns is the central novel proposition of new growth theory. And the implication of this simple and appealing idea is astonishing. Unlike the other two theories, new growth theory has no growth-stopping mechanism. As physical capital accumulates, the return to capital—the real interest rate—falls. But the incentive to innovate and earn a higher profit becomes stronger. So innovation occurs, capital becomes more productive, the demand for capital increases, and the real interest rate rises again.

Labor productivity grows indefinitely as people discover new technologies that yield a higher real interest rate. This growth rate depends on people's ability to innovate.

Over the years, the ability to innovate has changed. The invention of language and writing (the two most basic human capital tools) and later the development of the scientific method and the establishment of universities and research institutions brought huge increases in the pace of innovation. Today, a deeper understanding of genes is bringing profit in a growing biotechnology industry. And advances in computer technology are creating an explosion of profit opportunities in a wide range of information-age industries.

**A Perpetual Motion Economy** New growth theory sees the economy as a perpetual motion machine, which Fig. 6.11 illustrates.

No matter how rich we become, our wants will always exceed our ability to satisfy them. We will always want a higher standard of living. In the pursuit of a higher standard of living, human societies have developed incentive systems—markets, property rights, and money—that enable people to profit from innovation. Innovation leads to the development of new and better techniques of production and new and better products. To take advantage of new techniques and to produce new products, new firms start up and old firms go out of business—firms are born and die. As old firms die and new firms are born, some jobs are destroyed and others are created. The new jobs created are better than the old ones and they pay higher real wage rates. Also, with higher wage rates and more productive techniques, leisure increases. New and better jobs and new and better products lead to more consumption goods and services and, combined with increased leisure, bring a higher standard of living.

But our insatiable wants are still there, so the process continues, going round and round a circle of wants, incentives, innovation, and new and better products, and a yet higher standard of living.

## New Growth Theory Versus Malthusian Theory

The contrast between the Malthusian theory and new growth theory couldn't be more sharp. Malthusians see the end of prosperity as we know it today and new growth theorists see unending plenty. The contrast becomes clearest by thinking about the differing views about population growth.

To a Malthusian, population growth is part of the problem. To a new growth theorist, population growth is part of the solution. People are the ultimate economic resource. A larger population brings forth more wants, but it also brings a greater amount of scientific discovery and technological advance. So rather than

**FIGURE 6.11** A Perpetual Motion Machine

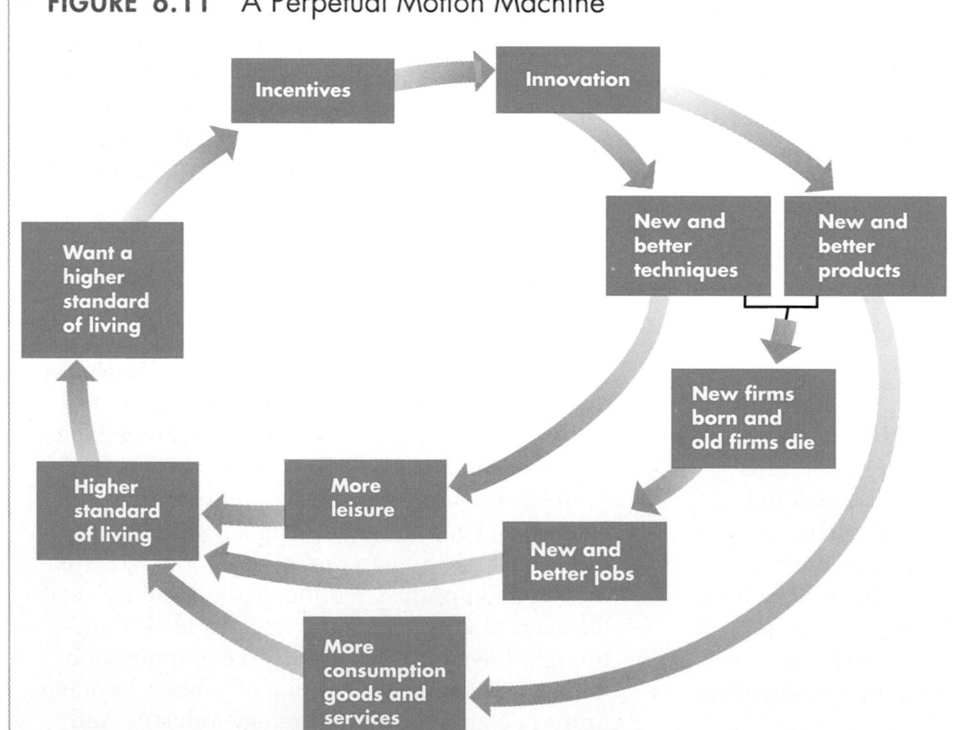


People want a higher standard of living and are spurred by profit incentives to make the innovations that lead to new and better techniques and new and better products. These new and better techniques and products, in turn, lead to the birth of new firms and the death of some old firms, new and better jobs, and more leisure and more consumption goods and services. The result is a higher standard of living. But people want a still higher standard of living, and the growth process continues.

*Source:* Based on a similar figure in *These Are the Good Old Days: A Report on U.S. Living Standards*, Federal Reserve Bank of Dallas 1993 Annual Report.

myeconlab animation

being the source of falling real GDP per person, population growth generates faster labor productivity growth and rising real GDP per person. Resources are limited, but the human imagination and ability to increase productivity are unlimited.

## Sorting Out the Theories

Which theory is correct? None of them tells us the whole story, but they all teach us something of value.

Classical growth theory reminds us that our physical resources are limited and that without advances in technology, we must eventually hit diminishing returns.

Neoclassical growth theory reaches the same conclusion but not because of a population explosion. Instead, it emphasizes diminishing returns to capital and reminds us that we cannot keep growth going just by accumulating physical capital. We must also advance technology and accumulate human capital. We must become more creative in our use of scarce resources.

New growth theory emphasizes the capacity of human resources to innovate at a pace that offsets diminishing returns. New growth theory fits the facts of today's world more closely than do either of the other two theories. But that doesn't make it correct.

## Achieving Faster Growth

Growth theory tells us that to achieve faster economic growth, we must increase the growth rate of physical capital, the pace of technological advance, or the growth rate of human capital.

The main suggestions for achieving these objectives are

- Stimulate saving
- Stimulate research and development
- Encourage international trade
- Improve the quality of education

**Stimulate Saving** Saving finances investment, which brings capital accumulation. So stimulating saving can increase economic growth. The East Asian economies have the highest growth rates and the highest saving rates. Some African economies have the lowest growth rates and the lowest saving rates.

Tax incentives can increase saving. Individual Retirement Accounts (IRAs) are a tax incentive to save. Economists claim that a tax on consumption rather than income provides the best saving incentive.

**Stimulate Research and Development** Everyone can use the fruits of *basic* research and development efforts. For example, all biotechnology firms can use advances in gene-splicing technology. Because basic inventions can be copied, the inventor's profit is limited and the market allocates too few resources to this activity.

Governments can direct public funds toward financing basic research, but this solution is not foolproof. It requires a mechanism for allocating the public funds to their highest-valued use. The National Science Foundation is one possibly efficient channel for allocating public funds to universities to finance and stimulate basic research.

**Encourage International Trade** Free international trade stimulates growth by extracting all the available gains from specialization and trade. The fastest-growing nations today are those with the fastest-growing exports and imports.

**Improve the Quality of Education** The free market produces too little education because it brings benefits beyond those valued by the people who receive the education. By funding basic education and by ensuring high standards in basic skills such as language, mathematics, and science, governments can contribute to a nation's growth potential. Education can also be stimulated and improved by using tax incentives to encourage improved private provision.

### Review Quiz

1. What is the key idea of classical growth theory that leads to the dismal outcome?
2. What, according to neoclassical growth theory, is the fundamental cause of economic growth?
3. What is the key proposition of new growth theory that makes economic growth persist?

Work Study Plan 6.5 and get instant feedback.

To complete your study of economic growth, take a look at *Reading Between the Lines* on pp. 154–155 and see how economic growth is transforming the economy of China.

READING BETWEEN THE LINES 

# Economic Growth in China

## China Industrial-Output Growth Is Slowest in 6 Years

http://www.bloomberg.com
September 12, 2008

China's industrial production grew at the slowest pace in six years on weaker export demand and factory shutdowns for the Olympics, increasing the likelihood the government will stimulate the economy.

Output rose 12.8 percent in August from a year earlier, the statistics bureau said today, after gaining 14.7 percent in July. That was less than the 14.5 percent median estimate of 22 economists surveyed by Bloomberg News. …

China's economic expansion slowed for a fourth quarter to 10.1 percent in the three months through June. Its growth remained the fastest of the world's 20 biggest economies. …

Power shortages are also restraining output. Aluminum Corp. of China Ltd. and 19 of its peers signed an accord in July to reduce production by as much as 10 percent until the end of the year to ease the shortages. Electricity output growth slowed in August for the fifth straight month to 5.1 percent. …

Still, the signs aren't all negative. Retail sales grew 23.2 percent last month, close to the fastest pace in nine years, the statistics bureau said today. While export growth slowed, the 21.1 percent increase was more than economists estimated.

Last month's industrial-output growth was the slowest since August 2002 after excluding the distortions in January and February each year caused by China's Lunar New Year holiday.



## Essence of the Story

- China's industrial production grew by 12.8 percent in the year to August 2008, its slowest pace since 2002.
- China's real GDP growth slowed to 10.1 percent in the second quarter—the fourth successive quarter of slower growth.
- China's real GDP growth is the fastest of the world's 20 biggest economies.
- Power shortages limited production.
- Retail sales grew 23.2 percent in August 2008, close to the fastest pace in nine years.
- Export growth slowed to 21.1 percent.

## Economic Analysis

- In 1978, under the leadership of Deng Xiaoping, China embarked on a program of economic reform.
- Gradually, state-owned monopolies were replaced by private competitive businesses, often financed with foreign capital and operated as joint ventures with foreign firms.
- By the early 1980s, China's real GDP was growing at one of the fastest rates in the world and the fastest ever known.
- In 2008, China's real GDP was more than $9 trillion (using U.S. dollars and PPP prices in 2000—see Chapter 21, p. 497).
- U.S. real GDP in 2008 was almost $12 trillion (2000 dollars).
- Although China's real GDP was not far behind U.S. real GDP in 2008, China used much more labor than the United States used.
- Aggregate labor hours in the United States in 2008 were about 250 billion.
- We don't know what China's aggregate labor hours were. But employment was 790 million and with an average workweek of 40 hours (an assumption), aggregate hours would be around 1,650 billion—more than 6 times the U.S. labor hours.
- So real GDP per hour of labor in China in 2008 was around $5 compared to about $48 in the United States.
- But China's real GDP is growing at about 10 percent a year. In contrast, U.S. real GDP is growing at about 2.5 percent a year.
- If these growth rates persist, China's real GDP will surpass that of the United States within the next decade.
- But China's real GDP per hour of labor will continue to lag well behind that of the United States.
- The figure shows the situation in China and the United States in 2008.

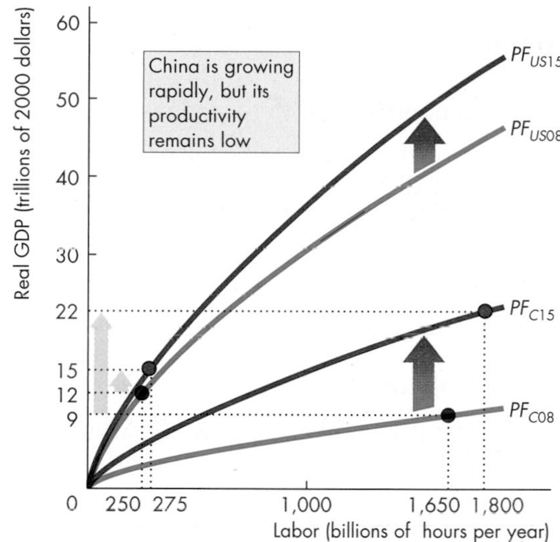


**Figure 1 Growth in China and the United States**

- The U.S. production function is $PF_{US08}$, and China's production function is $PF_{C08}$.
- With employment of 250 billion hours, the United States produces $12 trillion of real GDP, and with employment of 1,650 billion hours, China produces $9 trillion of real GDP.
- That is, an hour of labor in the United States produces around 10 times as much as an hour of labor in China produces.
- The figure also shows the situation in the United States and China in 2015 if current growth rates persist.
- The U.S. production function will be $PF_{US15}$, and China's production function will be $PF_{C15}$.
- With population growth at about 1 percent a year in both countries, labor hours will increase and so will real GDP.
- In 2015, China will be producing a larger real GDP than the United States but real GDP per hour of labor in China will still lag that in the United States.

## SUMMARY

### Key Points

#### The Basics of Economic Growth (pp. 134–135)

- Economic growth is the sustained expansion of production possibilities and is measured as the annual percentage rate of change of real GDP.
- The Rule of 70 tells us the number of years in which real GDP doubles—70 divided by the annual percentage growth rate.

#### Economic Growth Trends (pp. 136–138)

- Real GDP per person in the United States grows at an average rate of 2 percent a year. Growth was most rapid during the 1960s and the 1990s.
- The gap in real GDP per person between the United States and Central and South America has persisted. The gaps between the United States and Hong Kong, Korea, Taiwan, and China have narrowed. The gaps between the United States and Africa and Central Europe have widened.

#### How Potential GDP Grows (pp. 139–144)

- The aggregate production function and equilibrium in the aggregate labor market determine potential GDP.
- Potential GDP grows if the labor supply grows or if labor productivity grows.
- Only labor productivity growth makes real GDP per person and the standard of living grow.

#### Why Labor Productivity Grows (pp. 144–148)

- Labor productivity growth requires an incentive system created by firms, markets, property rights, and money.
- The sources of labor productivity growth are growth of physical capital and human capital and advances in technology.
- Growth accounting uses the one third rule to measure the contributions of capital accumulation and technological change to the growth of labor productivity.
- During the productivity growth slowdown of the 1970s, technological change did not stop growing but its focus changed to coping with energy price shocks and environmental protection.

#### Growth Theories and Policies (pp. 149–153)

- In classical theory, real GDP per person keeps returning to the subsistence level.
- In neoclassical growth theory, diminishing returns to capital limit economic growth.
- In new growth theory, economic growth persists indefinitely at a rate determined by decisions that lead to innovation and technological change.
- Policies for achieving faster growth include stimulating saving and research and development, encouraging international trade, and improving the quality of education.

### Key Figures



### Key Terms

## PROBLEMS and APPLICATIONS

Work problems 1–9 in Chapter 6 Study Plan and get instant feedback.
Work problems 10–19 as Homework, a Quiz, or a Test if assigned by your instructor.

1. Japan's real GDP was 561 trillion yen in 2007 and 569 trillion yen in 2008. Japan's population was 127.7 million in 2007 and 127.8 million in 2008. Calculate
   a. The economic growth rate.
   b. The growth rate of real GDP per person.
   c. The approximate number of years it takes for real GDP per person in Japan to double if the 2008 economic growth rate and population growth rate are maintained.
2. For three years, there was no technological change in Longland but capital per hour of labor increased from $10 to $20 to $30 and real GDP per hour of labor increased from $3.80 to $5.70 to $7.13. Then, in the fourth year, capital per hour of labor remained constant but real GDP per hour of labor increased to $10.
   a. Does Longland experience diminishing returns? Explain why or why not.
   b. Does Longland conform to the one third rule? If so, explain why. If not, explain why not and explain what rule, if any, it does conform to.
   c. Explain how you would do the growth accounting for Longland and calculate the effect of technological change on growth in the fourth year described above.
3. If the United States cracks down on illegal immigrants and returns millions of workers to their home countries, explain what happens to
   a. U.S. potential GDP.
   b. U.S. employment.
   c. The U.S. real wage rate.

   In the countries to which the immigrants return, explain what happens to
   d. Potential GDP.
   e. Employment.
   f. The real wage rate.
4. In the economy of Cape Despair, the subsistence real wage rate is $15 an hour. Whenever real GDP per hour rises above $15, the population grows, and whenever real GDP per hour of labor falls below this level, the population falls. The table shows Cape Despair's production function:

| Labor (billions of hours per year) | Real GDP (billions of 2000 dollars) |
|---|---|
| 0.5 | 8 |
| 1.0 | 15 |
| 1.5 | 21 |
| 2.0 | 26 |
| 2.5 | 30 |
| 3.0 | 33 |
| 3.5 | 35 |

   Initially, the population of Cape Despair is constant and real GDP per hour of labor is at the subsistence level of $15. Then a technological advance shifts the production function upward by 50 percent at each level of labor.
   a. What are the initial levels of real GDP and labor productivity?
   b. What happens to labor productivity immediately following the technological advance?
   c. What happens to the population growth rate following the technological advance?
   d. What are the eventual levels of real GDP and real GDP per hour of labor?
5. Explain the processes that will bring the growth of real GDP per person to a stop according to
   a. Classical growth theory.
   b. Neoclassical growth theory.
   c. New growth theory.
6. **U.S. Workers World's Most Productive**

   American workers stay longer in the office, at the factory, or on the farm than their counterparts in Europe and most other rich nations, and they produce more per person over the year. ... Productivity ... is found by dividing the country's gross domestic product by the number of people employed. ... Only part of the U.S. productivity growth, ... can be explained by the longer hours Americans are putting in. ... [The U.S.] also beats all 27 nations in the European Union, Japan, and Switzerland in the amount of wealth created per hour of work. ... The U.S. employee put in an average 1,804 hours of work in 2006 ... compared with 1,407.1 hours for the Norwegian worker and 1,564.4 for the French. It pales, however, in comparison with the annual hours worked per person in Asia, where seven economies—South Korea, Bangladesh, Sri Lanka, Hong Kong, China, Malaysia and Thailand—surpassed 2,200 average hours per worker. But those countries had lower productivity rates. …

*CBS News*, September 3, 2007

a. What is the difference between productivity in this article and per capita real GDP?
b. Identify and correct a confusion between levels and growth rates of productivity in the news article.
c. If workers in developing Asian economies work more hours than Americans, why are they not the world's most productive?

7. **You Have Seven Years to Learn Mandarin**

A recent study by the economist Angus Maddison projects that China will become the world's dominant economic superpower … in 2015. … If that happens, America will close out a 125-year run as the No. 1 economy. We assumed the title in 1890. … China was the largest economy for centuries because everyone had the same type of economy —subsistence— and so the country with the most people would be economically biggest. Then the Industrial Revolution sent the West on a more prosperous path. Now the world is returning to a common economy, this time technology-and information-based, so once again population triumphs.

*Fortune*, May 12, 2008

a. Why was China the world's largest economy until 1890?
b. Why did the United States surpass China in 1890 to become the world's largest economy?
c. Explain why China is predicted to become the world's largest economy again.
d. When China becomes the world's largest economy, does that mean that the standard of living in China will be higher than that in the United States? Explain.

8. **McCain Vows to Retool Training Programs**

John McCain … proposed updating the unemployment system and retooling training programs to help people who have lost their jobs—particularly older workers—adapt to a changing economy. "Change is hard, and while most of us gain, some industries, companies, and workers are forced to struggle with very difficult choices," the Republican presidential candidate said as he espoused free-market principles. … "But it is government's job to help workers get the education and training they need for the new jobs that will be created by new businesses in this new century," McCain added. … He said free people are the strongest economic force in the country. … [McCain] called for overhauling the unemployment insurance program so that it can retrain, relocate, and assist workers to find new jobs; replacing a half-dozen outmoded and redundant jobs programs with a single system; and drawing on the success of community colleges that he says does a better job than the federal government of giving workers [the] skills they need.

*The Washington Post*, October 9, 2007

a. Explain the rationale behind McCain's "free-market principles" and stance that "free people are the strongest economic force in the country."
b. Explain how the policies that McCain advocates can encourage greater growth in the changing U.S. economy.

9. **Aptera: Road Runner**

Steve Fambro was sick of people whizzing past him in the carpool lane, so he decided to do something about it. He set out to design a three-wheeled vehicle—technically a motorcycle—that would make it legal for him to drive alone in that lane and be cozy enough for daily commuting. While researching designs, he realized something important about fuel efficiency: It's all about aerodynamics. By tearing up the rule book, he found a shape that would nearly eliminate wind resistance, thereby reducing by two thirds the energy needed to move a car. With an infusion of $20 million from Idealab … Fambro's company, Aptera, is scheduled to begin production later this year. The vehicle gets an average of 300 miles per gallon. … Priced at around $30,000, Aptera's cars are already sold out.

*Fortune*, April 28, 2008

a. Explain which growth theory best describes the news article.
b. Use the model explained in this chapter to illustrate your answer in a.

10. If in 2008 China's real GDP is growing at 9 percent a year, its population is growing at 1 percent a year, and these growth rates continue, in what year will China's real GDP per person be twice what it is in 2008?
11. If a large increase in investment increases labor productivity, explain what happens to
    a. Potential GDP.
    b. Employment.
    c. The real wage rate.

    If a severe drought decreases labor productivity, explain what will happen to
    d. Potential GDP.
    e. Employment.
    f. The real wage rate.
12. **The New New World Order**

    "If you're a consumer sitting in Paris and you're ... watching TV, it looks like the world is coming to an end," says [international grocery store chain] Carrefour executive David Shriver. "But consumers in places like China and Brazil simply don't see it that way." Welcome to the new, precariously bipolar world. While gross domestic product growth is cooling a bit in emerging markets, the results are still tremendous compared with the U.S. and much of Western Europe. The 54 developing markets surveyed by Global Insight will post a 6.7% jump in real GDP this year, down from 7.5% last year. The 31 developed countries will grow an estimated 1.6%. The difference in growth rates represents the largest spread between developed and developing markets in the 37-year history of the survey.

    *Fortune*, July 14, 2008

    a. Explain the "bipolar world" that is revealed by recent economic growth rates.
    b. Do growth rates over the past few decades indicate that gaps in per capita real GDP around the world are shrinking, growing, or staying the same? Explain.
13. **Underinvesting in the Future**

    South Korea, Hong Kong, Taiwan, and Singapore have over 40 years averaged roughly the highest consistent economic growth rates in the world. ... But change the national accounting principles behind these rosy numbers and a different picture emerges, one that the societies concerned have barely begun to grapple with. In one vital respect these countries (soon to be joined by China) collectively may have the worst record of investment in the future since homo sapiens evolved: Investment in the next generation. They have the lowest fertility rates in the world. ... Economists forget that people as well as buildings depreciate at a roughly predictable rate. Child-rearing is at least as essential as building roads. Imagine if these four economies had invested less in infrastructure and ... more in people. ... They would not be facing a situation in which their workforces—unless replaced by immigrants—will decline dramatically within 20 years as the population over 65 continues to grow. The payback for years of what may well have been the misallocation of resources is not far in the future.

    *International Herald Tribune*, July 7, 2008

    a. Explain why the rapid growth rates of these Asian economies might be masking a "misallocation of resources" that will result in lower income per person in the future.
    b. Explain the difficulties in balancing goals for immediate economic growth and future economic growth.
14. **India's Economy Hits the Wall**

    Just six months ago, India was looking good. Annual growth was 9%, corporate profits were surging 20%, the stock market had risen 50% in 2007, consumer demand was huge, local companies were making ambitious international acquisitions, and foreign investment was growing. Nothing, it seemed, could stop the forward march of this Asian nation. But stop it has. ... The country is reeling from 11.4% inflation, large government deficits, and rising interest rates. Foreign investment in India's stock market is fleeing, the rupee is falling, and the stock market is down over 40% from the year's highs. Most economic forecasts expect growth to slow to 7%—a big drop for a country that needs to accelerate growth, not reduce it. ... India needs urgently to spend \$500 billion on new infrastructure and more on upgrading education and health-care facilities. ... A plan to build 30 Special Economic Zones is virtually suspended because New Delhi has not sorted out how to acquire the necessary land, a major issue in both urban and rural India, without a major social and political upheaval. Agriculture [is] ... technologically laggard ... [and] woefully unproductive.

Simple and nonpolitical reforms, like strengthening the legal system and adding more judges to the courtrooms, have been ignored. … A June 16 report by Goldman Sachs' Jim O'Neill and Tushar Poddar … urges India to improve governance, raise educational achievement, and control inflation. It also advises reining in profligate expenditures, liberalizing its financial markets, increasing agricultural productivity, and improving infrastructure, the environment, and energy use.

*BusinessWeek*, July 1, 2008

Explain five potential sources for faster economic growth in India suggested in this news clip.

15. **Makani Power: A Mighty Wind**

    Makani Power aims to generate energy from what are known as high-altitude wind-extraction technologies. And that's about all its 34-year-old Aussie founder, Saul Griffith, wants to say about it. … But Makani can't hide entirely, not when its marquee investor is Google.org, the tech company's philanthropic arm. Makani's plan is to capture that high-altitude wind … with a very old tool: kites. Harnessing higher-altitude wind, at least in theory, has greater potential than the existing wind industry … a thousand feet above ground, wind is stronger and more consistent.

    *Fortune*, April 28, 2008

    Explain which growth theory best describes the news article.

16. **The Productivity Watch**

    According to former Federal Reserve chairman Alan Greenspan, IT investments in the 1990s boosted productivity, which boosted corporate profits, which led to more IT investments, and so on, leading to a nirvana of high growth.

    *Fortune*, September 4, 2006

    Which of the growth theories that you've studied in this chapter best corresponds to the explanation given by Mr. Greenspan?

17. **Make Way for India—The Next China**

    … China … [is] growing at around 9 percent a year. … [China's] one-child policy will start to reduce the size of China's working population within the next 10 years. India, by contrast, will have an increasing working population for another generation at least.

    *The Independent*, March 1, 2006

    a. Given the expected population changes, do you think China or India will have the greater economic growth rate? Why?
    b. Would China's growth rate remain at 9 percent a year without the restriction on its population growth rate?
    c. India's population growth rate is 1.6 percent a year, and in 2005 its economic growth rate was 8 percent a year. China's population growth rate is 0.6 percent a year, and in 2005 its economic growth rate was 9 percent a year. In what year will real GDP per person double in each country?

18. Is faster economic growth always a good thing? Argue the case for faster growth and the case for slower growth. Then reach a conclusion on whether growth should be increased or slowed.

19. After studying *Reading Between the Lines* on pp. 154–155, answer the following questions:
    a. What was the growth rate of real GDP in China in the year ended August 2008?
    b. Is real GDP per hour of labor in China growing because labor productivity is increasing or only because the population is increasing? How would you determine the contribution of each factor?
    c. With the population growth in both countries at about 1 percent a year, is China narrowing the gap in real GDP per person between China and the United States?
    d. At the current rate of convergence in c, how long will it take for real GDP per person in China to equal that in the United States?

20. Use the link on MyEconLab (Chapter Resources, Chapter 6, Web links) to obtain data on real GDP per person for the United States, China, South Africa, and Mexico since 1960.
    a. Draw a graph of the data.
    b. Which country has the lowest real GDP per person and which has the highest?
    c. Which country has experienced the fastest growth rate since 1960 and which the slowest?
    d. Explain why the growth rates in these four countries are ranked in the order you have discovered.
    e. Return to the Web site and obtain data for any four other countries that interest you. Describe and explain the patterns that you find for these countries.

# 7 Finance, Saving, and Investment

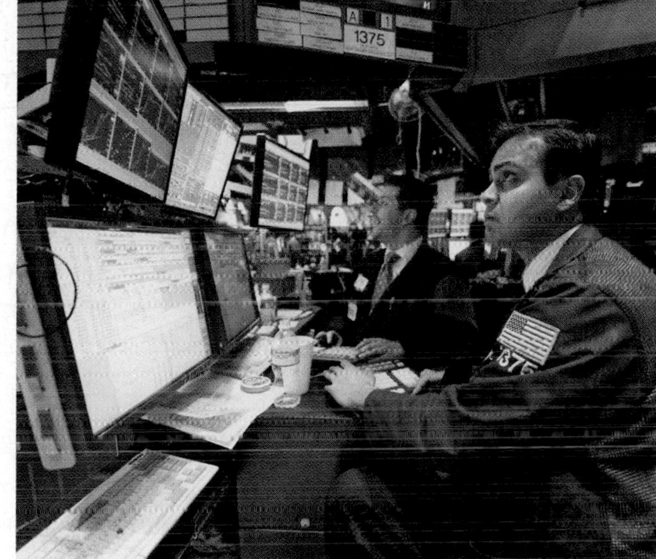


**After studying this chapter, you will be able to:**

- Describe and define the flows of funds through financial markets and the financial institutions
- Explain how investment and saving along with borrowing and lending decisions are made and how these decisions interact in the market for loanable funds
- Explain how a government deficit (or surplus) influences the real interest rate, saving, and investment in the market for loanable funds
- Explain how international borrowing or lending influences the real interest rate, saving, and investment in the global market for loanable funds

**During September 2008, Wall Street put** on a spectacular show. To prevent the collapse of Fannie Mae and Freddie Mac, the two largest lenders to home buyers, the U.S. government took over their risky debts. When Lehman Brothers, a venerable Wall Street investment bank, was on the verge of bankruptcy, secure phone lines and limousines worked overtime as the Federal Reserve Bank of New York, the U.S. Treasury, and senior officials of Bank of America and Barclays Bank (a British bank) tried to find ways to save the bank. The effort failed. On the same weekend, Bank of America bought Merrill Lynch, another big Wall Street investment bank. And a few days later, the U.S. government bought insurance giant AIG and tried to get Congress to provide $700 billion to buy just about every risky debt that anyone wanted to unload.

Behind such drama, Wall Street plays a crucial unseen role funneling funds from savers and lenders to investors and borrowers. This chapter explains how financial markets work and their place in the economy.

In *Reading Between the Lines* at the end of the chapter, we'll return to the events of September 2008 and apply what you've learned to better understand what was happening in those crucial days.

## Financial Institutions and Financial Markets

The financial institutions and markets that we study in this chapter play a crucial role in the economy. They provide the channels through which saving flows to finance the investment in new capital that makes the economy grow.

In studying the economics of financial institutions and markets, we distinguish between:

- Finance and money
- Physical capital and financial capital

### Finance and Money

In economics, we use the term *finance* to describe the activity of providing the funds that finance expenditures on capital. The study of finance looks at how households and firms obtain and use financial resources and how they cope with the risks that arise in this activity.

*Money* is what we use to pay for goods and services and factors of production and to make financial transactions. The study of money looks at how households and firms use it, how much of it they hold, how banks create and manage it, and how its quantity influences the economy.

In the economic lives of individuals and businesses, finance and money are closely interrelated. And some of the main financial institutions, such as banks, provide both financial services and monetary services. Nevertheless, by distinguishing between *finance* and *money* and studying them separately, we will better understand our financial and monetary markets and institutions.

For the rest of this chapter, we study finance. Money is the topic of the next chapter.

### Physical Capital and Financial Capital

Economists distinguish between physical capital and financial capital. *Physical capital* is the tools, instruments, machines, buildings, and other items that have been produced in the past and that are used today to produce goods and services. Inventories of raw materials, semifinished goods, and components are part of physical capital. When economists use the term capital, they mean *physical* capital. The funds that firms use to buy physical capital are called **financial capital**.

Along the *aggregate production function* in Chapter 6, the quantity of capital is fixed. An increase in the quantity of capital increases production possibilities and shifts the aggregate production function upward. You're going to see, in this chapter, how investment, saving, borrowing, and lending decisions influence the quantity of capital and make it grow, and as a consequence, make real GDP grow.

We begin by describing the links between capital and investment and between wealth and saving.

### Capital and Investment

The quantity of capital changes because of investment and depreciation. *Investment* (Chapter 4, p. 133) increases the quantity of capital and *depreciation* (Chapter 4, p. 140) decreases it. The total amount spent on new capital is called **gross investment**. The change in the value of capital is called **net investment**. Net investment equals gross investment minus depreciation.

Figure 7.1 illustrates these terms. On January 1, 2008, Ace Bottling Inc. had machines worth $30,000—Ace's initial capital. During 2008, the market value of Ace's machines fell by 67 percent—$20,000. After this depreciation, Ace's machines were valued at $10,000. During 2008, Ace spent $30,000 on new machines. This amount is Ace's gross investment. By December 31, 2008, Ace Bottling had capital valued at $40,000, so its capital had increased by $10,000. This amount is Ace's net investment. Ace's net investment equals its gross investment of $30,000 minus depreciation of its initial capital of $20,000.

### Wealth and Saving

**Wealth** is the value of all the things that people own. What people own is related to what they earn, but it is not the same thing. People earn an *income*, which is the amount they receive during a given time period from supplying the services of the resources they own. **Saving** is the amount of income that is not paid in taxes or spent on consumption goods and services. Saving increases wealth. Wealth also increases when the market value of assets rises—called *capital gains*—and decreases when the market value of assets falls—called *capital losses*.

For example, at the end of the school year you have $250 in the bank and a coin collection worth $300, so your wealth is $550. During the summer,

**FIGURE 7.1** Capital and Investment

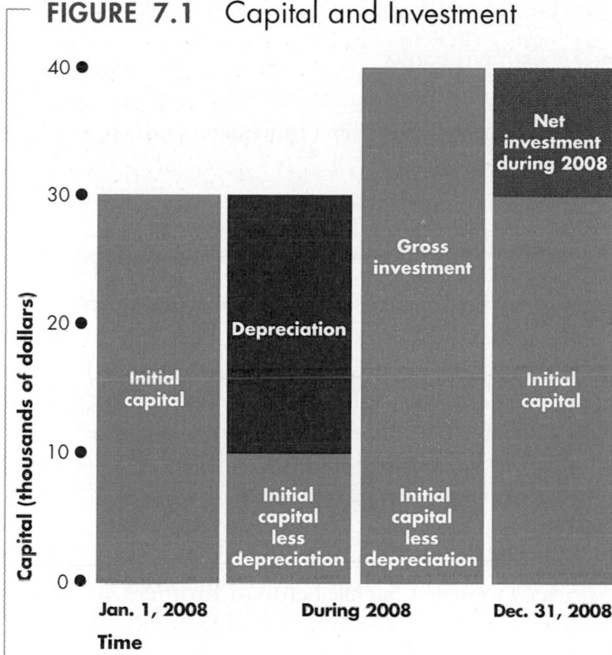


On January 1, 2008, Ace Bottling had capital worth $30,000. During the year, the value of Ace's capital fell by $20,000—depreciation and it spent $30,000 on new capital—gross investment. Ace's net investment was $10,000 ($30,000 gross investment minus $20,000 depreciation) so that at the end of 2008, Ace had capital worth $40,000.

myeconlab animation

you earn $5,000 (net of taxes) and spend $1,000 on consumption goods and services so your saving is $4,000. Your bank account increases to $4,250 and your wealth becomes $4,550. The $4,000 increase in wealth equals saving. If coins rise in value and your coin collection is now worth $500, you have a capital gain of $200, which is also added to your wealth.

National wealth and national saving work like this personal example. The wealth of a nation at the end of a year equals its wealth at the start of the year plus its saving during the year, which equals income minus consumption expenditure.

To make real GDP grow, saving and wealth must be transformed into investment and capital. This transformation takes place in the markets for financial capital and through the activities of financial institutions. We're now going to describe these markets and institutions.

## Markets for Financial Capital

Saving is the source of the funds that are used to finance investment, and these funds are supplied and demanded in three types of financial markets:

- Loan markets
- Bond markets
- Stock markets

**Loan Markets** Businesses often want short-term finance to buy inventories or to extend credit to their customers. Sometimes they get this finance in the form of a loan from a bank. Households often want finance to purchase big ticket items, such as automobiles or household furnishings and appliances. They get this finance as bank loans, often in the form of outstanding credit card balances.

Households also get finance to buy new homes. (Expenditure on new homes is counted as part of investment.) These funds are usually obtained as a loan that is secured by a **mortgage**—a legal contract that gives ownership of a home to the lender in the event that the borrower fails to meet the agreed loan payments (repayments and interest). Mortgage loans were at the center of the U.S. credit crisis of 2007–2008.

All of these types of financing take place in loan markets.

**Bond Markets** When Wal-Mart expands its business and opens new stores, it gets the finance it needs by selling bonds. Governments—federal, state, and municipal—also raise finance by issuing bonds.

A **bond** is a promise to make specified payments on specified dates. For example, you can buy a Wal-Mart bond that promises to pay $3.4375 every May and October until 2009 and then to make a final payment of $100 in October 2009.

The buyer of a bond from Wal-Mart makes a loan to the company and is entitled to the payments promised by the bond. When a person buys a newly issued bond, he or she may hold the bond until the borrower has repaid the amount borrowed or sell it to someone else. Bonds issued by firms and governments are traded in the **bond market.**

The term of a bond might be long (decades) or short (just a month or two). Firms often issue very short-term bonds as a way of getting paid for their sales before the buyer is able to pay. For example, when GM sells $100 million of railway locomotives to Union Pacific, GM wants to be paid when the items are shipped. But Union Pacific doesn't want to pay until the locomotives are earning an income. In this situation, Union Pacific might promise to pay GM $101 million three months in the future. A bank would be willing to buy this promise for (say) $100 million. GM gets $100 million immediately and the bank gets $101 million in three months when Union Pacific honors its promise. The U.S. Treasury issues promises of this type, called Treasury bills.

Another type of bond is a **mortgage-backed security**, which entitles its holder to the income from a package of mortgages. Mortgage lenders create mortgage-backed securities. They make mortgage loans to home buyers and then create securities that they sell to obtain more funds to make more mortgage loans. The holder of a mortgage-backed security is entitled to receive payments that derive from the payments received by the mortgage lender from the homebuyer–borrower.

Mortgage-backed securities were at the center of the storm in the financial markets in 2007–2008.

**Stock Markets** When Boeing wants finance to expand its airplane building business, it issues stock. A **stock** is a certificate of ownership and claim to the firm's profits. Boeing has issued about 900 million shares of its stock. So if you owned 900 Boeing shares, you would own one millionth of Boeing and be entitled to receive one millionth of its profits.

Unlike a stockholder, a bondholder does not own part the firm that issued the bond.

A **stock market** is a financial market in which shares of stocks of corporations are traded. The New York Stock Exchange, the London Stock Exchange (in England), the Frankfurt Stock Exchange (in Germany), and the Tokyo Stock Exchange (in Japan) are all examples of stock markets.

## Financial Institutions

Financial markets are highly competitive because of the role played by financial institutions in those markets. A **financial institution** is a firm that operates on both sides of the markets for financial capital. It is a borrower in one market and a lender in another.

Financial institutions also stand ready to trade so that households with funds to lend and firms or households seeking funds can always find someone on the other side of the market with whom to trade.

The key financial institutions are

- Investment banks
- Commercial banks
- Government-sponsored mortgage lenders
- Pension funds
- Insurance companies

**Investment Banks** Investment banks are firms that help other financial institutions and governments raise finance by issuing and selling bonds and stocks, as well as providing advice on transactions such as mergers and acquisitions. Until the late 1980s, the United States maintained a sharp separation between investment banking and commercial banking—a separation that was imposed by the *Glass-Steagall Act of 1933*.

Until 2008, five big Wall Street firms, Bear Stearns, Goldman Sachs, Lehman Brothers, Merrill Lynch, and Morgan Stanley, provided investment banking services. But in the financial meltdown of 2008, all of these firms disappeared and were absorbed into larger financial institutions that provide both investment banking and commercial banking services.

**Commercial Banks** The bank that you use for your own banking services and that issues your credit card is a commercial bank. We'll return to these banks and explain their role in Chapter 8 where we study the role of money in our economy.

**Government-Sponsored Mortgage Lenders** Two large financial institutions, the Federal National Mortgage Association, or Fannie Mae, and the Federal Home Loan Mortgage Corporation, or Freddie Mac, were government-sponsored enterprises that bought mortgages from banks, packaged them into mortgage-backed securities, and sold them. On September 7, 2008, Fannie Mae and Freddie Mac owned or guaranteed $6 trillion worth of mortgages (half of the U.S $12 trillion of mortgages) and were taken over by the federal government.

**Pension Funds** Pension funds are financial institutions that use the pension contributions of firms and workers to buy bonds and stocks. The mortgage-backed securities of Fannie Mae and Freddie Mac are among the assets of pension funds. Some pension funds are very large and play an active role in the firms whose stock they hold.

## Financial Failures

### The Institutions at the Center of the Storm

Bear Stearns: absorbed by JPMorgan Chase with help from the Federal Reserve. Lehman Brothers: gone. Fannie Mae and Freddie Mac: taken into government oversight with U.S. taxpayer guarantees. Merrill Lynch: absorbed by Bank of America. AIG: given an $85 billion lifeline by the Federal Reserve and sold off in parcels to financial institutions around the world. Wachovia: taken over by Wells Fargo. Washington Mutual: taken over by JPMorgan Chase. Morgan Stanley: 20 percent bought by Mitsubishi, a large Japanese bank. These are some of the events in the financial crisis of 2008. What is going on?

Between 2002 and 2005, mortgage lending exploded and home prices rose. Mortgage lenders bundled their loans into *mortgage-backed securities* and sold them to eager buyers around the world.

In 2006, interest rates began to rise and the values of financial assets fell. With lower asset values, financial institutions took big losses. Some losses of some institutions were too big to bear and these institutions became insolvent.

**Insurance Companies** Insurance companies provide risk-sharing services. They enter into agreements with households and firms to provide compensation in the event of accident, theft, fire, ill-health, and a host of other misfortunes. They receive premiums from their customers and make payments against claims.

Insurance companies use the funds they have received but not paid out as claims to buy bonds and stocks on which they earn an interest income.

Some insurance companies also insure bonds and other risky financial assets. In effect, they provide insurance that pays out if a firm fails and cannot meet its bond obligations. Some insurance companies insure other insurers in a complex network of reinsurance.

In normal times, insurance companies have a steady flow of funds coming in from premiums and interest on the financial assets they hold and a steady, but smaller, flow of funds paying claims. Their profit is the gap between the two flows. But in unusual times, when large and widespread losses are being incurred, insurance companies can run into difficulty in meeting their obligations. Such a situation arose in 2008 for one of the biggest insurers, AIG, and the firm was taken into public ownership.

## Insolvency and Illiquidity

A financial institution's **net worth** is the total market value of what it has lent minus the market value of what it has borrowed. If net worth is positive, the institution is *solvent* and can remain in business. But if net worth is negative, the institution is *insolvent* and goes out of business. The owners of an insolvent financial institution—usually its stockholders—bear the loss when the assets are sold and debts paid.

A financial institution both borrows and lends, so it is exposed to the risk that its net worth might become negative. To limit that risk, financial institutions are regulated and a minimum amount of their lending must be backed by their net worth.

Sometimes, a financial institution is solvent but illiquid. A firm is *illiquid* if it has made long-term loans with borrowed funds and is faced with a sudden demand to repay more of what it has borrowed than its available cash. In normal times, a financial institution that is illiquid can borrow from another institution. But if the all financial institutions are short of cash, the market for loans among financial institutions dries up.

Insolvency and illiquidity were at the core of the financial meltdown of 2007–2008.

## Interest Rates and Asset Prices

Stocks, bonds, short-term securities, and loans are collectively called *financial assets*. The interest rate on a financial asset is the interest received expressed as a percentage of the price of the asset.

Because the interest rate is a percentage of the price of an asset, if the asset price rises, other things remaining the same, the interest rate falls. Conversely, if the asset price falls, other things remaining the same, the interest rate rises.

To see this inverse relationship between an asset price and the interest rate, look at the example of a Microsoft share. In October 2008, the price of a Microsoft share was $26 and each share entitled its owner to 48 cents of Microsoft profit. The interest rate on a Microsoft share was

$$\text{Interest rate} = (\$0.48 \div \$26) \times 100 = 1.85 \text{ percent.}$$

If the price of a Microsoft share increased to $30 and each share still entitled its owner to 48 cents of Microsoft profit, the interest rate on a Microsoft share would become

$$\text{Interest rate} = (\$0.48 \div \$30) \times 100 = 1.6 \text{ percent.}$$

This relationship means that the price of an asset and the interest rate on that asset are determined simultaneously—one implies the other.

This relationship also means that if the interest rate on the asset rises, the price of the asset falls, debts become harder to pay, and the net worth of the financial institution falls. Insolvency can arise from previously unexpected large rises in the interest rate.

In the next part of this chapter, we learn how interest rates and asset prices are determined in the financial markets.

### Review Quiz

1. Distinguish between physical capital and financial capital and give two examples of each.
2. What is the distinction between gross investment and net investment?
3. What are the three main types of markets for financial capital?
4. Explain the connection between the price of a financial asset and its interest rate.

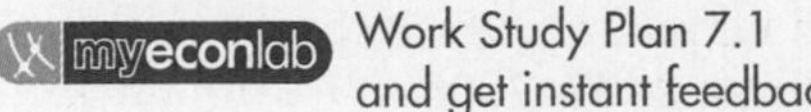

Work Study Plan 7.1 and get instant feedback.

## The Market for Loanable Funds

In macroeconomics, we group all the financial markets that we described in the previous section into a single market for loanable funds. The **market for loanable funds** is the aggregate of all the individual financial markets.

The circular flow model of Chapter 4 (see p. 87) can be extended to include flows in the market for loanable funds that finance investment.

### Funds that Finance Investment

Figure 7.2 shows the flows of funds that finance investment. They come from three sources:

1. Household saving
2. Government budget surplus
3. Borrowing from the rest of the world

Households' income, $Y$, is spent on consumption goods and services, $C$, saved, $S$, or paid in net taxes, $T$. **Net taxes** are the taxes paid to governments minus the cash transfers received from governments (such as Social Security and unemployment benefits). So income is equal to the sum of consumption expenditure, saving, and net taxes:

$$Y = C + S + T.$$

You saw in Chapter 4 (p. 88) that $Y$ also equals the sum of the items of aggregate expenditure: consumption expenditure, $C$, investment, $I$, government expenditure, $G$, and exports, $X$, minus imports, $M$. That is:

$$Y = C + I + G + X - M.$$

By using these two equations, you can see that

$$I + G + X = M + S + T.$$

Subtract $G$ and $X$ from both sides of the last equation to obtain

$$I = S + (T - G) + (M - X).$$

This equation tells us that investment, $I$, is financed by household saving, $S$, the government budget surplus, $(T - G)$, and borrowing from the rest of the world, $(M - X)$.

A government budget surplus $(T > G)$ contributes funds to finance investment, but a government budget deficit $(T < G)$, competes with investment for funds.

FIGURE 7.2 Financial Flows and the Circular Flow of Expenditure and Income

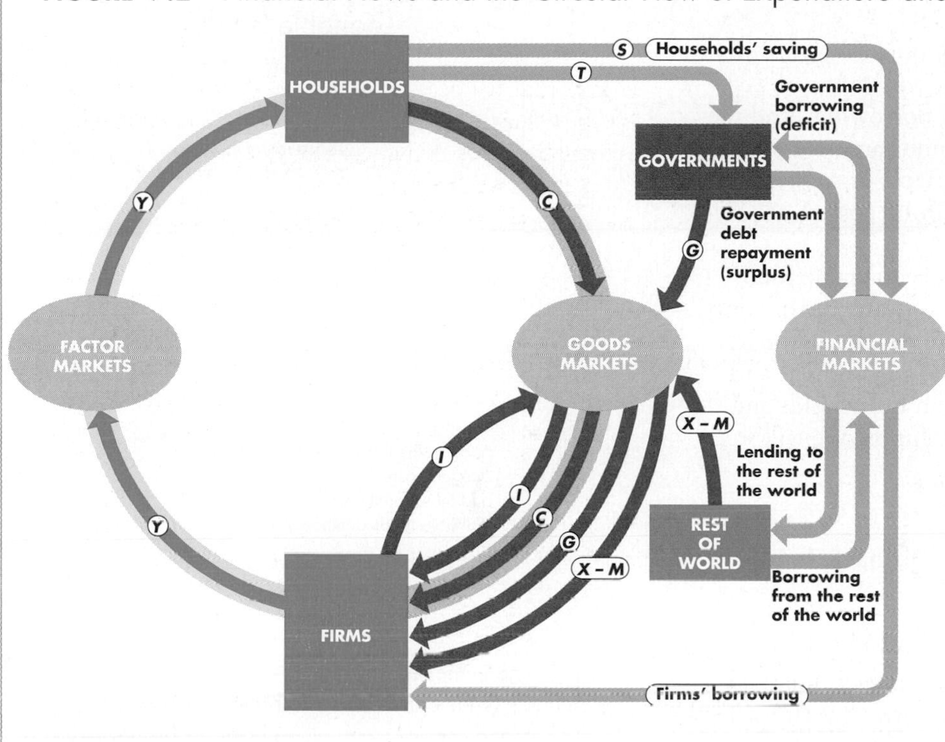


Households use their income for consumption expenditure (*C*), saving (*S*), and net taxes (*T*). Firms borrow to finance their investment expenditure. Governments borrow to finance a budget deficit or repay debt if they have a budget surplus. The rest of the world borrows to finance its deficit or lends its surplus.

myeconlab animation

If we export less than we import, we borrow $(M - X)$ from the rest of the world to finance some of our investment. If we export more than we import, we lend $(X - M)$ to the rest of the world and part of U.S. saving finances investment in other countries.

The sum of private saving, $S$, and government saving, $(T - G)$, is called **national saving.** National saving and foreign borrowing finance investment.

In 2008, U.S. investment was $2,056 billion. Governments (federal, state, and local combined) had a deficit of $707 billion. This total of $2,763 billion was financed by private saving of $2,045 billion and borrowing from the rest of the world (negative net exports) of $718 billion.

You're going to see how investment and saving and the flows of loanable funds—all measured in constant 2000 dollars—are determined. The price in the market for loanable funds that achieves equilibrium is an interest rate, which we also measure in real terms as the *real* interest rate. In the market for loanable funds, there is just one interest rate, which is an average of the interest rates on all the different types of financial securities that we described earlier. Let's see what we mean by the real interest rate.

## The Real Interest Rate

The **nominal interest rate** is the number of dollars that a borrower pays and a lender receives in interest in a year expressed as a percentage of the number of dollars borrowed and lent. For example, if the annual interest paid on a $500 loan is $25, the nominal interest rate is 5 percent per year: $25 ÷ $500 × 100 or 5 percent.

The **real interest rate** is the nominal interest rate adjusted to remove the effects of inflation on the buying power of money. The real interest rate is approximately equal to the nominal interest rate minus the inflation rate.

You can see why if you suppose that you have put $500 in a savings account that earns 5 percent a year. At the end of a year, you have $525 in your savings account. Suppose that the inflation rate is 2 percent per year—during the year, all prices increased by 2 percent. You need $510 to buy what a year earlier cost $500. So you can buy $15 worth more of goods and services than you could have bought a year earlier. You've earned goods and services worth $15, which is a real interest rate of 3 percent a year. And the bank has paid a real interest rate of 3 percent a year. So the real interest rate is the 5 percent nominal interest rate minus the 2 percent inflation rate[1].

The real interest rate is the opportunity cost of loanable funds. The real interest *paid* on borrowed funds is the opportunity cost of borrowing. And the real interest rate *forgone* when funds are used either to buy consumption goods and services or to invest in new capital goods is the opportunity cost of not saving or not lending those funds.

We're now going to see how the loanable funds market determines the real interest rate, the quantity of funds loaned, saving, and investment. In the rest of this section, we will ignore the government and the rest of the world and focus on households and firms in the market for loanable funds. We will study

- The demand for loanable funds
- The supply of loanable funds
- Equilibrium in the market for loanable funds

## The Demand for Loanable Funds

The *quantity of loanable funds demanded* is the total quantity of funds demanded to finance investment, the government budget deficit, and international investment or lending during a given period. Our focus here is on investment. We'll bring the other two items into the picture in later sections of this chapter.

What determines investment and the demand for loanable funds to finance it? Many details influence this decision, but we can summarize them in two factors:

1. The real interest rate
2. Expected profit

Firms invest in capital only if they expect to earn a profit and fewer projects are profitable at a high real interest rate than at a low real interest rate, so:

Other things remaining the same, the higher the real interest rate, the smaller is the quantity of loanable funds demanded; and the lower the real interest rate, the greater is the quantity of loanable funds demanded.

[1]The *exact* real interest rate formula, which allows for the change in the purchasing power of both the interest and the loan is: Real interest rate = (Nominal interest rate – Inflation rate) ÷ (1 + Inflation rate/100). If the nominal interest rate is 5 percent a year and the inflation rate is 2 percent a year, the real interest rate is (5 – 2) ÷ (1 + 0.02) = 2.94 percent a year.

**FIGURE 7.3** The Demand for Loanable Funds

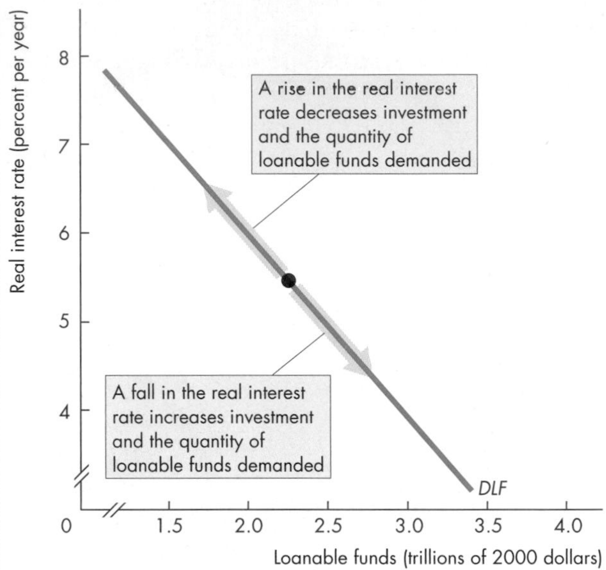
Real interest rate (percent per year)
8
7
6
5
4
0
A rise in the real interest rate decreases investment and the quantity of loanable funds demanded
A fall in the real interest rate increases investment and the quantity of loanable funds demanded
DLF
1.5
2.0
2.5
3.0
3.5
4.0
Loanable funds (trillions of 2000 dollars)

A change in the real interest rate changes the quantity of loanable funds demanded and brings a movement along the demand curve.

myeconlab animation

**Demand for Loanable Funds Curve** The **demand for loanable funds** is the relationship between the quantity of loanable funds demanded and the real interest rate, when all other influences on borrowing plans remain the same. The demand curve *DLF* in Fig. 7.3 is a demand for loanable funds curve.

To understand the demand for loanable funds, think about Amazon.com's decision to borrow $100 million to build some new warehouses. If Amazon expects to get a return of $5 million a year from this investment before paying interest costs and the interest rate is less than 5 percent a year, Amazon would make a profit, so it builds the warehouses. But if the interest rate is more than 5 percent a year, Amazon would incur a loss, so it doesn't build the warehouses. The quantity of loanable funds demanded is greater the lower is the real interest rate.

**Changes in the Demand for Loanable Funds** When the expected profit changes, the demand for loanable funds changes. Other things remaining the same, the greater the expected profit from new capital, the greater is the amount of investment and the greater the demand for loanable funds.

Expected profit rises during a business cycle expansion and falls during a recession; rises when technological change creates profitable new products; rises as a growing population brings increased demand for goods and services; and fluctuates with contagious swings of optimism and pessimism, called "animal spirits" by Keynes and "irrational exuberance" by Alan Greenspan.

When expected profit changes, the demand for loanable funds curve shifts.

## The Supply of Loanable Funds

The *quantity of loanable funds supplied* is the total funds available from private saving, the government budget surplus, and international borrowing during a given period. Our focus here is on saving. We'll bring the other two items into the picture later.

How do you decide how much of your income to save and supply in the market for loanable funds? Your decision is influenced by many factors, but chief among them are

1. The real interest rate
2. Disposable income
3. Expected future income
4. Wealth
5. Default risk

We begin by focusing on the real interest rate.

Other things remaining the same, the higher the real interest rate, the greater is the quantity of loanable funds supplied; and the lower the real interest rate, the smaller is the quantity of loanable funds supplied.

**The Supply of Loanable Funds Curve** The **supply of loanable funds** is the relationship between the quantity of loanable funds supplied and the real interest rate when all other influences on lending plans remain the same. The curve *SLF* in Fig. 7.4 is a supply of loanable funds curve.

Think about a student's decision to save some of what she earns from her summer job. With a real interest rate of 2 percent a year, she decides that it is not worth saving much—better to spend the income and take a student loan if funds run out during the semester. But if the real interest rate jumped to 10 percent a year, the payoff from saving would be high enough to encourage her to cut back on spending and increase the amount she saves.

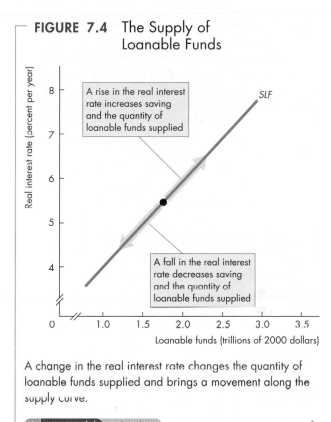

**FIGURE 7.4** The Supply of Loanable Funds

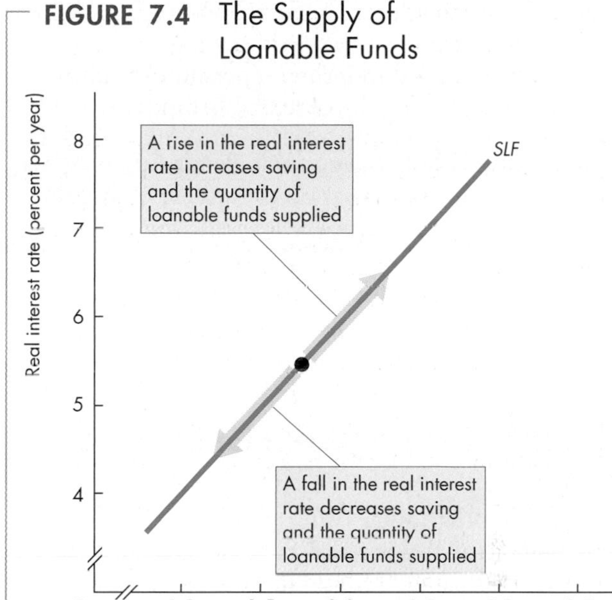
Real interest rate (percent per year)
8
7
6
5
4
0
A rise in the real interest rate increases saving and the quantity of loanable funds supplied
SLF
A fall in the real interest rate decreases saving and the quantity of loanable funds supplied
1.0
1.5
2.0
2.5
3.0
3.5
Loanable funds (trillions of 2000 dollars)

A change in the real interest rate changes the quantity of loanable funds supplied and brings a movement along the supply curve.

myeconlab animation

**Changes in the Supply of Loanable Funds** A change in disposable income, expected future income, wealth, or default risk changes the supply of loanable funds.

***Disposable Income*** A household's *disposable income* is the income earned minus net taxes. When disposable income increases, other things remaining the same, consumption expenditure increases but by less than the increase in income. Some of the increase in income is saved. So the greater a household's disposable income, other things remaining the same, the greater is its saving.

***Expected Future Income*** The higher a household's expected future income, other things remaining the same, the smaller is its saving today.

***Wealth*** The higher a household's wealth, other things remaining the same, the smaller is its saving. If a person's wealth increases because of a capital gain, the person sees less need to save. For example, from 2002 through 2006, when house prices were rising rapidly, wealth increased despite the fact that personal saving dropped close to zero.

***Default Risk*** Default risk is the risk that a loan will not be repaid. The greater that risk, the higher is the interest rate needed to induce a person to lend and the smaller is the supply of loanable funds.

**Shifts of the Supply of Loanable Funds Curve** When any of the four influences on the supply of loanable funds changes, the supply of loanable funds changes and the supply curve shifts. An increase in disposable income, a decrease in expected future income, a decrease in wealth, or a fall in default risk increases saving and increases the supply of loanable funds.

## Equilibrium in the Market for Loanable Funds

You've seen that other things remaining the same, the higher the real interest rate, the greater is the quantity of loanable funds supplied and the smaller is the quantity of loanable funds demanded. There is one real interest rate at which the quantities of loanable funds demanded and supplied are equal, and that interest rate is the equilibrium real interest rate.

Figure 7.5 shows how the demand for and supply of loanable funds determine the real interest rate. The *DLF* curve is the demand curve and the *SLF* curve is the supply curve. If the real interest rate exceeds 6 percent a year, the quantity of loanable funds supplied exceeds the quantity demanded. Borrowers find it easy to get funds, but lenders are unable to lend all the funds they have available. The real interest rate falls until the quantity of funds supplied equals the quantity of funds demanded.

If the real interest rate is less than 6 percent a year, the quantity of loanable funds supplied is less than the quantity demanded. Borrowers can't get the funds they want, but lenders are able to lend all the funds they have available. So the real interest rate rises and continues to rise until the quantity of funds supplied equals the quantity demanded.

Regardless of whether there is a surplus or a shortage of loanable funds, the real interest rate changes and is pulled toward an equilibrium level. In Fig. 7.5, the equilibrium real interest rate is 6 percent a year. At this interest rate, there is neither a surplus nor a shortage of loanable funds. Borrowers can get the funds they want, and lenders can lend all the funds they have available. The investment plans of borrowers and the saving plans of lenders are consistent with each other.

**FIGURE 7.5** Equilibrium in the Market for Loanable Funds

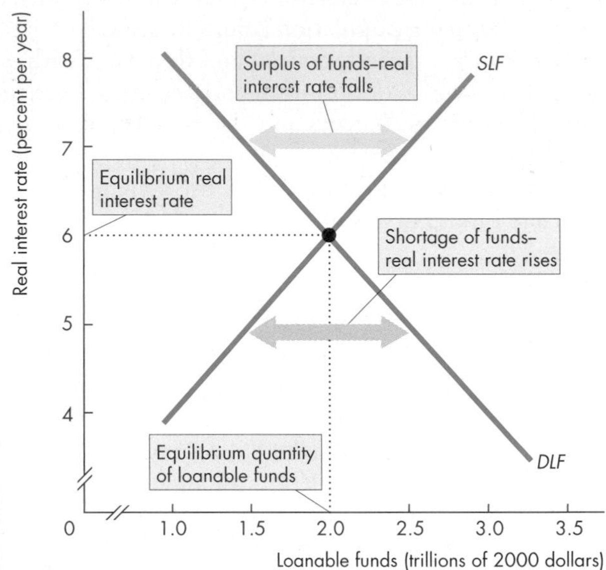


A surplus of funds lowers the real interest rate and a shortage of funds raises it. At an interest rate of 6 percent a year, the quantity of funds demanded equals the quantity supplied and the market is in equilibrium.

myeconlab animation

## Changes in Demand and Supply

Financial markets are highly volatile in the short run but remarkably stable in the long run. Volatility in the market comes from fluctuations in either the demand for loanable funds or the supply of loanable funds. These fluctuations bring fluctuations in the real interest rate and in the equilibrium quantity of funds lent and borrowed. They also bring fluctuations in asset prices.

Here we'll illustrate the effects of *increases* in demand and supply in the market for loanable funds.

**An Increase in Demand** If the profits that firms expect to earn increase, they increase their planned investment and increase their demand for loanable funds to finance that investment. With an increase in the demand for loanable funds, but no change in the supply of loanable funds, there is a shortage of funds. As borrowers compete for funds, the interest rate rises and lenders increase the quantity of funds supplied.

Figure 7.6(a) illustrates these changes. An increase in the demand for loanable funds shifts the demand curve rightward from $DLF_0$ to $DLF_1$. With no

**FIGURE 7.6** Changes in Demand and Supply

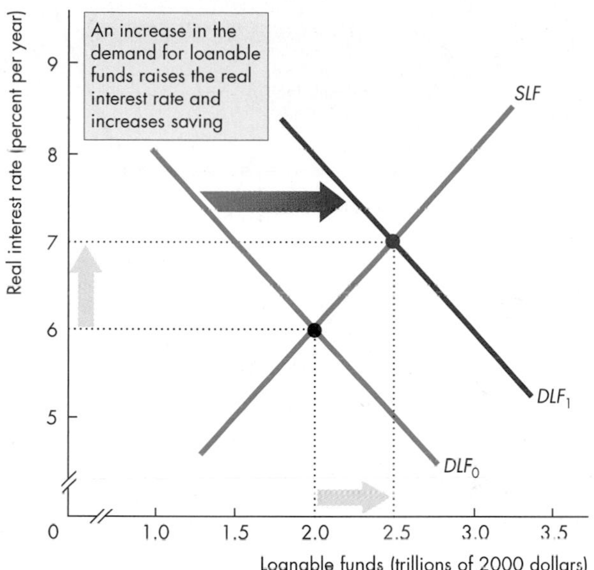


**(a) An increase in demand**

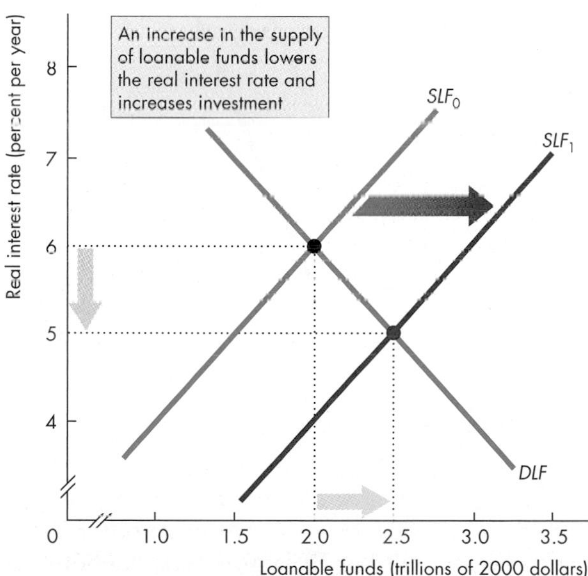


**(b) An increase in supply**

In part (a), the demand for loanable funds increases and supply doesn't change. The real interest rate rises (financial asset prices fall) and the quantity of funds increases.
In part (b), the supply of loanable funds increases and demand doesn't change. The real interest rate falls (financial asset prices rise) and the quantity of funds increases.

myeconlab animation

change in the supply of loanable funds, there is a shortage of funds at a real interest rate of 6 percent a year. The real interest rate rises until it is 7 percent a year. Equilibrium is restored and the equilibrium quantity of funds has increased.

**An Increase in Supply** If one of the influences on saving plans changes and increases saving, the supply of loanable funds increases. With no change in the demand for loanable funds, the market is flush with loanable funds. Borrowers find bargains and lenders find themselves accepting a lower interest rate. At the lower interest rate, borrowers find additional investment projects profitable and increase the quantity of loanable funds that they borrow.

Figure 7.6(b) illustrates these changes. An increase in supply shifts the supply curve rightward from $SLF_0$ to $SLF_1$. With no change in demand, there is a surplus of funds at a real interest rate of 6 percent a year. The real interest rate falls until it is 5 percent a year. Equilibrium is restored and the equilibrium quantity of funds has increased.

**Long-Run Growth of Demand and Supply** Over time, both demand and supply in the market for loanable funds fluctuate and the real interest rate rises and falls. Both the supply of loanable funds and the demand for loanable funds tend to increase over time. On the average, they increase at a similar pace, so although demand and supply trend upward, the real interest rate has no trend. It fluctuates around a constant average level.

## Review Quiz

1 What is the market for loanable funds?
2 Why is the real interest rate the opportunity cost of loanable funds?
3 How do firms make investment decisions?
4 What determines the demand for loanable funds and what makes it change?
5 How do households make saving decisions?
6 What determines the supply of loanable funds and what makes it change?
7 How do changes in the demand for and supply of loanable funds change the real interest rate and quantity of loanable funds?

Work Study Plan 7.2 and get instant feedback.

## The Origins of the 2007–2008 Financial Crisis

### Loanable Funds Fuel Home Price Bubble

The financial crisis that gripped the U.S. and global economies in 2007 and cascaded through the financial markets in 2008 had its origins much earlier in events taking place in the market for loanable funds.

Between 2001 and 2005, a massive injection of loanable funds occurred. Some funds came from the rest of the world, but that source of supply has been stable. The Federal Reserve provided funds to keep interest rates low and that was a major source of the increase in the supply of funds. (The next chapter explains how the Fed does this.)

Figure 1 illustrates the loanable funds market starting in 2001. In that year, the demand for loanable funds was $DLF_{01}$ and the supply of loanable funds was $SLF_{01}$. The equilibrium real interest rate was 4 percent a year and the equilibrium quantity of loanable funds was $29 trillion (in 2000 dollars).

During the ensuing four years, a massive increase in the supply of loanable funds shifted the supply curve rightward to $SLF_{05}$. A smaller increase in demand shifted the demand for loanable funds curve to $DLF_{05}$. The real interest rate fell to 1 percent a year and the quantity of loanable funds increased to $36 trillion—a 24 percent increase in just four years.

With this large increase in available funds, much of it in the form of mortgage loans to home buyers, the demand for homes increased by more than the increase in the supply of homes. Home prices rose and the expectation of further increases fueled the demand for loanable funds.

By 2006, the expectation of continued rapidly rising home prices brought a very large increase in the demand for loanable funds. At the same time, the Federal Reserve began to tighten credit. (Again, you'll learn how this is done in the next chapter). The result of the Fed's tighter credit policy was a slowdown in the pace of increase in the supply of loanable funds.

Figure 2 illustrates these events. In 2006, the demand for loanable funds increased from $DLF_{05}$ to $DLF_{06}$ and the supply of loanable funds increased by a smaller amount from $SLF_{05}$ to $SLF_{06}$. The real interest rate increased to 3 percent.

The rise in the real interest rate (and a much higher rise in the nominal interest rate) put many home owners in financial difficulty. Mortgage repayments increased and some borrowers stopped repaying their loans.

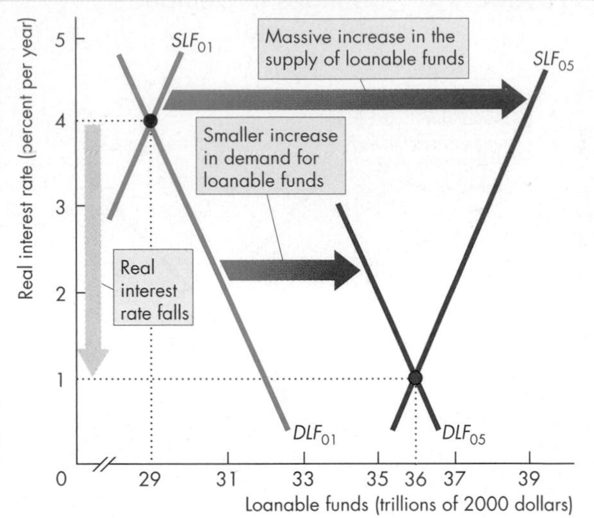


**Figure 1 The Foundation of the Crisis: 2001–2005**

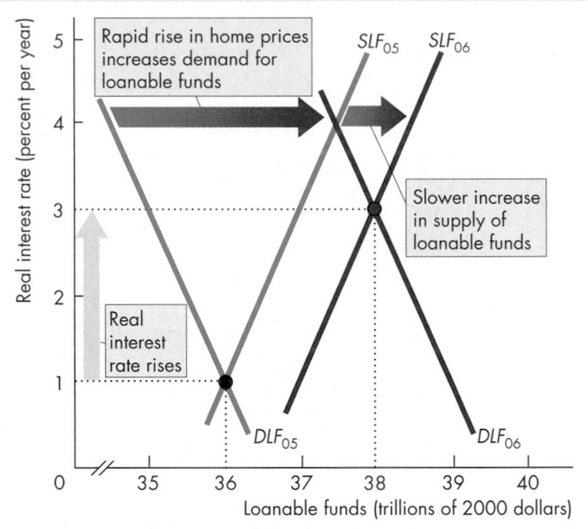


**Figure 2 The Start of the Crisis: 2005-2006**

By August 2007, the damage from mortgage default and foreclosure was so large that the credit market began to dry up. A large decrease in both demand and supply kept interest rates roughly constant but decreased the quantity of new business.

The total quantity of loanable funds didn't decrease, but the rate of increase slowed to a snail's pace and financial institutions most exposed to the bad mortgage debts and the securities that they backed (described on p. 566) began to fail.

These events illustrate the crucial role played by the loanable funds market in our economy.

## Government in the Market for Loanable Funds

Government enters the market for loanable funds when it has a budget surplus or budget deficit. A government budget surplus increases the supply of loanable funds and contributes to financing investment; a government budget deficit increases the demand for loanable funds and competes with businesses for funds. Let's study the effects of government on the market for loanable funds.

### A Government Budget Surplus

A government budget surplus increases the supply of loanable funds. The real interest rate falls, which decreases household saving and decreases the quantity of private funds supplied. The lower real interest rate increases the quantity of loanable funds demanded, and increases investment.

Figure 7.7 shows these effects of a government budget surplus. The private supply of loanable funds curve is *PSLF*. The supply of loanable funds curve, *SLF*, shows the sum of private supply and the government budget surplus. Here, the government budget surplus is $1 trillion, so at each real interest rate the *SLF* curve lies $1 trillion to the right of the *PSLF* curve. That is, the horizontal distance between the *PSLF* curve and the *SLF* curve equals the government budget surplus.

With no government surplus, the real interest rate is 6 percent a year, the quantity of loanable funds is $2 trillion a year and investment is $2 trillion a year. But with the government surplus of $1 trillion a year, the equilibrium real interest rate falls to 5 percent a year and the quantity of loanable funds increases to $2.5 trillion a year.

The fall in the interest rate decreases private saving to $1.5 trillion, but investment increases to $2.5 trillion, which is financed by private saving plus the government budget surplus (government saving).

**FIGURE 7.7** A Government Budget Surplus

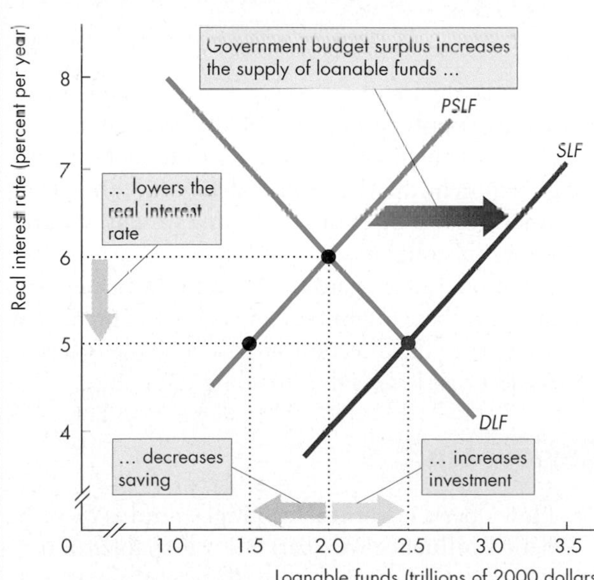


A government budget surplus of $1 trillion is added to private saving and the private supply of loanable funds (*PSLF*) to determine the supply of loanable funds, *SLF*. The real interest rate falls to 5 percent a year, private saving decreases, but investment increases to $2.5 trillion.

myeconlab animation

### A Government Budget Deficit

A government budget deficit increases the demand for loanable funds. The real interest rate rises, which increases household saving and increases the quantity of private funds supplied. But the higher real interest rate decreases investment and the quantity of loanable funds demanded by firms to finance investment.

Figure 7.8 shows these effects of a government budget deficit. The private demand for loanable funds curve is *PDLF*. The demand for loanable funds curve, *DLF*, shows the sum of private demand and the government budget deficit. Here, the government budget deficit is $1 trillion, so at each real interest rate the *DLF* curve lies $1 trillion to the right of the *PDLF* curve. That is, the horizontal distance between the *PDLF* curve and the *DLF* curve equals the government budget deficit.

With no government deficit, the real interest rate is 6 percent a year, the quantity of loanable funds is $2 trillion a year and investment is $2 trillion a year. But with the government budget deficit of $1 trillion a year, the equilibrium real interest rate rises to 7 percent a year and the quantity of loanable funds increases to $2.5 trillion a year.

The rise in the real interest rate increases private saving to $2.5 trillion, but investment decreases to $1.5 trillion because $1 trillion of private saving must finance the government budget deficit.

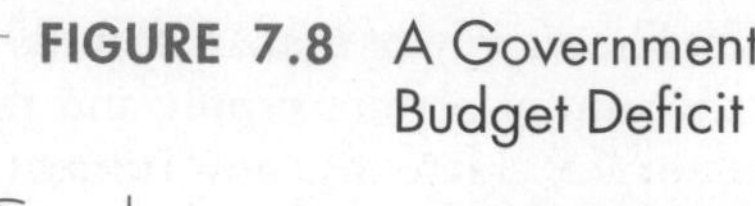

**FIGURE 7.8** A Government Budget Deficit

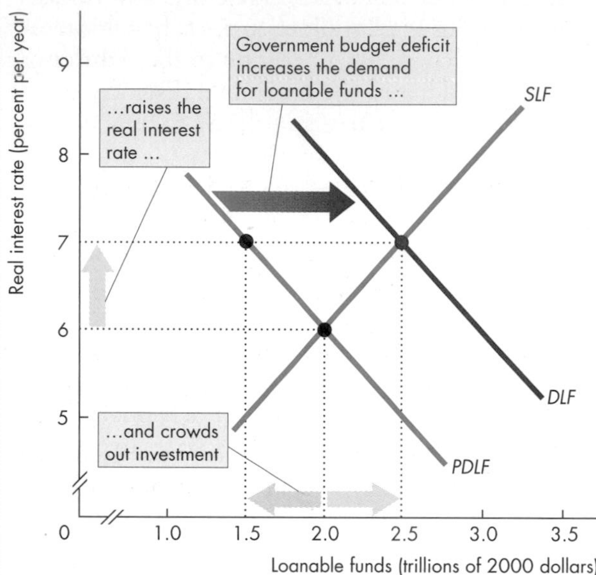


A government budget deficit adds to the private demand for loanable funds (*PDLF*) to determine the demand for loanable funds, *DLF*. The real interest rate rises, saving increases, but investment decreases—a crowding-out effect.

myeconlab animation

**FIGURE 7.9** The Ricardo-Barro Effect

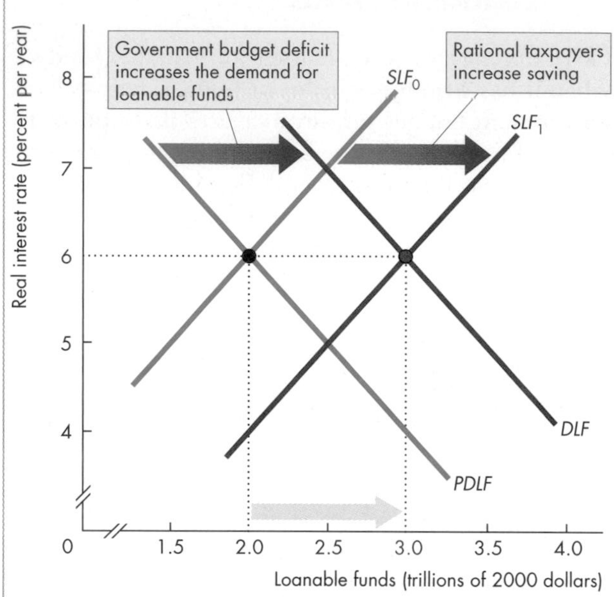


A budget deficit increases the demand for loanable funds to *DLF*. Rational taxpayers increase saving, which increases the supply of loanable funds from $SLF_0$ to $SLF_1$. Crowding out is avoided: Increased saving finances the budget deficit.

myeconlab animation

**The Crowding-Out Effect** The tendency for a government budget deficit to raise the real interest rate and decrease investment is called the **crowding-out effect**. The budget deficit crowds out investment by competing with businesses for scarce financial capital.

The crowding-out effect does not decrease investment by the full amount of the government budget deficit because the higher real interest rate induces an increase in private saving that partly contributes toward financing the deficit.

**The Ricardo-Barro Effect** First suggested by the English economist David Ricardo in the eighteenth century and refined by Robert J. Barro of Harvard University, the Ricardo-Barro effect holds that both of the effects we've just shown are wrong and the government budget, whether in surplus or deficit, has no effect on either the real interest rate or investment.

Barro says that taxpayers are rational. They can see that a budget deficit today means that future taxes will be higher and future disposable incomes will be smaller. With smaller expected future disposable incomes, saving increases today. Private saving and the private supply of loanable funds increase to match the quantity of loanable funds demanded by the government. So the budget deficit has no effect on either the real interest rate or investment. Figure 7.9 shows this outcome.

Most economists regard the Ricardo-Barro view as extreme. But there might be some change in private saving that goes in the direction suggested by the Ricardo-Barro effect that lessens the crowding-out effect.

## Review Quiz

1 How does a government budget surplus or deficit influence the market for loanable funds?
2 What is the crowding-out effect and how does it work?
3 What is the Ricardo-Barro effect and how does it modify the crowding-out effect?

Work Study Plan 7.3 and get instant feedback.

## The Global Loanable Funds Market

The loanable funds market is global, not national. Lenders on the supply side of the market want to earn the highest possible real interest rate and they will seek it by looking everywhere in the world. Borrowers on the demand side of the market want to pay the lowest possible real interest rate and they will seek it by looking everywhere in the world. Financial capital is mobile: It moves to the best advantage of lenders and borrowers.

### International Capital Mobility

If a U.S. supplier of loanable funds can earn a higher interest rate in Tokyo than in New York, funds supplied in Japan will increase and funds supplied in the United States will decrease—funds will flow from the United States to Japan.

If a U.S. demander of loanable funds can pay a lower interest rate in Paris than in New York, the demand for funds in France will increase and the demand for funds in the United States will decrease —funds will flow from France to the United States.

Because lenders are free to seek the highest real interest rate and borrowers are free to seek the lowest real interest rate, the loanable funds market is a single, integrated, global market. Funds flow into the country in which the interest rate is highest and out of the country in which the interest rate is lowest.

When funds leave the country with the lowest interest rate, a shortage of funds raises the real interest rate. When funds move into the country with the highest interest rate, a surplus of funds lowers the real interest rate. The free international mobility of financial capital pulls real interest rates around the world toward equality.

Only when the real interest rates in New York, Tokyo, and Paris are equal does the incentive to move funds from one country to another stop.

Equality of real interest rates does not mean that if you calculate the average real interest rate in New York, Tokyo, and Paris, you'll get the same number. To compare real interest rates, we must compare financial assets of equal risk.

Lending is risky. A loan might not be repaid. Or the price of a stock or bond might fall. Interest rates include a risk premium—the riskier the loan, other things remaining the same, the higher is the interest rate. The interest rate on a risky loan minus that on a safe loan is called the *risk premium*.

International capital mobility brings *real* interest rates in all parts of the world to equality except for differences that reflect differences in risk—differences in the risk premium.

### International Borrowing and Lending

A country's loanable funds market connects with the global market through net exports. If a country's net exports are negative ($X < M$), the rest of the world supplies funds to that country and the quantity of loanable funds in that country is greater than national saving. If a country's net exports are positive ($X > M$), the country is a net supplier of funds to the rest of the world and the quantity of loanable funds in that country is less than national saving.

### Demand and Supply in the Global and National Markets

The demand for and supply of funds in the global loanable funds market determines the world equilibrium real interest rate. This interest rate makes the quantity of loanable funds demanded equal the quantity supplied in the world economy. But it does not make the quantity of funds demanded and supplied equal in each national economy. The demand for and supply of funds in a national economy determine whether the country is a lender to or a borrower from the rest of the world.

**The Global Loanable Funds Market** Figure 7.10(a) illustrates the global market. The demand for loanable funds, $DLF_W$ is the sum of the demands in all countries. Similarly, the supply of loanable funds, $SLF_W$ is the sum of the supplies in all countries. The world equilibrium real interest rate makes the quantity of funds supplied in the world as a whole equal to the quantity demanded. In this example, the equilibrium real interest rate is 5 percent a year and the quantity of funds is $10 trillion.

**An International Borrower** Figure 7.10(b) shows the market for loanable funds in a country that borrows from the rest of the world. The country's demand for loanable funds, *DLF*, is part of the world demand in Fig. 7.10(a). The country's supply of loanable funds, $SLF_D$, is part of the world supply.

**FIGURE 7.10** Borrowing and Lending in the Global Loanable Funds Market

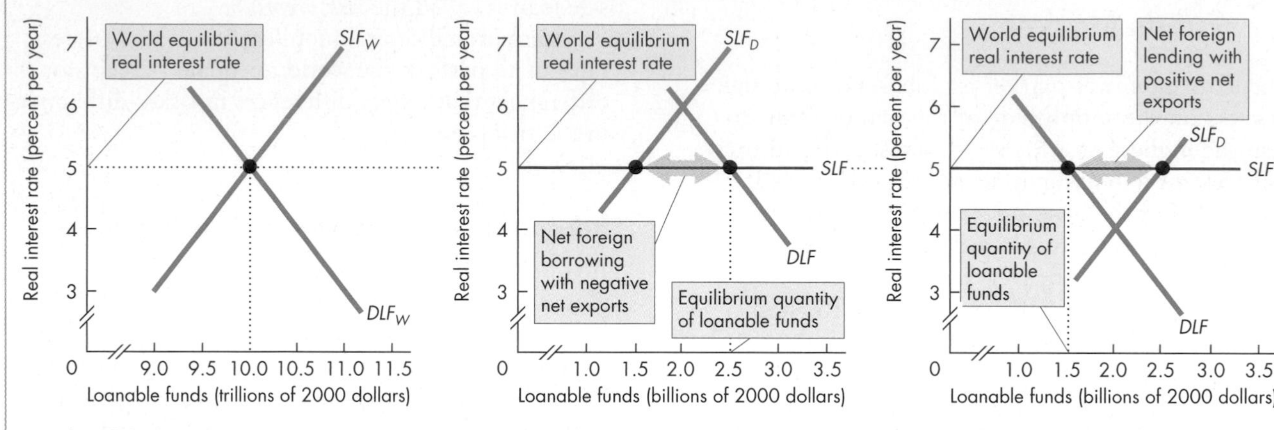


In part (a), the demand for loanable funds, *DLF*, and the supply of funds, *SLF*, determine the equilibrium real interest rate in the global loanable funds market.

The country in part (b) has a shortage of funds at the world equilibrium real interest rate and the country borrows from the rest of the world. The country has negative net exports.

The country in part (c) has a surplus of funds at the world equilibrium real interest rate and the country lends to the rest of the world. The country has positive net exports.

myeconlab animation

If this country were isolated from the global market, the real interest rate would be 6 percent a year (where the *DLF* and $SLF_D$ curves intersect). But if the country is integrated into the global economy, with an interest rate of 6 percent a year, funds would flood into it. With a real interest rate of 5 percent a year in the rest of the world, suppliers of loanable funds would seek the higher return in this country. In effect, the country faces the supply of loanable funds curve *SLF*, which is horizontal at the world equilibrium real interest rate.

The country's demand for loanable funds and the world interest rate determine the equilibrium quantity of loanable funds—\$2.5 billion in Fig. 7.10(b).

**An International Lender** Figure 7.10(c) shows the situation in a country that lends to the rest of the world. As before, the country's demand for loanable funds, *DLF*, is part of the world demand and the country's supply of loanable funds, $SLF_D$, is part of the world supply in Fig. 7.10(a).

If this country were isolated from the global economy, the real interest rate would be 4 percent a year (where the *DLF* and $SLF_D$ curves intersect). But if this country is integrated into the global economy, with an interest rate of 4 percent a year, funds would quickly flow out of it. With a real interest rate of 5 percent a year in the rest of the world, suppliers of loanable funds would seek the higher return in other countries. Again, the country faces the supply of loanable funds curve *SLF*, which is horizontal at the world equilibrium real interest rate.

The country's demand for loanable funds and the world interest rate determine the equilibrium quantity of loanable funds—\$1.5 billion in Fig. 7.10(c).

**Changes in Demand and Supply** A change in the demand or supply in the global market of loanable funds changes the real interest rate in the way shown in Fig. 7.6 (see p. 573). The effect of a change in demand or supply in a national market depends on the size of the country. A change in demand or supply in a small country has no significant effect on global demand or supply, so it leaves the world real interest rate unchanged and changes only the country's net exports and international borrowing or lending. A change in demand or supply in a large country has a significant effect on global demand or supply, so it changes the world real interest rate as well as the country's net exports and international borrowing or lending. Every country feels some of the effect of a large country's change in demand or supply.

## Greenspan's Interest Rate Puzzle

### The Role of the Global Market

The real interest rate paid by big corporations in the United States fell from 5.5 percent a year in 2001 to 2.5 percent a year in 2005. Alan Greenspan, then the Chairman of the Federal Reserve, said he was puzzled that the real interest rate was falling at a time when the U.S. government budget deficit was increasing.

Why did the real interest rate fall?

The answer lies in the global loanable funds market. Rapid economic growth in Asia and Europe brought a large increase in global saving, which in turn increased the global supply of loanable funds. The supply of loanable funds increased because Asian and European saving increased strongly.

The U.S. government budget deficit increased the U.S. and global demand for loanable funds. But this increase was very small compared to the increase in supply.

The result of a large increase in supply and a small increase in demand was a fall in the world average real interest rate and an increase in the equilibrium quantity of loanable funds.

The figure illustrates these events. The supply of loanable funds increased from $SLF_{01}$ in 2001 to $SLF_{05}$ in 2005. (In the figure, we ignore the change in the global demand for loanable funds because it was small relative to the increase in supply.)

With the increase in supply, the real interest rate fell from 5.5 percent to 2.5 percent a year and the quantity of loanable funds increased.

In the United States, borrowing from the rest of the world increased to finance the increased government budget deficit.

The interest rate puzzle illustrates the important fact that the loanable funds market is a global market, not a national market.

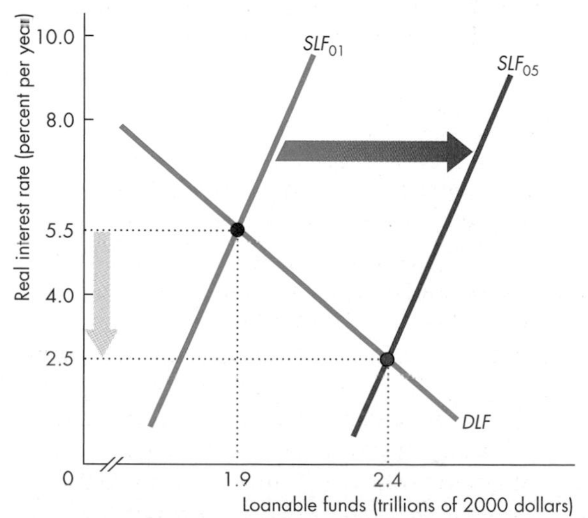


**The Global Loanable Funds Market**

## Review Quiz

1. Why do loanable funds flow among countries?
2. What determines the demand for and supply of loanable funds in an individual economy?
3. What happens if a country has a shortage of loanable funds at the world real interest rate?
4. What happens if a country has a surplus of loanable funds at the world real interest rate?
5. How is a government budget deficit financed in an open economy?

Work Study Plan 7.4 and get instant feedback.

To complete your study of financial markets, take a look at *Reading Between the Lines* on pp. 178–179 and see how you can use the model of the loanable funds market to understand the events in the financial market crisis of 2008.

READING BETWEEN THE LINES 

# Bailing Out Financial Markets

## Bailout Plan Wins Approval

http://www.nytimes.com
October 3, 2008

After the House reversed course and gave final approval to the $700 billion economic bailout package, President Bush quickly signed it into law on Friday, authorizing the Treasury to undertake what could become the most expensive government intervention in history.

But even as Mr. Bush declared that the measure would "help prevent the crisis on Wall Street from becoming a crisis in communities across our country," Congressional Democrats said that it was only a first step and pledged to carry out a sweeping overhaul of the nation's financial regulatory system. …

Some measures of the credit markets improved after the bill was approved, but only modestly. Analysts said it was too soon to tell whether borrowing rates—the interest rates banks charge each other for loans, and a key indicator of the flow of credit—would fall. …

Supporters said the bailout was needed to prevent economic collapse; opponents said it was hasty, ill conceived and risked too much taxpayer money to help Wall Street tycoons, while providing no guarantees of success. The rescue plan allows the Treasury to buy troubled securities from financial firms in an effort to ease a deepening credit crisis that is choking off business and consumer loans, the lifeblood of the economy, and contributing to a string of bank failures. …



## Essence of the Story

- In October 2008, Congress passed a $700 billion economic bailout package for troubled financial institutions.
- The plan allows the Treasury to buy troubled securities from financial firms.
- The goal was to unfreeze credit and make loan markets work normally.
- Analysts said it was too soon to tell whether interest rates would fall.
- Supporters of the bailout said it was needed to prevent economic collapse.
- Opponents of the bailout said it risked too much taxpayer money and provided no guarantees of success.

## Economic Analysis

- In the fall of 2008, the U.S. loanable funds market was in a distressed state.
- The spread in interest rates between safe U.S. government Treasury bills and risky commercial loans was unusually high and the quantity of loans was unusually low.
- Banks and other financial institutions were holding financial assets that they could sell only at a large loss—referred to as *toxic assets*.
- The financial markets were operating at an equilibrium that was hampering continued economic growth.
- The Congress and the Bush Administration hoped to inject some life into the markets by creating a $700 billion fund to buy up the toxic assets and enable financial institutions to start lending again.
- It was feared that without the $700 billion of funds, financial institutions would not only fail to provide the funds required to make the economy grow but also slide into a deeper state of stress with the quantity of funds available decreasing further.
- The figures illustrate the hope and the fear.
- In 2008 (both figures), the demand for loanable funds was $DLF_{08}$ and the supply is $SLF_{08}$. The real interest rate was 3 percent a year and quantity of funds was $40 trillion (2000 dollars).
- Figure 1 shows the hope. A rescue package increases the supply of loanable funds and increases optimism about the future. Increased optimism increases profit expectations and increases the demand for funds. The demand and supply curves shift rightward to $DLF_{09}$ and $SLF_{09}$. The quantity of funds increases and the economy begins to expand again.
- Figure 2 shows the fear. With no rescue package, the supply of loanable funds decreases and increases pessimism about the future. The increased pessimism decreases profit expectations and decreases the demand for funds. The demand and supply curves shift leftward to $DLF_{09}$ and $SLF_{09}$. The quantity of funds decreases and the economy goes into recession or worse.

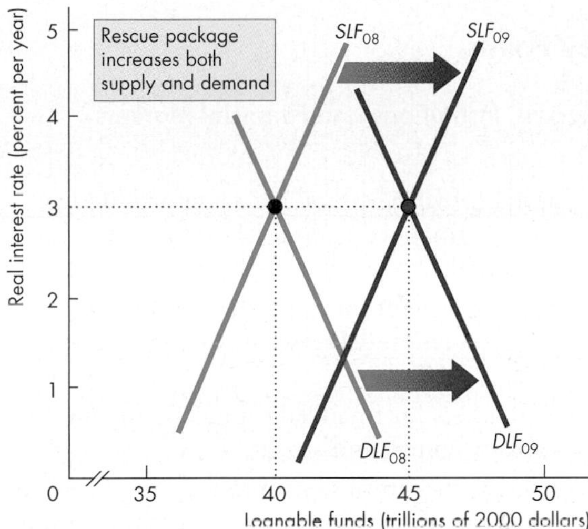


**Figure 1 The hope**

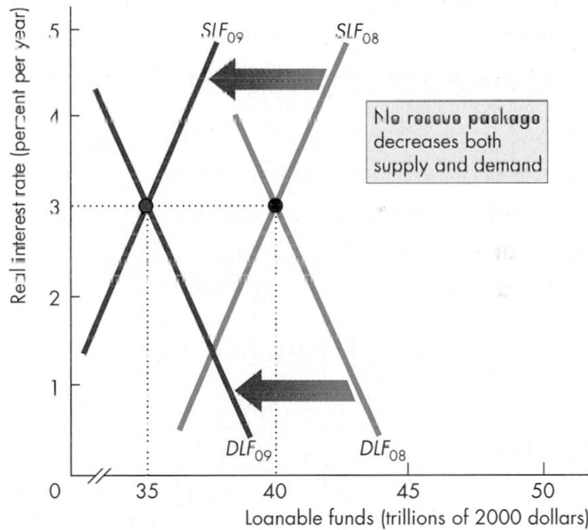


**Figure 2 The fear**

- Whether a rescue would work as hoped or whether the dire consequences of no rescue would occur as feared is not known. We have no direct experience of events like the ones described here on which to base solid predictions.

## SUMMARY

### Key Points

#### Financial Institutions and Financial Markets

(pp. 162–166)

- Capital (*physical capital*) is a real productive resource; financial capital is the funds used to buy capital.
- Gross investment increases the quantity of capital and depreciation decreases it. Saving increases wealth.
- The markets for financial capital are the markets for loans, bonds, and stocks.
- Financial institutions ensure that borrowers and lenders can always find someone with whom to trade.

#### The Market for Loanable Funds (pp. 166–172)

- Investment in capital is financed by household saving, a government budget surplus, and funds from the rest of the world.
- The quantity of loanable funds demanded depends negatively on the real interest rate and the demand for loanable funds changes when profit expectations change.
- The quantity of loanable funds supplied depends positively on the real interest rate and the supply of loanable funds changes when disposable income, expected future income, wealth, and default risk change.
- Equilibrium in the loanable funds market determines the real interest rate and quantity of funds.

#### Government in the Market for Loanable Funds

(pp. 173–174)

- A government budget surplus increases the supply of loanable funds, lowers the real interest rate, and increases investment and the equilibrium quantity of loanable funds.
- A government budget deficit increases the demand for loanable funds, raises the real interest rate, decreases investment in a crowding-out effect, and decreases the equilibrium quantity of loanable funds.
- The Ricardo-Barro effect is the response of rational taxpayers to a budget deficit: private saving increases to finance the budget deficit. The real interest rate remains constant and the crowding-out effect is avoided.

#### The Global Loanable Funds Market (pp. 175–177)

- The loanable funds market is a global market.
- The equilibrium real interest rate is determined in the global loanable funds market and national demand and supply determine the quantity of international borrowing or lending.

### Key Figures



### Key Terms

## PROBLEMS and APPLICATIONS

myeconlab Work problems 1–10 in Chapter 7 Study Plan and get instant feedback.
Work problems 11–19 as Homework, a Quiz, or a Test if assigned by your instructor.

1. Michael is an Internet service provider. On December 31, 2007, he bought an existing business with servers and a building worth $400,000. During his first year of operation, his business grew and he bought new servers for $500,000. The market value of some of his older servers fell by $100,000.
   a. What was Michael's gross investment, depreciation, and net investment during 2008?
   b. What is the value of Michael's capital at the end of 2008?
2. Lori is a student who teaches golf on the weekend and in a year earns $20,000 after paying her taxes. At the beginning of 2007, Lori owned $1,000 worth of books, CDs, and golf clubs and she had $5,000 in a savings account at the bank. During 2007, the interest on her savings account was $300 and she spent a total of $15,300 on consumption goods and services. There was no change in the market values of her books, CDs, and golf clubs.
   a. How much did Lori save in 2007?
   b. What was her wealth at the end of 2007?
3. First Call, Inc., is a cellular phone company. It plans to build an assembly plant that costs $10 million if the real interest rate is 6 percent a year. If the real interest rate is 5 percent a year, First Call will build a larger plant that costs $12 million. And if the real interest rate is 7 percent a year, First Call will build a smaller plant that costs $8 million.
   a. Draw a graph of First Call's demand for loanable funds curve.
   b. First Call expects its profit from the sale of cellular phones to double next year. If other things remain the same, explain how this increase in expected profit influences First Call's demand for loanable funds.
4. Draw a graph to illustrate how an increase in the supply of loanable funds and a decrease in the demand for loanable funds can lower the real interest rate and leave the equilibrium quantity of loanable funds unchanged.
5. The table at the top of the next column shows an economy's demand for loanable funds and the supply of loanable funds schedules, when the government's budget is balanced.

| Real interest rate (percent per year) | Loanable funds demanded (trillions of 2000 dollars) | Loanable funds supplied (trillions of 2000 dollars) |
|---|---|---|
| 4 | 8.5 | 5.5 |
| 5 | 8.0 | 6.0 |
| 6 | 7.5 | 6.5 |
| 7 | 7.0 | 7.0 |
| 8 | 6.5 | 7.5 |
| 9 | 6.0 | 8.0 |
| 10 | 5.5 | 8.5 |

   a. If the government has a budget surplus of $1 trillion, what are the real interest rate, the quantity of investment, and the quantity of private saving? Is there any crowding out in this situation?
   b. If the government has a budget deficit of $1 trillion, what are the real interest rate, the quantity of investment, and the quantity of private saving? Is there any crowding out in this situation?
   c. If the government has a budget deficit of $1 trillion and the Ricardo-Barro effect occurs, what are the real interest rate and the quantity of investment?
6. In the loanable funds market in problem 5, the quantity of loanable funds demanded increases by $1 trillion at each real interest rate and the quantity of loanable funds supplied increases by $2 trillion at each interest rate.
   a. If the government budget is balanced, what are the real interest rate, the quantity of loanable funds, investment, and private saving? Does any crowding out occur?
   b. If the government budget becomes a deficit of $1 trillion, what are the real interest rate, the quantity of loanable funds, investment, and private saving? Does any crowding out occur?
   c. If governments wants to stimulate the quantity of investment and increase it to $9 trillion, what must they do?

7. In a speech at the CFA Society of Nebraska in February 2007, William Poole, former Chairman of the St. Louis Federal Reserve said:

   Over most of the post-World War II period, the personal saving rate averaged about 6 percent, with some higher years from the mid 1970s to mid 1980s. The negative trend in the … saving rate started in the mid 1990s, about the same time the stock market boom started. Thus it is hard to dismiss the hypothesis that the decline in the measured saving rate in the late 1990s reflected the response of consumption to large capital gains from corporate equity [stock]. Evidence from panel data of households also supports the conclusion that the decline in the personal saving rate since 1984 is largely a consequence of capital gains on corporate equities [stocks].

   a. Is the purchase of corporate equities part of household consumption or saving? Explain your answer.
   b. Equities reap a capital gain in the same way that houses reap a capital gain. Does this mean that the purchase of equities is investment? If not, explain why it is not.
   c. U.S. household income has grown considerably since 1984. Has U.S. saving been on a downward trend because Americans feel wealthier?
   d. Explain why households preferred to buy corporate equities rather than bonds.

8. **The Global Saving Glut and the U.S. Current Account**, remarks by Ben Bernanke (when a governor of the Federal Reserve) on March 10, 2005:

   On most dimensions the U.S. economy appears to be performing well. Output growth has returned to healthy levels, the labor market is firming, and inflation appears to be well controlled. However, one aspect of U.S. economic performance still evokes concern among economists and policymakers: the nation's large and growing current account deficit [negative net exports]. … Most forecasters expect the nation's current account imbalance to decline slowly at best, implying a continued need for foreign credit and a concomitant decline in the U.S. net foreign asset position.

   Bernanke went on to ask the following questions. What are *your* answers to his questions:

   a. Why is the United States, with the world's largest economy, borrowing heavily on international capital markets—rather than lending, as would seem more natural?
   b. What implications do the U.S. current account deficit (negative net exports) and our consequent reliance on foreign credit have for economic performance in the United States?
   c. What policies, if any, should be used to address this situation?

9. **The New New World Order**

   … While gross domestic product growth is cooling a bit in emerging markets, the results are still tremendous compared with the United States and much of Western Europe. The 54 developing markets surveyed by Global Insight will post a 6.7% jump in real GDP this year, down from 7.5% last year. The 31 developed countries will grow an estimated 1.6%. The difference in growth rates represents the largest spread between developed and developing markets in the 37-year history of the survey.

   *Fortune*, July 14, 2008

   a. Do growth rates of real GDP over the past few decades indicate that world saving is shrinking, growing, or staying the same? Explain.
   b. If the world demand for loanable funds remains the same, will the world real interest rate rise, fall, or remain the same? Explain.

10. **IMF Warning Over Slowing Growth**

    The global economy may face a marked slowdown next year as a result of the turmoil in financial markets, the International Monetary Fund has warned. The IMF said the global credit squeeze would test the ability of the economy to continue expanding at recent rates. While future economic stability could not be taken for granted, there was plenty of evidence that the global economy remained durable, it added.

    *BBC News*, October 10, 2007

    a. Explain how turmoil in global financial markets might affect the demand for loanable funds, investment, and global economic growth in the future.
    b. What might be the evidence that the global economy will continue to grow?

11. Annie runs a fitness center. On December 31, 2008, she bought an existing business with exercise equipment and a building worth $300,000. During 2009, business improved and she bought some new equipment for $50,000. At the end of 2009, her equipment and buildings were worth $325,000. Calculate Annie's gross investment, depreciation, and net investment during 2009.
12. Karrie is a golf pro, and after she paid taxes, her income from golf and interest from financial assets was $1,500,000 in 2008. At the beginning of 2008, she owned $900,000 worth of financial assets. At the end of 2008, Karrie's financial assets were worth $1,900,000.
    a. How much did Karrie save during 2008?
    b. How much did she spend on consumption goods and services?
13. In 2008, the Lee family had disposable income of $80,000, wealth of $140,000, and an expected future income of $80,000 a year. At a real interest rate of 4 percent a year, the Lee family saves $15,000 a year; at a real interest rate of 6 percent a year, they save $20,000 a year; and at a real interest rate of 8 percent, they save $25,000 a year.
    a. Draw a graph of the Lee family's supply of loanable funds curve.
    b. In 2009, suppose that the stock market crash es and the default risk increases. Explain how this increase in default risk influences the Lee family's supply of loanable funds curve.
14. Draw a graph to illustrate the effect of an increase in the demand for loanable funds and an even larger increase in the supply of loanable funds on the real interest rate and the equilibrium quantity of loanable funds.
15. **India's Economy Hits the Wall**

    Just six months ago, India was looking good. Annual growth was 9%, corporate profits were surging 20%, the stock market had risen 50% in 2007, consumer demand was huge, local companies were making ambitious international acquisitions, and foreign investment was growing. Nothing, it seemed, could stop the forward march of this Asian nation. But stop it has. … The country is reeling from 11.4% inflation, large government deficits, and rising interest rates. … Most economic forecasts expect growth to slow to 7%—a big drop for a country that needs to accelerate growth, not reduce it. … A June 16 report by Goldman Sachs' Jim O'Neill and Tushar Poddar … urges India to improve governance, raise educational achievement, and control inflation. It also advises … liberalizing its financial markets. …

    *BusinessWeek*, July 1, 2008

    a. Suppose that the Indian government reduces its deficit and returns to a balanced budget. If other things remain the same, how will the demand or supply of loanable funds in India change?
    b. With economic growth forecasted to slow, future incomes are expected to fall. If other things remain the same, how will the demand or supply of loanable funds in India change?
16. **The Global Savings Glut and Its Consequences**

    The world is experiencing an unprecedented glut of savings, driving down real interest rates. It is a good time to borrow rather than lend. … Several developing countries are running large current account surpluses (representing an excess of savings over investment). … China has the biggest surplus of $1.2 trillion, but other developing countries put together have accumulated almost as much. … Rapid growth leads to high saving rates: people save a large fraction of additional income. In India, GDP growth has accelerated from 6% to 9%, lifting the saving rate from 23% a decade ago to 33% today. China's saving rate is a dizzy 55%. Not even the investment boom in Asia can absorb these huge savings, which are therefore put into U.S. bonds. When a poor country buys U.S. bonds, it is in effect lending to the United States.

    *The Cato Institute*, June 8, 2007

    a. Graphically illustrate and explain the impact of the "unprecedented glut of savings" on the real interest rate and the quantity of loanable funds.
    b. How do the high saving rates in China and India impact investment in the United States? How does this investment influence the production function and potential GDP in the United States?
17. … Most economists agree that the problems we are witnessing today developed over a long period of time. For more than a decade, a massive amount of money flowed into the United

States from investors abroad, because our country is an attractive and secure place to do business. This large influx of money to U.S. banks and financial institutions—along with low interest rates—made it easier for Americans to get credit. These developments allowed more families to borrow money for cars and homes and college tuition—some for the first time. They allowed more entrepreneurs to get loans to start new businesses and create jobs.

President George W. Bush, *Address to the Nation*, September 24, 2008

a. Explain why, for more than a decade, a massive amount of money flowed into the United States and compare and contrast your explanation with that of the President.
b. Explain why interest rates were low using the loanable funds analysis.
c. Provide a graphical analysis of the reasons why the interest rate was low.
d. Funds have been flowing into the United States since the early 1980s. Why might they have created problems in 2008 but not earlier?
e. Could the United States stop funds from flowing in from other countries? How?

18. **Greenspan's Conundrum Spells Confusion for Us All**

... At the beginning of the year, the consensus was that ... bond yields would rise. ... Gradually, over February, the consensus has started to reassert itself. ... Ten-year Treasury bond yields were hovering below 4 percent in the early part of the month but now they are around 4.3 percent.

Because the consensus was that bond yields should be 5 percent by the end of the year, most commentators have focused, not on why bond yields have suddenly risen, but on why they were so low before.

A number of explanations for this "conundrum" have been advanced. First, bond yields are being held artificially low by unusual buying. ... Another [is] ... bond yields reflect investors' expectations for an economic slowdown in 2005.

*Financial Times*, February 26, 2005

a. Explain how "unusual buying" might lead to a low real interest rate.
b. Explain how "investors' expectations for an economic slowdown" might lead to a lower real interest rate.

19. Study *Reading Between the Lines* on pp. 178–179 and then answer the following questions.
    a. What was the financial rescue package proposed by the Administration and what was it supposed to do?
    b. What did the government hope would occur after the rescue package was passed?
    c. Based on what happened in the stock market, do you think we can conclude that suppliers of loanable funds believed that the rescue package was needed and would work? Explain your answer.
    d. What did the government fear would occur if the rescue package was not passed?
    e. Again, based on what happened in the stock market, do you think we can conclude that suppliers of loanable funds shared the government's fears? Explain your answer.
    f. What other measures might the government take if it wants to boost supply and demand in the market for loanable funds?
    g. How do you think the global nature of the loanable funds markets influences how the U.S. market would have responded to no rescue package?

# 8 Money, the Price Level, and Inflation

**After studying this chapter, you will be able to:**

- Define money and describe its functions
- Explain the economic functions of banks and other depository institutions
- Describe the structure and functions of the Federal Reserve System (the Fed)
- Explain how the banking system creates money
- Explain what determines the demand for money, the supply of money, and the nominal interest rate
- Explain how the quantity of money influences the price level and the inflation rate in the long run

**Money, like fire and the wheel, has been around for** a long time, and it has taken many forms. Money was wampum (beads made from shells) for North American Indians, whale's teeth for Fijians, and tobacco for early American colonists. Cakes of salt served as money in Ethiopia and Tibet. Today, when we want to buy something, we use coins or dollar bills, write a check, or swipe a debit card or a credit card. Soon, we'll be using a "smart card" that keeps track of spending and that our pocket computer can read. Are all these things money?

When we deposit some coins or notes into a bank, is that still money? And what happens when the bank lends the money we've deposited to someone else? How can we get our money back if it has been lent out?

The quantity of money in our economy is regulated by the Federal Reserve—the Fed. How does the Fed influence the quantity of money? And what happens if the Fed creates too much money or too little money?

In this chapter, we study the functions of money, the banks that create it, the Federal Reserve and its influence on the quantity of money, and the long-run consequences of changes in the quantity of money. In *Reading Between the Lines* at the end of the chapter, we look at a spectacular example of money and inflation in action in the African nation Zimbabwe.

## What Is Money?

What do wampum, tobacco, and nickels and dimes have in common? They are all examples of **money**, which is defined as any commodity or token that is generally acceptable as a means of payment. A **means of payment** is a method of settling a debt. When a payment has been made, there is no remaining obligation between the parties to a transaction. So what wampum, tobacco, and nickels and dimes have in common is that they have served (or still do serve) as the means of payment. Money serves three other functions:

- Medium of exchange
- Unit of account
- Store of value

### Medium of Exchange

A *medium of exchange* is any object that is generally accepted in exchange for goods and services. Without a medium of exchange, goods and services must be exchanged directly for other goods and services—an exchange called **barter**. Barter requires a *double coincidence of wants*, a situation that rarely occurs. For example, if you want a hamburger, you might offer a CD in exchange for it. But you must find someone who is selling hamburgers and wants your CD.

A medium of exchange overcomes the need for a double coincidence of wants. Money acts as a medium of exchange because people with something to sell will always accept money in exchange for it. But money isn't the only medium of exchange. You can buy with a credit card, but a credit card isn't money. It doesn't make a final payment, and the debt it creates must eventually be settled by using money.

### Unit of Account

A *unit of account* is an agreed measure for stating the prices of goods and services. To get the most out of your budget, you have to figure out whether seeing one more movie is worth its opportunity cost. But that cost is not dollars and cents. It is the number of ice-cream cones, sodas, or cups of coffee that you must give up. It's easy to do such calculations when all these goods have prices in terms of dollars and cents (see Table 8.1). If the price of a movie is $8 and the price of a case of soda is $4, you know right away that seeing one movie costs you 2 cases of soda. If jelly beans are 50¢ a pack, one movie costs 16 packs of jelly beans. You need only one calculation to figure out the opportunity cost of any pair of goods and services.

**TABLE 8.1** The Unit of Account Function of Money Simplifies Price Comparisons

| Good | Price in money units | Price in units of another good |
|---|---|---|
| Movie | $8.00 each | 2 cases of soda |
| Soda | $4.00 per case | 2 ice-cream cones |
| Ice cream | $2 per cone | 4 packs of jelly beans |
| Jelly beans | $0.50 per pack | 2 sticks of gum |
| Gum | $0.25 per stick | |

*Money as a unit of account*: The price of a movie is $8 and the price of a stick of gum is 25¢, so the opportunity cost of a movie is 32 sticks of gum ($8.00 ÷ 25¢ = 32).
*No unit of account*: You go to a movie theater and learn that the price of a movie is 2 cases of soda. You go to a candy store and learn that a pack of jelly beans costs 2 sticks of gum. But how many sticks of gum does seeing a movie cost you? To answer that question, you go to the convenience store and find that a case of soda costs 2 ice-cream cones. Now you head for the ice-cream shop, where an ice-cream cone costs 4 packs of jelly beans. Now you get out your pocket calculator: 1 movie costs 2 cases of soda, or 4 ice-cream cones, or 16 packs of jelly beans, or 32 sticks of gum!

Imagine how troublesome it would be if your local movie theater posted its price as 2 cases of soda, the convenience store posted the price of a case of soda as 2 ice-cream cones, the ice-cream shop posted the price of an ice-cream cone as 4 packs of jelly beans, and the candy store priced a pack of jelly beans as 2 sticks of gum! Now how much running around and calculating will you have to do to find out how much that movie is going to cost you in terms of the soda, ice cream, jelly beans, or gum that you must give up to see it? You get the answer for soda right away from the sign posted on the movie theater. But for all the other goods, you're going to have to visit many different stores to establish the price of each commodity in terms of another and then calculate the prices in units that are relevant for your own decision. The hassle of doing all this research might be enough to make a person swear off movies! You can see how much simpler it is if all the prices are expressed in dollars and cents.

### Store of Value

Money is a *store of value* in the sense that it can be held and exchanged later for goods and services. If money were not a store of value, it could not serve as a means of payment.

Money is not alone in acting as a store of value. A house, a car, and a work of art are other examples.

The more stable the value of a commodity or token, the better it can act as a store of value and the more useful it is as money. No store of value has a completely stable value. The value of a house, a car, or a work of art fluctuates over time. The value of the commodities and tokens that are used as money also fluctuate over time.

Inflation lowers the value of money and the values of other commodities and tokens that are used as money. To make money as useful as possible as a store of value, a low inflation rate is needed.

### Money in the United States Today

In the United States today, money consists of

- Currency
- Deposits at banks and other depository institutions

**Currency** The notes and coins held by individuals and businesses are known as **currency**. Notes are money because the government declares them so with the words "This note is legal tender for all debts, public and private." You can see these words on every dollar bill. Notes and coins *inside* banks are not counted as currency because they are not held by individuals and businesses.

**Deposits** Deposits of individuals and businesses at banks and other depository institutions, such as savings and loan associations, are also counted as money. Deposits are money because the owners of the deposits can use them to make payments.

**Official Measures of Money** Two official measures of money in the United States today are known as M1 and M2. **M1** consists of currency and traveler's checks plus checking deposits owned by individuals and businesses. M1 does *not* include currency held by banks, and it does not include currency and checking deposits owned by the U.S. government. **M2** consists of M1 plus time deposits, savings deposits, and money market mutual funds and other deposits.

## Official Measures of U.S. Money

### Currency a Small Part of the Total

The figure shows the relative magnitudes of the items that make up M1 and M2. Notice that M2 is almost five times as large as M1 and that currency is a small part of our money.

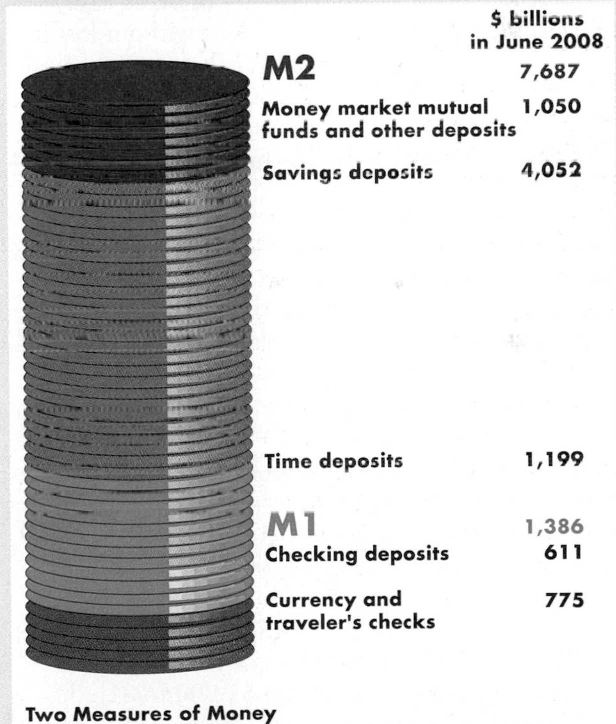


Two Measures of Money

**M1**
- Currency and traveler's checks
- Checking deposits at commercial banks, savings and loan associations, savings banks, and credit unions

**M2**
- M1
- Time deposits
- Savings deposits
- Money market mutual funds and other deposits

*Source of data:* The Federal Reserve Board.

**Are M1 and M2 Really Money?** Money is the means of payment. So the test of whether an asset is money is whether it serves as a means of payment. Currency passes the test. But what about deposits? Checking deposits are money because they can be transferred from one person to another by writing a check or using a debit card. Such a transfer of ownership is equivalent to handing over currency. Because M1 consists of currency plus checking deposits and each of these is a means of payment, *M1 is money*.

But what about M2? Some of the savings deposits in M2 are just as much a means of payment as the checking deposits in M1. You can use the ATM at the grocery store checkout or gas station and transfer funds directly from your savings account to pay for your purchase. But some savings deposits are not means of payment. These deposits are known as liquid assets. *Liquidity* is the property of being easily convertible into a means of payment without loss in value. Because the deposits in M2 that are not means of payment are quickly and easily converted into a means of payment—into currency or checking deposits—they are counted as money.

**Deposits Are Money but Checks Are Not** In defining money, we include, along with currency, deposits at banks and other depository institutions. But we do not count the checks that people write as money. Why are deposits money and checks not?

To see why deposits are money but checks are not, think about what happens when Colleen buys some roller-blades for $200 from Rocky's Rollers. When Colleen goes to Rocky's shop, she has $500 in her deposit account at the Laser Bank. Rocky has $1,000 in his deposit account—at the same bank, as it happens. The total deposits of these two people are $1,500. Colleen writes a check for $200. Rocky takes the check to the bank right away and deposits it. Rocky's bank balance rises from $1,000 to $1,200, and Colleen's balance falls from $500 to $300. The total deposits of Colleen and Rocky are still the same as before: $1,500. Rocky now has $200 more than before, and Colleen has $200 less.

This transaction has transferred money from Colleen to Rocky, but the check itself was never money. There wasn't an extra $200 of money while the check was in circulation. The check instructs the bank to transfer money from Colleen to Rocky.

If Colleen and Rocky use different banks, there is an extra step. Rocky's bank credits $200 to Rocky's account and then takes the check to a check-clearing center. The check is then sent to Colleen's bank, which pays Rocky's bank $200 and then debits Colleen's account $200. This process can take a few days, but the principles are the same as when two people use the same bank.

**Credit Cards Are Not Money** You've just seen that checks are not money. What about credit cards? Isn't having a credit card in your wallet and presenting the card to pay for your roller-blades the same thing as using money? Why aren't credit cards somehow valued and counted as part of the quantity of money?

When you pay by check, you are frequently asked to prove your identity by showing your driver's license. It would never occur to you to think of your driver's license as money. It's just an ID card. A credit card is also an ID card, but one that lets you take out a loan at the instant you buy something. When you sign a credit card sales slip, you are saying, "I agree to pay for these goods when the credit card company bills me." Once you get your statement from the credit card company, you must make at least the minimum payment due. To make that payment, you need money—you need to have currency or a checking deposit to pay the credit card company. So although you use a credit card when you buy something, the credit card is not the *means of payment* and it is not money.

## Review Quiz

1. What makes something money? What functions does money perform? Why do you think packs of chewing gum don't serve as money?
2. What are the problems that arise when a commodity is used as money?
3. What are the main components of money in the United States today?
4. What are the official measures of money? Are all the measures really money?
5. Why are checks and credit cards not money?

Work Study Plan 8.1 and get instant feedback.

We've seen that the main component of money in the United States is deposits at banks and other depository institutions. Let's take a closer look at these institutions.

## Depository Institutions

A **depository institution** is a financial firm that takes deposits from households and firms. These deposits are components of M1 and M2. You will learn what these institutions are, what they do, the economic benefits they bring, how they are regulated, and how they have innovated to create new financial products.

### Types of Depository Institution

The deposits of three types of financial firm make up the nation's money. They are

- Commercial banks
- Thrift institutions
- Money market mutual funds

**Commercial Banks** A *commercial bank* is a firm that is licensed to receive deposits and make loans. In 2008, about 7,000 commercial banks operated in the United States but mergers make this number fall each year as small banks disappear and big banks expand.

A few very large commercial banks offer a wide range of banking services and have extensive international operations. The largest of these banks are Bank of America, Citigroup, and JPMorgan Chase. Most commercial banks are small and serve their regional and local communities.

The deposits of commercial banks represent 37 percent of M1 and 61 percent of M2.

**Thrift Institutions** Savings and loan associations, savings banks, and credit unions are *thrift institutions.*

***Savings and Loan Association*** A *savings and loan association* (S&L) is a depository institution that receives deposits and makes personal, commercial, and home-purchase loans.

***Savings Bank*** A *savings bank* is a depository institution that accepts savings deposits and makes mostly home-purchase loans.

***Credit Union*** A *credit union* is a depository institution owned by a social or economic group, such as a firm's employees, that accepts savings deposits and makes mostly personal loans.

The deposits of the thrift institutions represent 10 percent of M1 and 18 percent of M2.

**Money Market Mutual Funds** A *money market mutual fund* is a fund operated by a financial institution that sells shares in the fund and holds assets such as U.S. Treasury bills and short-term commercial bills.

Money market mutual fund shares act like bank deposits. Shareholders can write checks on their money market mutual fund accounts, but there are restrictions on most of these accounts. For example, the minimum deposit accepted might be $2,500, and the smallest check a depositor is permitted to write might be $500.

Money market mutual funds do not feature in M1 and represent 13 percent of M2

### What Depository Institutions Do

Depository institutions provide services such as check clearing, account management, credit cards, and Internet banking, all of which provide an income from service fees.

But depository institutions earn most of their income by using the funds they receive from depositors to make loans and buy securities that earn a higher interest rate than that paid to depositors. In this activity, a depository institution must perform a balancing act weighing return against risk. To see this balancing act, we'll focus on the commercial banks.

A commercial bank puts the funds it receives from depositors and other funds that it borrows into four types of assets:

1. *Reserves* are notes and coins in a bank's vault or in a deposit account at the Federal Reserve. (We'll study the Federal Reserve later in this chapter.) These funds are used to meet depositors' currency withdrawals (such as when you use an ATM to get cash to buy your midnight pizza) and to make payments to other banks. In normal times, a bank keeps about a half of one percent of deposits as reserves.
2. *Liquid assets* are U.S. government Treasury bills and commercial bills. These assets are the banks' first line of defense if they need reserves. Liquid assets can be sold and instantly converted into reserves with virtually no risk of loss. Because they have a low risk, they also earn a low interest rate.
3. *Securities* are U.S. government bonds and other bonds such as mortgage-backed securities. These assets can be sold and converted into reserves but at prices that fluctuate. Because their prices

fluctuate, these assets are riskier than liquid assets, but they also have a higher interest rate.

4. *Loans* are commitments of funds for an agreed-upon period of time. Banks make loans to corporations to finance the purchase of capital. They also make mortgage loans to finance the purchase of homes, and personal loans to finance consumer durable goods, such as cars or boats. The outstanding balances on credit card accounts are also bank loans. Loans are the riskiest assets of a bank. They cannot be converted into reserves until they are due to be repaid. And some borrowers default and never repay. These riskiest of a bank's assets earn the highest interest rate.

Table 8.2 provides a snapshot of the sources and uses of funds of all the commercial banks in June 2008 that serves as a summary of the above account.

## Economic Benefits Provided by Depository Institutions

You've seen that a depository institution earns part of its profit because it pays a lower interest rate on deposits than what it earns on loans. What benefits do these institutions provide that make depositors willing to put up with a low interest rate and borrowers willing to pay a higher one?

**TABLE 8.2** Commercial Banks: Sources and Uses of Funds

| | $ billion June 2008 | Percentage of deposits |
|---|---|---|
| **Total funds** | 10,371 | 150.1 |
| ***Sources*** | | |
| Deposits | 6,911 | 100.0 |
| Borrowing | 2,322 | 33.6 |
| Own capital and other | 1,138 | 16.5 |
| ***Uses*** | | |
| Reserves | 44 | 0.6 |
| Liquid assets | 256 | 3.7 |
| Securities and other assets | 3,168 | 45.8 |
| Loans | 6,903 | 99.9 |

Commercial banks get two thirds of their funds from depositors and use a similar amount to make loans. In normal times (and the data here are for such a time) banks hold about a half of one percent as reserves and only a further almost 4 percent as liquid assets.

*Source of data*: The Federal Reserve Board.

Depository institutions provide four benefits:

- Create liquidity
- Pool risk
- Lower the cost of borrowing
- Lower the cost of monitoring borrowers

**Create Liquidity** Depository institutions create liquidity by *borrowing short and lending long*—taking deposits and standing ready to repay them on short notice or on demand and making loan commitments that run for terms of many years.

**Pool Risk** A loan might not be repaid—a default. If you lend to one person who defaults, you lose the entire amount loaned. If you lend to 1,000 people (through a bank) and one person defaults, you lose almost nothing. Depository institutions pool risk.

**Lower the Cost of Borrowing** Imagine there are no depository institutions and a firm is looking for $1 million to buy a new factory. It hunts around for several dozen people from whom to borrow the funds. Depository institutions lower the cost of this search. The firm gets its $1 million from a single institution that gets deposits from a large number of people but spreads the cost of this activity over many borrowers.

**Lower the Cost of Monitoring Borrowers** By monitoring borrowers, a lender can encourage good decisions that prevent defaults. But this activity is costly. Imagine how costly it would be if each household that lent money to a firm incurred the costs of monitoring that firm directly. Depository institutions can perform this task at a much lower cost.

## How Depository Institutions Are Regulated

Depository institutions are engaged in a risky business. And a failure, especially of a large bank, would have damaging effects on the entire financial system and economy. To make the risk of failure small, depository institutions are required to hold levels of reserves and owners' capital that equal or surpass ratios laid down by regulation. If a depository institution fails, its deposits are guaranteed up to $250,000 per depositor per bank by the *Federal Deposit Insurance Corporation* or FDIC. The FDIC can take over management of a bank that appears to be heading toward failure.

## Financial Innovation

Depository institutions are constantly seeking ways to improve their products and make larger profits. The process of developing new financial products is called *financial innovation*. Two influences on financial innovation are

- Economic environment
- Technology

The pace of financial innovation was remarkable during the 1980s and 1990s, and both of these forces played a role.

**Economic Environment** During the late 1970s and early 1980s, a high inflation rate brought high interest rates—the interest rate on home-purchase loans was as high as 15 percent a year. Traditional fixed interest rate mortgages became unprofitable and variable interest rate mortgages were introduced.

During the 2000s, when interest rates were extremely low and depository institutions were flush with funds, sub-prime mortgages were developed. These mortgages often exceeded the value of the home that secured the loan and usually had a low starter interest that escalated in later years.

To avoid the risk of carrying sub-prime mortgages, mortgage-backed securities were developed. The original lending institution sold these securities, lowered their own exposure to risk, and obtained funds to make more mortgage loans.

**Technology** The major technological influence on financial innovation is the development of low-cost computing and communication. Some examples of financial innovation that resulted from these technologies are the widespread use of credit cards and the spread of daily interest deposit accounts.

## Financial Innovation and Money

Financial innovation has brought changes in the composition of money. Checking deposits at thrift institutions—at S&Ls, savings banks, and credit unions—have become an increasing percentage of M1 while checking deposits at commercial banks have become a decreasing percentage. The composition of M2 has also changed as savings deposits have decreased, while time deposits and money market mutual funds have expanded. Surprisingly, the use of currency has not fallen much.

## Commercial Banks Under Stress

### The 2008 Credit Crisis

When Lehman Brothers (a New York investment bank) failed, panic spread through financial markets. Banks that are normally happy to lend to each other overnight for an interest rate barely above the rate they can earn on safe Treasury bills suddenly lost confidence and the interest rate in this market shot up to 3 percentage points above the Treasury bill rate. Banks wanted to be safe and to hold cash. Reserves increased to an unheard of level: They jumped to 2.6 percent and liquid assets to 4.1 percent of deposits.

But despite the credit crisis, bank deposits and bank lending kept expanding as you can see by comparing October 2008 in the table below with June 2008 in Table 8.2.

**Commercial Banks in October 2008**

| | $ billion October 2008 | Percentage of deposits |
|---|---|---|
| **Total funds** | 10,869 | 152.6 |
| **Sources** | | |
| Deposits | 7,124 | 100.0 |
| Borrowing | 2,521 | 35.4 |
| Own capital and other | 1,224 | 17.2 |
| **Uses** | | |
| Reserves | 184 | 2.6 |
| Liquid assets | 294 | 4.1 |
| Securities and other assets | 3,178 | 44.6 |
| Loans | 7,213 | 101.2 |

*Source of data*: The Federal Reserve Board.

## Review Quiz

1. What are depository institutions?
2. What are the functions of depository institutions?
3. How do depository institutions balance risk and return?
4. How do depository institutions create liquidity, pool risks, and lower the cost of borrowing?
5. How have depository institutions made innovations that have influenced the composition of money?

Work Study Plan 8.2 and get instant feedback.

You now know what money is. Your next task is to learn about the Federal Reserve System and the ways in which it can influence the quantity of money.

## The Federal Reserve System

The central bank of the United States is the **Federal Reserve System** (usually called the **Fed**). A **central bank** is a bank's bank and a public authority that regulates a nation's depository institutions and controls the quantity of money. As the banks' bank, the Fed provides banking services to commercial banks such as Citibank. A central bank is not a citizens' bank. That is, the Fed does not provide general banking services for businesses and individual citizens.

### The Fed's Goals and Targets

The Fed conducts the nation's *monetary policy,* which means that it adjusts the quantity of money in circulation. The Fed's goals are to keep inflation in check, maintain full employment, moderate the business cycle, and contribute toward achieving long-term growth. Complete success in the pursuit of these goals is impossible, and the Fed's more modest aim is to improve the performance of the economy and to get closer to the goals than a hands-off approach would achieve. Whether the Fed succeeds in improving economic performance is a matter on which there is a range of opinion.

In pursuit of its ultimate goals, the Fed pays close attention to interest rates and pays special attention to one interest rate, the **federal funds rate**, which is the interest rate that the banks charge each other on overnight loans of reserves. The Fed sets a target for the federal funds rate that is consistent with its ultimate goals and then takes actions to achieve its target.

This section examines the Fed's policy tools. Later in this chapter, we look at the long-run effects of the Fed's actions, and in Chapter 14, we look at the short-run context in which the Fed conducts monetary policy. We begin by describing the structure of the Fed.

### The Structure of the Fed

The key elements in the structure of the Federal Reserve System are

- The Board of Governors
- The regional Federal Reserve banks
- The Federal Open Market Committee

**The Board of Governors** The Board of Governors has seven members, who are appointed by the President of the United States and confirmed by the Senate, each for a 14-year term. The terms are staggered so that one seat on the board becomes vacant every two years. The President appoints one of the board members as chairman for a term of four years, which is renewable.

**The Federal Reserve Banks** There are 12 Federal Reserve banks, one for each of the 12 Federal Reserve districts shown in Fig. 8.1. These Federal Reserve banks provide check-clearing services to commercial banks and other depository institutions, hold the reserve accounts of commercial banks, lend reserves to banks, and issue the bank notes that circulate as currency.

One of the district banks, the Federal Reserve Bank of New York (known as the New York Fed), occupies a special place in the Federal Reserve System because it implements the policy decisions of the Federal Open Market Committee.

**The Federal Open Market Committee** The **Federal Open Market Committee** (FOMC) is the main policy-making organ of the Federal Reserve System. The FOMC consists of the following voting members:

- The chairman and the other six members of the Board of Governors
- The president of the Federal Reserve Bank of New York
- The presidents of the other regional Federal Reserve banks (of whom, on a yearly rotating basis, only four vote)

The FOMC meets approximately every six weeks to review the state of the economy and to decide the actions to be carried out by the New York Fed.

### The Fed's Power Center

A description of the formal structure of the Fed gives the impression that power in the Fed resides with the Board of Governors. In practice, it is the chairman of the Board of Governors who has the largest influence on the Fed's monetary policy actions, and some remarkable individuals have held this position. The current chairman is Ben Bernanke, a former eco-

FIGURE 8.1 The Federal Reserve System

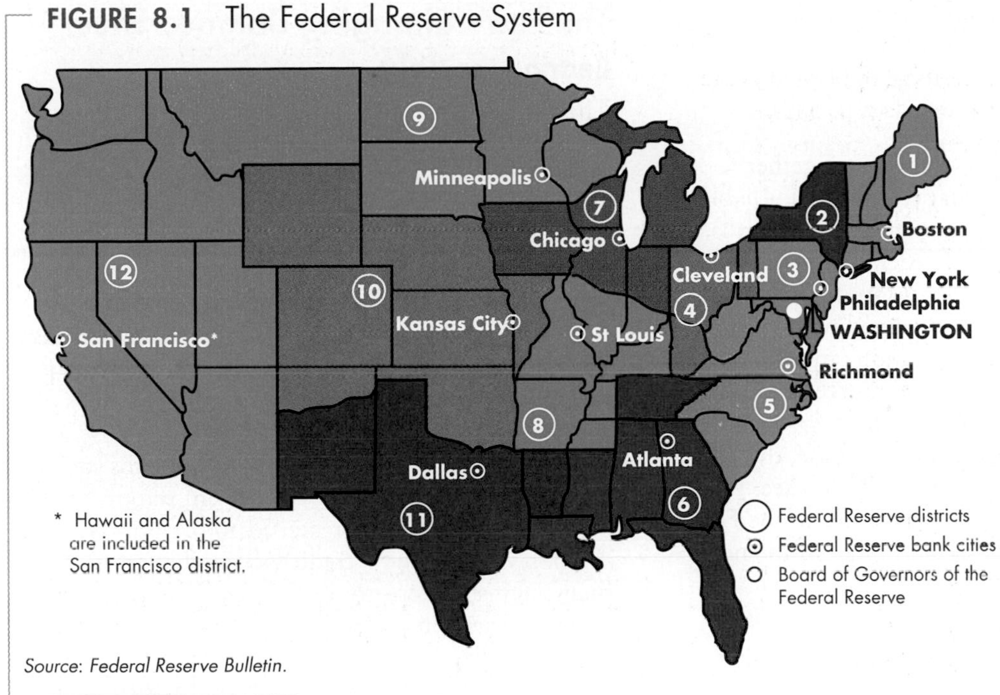


The nation is divided into 12 Federal Reserve districts, each having a Federal Reserve bank. (Some of the larger districts also have branch banks.) The Board of Governors of the Federal Reserve System is located in Washington, D.C.

*Source*: *Federal Reserve Bulletin*.

myeconlab animation

nomics professor at Princeton University, who was appointed by President George W. Bush in 2006. Bernanke followed Alan Greenspan (1987–2006) and Paul Volker (1979–1987).

The chairman's power and influence stem from three sources. First, it is the chairman who controls the agenda and who dominates the meetings of the FOMC. Second, day-to-day contact with a large staff of economists and other technical experts provides the chairman with detailed background briefings on monetary policy issues. Third, the chairman is the spokesperson for the Fed and the main liaison between the Fed, the President, and the U.S. government and with foreign central banks and governments.

## The Fed's Balance Sheet

The Fed influences the economy through the size and composition of its balance sheet—the assets that the Fed owns and the liabilities that it owes. You will learn *how* the Fed influences the economy in stages in the rest of this chapter and in Chapter 14. Here, you will learn about the items in the Fed's balance sheet.

**The Fed's Assets** The Fed has two main assets:

1. U.S. government securities
2. Loans to depository institutions

The Fed holds U.S. securities—Treasury bills and Treasury bonds—that it buys in the bond market. When the Fed buys or sells bonds, it participates in the *market for loanable funds* (see pp. 166–172).

The Fed makes loans to depository institutions. When these institutions in aggregate are short of reserves, they can borrow from the Fed. In normal times this item is small, but during 2007 and 2008, it grew as the Fed provided increasing amounts of relief from the sub-prime mortgage crisis. By October 2008, loans to depository institutions exceeded government securities in the Fed's balance sheet.

**The Fed's Liabilities** The Fed has two liabilities:

1. Federal Reserve notes
2. Depository institution deposits

Federal Reserve notes are the dollar bills that we use in our daily transactions. Some of these notes are held by individuals and businesses; others are in the tills and vaults of banks and other depository institutions.

Depository institution deposits at the Fed are part of the reserves of these institutions (see p. 189).

**The Monetary Base** The Fed's liabilities together with coins issued by the Treasury (coins are not liabilities of the Fed) make up the monetary base. That is, the **monetary base** is the sum of Federal Reserve notes, coins, and depository institution deposits at the Fed. The monetary base is so named because it acts like a base that supports the nation's money. Table 8.3 provides a snapshot of the sources and uses of the monetary base in October 2008.

When the Fed changes the monetary base, the quantity of money changes, as you will soon see. But first, we'll look at the policy tools available to the Fed for changing the monetary base and then, in the next section of this chapter, we'll see how banks create money and how the Fed can regulate its quantity.

## The Fed's Policy Tools

The Federal Reserve System has many responsibilities, but we'll examine its single most important one: regulating the amount of money floating around in the United States. How does the Fed control the quantity of money? It does so by adjusting the monetary base. Also, it is by adjusting the monetary base and by standing ready to make loans to banks that the Fed is able to prevent bank failures. The Fed uses three main policy tools to achieve its objectives.

These tools are

**TABLE 8.3** The Sources and Uses of the Monetary Base

| Sources (billions of dollars) | | Uses (billions of dollars) | |
|---|---|---|---|
| U.S. government securities | 491 | Currency | 805 |
| Loans to depository institutions | 543 | Reserves of depository institutions | 180 |
| Other items (net) | –49 | | |
| Monetary base | 985 | Monetary base | 985 |

*Source of data*: Federal Reserve Board: The data are for October 8, 2008.

## The Fed's Changing Balance Sheet

### Bearing the Risks

The Fed's balance sheet underwent some remarkable changes from mid-2007 to October 2008. The figure shows the effects of these changes on the size and composition of the monetary base.

In normal times, the Fed's holdings of U.S. government securities are almost as large as the monetary base (currency and depository institution reserves). But during the 2007–2008 sub-prime crisis, the Fed swapped a large volume of government securities for riskier loans to depository institutions. Holdings of government securities almost halved from close to $800 billion to less than $500 billion. Loans to depository institutions increased from zero to $1,000 billion. Some of this increase, $150 billion, was Term Auction Credit, a new credit facility that enables financial institutions to obtain high quality government securities in exchange for hard-to-sell risky private securities.

On the liabilities side of the Fed's balance sheet, reserves of depository institutions are usually a very small item. But during the sub-prime crisis, these institutions wanted to keep larger reserves and this item grew from $44 billion to $650 billion.

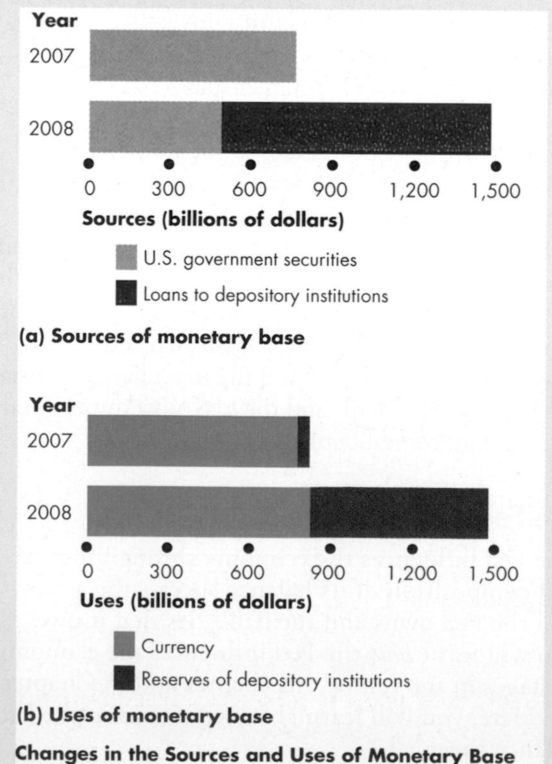


**Changes in the Sources and Uses of Monetary Base**

- Required reserve ratio
- Last resort loans
- Open market operations

**Required Reserve Ratio** Depository institutions are required to hold a minimum percentage of deposits as reserves, which is known as a **required reserve ratio.** In 2008, the Fed required banks to hold minimum reserves equal to 3 percent of checking deposits between $10.3 million and $44.4 million and 10 percent of these deposits in excess of $44.4 million. The required reserves on other types of deposits are zero.

**Last Resort Loans** The Fed is the **lender of last resort,** which means that if depository institutions are short of reserves, they can borrow from the Fed. But the Fed sets the interest rate on last resort loans and this interest rate is called the **discount rate.**

During the period since August 2007 when the first effects of the sub-prime mortgage crisis started to be felt, the Fed has been especially active as lender of last resort and has created, with the U.S. Treasury, a number of new lending facilities and initiatives to prevent banks from failing.

**Open Market Operations** An **open market operation** is the purchase or sale of government securities—U.S. Treasury bills and bonds—by the Federal Reserve System in the open market. When the Fed conducts an open market operation, it makes a transaction with a bank or some other business but it does not transact with the federal government.

## Review Quiz

1. What is the central bank of the United States and what functions does it perform?
2. What is the monetary base and how does it relate to the Fed's balance sheet?
3. What are the Fed's three policy tools?
4. What is the Federal Open Market Committee and what are its main functions?

Work Study Plan 8.3 and get instant feedback.

Next, we're going to see how the banking system—the banks and the Fed—creates money.

## How Banks Create Money

Banks create money. But this doesn't mean that they have smoke-filled back rooms in which counterfeiters are busily working. Remember, most money is bank deposits, not currency. What banks create is deposits, and they do so by making loans.

### Creating Deposits by Making Loans

The easiest way to see that banks create deposits is to think about what happens when Andy, who has a Visa card issued by Citibank, uses his card to buy a tank of gas from Chevron. When Andy signs the card sales slip, he takes a loan from Citibank and obligates himself to repay the loan at a later date. At the end of the business day, a Chevron clerk takes a pile of signed credit card sales slips, including Andy's, to Chevron's bank. For now, let's assume that Chevron also banks at Citibank. The bank immediately credits Chevron's account with the value of the slips (minus the bank's commission).

You can see that these transactions have created a bank deposit and a loan. Andy has increased the size of his loan (his credit card balance), and Chevron has increased the size of its bank deposit. Because bank deposits are money, Citibank has created money.

If, as we've just assumed, Andy and Chevron use the same bank, no further transactions take place. But the outcome is essentially the same when two banks are involved. If Chevron's bank is Bank of America, then Citibank uses its reserves to pay Bank of America. Citibank has an increase in loans and a decrease in reserves; Bank of America has an increase in reserves and an increase in deposits. The banking system as a whole has an increase in loans and deposits but no change in reserves.

If Andy had swiped his card at an automatic payment pump, all these transactions would have occurred at the time he filled his tank, and the quantity of money would have increased by the amount of his purchase (minus the bank's commission for conducting the transactions).

The quantity of deposits that the banking system can create is limited by three factors:

- The monetary base
- Desired reserves
- Desired currency holdings

**The Monetary Base** You've seen that the *monetary base* is the sum of Federal Reserve notes, coins, and banks' deposits at the Fed. The size of the monetary base limits the total quantity of money that the banking system can create. The reason is that banks have a desired level of reserves, households and firms have a desired holding of currency, and both of these desired holdings of the monetary base depend on the quantity of money.

**Desired Reserves** A bank's *actual* **reserves** consist of the notes and coins in its vaults and its deposit at the Federal Reserve. A bank uses its reserves to meet depositors' demand for currency and to make payments to other banks.

You've also seen that banks don't have $100 of reserves for every $100 that people have deposited with them. If the banks did behave that way, they wouldn't make a profit.

In September 2008, banks had reserves of $7.50 for every $100 of M1 deposits and $1.36 for every $100 of M2 deposits. Most of these reserves are currency. You saw in the previous section that reserves in the form of deposits at the Federal Reserve are tiny. But there's no need for panic. Banks hold the quantity of reserves that are adequate for their ordinary business needs.

The fraction of a bank's total deposits that are held in reserves is called the **reserve ratio**. So with reserves of $7.50 for every $100 of M1 deposits, the M1 reserve ratio is 0.075 or 7.5 percent, and with reserves of $1.36 for every $100 of M2 deposits, the M2 reserve ratio is 0.0136 or 1.36 percent.

A bank's desired reserves are the reserves that it wishes to hold. Banks are *required* to hold a quantity of reserves that does not fall below a specified percentage of total deposits. This percentage is the *required reserve ratio*.

The fraction of a bank's total deposits that it *wants* to hold in reserves is called the **desired reserve ratio**. This ratio exceeds the required reserve ratio by an amount that the banks determine to be prudent on the basis of their daily business requirements.

A bank's reserve ratio changes when its customers make a deposit or a withdrawal. If a bank's customer makes a deposit, reserves and deposits increase by the same amount, so the bank's reserve ratio increases. Similarly, if a bank's customer makes a withdrawal, reserves and deposits decrease by the same amount, so the bank's reserve ratio decreases.

A bank's **excess reserves** are its actual reserves minus its desired reserves. When a bank has excess reserves, it makes loans and creates money; and when it is short of reserves—when desired reserves exceed actual reserves—its loans and deposits shrink.

When the entire banking system has excess reserves, loans and deposits increase and when the banking system is short of reserves, loans and deposits decrease.

The greater the desired reserve ratio, the smaller is the quantity of money that the banking system can create from a given monetary base.

**Desired Currency Holding** We hold our money in the form of currency and bank deposits. The proportion of money held as currency isn't constant but at any given time, people have a definite view as to how much they want to hold in each form of money.

In 2008, for every dollar of M1 deposits held, we held $1.27 of currency and for every dollar of M2 deposits, we held 11¢ of currency.

Because households and firms want to hold some proportion of their money in the form of currency, when the total quantity of bank deposits increases, so does the quantity of currency that they want to hold. Because desired currency holding increases when deposits increase, currency leaves the banks when loans are made and deposits increase. We call the leakage of currency from the banking system the *currency drain*, and we call the ratio of currency to deposits the **currency drain ratio**.

The greater the currency drain ratio, the smaller is the quantity of deposits and money that the banking system can create from a given amount of monetary base.

## The Money Creation Process

The money creation process begins when the monetary base increases and the banking system has excess reserves. These excess reserves come from a purchase of securities by the Fed from a bank. (Chapter 14, pp. 357–358, explains exactly how the Fed conducts such a purchase—what is called an open market operation.)

When the Fed buys securities from a bank, the bank's reserves increase but its deposits do not change. So the bank has excess reserves. It lends those excess reserves and a sequence of events then plays out.

The sequence, which keeps repeating until all the

reserves held are desired and banks have no excess reserves, has eight steps:

1. Banks have excess reserves.
2. Banks lend excess reserves.
3. The quantity of money increases.
4. New money is used to make payments.
5. Some of the new money remains on deposit.
6. Some of the new money is a *currency drain*.
7. Desired reserves increase because deposits have increased.
8. Excess reserves decrease but remain positive.

The sequence repeats in a series of rounds, but each round begins with a smaller quantity of excess reserves than the quantity at the start of the previous one. The process of money creation continues until excess reserves have been eliminated. Figure 8.2 illustrates the first round in this process.

## The Money Multiplier

The **money multiplier** is the ratio of the change in the quantity of money to the change in monetary base. For example, if an increase in the monetary base by $100,000 increases the quantity of money by $250,000, then the money multiplier is 2.5.

The Mathematical Note on pp. 206–207 explains how the magnitude of the money multiplier depends on the reserve ratio and the currency drain ratio.

### Review Quiz

1. How do banks create money?
2. What limits the quantity of money that the banking system can create?
3. A bank manager tells you that she doesn't create money. She just lends the money that people deposit. Explain why she's wrong.

Work Study Plan 8.4 and get instant feedback.

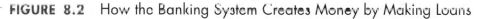

**FIGURE 8.2** How the Banking System Creates Money by Making Loans

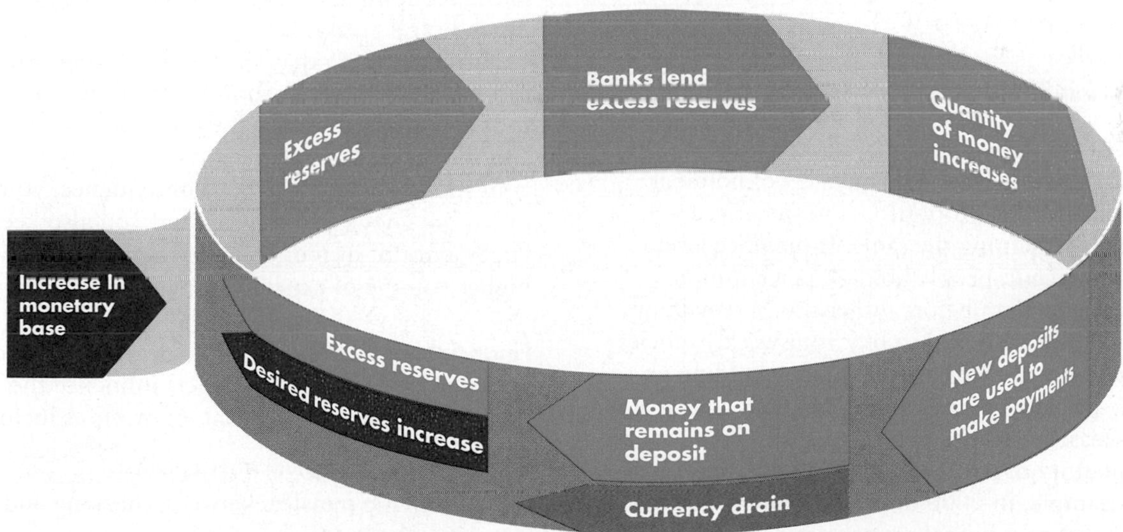


The Federal Reserve increases the monetary base which increases bank reserves and creates excess reserves. Banks lend the excess reserves and create new deposits. The quantity of money increases. New deposits are used to make payments. Some of the new money remains on deposit at banks and some leaves the banks in a currency drain. The increase in bank deposits increases banks' desired reserves. But the banks still have excess reserves, though less than before. The process repeats until excess reserves have been eliminated.

## The Market for Money

There is no limit to the amount of money we would like to *receive* in payment for our labor or as interest on our savings. But there *is* a limit to how big an inventory of money we would like to *hold* and neither spend nor use to buy assets that generate an income. The *quantity of money demanded* is the inventory of money that people plan to hold on any given day. It is the quantity of money in our wallets and in our deposit accounts at banks. The quantity of money held must equal the quantity supplied, and the forces that bring about this equality in the money market have powerful effects on the economy, as you will see in the rest of this chapter.

But first, we need to explain what determines the amount of money that people plan to hold.

### The Influences on Money Holding

The quantity of money that people plan to hold depends on four main factors:

- The price level
- The *nominal* interest rate
- Real GDP
- Financial innovation

**The Price Level** The quantity of money measured in dollars is *nominal money*. The quantity of nominal money demanded is proportional to the price level, other things remaining the same. If the price level rises by 10 percent, people hold 10 percent more nominal money than before, other things remaining the same. If you hold $20 to buy your weekly movies and soda, you will increase your money holding to $22 if the prices of movies and soda—and your wage rate—increase by 10 percent.

The quantity of money measured in constant dollars (for example, in 2000 dollars) is real money. *Real money* is equal to nominal money divided by the price level and is the quantity of money measured in terms of what it will buy. In the above example, when the price level rises by 10 percent and you increase your money holding by 10 percent, your *real* money holding is constant. Your $22 at the new price level buys the same quantity of goods and is the same quantity of *real money* as your $20 at the original price level. The quantity of real money demanded is independent of the price level.

**The *Nominal* Interest Rate** A fundamental principle of economics is that as the opportunity cost of something increases, people try to find substitutes for it. Money is no exception. The higher the opportunity cost of holding money, other things remaining the same, the smaller is the quantity of real money demanded. The nominal interest rate on other assets minus the nominal interest rate on money is the opportunity cost of holding money.

The interest rate that you earn on currency and checking deposits is zero. So the opportunity cost of holding these items is the nominal interest rate on other assets such as a savings bond or Treasury bill. By holding money instead, you forgo the interest that you otherwise would have received.

Money loses value because of inflation, so why isn't the inflation rate part of the cost of holding money? It is. Other things remaining the same, the higher the expected inflation rate, the higher is the nominal interest rate.

**Real GDP** The quantity of money that households and firms plan to hold depends on the amount they are spending, and the quantity of money demanded in the economy as a whole depends on aggregate expenditure—real GDP.

Again, suppose that you hold an average of $20 to finance your weekly purchases of movies and soda. Now imagine that the prices of these goods and of all other goods remain constant but that your income increases. As a consequence, you now buy more goods and services and you also keep a larger amount of money on hand to finance your higher volume of expenditure.

**Financial Innovation** Technological change and the arrival of new financial products influence the quantity of money held. Financial innovations include

1. Daily interest checking deposits
2. Automatic transfers between checking and saving deposits
3. Automatic teller machines
4. Credit cards and debit cards
5. Internet banking and bill paying

These innovations have occurred because of the development of computing power that has lowered the cost of calculations and record keeping.

We summarize the effects of the influences on money holding by using a demand for money curve.

## The Demand for Money

The **demand for money** is the relationship between the quantity of real money demanded and the nominal interest rate when all other influences on the amount of money that people wish to hold remain the same.

Figure 8.3 shows a demand for money curve, *MD*. When the interest rate rises, other things remaining the same, the opportunity cost of holding money rises and the quantity of real money demanded decreases—there is a movement up along the demand for money curve. Similarly, when the interest rate falls, the opportunity cost of holding money falls, and the quantity of real money demanded increases—there is a movement down along the demand for money curve.

When any influence on money holding other than the interest rate changes, there is a change in the demand for money and the demand for money curve shifts. Let's study these shifts.

## Shifts in the Demand for Money Curve

A change in real GDP or financial innovation changes the demand for money and shifts the demand for money curve.

Figure 8.4 illustrates the change in the demand for money. A decrease in real GDP decreases the demand for money and shifts the demand for money curve leftward from $MD_0$ to $MD_1$. An increase in real GDP has the opposite effect: It increases the demand for money and shifts the demand for money curve rightward from $MD_0$ to $MD_2$.

The influence of financial innovation on the demand for money curve is more complicated. It decreases the demand for currency and might increase the demand for some types of deposits and decrease the demand for others. But generally, financial innovation decreases the demand for money.

You can see the effects of changes in real GDP and financial innovation by looking at the demand for money in the United States on the next page.

**FIGURE 8.3** The Demand for Money

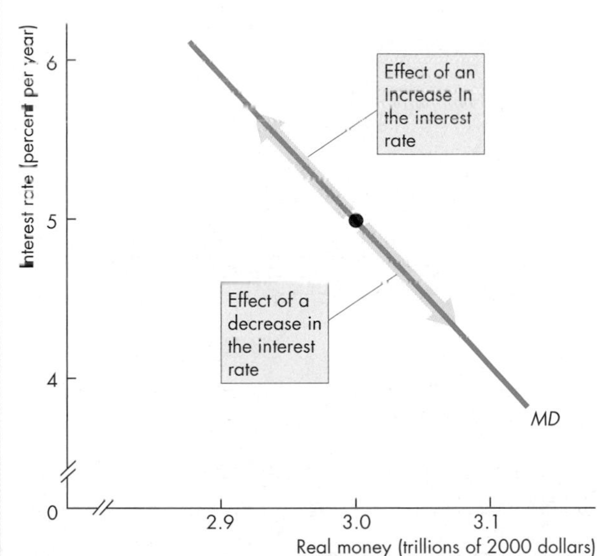


The demand for money curve, *MD*, shows the relationship between the quantity of real money that people plan to hold and the nominal interest rate, other things remaining the same. The interest rate is the opportunity cost of holding money. A change in the interest rate brings a movement along the demand for money curve.

myeconlab animation

**FIGURE 8.4** Changes in the Demand for Money

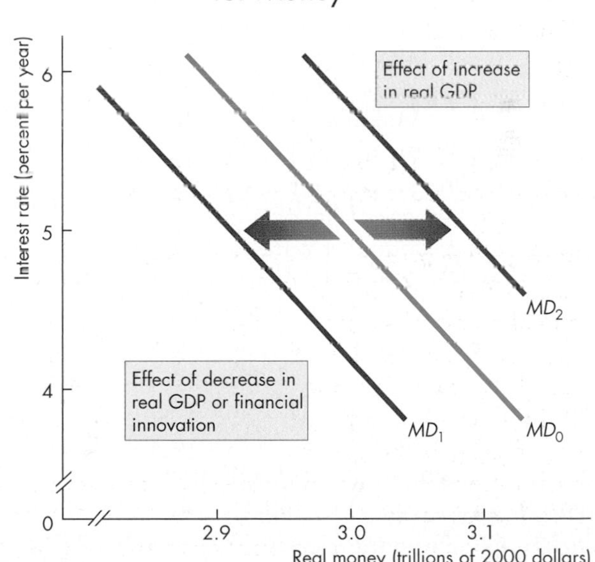


A decrease in real GDP decreases the demand for money. The demand for money curve shifts leftward from $MD_0$ to $MD_1$. An increase in real GDP increases the demand for money. The demand for money curve shifts rightward from $MD_0$ to $MD_2$. Financial innovation generally decreases the demand for money.

## Demand for Money in the United States

### How Money Holding Bounces Around

The growth of real GDP brings sustained growth in the demand for money. If real GDP were the only influence on the demand for money, the demand for money curve would shift rightward whenever real GDP increased, which is most of the time.

But financial innovation also influences the demand for money. During the early 1970s, the spread of credit cards decreased the demand for currency and checking deposits (M1).

A continued increase in the use of credit cards and the spread of ATMs further decreased the demand for M1 during the 1990s and 2000s.

Similarly, financial innovation has changed the demand for the savings deposits and money market funds that make up M2. New interest-bearing deposits increased the demand for M2 from 1970 through 1989. But between 1989 and 1994, innovations in financial products that compete with deposits of all kinds occurred and the demand for M2 decreased.

The figures illustrate the effects of the growth of real GDP and financial innovation on the demand for M1 in part (a) and M2 in part (b).

Each dot represents the quantity of real money and the interest rate in each year between 1970 and 2008. In 1970, the demand for M1 curve was $MD_0$ in part (a). The demand for M1 decreased during the early 1970s because of financial innovation, and the demand curve shifted leftward to $MD_1$. But real GDP growth increases the demand for M1, and by 1994, the demand curve had shifted rightward to $MD_2$. Further financial innovation decreased the demand for M1 during the 1990s and 2000s and shifted the demand curve leftward again to $MD_3$.

In 1970, the demand for M2 curve was $MD_0$ in part (b). The growth of real GDP increased the demand for M2, and by 1989, the demand curve had shifted rightward to $MD_1$. During the early 1990s, new substitutes for M2 decreased the demand for M2 and the demand curve shifted leftward to $MD_2$. But during the late 1990s, rapid growth of real GDP increased the demand for M2. By 2005, the demand curve had shifted rightward to $MD_3$.

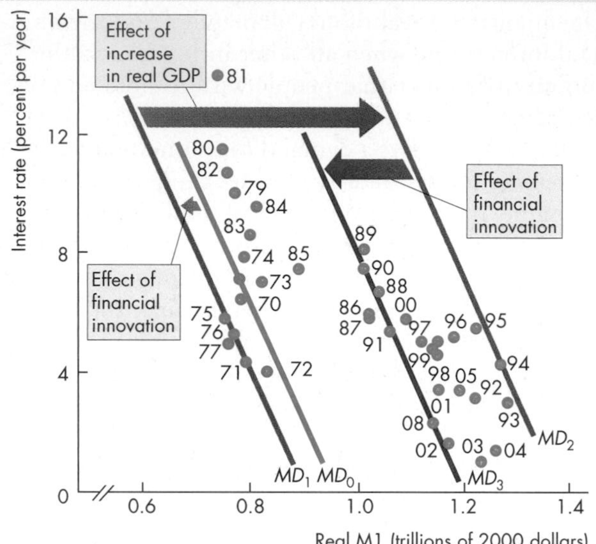


**(a) M1 demand**

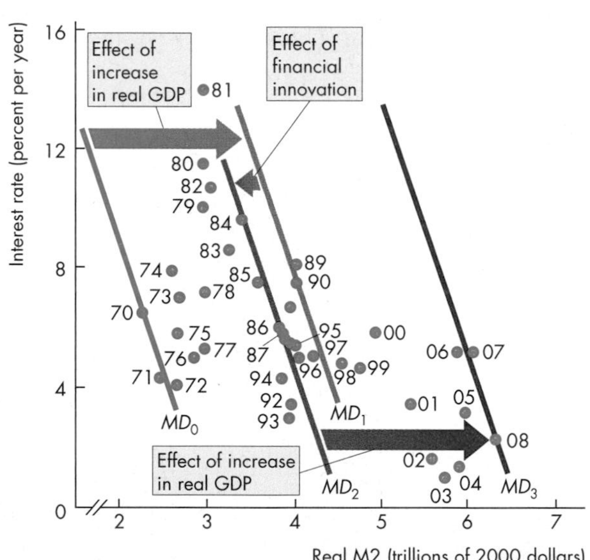


**(b) M2 demand**

**The U.S. Demand for Money**

*Sources of data*: Bureau of Economic Analysis and Federal Reserve Board.

You now know what determines the demand for money, and you've seen how the banking system creates money. Let's now see how the money market reaches an equilibrium.

## Money Market Equilibrium

Money market equilibrium occurs when the quantity of money demanded equals the quantity of money supplied. The adjustments that occur to bring money market equilibrium are fundamentally different in the short run and the long run. Our primary focus here is the long run. (We explore short-run issues in Chapters 10–14.) But we need to say a little bit about the short run so that you can appreciate how the long-run equilibrium comes about.

**Short-Run Equilibrium** The quantity of money supplied is determined by the actions of the banks and the Fed. Each day, the Fed adjusts the quantity of money to hit its interest rate target. In Fig. 8.5, with the demand for money curve *MD*, if the Fed wants the interest rate to be 5 percent a year, the Fed adjusts the quantity of money so that the quantity of real money supplied is $3.0 trillion and the supply of money curve is *MS*.

The equilibrium interest rate is 5 percent a year. If the interest rate were 4 percent a year, people would want to hold more money than is available. They would sell bonds, bid down their price, and the interest rate would rise. If the interest rate were 6 percent a year, people would want to hold less money than is available. They would buy bonds, bid up their price, and the interest rate would fall.

**Long-Run Equilibrium** In the long run, supply and demand in the loanable funds market determines the real interest rate. The nominal interest rate equals the equilibrium real interest rate plus the expected inflation rate. Real GDP, which influences the demand for money, equals potential GDP. So the *only* variable that is left to adjust in the long run is the price level. The price level adjusts to make the quantity of real money supplied equal to the quantity demanded. If the Fed changes the nominal quantity of money, the price level changes (in the long run) by a percentage equal to the percentage change in the quantity of nominal money. In the long run, the change in the price level is proportional to the change in the quantity of money.

**FIGURE 8.5** Money Market Equilibrium

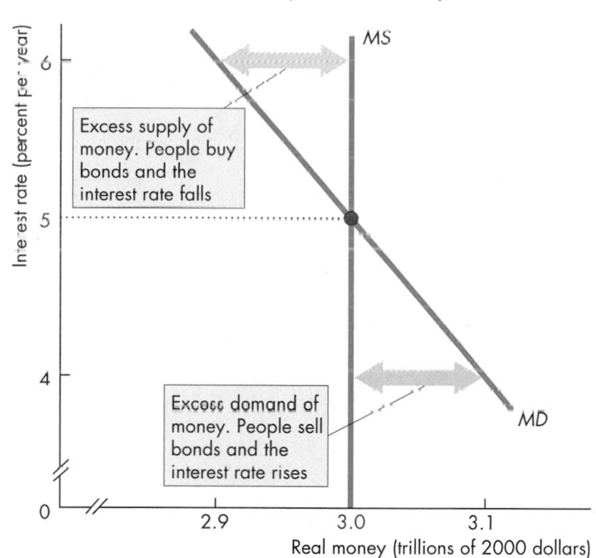


Money market equilibrium occurs when the quantity of money demanded equals the quantity supplied.

**Short run:** In the short run, the quantity of real money and real GDP are given and the interest rate adjusts to achieve equilibrium, here 5 percent a year.

**Long run:** In the long run, supply and demand in the loanable funds market determines the interest rate, real GDP equals potential GDP, and the price level adjusts to make the quantity of real money supplied equal the quantity demanded, here $3 trillion.

myeconlab animation

## Review Quiz

1. What are the main influences on the quantity of real money that people and businesses plan to hold?
2. How does a change in the nominal interest rate change the quantity of money demanded? Illustrate the effect by using the demand for money curve.
3. How does a change in real GDP change the demand for money? Illustrate the effect by using the demand for money curve.
4. How has financial innovation changed the demand for M1 and the demand for M2?
5. How is money market equilibrium determined in the short run and in the long run?

Work Study Plan 8.5 and get instant feedback.

Let's explore the long-run link between money and the price level a bit more thoroughly.

## The Quantity Theory of Money

In the long run, the price level adjusts to make the quantity of real money demanded equal the quantity supplied. A special theory of the price level and inflation—the quantity theory of money—explains this long-run adjustment of the price level.

The **quantity theory of money** is the proposition that in the long run, an increase in the quantity of money brings an equal percentage increase in the price level. To explain the quantity theory of money, we first need to define *the velocity of circulation.*

The **velocity of circulation** is the average number of times a dollar of money is used annually to buy the goods and services that make up GDP. But GDP equals the price level ($P$) multiplied by *real* GDP ($Y$). That is,

$$GDP = PY.$$

Call the quantity of money $M$. The velocity of circulation, $V$, is determined by the equation

$$V = PY/M.$$

For example, if GDP is $1,000 billion ($PY$ = $1,000 billion) and the quantity of money is $250 billion, then the velocity of circulation is 4.

From the definition of the velocity of circulation, the *equation of exchange* tells us how $M$, $V$, $P$, and $Y$ are connected. This equation is

$$MV = PY.$$

Given the definition of the velocity of circulation, the equation of exchange is always true—it is true by definition. It becomes the quantity theory of money if the quantity of money does not influence the velocity of circulation or real GDP. In this case, the equation of exchange tells us that in the long run, the price level is determined by the quantity of money. That is,

$$P = M(V/Y),$$

where $(V/Y)$ is independent of $M$. So a change in $M$ brings a proportional change in $P$.

We can also express the equation of exchange in growth rates,[1] in which form it states that

$$\text{Money growth rate} + \text{Rate of velocity change} = \text{Inflation rate} + \text{Real GDP growth rate}$$

## Does the Quantity Theory Work?

### Yes, on Average

On average, as predicted by the quantity theory of money, the inflation rate fluctuates in line with fluctuations in the money growth rate minus the real GDP growth rate. Figure 1 shows the relationship between money growth (M2 definition) and inflation in the United States. You can see a clear relationship between the two variables.

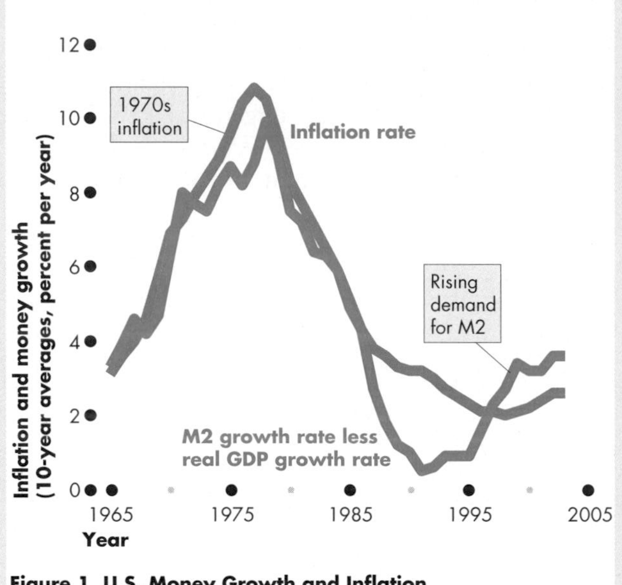


**Figure 1 U.S. Money Growth and Inflation**

*Source of data*: Federal Reserve and Bureau of Labor Statistics.

Solving this equation for the inflation rate gives

$$\text{Inflation rate} = \text{Money growth rate} + \text{Rate of velocity change} - \text{Real GDP growth rate}$$

In the long run, the rate of velocity change is not influenced by the money growth rate. More strongly, in the long run, the rate of velocity change is approxi-

[1] To obtain this equation, begin with

$$MV = PY.$$

and then changes in these variables are related by the equation

$$\Delta MV + M\Delta V = \Delta PY + P\Delta Y.$$

Divide this equation by the equation of exchange to obtain

$$\Delta M/M + \Delta V/V = \Delta P/P + \Delta Y/Y.$$

The term $\Delta M/M$ is the money growth rate, $\Delta V/V$ is the rate of velocity change, $\Delta P/P$ is the inflation rate, and $\Delta Y/Y$ is the real GDP growth rate.

International data also support the quantity theory. Figure 2 shows a scatter diagram of the inflation rate and the money growth rate in 134 countries and Fig. 3 shows the inflation rate and money growth rate in countries with inflation rates below 20 percent a year. You can see a general tendency for money growth and inflation to be correlated but the quantity theory (the red line) does not predict inflation precisely.

The correlation between money growth and inflation isn't perfect, and the correlation does not tell us that money growth *causes* inflation. Money growth might cause inflation; inflation might cause money growth; or some third variable might cause both inflation and money growth. Other evidence does confirm, though, that causation runs from money growth to inflation.

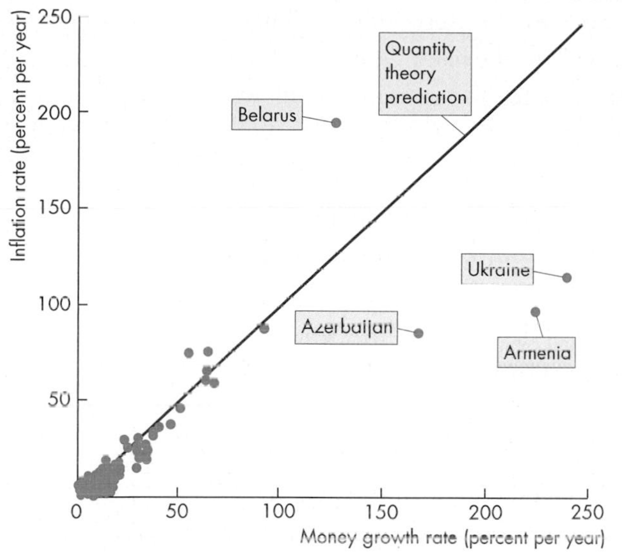


**Figure 2 134 Countries: 1990–2005**

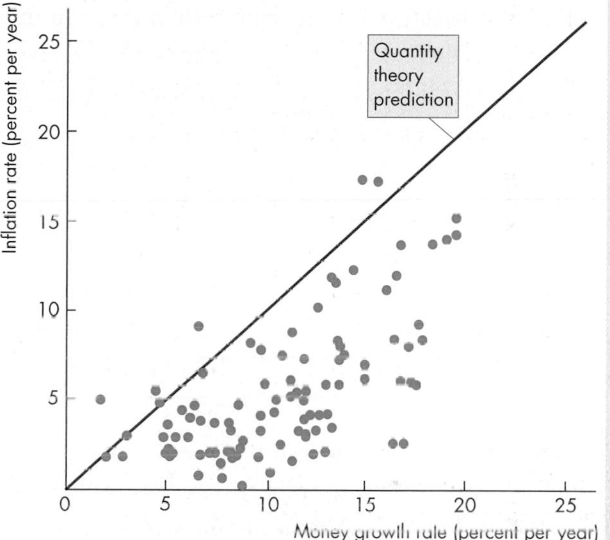


**Figure 3 104 Lower-inflation countries: 1990–2005**

*Sources of data*: International Financial Statistics Yearbook, 2008 and International Monetary Fund, *World Economic Outlook*, October, 2008.

mately zero. With this assumption, the inflation rate in the long run is determined as

$$\text{Inflation rate} = \text{Money growth rate} - \text{Real GDP growth rate}.$$

In the long run, fluctuations in the money growth rate minus the real GDP growth rate bring equal fluctuations in the inflation rate.

Also, in the long run, with the economy at full employment, real GDP equals potential GDP, so the real GDP growth rate equals the potential GDP growth rate. This growth rate might be influenced by inflation, but the influence is most likely small and the quantity theory assumes that it is zero. So the real GDP growth rate is given and doesn't change when the money growth rate changes—inflation is correlated with money growth.

## Review Quiz

1. What is the quantity theory of money?
2. How is the velocity of circulation calculated?
3. What is the equation of exchange? Can it be wrong?
4. Does the quantity theory correctly predict the effects of money growth on inflation?

Work Study Plan 8.6 and get instant feedback.

You now know what money is, how the banks create it, and how the quantity of money influences the nominal interest rate in the short-run and the price level in the long run. *Reading Between the Lines* rounds out the chapter by looking at the quantity theory of money in action in Zimbabwe today.

READING BETWEEN THE LINES

# The Quantity Theory of Money in Zimbabwe

## Life in Zimbabwe: Wait for Useless Money, Then Scour for Food

http://www.nytimes.com
October 2, 2008

Harare, Zimbabwe—Long before the rooster in their dirt yard crowed, Rose Moyo and her husband rolled out of bed … and took their daily moonlit stroll to the bank … hoping for a chance to withdraw the maximum amount of Zimbabwean currency the government allowed last month—the equivalent of just a dollar or two.

Zimbabwe is in the grip of one of the great hyperinflations in world history. The people of this once proud capital have been plunged into a Darwinian struggle to get by. Many have been reduced to peddlers and paupers, hawkers and black-market hustlers, eating just a meal or two a day, their hollowed cheeks a testament to their hunger.

… Mrs. Moyo has calculate the price of goods by the number of days she had to spend in line at the bank to withdraw cash to buy them: a day for a bar of soap; another for a bag of salt; and four for a sack of cornmeal.

The withdrawal limit rose on Monday, but with inflation surpassing what independent economists say is an almost unimaginable 40 million percent, she said the value of the new amount would quickly be a pittance, too.

"It's survival of the fittest," said Mrs. Moyo, 29, a hair braider who sells the greens she grows in her yard for a dime a bunch. "If you're not fit, you will starve."

Economists here and abroad say Zimbabwe's economic collapse is gaining velocity, radiating instability into the heart of southern Africa. As the bankrupt government prints ever more money, inflation has gone wild, rising from 1,000 percent in 2006 to 12,000 percent in 2007 to a figure so high the government had to lop 10 zeros off the currency in August to keep the nation's calculators from being overwhelmed. (Had it left the currency alone, $1 would now be worth about 10 trillion Zimbabwean dollars.) …



## Essence of the Story

- Hyperinflation in Zimbabwe is the worst in world history—40 million percent a year.
- $1 U.S. was heading toward $10 trillion Zimbabwean before 10 zeros were lopped off the currency unit.
- People get up in the middle of the night to stand in line for cash at the bank because the government limits cash withdrawals.
- Prices of goods are measured in the number of days spent in line to withdraw the cash to buy them: a day for a bar of soap or a bag of salt; four days for a sack of cornmeal.
- The people of Harare (the capital city) are on the edge of survival.
- The government fuels the inflation by printing ever more money.

## Economic Analysis

- Zimbabwe has the highest inflation rate in world history, so it provides a good example of the quantity theory of money in action.
- The quantity theory predicts that a low growth rate of the quantity of money keeps inflation low and a rapid growth rate of the quantity of money brings a high inflation rate.
- During 2008, the inflation rate in Zimbabwe was so high, it could not be measured accurately but it was reputed to be 231 million percent a year.
- To appreciate an inflation rate of 231 million percent a year, translate it to a monthly inflation rate. Every month, on average, prices rise by 239 percent. A cup of coffee that costs $3 in January costs $10 in February, $117 in April and $4,560 in July!
- Figure 1 shows Zimbabwe's reported inflation rate and money growth rate record from 2000 to 2007.
- The money growth rate increased from 52 percent a year in 2000 to 66,700 percent a year in 2007.
- The reported inflation rate increased slowly at first, from 56 percent a year in 2000 to 303 percent a year in 2005. In 2006, the inflation rate took off and climbed to a reported 1,100 percent in 2006 and 24,000 percent in 2007.
- The quantity theory predicts that inflation will outpace the money growth rate, not fall behind it as these reported inflation rates show.
- The reported inflation rate is almost certainly far lower than the true inflation rate.
- When people expect rapid inflation, they expect the money they hold to lose value rapidly, so they spend and hold goods rather than money.
- The velocity of circulation rises. The velocity of circulation is independent of the quantity of money but not independent of the money growth rate.
- We can measure the velocity of circulation in Zimbabwe by using the equation of exchange,

$$MV = PY$$

along with data on $M$, $P$, and $Y$.

- Real GDP, $Y$, has fallen every year since 2000, and in 2007 it stood at 70 percent of its 2000 level.

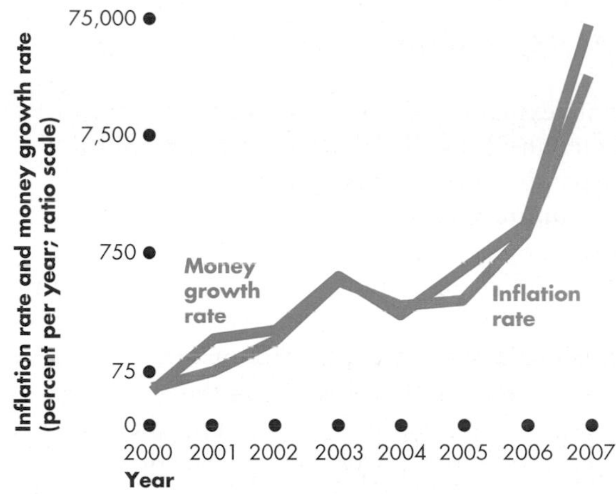


**Figure 1 Money growth and inflation**

- The velocity of circulation, based on the reported data, *fell* from 6.7 in 2000 to 0.6 in 2007.
- The true velocity of circulation could not have fallen. A lower velocity implies that people are hoarding more money.
- The explanation for the fall in the calculated velocity of circulation is that the true inflation rate is much higher than the reported rate.
- The unofficial reported inflation of 40 million percent a year in 2008 might be close to the truth. The inflation rate during the years 2003 through 2007 was almost certainly greater than the money growth rate.
- The reported change in the currency unit, lopping off 10 zeroes, has no effect on the inflation rate. It only changes the units in which prices are measured.
- To lower its inflation rate, the government of Zimbabwe must stop printing money to finance its expenditures.

## MATHEMATICAL NOTE

### The Money Multiplier

This note explains the basic math of the money multiplier and shows how the value of the multiplier depends on the banks' reserve ratio and the currency drain ratio.

To make the process of money creation concrete, we work through an example for a banking system in which each bank has a desired reserve ratio of 10 percent of deposits and the currency drain ratio is 50 percent of deposits or 0.5. (Although these ratios are larger than the ones in the U.S. economy, they make the process end more quickly and enable you to see more clearly the principles at work.)

The figure keeps track of the numbers. Before the process begins, the banks have no excess reserves. Then the monetary base increases by $100,000 and a bank has excess reserves of this amount.

The bank lends the $100,000 of excess reserves. When this loan is made, new money increases by $100,000.

With a currency drain ratio of 50 percent of deposits, $33,333 drains out of the banks as currency and $66,667 remains in the banks as deposits. The quantity of money has increased by $100,000—the increase in deposits plus the increase in currency holdings.

The increased bank deposits of $66,667 generate an increase in desired reserves of 10 percent of that amount, which is $6,667. Actual reserves have increased by the same amount as the increase in deposits: $66,667. So the banks now have excess reserves of $60,000.

The process we've just described repeats but begins with excess reserves of $60,000. The figure shows the next two rounds. At the end of the process, the quantity of money has increased by a multiple of the increase in the monetary base. In this case, the increase is $250,000, which is 2.5 times the increase in the monetary base.

The sequence in the figure is the first stages of the process that finally reaches the total shown in the final row of the "money" column.

To calculate what happens at the later stages in the process and the final increase in the quantity of money, look closely at the numbers in the figure. The

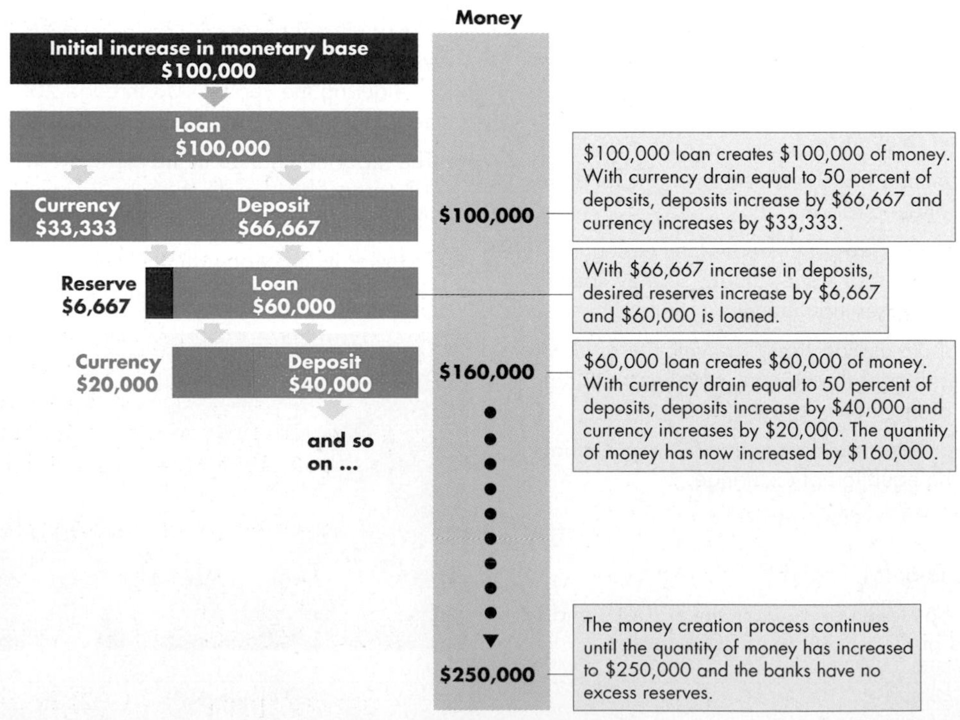


**Figure 1 The money creation process**

initial increase in reserves is \$100,000 (call it $A$). At each stage, the loan is 60 percent (0.6) of the previous loan and the quantity of money increases by 0.6 of the previous increase. Call that proportion $L$ ($L = 0.6$). We can write down the complete sequence for the increase in the quantity of money as

$$A + AL + AL^2 + AL^3 + AL^4 + AL^5 + \ldots .$$

Remember, $L$ is a fraction, so at each stage in this sequence, the amount of new loans and new money gets smaller. The total value of loans made and money created at the end of the process is the sum of the sequence, which is[1]

$$A/(1 - L).$$

If we use the numbers from the example, the total increase in the quantity of money is

$$\$100{,}000 + 60{,}000 + 36{,}000 + \ldots$$

$$= \$100{,}000\ (1 + 0.6 + 0.36 + \ldots)$$

$$= \$100{,}000\ (1 + 0.6 + 0.6^2 + \ldots)$$

$$= \$100{,}000 \times 1/(1 - 0.6)$$

$$= \$100{,}000 \times 1/(0.4)$$

$$= \$100{,}000 \times 2.5$$

$$= \$250{,}000.$$

The magnitude of the money multiplier depends on the desired reserve ratio and the currency drain ratio. Call the monetary base $MB$ and the quantity of money $M$. When there are no excess reserves,

$$MB = \text{Desired currency holding} + \text{Desired reserves.}$$

$$M = \text{Deposits} + \text{Desired currency holding.}$$

Call the currency drain ratio $a$ and the desired reserve ratio $b$. Then

$$\text{Desired currency holding} = a \times \text{Deposits}$$

$$\text{Desired reserves} = b \times \text{Deposits}$$

$$MB = (a + b) \times \text{Deposits}$$

$$M = (1 + a) \times \text{Deposits.}$$

Call the change in monetary base $\Delta MB$ and the change in the quantity of money $\Delta M$. Then

$$\Delta MB = (a + b) \times \text{Change in deposits}$$

$$\Delta M = (1 + a) \times \text{Change in deposits.}$$

The money multiplier is the ratio of $\Delta M$ to $\Delta MB$, so divide the above equation for $\Delta M$ by the one for $\Delta MB$. That is,

$$\text{Money multiplier} = (1 + a)/(a + b).$$

If we use the values of the example summarized in the figure, $a = 0.5$ and $b = 0.1$, the

$$\text{Money multiplier} = (1 + 0.5)/(0.5 + 0.1).$$

$$= 1.5/0.6 = 2.5.$$

## The U.S. Money Multiplier

The money multiplier in the United States can be found by using the formula above along with the values of $a$ and $b$ in the U.S. economy.

Because we have two definitions of money, M1 and M2, we have two money multipliers. The numbers for M1 in 2008 are $a = 1.24$ and $b = 0.28$. So

$$\text{M1 multiplier} = (1 + 1.24)/(1.24 + 0.28)$$

$$= 2.24/1.52 = 1.47.$$

For M2 in 2008, $a = 0.12$ and $b = 0.03$, so

$$\text{M2 multiplier} = (1 + 0.12)/(0.12 + 0.03)$$

$$= 1.12/0.15 = 7.5$$

[1] The sequence of values is called a convergent geometric series. To find the sum of a series such as this, begin by calling the sum $S$. Then write the sum as

$$S = A + AL + AL^2 + AL^3 + AL^4 + AL^5 + \ldots .$$

Multiply by $L$ to get

$$LS = AL + AL^2 + AL^3 + AL^4 + AL^5 + \ldots$$

and then subtract the second equation from the first to get

$$S(1 - L) = A$$

or

$$S = A/(1 - L).$$

## SUMMARY

### Key Points

**What Is Money?** (pp. 186–188)

- Money is the means of payment. It functions as a medium of exchange, a unit of account, and a store of value.
- Today, money consists of currency and deposits.

**Depository Institutions** (pp. 189–191)

- Commercial banks, S&Ls, savings banks, credit unions, and money market mutual funds are depository institutions whose deposits are money.
- Depository institutions provide four main economic services: They create liquidity, minimize the cost of obtaining funds, minimize the cost of monitoring borrowers, and pool risks.

**The Federal Reserve System** (pp. 192–195)

- The Federal Reserve System is the central bank of the United States.
- The Fed influences the quantity of money by setting the required reserve ratio, the discount rate, and by conducting open market operations.

**How Banks Create Money** (pp. 195–197)

- Banks create money by making loans.
- The total quantity of money that can be created depends on the monetary base, the desired reserve ratio, and the currency drain ratio.

**The Market for Money** (pp. 198–201)

- The quantity of money demanded is the amount of money that people plan to hold.
- The quantity of real money equals the quantity of nominal money divided by the price level.
- The quantity of real money demanded depends on the nominal interest rate, real GDP, and financial innovation. A rise in the nominal interest rate brings a decrease in the quantity of real money demanded.
- In the short run, the Fed sets the quantity of money to hit a target nominal interest rate.
- In the long run, the loanable funds market determines the real interest rate and money market equilibrium determines the price level.

**The Quantity Theory of Money** (pp. 202–203)

- The quantity theory of money is the proposition that money growth and inflation move up and down together in the long run.
- The U.S. and international evidence is consistent with the quantity theory, on average.

### Key Figures

Figure 8.2 How the Banking System Creates Money by Making Loans, 197
Figure 8.3 The Demand for Money, 199
Figure 8.5 Money Market Equilibrium, 201

### Key Terms

Barter, 186
Central bank, 192
Currency, 187
Currency drain ratio, 196
Demand for money, 199
Depository institution, 189
Desired reserve ratio, 196
Discount rate, 195
Excess reserves, 196
Federal funds rate, 192
Federal Open Market Committee, 192
Federal Reserve System (the Fed), 192
Lender of last resort, 195
M1, 187
M2, 187
Means of payment, 186
Monetary base, 194
Money, 186
Money multiplier, 197
Open market operation, 195
Quantity theory of money, 202
Required reserve ratio, 195
Reserve ratio, 196
Reserves, 196
Velocity of circulation, 202

## PROBLEMS and APPLICATIONS

myeconlab Work problems 1–12 in Chapter 8 Study Plan and get instant feedback.
Work problems 13–22 as Homework, a Quiz, or a Test if assigned by your instructor.

1. In the United States today, money includes which of the following items?
   a. Federal Reserve bank notes in Citibank's cash machines
   b. Your Visa card
   c. Coins inside a vending machine
   d. U.S. dollar bills in your wallet
   e. The check you have just written to pay for your rent
   f. The loan you took out last August to pay for your school fees
2. The commercial banks in Zap have

| | |
|---|---|
| Reserves | \$250 million |
| Loans | \$1,000 million |
| Deposits | \$2,000 million |
| Total assets | \$2,500 million |

   If banks have no excess reserves, calculate the banks' desired reserve ratio.
3. You are given the following information about the economy of Nocoin: The banks have deposits of \$300 billion. Their reserves are \$15 billion, two thirds of which is in deposits with the central bank. Households and firms hold \$30 billion in bank notes. There are no coins! Calculate
   a. The monetary base.
   b. The quantity of money.
   c. The banks' reserve ratio (as a percentage).
   d. The currency drain ratio (as a percentage).
4. [Study the Mathematical Note on pp. 206–207 to work this problem.] In problem 3, the banks have no excess reserves. Suppose that the Bank of Nocoin, the central bank, increases bank reserves by \$0.5 billion.
   a. What happens to the quantity of money?
   b. Explain why the change in the quantity of money is not equal to the change in the monetary base.
   c. Calculate the money multiplier.
5. In problem 3, the banks have no excess reserves. Suppose that the Bank of Nocoin, the central bank, decreases bank reserves by \$0.5 billion.
   a. Calculate the money multiplier.
   b. What happens to the quantity of money?
   c. What happens to the quantity of deposits?
   d. What happens to the quantity of currency?
6. The spreadsheet provides information about the demand for money in Minland. Column A is the nominal interest rate, *r*.

| | A | B | C |
|---|---|---|---|
| 1 | $r$ | $Y_0$ | $Y_1$ |
| 2 | 7 | 1.0 | 1.5 |
| 3 | 6 | 1.5 | 2.0 |
| 4 | 5 | 2.0 | 2.5 |
| 5 | 4 | 2.5 | 3.0 |
| 6 | 3 | 3.0 | 3.5 |
| 7 | 2 | 3.5 | 4.0 |
| 8 | 1 | 4.0 | 4.5 |

   Columns B and C show the quantity of money demanded at two different levels of real GDP: $Y_0$ is \$10 billion and $Y_1$ is \$20 billion. The quantity of money is \$3 billion. Initially, real GDP is \$20 billion. What happens in Minland if the interest rate
   a. Exceeds 4 percent a year?
   b. Is less than 4 percent a year?
   c. Equals 4 percent a year?
7. The Minland economy in problem 6 experiences a severe recession. Real GDP decreases to \$10 billion. If the quantity of money supplied does not change,
   a. What happens in Minland if the interest rate is 4 percent a year?
   b. Do people buy bonds or sell bonds?
   c. Will the interest rate rise or fall? Why?
8. Quantecon is a country in which the quantity theory of money operates. The country has a constant population, capital stock, and technology. In year 1, real GDP was \$400 million, the price level was 200, and the velocity of circulation was 20. In year 2, the quantity of money was 20 percent higher than in year 1. What was
   a. The quantity of money in year 1?
   b. The quantity of money in year 2?
   c. The price level in year 2?
   d. The level of real GDP in year 2?
   e. The velocity of circulation in year 2?

9. In Quantecon described in problem 8, in year 3, the quantity of money falls to one fifth of its level in year 2.
   a. What is the quantity of money in year 3?
   b. What is the price level in year 3?
   c. What is the level of real GDP in year 3?
   d. What is the velocity of circulation in year 3?
   e. If it takes more than one year for the full quantity theory effect to occur, what do you predict happens to real GDP in Quantecon in year 3? Why?

10. **Regulators Give Bleak Forecast for Banks**

    ... Federal Reserve Vice Chairman Donald Kohn, [told Congress] that banks have not allocated enough money to keep up with the growth of their problem assets. As a result, they may have to boost their skyrocketing loan loss reserves even further. ... Regulators added that they were bracing for an uptick in the number of bank failures, at least in the near term. Kohn declined to comment on the health of specific companies but said that Wall Street firms have learned a great deal from Bear Stearns and have reduced leverage and built up their liquidity. "I think we have a stronger set of investment banks than we had a month-and-a-half ago," said Kohn.

    *CNN*, June 5, 2008

   a. Explain a bank's "balancing act" and how the over-pursuit of profit or underestimation of risk can lead to a bank failure.
   b. During a time of uncertainty, why might it be necessary for a bank to build up its liquidity?

11. **Firms, Banks Using Fewer Emergency Loans**

    In a sign of some improvement in the credit crisis, Wall Street [investment] firms for the first time didn't borrow from the Federal Reserve's emergency lending program and commercial banks also scaled back. ... In the broadest use of the central bank's lending power since the 1930s, the Fed in March scrambled to avert a market meltdown by giving investment houses a place to go for emergency overnight loans. ... Commercial banks and investment companies now pay 2.25 percent in interest for the loans. Separately, as part of efforts to relieve credit strains, the Fed auctioned $21.3 billion in Treasury securities to investment companies Thursday. The auction drew bids for less than the $25 billion the Fed was making available, which was viewed as possible sign of some improvements in credit conditions. In exchange for the 28-day loans of Treasury securities, bidding companies can put up as collateral more risky investments. These include certain mortgage-backed securities and bonds secured by federally guaranteed student loans. The auction program, which began March 27, is intended to make investment companies more inclined to lend to each other. A second goal is providing relief to the distressed market for mortgage-linked securities and for student loans.

    *Time*, July 11, 2008

   a. What is the rationale behind allowing the Federal Reserve to make loans to banks?
   b. How might the Federal Reserve offering these "emergency loans" create a moral hazard problem in banking?

12. **Banks Drop on Higher Reserve Requirement**

    China's central bank will raise its reserve ratio requirement by a percentage point to a record 17.5 percent by June 25, stepping up a battle to contain lending growth. ... The increase will freeze up about 422 billion yuan of funds, equivalent to 91 percent of the value of new yuan-denominated loans extended in April. ... The latest move adds to the 614.7 billion yuan removed from the financial system through reserve ratio increases since January. China's banks had an average excess reserve deposit ratio of 2 percent as of March 31, down from 3.3 percent in December. The rate that banks charge each other for seven-day loans ... rose to 4.93 percent in Shanghai, the highest since Jan 24, according to China Bond Interbank Market. The gain suggests banks are hoarding cash in anticipation of further reserve ratio requirement increases. ... Every half-point increase in the reserve ratio requirement cuts banks' profits by as much as 1.5 percent, assuming they reduce lending to comply with it, said Li Qing, an analyst at CSC Securities HK Ltd.

    *People's Daily Online*, June 11, 2008

   a. Compare the required reserve ratio in China and in the United States.
   b. Explain how increasing the required reserve ratio can impact money creation in China's banking system.
   c. Why might higher required reserve ratios decrease bank profits?
   d. Explain how raising the required reserve ratio changes the interest rate in the short run and draw a graph to illustrate the change.

13. Sara withdraws $1,000 from her savings account at the Lucky S&L, keeps $50 in cash, and deposits the balance in her checking account at the Bank of Illinois. What is the immediate change in M1 and M2?
14. Banks in New Transylvania have a desired reserve ratio of 10 percent and no excess reserves. The currency drain ratio is 50 percent. Then the central bank increases bank reserves by $1,200.
    a. What is the initial increase in the monetary base?
    b. How much do the banks lend in the first round of the money creation process?
    c. How much of the amount initially lent does not return to the banks but is held as currency?
    d. Set out the transactions that take place and calculate the amount of deposits created and the increase in the amount of currency held after the second round of the money creation process.
15. [Study the Mathematical Note on pp. 206–207 to work this problem.] In the United Kingdom, the currency drain ratio is 0.38 of deposits and the desired reserve ratio is 0.002. In Australia, the quantity of money is $150 billion, the currency drain ratio is 33 percent of deposits and the desired reserve ratio is 8 percent.
    a. Calculate the U.K. money multiplier.
    b. Calculate the monetary base in Australia.
16. The table provides some data for the United States in the first decade following the Civil War.

| | 1869 | 1879 |
|---|---|---|
| Quantity of money | $1.3 billion | $1.7 billion |
| Real GDP (1929 dollars) | $7.4 billion | $Z$ |
| Price level (1929 = 100) | $X$ | 54 |
| Velocity of circulation | 4.50 | 4.61 |

*Source:* Milton Friedman and Anna J. Schwartz, *A Monetary History of the United States 1867-1960*

    a. Calculate the value of $X$ in 1869.
    b. Calculate the value of $Z$ in 1879.
    c. Are the data consistent with the quantity theory of money? Explain your answer.
17. **Fed to Curb Shady Lending Practices**
    The Federal Reserve will issue new rules next week aimed at protecting future home buyers from dubious lending practices, its most sweeping response to a housing crisis that has propelled foreclosures to record highs. ... To prevent a repeat of the current mortgage mess, [Chairman Ben] Bernanke said the Fed will adopt rules cracking down on a range of shady lending practices that have burned many of the nation's riskiest "sub-prime" borrowers—those with spotty credit or low incomes—who were hardest hit by the housing and credit debacles. ... Under the proposal unveiled last December, the rules would restrict lenders from penalizing risky borrowers who pay loans off early, require lenders to make sure these borrowers set aside money to pay for taxes and insurance and bar lenders from making loans without proof of a borrower's income. It also would prohibit lenders from engaging in a pattern or practice of lending without considering a borrower's ability to repay a home loan from sources other than the home's value.

    *Time*, July 9, 2008

    How are the proposed changes consistent with the overall purpose of the Federal Reserve System?
18. **What Bad Banking Means to You**
    Bad news about the banking industry may have you wondering about the safety of your hard earned cash at your own bank. In the past year there have been four bank failures.
    And the chairman of the Federal Deposit Insurance Corp and banking industry experts foresee many bank failures down the road. "Regulators are bracing for 100–200 bank failures over the next 12–24 months," says Jaret Seiberg, an analyst with the financial services firm, the Stanford Group. Expected loan losses, the deteriorating housing market and the credit squeeze are blamed for the drop in bank profits. ... The number of institutions categorized as "problem" institutions by the FDIC has also grown from 50 at the end of 2006 to 76 at the end of last year. But to put that in perspective—by the end of 1992—at the tail end of the banking crisis—there were 1,063 banks on that "trouble" list. ... Banking experts say there is one thing that will save your money if your bank goes under. That's FDIC insurance. "It's the gold standard," says banking consultant Bert Ely. "The FDIC has ample resources. It's never been an issue," he says. The FDIC insures deposits in banks and thrift institutions. The federal agency was created during the Great Depression in

response to thousands of bank failures. The FDIC maintains that not one depositor has lost a single cent of insured funds since 1934 as a result of a bank failure. …

*CNN*, February 28, 2008

a. Explain how bank attempts to maximize profits can sometimes lead to bank failures.
b. How does FDIC insurance help minimize bank failures and bring more stability to the banking system?
c. How might FDIC insurance create a moral hazard situation for banks?

19. **Fed at Odds with ECB over Value of Policy Tool**

Financial innovation and the spread of U.S. currency throughout the world has broken down relationships between money, inflation and growth, making monetary gauges a less useful tool for policy makers, the U.S. Federal Reserve chairman, Ben Bernanke, said. … The European Central Bank, Bank of Japan and Bank of England all use growth in the supply of money in formulating policy. "Heavy reliance on monetary aggregates as a guide to policy would seem to be unwise in the U.S. context," Bernanke said. … "The empirical relationship between money growth and variables such as inflation and nominal output growth has continued to be unstable. … " He said the Fed had "philosophical" and economic differences with European central bankers regarding the role of money and that debate between institutions was healthy. … "Unfortunately, forecast errors for money growth are often significant," reducing their effectiveness as a tool for policy, Bernanke said. "There are differences between the U.S. and Europe in terms of the stability of money demand and financial innovation," Bernanke said. … [Ultimately,] the risk of bad policy through a devoted following of money growth led the Fed to downgrade the importance of money measures.

*International Herald Tribune*, November 10, 2006

a. Explain how the debate surrounding the quantity theory of money could make "monetary gauges a less useful tool for policy makers."
b. What do Bernanke's statements reveal about his stance on the accuracy of the quantity theory of money?

20. Rapid inflation in Brazil in the early 1990s caused the cruzeiro to lose its ability to function as money. Which of the following commodities do you think would most likely have taken the place of the cruzeiro in the Brazilian economy? Explain why.

a. Tractor parts
b. Packs of cigarettes
c. Loaves of bread
d. Impressionist paintings
e. Baseball trading cards

21. **From Paper-Clip to House, in 14 Trades**

A 26-year-old Montreal man appears to have succeeded in his quest to barter a single, red paperclip all the way up to a house. It took almost a year and 14 trades. …

*CBC News*, 7 July 2006

a. Is barter a means of payment?
b. Is barter just as efficient as money when trading on e-Bay? Explain.

22. Study *Reading Between the Lines* on pp. 204–205 and then

a. Describe the money growth rate and the inflation rate in Zimbabwe since 2000.
b. How do we know that Zimbabwe's reported inflation between 2003 and 2007 is almost certainly below the true inflation rate?
c. What feature of Zimbabwe's economy provides a view of the cost of hyperinflation?
d. What must be done to stop Zimbabwe's inflation?
e. Why will knocking ten zeroes off all prices not stop Zimbabwe's inflation?

23. Use the link on MyEconLab (Textbook Resources, Chapter 8, Web links) to visit "Money—Past, Present, and Future" and study the section on e-money:

a. What is e-money and what are the alternative forms that it takes?
b. Do you think that the widespread use of e-money will limit the ability of the Federal Reserve to control the quantity of money? Why or why not?
c. When you buy an item on the Internet and pay for it using PayPal, are you using money? Explain why or why not.
d. Why might e-money be superior to cash as a means of payment?

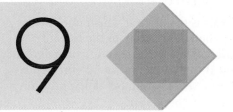

# 9 The Exchange Rate and the Balance of Payments

## After studying this chapter, you will be able to:

- Describe the foreign exchange market and distinguish between the nominal exchange rate and the real exchange rate
- Explain how the exchange rate is determined day by day
- Explain the long-run trends in the exchange rate and explain interest rate parity and purchasing power parity
- Describe the balance of payments accounts and explain what causes an international deficit
- Describe the alternative exchange rate policies and explain their long-run effects

**The dollar ($), the euro (€), and the yen (¥) are three** of the world's monies and most international payments are made using one of them. But the world has more than 100 different monies.

In October 2000, one U.S. dollar bought 1.17 euros, but from 2000 through 2008, the dollar sank against the euro and by July 2008 one U.S. dollar bought only 63 euro cents. Similarly, in February 2002, a dollar bought 134 yen, but since then, the dollar has fallen against the yen and in August 2008, one dollar bought only 107 yen. Why did the dollar fall against the euro and the yen? Can or should the United States do anything to stabilize the value of the dollar?

In 1988, the value of foreign assets owned by Americans equaled the value of the assets that foreigners owned in the United States. But every year since 1988, foreign entrepreneurs have roamed the United States with giant virtual shopping carts and loaded them up with Gerber, Firestone, Columbia Pictures, Ben & Jerry's, and Anheuser-Busch, all of which are now controlled by Japanese or European companies. Why have foreigners been buying U.S. businesses?

In this chapter, you're going to discover why the U.S. economy has become attractive to foreign investors, what determines the amount of international borrowing and lending, and why the dollar fluctuates against other currencies. In *Reading Between the Lines* at the end of the chapter, we'll look at China's foreign exchange rate policy and see why it troubles many Americans.

## Currencies and Exchange Rates

When Wal-Mart imports DVD players from Japan, it pays for them using Japanese yen. And when Japan Airlines buys an airplane from Boeing, it pays using U.S. dollars. Whenever people buy things from another country, they use the currency of that country to make the transaction. It doesn't make any difference what the item is that is being traded internationally. It might be a DVD player, an airplane, insurance or banking services, real estate, the stocks and bonds of a government or corporation, or even an entire business.

Foreign money is just like U.S. money. It consists of notes and coins issued by a central bank and mint and deposits in banks and other depository institutions. When we described U.S. money in Chapter 8, we distinguished between currency (notes and coins) and deposits. But when we talk about foreign money, we refer to it as foreign currency. **Foreign currency** is the money of other countries regardless of whether that money is in the form of notes, coins, or bank deposits.

We buy these foreign currencies and foreigners buy U.S. dollars in the foreign exchange market.

### The Foreign Exchange Market

The **foreign exchange market** is the market in which the currency of one country is exchanged for the currency of another. The foreign exchange market is not a place like a downtown flea market or a fruit and vegetable market. The foreign exchange market is made up of thousands of people—importers and exporters, banks, international travelers, and specialist traders called *foreign exchange brokers*.

The foreign exchange market opens on Monday morning in Sydney, Australia, and Hong Kong, which is still Sunday evening in New York. As the day advances, markets open in Singapore, Tokyo, Bahrain, Frankfurt, London, New York, Chicago, and San Francisco. As the West Coast markets close, Sydney is only an hour away from opening for the next day of business. The sun barely sets in the foreign exchange market. Dealers around the world are in continual contact by telephone and computer, and on a typical day in 2008, around $2 trillion (of all currencies) were traded in the foreign exchange market—or more than $400 trillion in a year.

### Exchange Rates

An **exchange rate** is the price at which one currency exchanges for another currency in the foreign exchange market. For example, on October 1, 2008, $1 would buy 106 Japanese yen or 72 euro cents. So the exchange rate was 106 yen per dollar or, equivalently, 72 euro cents per dollar.

The exchange rate fluctuates. Sometimes it rises and sometimes it falls. A rise in the exchange rate is called an *appreciation* of the dollar, and a fall in the exchange rate is called a *depreciation* of the dollar. For example, when the exchange rate rises from 106 yen to 130 yen per dollar, the dollar appreciates, and when the exchange rate falls from 106 yen to 100 yen per dollar, the dollar depreciates.

The quantity of foreign money that we can buy with our dollar changes when the dollar appreciates or depreciates. But a change in the value of the dollar might not change what we *really* pay for our imports and earn from our exports. The reason is that prices of goods and services might change to offset the change in the value of the dollar and leave the terms on which we trade with other countries unchanged.

To determine whether a change in the exchange rate changes what we earn from exports and pay for imports, we need to distinguish between the *nominal* exchange rate and the *real* exchange rate.

### Nominal and Real Exchange Rates

The **nominal exchange rate** is the value of the U.S. dollar expressed in units of foreign currency per U.S. dollar. It is a measure of how much of one money exchanges for a unit of another money.

The **real exchange rate** is the relative price of U.S.-produced goods and services to foreign-produced goods and services. It is a measure of the quantity of the real GDP of other countries that a unit of U.S. real GDP buys.

The exchange rates that we've just discussed are *nominal* exchange rates. To understand the real exchange rate, suppose that Japan produces only DVD players and the United States produces only airplanes. The price of a DVD player is 10,000 yen, and the price of an airplane is $100 million. Also suppose that the exchange rate—the *nominal* exchange rate—is 100 yen per dollar. With this information, we can calculate the *real* exchange rate, which is the number of DVD players that one airplane buys. Let's do this calculation.

## The Fluctuating U.S. Dollar

### More Down than Up

The figure shows the U.S. dollar exchange rate against the five currencies that feature most prominently in U.S. imports—the Canadian dollar, the Chinese yuan, the European euro, the Mexican peso, and the Japanese yen—between 1998 and 2008.

Against the Chinese yuan, the dollar was constant before 2005 and then started to depreciate. Against the Canadian dollar, the European euro, and the Japanese yen, the dollar appreciated until 2001 and then depreciated.

Against the Mexican peso, the dollar has appreciated but even against this currency, the dollar depreciated in 2007 and 2008.

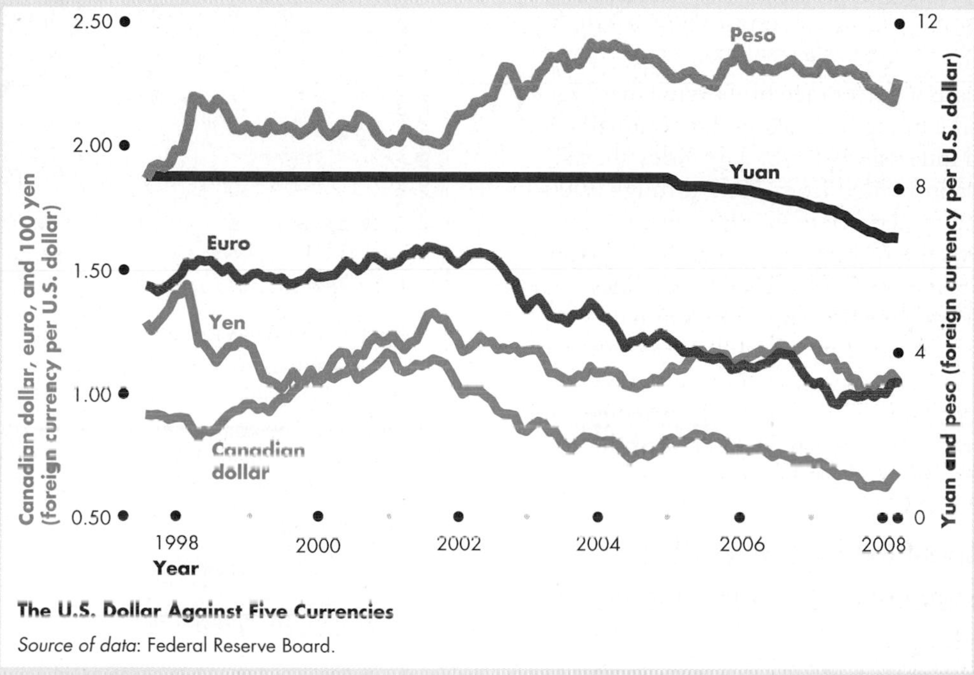


**The U.S. Dollar Against Five Currencies**

*Source of data*: Federal Reserve Board.

At the price of 10,000 yen and an exchange rate of 100 yen per dollar, the price of a DVD player is \$100. At a price of \$100 million for an airplane and \$100 for a DVD player, one airplane buys 1 million DVD players. The real exchange rate is 1 million DVD players per airplane.

In our example, airplanes represent U.S. real GDP, and DVD players represent Japanese real GDP. The price of a DVD player in Japan and the price of an airplane in the United States represent the price levels (GDP deflators) in the two countries.

Call the U.S. price level $P$, the Japanese price level $P^*$, the nominal exchange rate $E$ yen per dollar and the real exchange rate *RER* (Japanese real GDP per unit of U.S. real GDP). Then the real exchange rate is

$$RER = E \times (P/P^*).$$

In words, the real exchange rate equals the nominal exchange rate multiplied by the ratio of the U.S. price level to the foreign price level.

The real exchange rate changes if the nominal exchange rate changes and prices remain constant. But if the dollar appreciates ($E$ rises) and foreign prices rise ($P^*$ rises) by the same percentage, the real exchange rate doesn't change. In the above example, if the exchange rate rises to 120 yen per dollar and the price of a DVD player rises to 12,000 yen, one airplane still buys 1 million DVD players.

How has the real exchange rate changed over time? Has it changed in the same way as the nominal exchange rate? We could answer these questions by calculating a real exchange rate in terms of each of the individual currencies of the countries with which we trade. But there is a more efficient way of measuring the real exchange rate. Instead of looking at the exchange rates between many different currencies, we look at an average of the exchange rates against all the currencies in which the United States trades.

## Trade-Weighted Index

The average exchange rate of the U.S. dollar against other currencies, with individual currencies weighted by their importance in U.S. international trade, is called the **trade-weighted index.** The trade-weighted index is an index of a basket of major currencies—the European euro, the Australian and Canadian dollars, the Japanese yen, the Swedish krone, the Swiss franc, and the United Kingdom pound.

This index is defined to be 100 in 1998. So the index tells us the value of the U.S. dollar against these currencies as a percentage of its value in 1998.

The blue line in Fig. 9.1 shows the nominal trade-weighted index since 1998. The index shows that the dollar appreciated from 1999 through 2000 and then started to depreciate in 2001. The red line in Fig. 9.1 shows the real trade-weighted index. You can see that the nominal and real exchange rates moved in the same direction, but the nominal exchange rate appreciated by less and depreciated by more than the real exchange rate. The gap between the real exchange rate and the nominal exchange rate arises because the inflation rate in the rest of the world is less than the U.S. inflation rate.

## Questions About the Exchange Rate

The performance of the U.S. dollar in the foreign exchange market raises a number of questions that we address in the rest of this chapter.

First, how are the nominal exchange rate and real exchange rate determined? Why did the dollar appreciate through 2000 and then begin to depreciate? Why did the dollar appreciate against the Mexican peso but depreciate against many other currencies?

Second, how do exchange rate fluctuations influence our international trade and international payments? In particular, could we eliminate, or at least decrease, our international deficit by changing the exchange rate?

Third, how do the Fed and other central banks operate in the foreign exchange market? In particular, how was the exchange rate between the U.S. dollar and the Chinese yuan fixed and why did it remain constant for many years? Would an appreciation of the yuan change the balance of trade and payments between the United States and China?

We begin by learning how trading in the foreign exchange market determines the exchange rate.

**FIGURE 9.1** The Trade-Weighted Index

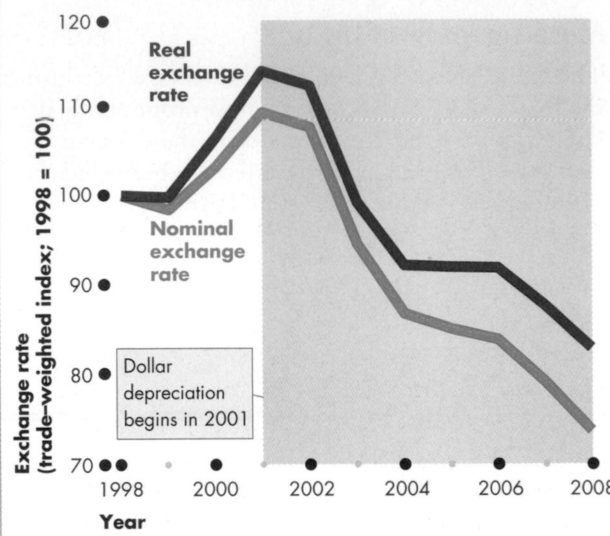


The nominal trade-weighted index of major currencies (blue line) and the real trade-weighted index of major currencies (red line) appreciated through the end of 2000 and then depreciated. The nominal exchange rate appreciated less and depreciated more than the real exchange rate because the U.S. inflation rate exceeded the inflation rate in the other major economies.

*Source of data*: Federal Reserve (rebased to 1998 = 100).

myeconlab animation

## Review Quiz

1. What is the foreign exchange market and what prices are determined in this market?
2. Distinguish between appreciation and depreciation of the dollar.
3. What are the world's major currencies?
4. Against which currencies and during which years has the U.S. dollar appreciated since 1998?
5. Against which currencies and during which years has the U.S. dollar depreciated since 1998?
6. What is the distinction between the nominal exchange rate and the real exchange rate?
7. What does the trade-weighted index measure?

Work Study Plan 9.1 and get instant feedback.

## The Foreign Exchange Market

An exchange rate is a price—the price of one currency in terms of another. And like all prices, an exchange rate is determined in a market—the *foreign exchange market.*

The U.S. dollar trades in the foreign exchange market and is supplied and demanded by tens of thousands of traders every hour of every business day. Because it has many traders and no restrictions on who may trade, the foreign exchange market is a *competitive market.*

In a competitive market, demand and supply determine the price. So to understand the forces that determine the exchange rate, we need to study the factors that influence demand and supply in the foreign exchange market. But there is a feature of the foreign exchange market that makes it special.

### The Demand for One Money Is the Supply of Another Money

When people who are holding the money of some other country want to exchange it for U.S. dollars, they demand U.S. dollars and supply that other country's money. And when people who are holding U.S. dollars want to exchange them for the money of some other country, they supply U.S. dollars and demand that other country's money.

So the factors that influence the demand for U.S. dollars also influence the supply of European Union euros, Canadian dollars, or Japanese yen. And the factors that influence the demand for that other country's money also influence the supply of U.S. dollars.

We'll first look at the influences on the demand for U.S. dollars in the foreign exchange market.

*Dealers in the foreign exchange market.*

### Demand in the Foreign Exchange Market

People buy U.S. dollars in the foreign exchange market so that they can buy U.S.-produced goods and services—U.S. exports. They also buy U.S. dollars so that they can buy U.S. assets such as bonds, stocks, businesses, and real estate or so that they can keep part of their money holding in a U.S. dollar bank account.

The quantity of U.S. dollars demanded in the foreign exchange market is the amount that traders plan to buy during a given time period at a given exchange rate. This quantity depends on many factors, but the main ones are

1. The exchange rate
2. World demand for U.S. exports
3. Interest rates in the United States and other countries
4. The expected future exchange rate

To see how the exchange rate is determined, we'll look first at the relationship between the quantity of U.S. dollars demanded in the foreign exchange market and the exchange rate when the other three influences remain the same. This relationship is called the law of demand in the foreign exchange market. Then in the next section, we'll consider what happens when these other influences change.

### The Law of Demand for Foreign Exchange

The law of demand applies to U.S. dollars just as it does to anything else that people value. Other things remaining the same, the higher the exchange rate, the smaller is the quantity of U.S. dollars demanded in the foreign exchange market. For example, if the price of the U.S. dollar rises from 100 yen to 120 yen but nothing else changes, the quantity of U.S. dollars that people plan to buy in the foreign exchange market decreases. The exchange rate influences the quantity of U.S. dollars demanded for two reasons:

- Exports effect
- Expected profit effect

**Exports Effect** The larger the value of U.S. exports, the larger is the quantity of U.S. dollars demanded in the foreign exchange market. But the value of U.S. exports depends on the prices of U.S.-produced goods and services *expressed in the currency of the foreign buyer*. And these prices depend on the exchange rate. The lower the exchange rate, other things remaining the same, the lower are the prices of U.S.-produced goods and services to foreigners and the greater is the volume of U.S. exports. So if the exchange rate falls (and other influences remain the same), the quantity of U.S. dollars demanded in the foreign exchange market increases.

To see the exports effect at work, think about orders for Boeing's new 787 airplane. If the price of a 787 is $100 million and the exchange rate is 90 euro cents per U.S. dollar, the price of this airplane to KLM, a European airline, is €90 million. KLM decides that this price is too high, so it doesn't buy a new 787. If the exchange rate falls to 80 euro cents per U.S. dollar and other things remain the same, the price of a 787 falls to €80 million. KLM now decides to buy a 787 and buys U.S. dollars in the foreign exchange market.

**Expected Profit Effect** The larger the expected profit from holding U.S. dollars, the greater is the quantity of U.S. dollars demanded in the foreign exchange market. But expected profit depends on the exchange rate. For a given expected future exchange rate, the lower the exchange rate today, the larger is the expected profit from buying U.S. dollars today and holding them, so the greater is the quantity of U.S. dollars demanded in the foreign exchange market today. Let's look at an example.

Suppose that Mizuho Bank, a Japanese bank, expects the exchange rate to be 120 yen per U.S. dollar at the end of the year. If today's exchange rate is also 120 yen per U.S. dollar, Mizuho Bank expects no profit from buying U.S. dollars and holding them until the end of the year. But if today's exchange rate is 100 yen per U.S. dollar and Mizuho Bank buys U.S. dollars, it expects to sell those dollars at the end of the year for 120 yen per dollar and make a profit of 20 yen per U.S. dollar.

The lower the exchange rate today, other things remaining the same, the greater is the expected profit from holding U.S. dollars and the greater is the quantity of U.S. dollars demanded in the foreign exchange market today.

## Demand Curve for U.S. Dollars

Figure 9.2 shows the demand curve for U.S. dollars in the foreign exchange market. A change in the exchange rate, other things remaining the same, brings a change in the quantity of U.S. dollars demanded and a movement along the demand curve. The arrows show such movements.

We will look at the factors that change demand in the next section of this chapter. But first, let's see what determines the supply of U.S. dollars.

**FIGURE 9.2** The Demand for U.S. Dollars

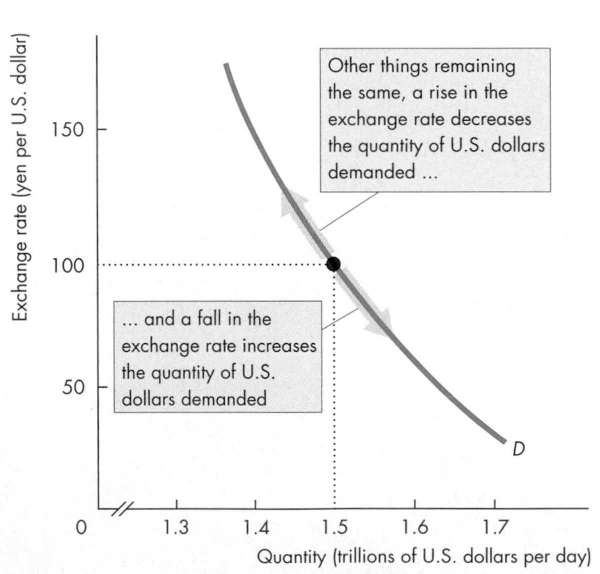


The quantity of U.S. dollars demanded depends on the exchange rate. Other things remaining the same, if the exchange rate rises, the quantity of U.S. dollars demanded decreases and there is a movement up along the demand curve for U.S. dollars. If the exchange rate falls, the quantity of U.S. dollars demanded increases and there is a movement down along the demand curve for U.S. dollars.

## Supply in the Foreign Exchange Market

People sell U.S. dollars and buy other currencies so that they can buy foreign-produced goods and services—U.S. imports. People also sell U.S. dollars and buy foreign currencies so that they can buy foreign assets such as bonds, stocks, businesses, and real estate or so that they can hold part of their money in bank deposits denominated in a foreign currency.

The quantity of U.S. dollars supplied in the foreign exchange market is the amount that traders plan to sell during a given time period at a given exchange rate. This quantity depends on many factors, but the main ones are

1. The exchange rate
2. U.S. demand for imports
3. Interest rates in the United States and other countries
4. The expected future exchange rate

Let's look at the law of supply in the foreign exchange market—the relationship between the quantity of U.S. dollars supplied in the foreign exchange market and the exchange rate when the other three influences remain the same.

## The Law of Supply of Foreign Exchange

Other things remaining the same, the higher the exchange rate, the greater is the quantity of U.S. dollars supplied in the foreign exchange market. For example, if the exchange rate rises from 100 yen to 120 yen per U.S. dollar and other things remain the same, the quantity of U.S. dollars that people plan to sell in the foreign exchange market increases.

The exchange rate influences the quantity of dollars supplied for two reasons:

- Imports effect
- Expected profit effect

**Imports Effect** The larger the value of U.S. imports, the larger is the quantity of U.S. dollars supplied in the foreign exchange market. But the value of U.S. imports depends on the prices of foreign-produced goods and services *expressed in U.S. dollars*. These prices depend on the exchange rate. The higher the exchange rate, other things remaining the same, the lower are the prices of foreign-produced goods and services to Americans and the greater is the volume of U.S. imports. So if the exchange rate rises (and other influences remain the same), the quantity of U.S. dollars supplied in the foreign exchange market increases.

**Expected Profit Effect** This effect works just like that on the demand for the U.S. dollar but in the opposite direction. The higher the exchange rate today, other things remaining the same, the larger is the expected profit from selling U.S. dollars today and holding foreign currencies, so the greater is the quantity of U.S. dollars supplied.

## Supply Curve for U.S. Dollars

Figure 9.3 shows the supply curve of U.S. dollars in the foreign exchange market. A change in the exchange rate, other things remaining the same, brings a change in the quantity of U.S. dollars supplied and a movement along the supply curve. The arrows show such movements.

**FIGURE 9.3** The Supply of U.S. Dollars

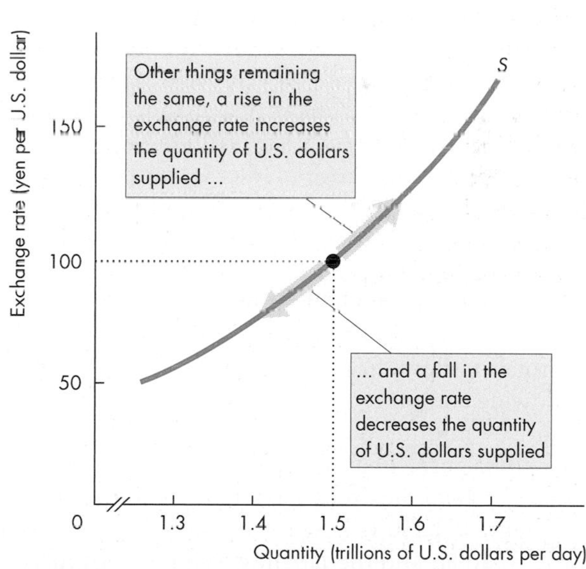
Exchange rate (yen per U.S. dollar)
150
100
50
0
S
Other things remaining the same, a rise in the exchange rate increases the quantity of U.S. dollars supplied ...
... and a fall in the exchange rate decreases the quantity of U.S. dollars supplied
1.3
1.4
1.5
1.6
1.7
Quantity (trillions of U.S. dollars per day)

The quantity of U.S. dollars supplied depends on the exchange rate. Other things remaining the same, if the exchange rate rises, the quantity of U.S. dollars supplied increases and there is a movement up along the supply curve of U.S. dollars. If the exchange rate falls, the quantity of U.S. dollars supplied decreases and there is a movement down along the supply curve of U.S. dollars.

myeconlab animation

## Market Equilibrium

Equilibrium in the foreign exchange market depends on how the Federal Reserve and other central banks operate. Here, we will study equilibrium when central banks keep out of this market. In a later section (on pp. 231–233), we examine the effects of alternative actions that the Fed or another central bank might take in the foreign exchange market.

Figure 9.4 shows the demand curve for U.S. dollars, *D*, from Fig. 9.2 and the supply curve of U.S. dollars, *S*, from Fig. 9.3, and the equilibrium exchange rate.

The exchange rate acts as a regulator of the quantities demanded and supplied. If the exchange rate is too high, there is a surplus—the quantity supplied exceeds the quantity demanded. For example, in Fig. 9.4, if the exchange rate is 150 yen per U.S. dollar, there is a surplus of U.S. dollars. If the exchange rate is too low, there is a shortage—the quantity supplied is less than the quantity demanded. For example, if the exchange rate is 50 yen per U.S. dollar, there is a shortage of U.S. dollars.

At the equilibrium exchange rate, there is neither a shortage nor a surplus—the quantity supplied equals the quantity demanded. In Fig. 9.4, the equilibrium exchange rate is 100 yen per U.S. dollar. At this exchange rate, the quantity demanded and the quantity supplied are each $1.5 trillion a day.

The foreign exchange market is constantly pulled to its equilibrium by the forces of supply and demand. Foreign exchange traders are constantly looking for the best price they can get. If they are selling, they want the highest price available. If they are buying, they want the lowest price available. Information flows from trader to trader through the worldwide computer network, and the price adjusts minute by minute to keep buying plans and selling plans in balance. That is, the price adjusts minute by minute to keep the exchange rate at its equilibrium.

Figure 9.4 shows how the exchange rate between the U.S. dollar and the Japanese yen is determined. The exchange rates between the U.S. dollar and all other currencies are determined in a similar way. So are the exchange rates among the other currencies. But the exchange rates are tied together so that no profit can be made by buying one currency, selling it for a second one, and then buying back the first one. If such a profit were available, traders would spot it, demand and supply would change, and the exchange rates would snap into alignment.

**FIGURE 9.4** Equilibrium Exchange Rate

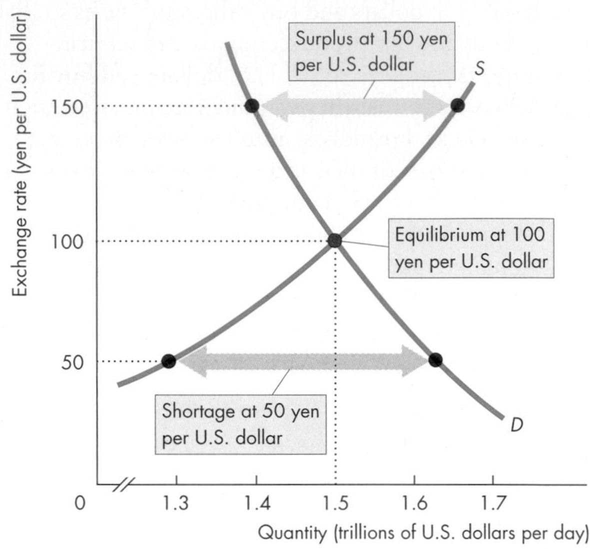


The demand curve for U.S. dollars is *D*, and the supply curve of U.S. dollars is *S*. If the exchange rate is 150 yen per U.S. dollar, there is a surplus of U.S. dollars and the exchange rate falls. If the exchange rate is 50 yen per U.S. dollar, there is a shortage of U.S. dollars and the exchange rate rises. If the exchange rate is 100 yen per U.S. dollar, there is neither a shortage nor a surplus of U.S. dollars and the exchange rate remains constant. The foreign exchange market is in equilibrium.

## Review Quiz

1. What are the influences on the demand for U.S. dollars in the foreign exchange market?
2. Provide an example of the exports effect on the demand for U.S. dollars.
3. What are the influences on the supply of U.S. dollars in the foreign exchange market?
4. Provide an example of the imports effect on the supply of U.S. dollars.
5. How is the equilibrium exchange rate determined?
6. What happens if there is a shortage or a surplus of U.S. dollars in the foreign exchange market?

Work Study Plan 9.2 and get instant feedback.

## Changes in Demand and Supply: Exchange Rate Fluctuations

When the demand for U.S. dollars or the supply of U.S. dollars changes, the exchange rate changes. We'll now look at the factors that make demand and supply change, starting with the demand side of the market.

### Changes in the Demand for U.S. Dollars

The demand for U.S. dollars in the foreign exchange market changes when there is a change in

- World demand for U.S. exports
- U.S. interest rate relative to the foreign interest rate
- The expected future exchange rate

**World Demand for U.S. Exports** An increase in world demand for U.S. exports increases the demand for U.S. dollars. To see this effect, think about Boeing's airplane sales. An increase in demand for air travel in Australia sends that country's airlines on a global shopping spree. They decide that the 787 is the ideal product, so they order 50 airplanes from Boeing. The demand for U.S. dollars now increases.

**U.S. Interest Rate Relative to the Foreign Interest Rate** People and businesses buy financial assets to make a return. The higher the interest rate that people can make on U.S. assets compared with foreign assets, the more U.S. assets they buy.

What matters is not the *level* of the U.S. interest rate, but the U.S. interest rate minus the foreign interest rate—a gap that is called the **U.S. interest rate differential.** If the U.S. interest rate rises and the foreign interest rate remains constant, the U.S. interest rate differential increases. The larger the U.S. interest rate differential, the greater is the demand for U.S. assets and the greater is the demand for U.S. dollars in the foreign exchange market.

**The Expected Future Exchange Rate** For a given current exchange rate, other things remaining the same, a rise in the expected future exchange rate increases the profit that people expect to make by holding U.S. dollars and the demand for U.S. dollars increases today.

Figure 9.5 summarizes the influences on the demand for U.S. dollars. An increase in the demand for U.S. exports, a rise in the U.S. interest rate differential, or a rise in the expected future exchange rate increases the demand for U.S. dollars today and shifts the demand curve rightward from $D_0$ to $D_1$. A decrease in the demand for U.S. exports, a fall in the U.S. interest rate differential, or a fall in the expected future exchange rate decreases the demand for U.S. dollars today and shifts the demand curve leftward from $D_0$ to $D_2$.

**FIGURE 9.5** Changes in the Demand for U.S. Dollars

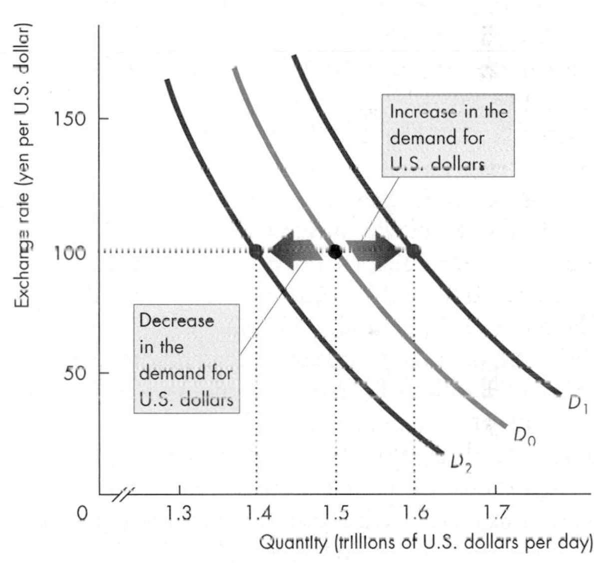


A change in any influence on the quantity of U.S. dollars that people plan to buy, other than the exchange rate, brings a change in the demand for U.S. dollars.

**The demand for U.S. dollars**

| *Increases if:* | *Decreases if:* |
|---|---|
| ■ World demand for U.S. exports increases | ■ World demand for U.S. exports decreases |
| ■ The U.S. interest rate differential rises | ■ The U.S. interest rate differential falls |
| ■ The expected future exchange rate rises | ■ The expected future exchange rate falls |

myeconlab animation

## Changes in the Supply of U.S. Dollars

The supply of U.S. dollars in the foreign exchange market changes when there is a change in

- U.S. demand for imports
- U.S. interest rate relative to the foreign interest rate
- The expected future exchange rate

**U.S. Demand for Imports** An increase in the U.S. demand for imports increases the supply of U.S. dollars in the foreign exchange market. To see why, think about Wal-Mart's purchase of DVD players. An increase in the demand for DVD players sends Wal-Mart out on a global shopping spree. Wal-Mart decides that Panasonic DVD players produced in Japan are the best buy, so Wal-Mart increases its purchases of these players. The supply of U.S. dollars now increases as Wal-Mart goes to the foreign exchange market for Japanese yen to pay Panasonic.

**U.S. Interest Rate Relative to the Foreign Interest Rate** The effect of the U.S. interest rate differential on the supply of U.S. dollars is the opposite of its effect on the demand for U.S. dollars. The larger the U.S. interest rate differential, the *smaller* is the supply of U.S. dollars in the foreign exchange market. The supply of U.S. dollars is smaller because the demand for *foreign* assets is smaller. If people spend less on foreign assets, the quantity of U.S. dollars they supply in the foreign exchange market decreases. So, a rise in the U.S. interest rate, other things remaining the same, increases the U.S. interest rate differential and decreases the supply of U.S. dollars in the foreign exchange market.

**The Expected Future Exchange Rate** For a given current exchange rate, other things remaining the same, a fall in the expected future exchange rate decreases the profit that can be made by holding U.S. dollars and decreases the quantity of U.S. dollars that people want to hold. To reduce their holdings of U.S. dollar assets, people must sell U.S. dollars. When they do so, the supply of U.S. dollars in the foreign exchange market increases.

Figure 9.6 summarizes the influences on the supply of U.S. dollars. If the supply of U.S. dollars decreases, the supply curve shifts leftward from $S_0$ to $S_1$. And if the supply of U.S. dollars increases, the supply curve shifts rightward from $S_0$ to $S_2$.

**FIGURE 9.6** Changes in the Supply of U.S. Dollars

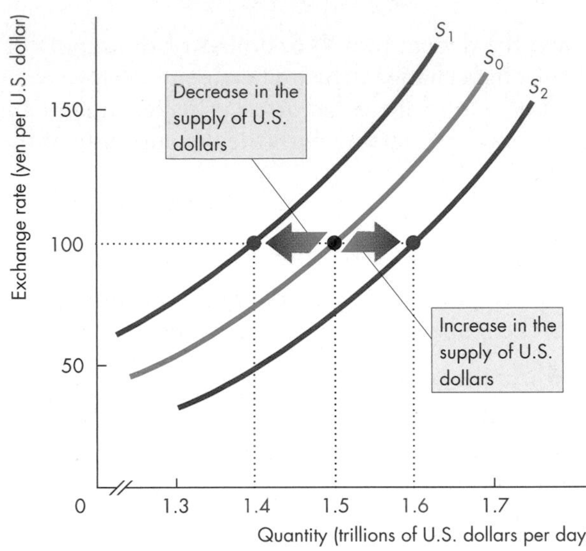


A change in any influence on the quantity of U.S. dollars that people plan to sell, other than the exchange rate, brings a change in the supply of dollars.

**The supply of U.S. dollars**

| *Increases if:* | *Decreases if:* |
|---|---|
| U.S. import demand increases | U.S. import demand decreases |
| The U.S. interest rate differential falls | The U.S. interest rate differential rises |
| The expected future exchange rate falls | The expected future exchange rate rises |

## Changes in the Exchange Rate

If the demand for U.S. dollars increases and the supply does not change, the exchange rate rises. If the demand for U.S. dollars decreases and the supply does not change, the exchange rate falls. Similarly, if the supply of U.S. dollars decreases and the demand does not change, the exchange rate rises. If the supply of U.S. dollars increases and the demand does not change, the exchange rate falls.

These predictions are exactly the same as those for any other market. Two episodes in the life of the U.S. dollar (next page) illustrate these predictions.

## Two Episodes in the Life of the Dollar

### A Currency on a Roller Coaster

The foreign exchange market is a striking example of a competitive market. The expectations of thousands of traders around the world influence this market minute-by-minute throughout the 24-hour global trading day.

Demand and supply rarely stand still and their fluctuations bring a fluctuating exchange rate. Two episodes in the life of the dollar illustrate these fluctuations: 2005–2007, when the dollar appreciated and 2007–2008, when the dollar depreciated.

**An Appreciating U.S. Dollar: 2005–2007** Between January 2005 and July 2007, the U.S. dollar appreciated against the yen. It rose from 103 yen to 123 yen per U.S. dollar. Part (a) of the figure provides an explanation for this appreciation.

In 2005, the demand and supply curves were those labeled $D_{05}$ and $S_{05}$. The exchange rate was 103 yen per U.S. dollar.

During 2005 and 2006, the Federal Reserve raised the interest rate, but the interest rate in Japan barely changed. With an increase in the U.S. interest rate differential, funds flowed into the United States. Also, currency traders, anticipating this increased flow of funds into the United States, expected the dollar to appreciate against the yen. The demand for U.S. dollars increased, and the supply of U.S. dollars decreased.

In the figure, the demand curve shifted rightward from $D_{05}$ to $D_{07}$ and the supply curve shifted leftward from $S_{05}$ to $S_{07}$. The exchange rate rose to 123 yen per U.S. dollar. In the figure, the equilibrium quantity remained unchanged—an assumption.

**A Depreciating U.S. Dollar: 2007–2008** Between July 2007 and September 2008, the U.S. dollar depreciated against the yen. It fell from 123 yen to 107 yen per U.S. dollar. Part (b) of the figure provides a possible explanation for this depreciation. The demand and supply curves labeled $D_{07}$ and $S_{07}$ are the same as in part (a).

During the last quarter of 2007 and the first three quarters of 2008, the U.S. economy entered a severe credit crisis and the Federal Reserve cut the interest rate in the United States. But the Bank of Japan kept the interest rate unchanged in Japan. With a narrowing of the U.S. interest rate differential, funds flowed out of the United States. Also, currency traders expected the U.S. dollar to depreciate against the yen. The demand for U.S. dollars decreased and the supply of U.S. dollars increased.

In part (b) of the figure, the demand curve shifted leftward from $D_{07}$ to $D_{08}$, the supply curve shifted rightward from $S_{07}$ to $S_{08}$, and the exchange rate fell to 107 yen per U.S. dollar.

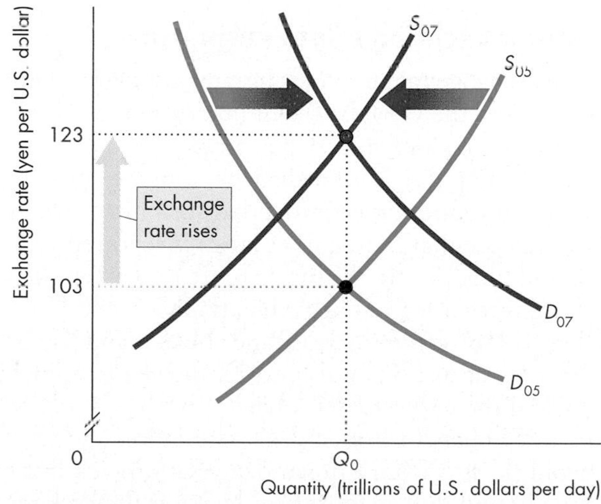


(a) 2005–2007

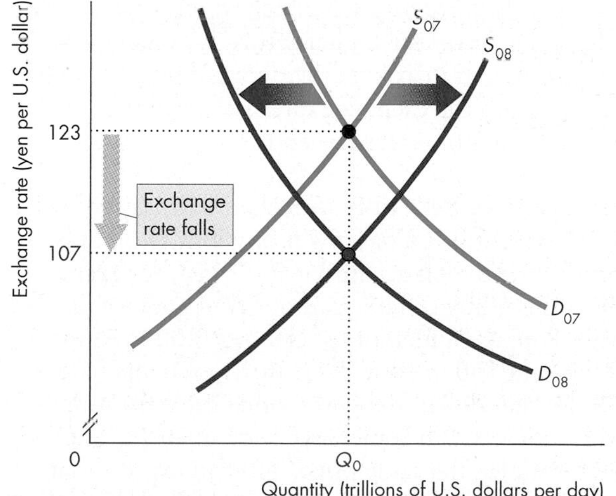


(b) 2007–2008

**The Rising and Falling U.S. Dollar**

## Exchange Rate Expectations

The changes in the exchange rate that we've just examined occurred in part because the exchange rate was *expected to change.* This explanation sounds a bit like a self-fulfilling prophecy. So what makes expectations change? The answer is new information about the deeper forces that influence the value of one money relative to the value of another money. There are two such forces:

- Interest rate parity
- Purchasing power parity

**Interest Rate Parity** One definition of what money is worth is what it can earn. Two kinds of money—U.S. dollars and Japanese yen, for example—might earn different amounts. Suppose a yen bank deposit in Tokyo earns 1 percent a year and a U.S. dollar bank deposit in New York earns 3 percent a year. In this situation, why does anyone deposit money in Tokyo? Why doesn't all the money flow to New York? The answer is because of exchange rate expectations. Suppose people expect the yen to appreciate by 2 percent a year. American investors expect that if they buy and hold yen for a year, they will earn 1 percent interest and 2 percent from the higher yen (lower dollar) to give a total return of 3 percent. So the interest rate in terms of U.S. dollars is the same in Tokyo and New York. This situation is one of **interest rate parity**, which means equal rates of return.

Adjusted for risk, interest rate parity always prevails. Funds move to get the highest return available. If for a few seconds a higher return is available in New York than in Tokyo, the demand for U.S. dollars increases and the exchange rate rises until the expected rates of return are equal.

**Purchasing Power Parity** Another definition of what money is worth is what it will buy. But two kinds of money—U.S. dollars and Japanese yen, for example—might buy different amounts of goods and services. Suppose a memory stick costs 5,000 yen in Tokyo and $50 in New York. If the exchange rate is 100 yen per dollar, the two monies have the same value. You can buy a memory stick in either Tokyo or New York for the same price. You can express that price as either 5,000 yen or $50, but the price is the same in the two currencies.

The situation we've just described is called **purchasing power parity**, which means *equal value of money.* If purchasing power parity does not prevail, some powerful forces go to work. To understand these forces, let's suppose that the price of a memory stick in New York rises to $60, but in Tokyo it remains at 5,000 yen. Further, suppose the exchange rate remains at 100 yen per dollar. In this case, a memory stick in Tokyo still costs 5,000 yen or $50, but in New York, it costs $60 or 6,000 yen. Money buys more in Japan than in the United States. Money is not of equal value in the two countries.

If all (or most) prices have increased in the United States and not increased in Japan, then people will generally expect that the value of the U.S. dollar in the foreign exchange market must fall. In this situation, the exchange rate is expected to fall. The demand for U.S. dollars decreases, and the supply of U.S. dollars increases. The exchange rate falls, as expected. If the exchange rate falls to 83.33 yen per dollar and there are no further price changes, purchasing power parity is restored. A memory stick that costs $60 in New York also costs the equivalent of $60 ($60 \times 83.33 = 5{,}000$) in Tokyo.

If prices increase in Japan and other countries but remain constant in the United States, then people will generally expect that the value of the U.S. dollar in the foreign exchange market is too low and that it is going to rise. In this situation, the exchange rate is expected to rise. The demand for U.S. dollars increases, and the supply of U.S. dollars decreases. The exchange rate rises, as expected.

## Instant Exchange Rate Response

The exchange rate responds instantly to news about changes in the variables that influence demand and supply in the foreign exchange market. You can see why the response is immediate by thinking about the expected profit opportunities that such news creates.

Suppose that the Bank of Japan is reported to be considering raising the interest rate next week. If this move is regarded as likely, then traders expect the demand for yen to increase and the demand for dollars to decrease. They also expect the yen to appreciate and the dollar to depreciate.

But to benefit from a yen appreciation and to avoid the loss from a dollar depreciation, yen must be bought and dollars must be sold *before* the exchange rate changes. Each trader knows that all the other traders share the same information and have similar expectations. And each trader knows that when people begin to sell dollars and buy yen, the exchange rate will change. To transact before the exchange rate changes means transacting right away, as soon as the information that changes expectations is received.

## The Nominal and Real Exchange Rates in the Short Run and in the Long Run

Earlier in this chapter, we distinguished between the nominal exchange rate and the real exchange rate. So far we've explained only how the nominal exchange rate is determined and we've focused on the day-to-day fluctuations in the nominal exchange rate. We're going to turn now to the real exchange rate and explain how it is determined. We're also going to distinguish between the short run and the long run.

Recall the equation that links the nominal and real exchange rates. That equation is

$$RER = E \times (P/P^*),$$

where $P$ is the U.S. price level, $P^*$ is the Japanese price level, $E$ is the nominal exchange rate (yen per U.S. dollar), and $RER$ is the real exchange rate (the quantity of Japanese real GDP per unit of U.S. real GDP).

In the short run, this equation determines the real exchange rate. The price levels in the United States and Japan don't change every time the nominal exchange rate changes. So a change in $E$ brings an equivalent change in $RER$.

But in the long run, the situation is radically different. In the long run, the equilibrium flows that determine the real exchange rate are determined by demand and supply in the markets for goods and services. If Japan and the United States produced identical goods (if GDP in both countries consisted only of memory sticks for example), purchasing power parity would make the real exchange rate equal 1. One Japanese memory stick would exchange for one U.S. memory stick. In reality, although there is overlap in what each country produces, U.S. real GDP is a different bundle of goods and services from Japanese real GDP. So the relative price of Japanese and U.S. real GDP—the real exchange rate—is not 1 and it fluctuates. The forces of demand and supply in the markets for the millions of goods and services that make up real GDP determine the relative prices of Japanese and U.S. real GDP.

In the long run, with the real exchange rate determined by the real forces of demand and supply in markets for goods and services, the above equation must be turned around to determine the nominal exchange rate. That is, the nominal exchange rate is

$$E = RER \times (P^*/P).$$

This equation tells us that in the long run, the nominal exchange rate is determined by the equilibrium real exchange rate and the price levels in the two countries. A rise in the Japanese price level, $P^*$, brings a rise in $E$ and dollar appreciation; and a rise in the U.S. price level, $P$, brings a fall in $E$ and dollar depreciation.

You learned in Chapter 8 (see pp. 202–203) that in the long run, the quantity of money determines the price level. But the quantity theory of money applies to all countries. So the quantity of money in Japan determines the price level in Japan, and the quantity of money in the United States determines the price level in the United States.

A nominal exchange rate, then, in the long run, is a monetary phenomenon. It is determined by the quantities of money in two countries.

The long-run forces that we've just described explain the broad trends in exchange rates. For example, the U.S dollar has generally appreciated against the Mexican peso because Mexico has created money at a faster pace than has the United States and the price level in Mexico has risen more rapidly than the U.S. price level. The U.S. dollar has depreciated since 2002 because U.S. prices have risen faster, on average, than European, Canadian, and Japanese prices.

### Review Quiz

1. Why does the demand for U.S. dollars change?
2. Why does the supply of U.S. dollars change?
3. What makes the U.S. dollar exchange rate fluctuate?
4. What is interest rate parity and what happens when this condition doesn't hold?
5. What is purchasing power parity and what happens when this condition doesn't hold?
6. What determines the real exchange rate and the nominal exchange rate in the short run?
7. What determines the real exchange rate and the nominal exchange rate in the long run?

myeconlab Work Study Plan 9.3 and get instant feedback.

# Financing International Trade

You now know how the exchange rate is determined, but what is the effect of the exchange rate? How does currency depreciation or currency appreciation influence our international trade and payments? We're going to lay the foundation for addressing these questions by looking at the scale of international trading, borrowing, and lending and at the way in which we keep our records of international transactions. These records are called the balance of payments accounts.

## Balance of Payments Accounts

A country's **balance of payments accounts** records its international trading, borrowing, and lending in three accounts:

1. Current account
2. Capital account
3. Official settlements account

The **current account** records receipts from exports of goods and services sold abroad, payments for imports of goods and services from abroad, net interest income paid abroad, and net transfers abroad (such as foreign aid payments). The *current account balance* equals the sum of exports minus imports, net interest income, and net transfers.

The **capital account** records foreign investment in the United States minus U.S. investment abroad. (This account also has a statistical discrepancy that arises from errors and omissions in measuring international capital transactions.)

The **official settlements account** records the change in **U.S. official reserves**, which are the government's holdings of foreign currency. If U.S. official reserves *increase*, the official settlements account balance is *negative*. The reason is that holding foreign money is like investing abroad. U.S. investment abroad is a minus item in the capital account and in the official settlements account.

The sum of the balances on the three accounts *always* equals zero. That is, to pay for our current account deficit, we must either borrow more from abroad than we lend abroad or use our official reserves to cover the shortfall.

Table 9.1 shows the U.S. balance of payments accounts in 2008. Items in the current account and the capital account that provide foreign currency to the United States have a plus sign; items that cost the United States foreign currency have a minus sign. The table shows that in 2008, U.S. imports exceeded U.S. exports and the current account had a deficit of $718 billion. How do we pay for imports that exceed the value of our exports? That is, how do we pay for our current account deficit?

We pay by borrowing from the rest of the world. The capital account tells us by how much. We borrowed $955 billion (foreign investment in the United States) but made loans of $300 billion (U.S. investment abroad). Our *net* foreign borrowing was $955 billion minus $300 billion, which equals $655 billion. There is almost always a statistical discrepancy between our capital account and current account transactions, and in 2008, the discrepancy was $66 billion. Combining the discrepancy with the measured net foreign borrowing gives a capital account balance of $721 billion.

**TABLE 9.1** U.S. Balance of Payments Accounts in 2008

| **Current account** | **Billions of dollars** |
|---|---|
| Exports of goods and services | +1,853 |
| Imports of goods and services | −2,561 |
| Net interest income | +121 |
| Net transfers | −123 |
| Current account balance | −718 |
| **Capital account** | |
| Foreign investment in the United States | +955 |
| U.S. investment abroad | −300 |
| Statistical discrepancy | 66 |
| Capital account balance | +721 |
| **Official settlements account** | |
| Official settlements account balance | −3 |

*Source of data:* Bureau of Economic Analysis.

Our capital account balance plus our current account balance equals the change in U.S. official reserves. In 2008, our capital account balance of $721 billion plus our current account balance of –$718 billion equaled $3 billion. Our official reserves *increased* in 2007 by $3 billion. Holding more foreign reserves is like lending to the rest of the world, so this amount appears in the official settlements account in Table 9.1 as –$3 billion. The sum of the current account balance, the capital account balance, and the official settlements balance equals 0.

To see more clearly what the nation's balance of payments accounts mean, think about your own balance of payments accounts. They are similar to the nation's accounts.

**An Individual's Balance of Payments Accounts** An individual's current account records the income from supplying the services of factors of production and the expenditure on goods and services. Consider Jackie, for example. She worked in 2005 and earned an income of $25,000. Jackie has $10,000 worth of investments that earned her an interest income of $1,000. Jackie's current account shows an income of $26,000. Jackie spent $18,000 buying consumption goods and services. She also bought a new house, which cost her $60,000. So Jackie's total expenditure was $78,000. Jackie's expenditure minus her income is $52,000 ($78,000 minus $26,000). This amount is Jackie's current account deficit.

## The U.S. Balance of Payments Since 1983

### Twenty-five Years of Deficits

The numbers that you reviewed in Table 9.1 give a snapshot of the balance of payments accounts in 2008. The figure below puts that snapshot into perspective by showing the balance of payments between 1983 and 2008.

Because the economy grows and the price level rises, changes in the dollar value of the balance of payments do not convey much information. To remove the influences of economic growth and inflation, the figure shows the balance of payments expressed as a percentage of nominal GDP.

As you can see, a large current account deficit emerged during the 1980s but declined from 1987 to 1991. The current account deficit then increased every year through 2000, decreased slightly in 2001, and then increased again through 2006 after which it dipped slightly again. The capital account balance is almost a mirror image of the current account balance. The official settlements balance is very small in comparison with the balances on the other two accounts

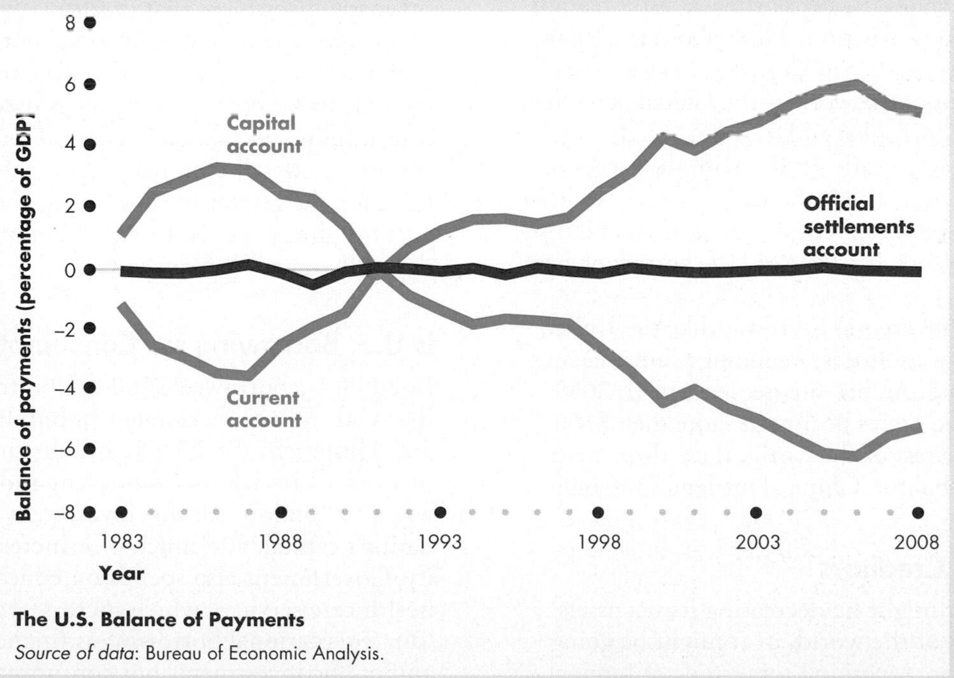


**The U.S. Balance of Payments**

*Source of data*: Bureau of Economic Analysis.

To pay for expenditure of $52,000 in excess of her income, Jackie must either use the money that she has in the bank or take out a loan. Suppose that Jackie took out a loan of $50,000 to help buy her house and that this loan was the only borrowing that she did. Borrowing is an *inflow* in the capital account, so Jackie's capital account *surplus* was $50,000. With a current account deficit of $52,000 and a capital account surplus of $50,000, Jackie was still $2,000 short. She got that $2,000 from her own bank account. Her cash holdings decreased by $2,000.

Jackie's income from her work is like a country's income from its exports. Her income from her investments is like a country's interest income from foreigners. Her purchases of goods and services, including her purchase of a house, are like a country's imports. Jackie's loan—borrowing from someone else—is like a country's borrowing from the rest of the world. The change in Jackie's bank account is like the change in the country's official reserves.

## Borrowers and Lenders

A country that is borrowing more from the rest of the world than it is lending to the rest of the world is called a **net borrower.** Similarly, a **net lender** is a country that is lending more to the rest of the world than it is borrowing from the rest of the world.

The United States is a net borrower, but it has not always been in this situation. Throughout the 1960s and most of the 1970s, the United States was a net lender to the rest of the world—the United States had a current account surplus and a capital account deficit. But from the early 1980s, with the exception of only a single year, 1991, the United States has been a net borrower from the rest of the world. And during the years since 1992, the scale of U.S. borrowing has mushroomed.

Most countries are net borrowers like the United States. But a few countries, including China, Japan, and oil-rich Saudi Arabia, are net lenders. In 2008, when the United States borrowed more than $700 billion from the rest of the world, these three countries lent $700 billion. China alone lent $380 billion.

## Debtors and Creditors

A net borrower might be decreasing its net assets held in the rest of the world, or it might be going deeper into debt. A nation's total stock of foreign investment determines whether it is a debtor or a creditor. A **debtor nation** is a country that during its entire history has borrowed more from the rest of the world than it has lent to it. It has a stock of outstanding debt to the rest of the world that exceeds the stock of its own claims on the rest of the world. A **creditor nation** is a country that during its entire history has invested more in the rest of the world than other countries have invested in it.

The United States was a debtor nation through the nineteenth century as we borrowed from Europe to finance our westward expansion, railroads, and industrialization. We paid off our debt and became a creditor nation for most of the twentieth century. But following a string of current account deficits, we became a debtor nation again in 1986.

Since 1986, the total stock of U.S. borrowing from the rest of the world has exceeded U.S. lending to the rest of the world. The largest debtor nations are the capital-hungry developing countries (such as the United States was during the nineteenth century). The international debt of these countries grew from less than a third to more than a half of their gross domestic product during the 1980s and created what was called the "Third World debt crisis."

Should we be concerned that the United States is a net borrower and a debtor? The answer to this question depends mainly on what the net borrower is doing with the borrowed money. If borrowing is financing investment that in turn is generating economic growth and higher income, borrowing is not a problem. It earns a return that more than pays the interest. But if borrowed money is used to finance consumption, to pay the interest and repay the loan, consumption will eventually have to be reduced. In this case, the greater the borrowing and the longer it goes on, the greater is the reduction in consumption that will eventually be necessary.

## Is U.S. Borrowing for Consumption?

In 2008, we borrowed $700 billion from abroad. In that year, private investment in buildings, plant, and equipment was $1,980 billion and government investment in defense equipment and social projects was $480 billion. All this investment added to the nation's capital, and much of it increased productivity. Government also spends on education and health care services, which increase *human capital.* Our international borrowing is financing private and public investment, not consumption.

## Current Account Balance

What determines a country's current account balance and net foreign borrowing? You've seen that net exports (*NX*) is the main item in the current account. We can define the current account balance (*CAB*) as

$$CAB = NX + \text{Net interest income} + \text{Net transfers}.$$

We can study the current account balance by looking at what determines net exports because the other two items are small and do not fluctuate much.

## Net Exports

Net exports are determined by the government budget and private saving and investment. To see how net exports are determined, we need to recall some of the things that we learned in Chapter 7 about the flows of funds that finance investment. Table 9.2 refreshes your memory and summarizes some calculations.

Part (a) lists the national income variables that are needed, with their symbols. Part (b) defines three balances. **Net exports** is exports of goods and services minus imports of goods and services.

The **government sector balance** is equal to net taxes minus government expenditures on goods and services. If that number is positive, a government sector surplus is lent to other sectors; if that number is negative, a government deficit must be financed by borrowing from other sectors. The government sector deficit is the sum of the deficits of the federal, state, and local governments.

The **private sector balance** is saving minus investment. If saving exceeds investment, a private sector surplus is lent to other sectors. If investment exceeds saving, a private sector deficit is financed by borrowing from other sectors.

Part (b) also shows the values of these balances for the United States in 2008. As you can see, net exports were –$737 billion, a deficit of $737 billion. The government sector's revenue from net taxes was $2,163 billion and its expenditure was $2,870 billion, so the government sector balance was –$707 billion—a deficit of $707 billion. The private sector saved $1,950 billion and invested $1,980 billion, so its balance was –$30 billion—a deficit of $30 billion.

Part (c) shows the relationship among the three balances. From the *National Income and Product Accounts*, we know that real GDP, *Y*, is the sum of consumption expenditure (*C*), investment, government expenditure, and net exports. Real GDP also equals the sum of consumption expenditure, saving, and net taxes. Rearranging these equations tells us that net exports is the sum of the government sector balance and the private sector balance. In the United States in 2008, the government sector balance was

**TABLE 9.2** Net Exports, the Government Budget, Saving, and Investment

| | Symbols and equations | United States in 2008 (billions of dollars) |
|---|---|---|
| **(a) Variables** | | |
| Exports* | $X$ | 1,908 |
| Imports* | $M$ | 2,645 |
| Government expenditures | $G$ | 2,870 |
| Net taxes | $T$ | 2,163 |
| Investment | $I$ | 1,980 |
| Saving | $S$ | 1,950 |
| **(b) Balances** | | |
| Net exports | $X - M$ | 1,908 – 2,645 = –737 |
| Government sector | $T - G$ | 2,163 – 2,870 = –707 |
| Private sector | $S - I$ | 1,950 – 1,980 = –30 |
| **(c) Relationship among balances** | | |
| National accounts | $Y = C + I + G + X - M$ | |
| | $= C + S + T$ | |
| Rearranging: | $X - M = S - I + T - G$ | |
| Net exports | $X - M$ | –737 |
| equals: | | |
| Government sector | $T - G$ | –707 |
| plus | | |
| Private sector | $S - I$ | –30 |

*Source of data*: Bureau of Economic Analysis. The data are for 2008, average of first two quarters, seasonally adjusted at annual rate.

* The *National Income and Product Accounts* measures of exports and imports are slightly different from the balance of payments accounts measures in Table 9.1 on p. 628.

## The Three Sector Balances

### Deficits and Surpluses

You've seen that net exports equal the sum of the government sector balance and the private sector balance. How do these three sector balances fluctuate over time?

The figure answers this question. It shows the government sector balance (the red line), net exports (the blue line), and the private sector balance (the green line).

The private sector balance and the government sector balance move in opposite directions. When the government sector deficit increased during the late 1980s and early 1990s, the private sector surplus increased. And when the government sector deficit decreased and became a surplus during the 1990s and early 2000s, the private sector's surplus decreased and became a deficit. And when the government deficit increased yet again in 2007 and 2008, the private sector deficit shrank and almost disappeared.

Sometimes, when the government sector deficit increases, as it did during the first half of the 1980s, net exports become more negative. But after the early 1990s, net exports did not follow the government sector balance closely. Rather, net exports respond to the *sum* of the government sector and private sector balances. When both the private sector and the government sector have a deficit, net exports are negative and the combined private and government deficit is financed by borrowing from the rest of the world. But the dominant trend in net exports is negative.

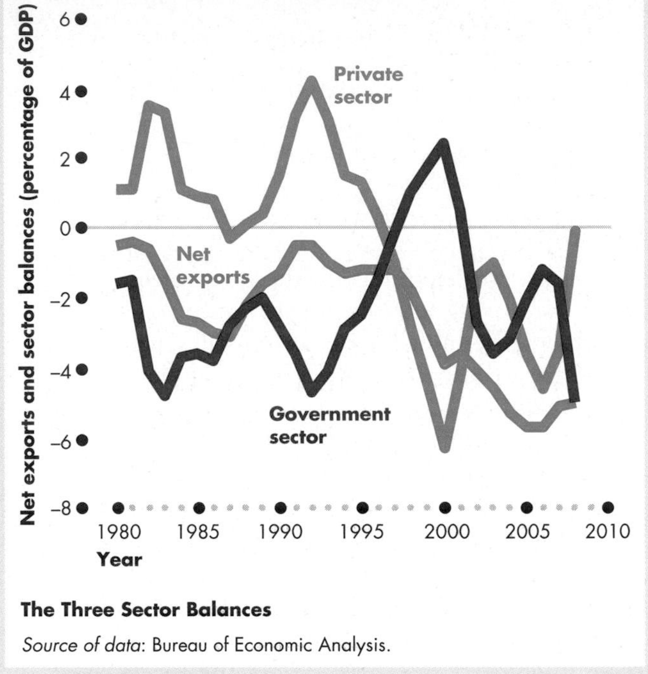


**The Three Sector Balances**

*Source of data*: Bureau of Economic Analysis.

–$707 billion and the private sector balance was –$30 billion. The government sector balance plus the private sector balance equaled net exports of –$737 billion.

## Where Is the Exchange Rate?

In explaining the current account balance, we have not mentioned the exchange rate. Doesn't the exchange rate play a role?

In the short run, a fall in the nominal exchange rate lowers the real exchange rate, which makes our imports more costly and our exports more competitive. A higher price of imported consumption goods and services might induce a decrease in consumption expenditure and an increase in saving. A higher price of imported capital goods might induce a decrease in investment. Other things remaining the same, an increase in saving or a decrease in investment decreases the private sector deficit and decreases the current account deficit.

But in the long run, a change in the nominal exchange rate leaves the real exchange rate and all other real variables unchanged. So in the long run, the nominal exchange rate plays no role in influencing the current account balance.

## Review Quiz

1 What are the transactions that the current account records?
2 What are the transactions that the capital account records?
3 What are the transactions that the official settlements account records?
4 Is the United States a net borrower or a net lender and a debtor or a creditor nation?
5 How are net exports and the government sector balance linked?

Work Study Plan 9.4 and get instant feedback.

## Exchange Rate Policy

Because the exchange rate is the price of a country's money in terms of another country's money, governments and central banks must have a policy toward the exchange rate. Three possible exchange rate policies are

- Flexible exchange rate
- Fixed exchange rate
- Crawling peg

### Flexible Exchange Rate

A **flexible exchange rate** policy is one that permits the exchange rate to be determined by demand and supply with no direct intervention in the foreign exchange market by the central bank. Most countries—and the United States is among them—operate a flexible exchange rate, and the foreign exchange market that we have studied so far in this chapter is an example of a flexible exchange rate regime.

But even a flexible exchange rate is influenced by central bank actions. If the Fed raises the U.S. interest rate and other countries keep their interest rates unchanged, the demand for U.S. dollars increases, the supply of U.S. dollars decreases, and the exchange rate rises. (Similarly, if the Fed lowers the U.S. interest rate, the demand for U.S. dollars decreases, the supply increases, and the exchange rate falls.)

In a flexible exchange rate regime, when the central bank changes the interest rate, its purpose is not to influence the exchange rate, but to achieve some other monetary policy objective. (We return to this topic at length in Chapter 14.)

### Fixed Exchange Rate

A **fixed exchange rate** policy is one that pegs the exchange rate at a value decided by the government or central bank and that blocks the unregulated forces of demand and supply by direct intervention in the foreign exchange market. The world economy operated a fixed exchange rate regime from the end of World War II to the early 1970s. China had a fixed exchange rate until recently. Hong Kong has had a fixed exchange rate for many years and continues with that policy today.

A fixed exchange rate requires active intervention in the foreign exchange market.

If the Fed wanted to fix the U.S. dollar exchange rate against the Japanese yen, the Fed would have to sell U.S. dollars to prevent the exchange rate from rising above the target value and buy U.S. dollars to prevent the exchange rate from falling below the target value.

There is no limit to the quantity of U.S. dollars that the Fed can *sell*. The Fed creates U.S. dollars and can create any quantity it chooses. But there is a limit to the quantity of U.S. dollars the Fed can *buy*. That limit is set by U.S. official foreign currency reserves because to buy U.S. dollars the Fed must sell foreign currency. Intervention to buy U.S. dollars stops when U.S. official foreign currency reserves run out.

Let's look at the foreign exchange interventions that the Fed can make.

Suppose the Fed wants the exchange rate to be steady at 100 yen per U.S. dollar. If the exchange rate rises above 100 yen, the Fed sells dollars. If the exchange rate falls below 100 yen, the Fed buys dollars. By these actions, the Fed keeps the exchange rate close to its target rate of 100 yen per U.S dollar.

Figure 9.7 shows the Fed's intervention in the foreign exchange market. The supply of dollars is $S$ and initially the demand for dollars is $D_0$. The equilibrium exchange rate is 100 yen per dollar. This exchange rate is also the Fed's target exchange rate, shown by the horizontal red line.

When the demand for U.S. dollars increases and the demand curve shifts rightward to $D_1$, the Fed sells \$10 billion. This action prevents the exchange rate from rising. When the demand for U.S. dollars decreases and the demand curve shifts leftward to $D_2$, the Fed buys \$10 billion. This action prevents the exchange rate from falling.

If the demand for U.S. dollars fluctuates between $D_1$ and $D_2$ and on average is $D_0$, the Fed can repeatedly intervene in the way we've just seen. Sometimes the Fed buys and sometimes it sells but, on average, it neither buys nor sells.

But suppose the demand for U.S. dollars *increases permanently* from $D_0$ to $D_1$. To maintain the exchange rate at 100 yen per U.S. dollar, the Fed must sell dollars and buy foreign currency, so U.S. official foreign currency reserves would be increasing. At some point, the Fed would abandon the exchange rate of 100 yen per U.S. dollar and stop piling up foreign currency reserves.

Now suppose the demand for U.S. dollars *decreases permanently* from $D_0$ to $D_2$. In this situation, the Fed

**FIGURE 9.7** Foreign Exchange Market Intervention

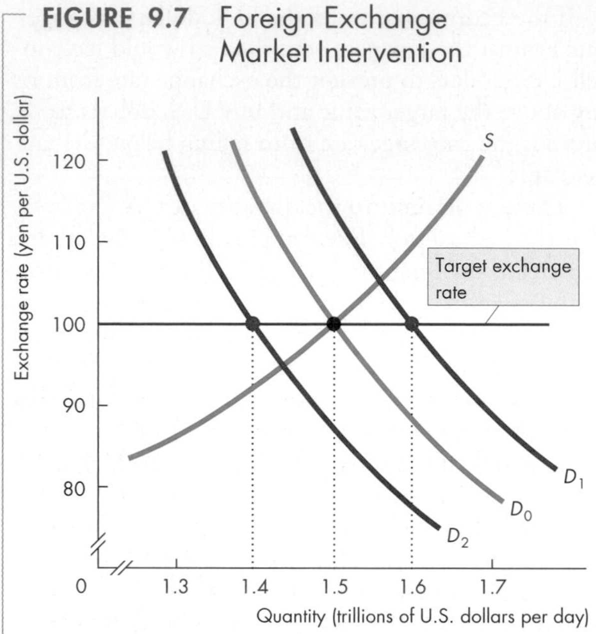


Initially, the demand for U.S. dollars is $D_0$, the supply of U.S. dollars is $S$, and the exchange rate is 100 yen per U.S. dollar. The Fed can intervene in the foreign exchange market to keep the exchange rate close to its target rate (100 yen in this example). If demand increases from $D_0$ to $D_1$, the Fed sells dollars. If demand decreases from $D_0$ to $D_2$, the Fed buys dollars. Persistent intervention on one side of the market cannot be sustained.

myeconlab animation

*cannot* maintain the exchange rate at 100 yen per U.S. dollar indefinitely. To hold the exchange rate at 100 yen, the Fed must *buy* U.S. dollars. When the Fed buys U.S. dollars in the foreign exchange market, it uses U.S. official foreign currency reserves. So the Fed's action decreases its foreign currency reserves. Eventually, the Fed would run out of foreign currency and would then have to abandon the target exchange rate of 100 yen per U.S. dollar.

## Crawling Peg

A **crawling peg** exchange rate policy is one that selects a target for the exchange rate that changes periodically, with intervention in the foreign exchange market to achieve the target.

A crawling peg works like a fixed exchange rate except that the target value changes. Sometimes the target changes once a month, and sometimes it changes every day.

The Fed has never operated a crawling peg. But some prominent countries do use this system. When China abandoned its fixed exchange rate, it replaced it with a crawling peg. China and some other developing countries use a crawling peg as a method of trying to control inflation—a role that we examine in Chapter 14, p. 368.

The ideal crawling peg sets a target for the exchange rate equal to the equilibrium exchange rate

## The People's Bank of China in the Foreign Exchange Market

### Fixed Rate Followed by Crawling Peg

You saw in the figure on p. 215 that the exchange rate between the U.S. dollar and the Chinese yuan was constant for several years. The reason for this near constant exchange rate is that China's central bank, the People's Bank of China, intervened to operate a fixed exchange rate policy. From 1997 until 2005, the yuan was pegged at 8.28 yuan per U.S. dollar. Since 2005, the yuan has appreciated slightly but it has not been permitted to fluctuate freely. Since 2005, the yuan has been on a crawling peg.

The immediate consequence of the fixed yuan exchange rate (and crawling exchange rate) is that since 2000, China has piled up U.S dollar reserves on a huge scale. By mid-2006, China's official foreign currency reserves approached \$1 trillion and by the end of 2007, they were fast approaching \$2 trillion!

Part (a) of the figure shows the scale of China's increase in official foreign currency reserves, some of which are euros and yen but most of which are U.S. dollars. You can see that China's reserves increased by \$200 billion in 2004 and in 2005, by a bit more than \$200 billion in 2006, and by \$460 billion in 2007.

The demand and supply curves in part (b) of the figure illustrate what is happening in the market for U.S. dollars priced in terms of the yuan and explains why China's reserves have increased. The demand curve $D$ and supply curve $S$ intersect at 5 yuan per U.S. dollar. If the People's Bank of China takes no actions in the market, this exchange rate is the equilibrium rate (an assumed value).

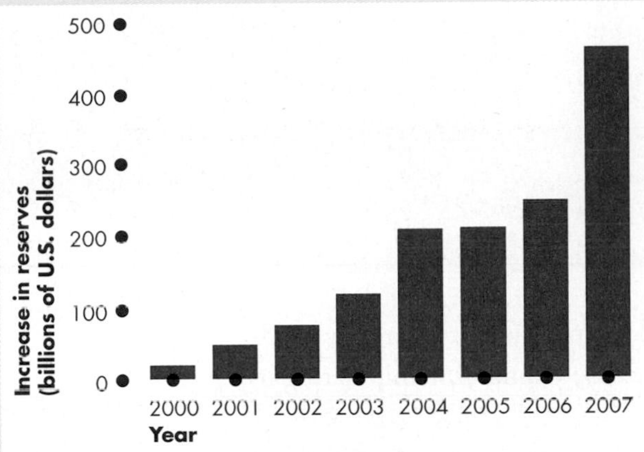


**(a) Increase in U.S. Dollar Reserves**

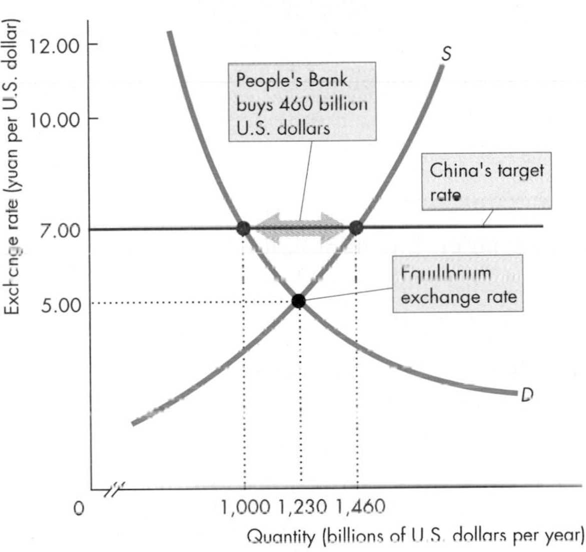


**(b) Pegging the Yuan**

**China's Foreign Exchange Market Intervention**

By intervening in the foreign exchange market and buying U.S. dollars, the People's Bank pegs the yuan at 7 yuan per U.S. dollar. But to do so, it must pile up U.S. dollars. To hold the exchange rate at 7 yuan per dollar, the People's Bank bought $460 billion in 2007.

If the People's Bank stopped buying U.S. dollars, the U.S. dollar would depreciate, the yuan would appreciate, and China would stop piling up U.S. dollar reserves.

**Why Does China Manage Its Exchange Rate?** The popular story is that China manages its exchange rate to keep its export prices low and to make it easier to compete in world markets. You've seen that this story is correct in the short run. With prices in China and the rest of the world given, a low yuan–U.S. dollar exchange rate brings lower U.S. dollar prices for China's exports. But the yuan–U.S. dollar exchange rate was fixed for almost 10 years and has been managed for three more years. This long period of a fixed exchange rate has long-run, not short-run, effects. In the long run, the exchange rate has no effect on competitiveness. The reason is that prices adjust to reflect the exchange rate and the real exchange rate is unaffected by the nominal exchange rate.

So why does China fix its exchange rate? The more convincing answer is that China sees a fixed exchange rate as a way of controlling its inflation rate. By making the yuan crawl against the U.S. dollar, China's inflation rate is anchored to the U.S. inflation rate and will not stray too far from that rate (see Chapter 14, p. 368).

The bottom line is that in the long run, exchange rate policy is monetary policy, not balance of payments policy. To change its balance of payments, a country must change its saving and investment.

on average. The peg seeks only to prevent large swings in the expected future exchange rate that change demand and supply and make the exchange rate fluctuate too wildly.

A crawling peg departs from the ideal if, as often happens with a fixed exchange rate, the target rate departs from the equilibrium exchange rate for too long. When this happens, the country either runs out of reserves or piles up reserves.

◆ *Reading Between the Lines* on pp. 234–235 looks further at China's crawling peg exchange rate policy.

## Review Quiz

1. What is a flexible exchange rate and how does it work?
2. What is a fixed exchange rate and how is its value fixed?
3. What is a crawling peg and how does it work?
4. How has China operated in the foreign exchange market, why, and with what effect?

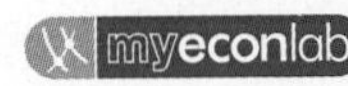


Work Study Plan 9.5 and get instant feedback.

READING BETWEEN THE LINES

# The Sinking Dollar

## Bush Aides Struggling with Yuan

http://www.nytimes.com
May 10, 2006

After nearly three years of pushing China to let its currency float more freely, with only modest results, the Bush administration still appears reluctant to accuse China of manipulating its exchange rate. …

American manufacturers and many members of Congress have complained for years that China has kept its currency, the yuan, at an artificially low exchange rate to the dollar as a way of selling its exports at cheap prices.

Treasury Secretary John W. Snow has resisted demands to threaten Beijing, arguing that Chinese leaders are making "progress" toward a more flexible exchange rate and a more open financial system.

This week, a Treasury official again emphasized China's steps toward openness.

"If you look at what China is doing in exercising their commitment on putting in place a foreign-exchange regime that has greater flexibility," Mr. Snow's principal spokesman, Tony Fratto, told reporters on Monday, "you see some evidence that they're doing that."

But changes in the yuan's value have been relatively minor. Chinese leaders let the yuan climb about 2 percent against the dollar last July, and another similarly small amount more recently.

When President Hu Jintao visited President Bush in Washington last month, top Chinese officials re-emphasized a need for "stability" and offered no hint of when they might let the yuan move more freely. …

The United States' trade deficit with China ballooned to $202 billion in 2005, an imbalance that might ordinarily have pushed up the value of the yuan in relation to the dollar. China has prevented the yuan from rising by buying hundreds of billions in dollar-denominated reserves. …



## Essence of the Story

- U.S. producers and members of Congress complain that China has kept the yuan artificially low to sell exports at low prices.
- Treasury Secretary John W. Snow says that China is moving toward a more flexible exchange rate.
- Changes in the yuan–dollar exchange rate have been small.
- The yuan appreciated in July 2005 and by small amounts more recently.
- The U.S. trade deficit with China was $202 billion in 2005.
- This imbalance should have pushed up the value of the yuan, but China prevented that from happening and increased its U.S. dollar reserves.

## Economic Analysis

- China's exchange rate was pegged at 8.28 yuan per U.S. dollar until July 2005.
- In July 2005, the yuan appreciated against the U.S. dollar (the U.S. dollar depreciated) by 2.1 percent.
- Since July 2005, the yuan has slowly but persistently appreciated against the dollar (the dollar has depreciated against the yuan).
- Figure 1 shows the path of the depreciating dollar against the yuan.
- To peg the yuan before July 2005 and since then to keep the exchange rate from rising more than it wants, the People's Bank of China buys U.S. dollars in the foreign exchange market.
- The result of these foreign exchange market transactions has been a strong growth in China's foreign reserves.
- Figure 2 shows the buildup of China's reserves, which, by 2008, were approaching $2 trillion.
- Americans are concerned about the yuan–U.S. dollar exchange rate because China has a large trade surplus with the United States.
- But China's overall current account surplus is not large and is a fraction of the large U.S. current account deficit.
- Figure 3 shows the U.S. current account deficit and China's current account surplus.
- The analysis in this chapter explains that a current account deficit results from too little private and government saving relative to investment.
- China saves more than it invests, and the United States invests more than it saves.
- A change in the nominal exchange rate between the U.S. dollar and the Chinese yuan cannot make a large contribution to changing these imbalances.
- The main effect of the appreciation of the yuan against the U.S. dollar will be to slow China's inflation rate relative to the U.S. inflation rate.

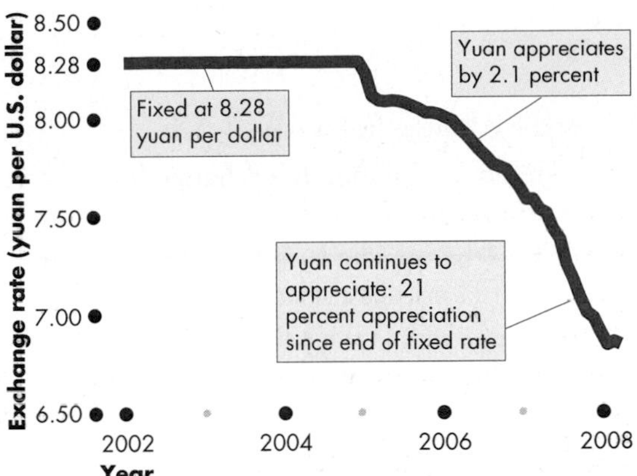


**Figure 1 The yuan–U.S. dollar exchange rate**

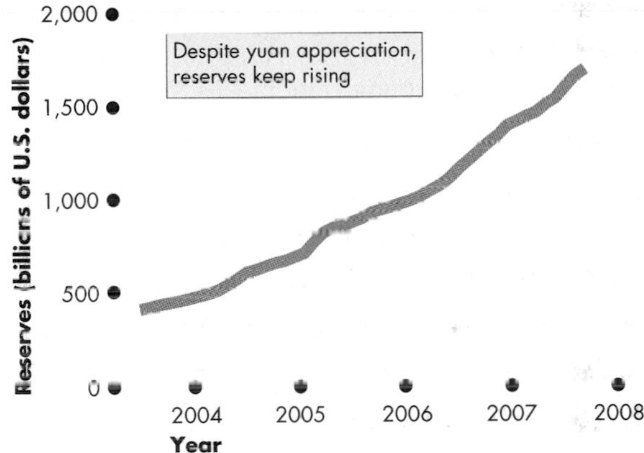


**Figure 2 China's reserves pile up**

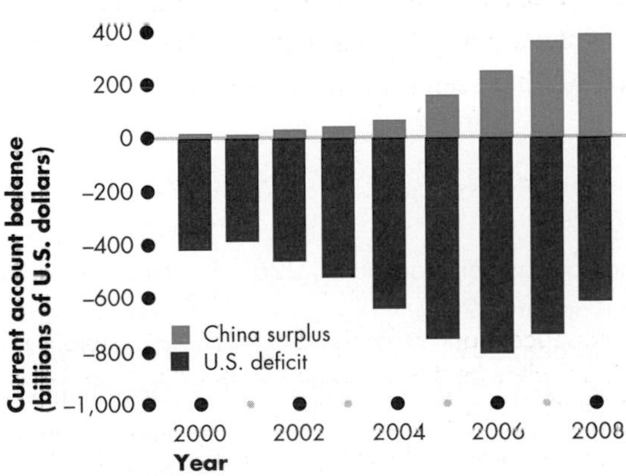


**Figure 3 Current account balances**

## SUMMARY

### Key Points

**Currencies and Exchange Rates** (pp. 214–216)

- Foreign currency is obtained in exchange for domestic currency in the foreign exchange market.
- The nominal exchange rate is the value of one currency in terms of another currency.
- The real exchange rate is the price of one country's real GDP in terms of another country's real GDP.

**The Foreign Exchange Market** (pp. 217–220)

- Demand and supply in the foreign exchange market determine the exchange rate.
- The higher the exchange rate, the smaller is the quantity of U.S. dollars demanded and the greater is the quantity of U.S. dollars supplied.
- The equilibrium exchange rate makes the quantity of U.S. dollars demanded equal the quantity of U.S. dollars supplied.

**Changes in Demand and Supply: Exchange Rate Fluctuations** (pp. 221–225)

- Changes in the the world demand for U.S. exports, the U.S. interest rate differential, or the expected future exchange rate change the demand for U.S. dollars.
- Changes in U.S. demand for imports, the U.S. interest rate differential, or the expected future exchange rate change the supply of U.S. dollars.
- Exchange rate expectations are influenced by purchasing power parity and interest rate parity.
- In the long run, the nominal exchange rate is a monetary phenomenon and the real exchange rate is independent of the nominal exchange rate.

**Financing International Trade** (pp. 226–230)

- International trade, borrowing, and lending are financed by using foreign currency.
- A country's international transactions are recorded in its current account, capital account, and official settlements account.
- The current account balance is similar to net exports and is determined by the government sector balance plus the private sector balance.

**Exchange Rate Policy** (pp. 231–233)

- An exchange rate can be flexible, fixed, or a crawling peg.
- To achieve a fixed or a crawling exchange rate, a central bank must intervene in the foreign exchange market and either buy or sell foreign currency.

### Key Figures and Table



### Key Terms

## PROBLEMS and APPLICATIONS

myeconlab Work problems 1–14 in Chapter 9 Study Plan and get instant feedback.
Work problems 15–21 as Homework, a Quiz, or a Test if assigned by your instructor.

1. The U.S. dollar exchange rate increased from $0.97 Canadian in 2007 to $1.06 Canadian in 2008, and it decreased from 115 Japanese yen in 2007 to 107 Japanese yen in 2008.
   a. Did the U.S. dollar appreciate or depreciate against the Canadian dollar?
   b. Did the U.S. dollar appreciate or depreciate against the Japanese yen?
   c. What was the value of the Canadian dollar in terms of U.S. dollars in 2007 and 2008?
   d. What was the value of 100 Japanese yen in terms of U.S. dollars in 2007 and 2008?
   e. Did the Canadian dollar appreciate or depreciate against the U.S. dollar in 2008?
   f. Did the Japanese yen appreciate or depreciate against the U.S. dollar in 2008?
2. In 2004, the price level in the Eurozone was 112.4, the price level in the United States was 109.1, and the nominal exchange rate was 80 euro cents per U.S. dollar. What was the real exchange rate expressed as Eurozone real GDP per unit of U.S. real GDP?
3. In 2003, the price level in the United States was 106.3, the price level in Japan was 95.4, and the real exchange rate expressed as Japanese real GDP per unit of U.S. real GDP was 103.6. What was the nominal exchange rate?
4. There is a large increase in the global demand for roses and Colombia is the biggest producer of roses. At the same time, the central bank of Colombia increases the interest rate. What happens in the foreign exchange market for Colombian pesos to
   a. The demand for pesos?
   b. The supply of pesos?
   c. The quantity of pesos demanded?
   d. The quantity of pesos supplied?
   e. The exchange rate of the pesos against the U.S. dollar?
5. If a euro deposit in a bank in Paris, France, earns interest of 4 percent a year and a yen deposit in Tokyo, Japan, earns 0.5 percent a year, everything else remaining the same and adjusted for risk, what is the exchange rate expectation of the Japanese yen?
6. The U.K. pound is trading at 1.82 U.S. dollars per U.K. pound. There is purchasing power parity at this exchange rate. The interest rate in the United States is 2 percent a year and the interest rate in the United Kingdom is 4 percent a year.
   a. Calculate the U.S. interest rate differential.
   b. What is the U.K. pound expected to be worth in terms of U.S. dollars one year from now?
   c. Which country more likely has the lower inflation rate? How can you tell?
7. You can purchase a laptop in Mexico City for 12,960 Mexican pesos. If the exchange rate is 10.8 Mexican pesos per U.S. dollar and if purchasing power parity prevails, at what price can you buy an identical computer in Dallas, Texas?
8. The table gives some information about the U.S. international transactions in 2003.

| Item | Billions of U.S. dollars |
|---|---|
| Imports of goods and services | 1,487 |
| Foreign investment in the United States | 1,051 |
| Exports of goods and services | 990 |
| U.S. investment abroad | 456 |
| Net interest income | 7 |
| Net transfers | –68 |
| Statistical discrepancy | –36 |

   a. Calculate the current account balance.
   b. Calculate the capital account balance.
   c. Did U.S. official reserves increase or decrease?
   d. Was the United States a net borrower or a net lender in 2003? Explain your answer.
9. A country has a lower inflation rate than all other countries. It has more rapid economic growth. The central bank does not intervene in the foreign exchange market. What can you say (and why) about:
   a. The exchange rate?
   b. The current account balance?
   c. The expected exchange rate?
   d. The interest rate differential?
   e. Interest rate parity?
   f. Purchasing power parity?

10. **The Lesson: Buy Ruffles in Myanmar**

    … A small bag of cheese-flavored Ruffles potato chips is $1.69 in Japan and only 8 cents in Myanmar. … The price of spending 1 hour at an Internet cafe in Vietnam is $0.62 U.S., in China is $1.48 U.S., and in South Africa is $3.40 U.S.

    *The Los Angeles Times*, April 23, 2006

    Do these prices indicate that purchasing power parity does not prevail? Why or why not?

11. **Peso's Party**

    It was bad enough when Canada's Loonie surpassed the dollar, but now the Mexican peso is gaining on the greenback, too. In April, the peso hit 10.44 to the dollar, its best rate in two years. Mexico's 4.2 percent GDP growth in January and February … finally convinced currency investors that the peso shouldn't be tethered to the dollar, as it has been in recent years. … At current levels, exports might soon become more expensive for gringos. In other words, time to stock up on Coronas.

    *Fortune*, May 12, 2008

    a. Is the news clip about the real exchange rate or the nominal exchange rate? Explain.
    b. Explain why "the Mexican peso is gaining on the greenback."
    c. Draw a graph to illustrate why "the Mexican peso is gaining on the greenback."
    d. Explain why Mexican goods might become more expensive to U.S. consumers.

12. **Double-Talking the Dollar**

    [The dollar] has lost 41% of its value against the euro, its main global competitor, since … 2001. The huge trade deficits that the country has been running for the past decade seem like a pretty good indication that the dollar was overvalued in global currency markets and needed to come down. … In the 1970s and '80s, the Treasury Department was constantly buying and selling foreign currencies to push the dollar this way or that. Since 1995 … [the] Treasury has made only a couple of token moves and since 2000 hasn't intervened at all. World currency markets are so huge and active, the thinking goes, that trying to manipulate the dollar is largely futile. … Over time, a currency's value reflects an economy's fundamentals—how well a country allocates resources, how productive its workers are, how it contains inflation, etc. … But for years on end, currencies can move in directions that seem to have little to do with fundamentals. They overshoot their correct values, in part because nobody is ever sure exactly what those correct values are.

    *Time*, May 5, 2008

    a. Evaluate the statement made about how huge trade deficits "seem like a pretty good indication that the dollar was overvalued in global currency markets and needed to come down."
    b. How has U.S. exchange rate policy evolved since the early '70s?
    c. Explain why "trying to manipulate the dollar is largely futile," especially in the long run.
    d. Draw a graph to illustrate and explain why a currency can experience short-run fluctuations "that seem to have little to do with fundamentals."

13. **The United States, Debtor Nation**

    The United States is a debtor nation, just like the poorest states in Africa, Latin America and Asia. … For most of the past 30 years the United States has been piling up large trade deficits. The current account … has now reached a deficit of 6 percent of GDP, and must be financed by capital inflows. Foreigners must purchase large amounts of US property, stocks, bonds, bank deposits and currency, or the current-account deficit cannot be financed. …

    *Asia Times*, September 28, 2006

    a. Explain why a current account deficit "must be financed by capital inflows."
    b. Under what circumstances should the debtor nation status of the United States be a concern?

14. The *Economist* magazine uses the price of a Big Mac to determine whether a currency is undervalued or overvalued. In May 2006, the price of a Big Mac was $3.10 in New York, 10.5 yuan in Beijing, and 6.30 Swiss francs in Geneva. The exchanges rates were 8.03 yuan per U.S. dollar and 1.21 Swiss francs per U.S. dollar.
    a. Was the yuan undervalued or overvalued relative to purchasing power parity?
    b. Was the Swiss franc undervalued or overvalued relative to purchasing power parity?
    c. Do you think the price of a Big Mac in different countries provides a valid test of purchasing power parity?

15. The table gives some information about the U.K. economy in 2003:

| Item | Billions of U.K. pounds |
|---|---|
| Consumption expenditure | 721 |
| Exports of goods and services | 277 |
| Government expenditure | 230 |
| Net taxes | 217 |
| Investment | 181 |
| Saving | 162 |

   a. Calculate the private sector balance.
   b. Calculate the government sector balance.
   c. Calculate net exports.
   d. What is the relationship between the government sector balance and net exports?

16. A country's currency appreciates, and its official holdings of foreign currency increase. What can you say about:
   a. The central bank's intervention in the foreign exchange market?
   b. The country's current account balance?
   c. The country's official settlements account?

17. **Top U.S. Real Estate Markets for Investment**

   Rahul Reddy … has been investing in commercial properties in Western Australia for the last two years. Now, with the Australian dollar growing in strength and the American housing market strained, he's got his eye on residential and commercial properties in Florida and California, areas he believes will recover over the long term. He's not alone. Encouraged by a weak dollar and a belief in the resiliency of the U.S. economy, individuals like Reddy, along with institutional investors such as pension funds and private equity groups, are seeking investment properties and development opportunities in the United States. … "The U.S. is good for speculative higher-risk investments from our perspective because the strong Australian dollar will enable us to gain hold of properties at prices we will probably not see for a long time," says Reddy. "The U.S. is an economic powerhouse that I think will recover, and if the exchange rate goes back to figures from a few years ago, that will benefit us. …"

   *Forbes*, July 10, 2008

   a. Explain why foreign individuals and institutions are "seeking investment properties and development opportunities in the United States."
   b. Explain what would happen if the speculation made by Reddy became widespread. Would expectations become self-fulfilling?
   c. Draw a graph of the foreign exchange market to illustrate your explanation in b.

18. **The Dollar's Short-Lived Comeback**

   After slipping to record lows against the euro in April, the greenback has recovered in recent weeks, helped in part by expectations that the Federal Reserve's aggressive rate-cutting campaign may have reached a stopping point. But with the U.S. economy under strain, resistance by foreign central banks to cut interest rates and a massive U.S. trade deficit, a number of currency experts are betting the dollar will stay under pressure at least through the remainder of the year. … The dollar's recent bounce will be short lived because of economic concerns. … Retail sales, which drive two thirds of economic activity in the United States, suffered a decline last month. At the same time, there has been further fallout in the housing market and unemployment is on the rise. Even though the weakened dollar has helped boost the nation's exports by making goods manufactured in the United States more attractive to foreign buyers, the nation's current account deficit … is still massive. The deficit was a whopping $738.6 billion at the end of last year. While that's down from $811.5 billion in 2006, it's still large enough to be a concern since the current account deficit has to be covered by borrowing from overseas investors. If these investors pull their money from the U.S., that could result in a cycle of falling stock and bond prices and ultimately a further decline in the value of the dollar. … In order for the dollar to get back to [previous] levels, experts say the U.S. trade deficit would have to drastically shrink and the Fed would need to aggressively raise interest rates to combat inflation.

   *CNN*, May 16, 2008

   a. Explain how expectations that the Federal Reserve will not cut the interest rate could make the U.S. dollar appreciate.
   b. Explain the factors identified in the news article that may keep the U.S. dollar from appreciating.
   c. Draw a graph to illustrate how the factors

identified in the news clip influence the exchange rate.

19. **U.S. Declines to Cite China as Currency Manipulator**

    The Bush administration has declined to cite China for manipulating its currency to gain unfair trade advantages against the United States … despite pressure in Congress for penalties. America's growing trade deficit with China, which last year hit an all-time high of $256.3 billion, [is] the largest deficit ever recorded with a single country. … Chinese currency, the yuan, has risen in value by 18.4 percent against the dollar since the Chinese government loosened its currency system in July 2005. However, American manufacturers contend the yuan is still undervalued by as much as 40 percent, making Chinese products more competitive in this country and U.S. goods more expensive in China. … China is a major holder of dollar-denominated investments such as U.S. Treasury securities, which it buys to keep the dollar from falling in value against the yuan.

    *MSN*, May 15, 2008

    a. Explain how China was able to maintain a fixed exchange rate with the dollar until July 2005.
    b. Draw a graph to illustrate how China kept the exchange rate fixed.
    c. Has China used a flexible exchange rate policy since July 2005?
    d. Explain how fixed and crawling peg exchange rates can be used to manipulate trade balances in the short-run, but not the long-run.
    e. What is the long-run rationale behind a fixed or crawling peg exchange rate?

20. **Inside the Mind of a Debtor Nation**

    Year after year, I am stunned by the decisions people make that get them into financial trouble. I've seen monthly car notes the size of mortgage payments. People take vacations or buy big-screen televisions and expensive jewelry while ignoring huge federal tax obligations. … Why do they continue to use credit even though they are already weighed down by so much debt? … What has made us into a nation of people who spend more than we earn? … Part of the problem is our economy's reliance on personal consumption. On some level, we all know our buying is out of control, but we are constantly bombarded with messages encouraging us to shop. The steady stream blunts our reasoning power. … Much of the difficulty stems from new retail technologies that make it easy to act without thinking. … What's the long-term effect of our overspending?

    *The Washington Post*, March 2, 2008

    a. Explain the effect on the dollar of "out of control" consumer spending and draw a graph of the foreign exchange market to illustrate your explanation.
    b. How can "out of control" spending be used to explain the trends in balance of payments since the 1990s?
    c. Explain whether or not we should be concerned that the United States is a net borrower and debtor nation.

21. Study *Reading Between the Lines* on pp. 234– 235 and then answer the following questions.
    a. Do you think the yuan–U.S. dollar exchange rate is a problem for Americans or the source of the U.S. current account deficit?
    b. Do you think that appreciation of the yuan against the U.S. dollar can help the United States to eliminate its current account deficit?
    c. What do you predict would be the main effects of an increase in the yuan–U.S. dollar exchange rate?
    d. What, if anything, could U.S. policy do to reduce the U.S. current account deficit?

22. Use the link in MyEconLab (Textbook resources, Chapter 9, Weblinks) to visit PACIFIC, an exchange rate service, and read the page on purchasing power parity.
    a. What is purchasing power parity?
    b. Which currencies are the most overvalued relative to the U.S. dollar today?
    c. Which currencies are the most undervalued relative to the U.S. dollar today?
    d. Give some suggestions as to why some currencies are overvalued and some undervalued.
    e. Do you think that the information on overvaluation and undervaluation is useful to currency speculators? Why or why not?

PART THREE

# UNDERSTANDING MACROECONOMIC TRENDS

## Expanding the Frontier

Economics is about how we cope with scarcity. We cope as individuals by making choices that balance marginal benefits and marginal costs so that we use our scarce resources efficiently. We cope as societies by creating incentive systems and social institutions that encourage specialization and exchange.

These choices and the incentive systems that guide them determine what we specialize in; how much work we do; how hard we work at school to learn the mental skills that form our human capital and that determine the kinds of jobs we get and the incomes we earn; how much we save for future big-ticket expenditures; how much businesses and governments spend on new capital—on auto assembly lines, computers and fiber cables for improved Internet services, shopping malls, highways, bridges, and tunnels; how intensively existing capital and natural resources are used and how quickly they wear out or are used up; and the problems that scientists, engineers, and other inventors work on to develop new technologies.

All the choices we've just described combine to determine the standard of living and the rate at which it improves—the economic growth rate.

Money that makes specialization and exchange in markets possible is a huge contributor to economic growth. But too much money brings a rising cost of living with no improvement in the standard of living.

**Joseph Schumpeter**, *the son of a textile factory owner, was born in Austria in 1883. He moved from Austria to Germany during the tumultuous 1920s when those two countries experienced hyperinflation. In 1932, in the depths of the Great Depression, he came to the United States and became a professor of economics at Harvard University.*

*This creative economic thinker wrote about economic growth and development, business cycles, political systems, and economic biography. He was a person of strong opinions who expressed them forcefully and delighted in verbal battles.*

*Schumpeter saw the development and diffusion of new technologies by profit-seeking entrepreneurs as the source of economic progress. But he saw economic progress as a process of creative destruction—the creation of new profit opportunities and the destruction of currently profitable businesses. For Schumpeter, economic growth and the business cycle were a single phenomenon.*

"Economic progress, in capitalist society, means turmoil."

**JOSEPH SCHUMPETER**
*Capitalism, Socialism, and Democracy*

# TALKING WITH

# Xavier Sala-i-Martin

**Xavier Sala-i-Martin** is Professor of Economics at Columbia University. He is also a Research Associate at the National Bureau of Economic Research, Senior Economic Advisor to the World Economic Forum, Associate Editor of the *Journal of Economic Growth,* founder and CEO of Umbele Foundation: A Future for Africa, and President of the Economic Commission of the Barcelona Football Club.

Professor Sala-i-Martin was an undergraduate at Universitat Autonoma de Barcelona and a graduate student at Harvard University, where he obtained his Ph.D. in 1990.

In 2004, he was awarded the Premio Juan Carlos I de Economía, a biannual prize given by the Bank of Spain to the best economist in Spain and Latin America. With Robert Barro, he is the author of *Economic Growth* Second Edition (MIT Press, 2003), the definitive graduate level text on this topic.

Michael Parkin talked with Xavier Sala-i-Martin about his work and the progress that economists have made in understanding economic growth.

*What attracted you to economics?*

It was a random event. I wanted to be rich, so I asked my mom, "In my family, who is the richest guy?" She said, "Your uncle John." And I asked, "What did he study?" And she said, "Economics." So I went into economics!

In Spain, there are no liberal arts colleges where you can study lots of things. At age 18, you must decide what career you will follow. If you choose economics, you go to economics school and take economics five years in a row. So you have to make a decision in a crazy way, like I did.

*How did economic growth become your major field of research?*

I studied economics. I liked it. I studied mathematical economics. I liked it too, and I went to graduate school. In my second year at Harvard, Jeffrey Sachs hired me to go to Bolivia. I saw poor people for the first time in my life. I was shocked. I decided I should try to answer the question "Why are these people so poor and why are we so rich, and what can we do to turn their state into our state?" We live in a bubble world in the United States and Europe, and we don't realize how poor people really are. When you see poverty at first hand, it is very hard to think about something else. So I decided to study economic growth. Coincidentally, when I returned from Bolivia, I was assigned to be Robert Barro's teaching assistant. He was teaching economic growth, so I studied with him and eventually wrote books and articles with him.

*In your first research on economic growth, you tested the neoclassical growth model using data for a number of countries and for the states of the United States. What did you discover?*

Neoclassical theory was criticized on two grounds. First, its source of growth, technological change, is exogenous—not explained. Second, its assumption of diminishing marginal returns to capital seems to imply that income per person should converge to the same level in every country. If you are poor, your marginal product should be high. Every cookie that you save should generate huge growth. If you are rich, your marginal product should be low. Every cookie you save should generate very little growth. Therefore poor countries should grow faster than rich countries, and convergence of income levels should occur. Convergence doesn't occur, so, said its critics, neoclassical theory must be wrong.

Growth through capital accumulation is very, very hard. Growth has to come from other things, such as technological change.

It turned out that it was this criticism that was wrong. Growth depends on the productivity of your cookies and on how many cookies you save. If you don't save any cookies, you don't grow, even if your marginal product is large.

Conditional convergence is the idea that income per person will converge only if countries have similar savings rates, similar technologies, and similar everything. That's what I tested. To hold every relevant factor equal, I tested the hypothesis using regions: states within the United States or countries that are similar. And once you're careful to hold other things equal, you see a perfect negative relationship between growth rates and income levels.

As predicted by neoclassical theory, poor countries grow faster than rich countries if they are similar. So my research shows that it is not so easy to reject neoclassical theory. The law of diminishing returns that comes from Adam Smith and Malthus and Ricardo is very powerful. Growth through capital accumulation is very, very hard. Growth has to come from other things, such as technological change.

*What do we know today about the nature and causes of the wealth of nations that Adam Smith didn't know?*

Actually, even though over the last two hundred years some of the best minds have looked at the question, we know surprisingly little. We have some general principles that are not very easy to apply in practice. We know, for example, that markets are good. We know that for the economy to work, we need property rights to be guaranteed. If there are thieves—government or private thieves—that can steal the proceeds of the investment, there's no investment and there's no growth. We know that the incentives are very important.

These are general principles. Because we know these principles we should ask: How come Africa is still poor? The answer is, it is very hard to translate "Markets are good" and "Property rights work" into practical actions. We know that Zimbabwe has to guarantee property rights. With the government it has, that's not going to work. The U.S. constitution works in the United States. If you try to copy the constitution and impose the system in Zimbabwe, it's not going to work.

*You've done a lot of work on distribution of income, and you say we've made a lot of progress. What is the evidence to support this conclusion?*

There are two issues: poverty and inequality. When in 2001 I said poverty is going down, everyone said I was crazy. The United Nations Development Report, which uses World Bank data, was saying the exact opposite. I said the World Bank methodology was flawed. After a big public argument that you can see in *The Economist*, the World Bank revised their poverty numbers and they now agree with me that poverty rates are falling.

Now why is poverty falling? In 1970, 80 percent of the world's poor were in Asia—in China, India, Bangladesh, and Indonesia. China's "Great Leap Forward" was a great leap backward. People were starving to death. Now, the growth of these countries has been spectacular and the global poverty rate has fallen. Yes, if you look at Africa, Africa is going backwards. But Africa has 700 million people. China has 1.3 billion. India has 1.1 billion. Indonesia has 300 million. Asia has 4 billion of the world's 6 billion people. These big guys are growing. It's impossible that global poverty is not going down.

But what we care about is poverty in different regions of the world. Asia has been doing very well, but Africa has not. Unfortunately, Africa is still going in the wrong direction.

*You've made a big personal commitment to Africa. What is the Africa problem? Why does this continent*

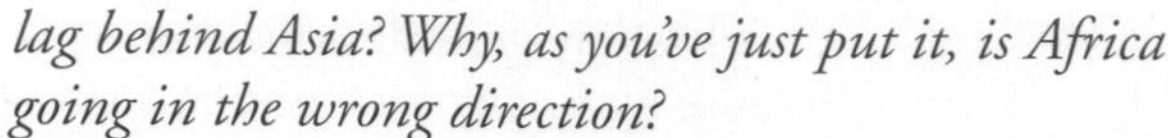

*lag behind Asia? Why, as you've just put it, is Africa going in the wrong direction?*

Number one, Africa is a very violent continent. There are twenty-two wars in Africa as we speak. Two, nobody will invest in Africa. Three, we in the rich world—the United States, Europe, and Japan—won't let them trade. Because we have agricultural subsidies, trade barriers, and tariffs for their products, they can't sell to us.

Africans should globalize themselves. They should open, and we should let them open. They should introduce markets. But to get markets, you need legal systems, police, transparency, less red tape. You need a lot of the things we have now. They have corrupt economies, very bureaucratic, with no property rights, the judiciary is corrupt. All of that has to change.

They need female education. One of the biggest rates of return that we have is educating girls. To educate girls, they'll need to build schools, they need to pay teachers, they need to buy uniforms, they need to provide the incentives for girls to go to school, which usually is like a string. You pull it, you don't push it. Pushing education doesn't work. What you need is: Let the girls know that the rate of return on education is very high by providing jobs after they leave school. So you need to change the incentives of the girls to go to school and educate themselves. That's going to increase the national product, but it will also increase health, and it will also reduce fertility.

*Returning to the problems of poverty and inequality, how can inequality be increasing within countries but decreasing globally—across countries?*

Because most inequality comes from the fact that some people live in rich countries and some people live in poor countries. The big difference across people is not that there are rich Americans and poor Americans. Americans are very close to each other relative to the difference between Americans and people from Senegal. What is closing today is the gap *across* countries—and for the first time in history. Before the Industrial Revolution, everybody was equal. Equal and poor. Equally poor. People were living at subsistence levels, which means you eat, you're clothed, you have a house, you die. No movies, no travel, no music, no toothbrush. Just subsist. And if the weather is not good, one third of the population dies. That was the history of the world between 10,000 B.C. and today.

Yes, there was a king, there was Caesar, but the majority of the population were peasants.

All of a sudden, the Industrial Revolution means that one small country, England, takes off and there is 2 percent growth every year. The living standard of the workers of England goes up and up and up. Then the United States, then France, then the rest of Europe, then Canada all begin to grow.

In terms of today's population, one billion people become rich and five billion remain poor. Now for the first time in history, the majority of these five billion people are growing more rapidly than the rich guys. They're catching up quickly. The incomes of the majority of poor citizens of the world are growing faster than those of Americans.

*What advice do you have for someone who is just beginning to study economics?*

Question! Question everything! Take some courses in history and math. And read my latest favorite book, Bill Easterly's *White Man's Burden.** It shows why we have not been doing the right thing in the aid business. I'm a little bit less dramatic than he is. He says that nothing has worked. I think some things have worked, and we have to take advantage of what has worked to build on it. But I agree with the general principle that being nice, being good, doesn't necessarily mean doing good. Lots of people with good intentions do harm. Economic science teaches us that incentives are the key.

Question!
Question everything!

*William Easterly, *The White Man's Burden: Why the West's Efforts to Aid the Rest Have Done So Much Ill and So Little Good.* New York, Penguin Books, 2006.

# 10 Aggregate Supply and Aggregate Demand

**After studying this chapter, you will be able to:**

- Explain what determines aggregate supply in the long run and in the short run
- Explain what determines aggregate demand
- Explain how real GDP and the price level are determined and how changes in aggregate supply and aggregate demand bring economic growth, inflation, and the business cycle
- Describe the main schools of thought in macroeconomics today

**Production grows and prices rise. But the pace at** which production grows and prices rise is uneven. In 2005, real GDP grew by 3 percent, but in 2008, growth slowed to less than 2 percent and was expected to stop growing or even shrink in 2009.

Similarly, during recent years, prices have increased at rates ranging from a barely perceptible 1 percent to a disturbing 5 percent a year.

The uneven pace of economic growth and inflation—the business cycle—is the subject of this chapter and the two that follow it. Here, you will discover the forces that bring fluctuations in the pace of real GDP growth and inflation and the associated fluctuations in employment and unemployment.

This chapter explains a model of real GDP and the price level—the *aggregate supply–aggregate demand model* or *AS-AD model*. This model represents the consensus view of macroeconomists on how real GDP and the price level are determined. The model provides a framework for understanding the forces that make our economy expand, that bring inflation, and that cause business cycle fluctuations. The *AS-AD* model also provides a framework within which we can see the range of views of macroeconomists in different schools of thought.

In *Reading Between the Lines* at the end of the chapter, we use the *AS-AD* model to interpret the course of U.S. real GDP and the price level in 2008.

## Aggregate Supply

The purpose of the aggregate supply–aggregate demand model that you study in this chapter is to explain how real GDP and the price level are determined and how they interact. The model uses similar ideas to those that you encountered in Chapter 3 when you learned how the quantity and price in a competitive market are determined. But the *aggregate* supply-*aggregate* demand model (*AS-AD* model) isn't just an application of the competitive market model. Some differences arise because the *AS-AD* model is a model of an imaginary market for the total of all the final goods and services that make up real GDP. The quantity in this "market" is real GDP and the price is the price level measured by the GDP deflator.

One thing that the *AS-AD* model shares with the competitive market model is that both distinguish between *supply* and the *quantity supplied*. We begin by explaining what we mean by the quantity of real GDP supplied.

### Quantity Supplied and Supply

The *quantity of real GDP supplied* is the total quantity of goods and services, valued in constant base-year (2000) dollars, that firms plan to produce during a given period. This quantity depends on the quantity of labor employed, the quantity of physical and human capital, and the state of technology.

At any given time, the quantity of capital and the state of technology are fixed. They depend on decisions that were made in the past. The population is also fixed. But the quantity of labor is not fixed. It depends on decisions made by households and firms about the supply of and demand for labor.

The labor market can be in any one of three states: at full employment, above full employment, or below full employment. At full employment, the quantity of real GDP supplied is *potential GDP*, which depends on the full-employment quantity of labor (see Chapter 6, pp. 139–141). Over the business cycle, employment fluctuates around full employment and the quantity of real GDP supplied fluctuates around potential GDP.

*Aggregate supply* is the relationship between the quantity of real GDP supplied and the price level. This relationship is different in the long run than in the short run and to study aggregate supply, we distinguish between two time frames:

- Long-run aggregate supply
- Short-run aggregate supply

### Long-Run Aggregate Supply

**Long-run aggregate supply** is the relationship between the quantity of real GDP supplied and the price level when the money wage rate changes in step with the price level to achieve full employment. The quantity of real GDP supplied at full employment equals potential GDP and this quantity is the same regardless of the price level.

The long-run aggregate supply curve in Fig. 10.1 illustrates long-run aggregate supply as the vertical line at potential GDP labeled *LAS*. Along the long-run aggregate supply curve, as the price level changes, the money wage rate also changes so the real wage rate is constant and real GDP remains at potential GDP. The long-run aggregate supply curve is always vertical and is always located at potential GDP.

The long-run aggregate supply curve is vertical because potential GDP is independent of the price level. The reason for this independence is that a movement along the *LAS* curve is accompanied by a change in *two* sets of prices: the prices of goods and services—the price level—and the prices of the factors of production, most notably, the money wage rate. A 10 percent increase in the prices of goods and services is matched by a 10 percent increase in the money wage rate. Because the price level and the money wage rate change by the same percentage, the *real wage rate* remains constant at its full-employment equilibrium level. So when the price level changes and the real wage rate remains constant, employment remains constant and real GDP remains constant at potential GDP.

**Production at a Pepsi Plant** You can see more clearly why real GDP remains constant when all prices change by the same percentage by thinking about production decisions at a Pepsi bottling plant. How does the quantity of Pepsi supplied change if the price of Pepsi changes and the wage rate of the workers and prices of all the other resources used vary by the same percentage? The answer is that the quantity supplied doesn't change. The firm produces the quantity that maximizes profit. That quantity depends on the price of Pepsi relative to the cost of producing it. With no change in price *relative to cost*, production doesn't change.

## Short-Run Aggregate Supply

**Short-run aggregate supply** is the relationship between the quantity of real GDP supplied and the price level *when the money wage rate, the prices of other resources, and potential GDP remain constant.* Figure 10.1 illustrates this relationship as the short-run aggregate supply curve *SAS* and the short-run aggregate supply schedule. Each point on the *SAS* curve corresponds to a row of the short-run aggregate supply schedule. For example, point *A* on the *SAS* curve and row *A* of the schedule tell us that if the price level is 105, the quantity of real GDP supplied is $11 trillion. In the short run, a rise in the price level brings an increase in the quantity of real GDP supplied. The short-run aggregate supply curve slopes upward.

With a given money wage rate, there is one price level at which the real wage rate is at its full-employment equilibrium level. At this price level, the quantity of real GDP supplied equals potential GDP and the *SAS* curve intersects the *LAS* curve. In this example, that price level is 115. If the price level rises above 115, the quantity of real GDP supplied increases along the *SAS* curve and exceeds potential GDP; if the price level falls below 115, the quantity of real GDP supplied decreases along the *SAS* curve and is less than potential GDP.

**Back at the Pepsi Plant** You can see why the short-run aggregate supply curve slopes upward by returning to the Pepsi bottling plant. If production increases, marginal cost rises and if production decreases, marginal cost falls (see Chapter 2, p. 35).

If the price of Pepsi rises with no change in the money wage rate and other costs, Pepsi can increase profit by increasing production. Pepsi is in business to maximize its profit, so it increases production.

Similarly, if the price of Pepsi falls while the money wage rate and other costs remain constant, Pepsi can avoid a loss by decreasing production. The lower price weakens the incentive to produce, so Pepsi decreases production.

What's true for Pepsi bottlers is true for the producers of all goods and services. When all prices rise, the *price level rises.* If the price level rises and the money wage rate and other factor prices remain constant, all firms increase production and the quantity of real GDP supplied increases. A fall in the price level has the opposite effect and decreases the quantity of real GDP supplied.

**FIGURE 10.1** Long-Run and Short-Run Aggregate Supply

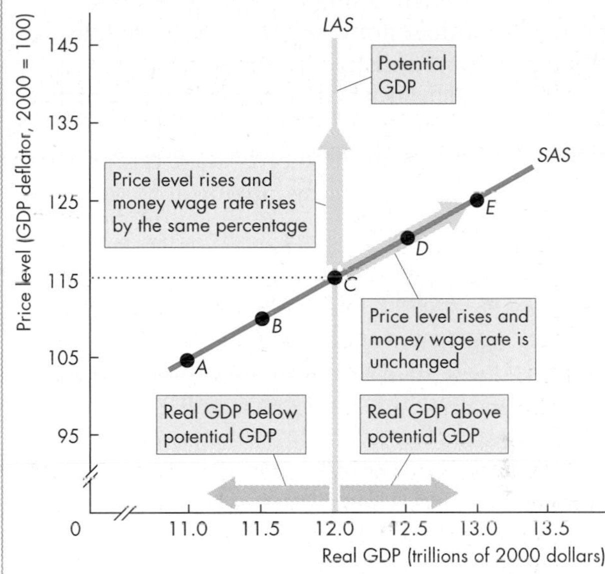


| | Price level (GDP deflator) | Real GDP supplied (trillions of 2000 dollars) |
|---|---|---|
| *A* | 105 | 11.0 |
| *B* | 110 | 11.5 |
| ***C*** | **115** | **12.0** |
| *D* | 120 | 12.5 |
| *E* | 125 | 13.0 |

In the long run, the quantity of real GDP supplied is potential GDP and the *LAS* curve is vertical at potential GDP.
In the short-run, the quantity of real GDP supplied increases if the price level rises, while all other influences on supply plans remain the same.
The short-run aggregate supply curve, *SAS*, slopes upward. The short-run aggregate supply curve is based on the aggregate supply schedule in the table. Each point *A* through *E* on the curve corresponds to the row in the table identified by the same letter.
When the price level is 115, the quantity of real GDP supplied is $12 trillion, which is potential GDP. If the price level rises above 115, the quantity of real GDP supplied increases and exceeds potential GDP; if the price level falls below 115, the quantity of real GDP supplied decreases below potential GDP.

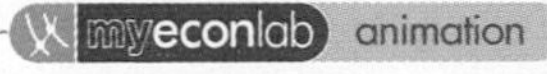

## Changes in Aggregate Supply

You've just seen that a change in the price level brings a movement along the aggregate supply curves but it does not change aggregate supply. Aggregate supply changes when an influence on production plans other than the price level changes. These other influences include a change in potential GDP and changes in the money wage rate and other factor prices. Let's begin by looking at factors that change potential GDP.

**Changes in Potential GDP** When potential GDP changes, aggregate supply changes. An increase in potential GDP increases both long-run aggregate supply and short-run aggregate supply.

Figure 10.2 shows the effects of an increase in potential GDP. Initially, the long-run aggregate supply curve is $LAS_0$ and the short-run aggregate supply curve is $SAS_0$. If potential GDP increases to $13 trillion, long-run aggregate supply increases and the long-run aggregate supply curve shifts rightward to $LAS_1$. Short-run aggregate supply also increases, and the short-run aggregate supply curve shifts rightward to $SAS_1$. The two supply curves shift by the same amount only if the full-employment price level remains constant, which we will assume to be the case.

Potential GDP can increase for any of three reasons:

- An increase in the full-employment quantity of labor
- An increase in the quantity of capital
- An advance in technology

Let's look at these influences on potential GDP and the aggregate supply curves.

***An Increase in the Full-Employment Quantity of Labor*** A Pepsi bottling plant that employs 100 workers bottles more Pepsi than does an otherwise identical plant that employs 10 workers. The same is true for the economy as a whole. The larger the quantity of labor employed, the greater is real GDP.

Over time, potential GDP increases because the labor force increases. But (with constant capital and technology) *potential* GDP increases only if the full-employment quantity of labor increases. Fluctuations in employment over the business cycle bring fluctuations in real GDP. But these changes in real GDP are fluctuations around potential GDP. They are not changes in potential GDP and long-run aggregate supply.

**FIGURE 10.2** A Change in Potential GDP

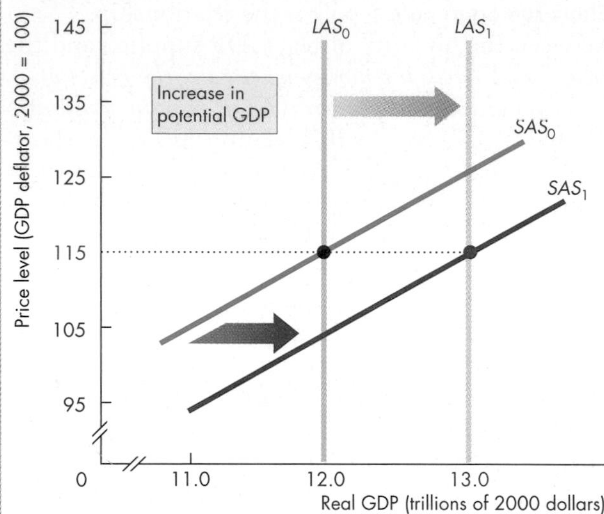


An increase in potential GDP increases both long-run aggregate supply and short-run aggregate supply and shifts both aggregate supply curves rightward from $LAS_0$ to $LAS_1$ and from $SAS_0$ to $SAS_1$.

***An Increase in the Quantity of Capital*** A Pepsi bottling plant with two production lines bottles more Pepsi than does an otherwise identical plant that has only one production line. For the economy, the larger the quantity of capital, the more productive is the labor force and the greater is its potential GDP. Potential GDP per person in the capital-rich United States is vastly greater than that in capital-poor China and Russia.

Capital includes *human capital.* One Pepsi plant is managed by an economics major with an MBA and has a labor force with an average of 10 years of experience. This plant produces a larger output than does an otherwise identical plant that is managed by someone with no business training or experience and that has a young labor force that is new to bottling. The first plant has a greater amount of human capital than the second. For the economy as a whole, the larger the quantity of *human capital*—the skills that people have acquired in school and through on-the-job training—the greater is potential GDP.

***An Advance in Technology*** A Pepsi plant that has pre-computer age machines produces less than one that uses the latest robot technology. Technological change enables firms to produce more from any given amount of factors of production. So even with fixed quantities of labor and capital, improvements in technology increase potential GDP.

Technological advances are by far the most important source of increased production over the past two centuries. As a result of technological advances, one farmer in the United States today can feed 100 people and in a year one autoworker can produce almost 14 cars and trucks.

Let's now look at the effects of changes in the money wage rate.

**Changes in the Money Wage Rate and Other Factor Prices** When the money wage rate (or the money price of any other factor of production such as oil) changes, short-run aggregate supply changes but long-run aggregate supply does not change.

Figure 10.3 shows the effect of an increase in the money wage rate. Initially, the short-run aggregate supply curve is $SAS_0$. A rise in the money wage rate *decreases* short-run aggregate supply and shifts the short-run aggregate supply curve leftward to $SAS_2$.

A rise in the money wage rate decreases short-run aggregate supply because it increases firms' costs. With increased costs, the quantity that firms are willing to supply at each price level decreases, which is shown by a leftward shift of the *SAS* curve.

A change in the money wage rate does not change long-run aggregate supply because on the *LAS* curve, the change in the money wage rate is accompanied by an equal percentage change in the price level. With no change in *relative* prices, firms have no incentive to change production and real GDP remains constant at potential GDP. With no change in potential GDP, the long-run aggregate supply curve *LAS* does not shift.

**What Makes the Money Wage Rate Change?** The money wage rate can change for two reasons: departures from full employment and expectations about inflation. Unemployment above the natural rate puts downward pressure on the money wage rate, and unemployment below the natural rate puts upward pressure on it. An expected rise in the inflation rate makes the money wage rate rise faster, and an expected fall in the inflation rate slows the rate at which the money wage rate rises.

**FIGURE 10.3** A Change in the Money Wage Rate

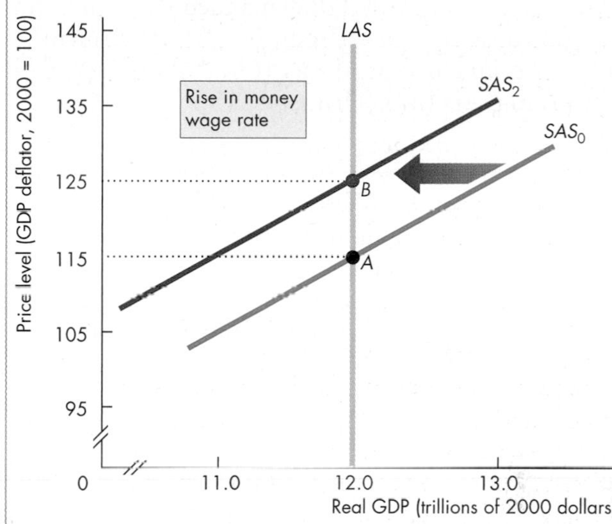


A rise in the money wage rate decreases short-run aggregate supply and shifts the short-run aggregate supply curve leftward from $SAS_0$ to $SAS_2$. A rise in the money wage rate does not change potential GDP, so the long-run aggregate supply curve does not shift.

myeconlab animation

## Review Quiz

1. If the price level and the money wage rate rise by the same percentage, what happens to the quantity of real GDP supplied? Along which aggregate supply curve does the economy move?
2. If the price level rises and the money wage rate remains constant, what happens to the quantity of real GDP supplied? Along which aggregate supply curve does the economy move?
3. If potential GDP increases, what happens to aggregate supply? Does the *LAS* curve shift or is there a movement along the *LAS* curve? Does the *SAS* curve shift or is there a movement along the *SAS* curve?
4. If the money wage rate rises and potential GDP remains the same, does the *LAS* curve or the *SAS* curve shift or is there a movement along the *LAS* curve or the *SAS* curve?

myeconlab Work Study Plan 10.1 and get instant feedback.

## Aggregate Demand

The quantity of real GDP demanded ($Y$) is the sum of real consumption expenditure ($C$), investment ($I$), government expenditure ($G$), and exports ($X$) minus imports ($M$). That is,

$$Y = C + I + G + X - M.$$

The *quantity of real GDP demanded* is the total amount of final goods and services produced in the United States that people, businesses, governments, and foreigners plan to buy.

These buying plans depend on many factors. Some of the main ones are

- The price level
- Expectations
- Fiscal policy and monetary policy
- The world economy

We first focus on the relationship between the quantity of real GDP demanded and the price level. To study this relationship, we keep all other influences on buying plans the same and ask: How does the quantity of real GDP demanded vary as the price level varies?

**FIGURE 10.4** Aggregate Demand

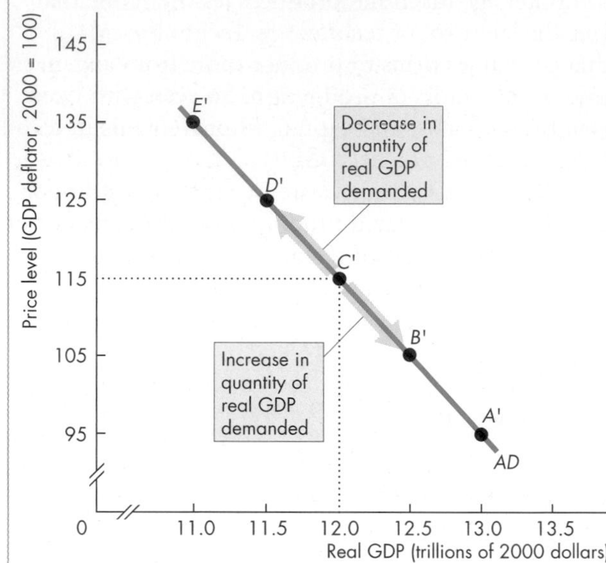


| | Price level (GDP deflator) | Real GDP demanded (trillions of 2000 dollars) |
|---|---|---|
| *A'* | 95 | 13.0 |
| *B'* | 105 | 12.5 |
| **C'** | **115** | **12.0** |
| *D'* | 125 | 11.5 |
| *E'* | 135 | 11.0 |

The aggregate demand curve (*AD*) shows the relationship between the quantity of real GDP demanded and the price level. The aggregate demand curve is based on the aggregate demand schedule in the table. Each point *A'* through *E'* on the curve corresponds to the row in the table identified by the same letter. When the price level is 115, the quantity of real GDP demanded is $12 trillion, as shown by point *C'* in the figure. A change in the price level, when all other influences on aggregate buying plans remain the same, brings a change in the quantity of real GDP demanded and a movement along the *AD* curve.

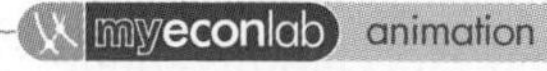


### The Aggregate Demand Curve

Other things remaining the same, the higher the price level, the smaller is the quantity of real GDP demanded. This relationship between the quantity of real GDP demanded and the price level is called **aggregate demand**. Aggregate demand is described by an *aggregate demand schedule* and an *aggregate demand curve*.

Figure 10.4 shows an aggregate demand curve (*AD*) and an aggregate demand schedule. Each point on the *AD* curve corresponds to a row of the schedule. For example, point *C'* on the *AD* curve and row *C'* of the schedule tell us that if the price level is 115, the quantity of real GDP demanded is $12 trillion.

The aggregate demand curve slopes downward for two reasons:

- Wealth effect
- Substitution effects

**Wealth Effect** When the price level rises but other things remain the same, *real* wealth decreases. Real wealth is the amount of money in the bank, bonds, stocks, and other assets that people own, measured not in dollars but in terms of the goods and services that the money, bonds, and stocks will buy.

People save and hold money, bonds, and stocks for many reasons. One reason is to build up funds for education expenses. Another reason is to build up enough funds to meet possible medical expenses or other big bills. But the biggest reason is to build up enough funds to provide a retirement income.

If the price level rises, real wealth decreases. People then try to restore their wealth. To do so, they must increase saving and, equivalently, decrease current consumption. Such a decrease in consumption is a decrease in aggregate demand.

***Maria's Wealth Effect*** You can see how the wealth effect works by thinking about Maria's buying plans. Maria lives in Moscow, Russia. She has worked hard all summer and saved 20,000 rubles (the ruble is the currency of Russia), which she plans to spend attending graduate school when she has finished her economics degree. So Maria's wealth is 20,000 rubles. Maria has a part-time job, and her income from this job pays her current expenses. The price level in Russia rises by 100 percent, and now Maria needs 40,000 rubles to buy what 20,000 once bought. To try to make up some of the fall in value of her savings, Maria saves even more and cuts her current spending to the bare minimum.

**Substitution Effects** When the price level rises and other things remain the same, interest rates rise. The reason is related to the wealth effect that you've just studied. A rise in the price level decreases the real value of the money in people's pockets and bank accounts. With a smaller amount of real money around, banks and other lenders can get a higher interest rate on loans. But faced with a higher interest rate, people and businesses delay plans to buy new capital and consumer durable goods and cut back on spending.

This substitution effect involves substituting goods in the future for goods in the present and is called an *intertemporal* substitution effect—a substitution across time. Saving increases to increase future consumption.

To see this intertemporal substitution effect more clearly, think about your own plan to buy a new computer. At an interest rate of 5 percent a year, you might borrow $1,000 and buy the new computer. But at an interest rate of 10 percent a year, you might decide that the payments would be too high. You don't abandon your plan to buy the computer, but you decide to delay your purchase.

A second substitution effect works through international prices. When the U.S. price level rises and other things remain the same, U.S.-made goods and services become more expensive relative to foreign-made goods and services. This change in *relative prices* encourages people to spend less on U.S.-made items and more on foreign-made items. For example, if the U.S. price level rises relative to the Japanese price level, Japanese buy fewer U.S.-made cars (U.S. exports decrease) and Americans buy more Japanese-made cars (U.S. imports increase). U.S. GDP decreases.

***Maria's Substitution Effects*** In Moscow, Russia, Maria makes some substitutions. She was planning to trade in her old motor scooter and get a new one. But with a higher price level and a higher interest rate, she decides to make her old scooter last one more year. Also, with the prices of Russian goods sharply increasing, Maria substitutes a low-cost dress made in Malaysia for the Russian-made dress she had originally planned to buy.

**Changes in the Quantity of Real GDP Demanded** When the price level rises and other things remain the same, the quantity of real GDP demanded decreases—a movement up along the *AD* curve as shown by the arrow in Fig. 10.4. When the price level falls and other things remain the same, the quantity of real GDP demanded increases—a movement down along the *AD* curve.

We've now seen how the quantity of real GDP demanded changes when the price level changes. How do other influences on buying plans affect aggregate demand?

## Changes in Aggregate Demand

A change in any factor that influences buying plans other than the price level brings a change in aggregate demand. The main factors are

- Expectations
- Fiscal policy and monetary policy
- The world economy

**Expectations** An increase in expected future income increases the amount of consumption goods (especially big-ticket items such as cars) that people plan to buy today and increases aggregate demand.

An increase in the expected future inflation rate increases aggregate demand today because people decide to buy more goods and services at today's relatively lower prices.

An increase in expected future profits increases the investment that firms plan to undertake today and increases aggregate demand.

**Fiscal Policy and Monetary Policy** The government's attempt to influence the economy by setting and changing taxes, making transfer payments, and purchasing goods and services is called **fiscal policy**. A tax cut or an increase in transfer payments—for example, unemployment benefits or welfare payments—increases aggregate demand. Both of these influences operate by increasing households' *disposable* income. **Disposable income** is aggregate income minus taxes plus transfer payments. The greater the disposable income, the greater is the quantity of consumption goods and services that households plan to buy and the greater is aggregate demand.

Government expenditure on goods and services is one component of aggregate demand. So if the government spends more on spy satellites, schools, and highways, aggregate demand increases.

**Monetary policy** consists of changes in the interest rate and in the quantity of money in the economy. The quantity of money is determined by the Federal Reserve (the Fed) and the banks (in a process described in Chapters 8 and 14). An increase in the quantity of money in the economy increases aggregate demand. To see why money affects aggregate demand, imagine that the Fed borrows the army's helicopters, loads them with millions of new $10 bills, and sprinkles them like confetti across the nation. People gather the newly available money and plan to spend some of it. So the quantity of goods and services demanded increases. But people don't plan to spend all the new money. They plan to save some of it and lend it to others through the banks. The interest rate falls, and with a lower interest rate, people plan to buy more consumer durables and firms plan to increase their investment.

**The World Economy** Two main influences that the world economy has on aggregate demand are the exchange rate and foreign income. The *exchange rate* is the amount of a foreign currency that you can buy with a U.S. dollar. Other things remaining the same, a rise in the exchange rate decreases aggregate

## Fiscal Policy to Fight Recession

### The 2008 Fiscal Stimulus Package

In February 2008, Congress passed legislation that gave $168 billion to businesses and low- and middle-income Americans—$600 to a single person and $1,200 to a couple with an additional $300 for each child. The benefit was scaled back for individuals with incomes above $75,000 a year and for families with incomes greater than $150,000 a year.

The idea of the package was to stimulate business investment and consumption expenditure and increase aggregate demand.

*Deal makers Senators Harry Reid and Mitch McConnell*

## Monetary Policy to Fight Recession

### Concerted Interest Rate Cuts

In October 2008, the Federal Reserve, in concert with the European Central Bank, the Bank of Canada, and the Bank of England, cut the interest rate and took other measures to ease credit and encourage banks and others to increase their lending. The U.S. interest rate was the lowest (see below).

Like the earlier fiscal stimulus package, the idea of these interest rate cuts and easier credit was to stimulate business investment and consumption expenditure and increase aggregate demand.

1.5%

Ben Bernake
Federal Reserve

4.5%

Marvyn King
Bank of England

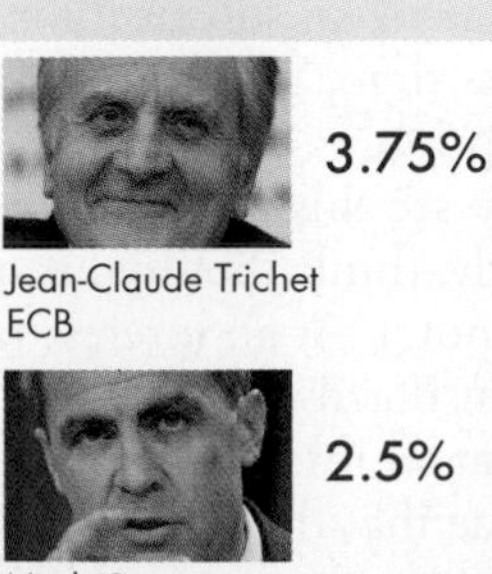

3.75%

Jean-Claude Trichet
ECB

2.5%

Mark Carrey
Bank of Canada

**FIGURE 10.5** Changes in Aggregate Demand

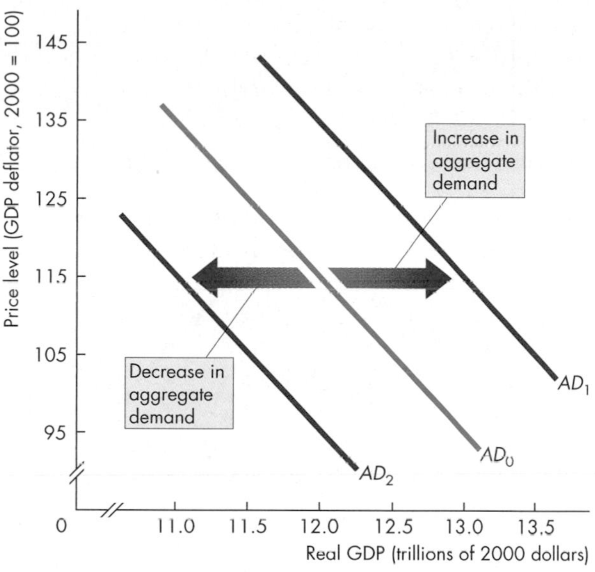


**Aggregate demand**

| *Decreases if:* | *Increases if:* |
|---|---|
| ■ Expected future income, inflation, or profits decrease | ■ Expected future income, inflation, or profits increase |
| ■ Fiscal policy decreases government expenditure, increases taxes, or decreases transfer payments | ■ Fiscal policy increases government expenditure, decreases taxes, or increases transfer payments |
| ■ Monetary policy decreases the quantity of money and increases interest rates | ■ Monetary policy increases the quantity of money and decreases interest rates |
| ■ The exchange rate increases or foreign income decreases | ■ The exchange rate decreases or foreign income increases |

myeconlab animation

demand. To see how the exchange rate influences aggregate demand, suppose that the exchange rate is 1.20 euros per U.S. dollar. A Nokia cell phone made in Finland costs 120 euros, and an equivalent Motorola phone made in the United States costs \$110. In U.S. dollars, the Nokia phone costs \$100, so people around the world buy the cheaper phone from Finland. Now suppose the exchange rate falls to 1 euro per U.S. dollar. The Nokia phone now costs \$120 and is more expensive than the Motorola phone. People will switch from the Nokia phone to the Motorola phone. U.S. exports will increase and U.S. imports will decrease, so U.S. aggregate demand will increase.

An increase in foreign income increases U.S. exports and increases U.S. aggregate demand. For example, an increase in income in Japan and Germany increases Japanese and German consumers' and producers' planned expenditures on U.S.-produced goods and services.

**Shifts of the Aggregate Demand Curve** When aggregate demand changes, the aggregate demand curve shifts. Figure 10.5 shows two changes in aggregate demand and summarizes the factors that bring about such changes.

Aggregate demand increases and the *AD* curve shifts rightward from $AD_0$ to $AD_1$ when expected future income, inflation, or profit increases; government expenditure on goods and services increases; taxes are cut; transfer payments increase; the quantity of money increases and the interest rate falls; the exchange rate falls; or foreign income increases.

Aggregate demand decreases and the *AD* curve shifts leftward from $AD_0$ to $AD_2$ when expected future income, inflation, or profit decreases; government expenditure on goods and services decreases; taxes increase; transfer payments decrease; the quantity of money decreases and the interest rate rises; the exchange rate rises; or foreign income decreases.

## Review Quiz

1. What does the aggregate demand curve show? What factors change and what factors remain the same when there is a movement along the aggregate demand curve?
2. Why does the aggregate demand curve slope downward?
3. How do changes in expectations, fiscal policy and monetary policy, and the world economy change aggregate demand and the aggregate demand curve?

Work Study Plan 10.2 and get instant feedback.

## Explaining Macroeconomic Fluctuations

The purpose of the *AS-AD* model is to explain changes in real GDP and the price level. The model's main purpose is to explain business cycle fluctuations in these variables. But the model also aids our understanding of economic growth and inflation trends. We begin by combining aggregate supply and aggregate demand to determine real GDP and the price level in equilibrium. Just as there are two time frames for aggregate supply, there are two time frames for macroeconomic equilibrium: a long-run equilibrium and a short-run equilibrium. We'll first look at short-run equilibrium.

### Short-Run Macroeconomic Equilibrium

The aggregate demand curve tells us the quantity of real GDP demanded at each price level, and the short-run aggregate supply curve tells us the quantity of real GDP supplied at each price level. **Short-run macroeconomic equilibrium** occurs when the quantity of real GDP demanded equals the quantity of real GDP supplied. That is, short-run macroeconomic equilibrium occurs at the point of intersection of the *AD* curve and the *SAS* curve. Figure 10.6 shows such an equilibrium at a price level of 115 and real GDP of $12 trillion (points *C* and *C'*).

To see why this position is the equilibrium, think about what happens if the price level is something other than 115. Suppose, for example, that the price level is 125 and that real GDP is $13 trillion (at point *E* on the *SAS* curve). The quantity of real GDP demanded is less than $13 trillion, so firms are unable to sell all their output. Unwanted inventories pile up, and firms cut both production and prices. Production and prices are cut until firms can sell all their output. This situation occurs only when real GDP is $12 trillion and the price level is 115.

Now suppose the price level is 105 and real GDP is $11 trillion (at point *A* on the *SAS* curve). The quantity of real GDP demanded exceeds $11 trillion, so firms are unable to meet the demand for their output. Inventories decrease, and customers clamor for goods and services, so firms increase production and raise prices. Production and prices increase until firms can meet the demand for their output. This situation occurs only when real GDP is $12 trillion and the price level is 115.

In the short run, the money wage rate is fixed. It does not adjust to move the economy to full employment. So in the short run, real GDP can be greater than or less than potential GDP. But in the long run, the money wage rate does adjust and real GDP moves toward potential GDP. We are going to study this adjustment process. But first, let's look at the economy in long-run equilibrium.

**FIGURE 10.6** Short-Run Equilibrium

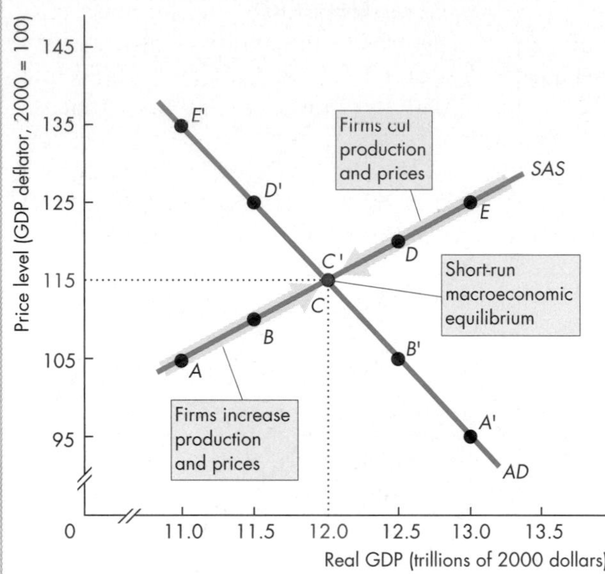


Short-run macroeconomic equilibrium occurs when real GDP demanded equals real GDP supplied—at the intersection of the aggregate demand curve (*AD*) and the short-run aggregate supply curve (*SAS*). Here, such an equilibrium occurs at points *C* and *C'*, where the price level is 115 and real GDP is $12 trillion.

If the price level is 125 and real GDP is $13 trillion (point *E*), firms will not be able to sell all their output. They will decrease production and cut prices. If the price level is 105 and real GDP is $11 trillion (point *A*), people will not be able to buy all the goods and services they demand. Firms will increase production and raise their prices.

Only when the price level is 115 and real GDP is $12 trillion can firms sell all that they produce and can people buy all the goods and services they demand. This is the short-run macroeconomic equilibrium.

## Long-Run Macroeconomic Equilibrium

**Long-run macroeconomic equilibrium** occurs when real GDP equals potential GDP—equivalently, when the economy is on its *LAS* curve. Figure 10.7 shows the long-run macroeconomic equilibrium, which occurs at the intersection of the *AD* curve and the *LAS* curve (the blue curves). Long-run macroeconomic equilibrium comes about because the money wage rate adjusts. Potential GDP and aggregate demand determine the price level, and the price level influences the money wage rate. In long-run equilibrium, the money wage rate has adjusted to put the *SAS* curve through the long-run equilibrium point.

We'll look at this money wage adjustment process later in this chapter. But first, let's see how the *AS-AD* model helps us to understand economic growth and inflation.

## Economic Growth in the *AS-AD* Model

Economic growth occurs because, the quantity of labor and labor productivity grow. Population growth is the source of labor growth, and capital accumulation and technological change are the sources of labor productivity growth. Chapter 6 explains and illustrates the effects of population growth as an increase in the supply of labor. That chapter also explains and illustrates the effects of labor productivity growth as an upward shift in the aggregate production function and an increase in the demand for labor. These changes increase potential GDP.

The *AS-AD* model explains and illustrates potential GDP growth as a rightward shift of the *LAS* curve. For example, in Fig. 10.8, potential GDP grows from \$12 trillion to \$13 trillion and the *LAS* curve shifts rightward from $LAS_0$ to $LAS_1$.

**FIGURE 10.7** Long-Run Equilibrium

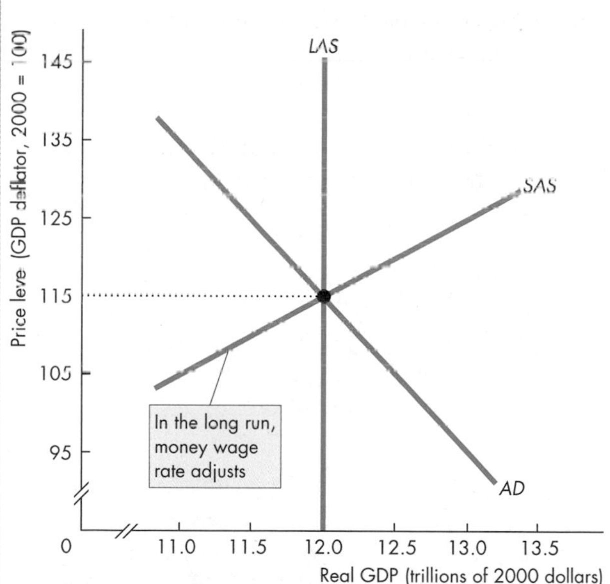


In long-run macroeconomic equilibrium, real GDP equals potential GDP. So long-run equilibrium occurs where the aggregate demand curve, *AD*, intersects the long-run aggregate supply curve, *LAS*. In the long run, aggregate demand determines the price level and has no effect on real GDP. The money wage rate adjusts in the long run, so that the *SAS* curve intersects the *LAS* curve at the long-run equilibrium price level.

myeconlab animation

**FIGURE 10.8** Economic Growth and Inflation

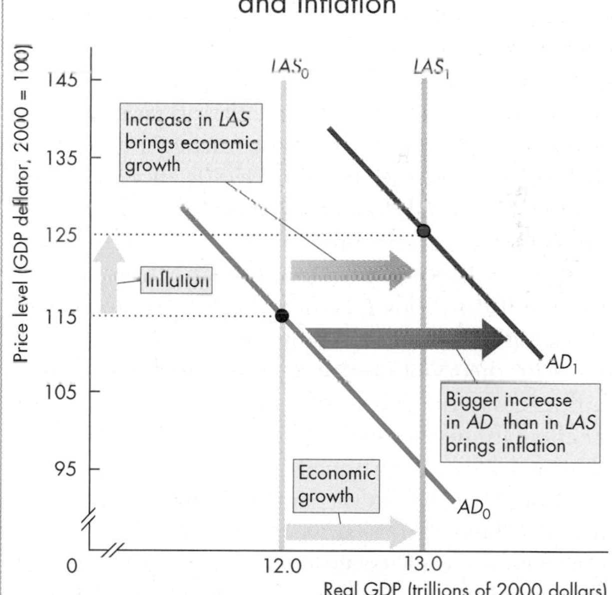


Economic growth is the persistent increase in potential GDP. Economic growth is shown as an ongoing rightward shift of the *LAS* curve. The pace at which the *LAS* curve shifts rightward depends on the growth rate of the labor force and the growth rate of labor productivity.

Inflation is a persistently rising price level and it occurs when the quantity of money grows to make the *AD* curve shift rightward at a faster pace than that of the *LAS* curve.

myeconlab animation

## Inflation in the *AS-AD* Model

Inflation occurs because the quantity of money grows more rapidly than potential GDP. In Chapter 8, the quantity theory of money, derived from the equation of exchange, explains inflation. With a constant velocity of circulation of money, the inflation rate equals the growth rate of the quantity of money minus the growth rate of real GDP. At full employment (in the macroeconomic long run), real GDP grows at the growth rate of potential GDP. So the inflation rate equals the growth rate of the quantity of money minus the growth rate of potential GDP.

We can explain and illustrate this inflation process using the *AS-AD* model. Inflation occurs when aggregate demand increases at a faster rate than the growth rate of potential GDP. That is, inflation occurs if the *AD* curve shifts rightward at a faster rate than the rate of rightward shift of the *LAS* curve. Figure 10.8 shows shifts of the *AD* and *LAS* curves that bring inflation.

If aggregate demand increases at the same rate as long-run aggregate supply, we experience real GDP growth with no inflation.

You've seen that the growth rate of potential GDP doesn't change much, but the inflation rate varies a great deal. During the 1970s, it reached a double-digit level and then during the 1980s, its rate fell to the low levels maintained through the 1990s and into the 2000s. Changes in the growth rate of aggregate demand explain the changes in the inflation rate.

Any of the influences on aggregate demand can change its growth rate. Using the ideas from the quantity theory of money, we can summarize those influences as the quantity of money and the velocity of circulation. Although either one can change, only the growth rate of the quantity of money can change by enough to explain the large and persistent changes in the inflation rate that we experience. When the quantity of money grows rapidly, aggregate demand grows rapidly and the inflation rate is high. When the growth rate of the quantity of money slows, the inflation rate eventually slows.

Our economy experiences periods of growth and inflation, like those shown in Fig. 10.8, but it does not experience *steady* growth and *steady* inflation. Real GDP fluctuates around potential GDP in a business cycle, and inflation fluctuates. When we study the business cycle, we ignore economic growth. By doing so, we see the business cycle more clearly.

## The Business Cycle in the *AS-AD* Model

The business cycle occurs because aggregate demand and short-run aggregate supply fluctuate but the money wage rate does not adjust quickly enough to keep real GDP at potential GDP. Figure 10.9 shows three types of short-run equilibrium.

Figure 10.9(a) shows an above full-employment equilibrium. An **above full-employment equilibrium** is an equilibrium in which real GDP exceeds potential GDP. The gap between real GDP and potential GDP is the **output gap.** When real GDP exceeds potential GDP, the output gap is called an **inflationary gap.**

The above full-employment equilibrium shown in Fig. 10.9(a) occurs where the aggregate demand curve $AD_0$ intersects the short-run aggregate supply curve $SAS_0$ at a real GDP of $12.2 trillion. There is an inflationary gap of $0.2 trillion.

## The Business Cycle in the U.S. Economy

### The Fluctuating Output Gap

The U.S. economy had an inflationary gap in 2000 (at *A* in the figure), full employment in 2001 (at *B*), and a recessionary gap in 2003 (at *C*). The fluctuating output gap in the figure is the real-world version of Fig. 10.9(d) and is generated by fluctuations in aggregate demand and short-run aggregate supply.

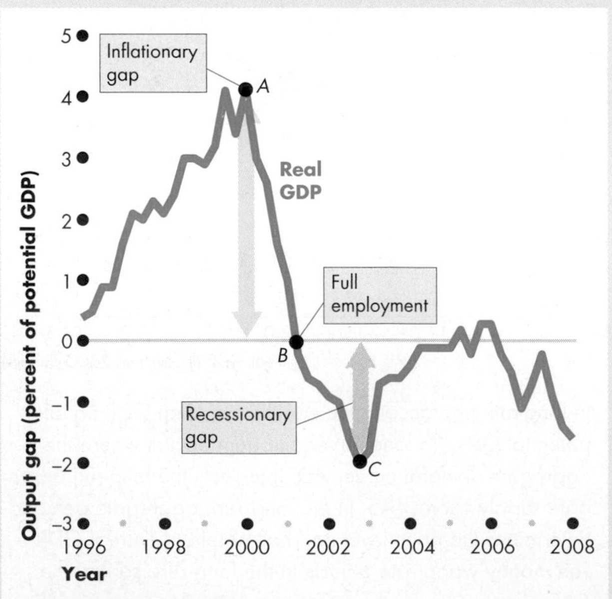


**The U.S. Output Gap**

*Sources of data:* Bureau of Economic Analysis and Congressional Budget Office.

Figure 10.9(b) is an example of **full-employment equilibrium,** in which real GDP equals potential GDP. In this example, the equilibrium occurs where the aggregate demand curve $AD_1$ intersects the short-run aggregate supply curve $SAS_1$ at an actual and potential GDP of $12 trillion.

In part (c), there is a below full-employment equilibrium. A **below full-employment equilibrium** is an equilibrium in which potential GDP exceeds real GDP. When potential GDP exceeds real GDP, the output gap is called a **recessionary gap**.

The below full-employment equilibrium shown in Fig. 10.9(c) occurs where the aggregate demand curve $AD_2$ intersects the short-run aggregate supply curve $SAS_2$ at a real GDP of $11.8 trillion. Potential GDP is $12 trillion, so the recessionary gap is $0.2 trillion.

The economy moves from one type of macroeconomic equilibrium to another as a result of fluctuations in aggregate demand and in short-run aggregate supply. These fluctuations produce fluctuations in real GDP. Figure 10.9(d) shows how real GDP fluctuates around potential GDP.

Let's now look at some of the sources of these fluctuations around potential GDP.

**FIGURE 10.9** The Business Cycle

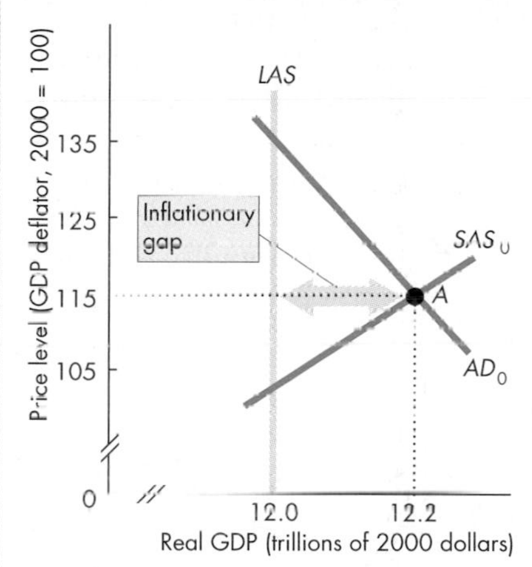


**(a) Above full employment equilibrium**

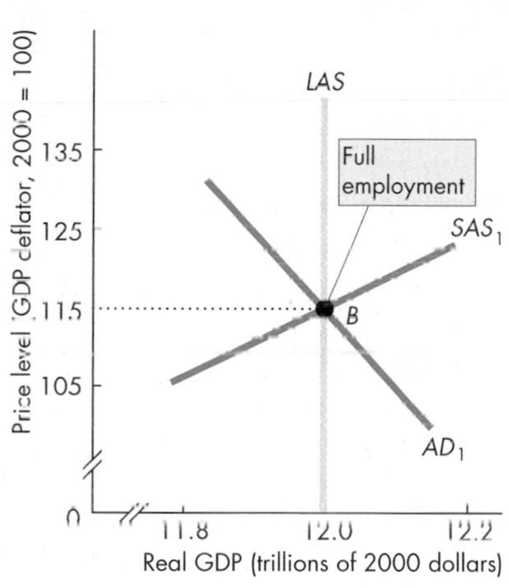


**(b) Full-employment equilibrium**

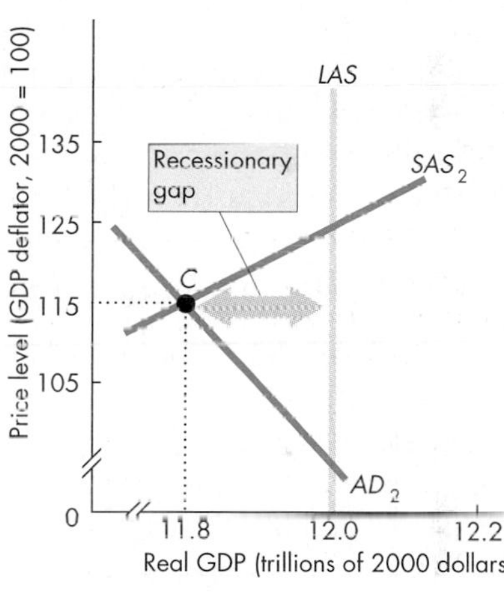


**(c) Below full-employment equilibrium**

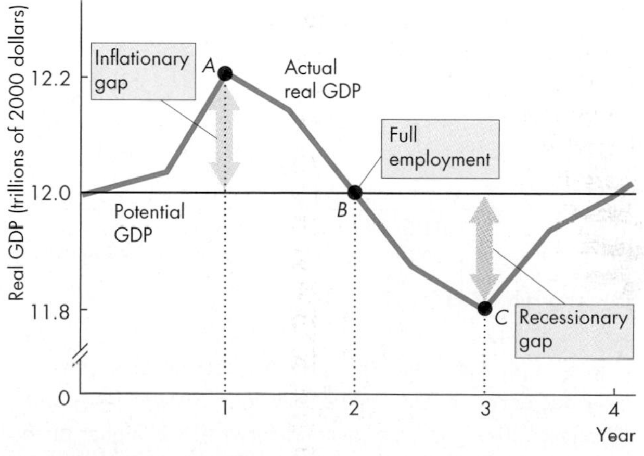


**(d) Fluctuations in real GDP**

Part (a) shows an above full-employment equilibrium in year 1; part (b) shows a full-employment equilibrium in year 2; and part (c) shows a below full-employment equilibrium in year 3. Part (d) shows how real GDP fluctuates around potential GDP in a business cycle.

In year 1, an inflationary gap exists and the economy is at point *A* in parts (a) and (d). In year 2, the economy is at full employment and the economy is at point *B* in parts (b) and (d). In year 3, a recessionary gap exists and the economy is at point *C* in parts (c) and (d).

myeconlab animation

## Fluctuations in Aggregate Demand

One reason real GDP fluctuates around potential GDP is that aggregate demand fluctuates. Let's see what happens when aggregate demand increases.

Figure 10.10(a) shows an economy at full employment. The aggregate demand curve is $AD_0$, the short-run aggregate supply curve is $SAS_0$, and the long-run aggregate supply curve is *LAS*. Real GDP equals potential GDP at $12 trillion, and the price level is 115.

Now suppose that the world economy expands and that the demand for U.S.-produced goods increases in Asia and Europe. The increase in U.S. exports increases aggregate demand in the United States, and the aggregate demand curve shifts rightward from $AD_0$ to $AD_1$ in Fig. 10.10(a).

Faced with an increase in demand, firms increase production and raise prices. Real GDP increases to $12.5 trillion, and the price level rises to 120. The economy is now in an above full-employment equilibrium. Real GDP exceeds potential GDP, and there is an inflationary gap.

The increase in aggregate demand has increased the prices of all goods and services. Faced with higher prices, firms have increased their output rates. At this stage, prices of goods and services have increased but the money wage rate has not changed. (Recall that as we move along the *SAS* curve, the money wage rate is constant.)

The economy cannot produce in excess of potential GDP forever. Why not? What are the forces at work that bring real GDP back to potential GDP?

Because the price level has increased and the money wage rate is unchanged, workers have experienced a fall in the buying power of their wages and firms' profits have increased. Under these circumstances, workers demand higher wages and firms, anxious to maintain their employment and output levels, meet those demands. If firms do not raise the money wage rate, they will either lose workers or have to hire less productive ones.

As the money wage rate rises, the short-run aggregate supply begins to decrease. In Fig. 10.10(b), the short-run aggregate supply curve begins to shift from

**FIGURE 10.10** An Increase in Aggregate Demand

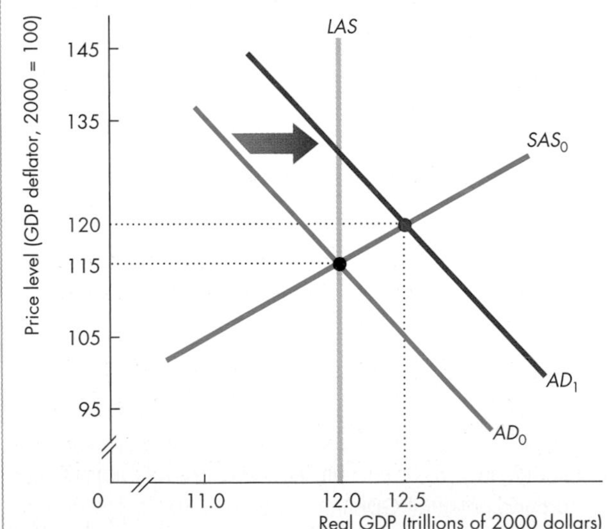


**(a) Short-run effect**

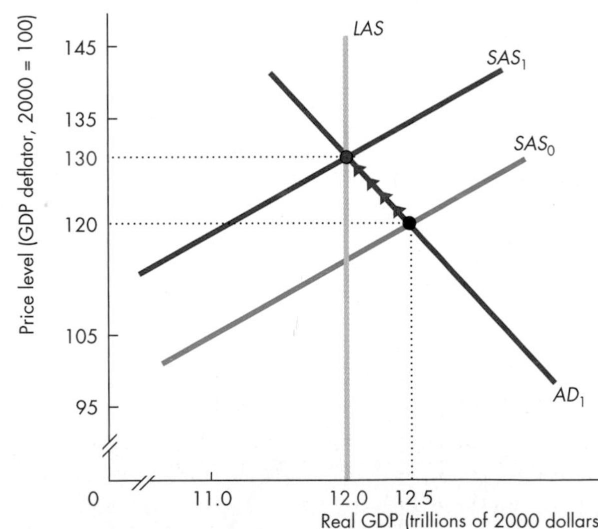


**(b) Long-run effect**

An increase in aggregate demand shifts the aggregate demand curve from $AD_0$ to $AD_1$. In short-run equilibrium, real GDP increases to $12.5 trillion and the price level rises to 120. In this situation, an inflationary gap exists. In the long run in part (b), the money wage rate rises and the short-run aggregate supply curve shifts leftward. As short-run aggregate supply decreases, the *SAS* curve shifts from $SAS_0$ to $SAS_1$ and intersects the aggregate demand curve $AD_1$ at higher price levels and real GDP decreases. Eventually, the price level rises to 130 and real GDP decreases to $12 trillion—potential GDP.

myeconlab animation

$SAS_0$ toward $SAS_1$. The rise in the money wage rate and the shift in the *SAS* curve produce a sequence of new equilibrium positions. Along the adjustment path, real GDP decreases and the price level rises. The economy moves up along its aggregate demand curve as shown by the arrows in the figure.

Eventually, the money wage rate rises by the same percentage as the price level. At this time, the aggregate demand curve $AD_1$ intersects $SAS_1$ at a new full-employment equilibrium. The price level has risen to 130, and real GDP is back where it started, at potential GDP.

A decrease in aggregate demand has effects similar but opposite to those of an increase in aggregate demand. That is, a decrease in aggregate demand shifts the aggregate demand curve leftward. Real GDP decreases to less than potential GDP, and a recessionary gap emerges. Firms cut prices. The lower price level increases the purchasing power of wages and increases firms' costs relative to their output prices because the money wage rate is unchanged. Eventually, the money wage rate falls and the short-run aggregate supply increases.

Let's now work out how real GDP and the price level change when aggregate supply changes.

## Fluctuations in Aggregate Supply

Fluctuations in short-run aggregate supply can bring fluctuations in real GDP around potential GDP. Suppose that initially real GDP equals potential GDP. Then there is a large but temporary rise in the price of oil. What happens to real GDP and the price level?

Figure 10.11 answers this question. The aggregate demand curve is $AD_0$, the short-run aggregate supply curve is $SAS_0$, and the long-run aggregate supply curve is *LAS*. Real GDP is $12 trillion, which equals potential GDP, and the price level is 115. Then the price of oil rises. Faced with higher energy and transportation costs, firms decrease production. Short-run aggregate supply decreases, and the short-run aggregate supply curve shifts leftward to $SAS_1$. The price level rises to 125, and real GDP decreases to $11.5 trillion. Because real GDP decreases, the economy experiences recession. Because the price level increases, the economy experiences inflation. A combination of recession and inflation, called **stagflation**, actually occurred in the United States in the mid-1970s and early 1980s, but events like this are not common.

When the price of oil returns to its original level, the economy returns to full employment.

**FIGURE 10.11** A Decrease in Aggregate Supply

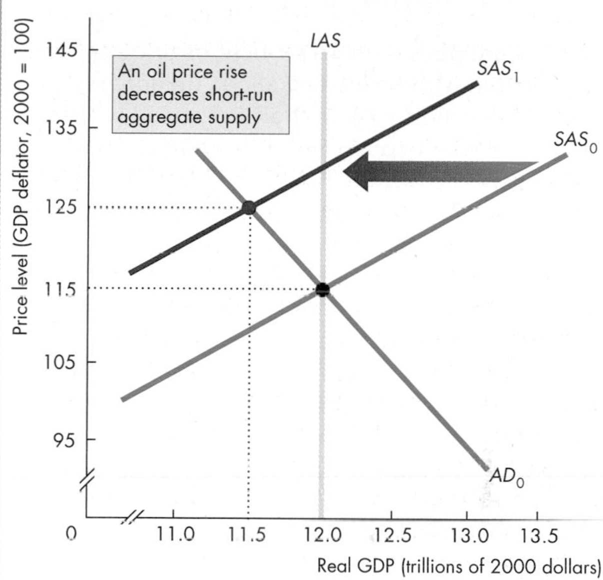


An increase in the price of oil decreases short-run aggregate supply and shifts the short-run aggregate supply curve from $SAS_0$ to $SAS_1$. Real GDP falls from $12 trillion to $11.5 trillion, and the price level rises from 115 to 125. The economy experiences stagflation.

myeconlab animation

## Review Quiz

1. Does economic growth result from increases in aggregate demand, short-run aggregate supply, or long-run aggregate supply?
2. Does inflation result from increases in aggregate demand, short-run aggregate supply, or long-run aggregate supply?
3. Describe three types of short-run macroeconomic equilibrium.
4. How do fluctuations in aggregate demand and short-run aggregate supply bring fluctuations in real GDP around potential GDP?

myeconlab Work Study Plan 10.3 and get instant feedback.

We can use the *AS-AD* model to explain and illustrate the views of the alternative schools of thought in macroeconomics. That is your next task.

## Macroeconomic Schools of Thought

Macroeconomics is an active field of research, and much remains to be learned about the forces that make our economy grow and fluctuate. There is a greater degree of consensus and certainty about economic growth and inflation—the longer-term trends in real GDP and the price level—than there is about the business cycle—the short-term fluctuations in these variables. Here, we'll look only at differences of view about short-term fluctuations.

The *AS-AD* model that you've studied in this chapter provides a good foundation for understanding the range of views that macroeconomists hold about this topic. But what you will learn here is just a first glimpse at the scientific controversy and debate. We'll return to these issues at various points later in the text and deepen your appreciation of the alternative views.

Classification usually requires simplification, and classifying macroeconomists is no exception to this general rule. The classification that we'll use here is simple, but it is not misleading. We're going to divide macroeconomists into three broad schools of thought and examine the views of each group in turn. The groups are

- Classical
- Keynesian
- Monetarist

### The Classical View

A **classical** macroeconomist believes that the economy is self-regulating and always at full employment. The term "classical" derives from the name of the founding school of economics that includes Adam Smith, David Ricardo, and John Stuart Mill.

A **new classical** view is that business cycle fluctuations are the efficient responses of a well-functioning market economy that is bombarded by shocks that arise from the uneven pace of technological change.

The classical view can be understood in terms of beliefs about aggregate demand and aggregate supply.

**Aggregate Demand Fluctuations** In the classical view, technological change is the most significant influence on both aggregate demand and aggregate supply. For this reason, classical macroeconomists don't use the *AS-AD* framework. But their views can be interpreted in this framework. A technological change that increases the productivity of capital brings an increase in aggregate demand because firms increase their expenditure on new plant and equipment. A technological change that lengthens the useful life of existing capital decreases the demand for new capital, which decreases aggregate demand.

**Aggregate Supply Response** In the classical view, the money wage rate that lies behind the short-run aggregate supply curve is instantly and completely flexible. The money wage rate adjusts so quickly to maintain equilibrium in the labor market that real GDP always adjusts to equal potential GDP.

Potential GDP itself fluctuates for the same reasons that aggregate demand fluctuates: technological change. When the pace of technological change is rapid, potential GDP increases quickly and so does real GDP. And when the pace of technological change slows, so does the growth rate of potential GDP.

**Classical Policy** The classical view of policy emphasizes the potential for taxes to stunt incentives and create inefficiency. By minimizing the disincentive effects of taxes, employment, investment, and technological advance are at their efficient levels and the economy expands at an appropriate and rapid pace.

### The Keynesian View

A **Keynesian** macroeconomist believes that left alone, the economy would rarely operate at full employment and that to achieve and maintain full employment, active help from fiscal policy and monetary policy is required.

The term "Keynesian" derives from the name of one of the twentieth century's most famous economists, John Maynard Keynes (see p. 321).

The Keynesian view is based on beliefs about the forces that determine aggregate demand and short-run aggregate supply.

**Aggregate Demand Fluctuations** In the Keynesian view, *expectations* are the most significant influence on aggregate demand. Those expectations are based on herd instinct, or what Keynes himself called "animal spirits." A wave of pessimism about future profit prospects can lead to a fall in aggregate demand and plunge the economy into recession.

**Aggregate Supply Response** In the Keynesian view, the money wage rate that lies behind the short-run aggregate supply curve is extremely sticky in the downward direction. Basically, the money wage rate doesn't fall. So if there is a recessionary gap, there is no automatic mechanism for getting rid of it. If it were to happen, a fall in the money wage rate would increase short-run aggregate supply and restore full employment. But the money wage rate doesn't fall, so the economy remains stuck in recession.

A modern version of the Keynesian view, known as the **new Keynesian** view, holds not only that the money wage rate is sticky but also that prices of goods and services are sticky. With a sticky price level, the short-run aggregate supply curve is horizontal at a fixed price level.

**Policy Response Needed** The Keynesian view calls for fiscal policy and monetary policy to actively offset changes in aggregate demand that bring recession.

By stimulating aggregate demand in a recession, full employment can be restored.

## The Monetarist View

A **monetarist** is a macroeconomist who believes that the economy is self-regulating and that it will normally operate at full employment, provided that monetary policy is not erratic and that the pace of money growth is kept steady.

The term "monetarist" was coined by an outstanding twentieth-century economist, Karl Brunner, to describe his own views and those of Milton Friedman (see p. 379).

The monetarist view can be interpreted in terms of beliefs about the forces that determine aggregate demand and short-run aggregate supply.

**Aggregate Demand Fluctuations** In the monetarist view, *the quantity of money* is the most significant influence on aggregate demand. The quantity of money is determined by the Federal Reserve (the Fed). If the Fed keeps money growing at a steady pace, aggregate demand fluctuations will be minimized and the economy will operate close to full employment. But if the Fed decreases the quantity of money or even just slows its growth rate too abruptly, the economy will go into recession. In the monetarist view, all recessions result from inappropriate monetary policy.

**Aggregate Supply Response** The monetarist view of short-run aggregate supply is the same as the Keynesian view: the money wage rate is sticky. If the economy is in recession, it will take an unnecessarily long time for it to return unaided to full employment.

**Monetarist Policy** The monetarist view of policy is the same as the classical view on fiscal policy. Taxes should be kept low to avoid disincentive effects that decrease potential GDP. Provided that the quantity of money is kept on a steady growth path, no active stabilization is needed to offset changes in aggregate demand.

## The Way Ahead

In the chapters that follow, you're going to encounter Keynesian, classical, and monetarist views again. In the next chapter, we study the original Keynesian model of aggregate demand. This model remains useful today because it explains how expenditure fluctuations are magnified and bring changes in aggregate demand that are larger than the changes in expenditure. We then go on to apply the *AS-AD* model to a deeper look at U.S. inflation and business cycles.

Our attention then turns to short-run macroeconomic policy—the fiscal policy of the Administration and Congress and the monetary policy of the Fed.

### Review Quiz

1. What are the defining features of classical macroeconomics and what policies do classical macroeconomists recommend?
2. What are the defining features of Keynesian macroeconomics and what policies do Keynesian macroeconomists recommend?
3. What are the defining features of monetarist macroeconomics and what policies do monetarist macroeconomists recommend?

Work Study Plan 10.4 and get instant feedback.

To complete your study of the *AS-AD* model, take a look at the U.S. economy in 2008 through the eyes of this model in *Reading Between the Lines* on pp. 262–263.

READING BETWEEN THE LINES

# Aggregate Supply and Aggregate Demand in Action

## GDP Figures Revised Downward

http://www.nytimes.com
September 26, 2008

Looks as if that brief burst of economic growth we saw wasn't as strong as it seemed.

Friday morning, the government said the economy grew at a rate of just 2.8 percent in the second quarter. That was less than forecasters had expected—and less than the government had previously estimated.

That doesn't bode well for future growth. As Joshua Shapiro, the chief United States economist for MFR Inc., put it in a note Friday, "The outlook remains grim."

Morgan Stanley said that it continued to expect no growth—0 percent—in the current quarter, which ends next week.

You can think of the economy as being made up of five parts: consumer spending, business spending on new factories and equipment, home building, government spending and trade. Trade is lifting growth right now, and home building activity, of course, is plunging. But as Goldman Sachs economists noted, the major reason for Friday's disappointing number was weaker-than-expected spending by consumers.

In the coming months, economists say, consumer spending is likely to weaken further. The spring coincided with the $100 billion in tax rebates the government sent out. And yet consumer spending still wasn't all that strong.



## Essence of the Story

- Real GDP grew at an annual rate of 2.8 percent in the second quarter of 2008.
- The growth rate was less than forecasters had expected and less than the previous estimate.
- Only exports lifted the growth rate in the second quarter. Consumer expenditure was less than expected despite a $100 billion tax rebate during the quarter.
- Economists expected consumer expenditure to decrease further and forecast zero growth in the third quarter of 2008.

## Economic Analysis

- U.S. real GDP grew at a 2.8 percent annual rate during the second quarter of 2008—a slower than average growth rate and slower than the original estimate a month earlier.
- In September 2008, most forecasters expected that real GDP growth would be zero in the third quarter and many forecasted a recession—falling real GDP—in the fourth quarter and the first half of 2009.
- The Congressional Budget Office (CBO) estimate of potential GDP implied a widening recessionary gap.
- Figure 1 illustrates the path of real GDP and the CBO estimate of potential GDP as well as the implied recessionary gap through 2007 and in the first half of 2008.
- Real GDP grew faster than potential GDP during 2007, so the recessionary gap narrowed, but it didn't disappear. In 2008, it widened.
- Another number estimated by the CBO places a question mark on the output gap estimate.
- The CBO estimate of the natural unemployment rate suggests that during 2007, the economy was above full employment and there was an inflationary gap.
- Figure 2 shows the actual unemployment rate and the CBO estimate of the natural rate.
- Whatever the true state of the output gap in 2007, by 2008 both the unemployment and real GDP data agreed that the output gap was a recessionary gap.
- In the second quarter of 2008, real GDP was $11.7 trillion and the price level (GDP deflator) was 122. In the third quarter of 2008, real GDP was expected to remain constant.
- Figure 3 illustrates the forecasted state of the economy in the fourth quarter of 2008.
- The CBO estimate of potential GDP was $12.1 trillion, which provides the location of the *LAS* curve.
- Aggregate demand, *AD*, and short-run aggregate supply, *SAS*, were expected to make real GDP decrease. In the outcome shown in Fig. 3, real GDP decreases to $11.5 trillion and the price level rises to 125. (These are assumptions.)

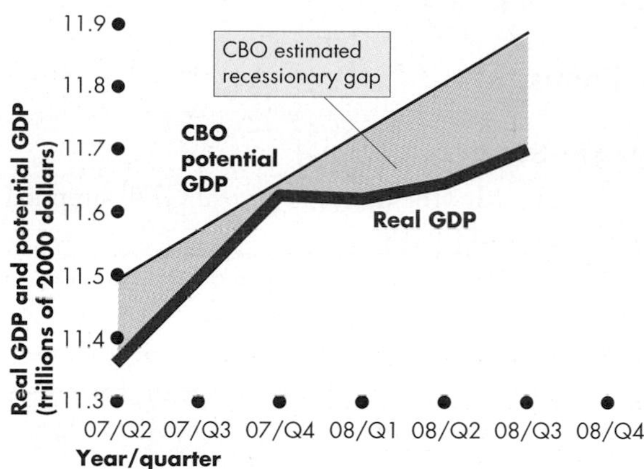


**Figure 1 Actual and potential real GDP**

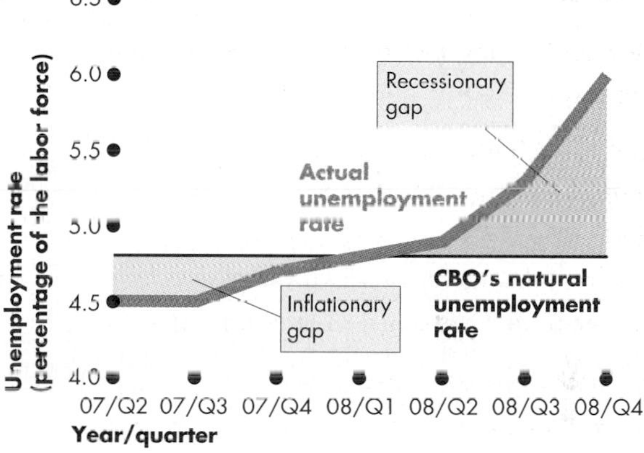


**Figure 2 Actual and natural unemployment rate**

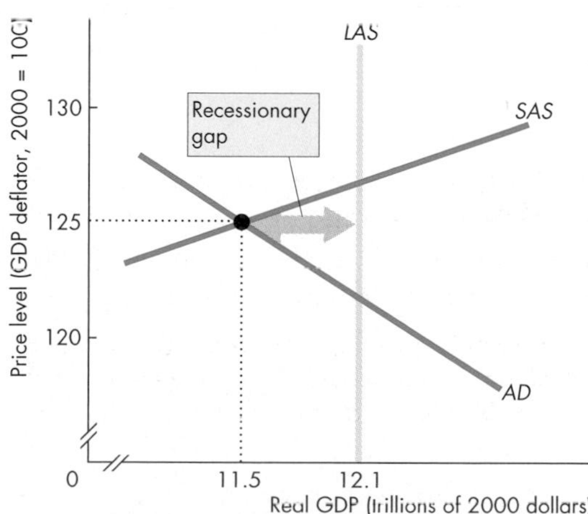


**Figure 3 Aggregate supply and aggregate demand in 2008**

# SUMMARY

## Key Points

### Aggregate Supply (pp. 246–249)

- In the long run, the quantity of real GDP supplied is potential GDP.
- In the short run, a rise in the price level increases the quantity of real GDP supplied.
- A change in potential GDP changes long-run and short-run aggregate supply. A change in the money wage rate changes only short-run aggregate supply.

### Aggregate Demand (pp. 250–253)

- A rise in the price level decreases the quantity of real GDP demanded.
- Changes in expected future income, inflation, and profits; in fiscal policy and monetary policy; and in foreign income and the exchange rate change aggregate demand.

### Explaining Macroeconomic Fluctuations (pp. 254–259)

- Aggregate demand and short-run aggregate supply determine real GDP and the price level.
- In the long run, real GDP equals potential GDP and aggregate demand determines the price level.
- The business cycle occurs because aggregate demand and aggregate supply fluctuate.

### Macroeconomic Schools of Thought (pp. 260–261)

- Classical economists believe that the economy is self-regulating and always at full employment.
- Keynesian economists believe that full employment can be achieved only with active policy.
- Monetarist economists believe that recessions result from inappropriate monetary policy.

## Key Figures



## Key Terms

## PROBLEMS and APPLICATIONS

Work problems 1–7 in Chapter 10 Study Plan and get instant feedback.
Work problems 8–15 as Homework, a Quiz, or a Test if assigned by your instructor.

1. The following events have occurred at times in the history of the United States:
   - A deep recession hits the world economy.
   - The world oil price rises sharply.
   - U.S. businesses expect future profits to fall.

   a. Explain for each event whether it changes short-run aggregate supply, long-run aggregate supply, aggregate demand, or some combination of them.

   b. Explain the separate effects of each event on U.S. real GDP and the price level, starting from a position of long-run equilibrium.

   c. Explain the combined effects of these events on U.S. real GDP and the price level, starting from a position of long-run equilibrium.

   d. Describe what a classical macroeconomist, a Keynesian, and a monetarist would want to do in response to each of the above events.

2. In the United Kingdom, potential GDP is 1,050 billion pounds and the table shows the aggregate demand and short-run aggregate supply schedules.

| Price level | Real GDP demanded | Real GDP supplied in the short run |
|---|---|---|
| | (billions of 2001 pounds) | |
| 100 | 1,150 | 1,050 |
| 110 | 1,100 | 1,100 |
| 120 | 1,050 | 1,150 |
| 130 | 1,000 | 1,200 |
| 140 | 950 | 1,250 |
| 150 | 900 | 1,300 |
| 160 | 850 | 1,350 |

   a. What is the short-run equilibrium real GDP and price level?

   b. Does the United Kingdom have an inflationary gap or a recessionary gap and what is its magnitude?

3. In September 2008, the Bureau of Economic Analysis reported that real GDP during the second quarter of 2008 was $11,727 billion compared to $11,491 billion in the same quarter of 2007. The GDP deflator was 121.9, up from 119.5 in the second quarter of 2007. The Congressional Budget Office estimated potential GDP to be $11,888 billion in the second quarter of 2008 and $11,568 billion a year earlier.

   a. Draw a graph of the aggregate demand curve, the short-run aggregate supply curve, and the long-run aggregate supply curve in 2007 that is consistent with these numbers.

   b. On the graph, show how the aggregate demand curve, the short-run aggregate supply curve, and the long-run aggregate supply curve shifted during the year to the second quarter of 2008.

4. Initially, the short-run aggregate supply curve is $SAS_0$ and the aggregate demand curve is $AD_0$. Some events change aggregate demand, and later, some other events change aggregate supply.

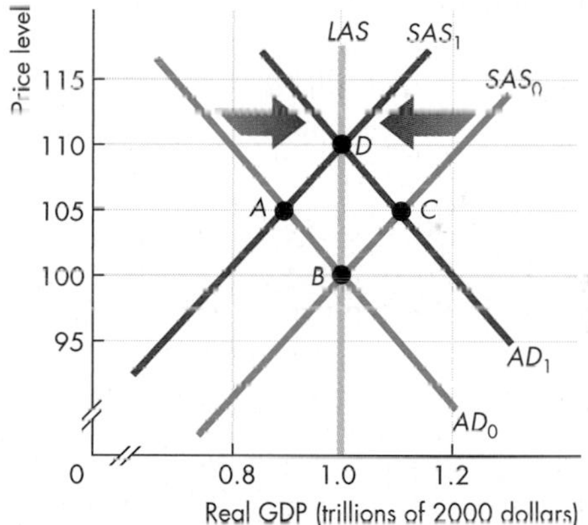


   a. What is the equilibrium after the change in aggregate demand?

   b. What is the equilibrium after the change in aggregate supply?

   c. Describe two events that could have changed aggregate demand from $AD_0$ to $AD_1$.

   d. Describe two events that could have changed aggregate supply from $SAS_0$ to $SAS_1$.

5. **It's a Recession—75 Percent of Americans Say**

   In a telephone poll of over 1,000 adult Americans, 75 percent said they believe the nation is now in a recession. … "From a consumers's perspective, the economy is bad, and the environment is going to be tough for a while," said Wachovia economist Mark Vitner. … Though growth was sluggish in the last quarter of 2007 and the first quarter of 2008, the U.S. economy has not yet shown retraction in the current slowdown. … "Whether the economy technically meets the definition of a recession matters more for economists and policy makers than it does for consumers," said Vitner. … Of those who think the economy is in a recession, 27 percent said they believe we are in a serious recession. … Americans are less confident in the future of the economy than they were in March. The poll showed that 23 percent believe the downturn will last more than two years, up from 19 percent in March. …

*CNN*, July 7, 2008

a. Explain the effects of a decrease in consumer confidence on the short-run macroeconomic equilibrium and draw a graph to illustrate the effects.
b. If the economy had been operating at a full-employment equilibrium, describe the state of equilibrium after the fall in consumer confidence. In what way might consumer expectations have a self-fulfilling prophecy?
c. Explain how the economy can adjust in the long run to restore a full-employment equilibrium and draw a graph to illustrate this adjustment process.

6. **Weak Dollar Helps Shrink Trade Deficit**

The United States trade deficit narrowed in May as exports, including industrial supplies and consumer goods, climbed to records. … Exports of American-made goods and services totaled $157.6 billion in May, a 0.9 percent increase from April. The declining value of the dollar relative to other currencies, especially the euro, is helping to make American exports cheaper and thus more attractive to foreign buyers. Growth in exports has been one of the few bright spots for the economy, which has been pounded by housing, credit and financial crises. … The stronger export figures should help bolster overall economic growth during the April-to-June quarter, which is already shaping up to be better than the grim projections made at the start of the year, when many feared the economy might contract. Tax rebates also are energizing shoppers, which should help second-quarter activity. "The narrowing trade deficit may be enough to keep second-quarter growth in the black," said Joel L. Naroff, president of Naroff Economic Advisors. The economy could grow to more than 2 percent, from 1 percent, in the second quarter. …

*The New York Times*, July 12, 2008

a. Explain and draw a graph to illustrate how depreciation of the dollar changes the short-run equilibrium real GDP and price level.
b. Explain the competing forces on aggregate demand in the second quarter that are identified in this article.
c. What will determine if aggregate demand increases or decreases as a result of the forces identified in the article? What prediction is made in the article concerning whether aggregate demand will increase or decrease?
d. Why would a recessionary gap eventually emerge even if aggregate demand remained constant?

7. **Adding Up the Cost of Obama's Agenda**

In more than a year of campaigning, Barack Obama has made a long list of promises for new federal programs costing tens of billions of dollars, many of them aimed at protecting people from the pain of a souring economy. … Obama has said he would strengthen the nation's bridges and dams ($6 billion a year) … extend health insurance to more people (part of a $65-billion-a-year health plan), develop cleaner energy sources ($15 billion a year), curb home foreclosures ($10 billion in one-time spending) and add $18 billion a year to education spending. … His $10-billion fund to reduce home foreclosures … is part of a $50-billion plan to stimulate the economy through increased government spending. … It is a far different blueprint than [John] McCain is offering. The senator from Arizona has proposed relatively little new spending, arguing that tax cuts and private business are more effective means of solving problems. … Unlike McCain, Obama [advocates] … rolling back the Bush tax cuts for families earning more than $250,000 annually.

*Los Angeles Times*, July 8, 2008

a. Based upon this news clip, explain what macroeconomic school of thought Barack Obama most likely follows.
b. Based upon this news clip, explain what macroeconomic school of thought John McCain most likely follows.

8. The following events have occurred at times in the history of the United States:
   - The world economy goes into an expansion.
   - U.S. businesses expect future profits to rise.
   - The government increases its expenditure on goods and services in a time of war or increased international tension.

   a. Explain for each event whether it changes short-run aggregate supply, long-run aggregate supply, aggregate demand, or some combination of them.
   b. Explain the separate effects of each event on U.S. real GDP and the price level, starting from a position of long-run equilibrium.
   c. Explain the combined effects of these events on U.S. real GDP and the price level, starting from a position of long-run equilibrium.
9. In Japan, potential GDP is 600 trillion yen and the table shows the aggregate demand and short-run aggregate supply schedules.

| Price level | Real GDP demanded | Real GDP supplied in the short run |
|---|---|---|
| | (trillions of 2000 yen) | |
| 75 | 600 | 400 |
| 85 | 550 | 450 |
| 95 | 500 | 500 |
| 105 | 450 | 550 |
| 115 | 400 | 600 |
| 125 | 350 | 650 |
| 135 | 300 | 700 |

   a. Draw a graph of the aggregate demand curve and the short-run aggregate supply curve.
   b. What is the short-run equilibrium real GDP and price level?
   c. Does Japan have an inflationary gap or a recessionary gap and what is its magnitude?
10. **Low Spending Is Taking Toll on Economy**

    For months, beleaguered American consumers have defied expert forecasts that they would soon succumb to the pressures of falling home prices, fewer jobs and shrinking paychecks. Now, they appear to have given in. On Wednesday, the Commerce Department reported that the economy continued to stagnate during the first three months of the year, with a sharp pullback in consumer spending the primary factor at play. … Americans cut back on a wide variety of discretionary purchases. … As real estate prices plunge, so does the ability of homeowners to borrow against the value of their homes, crimping a major artery of spending. As banks grow tighter with their dollars in a period of uncertainty, families are running up against credit limits, forcing many to live within their incomes. And as companies lay off employees and cut working hours, paychecks are effectively shrinking. … Consumer spending fell for a broad range of goods and services, including cars, auto parts, furniture, food and recreation, reflecting a growing inclination toward thrift. …

    *The New York Times*, May 1, 2008

    a. Explain and draw a graph to illustrate the effect of a fall in consumption expenditure on real GDP and the price level in the short run.
    b. If the economy had been operating at a full-employment equilibrium, describe the type of equilibrium after the fall in consumer spending in a.
    c. Why do changes in consumer spending play such a large role in the business cycle?
    d. Explain and draw a graph to illustrate how the economy can adjust in the long run to restore a full-employment equilibrium.
11. **It's Pinching Everyone**

    The rate of inflation [in India] has now touched a mind-boggling 11 per cent. … No one can predict when the process of spiraling prices will come to an end. … [T]he current inflationary process is a global phenomenon and practically every country is suffering. …

    Emerging and developing countries have been growing significantly faster than the rest of the world, and there has been a steep surge in demand in these countries. … Since there is no reason to believe that world production will rise miraculously at least in the immediate future, many people expect that prices will keep on rising. These expectations in turn exacerbate the inflationary process. Households buy more of non-perishable goods than they need for their immediate consumption because they expect prices to go up even further. What is worse is that traders withhold stocks from the market in the hope of being able to sell these at higher prices later on. In other words, expectations of higher prices become self-fulfilling.

    *The Times of India*, June 24, 2008

Explain and draw a graph to illustrate how inflation and inflation expectations "become self-fulfilling."

12. **Shoppers Stimulate Discount Stores**

    Consumers sought the biggest bang for their economic stimulus bucks in June, sending the sales of discount merchants such as Wal-Mart and Costco surging. … As the economy remains weak … shoppers—rich and poor—are flocking to discounters for low-cost goods. … Wal-Mart Stores Inc. trounced analyst expectations Thursday with a 5.8 percent jump in June sales, … attributing the increase to the government's economic stimulus payments. … The retailer said sales jumped across the board. But the most dramatic increases were in entertainment, particularly for flat-screen televisions, and apparel, especially in swimwear and sportswear. … Another major retailer, the warehouse club Costco Wholesale, beat analyst expectations with a 9 percent increase in same-store sales for June. … Target, a top competitor to Wal-Mart, said that its same-store sales edged up 0.4 percent, well above the 0.5 percent decline projected by analyst consensus. …

    *CNN*, July 10, 2008

    a. Explain and draw a graph to illustrate the effect of the fiscal stimulus payments on real GDP and the price level in the short run.
    b. At which type of short-run equilibrium would the government want to use this policy?
    c. Which macroeconomic school of thought would justify this policy?
    d. If the government used this policy when the economy was at full employment, explain what would happen in the long run.
    e. Draw a graph to illustrate your answer to d.

13. The International Monetary Fund's World Economic Outlook database provides the following data for India in 2004, 2005, and 2006.

| | 2004 | 2005 | 2006 |
|---|---|---|---|
| Real GDP growth rate | 8.1 | 8.3 | 7.3 |
| Inflation rate | 4.2 | 4.7 | 4.6 |

    a. What changes in long-run and short-run aggregate supply and aggregate demand are consistent with these numbers?
    b. Draw a graph to illustrate your answer to a.
    c. List the main factors that might have produced the changes in aggregate supply and aggregate demand that you have described in your answer to a.
    d. From the above data, do you think India has an inflationary gap, a recessionary gap, or is at full employment?

14. **That '70s Look: Stagflation**

    Lately, many people are hearing an echo—faintly perhaps but distinctly audible—of the stagflation of the 1970s. Even as economic growth sags, oil and gasoline prices are surging to new heights. Gold is on the rise, along with the prices of such basic commodities as wheat and steel. And on Wednesday, with the latest government report on consumer prices, there are signs that overall inflation, after years of only modest increases, may be breaking out of its box.

    *The New York Times*, February 21, 2008

    a. What is stagflation?
    b. Explain how the increase in the price of oil, gasoline, wheat, and steel can cause stagflation and draw a graph to illustrate this outcome.

15. After you have studied the account of the U.S. economy in 2008 in *Reading Between the Lines* on pp. 262–263,
    a. Describe the main features of the U.S. economy in the second quarter of 2008.
    b. Did the United States have a recessionary gap or an inflationary gap in 2008? How do you know?
    c. Use the *AS-AD* model to show the changes in aggregate demand and aggregate supply that brought the slow increase in real GDP and rise in the price level between the first and second quarters of 2008.
    d. Use the *AS-AD* model to show the changes in aggregate demand and aggregate supply that would occur if monetary policy cut the interest rate and increased the quantity of money.
    e. Use the *AS-AD* model to show the changes in aggregate demand and aggregate supply that would occur if the federal government increased its expenditure on goods and services or cut taxes further.

# 11 Expenditure Multipliers: The Keynesian Model

**After studying this chapter, you will be able to:**

- Explain how expenditure plans are determined when the price level is fixed
- Explain how real GDP is determined when the price level is fixed
- Explain the expenditure multiplier when the price level is fixed
- Explain the relationship between aggregate expenditure and aggregate demand and explain the multiplier when the price level changes

**Erykah Badu sings into a microphone in a barely** audible whisper. Increasing in volume, through the magic of electronic amplification, her voice fills Central Park.

Michael Bloomberg, the mayor of New York, and an assistant are being driven to a business meeting along one of the cobblestone streets of downtown Manhattan. The car's wheels bounce and vibrate over the uneven stone road, but its passengers are completely undisturbed and the assistant's notes are written without a ripple, thanks to the car's efficient shock absorbers.

Investment and exports fluctuate like the volume of Erykah Badu's voice and the uneven surface of a New York City street. How does the economy react to those fluctuations? Does it behave like an amplifier, blowing up the fluctuations and spreading them out to affect the many millions of participants in an economic rock concert? Or does it react like a limousine, absorbing the shocks and providing a smooth ride for the economy's passengers?

You will explore these questions in this chapter. You will learn how a recession or an expansion begins when a change in investment or exports induces an amplified change in aggregate expenditure and real GDP. *Reading Between the Lines* at the end of the chapter looks at the role played by consumption expenditure during 2008 as the economy began to shrink.

## Fixed Prices and Expenditure Plans

In the Keynesian model that we study in this chapter, all the firms are like your grocery store: They set their prices and sell the quantities their customers are willing to buy. If they persistently sell a greater quantity than they plan to and are constantly running out of inventory, they eventually raise their prices. And if they persistently sell a smaller quantity than they plan to and have inventories piling up, they eventually cut their prices. But on any given day, their prices are fixed and the quantities they sell depend on demand, not supply.

Because each firm's prices are fixed, for the economy as a whole:

1. The *price level* is fixed, and
2. *Aggregate demand* determines real GDP.

The Keynesian model explains fluctuations in aggregate demand at a fixed price level by identifying the forces that determine expenditure plans.

### Expenditure Plans

Aggregate expenditure has four components: consumption expenditure, investment, government expenditure on goods and services, and net exports (exports *minus* imports). These four components of aggregate expenditure sum to real GDP (see Chapter 4, pp. 87–88).

**Aggregate planned expenditure** is equal to the sum of the *planned* levels of consumption expenditure, investment, government expenditure on goods and services, and exports minus imports. Two of these components of planned expenditure, consumption expenditure and imports, change when income changes and so they depend on real GDP.

**A Two-Way Link Between Aggregate Expenditure and Real GDP** There is a two-way link between aggregate expenditure and real GDP. Other things remaining the same,

- An increase in real GDP increases aggregate expenditure, and
- An increase in aggregate expenditure increases real GDP.

You are now going to study this two-way link.

### Consumption and Saving Plans

Several factors influence consumption expenditure and saving plans. The more important ones are

- Disposable income
- Real interest rate
- Wealth
- Expected future income

**Disposable income** is aggregate income minus taxes plus transfer payments. Aggregate income equals real GDP, so disposable income depends on real GDP. To explore the two-way link between real GDP and planned consumption expenditure, we focus on the relationship between consumption expenditure and disposable income when the other three factors listed above are constant.

**Consumption Expenditure and Saving** The table in Fig. 11.1 lists the consumption expenditure and the saving that people plan at each level of disposable income. Households can only spend their disposable income on consumption or save it, so planned consumption expenditure plus planned saving *always* equals disposable income.

The relationship between consumption expenditure and disposable income, other things remaining the same, is called the **consumption function.** The relationship between saving and disposable income, other things remaining the same, is called the **saving function**.

**Consumption Function** Figure 11.1(a) shows a consumption function. The *y*-axis measures consumption expenditure, and the *x*-axis measures disposable income. Along the consumption function, the points labeled *A* through *F* correspond to the rows of the table. For example, point *E* shows that when disposable income is $8 trillion, consumption expenditure is $7.5 trillion. As disposable income increases, consumption expenditure also increases.

At point *A* on the consumption function, consumption expenditure is $1.5 trillion even though disposable income is zero. This consumption expenditure is called *autonomous consumption*, and it is the amount of consumption expenditure that would take place in the short run even if people had no current income. Consumption expenditure in excess of this amount is called *induced consumption*, which is the consumption expenditure that is induced by an increase in disposable income.

**45° Line** Figure 11.1(a) also contains a 45° line, the height of which measures disposable income. At each point on this line, consumption expenditure equals disposable income. Between *A* and *D* consumption expenditure exceeds disposable income, between *D* and *F* consumption expenditure is less than disposable income, and at point *D*, consumption expenditure equals disposable income.

**Saving Function** Figure 11.1(b) shows a saving function. Again, the points *A* through *F* correspond to the rows of the table. For example, point *E* shows that when disposable income is $8 trillion, saving is $0.5 trillion. As disposable income increases, saving increases. Notice that when consumption expenditure exceeds disposable income in part (a), saving is negative, called *dissaving,* in part (b).

**FIGURE 11.1** Consumption Function and Saving Function

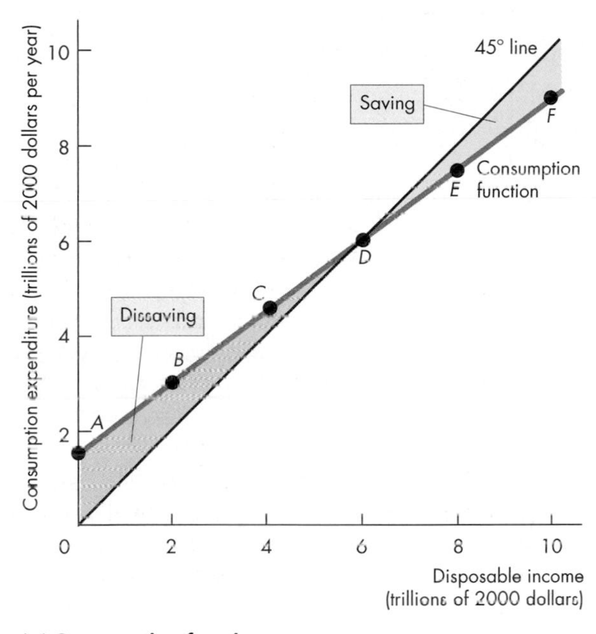


**(a) Consumption function**

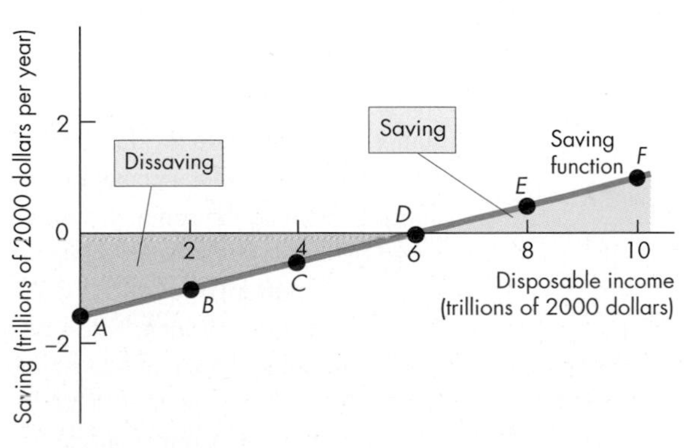


**(b) Saving function**

| | Disposable income | Planned consumption expenditure | Planned saving |
|---|---|---|---|
| | (trillions of 2000 dollars) | | |
| *A* | 0 | 1.5 | −1.5 |
| *B* | 2 | 3.0 | −1.0 |
| *C* | 4 | 4.5 | −0.5 |
| *D* | 6 | 6.0 | 0 |
| *E* | 8 | 7.5 | 0.5 |
| *F* | 10 | 9.0 | 1.0 |

The table shows consumption expenditure and saving plans at various levels of disposable income. Part (a) of the figure shows the relationship between consumption expenditure and disposable income (the consumption function). The height of the consumption function measures consumption expenditure at each level of disposable income. Part (b) shows the relationship between saving and disposable income (the saving function). The height of the saving function measures saving at each level of disposable income. Points *A* through *F* on the consumption and saving functions correspond to the rows in the table.

The height of the 45° line in part (a) measures disposable income. So along the 45° line, consumption expenditure equals disposable income. Consumption expenditure plus saving equals disposable income. When the consumption function is above the 45° line, saving is negative (dissaving occurs). When the consumption function is below the 45° line, saving is positive. At the point where the consumption function intersects the 45° line, all disposable income is spent on consumption and saving is zero.

myeconlab animation

## Marginal Propensities to Consume and Save

The **marginal propensity to consume** ($MPC$) is the fraction of a *change* in disposable income that is spent on consumption. It is calculated as the *change* in consumption expenditure ($\Delta C$) divided by the *change* in disposable income ($\Delta YD$). The formula is

$$MPC = \frac{\Delta C}{\Delta YD}.$$

In the table in Fig. 11.1, when disposable income increases by \$2 trillion, consumption expenditure increases by \$1.5 trillion. The $MPC$ is \$1.5 trillion divided by \$2 trillion, which equals 0.75.

The **marginal propensity to save** ($MPS$) is the fraction of a *change* in disposable income that is saved. It is calculated as the *change* in saving ($\Delta S$) divided by the *change* in disposable income ($\Delta YD$). The formula is

$$MPS = \frac{\Delta S}{\Delta YD}.$$

In the table in Fig. 11.1, when disposable income increases by \$2 trillion, saving increases by \$0.5 trillion. The $MPS$ is \$0.5 trillion divided by \$2 trillion, which equals 0.25.

Because an increase in disposable income is either spent on consumption or saved, the marginal propensity to consume plus the marginal propensity to save equals 1. You can see why by using the equation:

$$\Delta C + \Delta S = \Delta YD.$$

Divide both sides of the equation by the change in disposable income to obtain

$$\frac{\Delta C}{\Delta YD} + \frac{\Delta S}{\Delta YD} = 1.$$

$\Delta C/\Delta YD$ is the marginal propensity to consume ($MPC$), and $\Delta S/\Delta YD$ is the marginal propensity to save ($MPS$), so

$$MPC + MPS = 1.$$

## Slopes and Marginal Propensities

The slope of the consumption function is the marginal propensity to consume, and the slope of the saving function is the marginal propensity to save.

Figure 11.2(a) shows the $MPC$ as the slope of the consumption function. An increase in disposable income of \$2 trillion is the base of the red triangle. The increase in consumption expenditure that results from this increase in disposable income is \$1.5 trillion and is the height of the triangle. The slope of the consumption function is given by the formula "slope equals rise over run" and is \$1.5 trillion divided by \$2 trillion, which equals 0.75—the $MPC$.

Figure 11.2(b) shows the $MPS$ as the slope of the saving function. An increase in disposable income of \$2 trillion (the base of the red triangle) increases saving by \$0.5 trillion (the height of the triangle). The slope of the saving function is \$0.5 trillion divided by \$2 trillion, which equals 0.25—the $MPS$.

**FIGURE 11.2** The Marginal Propensities to Consume and Save

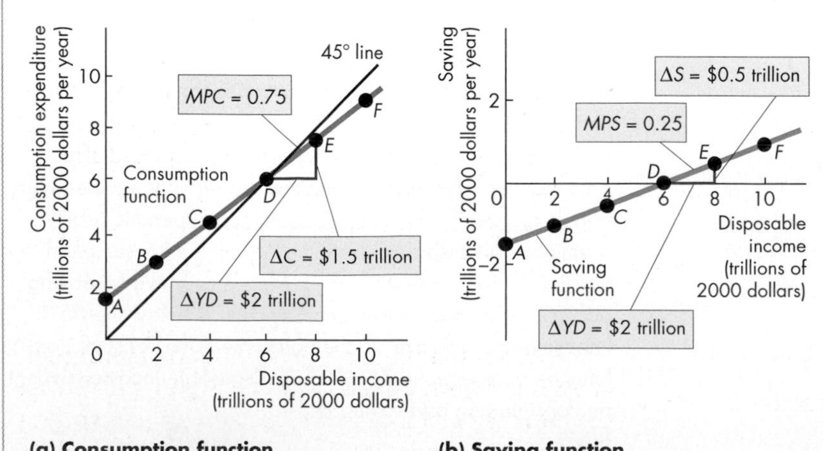


**(a) Consumption function** **(b) Saving function**

The marginal propensity to consume, $MPC$, is equal to the change in consumption expenditure divided by the change in disposable income, other things remaining the same. It is measured by the slope of the consumption function. In part (a), the $MPC$ is 0.75.

The marginal propensity to save, $MPS$, is equal to the change in saving divided by the change in disposable income, other things remaining the same. It is measured by the slope of the saving function. In part (b), the $MPS$ is 0.25.

myeconlab animation

## The U.S. Consumption Function

### Other Things Not Always Equal

The figure shows the U.S. consumption function. Each point identified by a blue dot represents consumption expenditure and disposable income for a particular year. (The dots are for the years 1968 to 2008, and the dots of five of the years are identified in the figure.)

The U.S. consumption function is $CF_0$ in 1968 and $CF_1$ in 2008.

The slope of the consumption function in the figure is 0.9, which means that a $1 increase in disposable income increases consumption expenditure by 90 cents. This slope, which is an estimate of the marginal propensity to consume, is an assumption that is at the upper end of the range of values that economists have estimated for the marginal propensity to consume.

The consumption function shifts upward over time as other influences on consumption expenditure change. Of these other influences, the real interest rate and wealth fluctuate and so bring upward and downward shifts in the consumption function.

But rising wealth and rising expected future income bring a steady upward shift in the consumption function. As the consumption function shifts upward, autonomous consumption increases.

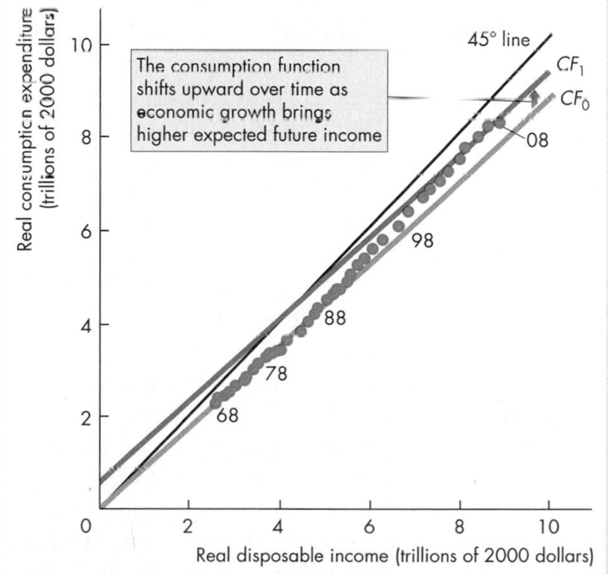


**The U.S. Consumption Function**

*Source of data*: Bureau of Economic Analysis.

### Consumption as a Function of Real GDP

Consumption expenditure changes when disposable income changes and disposable income changes when real GDP changes. So consumption expenditure depends not only on disposable income but also on real GDP. We use this link between consumption expenditure and real GDP to determine equilibrium expenditure. But before we do so, we need to look at one further component of aggregate expenditure: imports. Like consumption expenditure, imports are influenced by real GDP.

### Import Function

Of the many influences on U.S. imports in the short run, U.S. real GDP is the main influence. Other things remaining the same, an increase in U.S. real GDP increases the quantity of U.S. imports.

The relationship between imports and real GDP is determined by the **marginal propensity to import**, which is the fraction of an increase in real GDP that is spent on imports. It is calculated as the change in imports divided by the change in real GDP, other things remaining the same. For example, if an increase in real GDP of $1 trillion increases imports by $0.25 trillion, the marginal propensity to import is 0.25.

### Review Quiz

1. Which components of aggregate expenditure are influenced by real GDP?
2. Define and explain how we calculate the marginal propensity to consume and the marginal propensity to save.
3. How do we calculate the effects of real GDP on consumption expenditure and imports by using the marginal propensity to consume and the marginal propensity to import?

myeconlab Work Study Plan 11.1 and get instant feedback.

Real GDP influences consumption expenditure and imports, which in turn influence real GDP. Your next task is to study this second piece of the two-way link between aggregate expenditure and real GDP and see how all the components of aggregate planned expenditure interact to determine real GDP.

## Real GDP with a Fixed Price Level

You are now going to see how, at a given price level, aggregate expenditure plans determine real GDP. We start by looking at the relationship between aggregate planned expenditure and real GDP. This relationship can be described by an aggregate expenditure schedule or an aggregate expenditure curve. The *aggregate expenditure schedule* lists aggregate planned expenditure generated at each level of real GDP. The *aggregate expenditure curve* is a graph of the aggregate expenditure schedule.

### Aggregate Planned Expenditure

The table in Fig. 11.3 sets out an aggregate expenditure schedule. To calculate aggregate planned expenditure at a given real GDP, we add the expenditure components together. The first column of the table shows real GDP, and the second column shows the planned consumption at each level of real GDP. A $1 trillion increase in real GDP increases consumption expenditure by $0.7 trillion—the *MPC* is 0.7.

The next two columns show investment and government expenditure on goods and services, both of which are independent of the level of real GDP. Investment depends on the real interest rate and the expected profit (see Chapter 6, p. 141). At a given point in time, these factors generate a given level of investment. Suppose this level of investment is $2.0 trillion. Also, suppose that government expenditure is $2.2 trillion.

The next two columns show exports and imports. Exports are influenced by events in the rest of the world, prices of foreign-produced goods and services relative to the prices of similar U.S.-produced goods and services, and exchange rates. But they are not directly affected by U.S. real GDP. Exports are a constant $1.8 trillion. Imports increase as U.S. real GDP increases. A $1 trillion increase in U.S. real GDP generates a $0.2 trillion increase in imports—the marginal propensity to import is 0.2.

The final column shows aggregate planned expenditure—the sum of planned consumption expenditure, investment, government expenditure on goods and services, and exports minus imports.

Figure 11.3 plots an aggregate expenditure curve. Real GDP is shown on the *x*-axis, and aggregate planned expenditure is shown on the *y*-axis. The aggregate expenditure curve is the red line *AE*. Points *A* through *F* on that curve correspond to the rows of the table. The *AE* curve is a graph of aggregate planned expenditure (the last column) plotted against real GDP (the first column).

Figure 11.3 also shows the components of aggregate expenditure. The constant components—investment ($I$), government expenditure on goods and services ($G$), and exports ($X$)—are shown by the horizontal lines in the figure. Consumption expenditure ($C$) is the vertical gap between the lines labeled $I + G + X$ and $I + G + X + C$.

To construct the *AE* curve, subtract imports ($M$) from the $I + G + X + C$ line. Aggregate expenditure is expenditure on U.S.-produced goods and services. But the components of aggregate expenditure—$C$, $I$, and $G$—include expenditure on imported goods and services. For example, if you buy a new cell phone, your expenditure is part of consumption expenditure. But if the cell phone is a Nokia made in Finland, your expenditure on it must be subtracted from consumption expenditure to find out how much is spent on goods and services produced in the United States—on U.S. real GDP. Money paid to Nokia for cell phone imports from Finland does not add to aggregate expenditure in the United States.

Because imports are only a part of aggregate expenditure, when we subtract imports from the other components of aggregate expenditure, aggregate planned expenditure still increases as real GDP increases, as you can see in Fig. 11.3.

Consumption expenditure minus imports, which varies with real GDP, is called **induced expenditure**. The sum of investment, government expenditure, and exports, which does not vary with real GDP, is called **autonomous expenditure**. Consumption expenditure and imports can also have an autonomous component—a component that does not vary with real GDP. Another way of thinking about autonomous expenditure is that it would be the level of aggregate planned expenditure if real GDP were zero.

In Fig. 11.3, autonomous expenditure is $6 trillion—aggregate planned expenditure when real GDP is zero. For each $1 trillion increase in real GDP, induced expenditure increases by $0.5 trillion.

The aggregate expenditure curve summarizes the relationship between aggregate *planned* expenditure and real GDP. But what determines the point on the aggregate expenditure curve at which the economy operates? What determines *actual* aggregate expenditure?

FIGURE 11.3 Aggregate Planned Expenditure: The *AE* Curve

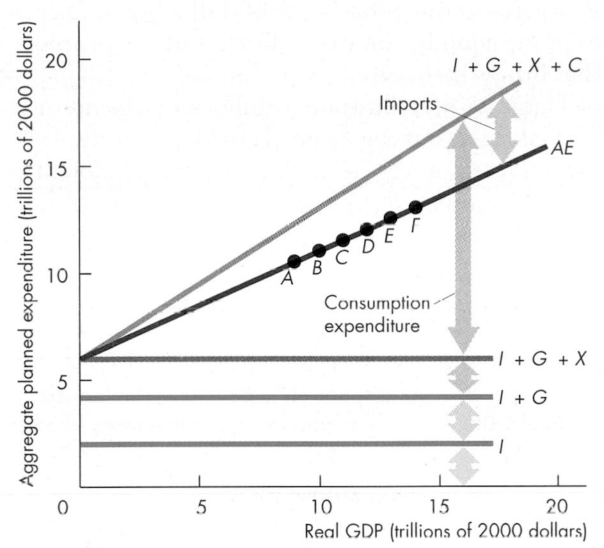


Aggregate planned expenditure is the sum of planned consumption expenditure, investment, government expenditure on goods and services, and exports minus imports. For example, in row *B* of the table, when real GDP is $10 trillion, planned consumption expenditure is $7.0 trillion, planned investment is $2.0 trillion, planned government expenditure is $2.2 trillion, planned exports are $1.8 trillion, and planned imports are $2.0 trillion. So when real GDP is $10 trillion, aggregate planned expenditure is $11 trillion ($7.0 + $2.0 + $2.2 + $1.8 – $2.0). The schedule shows that aggregate planned expenditure increases as real GDP increases. This relationship is graphed as the aggregate expenditure curve *AE*. The components of aggregate expenditure that increase with real GDP are consumption expenditure and imports. The other components—investment, government expenditure, and exports—do not vary with real GDP.

| | | Planned expenditure | | | | | |
|---|---|---|---|---|---|---|---|
| | Real GDP (*Y*) | Consumption expenditure (*C*) | Investment (*I*) | Government expenditure (*G*) | Exports (*X*) | Imports (*M*) | Aggregate planned expenditure (*AE* = *C* + *I* + *G* + *X* – *M*) |
| | | | | (trillions of 2000 dollars) | | | |
| | 0 | 0 | 2.0 | 2.2 | 1.8 | 0.0 | 6.0 |
| *A* | 9 | 6.3 | 2.0 | 2.2 | 1.8 | 1.8 | 10.5 |
| *B* | 10 | 7.0 | 2.0 | 2.2 | 1.8 | 2.0 | 11.0 |
| *C* | 11 | 7.7 | 2.0 | 2.2 | 1.8 | 2.2 | 11.5 |
| *D* | 12 | 8.4 | 2.0 | 2.2 | 1.8 | 2.4 | 12.0 |
| *E* | 13 | 9.1 | 2.0 | 2.2 | 1.8 | 2.6 | 12.5 |
| *F* | 14 | 9.8 | 2.0 | 2.2 | 1.8 | 2.8 | 13.0 |

myeconlab animation

## Actual Expenditure, Planned Expenditure, and Real GDP

*Actual* aggregate expenditure is always equal to real GDP, as we saw in Chapter 4 (p. 88). But aggregate *planned* expenditure is not always equal to actual aggregate expenditure and therefore is not always equal to real GDP. How can actual expenditure and planned expenditure differ? The answer is that firms can end up with inventories that are greater or smaller than planned. People carry out their consumption expenditure plans, the government implements its planned expenditure on goods and services, and net exports are as planned. Firms carry out their plans to purchase new buildings, plant, and equipment. But one component of investment is the change in firms' inventories. If aggregate planned expenditure is less than real GDP, firms sell less than they planned to sell and end up with unplanned inventories. If aggregate planned expenditure exceeds real GDP, firms sell more than they planned to sell and end up with inventories being too low.

## Equilibrium Expenditure

**Equilibrium expenditure** is the level of aggregate expenditure that occurs when aggregate *planned* expenditure equals real GDP. Equilibrium expenditure is a level of aggregate expenditure and real GDP at which spending plans are fulfilled. At a given price level, equilibrium expenditure determines real GDP. When aggregate planned expenditure and actual aggregate expenditure are unequal, a process of convergence toward equilibrium expenditure occurs. Throughout this process, real GDP adjusts. Let's examine equilibrium expenditure and the process that brings it about.

Figure 11.4(a) illustrates equilibrium expenditure. The table sets out aggregate planned expenditure at various levels of real GDP. These values are plotted as points *A* through *F* along the *AE* curve. The 45° line

**FIGURE 11.4** Equilibrium Expenditure

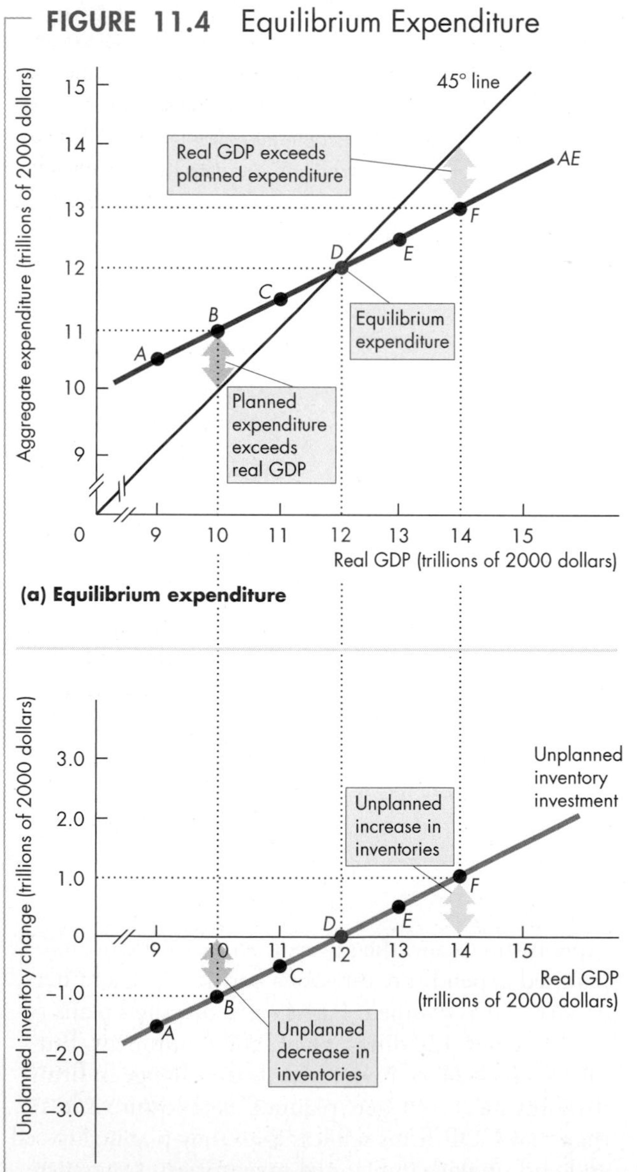


| | Real GDP ($Y$) | Aggregate planned expenditure ($AE$) | Unplanned inventory change ($Y - AE$) |
|---|---|---|---|
| | | (trillions of 2000 dollars) | |
| *A* | 9 | 10.5 | –1.5 |
| *B* | 10 | 11.0 | –1.0 |
| *C* | 11 | 11.5 | –0.5 |
| ***D*** | **12** | **12.0** | **0** |
| *E* | 13 | 12.5 | 0.5 |
| *F* | 14 | 13.0 | 1.0 |

The table shows expenditure plans at different levels of real GDP. When real GDP is $12 trillion, aggregate planned expenditure equals real GDP.

Part (a) of the figure illustrates equilibrium expenditure, which occurs when aggregate planned expenditure equals real GDP at the intersection of the 45° line and the *AE* curve. Part (b) of the figure shows the forces that bring about equilibrium expenditure. When aggregate planned expenditure exceeds real GDP, inventories decrease—for example, at point *B* in both parts of the figure. Firms increase production, and real GDP increases.

When aggregate planned expenditure is less than real GDP, inventories increase—for example, at point *F* in both parts of the figure. Firms decrease production, and real GDP decreases. When aggregate planned expenditure equals real GDP, there are no unplanned inventory changes and real GDP remains constant at equilibrium expenditure.

myeconlab animation

shows all the points at which aggregate planned expenditure equals real GDP. So where the *AE* curve lies above the 45° line, aggregate planned expenditure exceeds real GDP; where the *AE* curve lies below the 45° line, aggregate planned expenditure is less than real GDP; and where the *AE* curve intersects the 45° line, aggregate planned expenditure equals real GDP. Point *D* illustrates equilibrium expenditure. At this point, real GDP is $12 trillion.

## Convergence to Equilibrium

What are the forces that move aggregate expenditure toward its equilibrium level? To answer this question, we must look at a situation in which aggregate expenditure is away from its equilibrium level.

**From Below Equilibrium** Suppose that in Fig. 11.4, real GDP is $10 trillion. With real GDP at $10 trillion, actual aggregate expenditure is also $10 trillion. But aggregate *planned* expenditure is $11 trillion, point *B* in Fig. 11.4(a). Aggregate planned expenditure exceeds *actual* expenditure. When people spend $11 trillion and firms produce goods and services worth $10 trillion, firms' inventories fall by $1 trillion, point *B* in Fig. 11.4(b). Because the change in inventories is part of investment, *actual* investment is $1 trillion less than *planned* investment.

Real GDP doesn't remain at $10 trillion for very long. Firms have inventory targets based on their sales. When inventories fall below target, firms increase production to restore inventories to the target level. To increase inventories, firms hire additional labor and increase production. Suppose that they increase production in the next period by $1 trillion. Real GDP increases by $1.0 trillion to $11.0 trillion. But again, aggregate planned expenditure exceeds real GDP. When real GDP is $11.0 trillion, aggregate planned expenditure is $11.5 trillion, point *C* in Fig. 11.4(a). Again, inventories decrease, but this time by less than before. With real GDP of $11.0 trillion and aggregate planned expenditure of $11.5 trillion, inventories decrease by $0.5 trillion, point *C* in Fig. 11.4(b). Again, firms hire additional labor and production increases; real GDP increases yet further.

The process that we've just described—planned expenditure exceeds real GDP, inventories decrease, and production increases to restore inventories—ends when real GDP has reached $12 trillion. At this real GDP, there is equilibrium. Unplanned inventory changes are zero. Firms do not change their production.

**From Above Equilibrium** If in Fig. 11.4, real GDP is $14 trillion, the process that we've just described works in reverse. With real GDP at $14 trillion, actual aggregate expenditure is also $14 trillion. But aggregate planned expenditure is $13 trillion, point *F* in Fig. 11.4(a). Actual expenditure exceeds planned expenditure. When people spend $13 trillion and firms produce goods and services worth $14 trillion, firms' inventories rise by $1 trillion, point *F* in Fig. 11.4(b). Now, real GDP begins to fall. As long as actual expenditure exceeds planned expenditure, inventories rise, and production decreases. Again, the process ends when real GDP has reached $12 trillion, the equilibrium at which unplanned inventory changes are zero and firms do not change their production.

## Review Quiz

1. What is the relationship between aggregate planned expenditure and real GDP at equilibrium expenditure?
2. How does equilibrium expenditure come about? What adjusts to achieve equilibrium?
3. If real GDP and aggregate expenditure are less than equilibrium expenditure, what happens to firms' inventories? How do firms change their production? And what happens to real GDP?
4. If real GDP and aggregate expenditure are greater than equilibrium expenditure, what happens to firms' inventories? How do firms change their production? And what happens to real GDP?

Work Study Plan 11.2 and get instant feedback.

We've learned that when the price level is fixed, real GDP is determined by equilibrium expenditure. And we have seen how unplanned changes in inventories and the production response they generate bring a convergence toward equilibrium expenditure. We're now going to study *changes* in equilibrium expenditure and discover an economic amplifier called the *multiplier*.

## The Multiplier

Investment and exports can change for many reasons. A fall in the real interest rate might induce firms to increase their planned investment. A wave of innovation, such as occurred with the spread of multimedia computers in the 1990s, might increase expected future profits and lead firms to increase their planned investment. An economic boom in Western Europe and Japan might lead to a large increase in their expenditure on U.S.-produced goods and services—on U.S. exports. These are all examples of increases in autonomous expenditure.

When autonomous expenditure increases, aggregate expenditure increases and so does equilibrium expenditure and real GDP. But the increase in real GDP is *larger* than the change in autonomous expenditure. The **multiplier** is the amount by which a change in autonomous expenditure is magnified or multiplied to determine the change in equilibrium expenditure and real GDP.

To get the basic idea of the multiplier, we'll work with an example economy in which there are no income taxes and no imports. So we'll first assume that these factors are absent. Then, when you understand the basic idea, we'll bring these factors back into play and see what difference they make to the multiplier.

### The Basic Idea of the Multiplier

Suppose that investment increases. The additional expenditure by businesses means that aggregate expenditure and real GDP increase. The increase in real GDP increases disposable income, and with no income taxes, real GDP and disposable income increase by the same amount. The increase in disposable income brings an increase in consumption expenditure. And the increased consumption expenditure adds even more to aggregate expenditure. Real GDP and disposable income increase further, and so does consumption expenditure. The initial increase in investment brings an even bigger increase in aggregate expenditure because it induces an increase in consumption expenditure. The magnitude of the increase in aggregate expenditure that results from an increase in autonomous expenditure is determined by the *multiplier*.

The table in Fig. 11.5 sets out an aggregate planned expenditure schedule. Initially, when real GDP is \$11 trillion, aggregate planned expenditure is \$11.25 trillion. For each \$1 trillion increase in real GDP, aggregate planned expenditure increases by \$0.75 trillion. This aggregate expenditure schedule is shown in the figure as the aggregate expenditure curve $AE_0$. Initially, equilibrium expenditure is \$12 trillion. You can see this equilibrium in row *B* of the table and in the figure where the curve $AE_0$ intersects the 45° line at the point marked *B*.

Now suppose that autonomous expenditure increases by \$0.5 trillion. What happens to equilibrium expenditure? You can see the answer in Fig. 11.5. When this increase in autonomous expenditure is added to the original aggregate planned expenditure, aggregate planned expenditure increases by \$0.5 trillion at each level of real GDP. The new aggregate expenditure curve is $AE_1$. The new equilibrium expenditure, highlighted in the table (row *D*'), occurs where $AE_1$ intersects the 45° line and is \$14 trillion (point *D*'). At this real GDP, aggregate planned expenditure equals real GDP.

### The Multiplier Effect

In Fig. 11.5, the increase in autonomous expenditure of \$0.5 trillion increases equilibrium expenditure by \$2 trillion. That is, the change in autonomous expenditure leads, like Erykah Badu's electronic equipment, to an amplified change in equilibrium expenditure. This amplified change is the *multiplier effect*—equilibrium expenditure increases by *more than* the increase in autonomous expenditure. The multiplier is greater than 1.

Initially, when autonomous expenditure increases, aggregate planned expenditure exceeds real GDP. As a result, inventories decrease. Firms respond by increasing production so as to restore their inventories to the target level. As production increases, so does real GDP. With a higher level of real GDP, *induced expenditure* increases. Equilibrium expenditure increases by the sum of the initial increase in autonomous expenditure and the increase in induced expenditure. In this example, equilibrium expenditure increases by \$2 trillion following the increase in autonomous expenditure of \$0.5 trillion, so induced expenditure increases by \$1.5 trillion.

Although we have just analyzed the effects of an *increase* in autonomous expenditure, this analysis applies to a decrease in autonomous expenditure. If initially the aggregate expenditure curve is $AE_1$, equilibrium expenditure and real GDP are \$14 trillion. A decrease in autonomous expenditure of \$0.5 trillion shifts the aggregate expenditure curve downward by

**FIGURE 11.5** The Multiplier

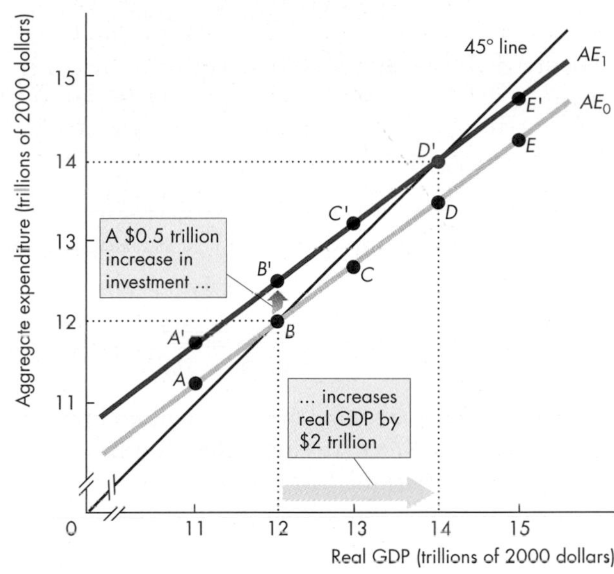


| Real GDP ($Y$) | Aggregate planned expenditure: Original ($AE_0$) | | New ($AE_1$) | |
|---|---|---|---|---|
| | (trillions of 2000 dollars) | | | |
| 11 | *A* | 11.25 | *A'* | 11.75 |
| **12** | ***B*** | **12.00** | ***B'*** | **12.50** |
| 13 | *C* | 12.75 | *C'* | 13.25 |
| **14** | *D* | 13.50 | ***D'*** | **14.00** |
| 15 | *E* | 14.25 | *E'* | 14.75 |

A $0.5 trillion increase in autonomous expenditure shifts the *AE* curve upward by $0.5 trillion from $AE_0$ to $AE_1$. Equilibrium expenditure increases by $2 trillion from $12 trillion to $14 trillion. The increase in equilibrium expenditure is 4 times the increase in autonomous expenditure, so the multiplier is 4.

$0.5 trillion to $AE_0$. Equilibrium expenditure decreases from $14 trillion to $12 trillion. The decrease in equilibrium expenditure ($2 trillion) is larger than the decrease in autonomous expenditure that brought it about ($0.5 trillion).

## Why Is the Multiplier Greater Than 1?

We've seen that equilibrium expenditure increases by more than the increase in autonomous expenditure. This makes the multiplier greater than 1. How come? Why does equilibrium expenditure increase by more than the increase in autonomous expenditure?

The multiplier is greater than 1 because induced expenditure increases—an increase in autonomous expenditure *induces* further increases in expenditure. The NASA space shuttle program costs about $5 billion a year. This expenditure adds $5 billion a year directly to real GDP. But that is not the end of the story. Astronauts and engineers now have more income, and they spend part of the extra income on goods and services. Real GDP now rises by the initial $5 billion plus the extra consumption expenditure induced by the $5 billion increase in income. The producers of cars, flat-screen TVs, vacations, and other goods and services now have increased incomes, and they, in turn, spend part of the increase in their incomes on consumption goods and services. Additional income induces additional expenditure, which creates additional income.

How big is the multiplier effect?

## The Size of the Multiplier

Suppose that the economy is in a recession. Profit prospects start to look better, and firms are planning a large increase in investment. The world economy is also heading toward expansion. The question on everyone's lips is: How strong will the expansion be? This is a hard question to answer, but an important ingredient in the answer is the size of the multiplier.

The *multiplier* is the amount by which a change in autonomous expenditure is multiplied to determine the change in equilibrium expenditure that it generates. To calculate the multiplier, we divide the change in equilibrium expenditure by the change in autonomous expenditure.

Let's calculate the multiplier for the example in Fig. 11.5. Initially, equilibrium expenditure is $12 trillion. Then autonomous expenditure increases by $0.5 trillion, and equilibrium expenditure increases by $2 trillion, to $14 trillion. Then

$$\text{Multiplier} = \frac{\text{Change in equilibrium expenditure}}{\text{Change in autonomous expenditure}}$$

$$\text{Multiplier} = \frac{\$2 \text{ trillion}}{\$0.5 \text{ trillion}} = 4.$$

## The Multiplier and the Slope of the *AE* Curve

The magnitude of the multiplier depends on the slope of the *AE* curve. In Fig. 11.6, the *AE* curve in part (a) is steeper than the *AE* curve in part (b), and the multiplier is larger in part (a) than in part (b). To see why, let's do a calculation.

Aggregate expenditure and real GDP change because induced expenditure and autonomous expenditure change. The change in real GDP ($\Delta Y$) equals the change in induced expenditure ($\Delta N$) plus the change in autonomous expenditure ($\Delta A$). That is,

$$\Delta Y = \Delta N + \Delta A.$$

But the change in induced expenditure is determined by the change in real GDP and the slope of the *AE* curve. To see why, begin with the fact that the slope of the *AE* curve equals the "rise," $\Delta N$, divided by the "run," $\Delta Y$. That is

$$\text{Slope of } AE \text{ curve} = \Delta N \div \Delta Y.$$

So

$$\Delta N = \text{Slope of } AE \text{ curve} \times \Delta Y.$$

Now, use this equation to replace $\Delta N$ in the first equation above to give

$$\Delta Y = \text{Slope of } AE \text{ curve} \times \Delta Y + \Delta A.$$

Now, solve for $\Delta Y$ as

$$(1 - \text{Slope of } AE \text{ curve}) \times \Delta Y = \Delta A$$

and rearrange to give

$$\Delta Y = \frac{\Delta A}{1 - \text{Slope of } AE \text{ curve}}.$$

Finally, divide both sides of this equation by $\Delta A$ to give

$$\text{Multiplier} = \frac{\Delta Y}{\Delta A} = \frac{1}{1 - \text{Slope of } AE \text{ curve}}.$$

If we use the example in Fig. 11.5, the slope of the *AE* curve is 0.75, so

$$\text{Multiplier} = \frac{1}{1 - 0.75} = \frac{1}{0.25} = 4.$$

Where there are no income taxes and no imports, the slope of the *AE* curve equals the marginal propensity to consume (*MPC*). So

$$\text{Multiplier} = \frac{1}{1 - MPC}.$$

But (1 – *MPC*) equals *MPS*. So another formula is

$$\text{Multiplier} = \frac{1}{MPS}.$$

Again using the numbers in Fig. 11.5, we have

$$\text{Multiplier} = \frac{1}{0.25} = 4.$$

Because the marginal propensity to save (*MPS*) is a fraction—a number between 0 and 1—the multiplier is greater than 1.

**FIGURE 11.6** The Multiplier and the Slope of the *AE* Curve

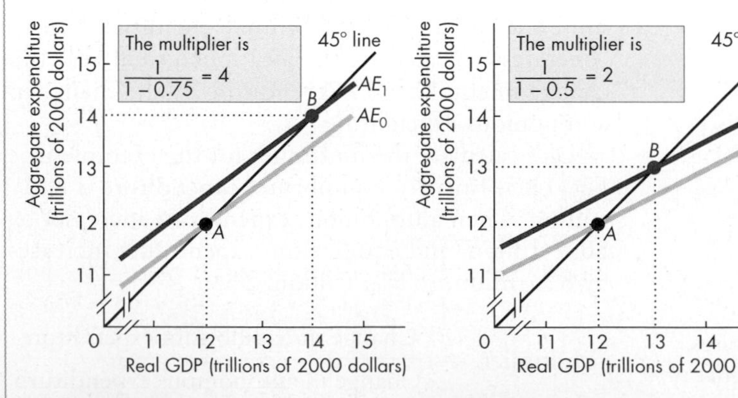


**(a) Multiplier is 4** **(b) Multiplier is 2**

Imports and income taxes make the *AE* curve less steep and reduce the value of the multiplier. In part (a), with no imports and no income taxes, the slope of the *AE* curve is 0.75 (the marginal propensity to consume) and the multiplier is 4. But with imports and income taxes, the slope of the *AE* curve is less than the marginal propensity to consume. In part (b), the slope of the *AE* curve is 0.5. In this case, the multiplier is 2.

myeconlab animation

## Imports and Income Taxes

Imports and income taxes influence the size of the multiplier and make it smaller than it otherwise would be.

To see why imports make the multiplier smaller, think about what happens following an increase in investment. The increase in investment increases real GDP, which in turn increases consumption expenditure. But part of the increase in expenditure is on imported goods and services. Only expenditure on U.S.-produced goods and services increases U.S. real GDP. The larger the marginal propensity to import, the smaller is the change in U.S. real GDP.*

Income taxes also make the multiplier smaller than it otherwise would be. Again, think about what happens following an increase in investment. The increase in investment increases real GDP. Income tax payments increase so disposable income increases by less than the increase in real GDP and consumption expenditure increases by less than it would if taxes had not changed. The larger the income tax rate, the smaller is the change in real GDP.

The marginal propensity to import and the income tax rate together with the marginal propensity to consume determine the multiplier. And their combined influence determines the slope of the *AE* curve.

Over time, the value of the multiplier changes as tax rates change and as the marginal propensity to consume and the marginal propensity to import change. These ongoing changes make the multiplier hard to predict. But they do not change the fundamental fact that an initial change in autonomous expenditure leads to a magnified change in aggregate expenditure and real GDP.

## The Multiplier Process

The multiplier effect isn't a one-shot event. It is a process that plays out over a few months. Figure 11.7 illustrates the multiplier process. Autonomous expenditure increases by $0.5 trillion and real GDP increases by $0.5 trillion (the green bar in round 1). This increase in real GDP increases induced expenditure in round 2. With the slope of the *AE* curve equal to 0.75, induced expenditure increases by 0.75 times the increase in real GDP, so the increase in real GDP of $0.5 trillion induces a further increase in expenditure of $0.375 trillion. This change in induced expenditure (the green bar in round 2) when added to the previous increase in expenditure (the blue bar in round 2) increases real GDP by $0.875 trillion. The round 2 increase in real GDP induces a round 3 increase in induced expenditure. The process repeats through successive rounds. Each increase in real GDP is 0.75 times the previous increase and eventually real GDP increases by $2 trillion.

*The Mathematical Note, pp. 290–293, shows the effects of imports and income taxes on the multiplier.

**FIGURE 11.7** The Multiplier Process

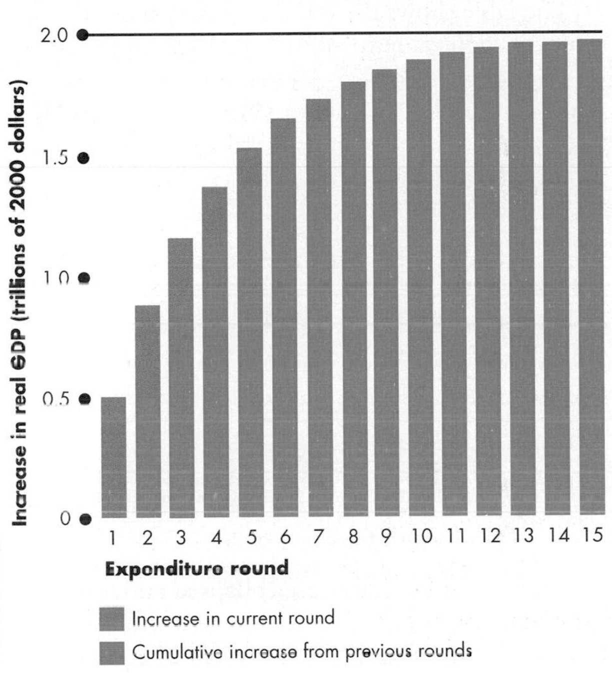


Autonomous expenditure increases by $0.5 trillion. In round 1, real GDP increases by the same amount. With the slope of the *AE* curve equal to 0.75, each additional dollar of real GDP induces an additional 0.75 of a dollar of induced expenditure. The round 1 increase in real GDP brings an increase in induced expenditure of $0.375 trillion in round 2. At the end of round 2, real GDP has increased by $0.875 trillion. The extra $0.375 trillion of real GDP in round 2 brings a further increase in induced expenditure of $0.281 trillion in round 3. Real GDP increases yet further to $1.156 trillion. This process continues with real GDP increasing by ever-smaller amounts. When the process comes to an end, real GDP has increased by a total of $2 trillion.

## The Multiplier in the Great Depression

### Investment Collapse Kills the Economy

The aggregate expenditure model and its multiplier were developed during the 1930s by John Maynard Keynes to understand the most traumatic event in economic history, the *Great Depression*.

In 1929, the U.S. and global economies were booming. U.S. real GDP and real GDP per person had never been higher. By 1933, real GDP had fallen to 73 percent of its 1929 level and more than a quarter of the labor force was unemployed.

The table shows the GDP numbers and components of aggregate expenditure in 1929 and 1933.

| | 1929 | | 1933 | |
|---|---|---|---|---|
| | (billions of 1929 dollars) | | | |
| Consumption expenditure | 77 | | 64 | |
| Imports | 6 | | 4 | |
| *Induced expenditure* | | 71 | | 60 |
| Investment | 17 | | 3 | |
| Government expenditure | 10 | | 10 | |
| Exports | 6 | | 3 | |
| *Autonomous expenditure* | | 33 | | 16 |
| **GDP** | | 104 | | 76 |

*Source of data*: Bureau of Economic Analysis.

Autonomous expenditure collapsed and most of the decrease was in investment, which fell from $17 billion to $3 billion. Exports also fell by a large amount. Government expenditure held steady.

The figure uses the aggregate expenditure model to illustrate the Great Depression.

In 1929, with autonomous expenditure of $33 billion, the *AE* curve was $AE_{29}$. Equilibrium expenditure and real GDP were $104 billion.

By 1933, autonomous expenditure had fallen by $17 billion to $16 billion and the *AE* curve had shifted downward to $AE_{33}$. Equilibrium expenditure and real GDP had fallen to $76 billion.

The decrease in autonomous expenditure of $17 billion brought a decrease in real GDP of $28 billion. The multiplier was $28/$17 = 1.6. The slope of the *AE* curve is the change in induced expenditure, a fall of $11 billion, divided by the change in real GDP, a fall of $28 billion, and is 0.39. You can check that the multiplier formula, 1/(1 – Slope of *AE* curve), delivers a multiplier equal to 1.6.

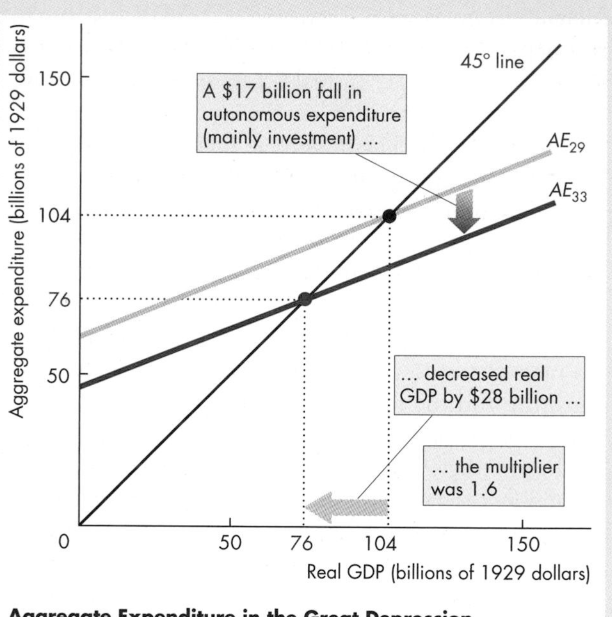


**Aggregate Expenditure in the Great Depression**

## Business Cycle Turning Points

At business cycle turning points, the economy moves from expansion to recession or from recession to expansion. Economists understand these turning points as seismologists understand earthquakes. They know quite a lot about the forces and mechanisms that produce them, but they can't predict them. The forces that bring business cycle turning points are the swings in autonomous expenditure, such as investment and exports. The multiplier that you've just studied is the mechanism that gives momentum to the economy's new direction.

### Review Quiz

1. What is the multiplier? What does it determine? Why does it matter?
2. How do the marginal propensity to consume, the marginal propensity to import, and the income tax rate influence the multiplier?
3. How do fluctuations in autonomous expenditure influence real GDP?

Work Study Plan 11.3 and get instant feedback.

## The Multiplier and the Price Level

We have just considered adjustments in spending that occur in the very short run when the price level is fixed. In this time frame, the economy's cobblestones, which are changes in investment and exports, are not smoothed by shock absorbers like those on Michael Bloomberg's car. Instead, they are amplified like Erykah Badu's voice. But these outcomes occur only when the price level is fixed. We now investigate what happens after a long enough time lapse for the price level to change.

### Adjusting Quantities and Prices

When firms can't keep up with sales and their inventories fall below target, they increase production, but at some point, they raise their prices. Similarly, when firms find unwanted inventories piling up, they decrease production, but eventually they cut their prices. So far, we've studied the macroeconomic consequences of firms changing their production levels when their sales change, but we haven't looked at the effects of price changes. When individual firms change their prices, the economy's price level changes.

To study the simultaneous determination of real GDP and the price level, we use the *AS-AD model*, which is explained in Chapter 10. But to understand how aggregate demand adjusts, we need to work out the connection between the *AS-AD* model and the aggregate expenditure model that we've used in this chapter. The key to understanding the relationship between these two models is the distinction between the aggregate *expenditure* and aggregate *demand* and the related distinction between the aggregate *expenditure curve* and the aggregate *demand curve*.

### Aggregate Expenditure and Aggregate Demand

The aggregate expenditure curve is the relationship between the aggregate planned expenditure and real GDP, all other influences on aggregate planned expenditure remaining the same. The aggregate demand curve is the relationship between the aggregate quantity of goods and services demanded and the price level, all other influences on aggregate demand remaining the same. Let's explore the links between these two relationships.

### Deriving the Aggregate Demand Curve

When the price level changes, aggregate planned expenditure changes and the quantity of real GDP demanded changes. The aggregate demand curve slopes downward. Why? There are two main reasons:

- Wealth effect
- Substitution effects

**Wealth Effect** Other things remaining the same, the higher the price level, the smaller is the purchasing power of wealth. For example, suppose you have $100 in the bank and the price level is 105. If the price level rises to 125, your $100 buys fewer goods and services. You are less wealthy. With less wealth, you will probably want to try to spend a bit less and save a bit more. The higher the price level, other things remaining the same, the lower is aggregate planned expenditure.

**Substitution Effects** For a given expected future price level, a rise in the price level today makes current goods and services more expensive relative to future goods and services and results in a delay in purchases—an *intertemporal substitution*. A rise in the U.S. price level, other things remaining the same, makes U.S.-produced goods and services more expensive relative to foreign-produced goods and services. As a result, U.S. imports increase and U.S. exports decrease—an *international substitution*.

When the price level rises, each of these effects reduces aggregate planned expenditure at each level of real GDP. As a result, when the price level *rises*, the aggregate expenditure curve shifts *downward*. A fall in the price level has the opposite effect. When the price level *falls*, the aggregate expenditure curve shifts *upward*.

Figure 11.8(a) shows the shifts of the *AE* curve. When the price level is 115, the aggregate expenditure curve is $AE_0$, which intersects the 45° line at point *B*. Equilibrium expenditure is $12 trillion. If the price level increases to 135, the aggregate expenditure curve shifts downward to $AE_1$, which intersects the 45° line at point *A*. Equilibrium expenditure decreases to $11 trillion. If the price level decreases to 95, the aggregate expenditure curve shifts upward to $AE_2$, which intersects the 45° line at point *C*. Equilibrium expenditure increases to \$13 trillion.

We've just seen that when the price level changes, other things remaining the same, the aggregate expenditure curve shifts and the equilibrium expenditure changes. But when the price level changes, other things remaining the same, there is a movement along the aggregate demand curve.

Figure 11.8(b) shows the movements along the aggregate demand curve. At a price level of 115, the aggregate quantity of goods and services demanded is \$12 trillion—point *B* on the *AD* curve. If the price level rises to 135, the aggregate quantity of goods and services demanded decreases to \$11 trillion. There is a movement up along the aggregate demand curve to point *A*. If the price level falls to 95, the aggregate quantity of goods and services demanded increases to \$13 trillion. There is a movement down along the aggregate demand curve to point *C*.

Each point on the aggregate demand curve corresponds to a point of equilibrium expenditure. The equilibrium expenditure points *A, B,* and *C* in Fig. 11.8(a) correspond to the points *A, B,* and *C* on the aggregate demand curve in Fig. 11.8(b).

## Changes in Aggregate Expenditure and Aggregate Demand

When any influence on aggregate planned expenditure other than the price level changes, both the aggregate expenditure curve and the aggregate demand curve shift. For example, an increase in investment or exports increases both aggregate planned expenditure and aggregate demand and shifts both the *AE* curve and the *AD* curve. Figure 11.9 illustrates the effect of such an increase.

Initially, the aggregate expenditure curve is $AE_0$ in part (a) and the aggregate demand curve is $AD_0$ in part (b). The price level is 115, real GDP is \$12 trillion, and the economy is at point *A* in both parts of Fig. 11.9. Now suppose that investment increases by \$1 trillion. At a constant price level of 115, the aggregate expenditure curve shifts upward to $AE_1$. This curve intersects the 45° line at an equilibrium expenditure of \$14 trillion (point *B*). This equilibrium expenditure of \$14 trillion is the aggregate quantity of goods and services demanded at a price level of 115, as shown by point *B* in part (b). Point *B* lies on

**FIGURE 11.8** Equilibrium Expenditure and Aggregate Demand

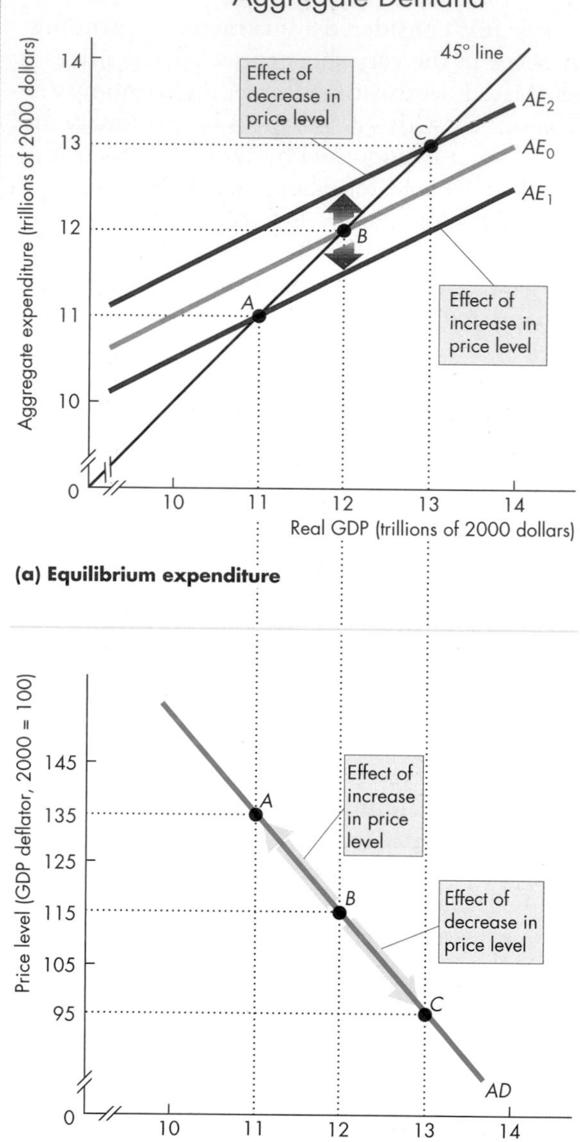


A change in the price level *shifts* the *AE* curve and results in a *movement along* the *AD* curve. When the price level is 115, the *AE* curve is $AE_0$ and equilibrium expenditure is \$12 trillion at point *B*. When the price level rises to 135, the *AE* curve is $AE_1$ and equilibrium expenditure is \$11 trillion at point *A*. When the price level falls to 95, the *AE* curve is $AE_2$ and equilibrium expenditure is \$13 trillion at point *C*. Points *A, B,* and *C* on the *AD* curve in part (b) correspond to the equilibrium expenditure points *A, B,* and *C* in part (a).

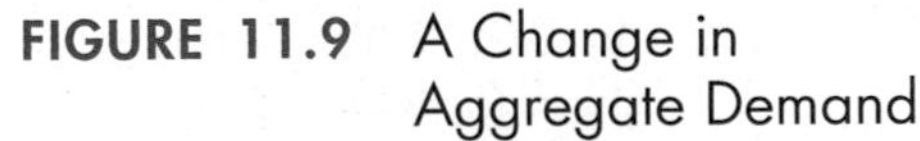


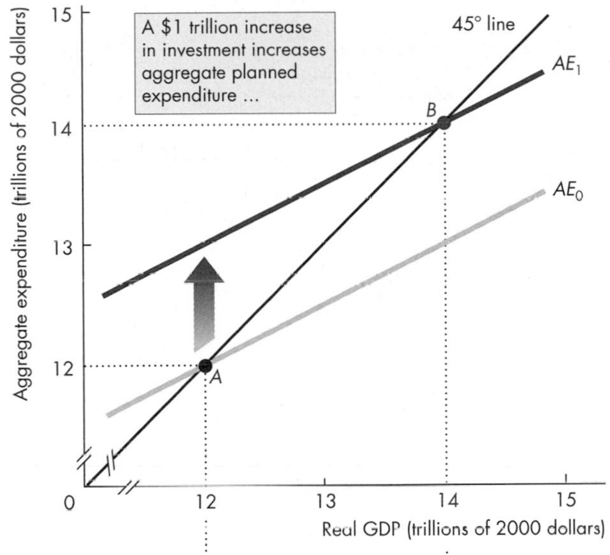


(a) Aggregate expenditure

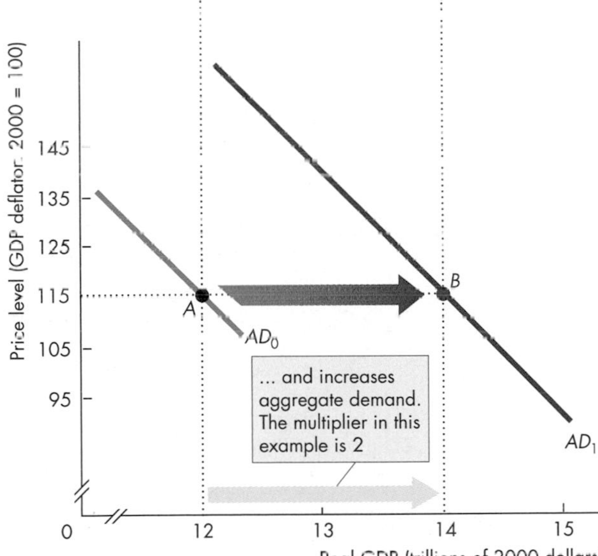


**(b) Aggregate demand**

The price level is 115. When the aggregate expenditure curve is $AE_0$ in part (a), the aggregate demand curve is $AD_0$ in part (b). An increase in autonomous expenditure shifts the *AE* curve upward to $AE_1$. In the new equilibrium, real GDP is $14 trillion (at point *B*). Because the quantity of real GDP demanded at a price level of 115 increases to $14 trillion, the *AD* curve shifts rightward to $AD_1$.

myeconlab animation

a new aggregate demand curve. The aggregate demand curve has shifted rightward to $AD_1$.

But how do we know by how much the *AD* curve shifts? The multiplier determines the answer. The larger the multiplier, the larger is the shift in the aggregate demand curve that results from a given change in autonomous expenditure. In this example, the multiplier is 2. A $1 trillion increase in investment produces a $2 trillion increase in the aggregate quantity of goods and services demanded at each price level. That is, a $1 trillion increase in autonomous expenditure shifts the aggregate demand curve rightward by $2 trillion.

A decrease in autonomous expenditure shifts the aggregate expenditure curve downward and shifts the aggregate demand curve leftward. You can see these effects by reversing the change that we've just described. If the economy is initially at point *B* on the aggregate expenditure curve $AE_1$ and on the aggregate demand curve $AD_1$, a decrease in autonomous expenditure shifts the aggregate expenditure curve downward to $AE_0$. The aggregate quantity of goods and services demanded decreases from $14 trillion to $12 trillion, and the aggregate demand curve shifts leftward to $AD_0$.

Let's summarize what we have just discovered:

> If some factor other than a change in the price level increases autonomous expenditure, the *AE* curve shifts upward and the *AD* curve shifts rightward. The size of the *AD* curve shift equals the change in autonomous expenditure multiplied by the multiplier.

## Equilibrium Real GDP and the Price Level

In Chapter 10, we learned that aggregate demand and short-run aggregate supply determine equilibrium real GDP and the price level. We've now put aggregate demand under a more powerful microscope and have discovered that a change in investment (or in any component of autonomous expenditure) changes aggregate demand and shifts the aggregate demand curve. The magnitude of the shift depends on the multiplier. But whether a change in autonomous expenditure results ultimately in a change in real GDP, a change in the price level, or a combination of the two depends on aggregate supply. There are two time frames to consider: the short run and the long run. First we'll see what happens in the short run.

### An Increase in Aggregate Demand in the Short Run

Figure 11.10 describes the economy. Initially, in part (a), the aggregate expenditure curve is $AE_0$ and equilibrium expenditure is \$12 trillion—point *A*. In part (b), aggregate demand is $AD_0$ and the short-run aggregate supply curve is *SAS*. (Chapter 10, pp. 247–249, explains the *SAS* curve.) Equilibrium is at point *A* in part (b), where the aggregate demand and short-run aggregate supply curves intersect. The price level is 115, and real GDP is \$12 trillion.

Now suppose that investment increases by \$1 trillion. With the price level fixed at 115, the aggregate expenditure curve shifts upward to $AE_1$. Equilibrium expenditure increases to \$14 trillion—point *B* in part (a). In part (b), the aggregate demand curve shifts rightward by \$2 trillion, from $AD_0$ to $AD_1$. How far the aggregate demand curve shifts is determined by the multiplier when the price level is fixed.

But with this new aggregate demand curve, the price level does not remain fixed. The price level rises, and as it does, the aggregate expenditure curve shifts downward. The short-run equilibrium occurs when the aggregate expenditure curve has shifted downward to $AE_2$ and the new aggregate demand curve, $AD_1$, intersects the short-run aggregate supply curve at point *C* in both part (a) and part (b). Real GDP is \$13.3 trillion, and the price level is 128.

When price level effects are taken into account, the increase in investment still has a multiplier effect on real GDP, but the multiplier is smaller than it would be if the price level were fixed. The steeper the slope of the short-run aggregate supply curve, the larger is the increase in the price level and the smaller is the multiplier effect on real GDP.

### An Increase in Aggregate Demand in the Long Run

Figure 11.11 illustrates the long-run effect of an increase in aggregate demand. In the long run, real GDP equals potential GDP and there is full employment. Potential GDP is \$12 trillion, and the long-run aggregate supply curve is *LAS*. Initially, the economy is at point *A* in parts (a) and (b).

Investment increases by \$1 trillion. In Fig. 11.11, the aggregate expenditure curve shifts to $AE_1$ and the aggregate demand curve shifts to $AD_1$. With no change in the price level, the economy would move to point *B* and real GDP would increase to \$14 trillion. But in the short run, the price level rises to 128 and real GDP increases to only \$13.3 trillion. With the higher price level, the *AE* curve shifts from $AE_1$ to

**FIGURE 11.10** The Multiplier in the Short Run

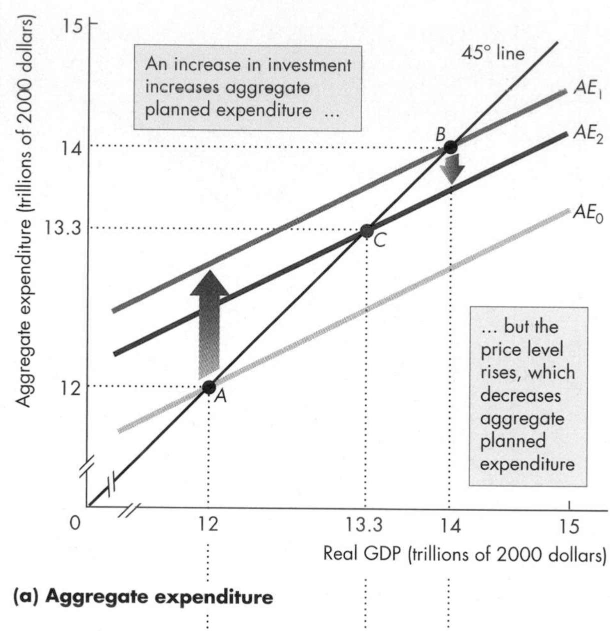


**(a) Aggregate expenditure**

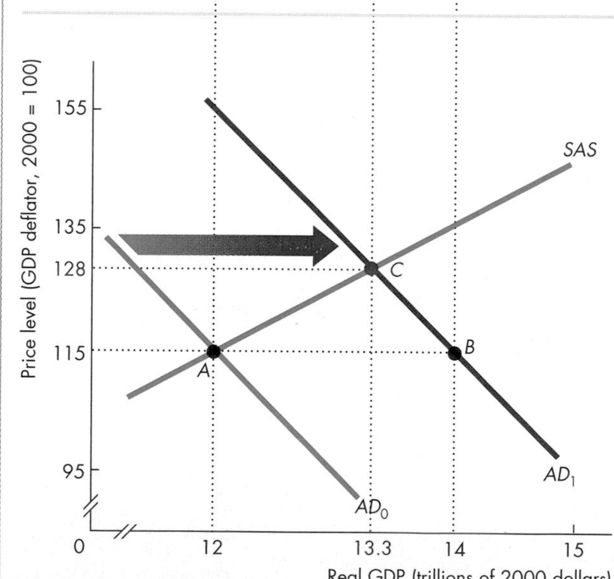


**(b) Aggregate demand**

An increase in investment shifts the *AE* curve from $AE_0$ to $AE_1$ and the *AD* curve from $AD_0$ to $AD_1$. The price level rises, and the higher price level shifts the *AE* curve downward from $AE_1$ to $AE_2$. The economy moves to point *C* in both parts. In the short run, when prices are flexible, the multiplier effect is smaller than when the price level is fixed.

**FIGURE 11.11** The Multiplier in the Long Run

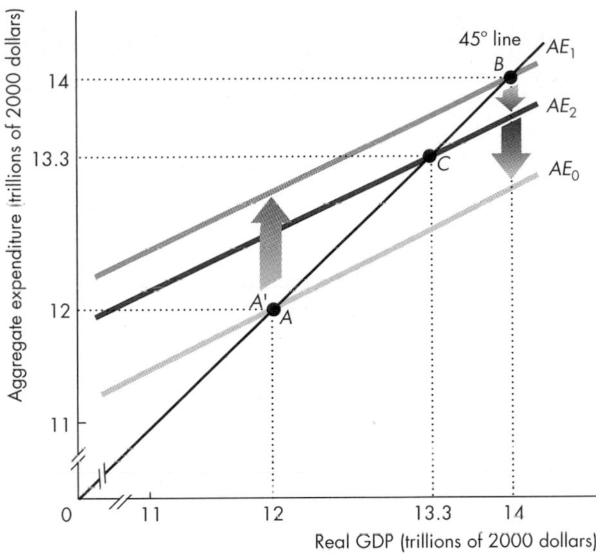


**(a) Aggregate expenditure**

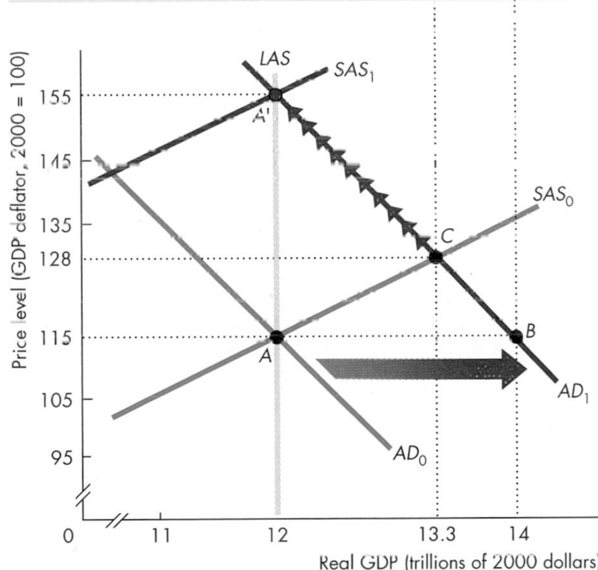


**(b) Aggregate demand**

Starting from point *A*, an increase in investment shifts the *AE* curve to $AE_1$ and the *AD* curve to $AD_1$. In the short run, the economy moves to point *C*. In the long run, the money wage rate rises and the *SAS* curve shifts to $SAS_1$. As the price level rises, the *AE* curve shifts back to $AE_0$ and the economy moves to point *A*'. In the long run, the multiplier is zero.

myeconlab animation

$AE_2$. The economy is now in a short-run equilibrium at point *C* in both part (a) and part (b).

Real GDP now exceeds potential GDP. The labor force is more than fully employed, and in the long run, shortages of labor increase the money wage rate. The higher money wage rate increases firms' costs, which decreases short-run aggregate supply and shifts the *SAS* curve leftward to $SAS_1$. The price level rises further, and real GDP decreases. There is a movement along $AD_1$, and the *AE* curve shifts downward from $AE_2$ toward $AE_0$. When the money wage rate and the price level have increased by the same percentage, real GDP is again equal to potential GDP and the economy is at point *A*'. In the long run, the multiplier is zero.

## Review Quiz

1 How does a change in the price level influence the *AE* curve and the *AD* curve?
2 If autonomous expenditure increases with no change in the price level, what happens to the *AE* curve and the *AD* curve? Which curve shifts by an amount that is determined by the multiplier and why?
3 How does an increase in autonomous expenditure change real GDP in the short run? Does real GDP change by the same amount as the change in aggregate demand? Why or why not?
4 How does real GDP change in the long run when autonomous expenditure increases? Does real GDP change by the same amount as the change in aggregate demand? Why or why not?

myeconlab Work Study Plan 11.4 and get instant feedback.

You are now ready to build on what you've learned about aggregate expenditure fluctuations. We'll study the business cycle and the roles of fiscal policy and monetary policy in smoothing the cycle while achieving price stability and sustained economic growth. In Chapter 12 we study the U.S. business cycle and inflation, and in Chapters 13 and 14 we study fiscal policy and monetary policy, respectively. But before you leave the current topic, look at *Reading Between the Lines* on pp. 288–289 and see the aggregate expenditure model in action in the U.S. economy during 2008.

READING BETWEEN THE LINES 

# Consumption Expenditure in the 2008 Downturn

## In Tightfisted Turn, Economy Contracts; Drop in Spending Is Drag on Growth

http://www.washingtonpost.com
October 31, 2008

Through recession, countless natural disasters and a major terrorist attack, there has been one constant in the U.S. economy: American consumers have bought more stuff in any given quarter than they did in the previous one.

Not anymore. Personal consumption expenditure fell at a 3.1 percent annual rate in the third quarter, the government said yesterday, the worst decline since 1980. The data show that even before the financial crisis deepened in October, American households were being walloped to a degree that has no recent precedent. Conditions, economists said, are almost certain to get worse before getting better.

"This is a major about-face in consumer spending," said Robert A. Dye, a senior economist with PNC Financial Services Group. "It's no surprise why. We've had a drop in the value of houses and stock portfolios, a very weak labor market and a tightening of credit."

Overall, the nation's gross domestic product, the broadest measure of economic growth, declined at a 0.3 percent annual rate in the three months ended Sept. 30, the Commerce Department said. The economy would have shrunk even more had it not been for strong export growth and government spending, as well as a buildup in business inventories—all factors that are poised to offer less of a boost in the future. …

Exports proved to be a major bright spot in the report, rising at a 5.9 percent annual pace. But that growth was driven by two trends that seem to be dissipating. First, economies in the rest of the world are deteriorating rapidly, meaning foreigners will be less able to buy American goods in the months ahead. And the value of the dollar has been rising relative to other currencies in recent weeks, making U.S. exports less competitive on price. …



## Essence of the Story

- Real GDP shrank at a 0.3 percent annual rate in the three months ended Sept. 30, 2008.
- Personal consumption expenditure fell at a 3.1 percent annual rate, the largest decrease since 1980.
- A fall in the value of houses and stocks, falling employment, and tight credit were seen as the reason for the fall in personal consumption expenditure.
- Government expenditure, business inventories, and exports increased.
- A slowing global economy and strong dollar will weaken exports growth in the near future.

## Economic Analysis

- We can use the aggregate expenditure model to interpret this news article.
- The article reports that the economy was shrinking in the third quarter of 2008 and consumption expenditure decreased most.
- Table 1 shows the real GDP and aggregate expenditure numbers for the second and third quarters of 2008 along with the change.
- Consumption expenditure was the component that decreased most—by $66 billion.
- Investment and imports also decreased but government expenditure and exports increased.
- Consumption expenditure is partly autonomous and partly induced.
- When real GDP falls, disposable income falls and induces a fall in consumption expenditure.
- A $7-billion fall in real GDP, which occurred in the third quarter of 2008, decreases disposable income by about $5 billion, which in turn decreases induced consumption expenditure by about $4 billion.
- The decrease in consumption expenditure of $66 billion is mainly a decrease in autonomous consumption expenditure.
- A decrease in household wealth resulting from lower house prices and lower stock prices decreased autonomous consumption expenditure. Lower expected future income might also have played a role.
- Figure 1 illustrates the change in aggregate planned expenditure that brought about the fall in real GDP.
- In the second quarter of 2008, aggregate planned expenditure was $AE_0$ and equilibrium expenditure was $11,727 billion.
- In the third quarter of 2008, autonomous expenditure decreased and the aggregate expenditure curve shifted downward to $AE_1$. Equilibrium expenditure decreased to $11,720 billion.
- The news article reports and Table 1 shows that during the third quarter business inventories decreased by $39 billion.

**Table 1 The Components of Aggregate Expenditure**

| | 2008 Q2 | 2008 Q3 | Change |
|---|---|---|---|
| | (billions of 2000 dollars) | | |
| Consumption expenditure | 8,341 | 8,275 | –66 |
| Investment | 1,702 | 1,694 | –8 |
| Government expenditure | 2,059 | 2,088 | 29 |
| Exports | 1,545 | 1,567 | 22 |
| Imports | 1,926 | 1,917 | –9 |
| Residual* | –44 | –19 | 25 |
| **Real GDP** | **11,727** | **11,720** | **–7** |
| Change in inventories | –51 | –39 | |

*The residual arises because chain-dollar real variables are calculated for each expenditure component independently of chain-dollar real GDP and the components don't exactly sum to real GDP.

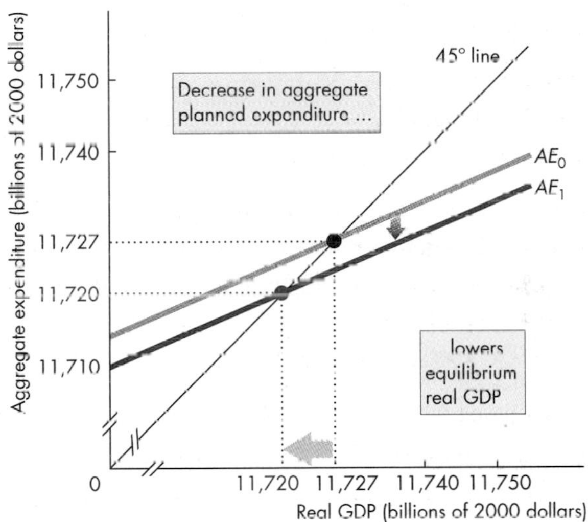


**Figure 1 Equilibrium expenditure**

- This decrease in inventories was mostly planned because with real GDP decreasing, any unplanned inventory changes would have been positive.
- If exports stop increasing, and if investment decreases further, aggregate planned expenditure will fall again in the fourth quarter of 2008 and real GDP will decrease further.

# MATHEMATICAL NOTE

## The Algebra of the Keynesian Model

This mathematical note derives formulas for equilibrium expenditure and the multipliers. We begin by defining the symbols we need:

- Aggregate planned expenditure, $AE$
- Real GDP, $Y$
- Consumption expenditure, $C$
- Disposable income, $YD$
- Investment, $I$
- Government expenditure, $G$
- Exports, $X$
- Imports, $M$
- Net taxes, $T$
- Autonomous consumption expenditure, $a$
- Autonomous taxes, $T_a$
- Marginal propensity to consume, $b$
- Marginal propensity to import, $m$
- Marginal tax rate, $t$
- Autonomous expenditure, $A$

### Aggregate Expenditure

Aggregate planned expenditure ($AE$) is the sum of the planned amounts of consumption expenditure ($C$), investment ($I$), government expenditure ($G$), and exports ($X$) minus the planned amount of imports ($M$).

$$AE = C + I + G + X - M.$$

**Consumption Function** Consumption expenditure ($C$) depends on disposable income ($YD$), and we write the consumption function as

$$C = a + bYD.$$

Disposable income ($YD$) equals real GDP minus net taxes ($Y - T$). So if we replace $YD$ with ($Y - T$), the consumption function becomes

$$C = a + b(Y - T).$$

Net taxes, $T$, equal autonomous taxes (that are independent of income), $T_a$, plus induced taxes (that vary with income), $tY$.

So we can write net taxes as

$$T = T_a + tY.$$

Use this last equation to replace $T$ in the consumption function. The consumption function becomes

$$C = a - bT_a + b(1 - t)Y.$$

This equation describes consumption expenditure as a function of real GDP.

**Import Function** Imports depend on real GDP, and the import function is

$$M = mY.$$

**Aggregate Expenditure Curve** Use the consumption function and the import function to replace $C$ and $M$ in the $AE$ equation. That is,

$$AE = a - bT_a + b(1 - t)Y + I + G + X - mY.$$

Collect the terms that involve $Y$ on the right side of the equation to obtain

$$AE = (a - bT_a + I + G + X) + [b(1 - t) - m]Y.$$

Autonomous expenditure ($A$) is $(a - bT_a + I + G + X)$, and the slope of the $AE$ curve is $[b(1 - t) - m]$. So the equation for the $AE$ curve, which is shown in Fig. 1, is

$$AE = A + [b(1 - t) - m]Y.$$

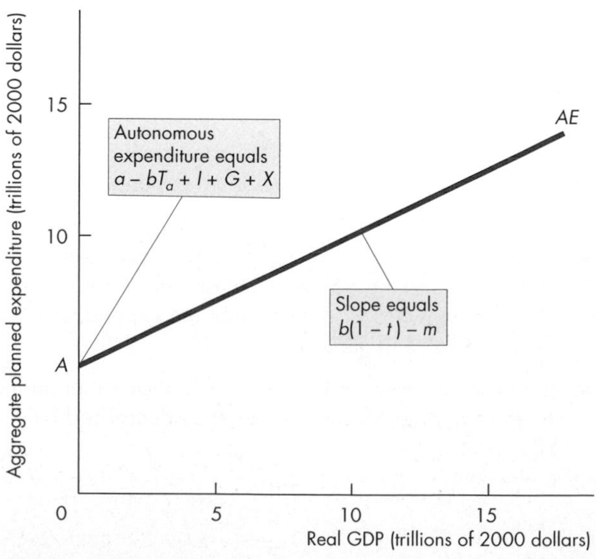


**Figure 1 The *AE* curve**

## Equilibrium Expenditure

*Equilibrium expenditure* occurs when aggregate planned expenditure ($AE$) equals real GDP ($Y$). That is,

$$AE = Y.$$

In Fig. 2, the scales of the $x$-axis (real GDP) and the $y$-axis (aggregate planned expenditure) are identical, so the 45° line shows the points at which aggregate planned expenditure equals real GDP.

Figure 2 shows the point of equilibrium expenditure at the intersection of the $AE$ curve and the 45° line.

To calculate equilibrium expenditure, solve the equations for the $AE$ curve and the 45° line for the two unknown quantities $AE$ and $Y$. So starting with

$$AE = A + [b(1 - t) - m]Y$$
$$AE = Y,$$

replace $AE$ with $Y$ in the $AE$ equation to obtain

$$Y = A + [b(1 - t) - m]Y.$$

The solution for $Y$ is

$$Y = \frac{1}{1 - [b(1 - t) - m]}A.$$

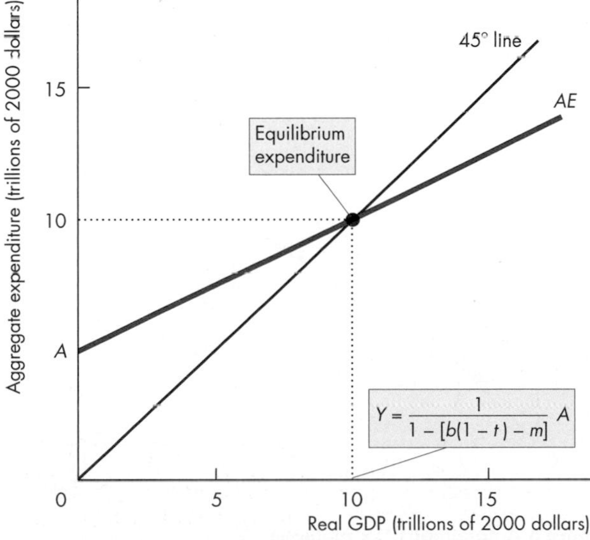


**Figure 2 Equilibrium expenditure**

## The Multiplier

The *multiplier* equals the change in equilibrium expenditure and real GDP ($Y$) that results from a change in autonomous expenditure ($A$) divided by the change in autonomous expenditure.

A change in autonomous expenditure ($\Delta A$) changes equilibrium expenditure and real GDP by

$$\Delta Y = \frac{1}{1 - [b(1 - t) - m]}\Delta A.$$

$$\text{Multiplier} = \frac{1}{1 - [b(1 - t) - m]}.$$

The size of the multiplier depends on the slope of the $AE$ curve, $b(1 - t) - m$. The larger the slope, the larger is the multiplier. So the multiplier is larger,

- The greater the marginal propensity to consume ($b$)
- The smaller the marginal tax rate ($t$)
- The smaller the marginal propensity to import ($m$)

An economy with no imports and no income taxes has $m = 0$ and $t = 0$. In this special case, the multiplier equals $1/(1 - b)$. If $b$ is 0.75, then the multiplier is 4, as shown in Fig. 3.

In an economy with imports and income taxes, if $b = 0.75$, $t = 0.2$, and $m = 0.1$, the multiplier equals 1 divided by $[1 - 0.75(1 - 0.2) - 0.1]$, which equals 2. Make up some more examples to show the effects of $b$, $t$, and $m$ on the multiplier.

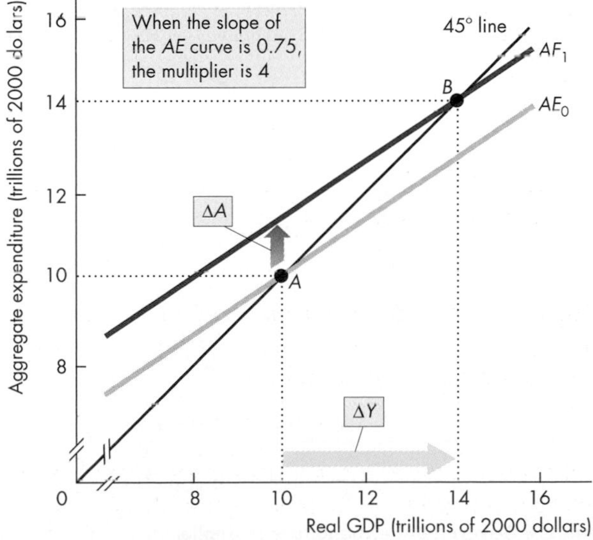


**Figure 3 The multiplier**

## Government Expenditure Multiplier

The **government expenditure multiplier** equals the change in equilibrium expenditure ($Y$) that results from a change in government expenditure ($G$) divided by the change in government expenditure. Because autonomous expenditure is equal to

$$A = a - bT_a + I + G + X,$$

the change in autonomous expenditure equals the change in government expenditure. That is,

$$\Delta A = \Delta G.$$

You can see from the solution for equilibrium expenditure $Y$ that

$$\Delta Y = \frac{1}{1 - [b(1 - t) - m]}\Delta G.$$

The government expenditure multiplier equals

$$\frac{1}{1 - [b(1 - t) - m]}.$$

In an economy in which $t = 0$ and $m = 0$, the government expenditure multiplier is $1/(1 - b)$. With $b = 0.75$, the government expenditure multiplier is 4, as Fig. 4 shows. Make up some examples and use the above formula to show how $b$, $m$, and $t$ influence the government expenditure multiplier.

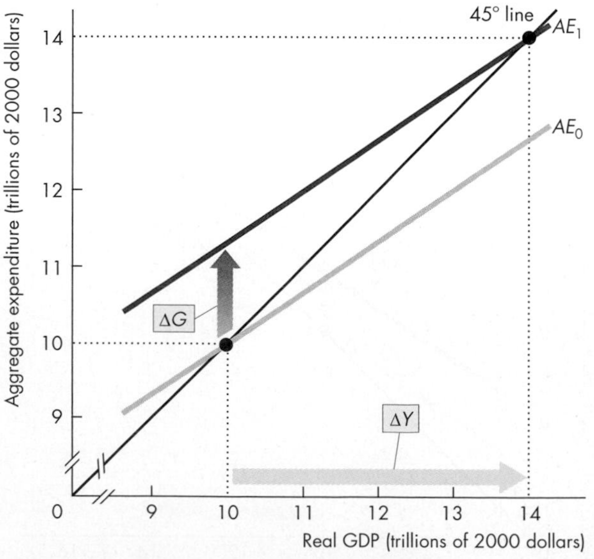


**Figure 4 Government expenditure multiplier**

## Autonomous Tax Multiplier

The **autonomous tax multiplier** equals the change in equilibrium expenditure ($Y$) that results from a change in autonomous taxes ($T_a$) divided by the change in autonomous taxes. Because autonomous expenditure is equal to

$$A = a - bT_a + I + G + X,$$

the change in autonomous expenditure equals *minus* $b$ multiplied by the change in autonomous taxes. That is,

$$\Delta A = -b\Delta T_a.$$

You can see from the solution for equilibrium expenditure $Y$ that

$$\Delta Y = \frac{-b}{1 - [b(1 - t) - m]}\Delta T_a.$$

The autonomous tax multiplier equals

$$\frac{-b}{1 - [b(1 - t) - m]}.$$

In an economy in which $t = 0$ and $m = 0$, the autonomous tax multiplier is $-b/(1 - b)$. In this special case, with $b = 0.75$, the autonomous tax multiplier equals $-3$, as Fig. 5 shows. Make up some examples and use the above formula to show how $b$, $m$, and $t$ influence the autonomous tax multiplier.

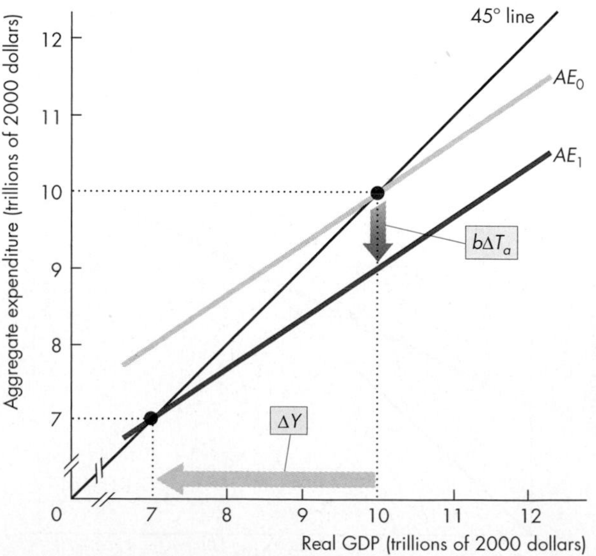


**Figure 5 Autonomous tax multiplier**

## Balanced Budget Multiplier

The **balanced budget multiplier** equals the change in equilibrium expenditure ($Y$) that results from equal changes in government expenditure and lump-sum taxes divided by the change in government expenditure. Because government expenditure and autonomous taxes change by the same amount, the budget balance does not change.

The change in equilibrium expenditure that results from the change in government expenditure is

$$\Delta Y = \frac{1}{1 - [b(1 - t) - m]}\Delta G.$$

And the change in equilibrium expenditure that results from the change in autonomous taxes is

$$\Delta Y = \frac{-b}{1 - [b(1 - t) - m]}\Delta T_a.$$

So the change in equilibrium expenditure resulting from the changes in government expenditure and autonomous taxes is

$$\Delta Y = \frac{1}{1 - [b(1 - t) - m]}\Delta G + \frac{-b}{1-[b(1 - t)-m]}\Delta T_a.$$

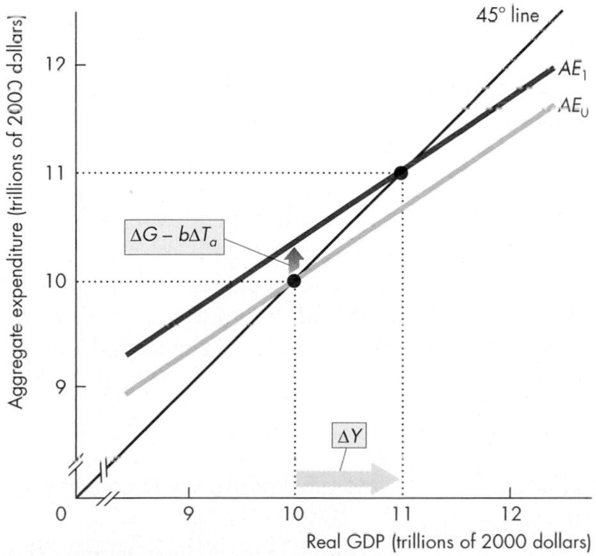


**Figure 6 Balanced budget multiplier**

Notice that

$$\frac{1}{1-[b(1 - t)-m]}$$

is common to both terms on the right side. So we can rewrite the equation as

$$\Delta Y = \frac{1}{1 - [b(1 - t) - m]}(\Delta G - b\Delta T_a)$$

The $AE$ curve shifts upward by $\Delta G - b\Delta T_a$ as shown in Fig. 6.

But the change in government expenditure equals the change in autonomous taxes. That is,

$$\Delta G = \Delta T_a.$$

So we can write the equation as

$$\Delta Y = \frac{1 - b}{1 - [b(1 - t) - m]}\Delta G.$$

The balanced budget multiplier equals

$$\frac{1 - b}{1 - [b(1 - t) - m]}.$$

In an economy in which $t = 0$ and $m = 0$, the balanced budget multiplier is $(1 - b)/(1 - b)$, which equals 1, as Fig. 6 shows. Make up some examples and use the above formula to show how $b$, $m$, and $t$ influence the balanced budget multiplier.

## SUMMARY

### Key Points

**Fixed Prices and Expenditure Plans** (pp. 270–273)

- When the price level is fixed, expenditure plans determine real GDP.
- Consumption expenditure is determined by disposable income, and the marginal propensity to consume (*MPC*) determines the change in consumption expenditure brought about by a change in disposable income. Real GDP determines disposable income.
- Imports are determined by real GDP, and the marginal propensity to import determines the change in imports brought about by a change in real GDP.

**Real GDP with a Fixed Price Level** (pp. 274–277)

- Aggregate *planned* expenditure depends on real GDP.
- Equilibrium expenditure occurs when aggregate planned expenditure equals actual expenditure and real GDP.

**The Multiplier** (pp. 278–282)

- The multiplier is the magnified effect of a change in autonomous expenditure on equilibrium expenditure and real GDP.
- The multiplier is determined by the slope of the *AE* curve.
- The slope of the *AE* curve is influenced by the marginal propensity to consume, the marginal propensity to import, and the income tax rate.

**The Multiplier and the Price Level** (pp. 283–287)

- The *AD* curve is the relationship between the quantity of real GDP demanded and the price level, other things remaining the same.
- The *AE* curve is the relationship between aggregate planned expenditure and real GDP, other things remaining the same.
- At a given price level, there is a given *AE* curve. A change in the price level changes aggregate planned expenditure and shifts the *AE* curve. A change in the price level also creates a movement along the *AD* curve.
- A change in autonomous expenditure that is not caused by a change in the price level shifts the *AE* curve and shifts the *AD* curve. The magnitude of the shift of the *AD* curve depends on the multiplier and on the change in autonomous expenditure.
- The multiplier decreases as the price level changes, and the long-run multiplier is zero.

### Key Figures



### Key Terms

## PROBLEMS and APPLICATIONS

Work problems 1–8 in Chapter 11 Study Plan and get instant feedback.
Work problems 9–15 as Homework, a Quiz, or a Test if assigned by your instructor.

1. You are given the following information about the economy of the United Kingdom.

| Disposable income | Consumption expenditure |
|---|---|
| (billions of pounds per year) | |
| 300 | 340 |
| 400 | 420 |
| 500 | 500 |
| 600 | 580 |
| 700 | 660 |

   a. Calculate the marginal propensity to consume.
   b. Calculate saving at each level of disposable income.
   c. Calculate the marginal propensity to save.

2. The figure illustrates the components of aggregate planned expenditure on Turtle Island. Turtle Island has no imports or exports, the people of Turtle Island pay no incomes taxes, and the price level is fixed.

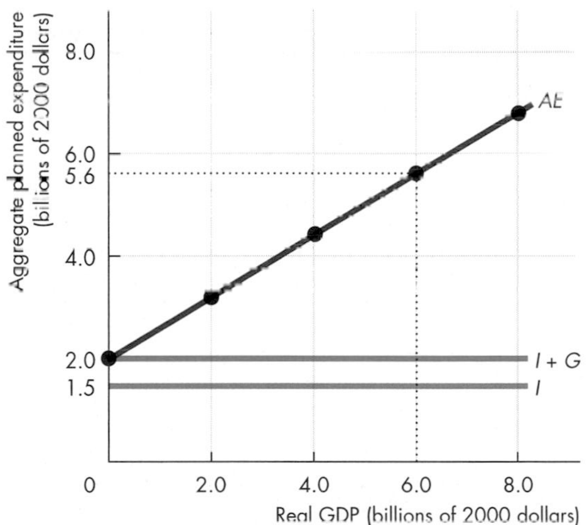


   a. Calculate autonomous expenditure.
   b. Calculate the marginal propensity to consume.
   c. What is aggregate planned expenditure when real GDP is $6 billion?
   d. If real GDP is $4 billion, what is happening to inventories?
   e. If real GDP is $6 billion, what is happening to inventories?
   f. Calculate the multiplier.

3. You are given the following information about the Canadian economy: Autonomous consumption expenditure is $50 billion, investment is $200 billion, and government expenditure is $250 billion. The marginal propensity to consume is 0.7 and net taxes are $250 billion—net taxes are assumed to be constant and not vary with income. Exports are $500 billion and imports are $450 billion.
   a. What is the consumption function?
   b. What is the equation of the *AE* curve?
   c. Calculate equilibrium expenditure.
   d. Calculate the multiplier.
   e. If investment decreases to $150 billion, what is the change in equilibrium expenditure?
   f. Describe the process in e that moves the economy to its new equilibrium expenditure.

4. Suppose that the economy is at full employment, the price level is 100, and the multiplier is 2. Investment increases by $100 billion.
   a. What is the change in equilibrium expenditure if the price level remains at 100?
   b. What is the immediate change in the quantity of real GDP demanded?
   c. In the short run, does real GDP increase by more than, less than, or the same amount as the increase in the quantity of real GDP demanded in b?
   d. In the short run, does the price level remain at 100? Explain why or why not.
   e. In the long run, does real GDP increase by more than, less than, or the same amount as the increase in the quantity of real GDP demanded in b?
   f. Explain how the price level changes in the long run.
   g. Are the values of the multipliers in the short run and the long run larger or smaller than 2?

5. **Understimulated**

   The Senate seems to have agreed on a deal for a stimulus package that would send more than $100 billion in cash to American taxpayers later this spring. ... The theory behind the rebates is that American taxpayers, being Americans, will take the $100-plus billion, and spend it—thus providing a jolt of stimulus to the economy. But will they? ... In 2001, Washington sought to jolt the economy back into life with tax rebates. ... In all, 90 million households received some $38 billion in cash. ... When economists delved into consumption and spending data in the months after the rebates, they discovered that ... households spent 20-40 percent of their rebates ... during the three-month period in which their rebates were received and roughly another third of their rebates during the subsequent three-month period. ... People with low income and low levels of liquid assets spent more.

*Newsweek*, February 7, 2008

a. Will $100 billion worth of tax rebates to American consumers increase aggregate expenditure by more than, less than, or exactly $100 billion? Explain.
b. Explain and draw a graph to illustrate how this fiscal stimulus will influence aggregate expenditure and aggregate demand in both the short run and the long run.
c. Explain what this article implies about the *MPC* and *MPS* of low-income individuals.

6. **The U.S. and China's Savings Problems**

Last year China saved about half of its gross domestic product. ... At the same time, the U.S. saved only 13 percent of its national income. ... And that's just looking at national averages that include saving by consumers, businesses, and governments. The contrast is even starker at the household level—a personal saving rate in China of about 30 percent of household income, compared with a U.S. rate that dipped into negative territory last year (–0.4% of after-tax household income). ... Similar extremes show up in the consumption shares of the two economies. ...

*Fortune*, March 8, 2006

Compare the *MPC* and *MPS* in the United States and China. Why might they differ?

7. **Working Poor More Pinched as Rich Cut Back**

Cutbacks by the wealthy have a ripple effect across all consumer spending, said Michael P. Niemira, chief economist at the International Council of Shopping Centers. That's because American households in the top 20 percent by income—those making at least $150,000 a year—account for about 40 percent of overall consumer spending, which makes up two-thirds of economic activity. ... Soaring home values had made upper-middle class shoppers feel wealthy in recent years, causing them to trade up to $500 Coach handbags and $1,000 espresso makers, but a housing slump has wiped away their paper wealth. ... The economy needs affluent shoppers to spend with enthusiasm. ... the top 20 percent of households spend about $94,000 annually, almost five times the bottom 20 percent and more per year than the bottom sixty percent combined. Then there's also the multiplier effect. When shoppers splurge on $1,000 dinners and $300 limousine rides, that means fatter tips for the waiter and the driver. Sales clerks at upscale stores, who typically earn sales commissions, also depend on spending sprees of mink coats and jewelry. But the trickling down is starting to dry up, threatening to hurt a broad base of low-paid workers.

*MSNBC*, January 28, 2008

a. Explain and draw a graph to illustrate the process by which a recession can occur as a result of "cutbacks by the wealthy."
b. Explain and draw a graph to illustrate how real GDP will be driven back to potential GDP in the long run.
c. Why is the multiplier only a short-run influence on GDP?

8. **Inflation: Price Jump Worst Since '91**

Record gas and higher food prices drove inflation to the biggest annual jump since 1991 and fanned fears about growing pressures on consumers. ... "Rapid increases in the prices of energy and other commodities ... have sapped household purchasing power ..." [Ben Bernanke] said in testimony. He also warned that spending by consumers, which provides nearly three-quarters of the nation's economic activity, "seems likely to be restrained over coming quarters" and that price increases could also make businesses cautious about their own spending plans.

*CNN*, July 16, 2008

a. Explain and draw a graph to illustrate how the events described above influence aggregate planned expenditure.
b. Why might aggregate planned expenditure and actual aggregate expenditure become unequal in the situation described?
c. If actual aggregate expenditure and aggregate planned expenditure become unequal, how will they return to equilibrium expenditure?

9. You are given the following information about the economy of Australia.

| Disposable income | Saving |
|---|---|
| (billions of dollars per year) | |
| 0 | –5 |
| 100 | 20 |
| 200 | 45 |
| 300 | 70 |
| 400 | 95 |

a. Calculate the marginal propensity to save.
b. Calculate consumption at each level of disposable income.
c. Calculate the marginal propensity to consume.

10. The spreadsheet lists the components of aggregate planned expenditure in the United Kingdom. The numbers are in billions of pounds.

| | A | B | C | D | E | F | G |
|---|---|---|---|---|---|---|---|
| 1 | | Y | C | I | G | X | M |
| 2 | A | 100 | 110 | 50 | 60 | 60 | 15 |
| 3 | B | 200 | 170 | 50 | 60 | 60 | 30 |
| 4 | C | 300 | 230 | 50 | 60 | 60 | 45 |
| 5 | D | 400 | 290 | 50 | 60 | 60 | 60 |
| 6 | E | 500 | 350 | 50 | 60 | 60 | 75 |
| 7 | F | 600 | 410 | 50 | 60 | 60 | 90 |

a. Calculate autonomous expenditure.
b. Calculate the marginal propensity to consume.
c. What is aggregate planned expenditure when real GDP is 200 billion pounds?
d. If real GDP is 200 billion pounds, what is happening to inventories?
e. If real GDP is 500 billion pounds, what is happening to inventories?
f. Calculate the multiplier.

11. **The Stimulus Strategy**

When President Bush signed into law last week a fiscal stimulus package of income-tax rebates and business tax breaks, it was the first good news for American consumers in a while. The plan will give many families a $1,200 windfall. ... It's not ideal in its targeting—Congress omitted policies that are especially effective in generating spending, including the extension of unemployment benefits and food stamps—but it does limit the rebates to families with incomes under $174,000 ... [which] should make the stimulus plan more effective, because the people getting the rebates are not, for the most part, the people who will be paying for them. And since the wealthy save a far higher percentage of their incomes than the less well-off, the plan essentially takes money from people who would probably save it and gives it to those who will likely spend it. In the long run, this isn't sustainable—the current crisis has shown that Americans need to save more and borrow less. But in the short run a little spending spree could be just what an idling, anxious economy needs.

*MSNBC*, February 18, 2008

a. Explain and draw a graph to illustrate how this fiscal stimulus will influence aggregate expenditure and aggregate demand in both the short run and the long run.
b. Explain why some types of fiscal stimulus are more "effective in generating spending" than others.
c. What does this article imply about the *MPS* in the United State? Why might this be good in the short-run in this situation, but not "sustainable" in the long-run?

12. **Americans $1.7 trillion Poorer**

Americans saw their net worth decline by $1.7 trillion in the first quarter—the biggest drop since 2002—as declines in home values and the stock market ravaged their holdings. ... Until then, net worth had been rising steadily since 2003. ...

The recent declines, however, may not affect consumer spending, said Michael Englund, senior economist with Action Economics. Americans have actually spent more in recent months. ... Americans "are spending everything in their wallet and borrowing more," Englund said. ... Household debt grew by 3.5 percent in the first quarter. ... Consumer credit, which includes credit cards, rose at an annual rate of 5.75 percent. ...

*CNN*, June 5, 2008

a. Explain and draw a graph to illustrate how a decrease in household wealth theoretically impacts the consumption function and saving function.
b. According to this article, how has consumption expenditure actually responded in the first quarter?
c. What other factors could explain the discrepancy between what is predicted in a and how consumers are actually responding in b?

d. Draw a graph of a consumption function and show at what point consumers were actually operating at in the first quarter. Explain your answer.

13. **Americans Spend Every Cent—and More**

For the last 19 months ... American consumers [have been] spending more than they're taking home after taxes. The savings rate was a negative 0.6 percent in October. In other words, the typical American spent $100.60 for every $100 of take home pay. ... Dean Baker, co-director of the Center for Economic and Policy Research, said the negative savings rate ... will end when consumers cut back on spending, which in turn will spark a recession. ... Largely to blame for the negative rate, Baker said, is the spike in home prices over the last five years that convinced many Americans they no longer needed to save. ... But since Baker believes the current housing slump will worsen next year, he's forecasting a drop in spending as well. "People will have to cut back their consumption because people can't spend at the same rate," he said. ... [Economist Steven] Wieting said it will take more than the recent slump in housing prices to change consumer behavior and put the brakes on spending. "I don't think attitudes change very rapidly," he said. "They'll look at the totality of their household balance sheet along with income and savings. I would expect there to be only a very gradual recovery in the true level of personal saving."

*CNN*, December 21, 2006

a. How is it possible for households to have a negative savings rate? What has caused this negative household savings rate?
b. Is this negative household savings rate sustainable in the long-run?
c. Explain and draw a graph to illustrate Baker's claim that this "will end when consumers cut back on spending, which in turn will spark a recession."
d. Compare the predictions offered by Baker and Wieting. Why might Wieting's predictions have different business cycle implications than Baker's in c?

14. **Where Americans Will (and Won't) Cut Back**

Consumer confidence is in the gutter ... but even as consumers cut back on spending, there are some things they refuse to give up. ... Even in a time of belt-tightening, Americans are demonstrating a strong "reluctance to give up on everyday pleasures," [market researcher Jon Berry] said. But still, many are forced to prioritize and scale back spending somewhere in their lives. "There are clear priorities with dining out, out-of-the-home entertainment, clothes, vacations and buying lunch the first to be cut," Berry said. ... Many Americans are leaving the car in the garage and staying on their living room couch. A whopping 50 percent of Americans plan to buy an HD or flat-panel TV in the next year. ... Cable and satellite TV subscriptions are also way down the list on cutbacks. Despite the expense, another thing consumers refuse to give up altogether is vacationing and travel. Even in these tough times, 59 percent of Americans plan to take a trip ... in the next six months. ...

*CNN*, July 16, 2008

a. Explain the difference between induced consumption expenditure and autonomous consumption expenditure. Why isn't all consumption expenditure induced expenditure?
b. Explain and draw a graph to illustrate how declining consumer confidence influences aggregate expenditure and aggregate demand in the short-run.
c. Explain and draw a graph to illustrate the long-run effect on aggregate expenditure and aggregate demand of the decline in consumer confidence.

15. Study *Reading Between the Lines* on pp. 288–289 and then answer the following questions:
a. If the 2008 third quarter changes in inventories were mainly *planned* changes, what role did they play in shifting the *AE* curve and changing equilibrium expenditure? Use a figure similar to that on p. 276 to answer this question.
b. If , as the news article reports, the world economy is slowing and U.S. exports stop growing, what will happen to the *AE* curve in future quarters and how will real GDP change?
c. What do you think will happen to real GDP, aggregate expenditure, and inventory investment in 2009? What clues do you get from the news article?

# 12 U.S. Inflation, Unemployment, and Business Cycle

**After studying this chapter, you will be able to:**

- Explain how demand-pull and cost-push forces bring cycles in inflation and output
- Explain the short-run and long-run tradeoff between inflation and unemployment
- Explain how the mainstream business cycle theory and real business cycle theory account for fluctuations in output and employment

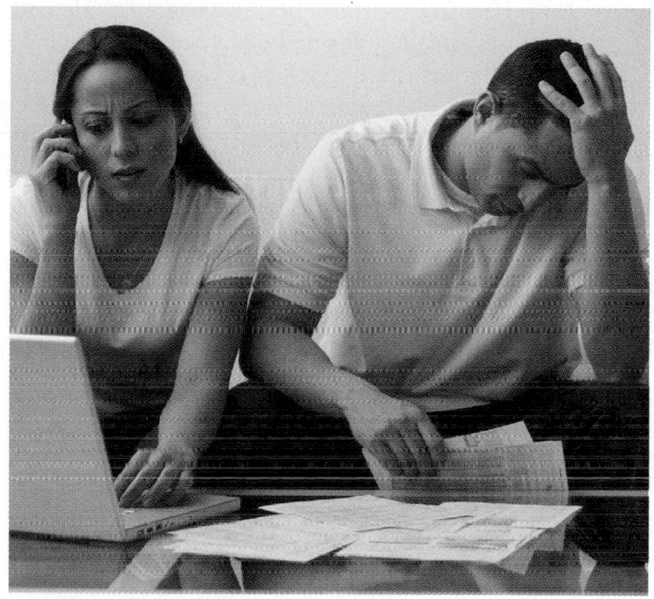

**Back in the 1970s, when inflation was** raging at a double-digit rate, economist Arthur M. Okun proposed what he called the "misery index." Misery, he suggested, could be measured as the sum of the inflation rate and the unemployment rate. At its peak, in 1980, the misery index hit 22. At its lowest, in 1953, the misery index was 3.

Inflation and unemployment make us miserable for good reasons. We care about inflation because it raises our cost of living. And we care about unemployment because either it hits us directly and takes our jobs or it scares us into thinking that we might lose our jobs.

We want rapid income growth, low unemployment, and low inflation. But can we have all these things at the same time? Or do we face a tradeoff among them? As this chapter explains, we face a tradeoff in the short run but not in the long run.

We use the *AS-AD* model that you studied in Chapter 10 to explain the patterns in inflation and output that occur in our economy. We also look at a related model, the Phillips curve, that illustrates the short-run tradeoff between inflation and unemployment. We then use the potential GDP model of Chapter 6 to explain how business cycle fluctuations can arise from the normal working of the economy and indepen-dently of fluctuations in cost-push forces or aggregate demand.

At the end of the chapter, in *Reading Between the Lines*, we examine the state of the economy in 2008 as the misery index returned to the news.

## Inflation Cycles

In the long run, inflation is a monetary phenomenon. It occurs if the quantity of money grows faster than potential GDP. But in the short run, many factors can start an inflation, and real GDP and the price level interact. To study these interactions, we distinguish between two sources of inflation:

- Demand-pull inflation
- Cost-push inflation

### Demand-Pull Inflation

An inflation that starts because aggregate demand increases is called **demand-pull inflation**. Demand-pull inflation can be kicked off by *any* of the factors that change aggregate demand. Examples are a cut in the interest rate, an increase in the quantity of money, an increase in government expenditure, a tax cut, an increase in exports, or an increase in investment stimulated by an increase in expected future profits.

**Initial Effect of an Increase in Aggregate Demand** Suppose that last year the price level was 115 and real GDP was $12 trillion. Potential GDP was also $12 trillion. Figure 12.1(a) illustrates this situation. The aggregate demand curve is $AD_0$, the short-run aggregate supply curve is $SAS_0$, and the long-run aggregate supply curve is *LAS*.

Now suppose that the Fed cuts the interest rate and increases the quantity of money and aggregate demand increases to $AD_1$. With no change in potential GDP and no change in the money wage rate, the long-run aggregate supply curve and the short-run aggregate supply curve remain at *LAS* and $SAS_0$, respectively.

The price level and real GDP are determined at the point where the aggregate demand curve $AD_1$ intersects the short-run aggregate supply curve. The price level rises to 118, and real GDP increases above potential GDP to $12.5 trillion. Unemployment falls below its natural rate. The economy is at an above full-employment equilibrium and there is an inflationary gap.The next step in the unfolding story is a rise in the money wage rate.

**FIGURE 12.1** A Demand-Pull Rise in the Price Level

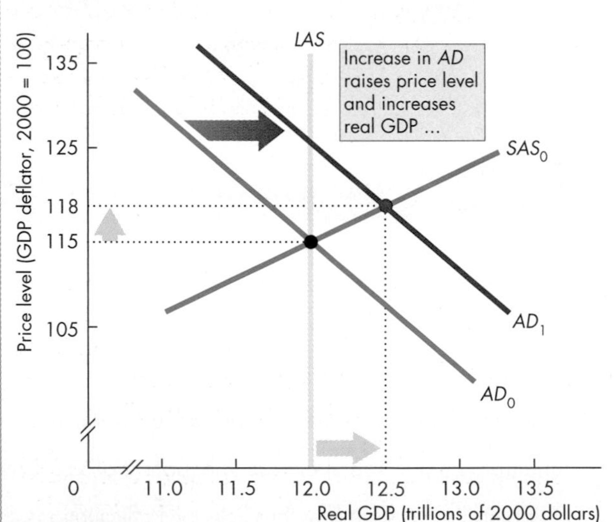


**(a) Initial effect**

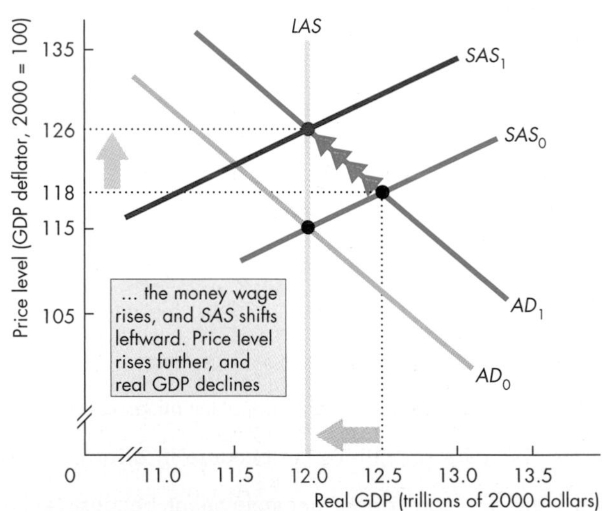


**(b) The money wage adjusts**

In part (a), the aggregate demand curve is $AD_0$, the short-run aggregate supply curve is $SAS_0$, and the long-run aggregate supply curve is *LAS*. The price level is 115, and real GDP is $12 trillion, which equals potential GDP. Aggregate demand increases to $AD_1$. The price level rises to 118, and real GDP increases to $12.5 trillion.

In part (b), starting from the above full-employment equilibrium, the money wage rate begins to rise and the short-run aggregate supply curve shifts leftward toward $SAS_1$. The price level rises further, and real GDP returns to potential GDP.

myeconlab animation

**Money Wage Rate Response** Real GDP cannot remain above potential GDP forever. With unemployment below its natural rate, there is a shortage of labor. In this situation, the money wage rate begins to rise. As it does so, short-run aggregate supply decreases and the *SAS* curve starts to shift leftward. The price level rises further, and real GDP begins to decrease.

With no further change in aggregate demand—that is, the aggregate demand curve remains at $AD_1$—this process ends when the short-run aggregate supply curve has shifted to $SAS_1$ in Fig. 12.1(b). At this time, the price level has increased to 126 and real GDP has returned to potential GDP of $12 trillion, the level at which it started.

**A Demand-Pull Inflation Process** The events that we've just described bring a *one-time rise in the price level,* not an inflation. For inflation to proceed, aggregate demand must *persistently* increase.

The only way in which aggregate demand can persistently increase is if the quantity of money persistently increases. Suppose the government has a budget deficit that it finances by selling bonds. Also suppose that the Fed buys some of these bonds. When the Fed buys bonds, it creates more money. In this situation, aggregate demand increases year after year. The aggregate demand curve keeps shifting rightward. This persistent increase in aggregate demand puts continual upward pressure on the price level. The economy now experiences demand-pull inflation.

Figure 12.2 illustrates the process of demand-pull inflation. The starting point is the same as that shown in Fig. 12.1. The aggregate demand curve is $AD_0$, the short-run aggregate supply curve is $SAS_0$, and the long-run aggregate supply curve is *LAS*. Real GDP is $12 trillion, and the price level is 115. Aggregate demand increases, shifting the aggregate demand curve to $AD_1$. Real GDP increases to $12.5 trillion, and the price level rises to 118. The economy is at an above full-employment equilibrium. There is a shortage of labor, and the money wage rate rises. The short-run aggregate supply curve shifts to $SAS_1$. The price level rises to 126, and real GDP returns to potential GDP.

But the Fed increases the quantity of money again, and aggregate demand continues to increase. The aggregate demand curve shifts rightward to $AD_2$. The price level rises further to 130, and real GDP again exceeds potential GDP at $12.5 trillion. Yet again,

**FIGURE 12.2** A Demand-Pull Inflation Spiral

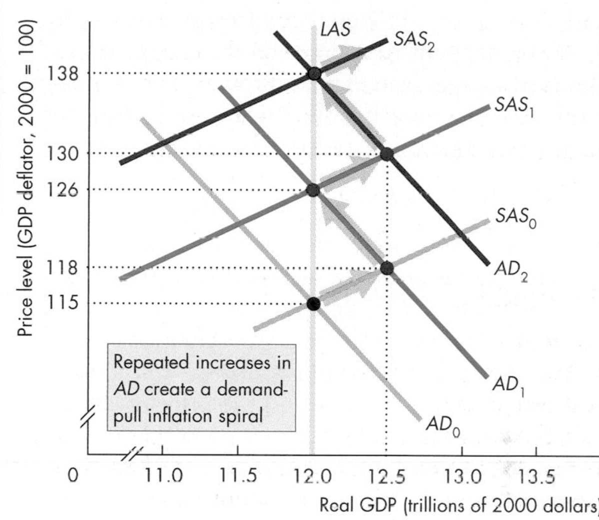


Each time the quantity of money increases, aggregate demand increases and the aggregate demand curve shifts rightward from $AD_0$ to $AD_1$ to $AD_2$, and so on. Each time real GDP increases above potential GDP, the money wage rate rises and the short-run aggregate supply curve shifts leftward from $SAS_0$ to $SAS_1$ to $SAS_2$, and so on. The price level rises from 115 to 118, 126, 130, 138, and so on. There is a demand-pull inflation spiral. Real GDP fluctuates between $12 trillion and $12.5 trillion.

myeconlab animation

the money wage rate rises and decreases short-run aggregate supply. The *SAS* curve shifts to $SAS_2$, and the price level rises further, to 138. As the quantity of money continues to grow, aggregate demand increases and the price level rises in an ongoing demand-pull inflation process.

The process you have just studied generates inflation—an ongoing process of a rising price level.

**Demand-Pull Inflation in Kalamazoo** You may better understand the inflation process that we've just described by considering what is going on in an individual part of the economy, such as a Kalamazoo soda-bottling plant. Initially, when aggregate demand increases, the demand for soda increases and the price of soda rises. Faced with a higher price, the soda plant works overtime and increases production. Conditions are good for workers in Kalamazoo, and the soda factory finds it hard to hang on to its best people. To do so, it offers a higher money wage rate. As the wage rate rises, so do the soda factory's costs.

What happens next depends on aggregate demand. If aggregate demand remains constant, the firm's costs increase but the price of soda does not increase as quickly as its costs. In this case, the firm cuts production. Eventually, the money wage rate and costs increase by the same percentage as the rise in the price of soda. In real terms, the soda factory is in the same situation as it was initially. It produces the same amount of soda and employs the same amount of labor as before the increase in demand.

But if aggregate demand continues to increase, so does the demand for soda and the price of soda rises at the same rate as wages. The soda factory continues to operate at above full employment and there is a persistent shortage of labor. Prices and wages chase each other upward in a demand-pull inflation spiral.

**Demand-Pull Inflation in the United States** A demand-pull inflation like the one you've just studied occurred in the United States during the late 1960s. In 1960, inflation was a moderate 2 percent a year, but its rate increased slowly to 3 percent by 1966. Then, in 1967, a large increase in government expenditure on the Vietnam War and an increase in spending on social programs, together with an increase in the growth rate of the quantity of money, increased aggregate demand more quickly. Consequently, the rightward shift of the aggregate demand curve accelerated and the price level increased more quickly. Real GDP moved above potential GDP, and the unemployment rate fell below its natural rate.

With unemployment below its natural rate, the money wage rate started to rise more quickly and the short-run aggregate supply curve shifted leftward. The Fed responded with a further increase in the money growth rate, and a demand-pull inflation spiral unfolded. By 1970, the inflation rate had reached 5 percent a year.

For the next few years, aggregate demand grew even more quickly and the inflation rate kept rising. By 1974, the inflation rate had reached 11 percent a year.

Next, let's see how shocks to aggregate supply can create cost-push inflation.

## Cost-Push Inflation

An inflation that is kicked off by an increase in costs is called **cost-push inflation**. The two main sources of cost increases are

1. An increase in the money wage rate
2. An increase in the money prices of raw materials

At a given price level, the higher the cost of production, the smaller is the amount that firms are willing to produce. So if the money wage rate rises or if the prices of raw materials (for example, oil) rise, firms decrease their supply of goods and services. Aggregate supply decreases, and the short-run aggregate supply curve shifts leftward.[1] Let's trace the effects of such a decrease in short-run aggregate supply on the price level and real GDP.

**Initial Effect of a Decrease in Aggregate Supply** Suppose that last year the price level was 115 and real GDP was $12 trillion. Potential real GDP was also $12 trillion. Figure 12.3(a) illustrates this situation. The aggregate demand curve was $AD_0$, the short-run aggregate supply curve was $SAS_0$, and the long-run aggregate supply curve was *LAS*. In the current year, the world's oil producers form a price-fixing organization that strengthens their market power and increases the relative price of oil. They raise the price of oil, and this action decreases short-run aggregate supply. The short-run aggregate supply curve shifts leftward to $SAS_1$. The price level rises to 122, and real GDP decreases to $11.5 trillion. The economy is at a below full-employment equilibrium and there is a recessionary gap.

This event is a *one-time rise in the price level*. It is not inflation. In fact, a supply shock on its own cannot cause inflation. Something more must happen to enable a one-time supply shock, which causes a one-time rise in the price level, to be converted into a process of ongoing inflation. The quantity of money must persistently increase. And it sometimes does increase, as you will now see.

[1] Some cost-push forces, such as an increase in the price of oil accompanied by a decrease in the availability of oil, can also decrease long-run aggregate supply. We'll ignore such effects here and examine cost-push factors that change only short-run aggregate supply. Later in the chapter, we study the effects of shocks to long-run aggregate supply.

FIGURE 12.3 A Cost-Push Rise in the Price Level

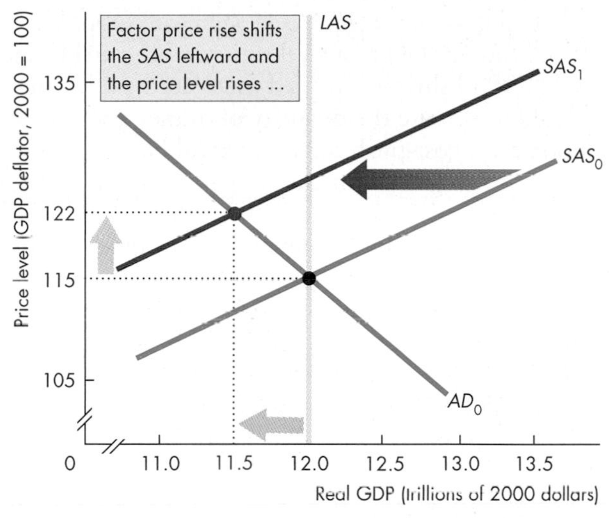


**(a) Initial cost push**

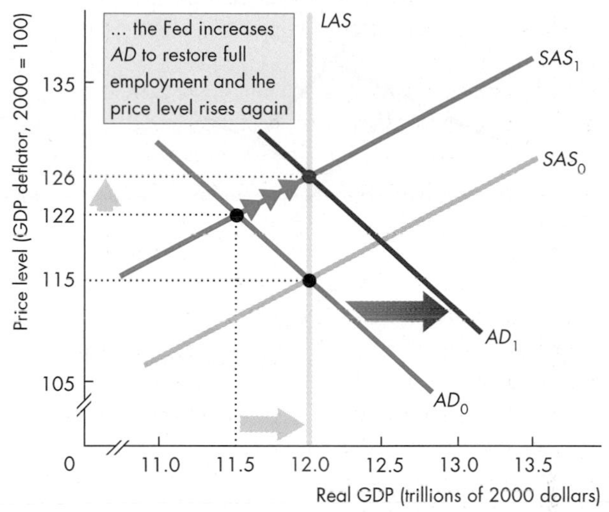


**(b) The Fed responds**

Initially, the aggregate demand curve is $AD_0$, the short-run aggregate supply curve is $SAS_0$, and the long-run aggregate supply curve is *LAS*. A decrease in aggregate supply (for example, resulting from a rise in the world price of oil) shifts the short-run aggregate supply curve to $SAS_1$. The economy moves to the point where the short-run aggregate supply curve $SAS_1$ intersects the aggregate demand curve $AD_0$. The price level rises to 122, and real GDP decreases to $11.5 trillion.

In part (b), if the Fed responds by increasing aggregate demand to restore full employment, the aggregate demand curve shifts rightward to $AD_1$. The economy returns to full employment, but the price level rises further to 126.

**Aggregate Demand Response** When real GDP decreases, unemployment rises above its natural rate. In such a situation, there is often an outcry of concern and a call for action to restore full employment. Suppose that the Fed cuts the interest rate and increases the quantity of money. Aggregate demand increases. In Fig. 12.3(b), the aggregate demand curve shifts rightward to $AD_1$ and full employment is restored. But the price level rises further to 126.

**A Cost-Push Inflation Process** The oil producers now see the prices of everything they buy increasing, so oil producers increase the price of oil again to restore its new high relative price. Figure 12.4 continues the story. The short-run aggregate supply curve now shifts to $SAS_2$. The price level rises and real GDP decreases.

The price level rises further, to 134, and real GDP decreases to $11.5 trillion. Unemployment increases above its natural rate. If the Fed responds yet again with an increase in the quantity of money, aggregate demand increases and the aggregate demand curve shifts to $AD_2$. The price level rises even higher—to 138—and full employment is again restored. A cost-push inflation spiral results. The combination of a rising price level and decreasing real GDP is called **stagflation.**

You can see that the Fed has a dilemma. If it does not respond when producers raises the oil price, the economy remains below full employment. If the Fed increases the quantity of money to restore full employment, it invites another oil price hike that will call forth yet a further increase in the quantity of money.

If the Fed responds to each oil price hike by increasing the quantity of money, inflation will rage along at a rate decided by oil producers. But if the Fed keeps the lid on money growth, the economy remains below full employment.

**FIGURE 12.4** A Cost-Push Inflation Spiral

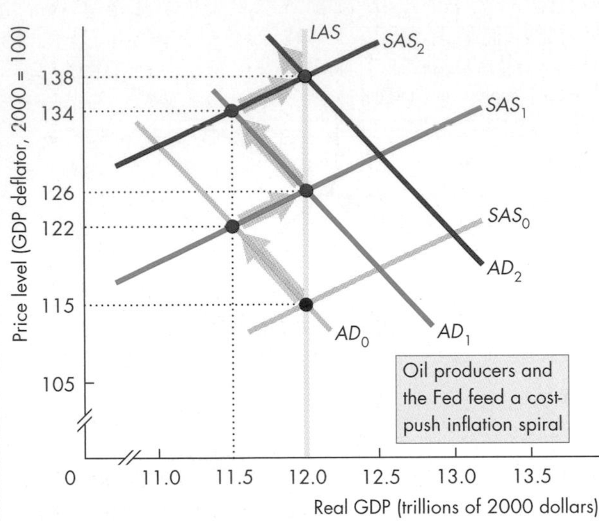


Each time a cost increase occurs, the short-run aggregate supply curve shifts leftward from $SAS_0$ to $SAS_1$ to $SAS_2$, and so on. Each time real GDP decreases below potential GDP, the Fed increases the quantity of money and the aggregate demand curve shifts rightward from $AD_0$ to $AD_1$ to $AD_2$, and so on. The price level rises from 115 to 122, 126, 134, 138, and so on. There is a cost-push inflation spiral. Real GDP fluctuates between \$12 trillion and \$11.5 trillion.

myeconlab animation

**Cost-Push Inflation in Kalamazoo** What is going on in the Kalamazoo soda-bottling plant when the economy is experiencing cost-push inflation?

When the oil price increases, so do the costs of bottling soda. These higher costs decrease the supply of soda, increasing its price and decreasing the quantity produced. The soda plant lays off some workers.

This situation persists until either the Fed increases aggregate demand or the price of oil falls. If the Fed increases aggregate demand, the demand for soda increases and so does its price. The higher price of soda brings higher profits, and the bottling plant increases its production. The soda factory rehires the laid-off workers.

**Cost-Push Inflation in the United States** A cost-push inflation like the one you've just studied occurred in the United States during the 1970s. It began in 1974 when the Organization of the Petroleum Exporting Countries (OPEC) raised the price of oil fourfold. The higher oil price decreased aggregate supply, which caused the price level to rise more quickly and real GDP to shrink. The Fed then faced a dilemma: Would it increase the quantity of money and accommodate the cost-push forces, or would it keep aggregate demand growth in check by limiting money growth? In 1975, 1976, and 1977, the Fed repeatedly allowed the quantity of money to grow quickly and inflation proceeded at a rapid rate. In 1979 and 1980, OPEC was again able to push oil prices higher. On that occasion, the Fed decided not to respond to the oil price hike with an increase in the quantity of money. The result was a recession but also, eventually, a fall in inflation.

## Expected Inflation

If inflation is expected, the fluctuations in real GDP that accompany demand-pull and cost-push inflation that you've just studied don't occur. Instead, inflation proceeds as it does in the long run, with real GDP equal to potential GDP and unemployment at its natural rate. Figure 12.5 explains why.

Suppose that last year the aggregate demand curve was $AD_0$, the aggregate supply curve was $SAS_0$, and the long-run aggregate supply curve was *LAS*. The price level was 115, and real GDP was \$12 trillion, which is also potential GDP.

To keep things as simple as possible, suppose that potential GDP does not change, so the *LAS* curve doesn't shift. Also suppose that aggregate demand is *expected to increase* to $AD_1$.

In anticipation of this increase in aggregate demand, the money wage rate rises and the short-run aggregate supply curve shifts leftward. If the money wage rate rises by the same percentage as the price level is expected to rise, the short-run aggregate supply curve for next year is $SAS_1$.

If aggregate demand turns out to be the same as expected, the aggregate demand curve is $AD_1$. The short-run aggregate supply curve, $SAS_1$, and $AD_1$ determine the actual price level at 126. Between last year and this year, the price level increased from 115 to 126 and the economy experienced an inflation rate equal to that expected. If this inflation is ongoing, aggregate demand increases (as expected) in the following year and the aggregate demand curve shifts to $AD_2$. The money wage rate rises to reflect the expected inflation, and the short-run aggregate sup-

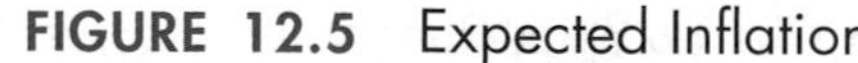

**FIGURE 12.5** Expected Inflation

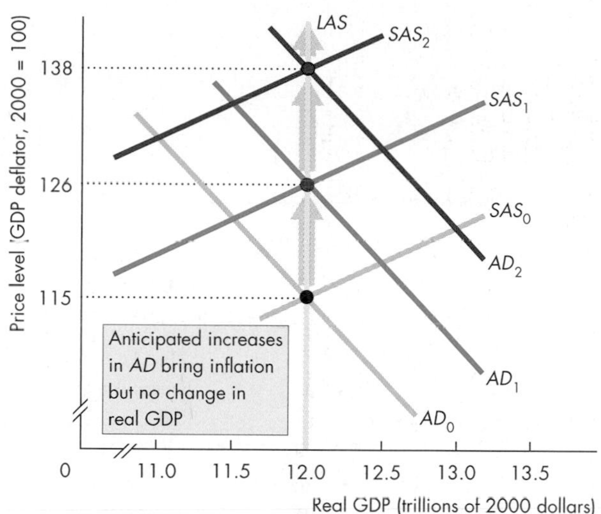


Potential real GDP is \$12 trillion. Last year, aggregate demand was $AD_0$ and the short-run aggregate supply curve was $SAS_0$. The actual price level was the same as the expected price level: 115. This year, aggregate demand is expected to increase to $AD_1$ and the price level is expected to rise from 115 to 126. As a result, the money wage rate rises and the short-run aggregate supply curve shifts to $SAS_1$. If aggregate demand actually increases as expected, the actual aggregate demand curve $AD_1$ is the same as the expected aggregate demand curve. Real GDP is \$12 trillion, and the actual price level rises to 126. The inflation is expected. Next year, the process continues with aggregate demand increasing as expected to $AD_2$ and the money wage rate rising to shift the short-run aggregate supply curve to $SAS_2$. Again, real GDP remains at \$12 trillion, and the price level rises, as expected, to 138.

myeconlab animation

ply curve shifts to $SAS_2$. The price level rises, as expected, to 138.

What caused this inflation? The immediate answer is that because people expected inflation, the money wage rate increased and the price level increased. But the expectation was correct. Aggregate demand was expected to increase, and it did increase. It is the actual and expected increase in aggregate demand that caused the inflation.

An expected inflation at full employment is exactly the process that the quantity theory of money predicts. To review the quantity theory of money, see Chapter 8, pp. 202–203.

This broader account of the inflation process and its short-run effects show why the quantity theory of money doesn't explain the *fluctuations* in inflation. The economy follows the course described in Fig. 12.5, and as predicted by the quantity theory, only if aggregate demand growth is forecasted correctly.

## Forecasting Inflation

To anticipate inflation, people must forecast it. Some economists who work for macroeconomic forecasting agencies, banks, insurance companies, labor unions, and large corporations specialize in inflation forecasting. The best forecast available is one that is based on all the relevant information and is called a **rational expectation**. A rational expectation is not necessarily a correct forecast. It is simply the best forecast with the information available. It will often turn out to be wrong, but no other forecast that could have been made with the information available could do better.

## Inflation and the Business Cycle

When the inflation forecast is correct, the economy operates at full employment. If aggregate demand grows faster than expected, real GDP rises above potential GDP, the inflation rate exceeds its expected rate, and the economy behaves like it does in a demand-pull inflation. If aggregate demand grows more slowly than expected, real GDP falls below potential GDP and the inflation rate slows.

## Review Quiz

1. How does demand-pull inflation begin?
2. What must happen to create a demand-pull inflation spiral?
3. How does cost-push inflation begin?
4. What must happen to create a cost-push inflation spiral?
5. What is stagflation and why does cost-push inflation cause stagflation?
6. How does expected inflation occur?
7. How do real GDP and the price level change if the forecast of inflation is incorrect?

myeconlab Work Study Plan 12.1 and get instant feedback.

## Inflation and Unemployment: The Phillips Curve

Another way of studying inflation cycles focuses on the relationship and the short-run tradeoff between inflation and unemployment, a relationship called the **Phillips curve**—so named because it was first suggested by New Zealand economist A.W. Phillips.

Why do we need another way of studying inflation? What is wrong with the *AS-AD* explanation of the fluctuations in inflation and real GDP? The first answer to both questions is that we often want to study changes in both the expected and actual inflation rates and for this purpose, the Phillips curve provides a simpler tool and clearer insights than the *AS-AD* model provides. The second answer to both questions is that we often want to study changes in the short-run tradeoff between inflation and real economic activity (real GDP and unemployment) and again, the Phillips curve serves this purpose well.

To begin our explanation of the Phillips curve, we distinguish between two time frames (similar to the two aggregate supply time frames). We study

- The short-run Phillips curve
- The long-run Phillips curve

### The Short-Run Phillips Curve

The **short-run Phillips curve** shows the relationship between inflation and unemployment, holding constant:

1. The expected inflation rate
2. The natural unemployment rate

You've just seen what determines the expected inflation rate. The natural unemployment rate and the factors that influence it are explained in Chapter 5, pp. 112–114.

Figure 12.6 shows a short-run Phillips curve, *SRPC*. Suppose that the expected inflation rate is 10 percent a year and the natural unemployment rate is 6 percent, point *A* in the figure. A short-run Phillips curve passes through this point. If inflation rises above its expected rate, unemployment falls below its natural rate. This joint movement in the inflation rate and the unemployment rate is illustrated as a movement up along the short-run Phillips curve from point *A* to point *B*. Similarly, if inflation falls below its expected rate, unemployment rises above its natural rate. In this case, there is movement down along the short-run Phillips curve from point *A* to point *C*.

The short-run Phillips curve is like the short-run aggregate supply curve. A movement along the *SAS* curve that brings a higher price level and an increase in real GDP is equivalent to a movement along the short-run Phillips curve from *A* to *B* that brings an increase in the inflation rate and a decrease in the unemployment rate.

Similarly, a movement along the *SAS* curve that brings a lower price level and a decrease in real GDP is equivalent to a movement along the short-run Phillips curve from *A* to *C* that brings a decrease in the inflation rate and an increase in the unemployment rate.

**FIGURE 12.6** A Short-Run Phillips Curve

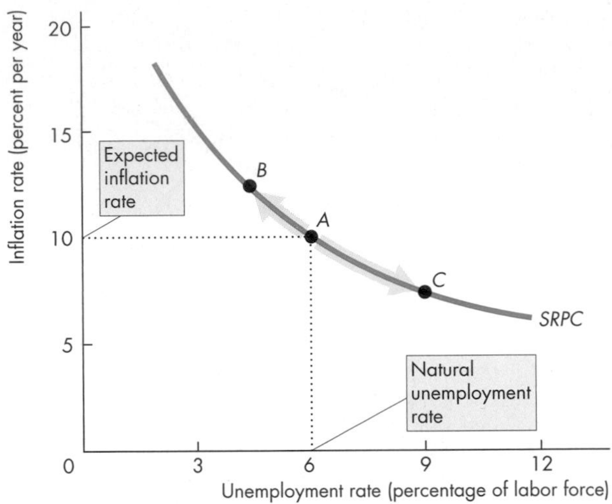


The short-run Phillips curve (*SRPC*) shows the relationship between inflation and unemployment at a given expected inflation rate and a given natural unemployment rate. With an expected inflation rate of 10 percent a year and a natural unemployment rate of 6 percent, the short-run Phillips curve passes through point *A*.

An unexpected increase in aggregate demand lowers unemployment and increases the inflation rate—a movement up along the short-run Phillips curve to point *B*. An unexpected decrease in aggregate demand increases unemployment and lowers the inflation rate—a movement down along the short-run Phillips curve to point *C*.

## The Long-Run Phillips Curve

The **long-run Phillips curve** shows the relationship between inflation and unemployment when the actual inflation rate equals the expected inflation rate. The long-run Phillips curve is vertical at the natural unemployment rate. In Fig. 12.7, it is the vertical line *LRPC*.

The long-run Phillips curve tells us that any expected inflation rate is possible at the natural unemployment rate. This proposition is consistent with the *AS-AD* model, which predicts (and which Fig. 12.5 illustrates) that when inflation is expected, real GDP equals potential GDP and unemployment is at its natural rate.

The short-run Phillips curve intersects the long-run Phillips curve at the expected inflation rate. A change in the expected inflation rate shifts the short-run Phillips curve but it does not shift the long-run Phillips curve.

In Fig. 12.7, if the expected inflation rate is 10 percent a year, the short-run Phillips curve is $SRPC_0$. If the expected inflation rate falls to 6 percent a year, the short-run Phillips curve shifts downward to $SRPC_1$. The vertical distance by which the short-run Phillips curve shifts from point *A* to point *D* is equal to the change in the expected inflation rate. If the actual inflation rate also falls from 10 percent to 6 percent, there is a movement down the long-run Phillips curve from *A* to *D*. An increase in the expected inflation rate has the opposite effect to that shown in Fig. 12.7.

The other source of a shift in the Phillips curve is a change in the natural unemployment rate.

## Changes in the Natural Unemployment Rate

The natural unemployment rate changes for many reasons (see Chapter 5, pp. 112–114). A change in the natural unemployment rate shifts both the short-run and long-run Phillips curves. Figure 12.8 illustrates such shifts.

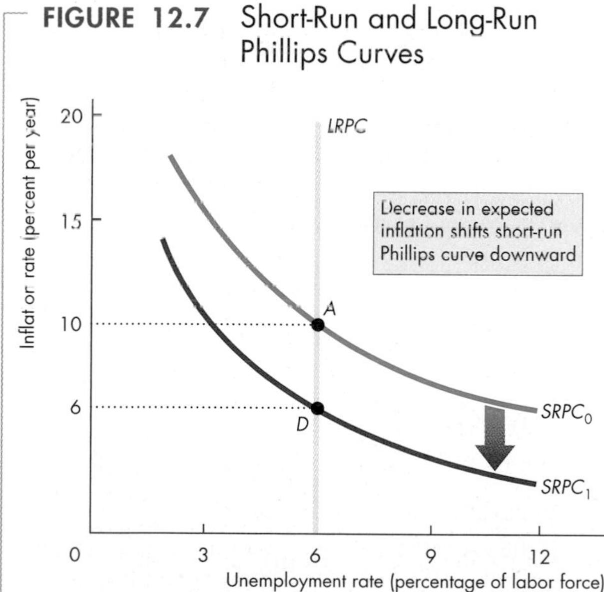


The long-run Phillips curve is *LRPC*. A fall in expected inflation from 10 percent a year to 6 percent a year shifts the short-run Phillips curve downward from $SRPC_0$ to $SRPC_1$. The long-run Phillips curve does not shift. The new short-run Phillips curve intersects the long-run Phillips curve at the new expected inflation rate—point *D*.

myeconlab animation

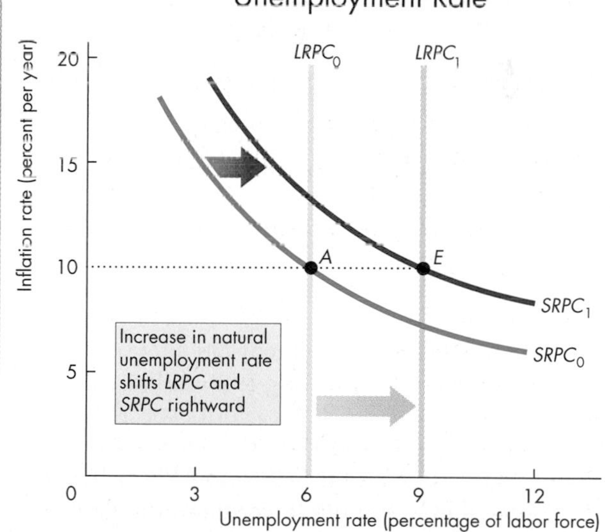


A change in the natural unemployment rate shifts both the short-run and long-run Phillips curves. An increase in the natural unemployment rate from 6 percent to 9 percent shifts the Phillips curves rightward to $SRPC_1$ and $LRPC_1$. The new long-run Phillips curve intersects the new short-run Phillips curve at the expected inflation rate—point *E*.

myeconlab animation

## The U.S. Phillips Curve

### The Shifting Short-Run Tradeoff

Figure 1 is a scatter diagram of the U.S. inflation rate (measured by the GDP deflator) and the unemployment rate since 1961. We can interpret the data in terms of the shifting short-run Phillips curve in Fig. 2.

During the 1960s, the short-run Phillips curve was $SRPC_0$, with a natural unemployment rate of 4.5 percent and an expected inflation rate of 2 percent a year (point *A*).

During the early 1970s, the short-run Phillips curve was $SRPC_1$, with a natural unemployment rate of 5 percent and an expected inflation rate of 6 percent a year (point *B*).

During the late 1970s, the natural unemployment rate increased to 8 percent (point *C*) and the short-run Phillips curve shifted to $SRPC_2$. Briefly in 1975 and again in 1981, the expected inflation rate surged to 9 percent a year (point *D*) and the short-run Phillips curve shifted to $SRPC_3$.

During the 1980s and 1990s, the expected inflation rate and the natural unemployment rate decreased and the short-run Phillips curve shifted leftward back to $SRPC_1$ and, by the mid-1990s, back to $SRPC_0$, where it remained into the 2000s.

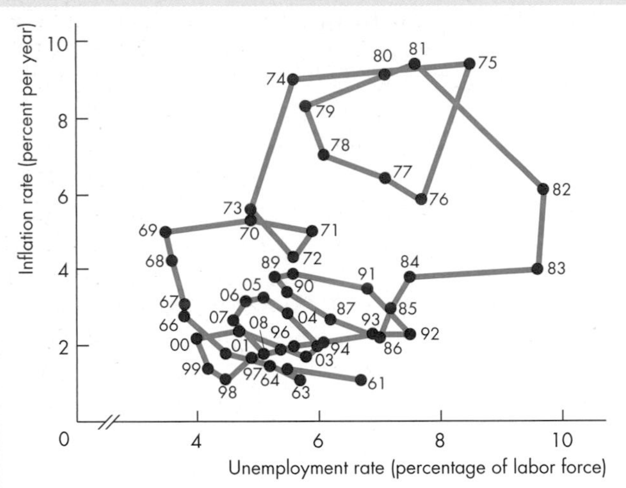


**Figure 1 Phillips Curve Data in the United States: The Time Sequence**

*Source of data*: Bureau of Labor Statistics.

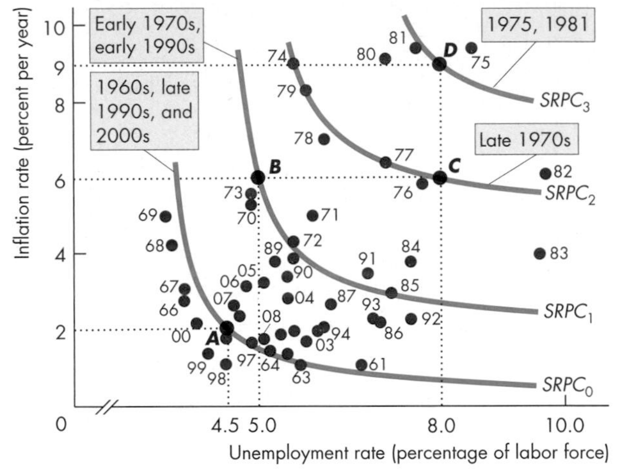


**Figure 2 The Shifting Phillips Curves**

If the natural unemployment rate increases from 6 percent to 9 percent, the long-run Phillips curve shifts from $LRPC_0$ to $LRPC_1$, and if expected inflation is constant at 10 percent a year, the short-run Phillips curve shifts from $SRPC_0$ to $SRPC_1$. Because the expected inflation rate is constant, the short-run Phillips curve $SRPC_1$ intersects the long-run curve $LRPC_1$ (point *E*) at the same inflation rate at which the short-run Phillips curve $SRPC_0$ intersects the long-run curve $LRPC_0$ (point *A*).

Changes in both the expected inflation rate and the natural unemployment rate have shifted the U.S. Phillips curve but the expected inflation rate has had the greater effect.

## Review Quiz

1. How would you use the Phillips curve to illustrate an unexpected change in inflation?
2. If the expected inflation rate increases by 10 percentage points, how do the short-run Phillips curve and the long-run Phillips curve change?
3. If the natural unemployment rate increases, what happens to the short-run Phillips curve and the long-run Phillips curve?
4. Does the United States have a stable short-run Phillips curve? Explain why or why not.

Work Study Plan 12.2 and get instant feedback.

## The Business Cycle

The business cycle is easy to describe but hard to explain and business cycle theory remains unsettled and a source of controversy. We'll look at two approaches to understanding the business cycle:

- Mainstream business cycle theory
- Real business cycle theory

### Mainstream Business Cycle Theory

The mainstream business cycle theory is that potential GDP grows at a steady rate while aggregate demand grows at a fluctuating rate. Because the money wage rate is sticky, if aggregate demand grows faster than potential GDP, real GDP moves above potential GDP and an inflationary gap emerges. And if aggregate demand grows slower than potential GDP, real GDP moves below potential GDP and a recessionary gap emerges. If aggregate demand decreases, real GDP also decreases in a recession.

Figure 12.9 illustrates this business cycle theory. Initially, actual and potential GDP are \$9 trillion. The long-run aggregate supply curve is $LAS_0$, the aggregate demand curve is $AD_0$, and the price level is 105. The economy is at full employment at point *A*.

An expansion occurs when potential GDP increases and the *LAS* curve shifts rightward to $LAS_1$. During an expansion, aggregate demand also increases, and usually by more than potential GDP, so the price level rises. Assume that in the current expansion, the price level is expected to rise to 115 and that the money wage rate has been set on that expectation. The short-run aggregate supply curve is $SAS_1$.

If aggregate demand increases to $AD_1$, real GDP increases to \$12 trillion, the new level of potential GDP, and the price level rises, as expected, to 115. The economy remains at full employment but now at point *B*.

If aggregate demand increases more slowly to $AD_2$, real GDP grows by less than potential GDP and the economy moves to point *C*, with real GDP at \$11.5 trillion and the price level at 112. Real GDP growth is slower and inflation is lower than expected.

If aggregate demand increases more quickly to $AD_3$, real GDP grows by more than potential GDP and the economy moves to point *D*, with real GDP at \$12.5 trillion and the price level at 118. Real GDP growth is faster and inflation is higher than expected.

Growth, inflation, and the business cycle arise from the relentless increases in potential GDP, faster (on average) increases in aggregate demand, and fluctuations in the pace of aggregate demand growth.

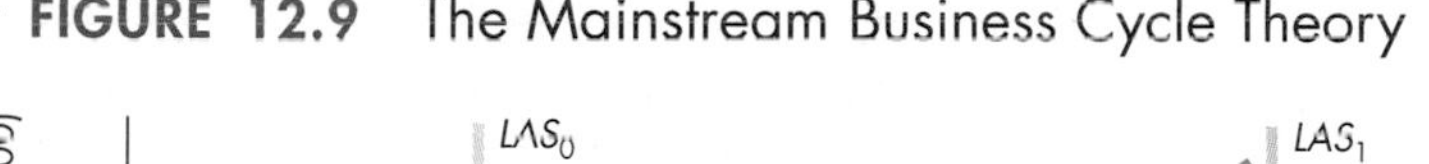

**FIGURE 12.9** The Mainstream Business Cycle Theory

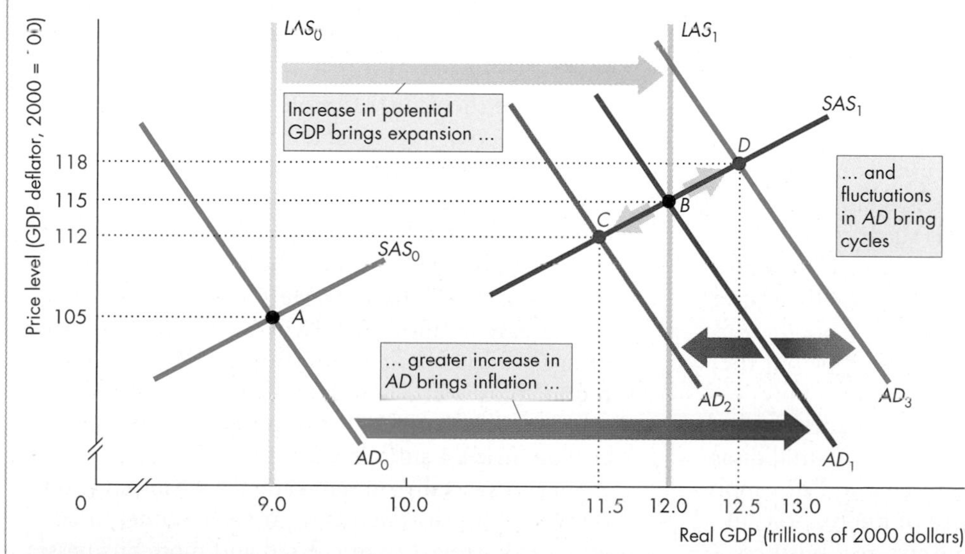


In a business cycle expansion, potential GDP increases and the *LAS* curve shifts rightward from $LAS_0$ to $LAS_1$. A greater than expected increase in aggregate demand brings inflation.

If the aggregate demand curve shifts to $AD_1$, the economy remains at full employment. If the aggregate demand curve shifts to $AD_2$, a recessionary gap arises. If the aggregate demand curve shifts to $AD_3$, an inflationary gap arises.

myeconlab animation

This mainstream theory comes in a number of special forms that differ regarding the source of fluctuations in aggregate demand growth and the source of money wage stickiness.

**Keynesian Cycle Theory** In **Keynesian cycle theory**, fluctuations in investment driven by fluctuations in business confidence—summarized by the phrase "animal spirits"—are the main source of fluctuations in aggregate demand.

**Monetarist Cycle Theory** In **monetarist cycle theory**, fluctuations in both investment and consumption expenditure, driven by fluctuations in the growth rate of the quantity of money, are the main source of fluctuations in aggregate demand.

Both the Keynesian and monetarist cycle theories simply assume that the money wage rate is rigid and don't explain that rigidity.

Two newer theories seek to explain money wage rate rigidity and to be more careful about working out its consequences.

**New Classical Cycle Theory** In **new classical cycle theory**, the rational expectation of the price level, which is determined by potential GDP and *expected* aggregate demand, determines the money wage rate and the position of the *SAS* curve. In this theory, only *unexpected* fluctuations in aggregate demand bring fluctuations in real GDP around potential GDP.

**New Keynesian Cycle Theory** The **new Keynesian cycle theory** emphasizes the fact that today's money wage rates were negotiated at many past dates, which means that *past* rational expectations of the current price level influence the money wage rate and the position of the *SAS* curve. In this theory, both unexpected and currently expected fluctuations in aggregate demand bring fluctuations in real GDP around potential GDP.

The mainstream cycle theories don't rule out the possibility that occasionally an aggregate supply shock might occur. An oil price rise, a widespread drought, a major hurricane, or another natural disaster, could, for example, bring a recession. But supply shocks are not the normal source of fluctuations in the mainstream theories. In contrast, real business cycle theory puts supply shocks at center stage.

## Real Business Cycle Theory

The newest theory of the business cycle, known as **real business cycle theory** (or RBC theory), regards random fluctuations in productivity as the main source of economic fluctuations. These productivity fluctuations are assumed to result mainly from fluctuations in the pace of technological change, but they might also have other sources, such as international disturbances, climate fluctuations, or natural disasters. The origins of RBC theory can be traced to the rational expectations revolution set off by Robert E. Lucas, Jr., but the first demonstrations of the power of this theory were given by Edward Prescott and Finn Kydland and by John Long and Charles Plosser. Today, RBC theory is part of a broad research agenda called dynamic general equilibrium analysis, and hundreds of young macroeconomists do research on this topic.

We'll explore RBC theory by looking first at its impulse and then at the mechanism that converts that impulse into a cycle in real GDP.

**The RBC Impulse** The impulse in RBC theory is the growth rate of productivity that results from technological change. RBC theorists believe this impulse to be generated mainly by the process of research and development that leads to the creation and use of new technologies.

To isolate the RBC theory impulse, economists use growth accounting, which is explained in Chapter 6, p. 146. Figure 12.10 shows the RBC impulse for the United States from 1962 through 2007. You can see that fluctuations in productivity growth are correlated with real GDP fluctuations.

Most of the time, technological change is steady and productivity grows at a moderate pace. But sometimes productivity growth speeds up, and occasionally productivity *decreases*—labor becomes less productive, on average. A period of rapid productivity growth brings a business cycle expansion, and a *decrease* in productivity triggers a recession.

It is easy to understand why technological change brings productivity growth. But how does it *decrease* productivity? All technological change eventually increases productivity. But if initially, technological change makes a sufficient amount of existing capital—especially human capital—obsolete, productivity temporarily decreases. At such a time, more jobs are destroyed than created and more businesses fail than start up.

**FIGURE 12.10** The Real Business Cycle Impulse

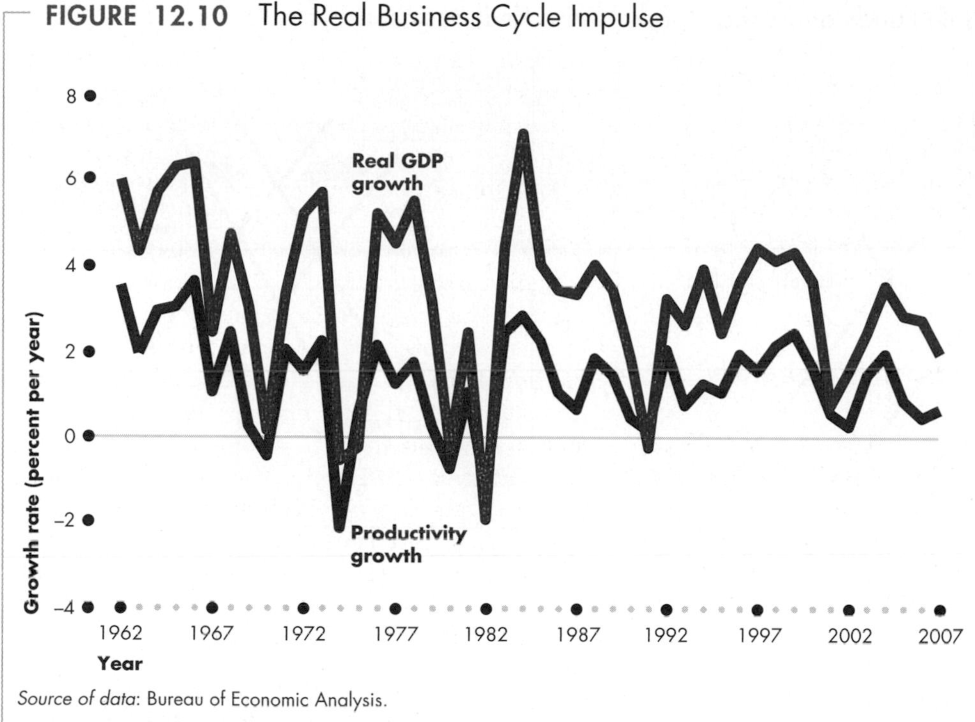


*Source of data*: Bureau of Economic Analysis.

The real business cycle is caused by changes in technology that bring fluctuations in the growth rate of productivity. The fluctuations in productivity growth shown here are calculated by using growth accounting (the one third rule) to remove the contribution of capital accumulation to productivity growth. Productivity fluctuations are correlated with real GDP fluctuations. Economists are not sure what the productivity variable actually measures or what causes it to fluctuate.

myeconlab animation

**The RBC Mechanism** Two effects follow from a change in productivity that gets an expansion or a contraction going:

1. Investment demand changes.
2. The demand for labor changes.

We'll study these effects and their consequences during a recession. In an expansion, they work in the direction opposite to what is described here.

Technological change makes some existing capital obsolete and temporarily decreases productivity. Firms expect the future profits to fall and see their labor productivity falling. With lower profit expectations, they cut back their purchases of new capital, and with lower labor productivity, they plan to lay off some workers. So the initial effect of a temporary fall in productivity is a decrease in investment demand and a decrease in the demand for labor.

Figure 12.11 illustrates these two initial effects of a decrease in productivity. Part (a) shows the effects of a decrease in investment demand in the loanable funds market. The demand for loanable funds is *DLF* and the supply of loanable funds is *SLF* (both of which are explained in Chapter 7, pp. 166–172). Initially, the demand for loanable funds is $DLF_0$ and the equilibrium quantity of funds is \$2 trillion at a real interest rate of 6 percent a year. A decrease in productivity decreases investment demand, and the demand for loanable funds curve *DLF* shifts leftward to $DLF_1$. The real interest rate falls to 4 percent a year, and the equilibrium quantity of loanable funds decreases to \$1.7 trillion.

Figure 12.11(b) shows the demand for labor curve *LD* and the supply of labor curve *LS* (which are explained in Chapter 6, pp. 139–140). Initially, the demand for labor curve is $LD_0$, and equilibrium employment is 200 billion hours a year at a real wage rate of \$35 an hour. The decrease in productivity decreases the demand for labor, and the *LD* curve shifts leftward to $LD_1$.

Before we can determine the new level of employment and real wage rate, we need to take a ripple effect into account—the key effect in RBC theory.

**The Key Decision: When to Work?** According to RBC theory, people decide *when* to work by doing a cost-benefit calculation. They compare the return

**FIGURE 12.11** Loanable Funds and Labor Markets in a Real Business Cycle

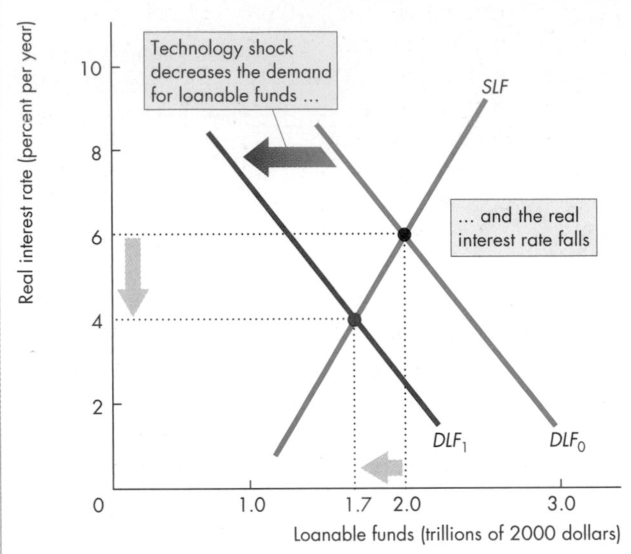


**(a) Loanable funds and interest rate**

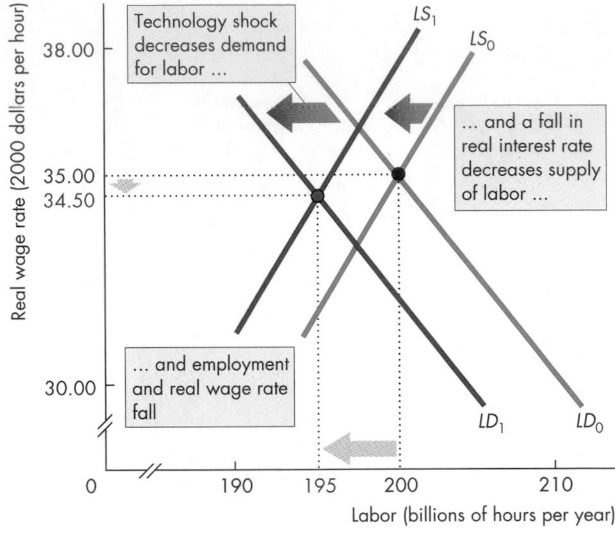


**(b) Labor and wage rate**

In part (a), the supply of loanable funds *SLF* and initial demand for loanable funds $DLF_0$ determine the real interest rate at 6 percent a year. In part (b), the initial demand for labor $LD_0$ and supply of labor, $LS_0$, determine the real wage rate at \$35 an hour and employment at 200 billion hours. A technological change temporarily decreases productivity, and both the demand for loanable funds and the demand for labor decrease. The two demand curves shift leftward to $DLF_1$ and $LD_1$. In part (a), the real interest rate falls to 4 percent a year. In part (b), the fall in the real interest rate decreases the supply of labor (the when-to-work decision) and the supply of labor curve shifts leftward to $LS_1$. Employment decreases to 195 billion hours, and the real wage rate falls to \$34.50 an hour. A recession is underway.

from working in the current period with the *expected* return from working in a later period. You make such a comparison every day in school. Suppose your goal in this course is to get an A. To achieve this goal, you work hard most of the time. But during the few days before the midterm and final exams, you work especially hard. Why? Because you believe that the return from studying close to the exam is greater than the return from studying when the exam is a long time away. So during the term, you take time off for the movies and other leisure pursuits, but at exam time, you study every evening and weekend.

RBC theory says that workers behave like you. They work fewer hours, sometimes zero hours, when the real wage rate is temporarily low, and they work more hours when the real wage rate is temporarily high. But to properly compare the current wage rate with the expected future wage rate, workers must use the real interest rate. If the real interest rate is 6 percent a year, a real wage of \$1 an hour earned this week will become \$1.06 a year from now. If the real wage rate is expected to be \$1.05 an hour next year, today's real wage of \$1 looks good. By working longer hours now and shorter hours a year from now, a person can get a 1 percent higher real wage. But suppose the real interest rate is 4 percent a year. In this case, \$1 earned now is worth \$1.04 next year. Working fewer hours now and more next year is the way to get a 1 percent higher real wage.

So the when-to-work decision depends on the real interest rate. The lower the real interest rate, other things remaining the same, the smaller is the supply of labor today. Many economists believe this *intertemporal substitution* effect to be of negligible size. RBC theorists believe that the effect is large, and it is the key feature of the RBC mechanism.

You saw in Fig. 12.11(a) that the decrease in the demand for loanable funds lowers the real interest rate. This fall in the real interest rate lowers the return to current work and decreases the supply of labor.

In Fig. 12.11(b), the labor supply curve shifts leftward to $LS_1$. The effect of the decrease in productivity on the demand for labor is larger than the effect of the fall in the real interest rate on the supply of labor. That is, the *LD* curve shifts farther leftward than does the *LS* curve. As a result, the real wage rate falls to $34.50 an hour and employment decreases to 195 billion hours. A recession has begun and is intensifying.

**What Happened to Money?** The name *real* business cycle theory is no accident. It reflects the central prediction of the theory. Real things, not nominal or monetary things, cause the business cycle. If the quantity of money changes, aggregate demand changes. But if there is no real change—with no change in the use of resources and no change in potential GDP—the change in the quantity of money changes only the price level. In RBC theory, this outcome occurs because the aggregate supply curve is the *LAS* curve, which pins real GDP down at potential GDP, so when aggregate demand changes, only the price level changes.

**Cycles and Growth** The shock that drives the business cycle of RBC theory is the same as the force that generates economic growth: technological change. On average, as technology advances, productivity grows. But it grows at an uneven pace. You saw this fact when you studied growth accounting in Chapter 6, p. 146. There, we focused on slow-changing trends in productivity growth. RBC theory uses the same idea but says that there are frequent shocks to productivity that are mostly positive but that are occasionally negative.

**Criticisms and Defenses of RBC Theory** The three main criticisms of RBC theory are that (1) the money wage rate *is* sticky, and to assume otherwise is at odds with a clear fact; (2) intertemporal substitution is too weak a force to account for large fluctuations in labor supply and employment with small real wage rate changes; and (3) productivity shocks are as likely to be caused by *changes in aggregate demand* as by technological change.

If aggregate demand fluctuations cause the fluctuations in productivity, then the traditional aggregate demand theories are needed to explain them. Fluctuations in productivity do not cause the business cycle but are caused by it!

Building on this theme, the critics point out that the so-called productivity fluctuations that growth accounting measures are correlated with changes in the growth rate of money and other indicators of changes in aggregate demand.

The defenders of RBC theory claim that the theory explains the macroeconomic facts about the business cycle and is consistent with the facts about economic growth. In effect, a single theory explains *both growth and the business cycle*. The growth accounting exercise that explains slowly changing trends also explains the more frequent business cycle swings. Its defenders also claim that RBC theory is consistent with a wide range of *micro*economic evidence about labor supply decisions, labor demand and investment demand decisions, and information on the distribution of income between labor and capital.

## Review Quiz

1 Explain the mainstream theory of the business cycle.
2 What are the four varieties of the mainstream theory of the business cycle and how do they differ?
3 According to RBC theory, what is the source of the business cycle? What is the role of fluctuations in the rate of technological change?
4 According to RBC theory, how does a fall in productivity growth influence investment demand, the market for loanable funds, the real interest rate, the demand for labor, the supply of labor, employment, and the real wage rate?
5 What are the main criticisms of RBC theory and how do its supporters defend it?

myeconlab Work Study Plan 12.3 and get instant feedback.

You can complete your study of economic fluctuations in *Reading Between the Lines* on pp. 314–315, which looks at the shifting inflation–unemployment tradeoff and misery index in the United States.

READING BETWEEN THE LINES 

# The Shifting Short-Run Inflation–Unemployment Tradeoff in 2008

## The Return of the Misery Index

http://www.nytimes.com
September 13, 2008

It has been almost three decades since the term "misery index" gained political currency, as President Jimmy Carter confronted the twin problems of rising inflation and unemployment. Now that almost-forgotten index is rising more rapidly than at any time since Mr. Carter's last year in office—1980.

The index is the sum of the unemployment rate and the inflation rate over the preceding 12 months. In normal times, the two indexes are likely to move in different directions, with inflation easing when unemployment rises, and climbing as the economy gets stronger and unemployment ebbs.

This year, however, both have been rising.

On Tuesday, the Labor Department will report on the inflation rate, as measured by the Consumer Price Index, for August. The consensus forecast of economists, according to Bloomberg News, is for a 5.6 percent rate. With the unemployment rate already reported at 6.1 percent, that would produce a misery index of 11.7 percent, up from July's figure of 11.2 percent.

That rate has been rising rapidly, and in July was up 4.2 percentage points from a year earlier. If the consensus forecast is accurate, the August year-over-year rise will be 5.1 percentage points.

Before the Bush administration, there were only three presidential terms in which the misery index rose at least 4 percentage points over a 12-month span. The first was in 1949–53, and the second in 1973-77. In each case, the incumbent party lost the following election.

The third was President Carter's term, from 1977 to 1981, when the combination of soaring oil prices and recession caused the misery index to peak at 21.9 percent. Ronald Reagan famously asked voters, "Are you better off than you were four years ago?" and defeated President Carter.



## Essence of the Story

- The misery index is the sum of the unemployment rate and the inflation rate.
- Normally inflation eases when unemployment rises but in 2008, both rose together to give a misery index of 11.2 percent in July and 11.7 percent in August.
- Only three previous presidential terms saw the misery index rise at least 4 percentage points over a 12-month span and in each case, the incumbent party lost the following election.

# Economic Analysis

- In the year to August 2008, the CPI inflation rate was 5.4 percent (a bit less than the forecast in the news article) and the unemployment rate was 6.1 percent. Combining these numbers generates a misery index of 11.5 percent.
- The news article compares the rise of 4 or more percentage points with earlier episodes of rising "misery."
- Figure 1 puts 2008 in a longer perspective.
- By the standards of the mid-1970s and early 1980s, 2008 was a time of low inflation and moderate unemployment.
- The peak value of the misery index occurred in mid-1980 when it reached 22 percent (the sum of an unemployment rate of 7.6 percent and an inflation rate of 14.4 percent a year).
- The misery index increases when the expected inflation rate rises, which shifts the short-run Phillips curve upward, and the natural unemployment rate rises, which shifts the short-run Phillips curve rightward.
- Figure 2 shows the short-run Phillips curves for four years: 1976, 1980, 2007, and 2008 ($SRPC_{76}$, $SRPC_{80}$, $SRPC_{07}$, and $SRPC_{08}$, respectively).
- In 1976, on the eve of Jimmy Carter's term as president, the economy was at point *A*. The unemployment rate was 7.5 percent and the inflation rate was 5.2 percent a year.
- By 1980, when Jimmy Carter left office (and lost the election to Ronald Reagan), the economy was at point *B*. The unemployment rate was 7.6 percent and the inflation rate had leapt to 14.4 percent a year.
- In August 2007, discussed in the news article, the economy was at point *C*. The unemployment rate was 4.7 percent and the inflation rate was 2.8 percent a year.
- By August 2008, the economy was at point *D*. The unemployment rate was 6.1 percent and the inflation rate was 5.4 percent a year.
- The rise in the inflation rate and the increase in the unemployment rate in the year to August 2008 increased the misery index by 4 percentage points, but the situation in 2008 was not nearly as "miserable" as 1976 through 1980.

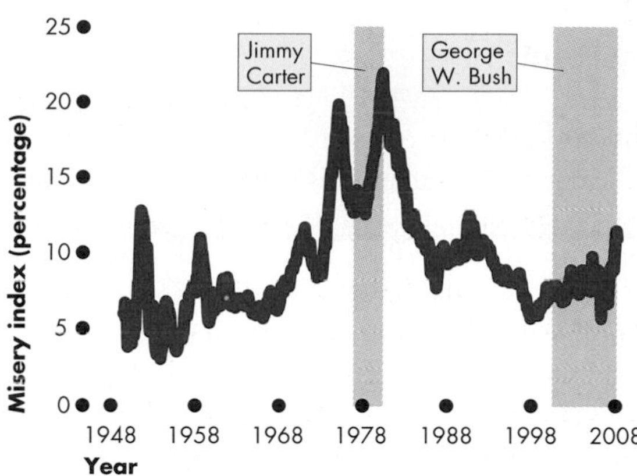


**Figure 1 The U.S. misery index**

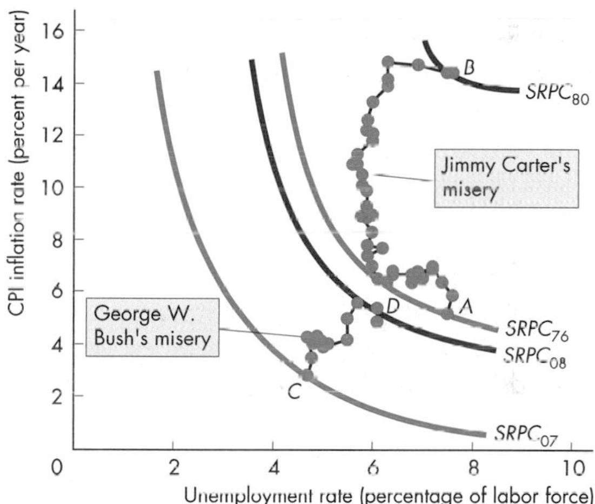


**Figure 2 The shifting Phillips curve**

## SUMMARY

### Key Points

#### Inflation Cycles (pp. 300 305)

- Demand-pull inflation is triggered by an increase in aggregate demand and fueled by ongoing money growth. Real GDP cycles above full employment.
- Cost-push inflation is triggered by an increase in the money wage rate or raw material prices and is fueled by ongoing money growth. Real GDP cycles below full employment in a stagflation.
- When the forecast of inflation is correct, real GDP remains at potential GDP.

#### Inflation and Unemployment: The Phillips Curve (pp. 306–308)

- The short-run Phillips curve shows the tradeoff between inflation and unemployment when the expected inflation rate and the natural unemployment rate are constant.
- The long-run Phillips curve, which is vertical, shows that when the actual inflation rate equals the expected inflation rate, the unemployment rate equals the natural unemployment rate.

#### The Business Cycle (pp. 309–313)

- The mainstream business cycle theory explains the business cycle as fluctuations of real GDP around potential GDP and as arising from a steady expansion of potential GDP combined with an expansion of aggregate demand at a fluctuating rate.
- Real business cycle theory explains the business cycle as fluctuations of potential GDP, which arise from fluctuations in the influence of technological change on productivity growth.

### Key Figures



### Key Terms

Cost-push inflation, 302
Demand-pull inflation, 300
Keynesian cycle theory, 310
Long-run Phillips curve, 307
Monetarist cycle theory, 310
New classical cycle theory, 310
New Keynesian cycle theory, 310
Phillips curve, 306
Rational expectation, 305
Real business cycle theory, 310
Short-run Phillips curve, 306
Stagflation, 303

## PROBLEMS and APPLICATIONS

Work problems 1–9 in Chapter 12 Study Plan and get instant feedback.
Work problems 10–17 as Homework, a Quiz, or a Test if assigned by your instructor.

1. The spreadsheet provides information about the economy in Argentina. Column A is the year, Column B is real GDP in billions of 2000 pesos, and Column C is the price level.

| | A | B | C |
|---|---|---|---|
| 1 | 1997 | 277 | 105.6 |
| 2 | 1998 | 288 | 103.8 |
| 3 | 1999 | 278 | 101.9 |
| 4 | 2000 | 276 | 102.9 |
| 5 | 2001 | 264 | 101.8 |
| 6 | 2002 | 235 | 132.9 |
| 7 | 2003 | 256 | 146.8 |
| 8 | 2004 | 279 | 160.4 |
| 9 | 2005 | 305 | 174.5 |
| 10 | 2006 | 331 | 198.0 |
| 11 | 2007 | 359 | 226.1 |
| 12 | 2008 | 384 | 267.7 |

   a. In which years did Argentina experience inflation? In which years did it experience deflation (a falling price level)?
   b. In which years did recessions occur? In which years did expansions occur?
   c. In which years do you expect the unemployment rate was highest? Why?
   d. Do these data show a relationship between unemployment and inflation in Argentina?

Use the following figure to answer problems 2, 3, 4, and 5. In each question the economy starts out on the curves $AD_0$ and $SAS_0$.

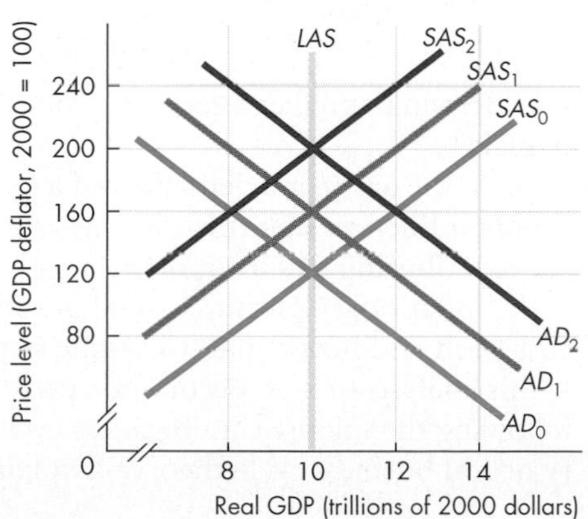


2. Some events occur and the economy experiences a demand-pull inflation.
   a. List the events that might cause a demand-pull inflation.
   b. Describe the initial effects of a demand-pull inflation.
   c. Describe what happens as a demand-pull inflation spiral proceeds.
3. Some events occur and the economy experiences a cost-push inflation.
   a. List the events that might cause a cost-push inflation.
   b. Describe the initial effects of a cost-push inflation.
   c. Describe what happens as a cost-push inflation spiral proceeds.
4. Some events occur and the economy is expected to experience inflation.
   a. List the events that might cause an expected inflation.
   b. Describe the initial effects of an expected inflation.
   c. Describe what happens as an expected inflation proceeds.
5. Suppose that people expect deflation (a falling price level), but aggregate demand remains at $AD_0$.
   a. What happens to the short-run and long-run aggregate supply curves? (Draw some new curves if you need to.)
   b. Describe the initial effects of an expected deflation.
   c. Describe what happens as it becomes obvious to everyone that the expected deflation is not going to occur.
6. **The Right Way to Beat Chinese Inflation**

   High inflation is threatening social stability in China, soaring from 3.3 percent in March 2007 to 8.3 percent in March 2008. … China's accelerating inflation reflects a similar climb in its GDP growth rate, from the already high 11 percent in 2006 to 11.5 percent in 2007. The proximate cause of price growth since mid-2007 is the appearance of production bottlenecks as domestic demand exceeds supply in an increasing number of sectors, such as power generation, transportation, and intermediate-goods industries. … [T]he prolonged rapid increase in Chinese aggregate demand has been fueled by an investment boom, as well as a growing trade surplus. …

Brookings Institution, July 2, 2008

a. Is China experiencing demand-pull or cost-push inflation? Explain.
b. Draw a graph to illustrate the initial rise in the price level and the money wage rate response to a one-time rise in the price level.
c. Draw a graph to illustrate and explain how China might experience an inflation spiral.

7. **Recession? Maybe. Depression? Get Real.**

The unemployment rate skyrocketed during the Depression, peaking at nearly 25 percent in 1933. The current unemployment rate is just 5 percent. And that's only up from 4.5 percent a year ago. Contrast that with the far more explosive spike at the beginning of the Great Depression—from about 3 percent in 1929 to nearly 8.7 percent in 1930. … Another hallmark of the Depression was deflation, which is obviously not happening today. …

*CNN*, May 28, 2008

a. Has the U.S. economy experienced inflation or deflation during recent recessions? Explain.
b. Can the inflation and unemployment trends during the Great Depression be explained by a movement along a short-run Phillips curve?
c. Can the inflation and unemployment trends during 2008 be explained by a movement along a short-run Phillips curve?

8. **Tight Money Won't Slay Food, Energy Inflation**

… It's important to differentiate between a general increase in prices—a situation in which the cumulative demand for goods and services exceeds their aggregate supply—and a relative price shock. … Take higher energy prices. … A specific price shock can become generalized if producers are able to pass on the higher costs. So far, global competition has made that difficult for companies, while higher input costs have largely been neutralized by rising labor productivity and corporate efficiencies. Since 2003, core inflation, which excludes food and energy, has averaged less than 2 percent a year in the 30 [industrial countries]. … History also suggests the Fed's gamble that slowing growth will shackle core inflation is a winning wager. The risk is that if U.S. consumers don't believe price increases will slow, growing inflation expectations may become self-fulfilling.

*Bloomberg*, May 9, 2008

a. Explain the two types of inflation that are described in this article.
b. Explain why "rising labor productivity" can neutralize the effect on inflation of "higher input costs."
c. Explain how "slowing growth" can reduce inflationary pressure.
d. Draw a graph to illustrate and explain how "growing inflation expectations may become self-fulfilling."

9. **Economists See Growth Remaining Feeble**

The economy's growth slowed sharply in the final quarter of 2007 and remained stuck in a rut in the first quarter of this year. … Federal Reserve Chairman Ben Bernanke … warned that over the rest of this year, the economy will grow "appreciably below its trend rate" mostly because of continued weakness in housing markets, high energy prices and tight credit conditions. Normal activity would be along the lines of a 2.5 percent to 3 percent growth rate for the economy. Not only is the country slogging through lethargic growth, but it is also confronted by rising prices that threaten to spread inflation. … [Businesses are] paying more for raw materials, such as fuel and steel. … Those higher prices are squeezing profit margins and leading some firms … to boost their prices. … Grappling with fallout from housing and credit troubles and stung by high costs for energy and other raw materials, employers have cut jobs in each of the first six months of this year.

*CNN*, July 21, 2008

a. Did Bernanke predict a recession for 2008? Explain.
b. Explain the aggregate demand and aggregate supply influences identified in this article that are contributing to slow growth.
c. Is the inflationary pressure a demand-pull or a cost-push and how could it become a spiral?
d. Is this analysis of macroeconomic performance following the mainstream business cycle theory or real business cycle theory? Explain.

10. The Reserve Bank of New Zealand signed an agreement with the New Zealand government in which the Bank agreed to maintain inflation inside a low target range. Failure to achieve the target would result in the governor of the Bank (the equivalent of the chairman of the Fed) losing his job.
    a. Explain how this arrangement might have influenced New Zealand's short-run Phillips curve.
    b. Explain how this arrangement might have influenced New Zealand's long-run Phillips curve.
11. An economy has an unemployment rate of 4 percent and an inflation rate of 5 percent a year at point *A* in the figure.

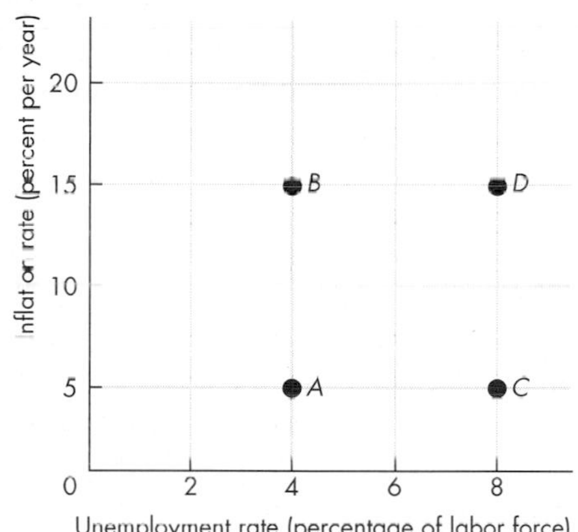


Some events occur that move the economy in a clockwise loop from *A* to *B* to *D* to *C* and back to *A*.
    a. Describe the events that could create this sequence.
    b. Draw in the figure the sequence of the economy's short-run and long-run Phillips curves.
    c. Has the economy experienced demand-pull inflation, cost-push inflation, expected inflation, or none of these?
12. Suppose that the business cycle in the United States is best described by RBC theory. An advance in technology increases productivity.
    a. Draw a diagram to show the effect of the advance in technology in the market for loanable funds.
    b. Draw a diagram to show the effect of the advance in technology in the labor market.
    c. Explain the when-to-work decision when technology advances.
13. **Fed Pause Promises Financial Disaster**

    The indication is that inflationary expectations have become entrenched and strongly footed in world markets. … With inflationary expectations becoming strongly entrenched, the risk of global stagflation has become significant. A drawn-out inflationary process always precedes stagflation, anathema to the so-called Phillips Curve. Following the attritional effect of inflation, the economy starts to grow below its potential. It experiences a persistent output gap, rising unemployment, and increasingly entrenched inflationary expectations.

    *Asia Times Online*, May 20, 2008
    a. Evaluate the claim that stagflation is anathema to the Phillips Curve.
    b. Evaluate the claim made in this article that if "inflationary expectations" become "strongly entrenched" an economy will experience "a persistent output gap."
14. **Bernanke Sees No Repeat of '70s-Style Inflation**

    "We see little indication today of the beginnings of a 1970s style wage-price spiral, in which wages and prices chased each other ever upward," [Federal Reserve Chairman Ben] Bernanke said. … Then, as now, the U.S. endured a serious oil price shock, sharply rising prices for food and other commodities and subpar economic growth, he said. Today's economy, however, is more flexible in responding to difficulties and the country is more energy efficient than a generation ago, Bernanke said. "Since 1975, the energy required to produce a given amount of output in the United States has fallen by half," he said. … The Fed is paying attention to the extent to which consumers, investors, and businesses believe prices will rise in the future. Monitoring those "inflation expectations" is important. If people believe inflation will keep going up, they will change their behavior in ways that aggravate inflation—thus, a self-fulfilling prophecy. … In the 1970s, people were demanding—and getting—higher wages in anticipation of rapidly rising prices; hence, the "wage-price" spiral Bernanke cited. The inflation rate has averaged about 3.5 percent over the past four quarters. That is "significantly higher" than the Fed would like but much less than the double-digit inflation rates of the mid-1970s and 1980, Bernanke said.

    *USA Today*, June 4, 2008

a. Draw a graph to illustrate and explain the inflation spiral that the U.S. experienced in the 1970s.
b. Explain the role that inflation expectations play in creating a self-fulfilling prophecy.
c. Explain Bernanke's predictions about the impact of the current oil price shock as compared to the '70s.

15. **Stagflation Is Back. Here's How to Beat It**

Three decades ago, in a bleak stretch of the 1970s, an economic phenomenon emerged that was as ugly as its name: stagflation. … It created an existential crisis for the global economy, leading many to argue that the world had reached its limits of growth and prosperity. … Fortunately, there is a better way forward than we took after 1974. We need to adopt coherent national and global technology policies to address critical needs in energy, food, water, and climate change. … There is certainly no shortage of promising ideas, merely a lack of federal commitment to support their timely development, demonstration, and diffusion. Solar power … high-mileage automobiles (like plug-in hybrids with advanced batteries), green buildings, carbon capture, cellulose-based ethanol, safe nuclear power, and countless other technologies on the horizon can reconcile a world of growing energy demands with increasingly scarce fossil fuels and rising threats of human-made climate change. As for food supplies, new drought-resistant crop varieties have the potential to bolster global food security in the face of an already changing climate. New irrigation technologies can help impoverished farmers move from one subsistence crop to several high-value crops year round. Yet as promising as these alternatives are, we have not been investing enough to bring them to fruition. …

*Fortune*, May 28, 2008

Does this analysis of macroeconomic performance reflect the mainstream business cycle theory or real business cycle theory? Explain.

16. **Real Wages Fail to Match a Rise in Productivity**

For most of the last century, wages and productivity—the key measure of the economy's efficiency—have risen together, increasing rapidly through the 1950s and '60s and far more slowly in the 1970s and '80s. But in recent years, the productivity gains have continued while the pay increases have not kept up.

*The New York Times*, August 28, 2006

Explain the relationship between wages and productivity in this news article in terms of real business cycle theory.

17. Study the account of the U.S. misery index in *Reading Between the Lines* on pp. 314–315, then answer the following questions.
    a. What are the main features of U.S. inflation and unemployment since 1948 that brought fluctuations in the misery index?
    b. When the misery index was at its peak in 1980, did inflation or unemployment contribute most to the high index?
    c. Do you think the U.S. economy had a recessionary gap or an inflationary gap or no gap in 1980? How might you be able to tell?
    d. Use the *AS-AD* model to show the changes in aggregate demand and aggregate supply that are consistent with the rise of the misery index in 1980.
    e. Use the *AS-AD* model to show the changes in aggregate demand and aggregate supply that are consistent with the rise of the misery index in 2008.
18. Use the links on MyEconLab (Textbook Resources, Chapter 12, Weblinks) to find data on recent changes in and forecasts of real GDP and the price level in the United States.
    a. What is your forecast of next year's real GDP?
    b. What is your forecast of next year's price level?
    c. What is your forecast of the inflation rate?
    d. What is your forecast of the growth rate of real GDP?
    e. Do you think there will be a recessionary gap or an inflationary gap next year?

PART FOUR

# UNDERSTANDING MACROECONOMIC FLUCTUATIONS

## Boom and Bust

To cure a disease, doctors must first understand how the disease responds to different treatments. It helps to understand the mechanisms that operate to cause the disease, but sometimes, a workable cure can be found even before the full story of the causes has been told.

Curing economic ills is similar to curing our medical ills. We need to understand how the economy responds to the treatments we might prescribe for it. And sometimes, we want to try a cure even though we don't fully understand the reasons for the problem we're trying to control.

You've seen how the pace of capital accumulation and technological change determine the long-term growth trend. You've learned how fluctuations around the long-term trend can be generated by changes in aggregate demand and aggregate supply. And you've learned about the key sources of fluctuations in aggregate demand and aggregate supply.

The *AS-AD* model explains the forces that determine real GDP and the price level in the short run. The model also enables us to see the big picture or grand vision of the different schools of macroeconomic thought concerning the sources of aggregate fluctuations. The Keynesian aggregate expenditure model provides an account of the factors that determine aggregate demand and make it fluctuate.

An alternative real business cycle theory puts all the emphasis on fluctuations in long-run aggregate supply. According to this theory, money changes aggregate demand and the price level but leaves the real economy untouched. The events of 2008 and 2009 will provide a powerful test of this theory.

**John Maynard Keynes,** *born in England in 1883, was one of the outstanding minds of the twentieth century. He represented Britain at the Versailles peace conference at the end of World War I, was a master speculator on international financial markets (an activity he conducted from bed every morning and which made and lost him several fortunes), and played a prominent role in creating the International Monetary Fund.*

*He was a member of the Bloomsbury Group, a circle of outstanding artists and writers that included E. M. Forster, Bertrand Russell, and Virginia Woolf.*

*Keynes was a controversial and quick-witted figure. A critic once complained that Keynes had changed his opinion on some matter, to which Keynes retorted: "When I discover I am wrong, I change my mind. What do you do?"*

*Keynes' book,* The General Theory of Employment, Interest and Money, *written during the Great Depression and published in 1936, revolutionanized macroeconomics.*

"The ideas of economists and political philosophers, both when they are right and when they are wrong, are more powerful than is commonly understood. Indeed the world is ruled by little else."

**JOHN MAYNARD KEYNES**
*The General Theory of Employment, Interest and Money*

# TALKING WITH

# Ricardo J. Caballero

**Ricardo J. Caballero** is Ford Professor of International Economics at MIT. He has received many honors, the most notable of which are the Frisch Medal of the Econometric Society (2002) and being named Chile's Economist of the Year (2001). A highly regarded teacher, he is much sought as a special lecturer and in 2005 gave the prestigious Yrjo Jahnsson Lecture at the University of Helsinki.

Professor Caballero earned his B.S. degree in 1982 and M.A. in 1983 at Pontificia Universidad Católica de Chile. He then moved to the United States and obtained his Ph.D. at MIT in 1988.

Michael Parkin talked with Ricardo Caballero about his work and the progress that economists have made in understanding economic fluctuations.

*Professor Caballero, why did you decide to become an economist?*

Did I decide? I'm convinced that one is either born an economist or not. I began studying business, but as soon as I took the first course in economics, I was captivated by the simple but elegant logic of (good) economic reasoning. Given the complexity of the real world, economic analysis is necessarily abstract. But at the same time, economics is mostly about concrete and important issues that affect the lives of millions of people. Abstraction and relevance—this is a wonderful but strange combination. Not everybody feels comfortable with it, but if you do, economics is for you.

*Most of your work has been on business cycles and other high-frequency phenomena. Can we begin by reviewing the costs of recessions? Robert Lucas says that postwar U.S. recessions have cost very little. Do you agree?*

No . . . but I'm not sure Robert Lucas was really trying to say that. My sense is that he was trying to push the profession to focus a bit more on long-run growth issues. Putting down the costs of recessions was a useful debating device to make his important point.

I believe that the statement that recessions are not costly is incorrect. First, I think his calculation of this magnitude reflects some fundamental flaw in the way the workhorse models we use in economics fail to account for the costs of risk and volatility. This flaw shows up in many different puzzles in economics, including the well-known equity premium puzzle. Economic models underestimate, by an order of magnitude, how unhappy agents are about facing uncertainty. Second, it is highly unlikely that recessions and medium-term growth are completely separable. In particular, the ongoing process of restructuring, which is central to productivity growth, is severely hampered by deep recessions.

Recessions are costly because they waste enormous resources, affect physical and human investment decisions, have large negative distributional consequences, influence political outcomes, and so on.

*What about the costs of recessions in other parts of the world, especially Latin America?*

The cost of recessions grows exponentially with their

size and the country's inability to soften the impact on the most affected. Less developed economies suffer much larger shocks because their economies are not well diversified, and they experience capital outflows that exacerbate the impact of recessionary shocks. Their domestic financial sectors are small and often become strained during recessions, making it difficult to reallocate scarce resources toward those who need them the most. To make matters worse, the government's ability to use fiscal policy becomes impaired by the capital outflows, and monetary policy is also out of the question when the currency is in free fall and liabilities are dollarized. There are many things that we take for granted in the United States that simply are not feasible for emerging markets in distress. One has to be careful with extrapolating too directly the countercyclical recipes used for developed economies to these countries.

> Recessions are costly because they waste enormous resources [and] affect physical and human investment decisions.

*Your first work, in your M.A. dissertation, was to build a macroeconomic model of the economy of Chile. What do we learn by comparing economies? Does the Chilean economy behave essentially like the U.S. economy or are there fundamental differences?*

Chile is a special economy among emerging markets. It began pro-market reforms many years before the rest and has had very prudent macroeconomic management for several decades by now. For that reason, it is a bit more "like the U.S. economy" than most other emerging market economies. However, there are still important differences, of the sort described in my answer to the previous question.

Beyond the specifics of Chile, at some deep level, macroeconomic principles, and economic principles more generally, are the same everywhere. It is all about incentives, tradeoffs, effort, commitment, discipline, transparency, insurance, and so on. But different economies hurt in different places, and hence the practice of economics has plenty of diversity.

*During the most recent U.S. expansion, some asset prices—especially house prices—have looked as if they might be experiencing a speculative bubble, and you've done some recent work on bubbles. How can we tell whether we're seeing a bubble or just a rapid increase that is being driven by fundamental market forces?*

First things first. I think we need to get used to the presence of speculative bubbles. The reason is that the world today has a massive shortage of financial assets that savers can use to store value. Because of this shortage, "artificial" assets are ready to emerge at all times. Specific bubbles come and go—from the NASDAQ, to real estate, to commodities—but the total is much more stable.

I do not think the distinction between bubbles and fundamentals is as clear-cut as people describe. Probably outside periods of liquidity crises, all assets have some bubble component in them. The question is how much.

*You've studied situations in which capital suddenly stops flowing into an economy from abroad. What are the lessons you've learned from this research?*

The most basic lesson for emerging markets is that capital flows are volatile. Sometimes they simply magnify domestic problems, but in many other cases, they are the direct source of volatility. However, the conclusion from this observation is not that capital flows should be limited, just as we do not close the banks in the United States to eliminate the possibility of bank runs. On the contrary, much of the volatility comes from insufficient integration with international capital markets, which makes emerging markets illiquid and the target of specialists and speculators. For the short and medium run, the main policy lesson is that sudden stops to the inflow of capital must be put at the center of macroeconomic policy design in emerging markets. This has deep implications for the design of monetary and fiscal policy, as well as for international reserves

> The most basic lesson for emerging markets is that capital flows are volatile.

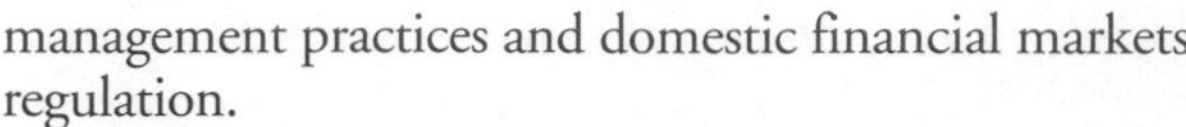

management practices and domestic financial markets regulation.

*The U.S. current account deficit has been large and increasing for many years, and dollar debt levels around the world have increased. Do you see any danger in this process for either the United States or the rest of the world?*

I believe the persistent current account deficits in the United States are not the result of an anomaly that, as such, must go away in a sudden crash, as the conventional view has it. Instead, my view is that these deficits are just the counterpart of large capital inflows resulting from the global shortage of financial assets that I mentioned earlier. Good growth potential in the United States over that of Europe and Japan and the much better quality of its financial assets over those of emerging Asian and oil-producing countries make the United States very attractive to international private and public investors.

. . . Good growth potential in the United States over that of Europe and Japan and the much better quality of its financial assets over those of emerging Asian and oil-producing countries make the United States very attractive to international private and public investors.

Absent major shocks, this process may still last for quite some time. But of course shocks do happen, and in that sense, leverage is dangerous. However, there isn't much we can or should do, short of implementing structural reforms around the world aimed at improving growth potential in some cases and domestic financial development in others.

*What advice do you have for someone who is just beginning to study economics but who wants to become an economist? If they are not in the United States, should they come here for graduate work as you did?*

There is no other place in the world like the United States to pursue a Ph.D. and do research in economics. However, this is only the last stage in the process of becoming an economist. There are many superb economists, especially applied ones, all around the world.

I believe the most important step is to learn to think like an economist. I heard Milton Friedman say that he knows many economists who have never gone through a Ph.D. program, and equally many who have completed their Ph.D. but are not really economists. I agree with him on this one. A good undergraduate program and talking about economics is a great first step. Almost everything in life has an economic angle to it—look for it and discuss it with your friends. It will not improve your social life, but it will make you a better economist.

Almost everything in life has an economic angle to it—look for it . . .

# 13 Fiscal Policy

**After studying this chapter, you will be able to:**

- Describe the federal budget process and the recent history of outlays, tax revenues, deficits, and debt
- Explain the supply-side effects of fiscal policy
- Explain how fiscal policy choices redistribute benefits and costs across generations
- Explain how fiscal policy is used to stabilize the business cycle

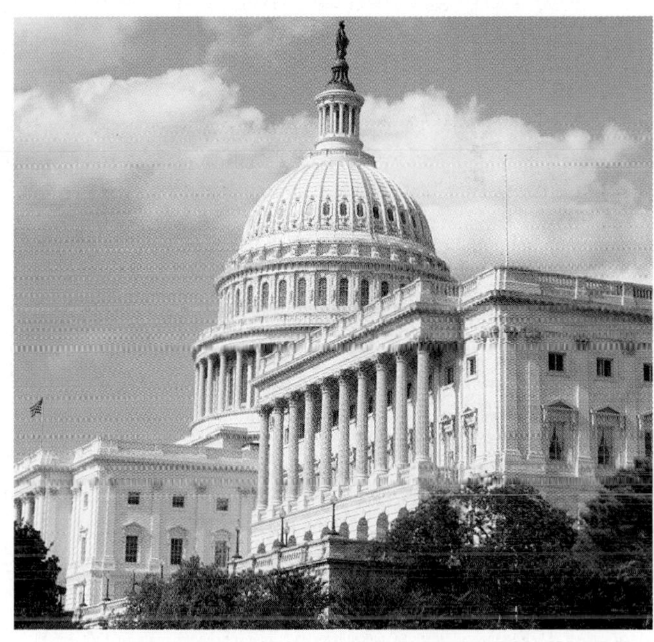

**In 2009, the federal government planned to collect** taxes of 20 cents on every dollar Americans earned and spend 23 cents of every dollar that Americans earned. So the government planned a deficit of 3 cents on every dollar earned—a total deficit of $393 billion. Federal government deficits are not new. Aside from the four years 1998–2001, the government's budget has been in deficit every year since 1970. Deficits bring debts, and your share of the federal government's debt is around $30,000.

What are the effects of taxes on the economy? Do they harm employment and production?

Does it matter if the government doesn't balance its books? What are the effects of an ongoing government deficit and accumulating debt? Do they slow economic growth? Do they impose a burden on future generations—on you and your children?

What are the effects of government spending on the economy? Does a dollar spent by the government on goods and services have the same effect as a dollar spent by someone else? Does it create jobs, or does it destroy them?

These are the fiscal policy issues that you will study in this chapter. In *Reading Between the Lines* at the end of the chapter, we look at fiscal policy actions that the new president-elect Obama outlined in his first post-election news conference in November 2008.

## The Federal Budget

The annual statement of the outlays and tax revenues of the government of the United States together with the laws and regulations that approve and support those outlays and tax revenues make up the **federal budget**. The federal budget has two purposes:

1. To finance the activities of the federal government
2. To achieve macroeconomic objectives

The first purpose of the federal budget was its only purpose before the Great Depression of the 1930s. The second purpose arose as a reaction to the Great Depression. The use of the federal budget to achieve macroeconomic objectives such as full employment, sustained economic growth, and price level stability is called **fiscal policy**. In this chapter, we focus on this second purpose—U.S. fiscal policy.

### The Institutions and Laws

Fiscal policy is made by the president and Congress on an annual timeline that is shown in Fig. 13.1 for the 2009 budget.

**The Roles of the President and Congress** The president *proposes* a budget to Congress each February. Congress debates the proposed budget and passes the budget acts in September. The president either signs those acts into law or vetoes the *entire* budget bill. The president does not have the veto power to eliminate specific items in a budget bill and approve others—known as a *line-item veto*. Many state governors have long had line-item veto authority. Congress attempted to grant these powers to the president of the United States in 1996, but in a 1998 Supreme Court ruling, the line-item veto for the president was declared unconstitutional. Although the president proposes and ultimately approves the budget, the task of making the tough decisions on spending and taxes rests with Congress.

Congress begins its work on the budget with the president's proposal. The House of Representatives and the Senate develop their own budget ideas in their respective House and Senate Budget Committees. Formal conferences between the two houses eventually resolve differences of view, and a series of spending acts and an overall budget act are usually passed by both houses before the start of the fiscal year. A *fiscal year* is a year that runs from October 1 to September 30 in the next calendar year. *Fiscal* 2009 is the fiscal year that *begins* on October 1, 2008.

**FIGURE 13.1 The Federal Budget Timeline in Fiscal 2009**

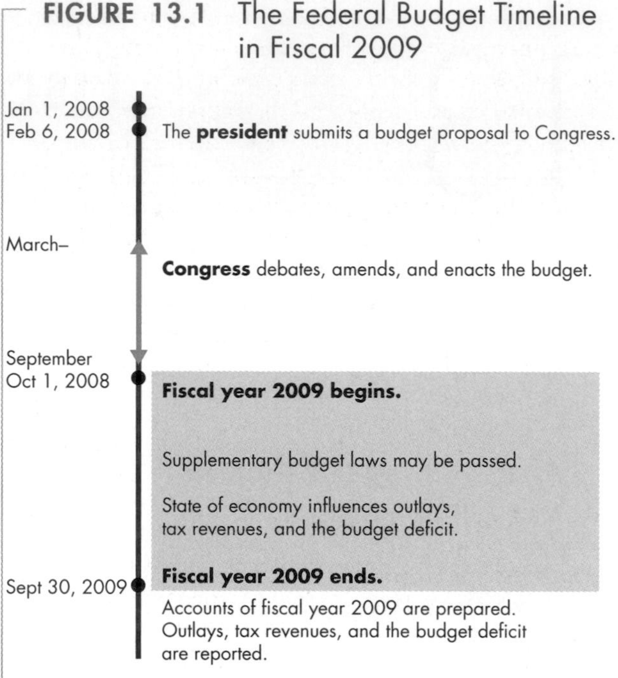

Jan 1, 2008
Feb 6, 2008
The **president** submits a budget proposal to Congress.
March–
**Congress** debates, amends, and enacts the budget.
September
Oct 1, 2008
**Fiscal year 2009 begins.**
Supplementary budget laws may be passed.
State of economy influences outlays, tax revenues, and the budget deficit.
Sept 30, 2009
**Fiscal year 2009 ends.**
Accounts of fiscal year 2009 are prepared. Outlays, tax revenues, and the budget deficit are reported.

The federal budget process begins with the president's proposals in February. Congress debates and amends these proposals and enacts a budget before the start of the fiscal year on October 1. The president signs the budget acts into law or vetoes the entire budget bill. Throughout the fiscal year, Congress might pass supplementary budget laws. The budget outcome is calculated after the end of the fiscal year.

myeconlab animation

During a fiscal year, Congress often passes supplementary budget laws, and the budget outcome is influenced by the evolving state of the economy. For example, if a recession begins, tax revenues fall and welfare payments increase.

**The Employment Act of 1946** Fiscal policy operates within the framework of the landmark **Employment Act of 1946** in which Congress declared that

> . . . it is the continuing policy and responsibility of the Federal Government to use all practicable means . . . to coordinate and utilize all its plans, functions, and resources . . . to promote maximum employment, production, and purchasing power.

This act recognized a role for government actions to keep unemployment low, the economy expanding, and inflation in check. The *Full Employment and Balanced Growth Act of 1978*, more commonly known as the *Humphrey-Hawkins Act*, went farther than the Employment Act of 1946 and set a specific target of 4 percent for the unemployment rate. But this target has never been treated as an unwavering policy goal. Under the 1946 act, the president must describe the current economic situation and the policies he believes are needed in the annual *Economic Report of the President*, which the Council of Economic Advisers writes.

**The Council of Economic Advisers** The president's Council of Economic Advisers was established in the Employment Act of 1946. The Council consists of a chairperson and two other members, all of whom are economists on a one- or two-year leave from their regular university or public service jobs. In 2006, the chair of President Bush's Council of Economic Advisers was Edward P. Lazear of Stanford University. The **Council of Economic Advisers** monitors the economy and keeps the President and the public well informed about the current state of the economy and the best available forecasts of where it is heading. This economic intelligence activity is one source of data that informs the budget making process.

Let's look at the most recent federal budget.

## Highlights of the 2009 Budget

Table 13.1 shows the main items in the federal budget proposed by President Bush for 2009. The numbers are projected amounts for the fiscal year beginning on October 1, 2008—fiscal 2009. Notice the three main parts of the table: *Tax revenues* are the government's receipts, *outlays* are the government's payments, and the *deficit* is the amount by which the government's outlays exceed its tax revenues.

**Tax Revenues** Tax revenues were projected to be $2,805 billion in fiscal 2009. These revenues come from four sources:

1. Personal income taxes
2. Social Security taxes
3. Corporate income taxes
4. Indirect taxes

The largest source of revenue is *personal income taxes*, which in 2009 are expected to be $1,234 billion. These taxes are paid by individuals on their incomes. The second largest source is *Social Security taxes*. These taxes are paid by workers and their employers to finance the government's Social Security programs. Third in size are *corporate income taxes*. These taxes are paid by companies on their profits. Finally, the smallest source of federal revenue is what are called *indirect taxes*. These taxes are on the sale of gasoline, alcoholic beverages, and a few other items.

**Outlays** Outlays are classified into three categories:

1. Transfer payments
2. Expenditure on goods and services
3. Debt interest

The largest item of outlays, *transfer payments*, are payments to individuals, businesses, other levels of government, and the rest of the world. In 2009, this item is expected to be $1,855 billion. It includes Social Security benefits, Medicare and Medicaid, unemployment checks, welfare payments, farm subsidies, grants to state and local governments, aid to developing countries, and dues to international organizations such as the United Nations. Transfer

**TABLE 13.1** Federal Budget in Fiscal 2009

| Item | Projections (billions of dollars) | |
|---|---|---|
| **Tax Revenues** | **2,805** | |
| Personal income taxes | | 1,234 |
| Social security taxes | | 1,033 |
| Corporate income taxes | | 352 |
| Indirect taxes | | 186 |
| **Outlays** | **3,198** | |
| Transfer payments | | 1,854 |
| Expenditure on goods and services | | 1,006 |
| Debt interest | | 338 |
| **Deficit** | **393** | |

*Source of data: Budget of the United States Government, Fiscal Year 2009*, Table 14.1.

payments, especially those for Medicare and Medicaid, are sources of persistent growth in government expenditures and are a major source of concern and political debate.

*Expenditure on goods and services* is the expenditure on final goods and services, and in 2009, it is expected to total $1,006 billion. This expenditure, which includes that on national defense, homeland security, research on cures for AIDS, computers for the Internal Revenue Service, government cars and trucks, federal highways, and dams, has decreased in recent years. This component of the federal budget is the *government expenditure on goods and services* that appears in the circular flow of expenditure and income and in the National Income and Product Accounts (see Chapter 4, pp. 87–88).

*Debt interest* is the interest on the government debt. In 2009, this item is expected to be $338 billion—about 10 percent of total expenditure. This interest payment is large because the government has a debt of more than $4.4 trillion, which has arisen from many years of budget deficits during the 1970s, 1980s, 1990s, and 2000s.

**Surplus or Deficit** The government's budget balance is equal to tax revenues minus outlays.

Budget balance = Tax revenues – Outlays.

If tax revenues exceed outlays, the government has a **budget surplus**. If outlays exceed tax revenues, the government has a **budget deficit**. If tax revenues equal outlays, the government has a **balanced budget**. For fiscal 2009, with projected outlays of $3,198 billion and tax revenues of $2,805 billion, the government projected a budget deficit of $393 billion.

Big numbers like these are hard to visualize and hard to compare over time. To get a better sense of the magnitude of tax revenues, outlays, and the deficit, we often express them as percentages of GDP. Expressing them in this way lets us see how large government is relative to the size of the economy and also helps us to study *changes* in the scale of government over time.

How typical is the federal budget of 2009? Let's look at the recent history of the budget.

## The Budget in Historical Perspective

Figure 13.2 shows the government's tax revenues, outlays, and budget surplus or deficit since 1980. Through 1997, there was a budget deficit. The federal government began running a deficit in 1970, and the 1983 deficit shown in the figure was the highest on record at 5.2 percent of GDP. The deficit declined through 1989 but climbed again during the 1990–1991 recession. During the 1990s expansion,

**FIGURE 13.2** The Budget Surplus and Deficit

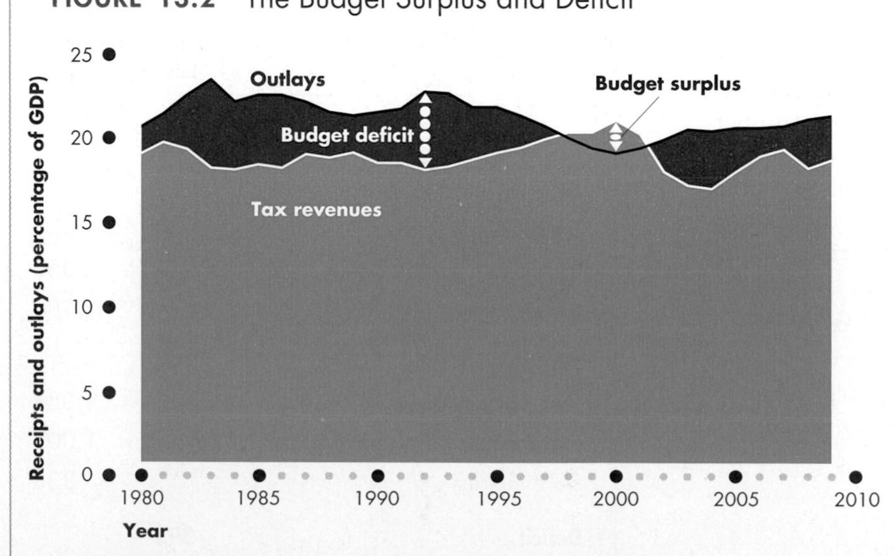


The figure records the federal government's outlays, tax revenues, and budget balance from 1980 to 2009. During the 1980s, a large and persistent budget deficit arose from the combination of falling tax revenues and rising outlays. In 1998, rising tax revenues and falling outlays (as percentages of GDP) created a budget surplus, but a deficit emerged again in 2002 as expenditure on security increased and taxes were cut.

*Source of data: Budget of the United States Government, Fiscal Year 2009,* Table 14.2.

myeconlab animation

the deficit gradually shrank, and in 1998, the first budget surplus since 1969 emerged. But by 2002, the budget was again in deficit.

Why did the budget deficit grow during the 1980s and vanish in the late 1990s? The answer lies in the changes in outlays and tax revenues. But which components of outlays and tax revenues changed to swell and then shrink the deficit? Let's look at tax revenues and outlays in a bit more detail.

**Tax Revenues** Figure 13.3(a) shows the components of tax revenues as percentages of GDP from 1980 to 2009. Cuts in corporate and personal income taxes lowered total tax revenues between 1983 and 1986. The decline resulted from tax cuts that had been passed during 1981. From 1986 through 1991, tax revenues did not change much as a percentage of GDP. Personal income tax payments increased through the 1990s but fell after 2000.

**FIGURE 13.3** Federal Government Tax Revenues and Outlays

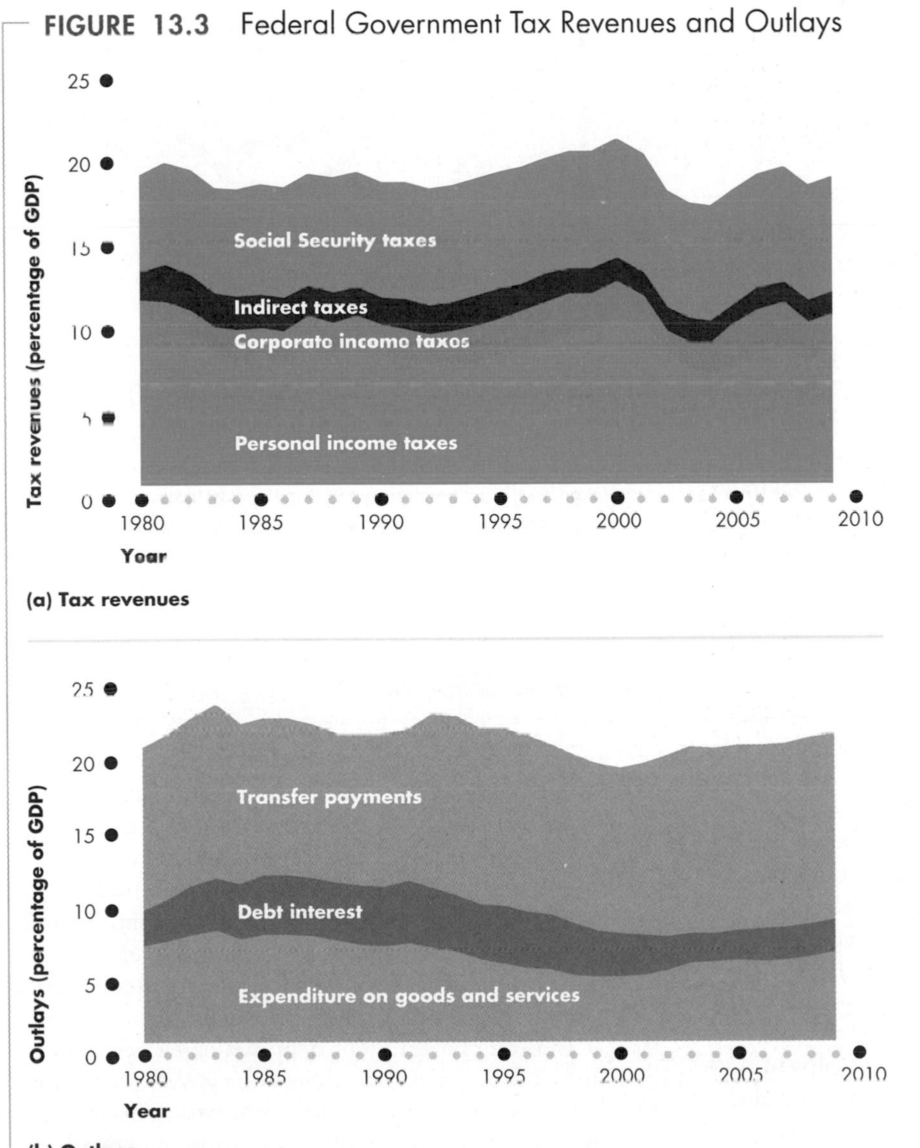


In part (a), revenues from personal and corporate income taxes as a percentage of GDP were approximately constant during the 1980s, increased during the 1990s, and decreased sharply from 2000 to 2004 but then increased again. The other components of tax revenues remained steady.

In part (b), expenditure on goods and services as a percentage of GDP decreased through 2001 but then increased because expenditure on security-related goods and services increased sharply after 2001. Transfer payments increased over the entire period. Debt interest held steady during the 1980s and decreased during the 1990s and 2000s, helped by a shrinking budget deficit during the 1990s and low interest rates during 2002 and 2003.

*Source of data: Budget of the United States Government, Fiscal Year 2009* Table 14.2.

myeconlab animation

**Outlays** Figure 13.3(b) shows the components of government outlays as percentages of GDP from 1980 to 2009. Total outlays decreased slightly through 1989, increased during the early 1990s, decreased steadily until 2000, and then increased again. Expenditure on goods and services decreased through 2001. It increased when expenditure on security-related goods and services increased sharply in 2002 in the wake of the attacks that occurred on September 11, 2001. Transfer payments increased over the entire period. Debt interest was a constant percentage of GDP during the 1980s and fell slightly during the late 1990s and 2000s. To understand the role of debt interest, we need to see the connection between the government's budget balance and debt.

**Budget Balance and Debt** The government borrows when it has a budget deficit and makes repayments when it has a budget surplus. **Government debt** is the total amount that the government has borrowed. It is the sum of past budget deficits minus the sum of past budget surpluses. A government budget deficit increases government debt. A persistent budget deficit feeds itself: The budget deficit leads to increased borrowing; increased borrowing leads to larger interest payments; and larger interest payments lead to a larger deficit. That is the story of the increasing budget deficit during the 1970s and 1980s.

Figure 13.4 shows two measures of government debt since 1940. Gross debt includes the amounts that the government owes to future generations in Social Security payments. Net debt is the debt held by the public, and it excludes social security obligations.

Government debt (as a percentage of GDP) was at an all-time high at the end of World War II. Budget surpluses and rapid economic growth lowered the debt-to-GDP ratio through 1974. Small budget deficits increased the debt-to-GDP ratio slightly through the 1970s, and large budget deficits increased it dramatically during the 1980s and the 1990–1991 recession. The growth rate of the debt-to-GDP ratio slowed as the economy expanded during the mid-1990s, fell when the budget went into surplus in the late 1990s and early 2000s, and began to rise again as the budget turned in to a deficit.

**Debt and Capital** Businesses and individuals incur debts to buy capital—assets that yield a return. In fact, the main point of debt is to enable people to buy assets that will earn a return that exceeds the interest paid on the debt. The government is similar to individuals and businesses in this regard. Much government expenditure is on public assets that yield a return. Highways, major irrigation schemes, public schools and universities, public libraries, and the stock of national defense capital all yield a social rate of return that probably far exceeds the interest rate the government pays on its debt.

But total government debt, which exceeds $4 trillion, is four times the value of the government's capital stock. So some government debt has been incurred to finance public consumption expenditure and transfer payments, which do not have a social return. Future generations bear the cost of this debt.

How does the U.S. government budget balance compare with those in other countries?

**FIGURE 13.4** The Federal Government Debt

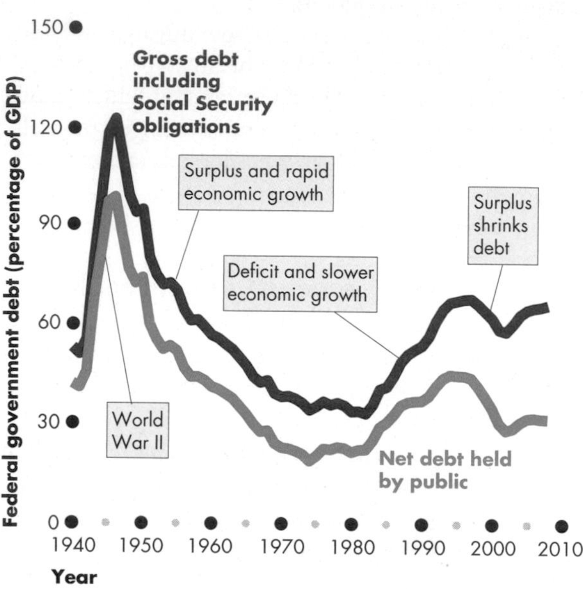


Gross and net government debt (the accumulation of past budget deficits less past budget surpluses) was at its highest at the end of World War II. Debt as a percentage of GDP fell through 1974 but then started to increase. After a further brief decline during the late 1970s, it exploded during the 1980s and continued to increase through 1995, after which it fell. After 2002, it began to rise again.

*Source of data: Budget of the United States Government, Fiscal Year 2009*, Table 7.1.

myeconlab animation

## The U.S. Government Budget in Global Perspective

### More Deficits than Surpluses

The U.S. government budget deficit in Fiscal 2009 was projected to be almost $400 billion, or close to 3 percent of GDP. How does this U.S. budget deficit compare with the deficits of other countries?

To compare the deficits of governments across countries, we must take into account the differences in local and regional government arrangements. Some countries, and the United States is one of them, have large state and local governments. Other countries, and the United Kingdom is one, have larger central government and small local governments. These differences make the international comparison more valid at the level of total government. The figure shows the budget balances of all levels of government in the United States and other countries.

Of the countries shown here, the United States has the largest deficit, as a percentage of GDP. Japan, the United Kingdom, France, and Italy come next, followed by the European Union as a whole and Germany.

Canada, the newly industrialized economies of Asia (Hong Kong, South Korea, Singapore, and Taiwan), and other advanced economies as a group, had projected surpluses in 2009. One country, Norway, which has substantial oil wealth, dominates the other advanced countries surplus.

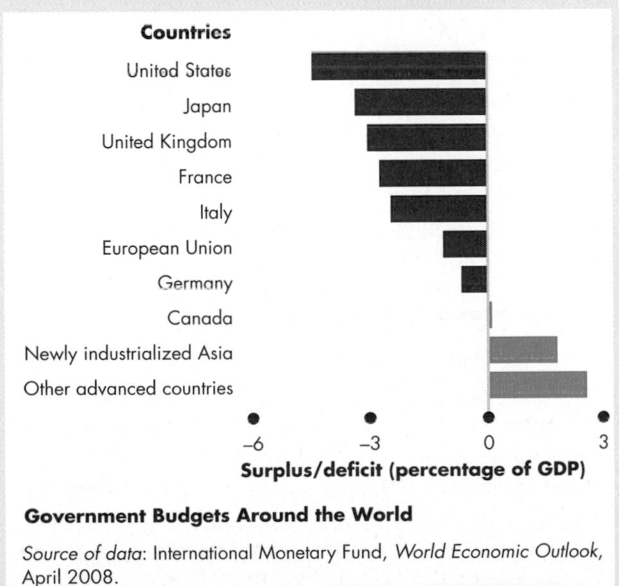


**Government Budgets Around the World**

*Source of data*: International Monetary Fund, *World Economic Outlook*, April 2008.

### State and Local Budgets

The *total government* sector of the United States includes state and local governments as well as the federal government. In 2008, when federal government outlays were $3,200 billion, state and local outlays were a further $2,000 billion. Most of these expenditures were on public schools, colleges, and universities ($550 billion); local police and fire services; and roads.

It is the combination of federal, state, and local government tax revenues, outlays, and budget deficits that influences the economy. But state and local budgets are not designed to stabilize the aggregate economy. So sometimes, when the federal government cuts taxes or outlays, state and local governments do the reverse and, to a degree, cancel out the effects of the federal actions. For example, since 2000, federal taxes decreased as a percentage of GDP, but state and local taxes and total government taxes increased.

## Review Quiz

1. What is fiscal policy, who makes it, and what is it designed to influence?
2. What special role does the president play in creating fiscal policy?
3. What special roles do the Budget Committees of the House of Representatives and the Senate play in creating fiscal policy?
4. What is the timeline for the U.S. federal budget each year? When does a fiscal year begin and end?
5. Is the federal government budget today in surplus or deficit?

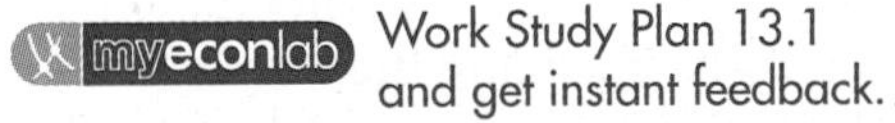


Work Study Plan 13.1 and get instant feedback.

Now that you know what the federal budget is and what the main components of tax revenues and outlays are, it is time to study the *effects* of fiscal policy. We'll begin by learning about the effects of taxes on employment, aggregate supply, and potential GDP. Then we'll study the effects of budget deficits and see how fiscal policy brings redistribution across generations. Finally, we'll look at the demand-side effects of fiscal policy and see how it provides a tool for stabilizing the business cycle.

## Supply-Side Effects of Fiscal Policy

Fiscal policy has important effects on employment, potential GDP, and aggregate supply that we'll now examine. These effects are known as **supply-side effects**, and economists who believe these effects to be large ones are generally referred to as *supply-siders*. To study these effects, we'll begin with a refresher on how full employment and potential GDP are determined in the absence of taxes. Then we'll introduce an income tax and see how it changes the economic outcome.

### Full Employment and Potential GDP

You learned in Chapter 6 (pp. 139–141) how the full-employment quantity of labor and potential GDP are determined. At full employment, the real wage rate adjusts to make the quantity of labor demanded equal the quantity of labor supplied. Potential GDP is the real GDP that the full-employment quantity of labor produces.

Figure 13.5 illustrates a full-employment situation. In part (a), the demand for labor curve is *LD*, and the supply of labor curve is *LS*. At a real wage rate of $30 an hour and 250 billion hours of labor a year employed, the economy is at full employment.

In Fig. 13.5(b), the production function is *PF*. When 250 billion hours of labor are employed, real GDP—which is also potential GDP—is $13 trillion.

Let's now see how an income tax changes potential GDP.

### The Effects of the Income Tax

The tax on labor income influences potential GDP and aggregate supply by changing the full-employment quantity of labor. The income tax weakens the incentive to work and drives a wedge between the take-home wage of workers and the cost of labor to firms. The result is a smaller quantity of labor and a lower potential GDP.

Figure 13.5 shows this outcome. In the labor market, the income tax has no effect on the demand for labor, which remains at *LD*. The reason is that the quantity of labor that firms plan to hire depends only on how productive labor is and what it costs—its real wage rate.

**FIGURE 13.5** The Effects of the Income Tax on Aggregate Supply

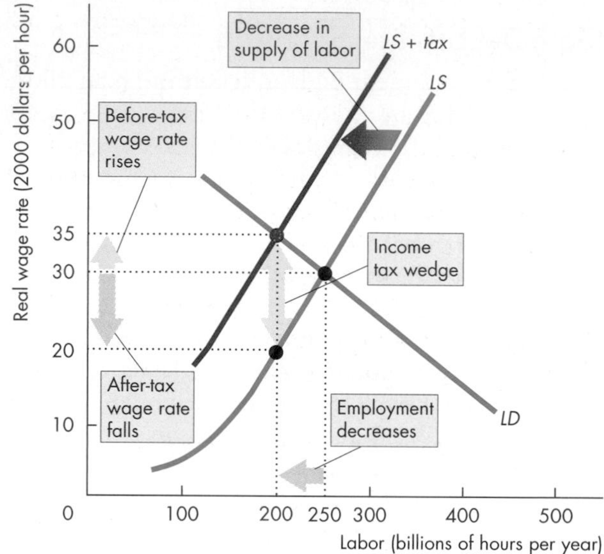


**(a) Income tax and the labor market**

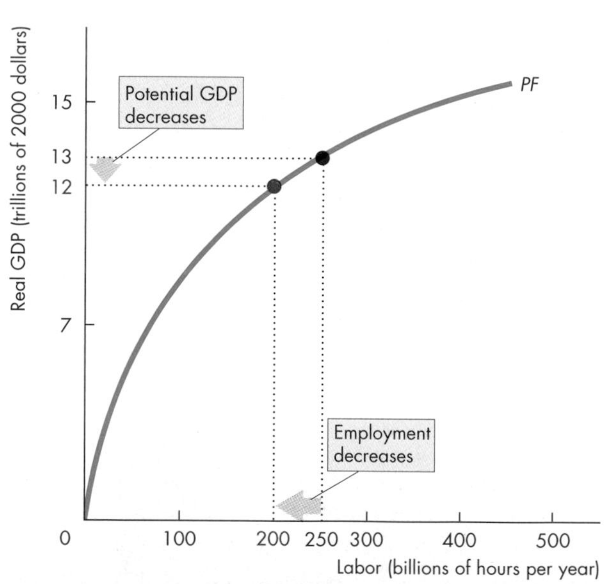


**(b) Income tax and potential GDP**

In part (a), with no income tax, the real wage rate is $30 an hour and employment is 250 billion hours. In part (b), potential GDP is $13 trillion. An income tax shifts the supply of labor curve leftward to *LS + tax*. The before-tax wage rate rises to $35 an hour, the after-tax wage rate falls to $20 an hour, and the quantity of labor employed decreases to 200 billion hours. With less labor, potential GDP decreases.

myeconlab animation

But the supply of labor *does* change. With no income tax, the real wage rate is $30 an hour and 250 billion hours of labor a year are employed. An income tax weakens the incentive to work and decreases the supply of labor. The reason is that for each dollar of before-tax earnings, workers must pay the government an amount determined by the income tax code. So workers look at the after-tax wage rate when they decide how much labor to supply. An income tax shifts the supply curve leftward to *LS* + *tax*. The vertical distance between the *LS* curve and the *LS* + *tax* curve measures the amount of income tax. With the smaller supply of labor, the *before-tax* wage rate rises to $35 an hour but the *after-tax* wage rate falls to $20 an hour. The gap created between the before-tax and after-tax wage rates is called the **tax wedge**.

The new equilibrium quantity of labor employed is 200 billion hours a year—less than in the no-tax case. Because the full-employment quantity of labor decreases, so does potential GDP. And a decrease in potential GDP decreases aggregate supply.

In this example, the tax rate is high—$15 tax on a $35 wage rate, about 43 percent. A lower tax rate would have a smaller effect on employment and potential GDP.

An increase in the tax rate to above 43 percent would decrease the supply of labor by more than the decrease shown in Fig. 13.5. Equilibrium employment and potential GDP would also decrease still further. A tax cut would increase the supply of labor, increase equilibrium employment, and increase potential GDP.

## Taxes on Expenditure and the Tax Wedge

The tax wedge that we've just considered is only a part of the wedge that affects labor-supply decisions. Taxes on consumption expenditure add to the wedge. The reason is that a tax on consumption raises the prices paid for consumption goods and services and is equivalent to a cut in the real wage rate.

The incentive to supply labor depends on the goods and services that an hour of labor can buy. The higher the taxes on goods and services and the lower the after-tax wage rate, the less is the incentive to supply labor. If the income tax rate is 25 percent and the tax rate on consumption expenditure is 10 percent, a dollar earned buys only 65 cents worth of goods and services. The tax wedge is 35 percent.

## Some Real World Tax Wedges

### Why Americans Work Longer Hours than Europeans

Edward C. Prescott of Arizona State University, who shared the 2004 Nobel Prize for Economic Science, has estimated the tax wedges for a number of countries, among them the United States, the United Kingdom, and France.

The U.S. tax wedge is a combination of 13 percent tax on consumption and 32 percent tax on incomes. The income tax component of the U.S. tax wedge includes Social Security taxes and is the *marginal* tax rate—the tax rate paid on the marginal dollar earned.

Prescott estimates that in France, taxes on consumption are 33 percent and taxes on incomes are 49 percent.

The estimates for the United Kingdom fall between those for the United States and France. The figure shows these components of the tax wedges in the three countries.

### Does the Tax Wedge Matter?

According to Prescott's estimates, the tax wedge has a powerful effect on employment and potential GDP. Potential GDP in France is 14 percent below that of the United States (per person), and the entire difference can be attributed to the difference in the tax wedge in the two countries.

Potential GDP in the United Kingdom is 41 percent below that of the United States (per person), and about a third of the difference arises from the different tax wedges. (The rest is due to different productivities.)

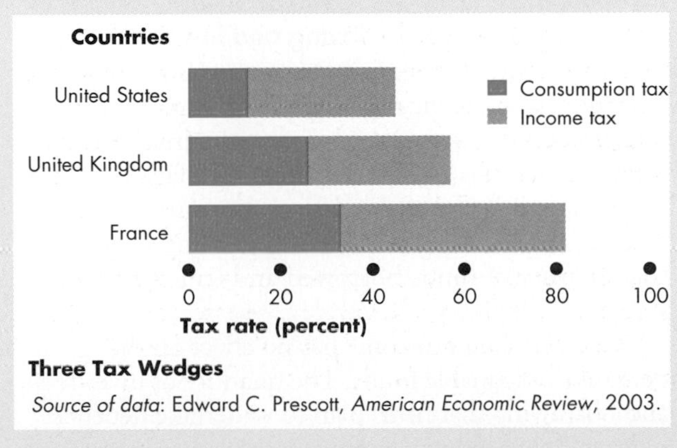


**Three Tax Wedges**

*Source of data*: Edward C. Prescott, *American Economic Review*, 2003.

## Taxes and the Incentive to Save

A tax on interest income weakens the incentive to save and drives a wedge between the after-tax interest rate earned by savers and the interest rate paid by firms. These effects are analogous to those of a tax on labor income. But they are more serious for two reasons.

First, a tax on labor income lowers the quantity of labor employed and lowers potential GDP, while a tax on capital income lowers the quantity of saving and investment and *slows the growth rate of real GDP*.

Second, the true tax rate on interest income is much higher than that on labor income because of the way in which inflation and taxes on interest income interact. Let's examine this interaction.

**Effect of Tax Rate on Real Interest Rate** The interest rate that influences investment and saving plans is the *real after-tax interest rate*. The real *after-tax* interest rate subtracts the income tax rate paid on interest income from the real interest rate. But the taxes depend on the nominal interest rate, not the real interest rate. So the higher the inflation rate, the higher is the true tax rate on interest income. Here is an example. Suppose the real interest rate is 4 percent a year and the tax rate is 40 percent.

If there is no inflation, the nominal interest rate equals the real interest rate. The tax on 4 percent interest is 1.6 percent (40 percent of 4 percent), so the real after-tax interest rate is 4 percent minus 1.6 percent, which equals 2.4 percent.

If the inflation rate is 6 percent a year, the nominal interest rate is 10 percent. The tax on 10 percent interest is 4 percent (40 percent of 10 percent), so the real after-tax interest rate is 4 percent minus 4 percent, which equals zero. The true tax rate in this case is not 40 percent but 100 percent!

**Effect of Income Tax on Saving and Investment** In Fig. 13.6, initially there are no taxes. Also, the government has a balanced budget. The demand for loanable funds curve, which is also the investment demand curve, is *DLF*. The supply of loanable funds curve, which is also the saving supply curve, is *SLF*. The equilibrium interest rate is 3 percent a year, and the quantity of funds borrowed and lent is $2 trillion a year.

A tax on interest income has no effect on the demand for loanable funds. The quantity of investment and borrowing that firms plan to undertake depends only on how productive capital is and what it costs—its real interest rate. But a tax on interest income weakens the incentive to save and lend and decreases the supply of loanable funds. For each dollar of before-tax interest, savers must pay the government an amount determined by the tax code. So savers look at the after-tax real interest rate when they decide how much to save.

When a tax is imposed, saving decreases and the supply of loanable funds curve shifts leftward to *SLF + tax*. The amount of tax payable is measured by the vertical distance between the *SLF* curve and the *SLF + tax* curve. With this smaller supply of loanable funds, the interest rate rises to 4 percent a year but the *after-tax* interest rate falls to 1 percent a year. A tax wedge is driven between the interest rate and the after-tax interest rate, and the equilibrium quantity of loanable funds decreases. Saving and investment also decrease.

**FIGURE 13.6** The Effects of a Tax on Capital Income

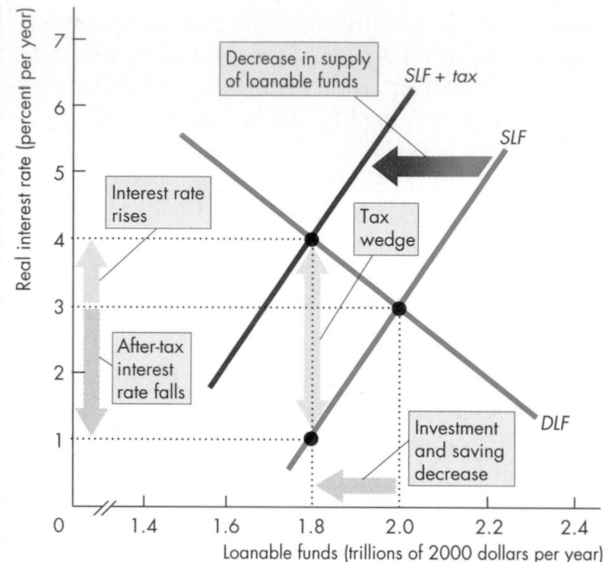


The demand for loanable funds and investment demand curve is *DLF*, and the supply of loanable funds and saving supply curve is *SLF*. With no income tax, the real interest rate is 3 percent a year and investment is $2 trillion. An income tax shifts the supply curve leftward to *SLF + tax*. The interest rate rises to 4 percent a year, the after-tax interest rate falls to 1 percent a year, and investment decreases to $1.8 trillion. With less investment, the real GDP growth rate decreases.

myeconlab animation

## Tax Revenues and the Laffer Curve

An interesting consequence of the effect of taxes on employment and saving is that a higher tax *rate* does not always bring greater tax *revenue*. A higher tax rate brings in more revenue per dollar earned. But because a higher tax rate decreases the number of dollars earned, two forces operate in opposite directions on the tax revenue collected.

The relationship between the tax rate and the amount of tax revenue collected is called the **Laffer curve**. The curve is so named because Arthur B. Laffer, a member of President Reagan's Economic Policy Advisory Board, drew such a curve on a table napkin and launched the idea that tax *cuts* could *increase* tax revenue.

Figure 13.7 shows a Laffer curve. The tax *rate* is on the $x$-axis, and total tax *revenue* is on the $y$-axis. For tax rates below $T^*$, an increase in the tax rate increases tax revenue; at $T^*$, tax revenue is maximized; and a tax rate increase above $T^*$ decreases tax revenue.

Most people think that the United States is on the upward-sloping part of the Laffer curve; so is the United Kingdom. But France might be close to the maximum point or perhaps even beyond it.

**FIGURE 13.7** A Laffer Curve

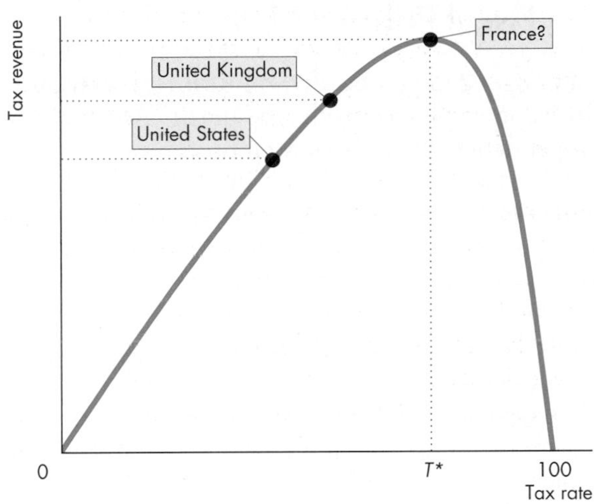


A Laffer curve shows the relationship between the tax rate and tax revenues. For tax rates below $T^*$, an increase in the tax rate increases tax revenue. At the tax rate $T^*$, tax revenue is maximized. For tax rates above $T^*$, an increase in the tax rate decreases tax revenue.

## The Supply-Side Debate

Before 1980, few economists paid attention to the supply-side effects of taxes on employment and potential GDP. Then, when Ronald Reagan took office as president, a group of supply-siders began to argue the virtues of cutting taxes. Arthur Laffer was one of them. Laffer and his supporters were not held in high esteem among mainstream economists, but they were influential for a period. They correctly argued that tax cuts would increase employment and increase output. But they incorrectly argued that tax cuts would increase tax revenues and decrease the budget deficit. For this prediction to be correct, the United States would have had to be on the "wrong" side of the Laffer curve. Given that U.S. tax rates are among the lowest in the industrial world, it is unlikely that this condition was met. And when the Reagan administration did cut taxes, the budget deficit increased, a fact that reinforces this view.

Supply-side economics became tarnished because of its association with Laffer and came to be called "voodoo economics." But mainstream economists, including Martin Feldstein, a Harvard professor who was Reagan's chief economic advisor, recognized the power of tax cuts as incentives but took the standard view that tax cuts without spending cuts would swell the budget deficit and bring serious further problems. This view is now widely accepted by economists of all political persuasions.

## Review Quiz

1. How does a tax on labor income influence the equilibrium quantity of employment?
2. How does the tax wedge influence potential GDP?
3. Why are consumption taxes relevant for measuring the tax wedge?
4. Why are income taxes on capital income more powerful than those on labor income?
5. What is the Laffer curve and why is it unlikely that the United States is on the "wrong" side of it?

myeconlab Work Study Plan 13.2 and get instant feedback.

You now know how taxes influence potential GDP and saving and investment. Next we look at the intergenerational effects of fiscal policy.

## Generational Effects of Fiscal Policy

Is a budget deficit a burden on future generations? If it is, how will the burden be borne? And is the budget deficit the only burden on future generations? What about the deficit in the Social Security fund? Does it matter who owns the bonds that the government sells to finance its deficit? What about the bonds owned by foreigners? Won't repaying those bonds impose a bigger burden than repaying bonds owned by Americans?

To answer questions like these, we use a tool called **generational accounting**—an accounting system that measures the lifetime tax burden and benefits of each generation. This accounting system was developed by Alan Auerbach of the University of Pennsylvania and Laurence Kotlikoff of Boston University. Generational accounts for the United States have been prepared by Jagadeesh Gokhale of the Federal Reserve Bank of Cleveland and Kent Smetters of the University of Pennsylvania.

### Generational Accounting and Present Value

Income taxes and Social Security taxes are paid by people who have jobs. Social Security benefits are paid to people after they retire. So to compare taxes and benefits, we must compare the value of taxes paid by people during their working years with the benefits received in their retirement years. To compare the value of an amount of money at one date with that at a later date, we use the concept of present value. A **present value** is an amount of money that, if invested today, will grow to equal a given future amount when the interest that it earns is taken into account. We can compare dollars today with dollars in 2030 or any other future year by using present values.

For example, if the interest rate is 5 percent a year, $1,000 invested today will grow, with interest, to $11,467 after 50 years. So the present value (in 2008) of $11,467 in 2058 is $1,000.

By using present values, we can assess the magnitude of the government's debts to older Americans in the form of pensions and medical benefits.

But the assumed interest rate and growth rate of taxes and benefits critically influence the answers we get. For example, at an interest rate of 3 percent a year, the present value (in 2008) of $11,467 in 2058 is $2,616. The lower the interest rate, the greater is the present value of a given future amount.

Because there is uncertainty about the proper interest rate to use to calculate present values, plausible alternative numbers are used to estimate a range of present values.

Using generational accounting and present values, economists have studied the situation facing the federal government arising from its Social Security obligations, and they have found a time bomb!

### The Social Security Time Bomb

When Social Security was introduced in the New Deal of the 1930s, today's demographic situation was not envisaged. The age distribution of the U.S. population today is dominated by the surge in the birth rate after World War II that created what is called the "baby boom generation." There are 77 million "baby boomers."

In 2008, the first of the baby boomers will start collecting Social Security pensions and in 2011, they will become eligible for Medicare benefits. By 2030, all the baby boomers will have retired and, compared to 2008, the population supported by social security will have doubled.

Under the existing Social Security laws, the federal government has an obligation to these citizens to pay pensions and Medicare benefits on an already declared scale. These obligations are a debt owed by the government and are just as real as the bonds that the government issues to finance its current budget deficit.

To assess the full extent of the government's obligations, economists use the concept of fiscal imbalance. **Fiscal imbalance** is the present value of the government's commitments to pay benefits minus the present value of its tax revenues. Fiscal imbalance is an attempt to measure the scale of the government's true liabilities.

Gokhale and Smetters estimated that the fiscal imbalance was $45 trillion in 2003. (Using alternative assumptions about interest rates and growth rates, the number might be as low as $29 trillion or as high as $65 trillion.) To put the $45 trillion in perspective, note that U.S. GDP in 2003 was $11 trillion. So the fiscal imbalance was four times the value of one year's production.

How can the federal government meet its social security obligations? Gokhale and Smetters consider four alternative fiscal policy changes that might be made:

- Raise income taxes
- Raise Social Security taxes
- Cut Social Security benefits
- Cut federal government discretionary spending

They estimated that starting in 2003 and making only one of these changes, income taxes would need to be raised by 69 percent, or Social Security taxes raised by 95 percent, or Social Security benefits cut by 56 percent. Even if the government stopped all its discretionary spending, including that on national defense, it would not be able to pay its bills.

Of course, by combining the four measures, the pain from each could be lessened. But the pain would still be severe. And worse, delay makes all these numbers rise. With no action, the fiscal imbalance climbs from the $45 trillion of 2003 to $54 trillion in 2008.

## Generational Imbalance

A fiscal imbalance must eventually be corrected and when it is, people either pay higher taxes or receive lower benefits. The concept of generational imbalance tells us who will pay. **Generational imbalance** is the division of the fiscal imbalance between the current and future generations, assuming that the current generation will enjoy the existing levels of taxes and benefits.

Figure 13.8 shows an estimate of how the fiscal imbalance is distributed across the current (born before 1988) and future (born in or after 1988) generations. It also shows that the major source of the imbalances is Medicare. Social Security pension benefits create a fiscal imbalance, but these benefits will be more than fully paid for by the current generation. But the current generation will pay less than 50 percent of its Medicare costs, and the balance will fall on future generations. If we sum all the items, the current generation will pay 43 percent and future generations will pay 57 percent of the fiscal imbalance.

Because the estimated fiscal imbalance is so large, it is not possible to predict how it will be resolved. But we can predict that the outcome will involve both lower benefits and higher taxes. One of these taxes could be the inflation tax—paying bills with new money and creating inflation. But the Fed will resist inflation being used to deal with the imbalance, as you will see in the next chapter.

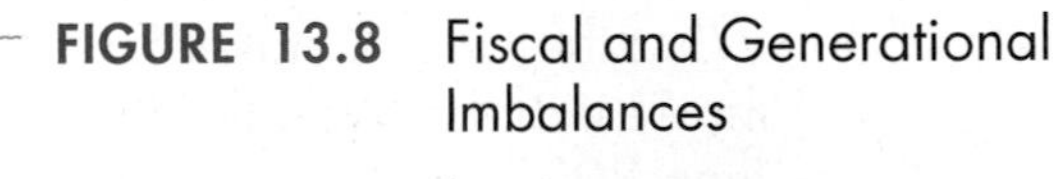

**FIGURE 13.8** Fiscal and Generational Imbalances

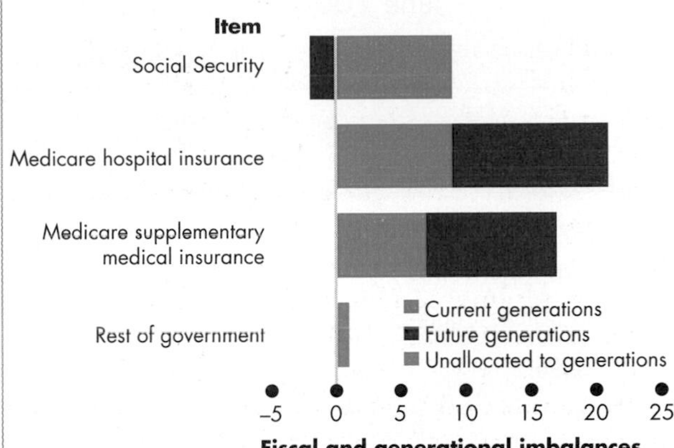


The bars show the scale of the fiscal imbalance. The largest component is the more than $20 trillion of Medicare benefits. These benefits are also the main component of the generational imbalance. Social Security pensions are paid for entirely by the current generation.

*Source of data*: Jagadeesh Gokhale and Kent Smetters, *Fiscal and Generational Imbalances: New Budget Measures for New Budget Priorities*, Washington, D.C: The AEI Press, April 2003.

myeconlab animation

## International Debt

So far in our discussion of government deficits and debts, we've ignored the role played by the rest of the world. We'll conclude this discussion by considering the role and magnitude of international debt.

You've seen that borrowing from the rest of the world is one source of investment finance. And you've also seen that this source of investment finance became larger during the late 1990s and 2000s.

How large is the contribution of the rest of the world? How much investment have we paid for by borrowing from the rest of the world? And how much U.S. government debt is held abroad?

Table 13.2 answers these questions. In June 2008, the United States had a net debt to the rest of the world of $8.1 trillion. Of that debt, $4.7 trillion was U.S. government debt. U.S. corporations had used $5.9 trillion of foreign funds ($3.1 trillion in bonds and $2.8 trillion in equities). Almost 90 percent of government debt is held by foreigners.

The international debt of the United States is important because, when that debt is repaid, the United States will transfer real resources to the rest of

**TABLE 13.2** What the United States Owed the Rest of the World in June 2008

| | $ trillions |
|---|---|
| **(a) U.S. Liabilities** | |
| Deposits in U.S. banks | 1.5 |
| U.S. government securities | 4.7 |
| U.S. corporate bonds | 3.1 |
| U.S. corporate equities | 2.8 |
| Other (net) | –4.0 |
| **Total** | 8.1 |
| **(b) U.S. government securities** | |
| Held by rest of world | 4.7 |
| Held in the United States | 0.6 |
| **Total** | 5.3 |

*Source of data*: Federal Reserve Board.

the world. Instead of running a large net exports deficit, the United States will need a surplus of exports over imports. To make a surplus possible, U.S. saving must increase and consumption must decrease. Some tough choices lie ahead.

## Review Quiz

1. What is a present value?
2. Distinguish between fiscal imbalance and generational imbalance.
3. How large was the estimated U.S. fiscal imbalance in 2003 and how did it divide between current and future generations?
4. What is the source of the U.S. fiscal imbalance and what are the painful choices that face current and future generations?
5. How much of U.S. government debt is held by the rest of the world?

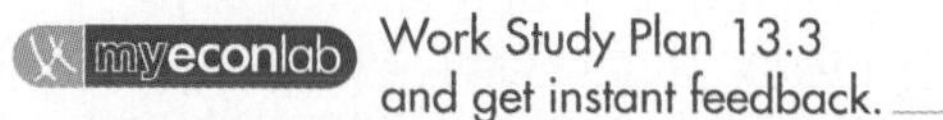

Work Study Plan 13.3 and get instant feedback.

You now know how economists assess fiscal imbalance and how they divide the cost of covering an imbalance across generations. And you've seen the extent and implication of U.S. debt held in the rest of the world. We conclude this chapter by looking at fiscal policy as a tool for stabilizing the business cycle.

# Stabilizing the Business Cycle

Fiscal policy actions that seek to stabilize the business cycle work by changing aggregate demand and are either

- Discretionary or
- Automatic

A fiscal action initiated by an act of Congress is called **discretionary fiscal policy**. It requires a change in a spending program or in a tax law. For example, an increase in defense spending or a cut in the income tax rate is a discretionary fiscal policy.

A fiscal action that is triggered by the state of the economy is called **automatic fiscal policy**. For example, an increase in unemployment induces an increase in payments to the unemployed. A fall in incomes induces a decrease in tax revenues.

Changes in government expenditure and changes in taxes have multiplier effects on aggregate demand. Chapter 11 explains the basic idea of the multiplier and the Mathematical Note on pp. 290–293 shows the algebra of the fiscal policy multipliers that we'll now study.

## Government Expenditure Multiplier

The **government expenditure multiplier** is the magnification effect of a change in government expenditure on goods and services on aggregate demand. Government expenditure is a component of aggregate expenditure, so when government expenditure changes, aggregate demand changes. Real GDP changes and induces a change in consumption expenditure, which brings a further change in aggregate expenditure. A multiplier process ensues.

**A Homeland Security Multiplier** The terrorist attacks of September 11, 2001, brought a reappraisal of the nation's homeland security requirements and an increase in government expenditure. This increase initially increased the incomes of producers of airport and border security equipment and security workers. Better-off security workers increased their consumption expenditure. With rising revenues, other businesses in all parts of the nation boomed and expanded their payrolls. A second round of increased consumption expenditure increased incomes yet further. This multiplier effect helped to end the 2001 recession.

## The Autonomous Tax Multiplier

The **autonomous tax multiplier** is the magnification effect of a change in autonomous taxes on aggregate demand. A *decrease* in taxes *increases* disposable income, which increases consumption expenditure. A decrease in taxes works like an increase in government expenditure. But the magnitude of the autonomous tax multiplier is smaller than the government expenditure multiplier. The reason is that a $1 tax cut generates *less than* $1 of additional expenditure. The marginal propensity to consume determines the increase in consumption expenditure induced by a tax cut. For example, if the marginal propensity to consume is 0.75, then a $1 tax cut increases consumption expenditure by only 75 cents. In this case, the tax multiplier is 0.75 times the magnitude of the government expenditure multiplier.

**A Bush Tax Cut Multiplier** Congress enacted the Bush tax cut package that lowered taxes starting in 2002. These tax cuts had a multiplier effect. With more disposable income, people increased consumption expenditure. This spending increased other people's incomes, which spurred yet more consumption expenditure. Like the increase in security expenditures, the tax cut and its multiplier effect helped to end the 2001 recession.

## The Balanced Budget Multiplier

The **balanced budget multiplier** is the magnification effect on aggregate demand of a *simultaneous* change in government expenditure and taxes that leaves the budget balance unchanged. The balanced budget multiplier is positive because a $1 increase in government expenditure increases aggregate demand by more than a $1 increase in taxes decreases aggregate demand. So when both government expenditure and taxes increase by $1, aggregate demand increases.

## Discretionary Fiscal Stabilization

If real GDP is below potential GDP, discretionary fiscal policy might be used in an attempt to restore full employment. The government might increase its expenditure on goods and services, cut taxes, or do some of both. These actions would increase aggregate demand. If they were timed correctly and were of the correct magnitude, they could restore full employment. Figure 13.9 shows how. Potential GDP is $12 trillion, but real GDP is below potential at $11 trillion and there is a $1 trillion *recessionary gap* (see Chapter 10, p. 257). To restore full employment, the government takes a discretionary fiscal policy action. An increase in government expenditure or a tax cut increases aggregate expenditure by $\Delta E$. If this were the only change in spending plans, the *AD* curve would become $AD_0 + \Delta E$ in Fig. 13.9. But the fiscal policy action sets off a multiplier process, which increases consumption expenditure. As the multiplier process plays out, aggregate demand increases further and the *AD* curve shifts rightward to $AD_1$.

With no change in the price level, the economy would move from point *A* to point *B* on $AD_1$. But the increase in aggregate demand combined with the upward-sloping *SAS* curve brings a rise in the price level. The economy moves to point *C*, and the economy returns to full employment.

Figure 13.10 illustrates the opposite case in which discretionary fiscal policy is used to eliminate inflationary pressure. The government decreases its expenditure on goods and services or raises taxes to

**FIGURE 13.9** Expansionary Fiscal Policy

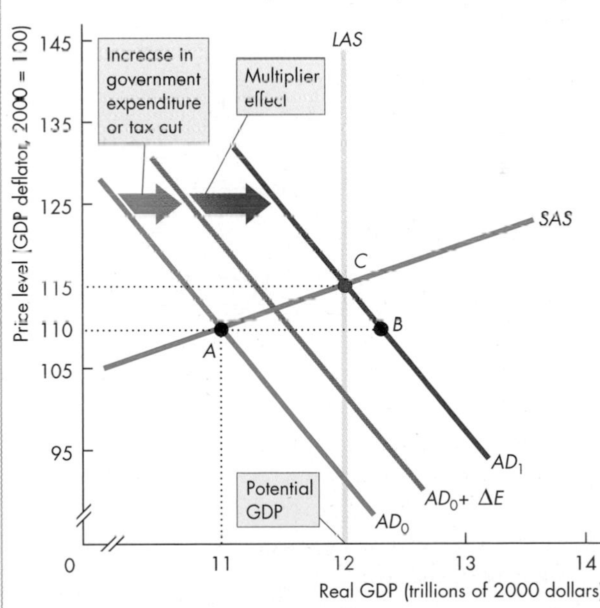


Potential GDP is $12 trillion, real GDP is $11 trillion, and there is a $1 trillion recessionary gap. An increase in government expenditure or a tax cut increases expenditure by $\Delta E$. The multiplier increases induced expenditure. The *AD* curve shifts rightward to $AD_1$, the price level rises to 115, real GDP increases to $12 trillion, and the recessionary gap is eliminated.

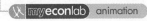

myeconlab animation

decrease aggregate demand. In the figure, the fiscal policy action decreases aggregate expenditure by $\Delta E$ and the $AD$ curve shifts to $AD_0 - \Delta E$. The initial decrease in aggregate expenditure sets off a multiplier process, which decreases consumption expenditure. The multiplier process decreases aggregate demand further and the $AD$ curve shifts leftward to $AD_1$.

With no change in the price level, the economy would move from point *A* to point *B* on $AD_1$ in Fig. 13.10. But the decrease in aggregate demand combined with the upward-sloping *SAS* curve brings a fall in the price level. So the economy moves to point *C*, where the inflationary gap has been eliminated, inflation has been avoided, and the economy is back at full employment.

Figures 13.9 and 13.10 make fiscal policy look easy: Calculate the recessionary gap or the inflationary gap and the multiplier, change government expenditure or taxes, and eliminate the gap. In reality, things are not that easy.

**FIGURE 13.10** Contractionary Fiscal Policy

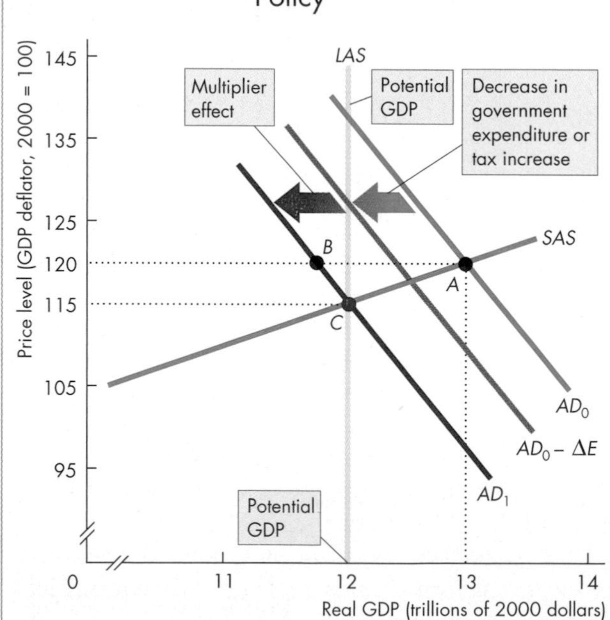


Potential GDP is \$12 trillion, real GDP is \$13 trillion, and there is a \$1 trillion inflationary gap. A decrease in government expenditure or a rise in taxes decreases expenditure by $\Delta E$. The multiplier decreases induced expenditure. The *AD* curve shifts leftward to $AD_1$, the price level falls to 115, real GDP decreases to \$12 trillion, and the inflationary gap is eliminated.

myeconlab animation

## Limitations of Discretionary Fiscal Policy

The use of discretionary fiscal policy is seriously hampered by three time lags:

- Recognition lag
- Law-making lag
- Impact lag

**Recognition Lag** The *recognition lag* is the time it takes to figure out that fiscal policy actions are needed. This process has two aspects: assessing the current state of the economy and forecasting its future state.

**Law-Making Lag** The *law-making lag* is the time it takes Congress to pass the laws needed to change taxes or spending. This process takes time because each member of Congress has a different idea about what is the best tax or spending program to change, so long debates and committee meetings are needed to reconcile conflicting views. The economy might benefit from fiscal stimulation today, but by the time Congress acts, a different fiscal medicine is needed.

**Impact Lag** The *impact lag* is the time it takes from passing a tax or spending change to its effects on real GDP being felt. This lag depends partly on the speed with which government agencies can act and partly on the timing of changes in spending plans by households and businesses.

Economic forecasting has improved in recent years, but it remains inexact and subject to error. So because of these three time lags, discretionary fiscal action might end up moving real GDP *away* from potential GDP and creating the problem it seeks to correct.

Let's now look at automatic fiscal policy.

## Automatic Stabilizers

Automatic fiscal policy is a consequence of tax revenues and outlays that fluctuate with real GDP. These features of fiscal policy are called **automatic stabilizers** because they work to stabilize real GDP without explicit action by the government. Their name is borrowed from engineering and conjures up images of shock absorbers, thermostats, and sophisticated devices that keep airplanes and ships steady in turbulent air and seas.

## The 2008 Fiscal Stimulus Package

### Congress Aims to Close the Output Gap

As recession fears grew in the wake of the sub-prime mortgage crisis, Congress passed the *Economic Stimulus Act of 2008*. This act of *discretionary fiscal policy* was designed to increase aggregate demand and close a recessionary gap.

Tax rebates were the key component of the package and their effect on aggregate demand depends on the extent to which they are spent and saved.

The last time the federal government boosted aggregate demand with a tax rebate was in 2001 and a statistical investigation of the effects estimated that 70 percent of the rebates were spent within six months of being received.

The rebates in the 2008 fiscal package were targeted predominantly at low-income individuals and families, so the experience of 2001 would be likely to apply: Most of the rebates would be spent.

The cost of the package in 2008 was about $160 billion, so aggregate demand would be expected to increase by close to this amount and then by a multiplier as the initial spending became someone else's income and so boosted their spending.

The figure illustrates the effects of the package. Before the rebates, aggregate demand was $AD_0$ and real GDP was $11.7 trillion. The rebates increased aggregate demand to $AD_0 + \Delta E$, and a multiplier increased it to $AD_1$. Real GDP and the price level increased and the recessionary gap narrowed.

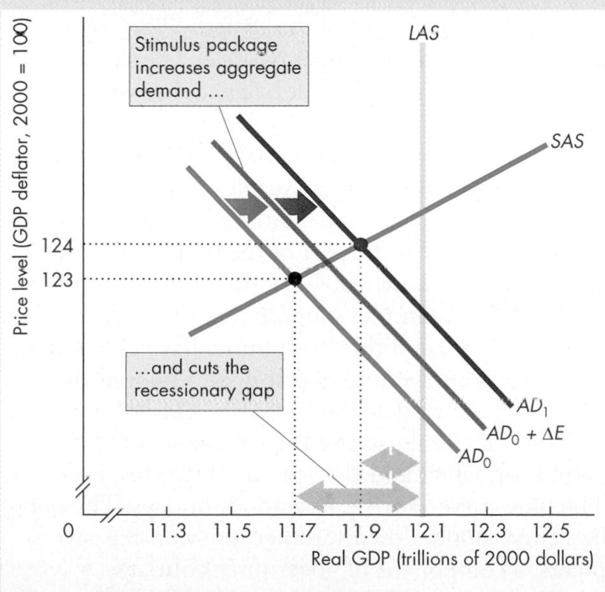


**Effects of Fiscal Stimulus Act of 2008**

**Induced Taxes** On the revenues side of the budget, tax laws define tax *rates*, not tax *dollars*. Tax dollars paid depend on tax rates and incomes. But incomes vary with real GDP, so tax revenues depend on real GDP. Taxes that vary with real GDP are called **induced taxes.** When real GDP increases in an expansion, wages and profits rise, so the taxes on these incomes—induced taxes—rise. When real GDP decreases in a recession, wages and profits fall, so the induced taxes on these incomes fall.

**Needs-Tested Spending** On the outlays side of the budget, the government creates programs that pay benefits to suitably qualified people and businesses. The spending on such programs is called **needs-tested spending**, and it results in transfer payments that depend on the economic state of individual citizens and businesses. When the economy is in a recession, unemployment is high and the number of people experiencing economic hardship increases, and needs-tested spending on unemployment benefits and food stamps also increases. When the economy expands, unemployment falls, the number of people experiencing economic hardship decreases, and needs-tested spending decreases.

Induced taxes and needs-tested spending decrease the multiplier effects of changes in autonomous expenditure (such as investment and exports). So they moderate both expansions and recessions and make real GDP more stable. They achieve this outcome by weakening the link between real GDP and disposable income and so reduce the effect of a change in real GDP on consumption expenditure. When real GDP increases, induced taxes increase and needs-tested spending decreases, so disposable income does not increase by as much as the increase in real GDP. As a result, consumption expenditure does not increase by as much as it otherwise would and the multiplier effect is reduced.

We can see the effects of automatic stabilizers by looking at the way in which the government budget deficit fluctuates over the business cycle.

**Budget Deficit Over the Business Cycle** Figure 13.11 shows the business cycle in part (a) and fluctuations in the budget deficit in part (b) between 1998 and 2008. Both parts highlight recessions by shading those periods. By comparing the two parts of the figure, you can see the relationship between the business cycle and the budget deficit. When the economy is in

**FIGURE 13.11** The Business Cycle and the Budget Deficit

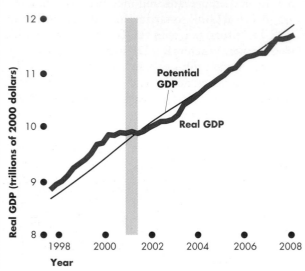

Real GDP (trillions of 2000 dollars)

12 11 10 9 8

Potential GDP

Real GDP

1998 2000 2002 2004 2006 2008

Year

**(a) Growth and recessions**

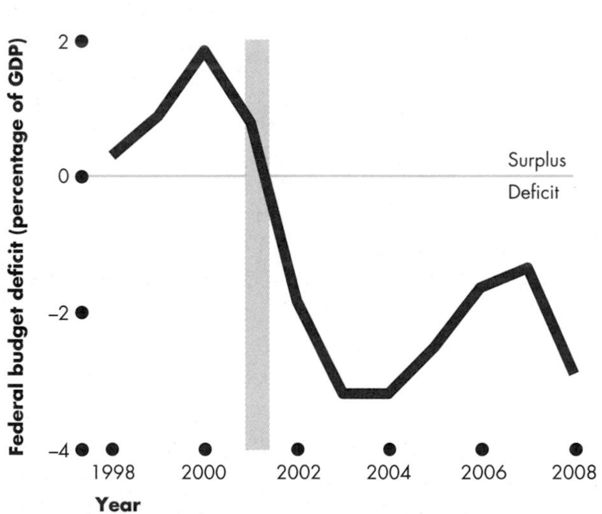


**(b) Federal budget deficit**

As real GDP fluctuates around potential GDP (part a), the budget deficit fluctuates (part b). During a recession (shaded years), tax revenues decrease, transfer payments increase, and the budget deficit increases. The deficit also increases before a recession as real GDP growth slows and after a recession before real GDP growth speeds up.

*Sources of data:* Bureau of Economic Analysis, Congressional Budget Office, and Office of Management and Budget.

myeconlab animation

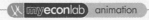

an expansion, the budget deficit declines. (In the figure, a declining deficit means a deficit that is getting closer to zero.) As the expansion slows before the recession begins, the budget deficit increases. It continues to increase during the recession and for a period after the recession is over. Then, when the expansion is well under way, the budget deficit declines again.

The budget deficit fluctuates with the business cycle because both tax revenues and outlays fluctuate with real GDP. As real GDP increases during an expansion, tax revenues increase and transfer payments decrease, so the budget deficit automatically decreases. As real GDP decreases during a recession, tax revenues decrease and transfer payments increase, so the budget deficit automatically increases. Fluctuations in investment and exports have a multiplier effect on real GDP. But fluctuations in the budget deficit decrease the swings in disposable income and make the multiplier effect smaller. They dampen both expansions and recessions.

**Cyclical and Structural Balances** Because the government budget balance fluctuates with the business cycle, we need a method of measuring the balance that tells us whether it is a temporary cyclical phenomenon or a persistent phenomenon. A temporary cyclical surplus or deficit vanishes when full employment returns. A persistent surplus or deficit requires government action to remove it.

To determine whether the budget balance is persistent or temporary and cyclical, economists have developed the concepts of the structural budget balance and the cyclical budget balance. The **structural surplus or deficit** is the budget balance that would occur if the economy were at full employment and real GDP were equal to potential GDP. The **cyclical surplus or deficit** is the actual surplus or deficit minus the structural surplus or deficit. That is, the cyclical surplus or deficit is the part of the budget balance that arises purely because real GDP does not equal potential GDP. For example, suppose that the budget deficit is \$100 billion, and that economists have determined that there is a structural deficit of \$25 billion. In that case, there is a cyclical deficit of \$75 billion.

Figure 13.12 illustrates the concepts of the cyclical surplus or deficit and the structural surplus or deficit. The blue curve shows government outlays. The outlays curve slopes downward because transfer payments, a component of government outlays, decreases as real GDP increases. The green curve

**FIGURE 13.12** Cyclical and Structural Surpluses and Deficits

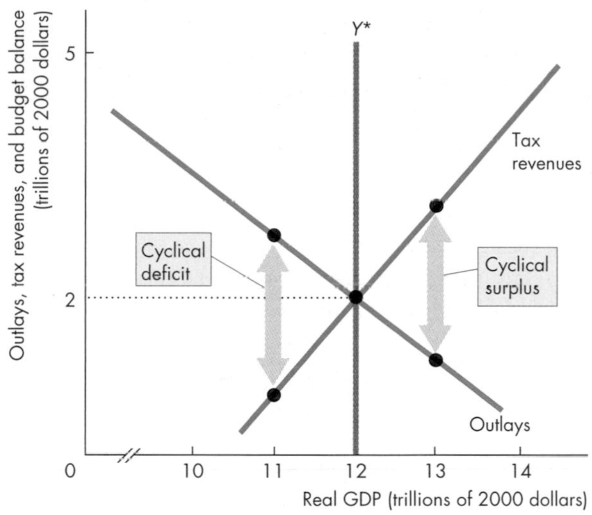


**(a) Cyclical deficit and cyclical surplus**

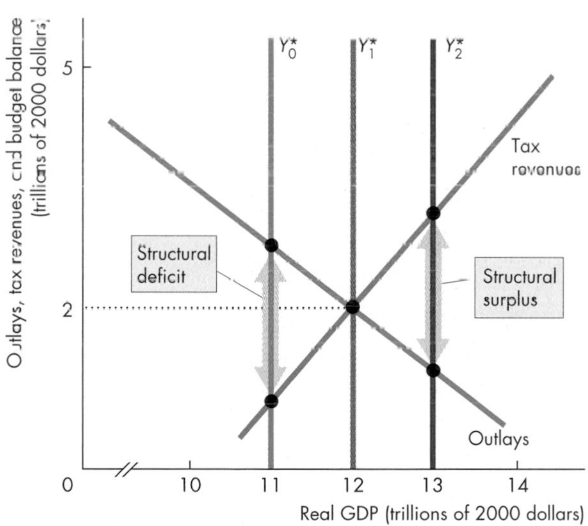


**(b) Structural deficit and structural surplus**

In part (a), potential GDP is $12 trillion. When real GDP is less than potential GDP, the budget is in a *cyclical deficit.* When real GDP exceeds potential GDP, the budget is in a *cyclical surplus*. The government has a *balanced budget* when real GDP equals potential GDP. In part (b), if real GDP and potential GDP are $11 trillion, there is a *structural deficit.* But if real GDP and potential GDP are $13 trillion, there is a *structural surplus.*

myeconlab animation

shows tax revenues. The tax revenues curve slopes upward because most components of tax revenues increase as incomes and real GDP increase.

In Fig. 13.12(a), potential GDP is $12 trillion. If real GDP equals potential GDP, the government has a *balanced budget*. Outlays and tax revenues each equal $2 trillion. If real GDP is less than potential GDP, outlays exceed tax revenues and there is a *cyclical deficit*. If real GDP is greater than potential GDP, outlays are less than tax revenues and there is a *cyclical surplus*.

In Fig. 13.12(b), if both real GDP and potential GDP are $11 trillion ($Y^*_0$), the government has a budget deficit and it is a *structural deficit*. If both real GDP and potential GDP are $12 trillion ($Y^*_1$), the budget is balanced—a *structural balance* of zero. If both real GDP and potential GDP are $13 trillion ($Y^*_2$), the government has a budget surplus and it is a *structural surplus*.

The U.S. federal budget is a structural deficit and has been in that state since the early 1970s. The structural deficit decreased from 1992 to 2000 and was almost eliminated in 2000. But since 2000, the structural deficit has increased. The cyclical deficit is estimated to be small relative to the structural deficit.

The federal government faces some tough fiscal policy challenges.

## Review Quiz

1. How can the federal government use fiscal policy to stabilize the business cycle?
2. Why is the government expenditure multiplier larger than the autonomous tax multiplier?
3. Why does a balanced budget increase in spending and taxes increase aggregate demand?
4. How do induced taxes and needs-tested spending programs work as automatic stabilizers to dampen the business cycle?
5. How do we tell whether a budget deficit needs government action to remove it?

myeconlab Work Study Plan 13.4 and get instant feedback.

You've seen how fiscal policy influences potential GDP, the growth rate of real GDP, and real GDP fluctuations. *Reading Between the Lines* on pp. 344–345 looks further at the fiscal policy actions proposed by President Obama.

# Obama Fiscal Policy

## "I'm going to confront this economic crisis," Obama says

http://www.cnn.com
November 7, 2008

Sen. Barack Obama spoke at his first news conference as president-elect Friday afternoon. The following is a transcript of the conference:

President-elect Barack Obama emphasized the economy in a news conference in Chicago, Illinois, on Friday.

Obama: Thank you very much, everybody. Thank you very much.

This morning, we woke up to more sobering news about the state of our economy. The 240,000 jobs lost in October marks the 10th consecutive month that our economy has shed jobs. In total, we've lost nearly 1.2 million jobs this year, and more than 10 million Americans are now unemployed. …

First of all, we need a rescue plan for the middle class that invests in immediate efforts to create jobs and provide relief to families that are watching their paychecks shrink and their life savings disappear.

A particularly urgent priority is a further extension of unemployment insurance benefits for workers who cannot find work in the increasingly weak economy.

A fiscal stimulus plan that will jump-start economic growth is long overdue. I've talked about it throughout this—the last few months of the campaign. We should get it done.

Second, we have to address the spreading impact of the financial crisis on the other sectors of our economy: small businesses that are struggling to meet their payrolls and finance their holiday inventories; and state and municipal governments facing devastating budget cuts and tax increases. …



## Essence of the Story

- Barack Obama gave his first news conference as president-elect November 7, 2008.
- The economy lost 240,000 jobs in October and nearly 1.2 million jobs in 2008.
- More than 10 million Americans are unemployed.
- We need a rescue plan for the middle class that creates jobs and provides income to families.
- A further extension of unemployment insurance benefits is an urgent priority.
- A fiscal stimulus plan that will jump-start economic growth is overdue.
- Small businesses are struggling to meet payrolls.
- State and municipal governments are facing devastating budget cuts and tax increases.

## Economic Analysis

- The transcript of president-elect Obama's first post-election news conference included a preview of the new president's fiscal policy priorities.
- Two urgent changes are described: (1) an extension of unemployment insurance benefits, and (2) a fiscal stimulus package.
- In November 2008, the economy had not yet entered the worst of the predicted recession of 2009, but the labor market was already showing serious weakness and real GDP had just begun to shrink.
- With no further policy action, most likely real GDP would shrink further during 2009 and an output gap of as much as $800 billion (more than 6 percent of potential GDP) would emerge.
- The new president wanted to avoid this bleak outcome.
- Figure 1 shows what might happen in the labor market with an extension of unemployment insurance benefits.
- Extended benefits increase the incentive to spend longer in job search looking for the best available job. The supply of labor decreases, the labor supply curve shifts leftward from $LS_0$ to $LS_1$. Equilibrium employment decreases.
- Figure 2 shows the effects of both an extension of unemployment insurance benefits and a fiscal stimulus package.
- The extension of unemployment benefits decreases aggregate supply and the *SAS* curve shifts leftward from $SAS_0$ to $SAS_1$.
- When people spend their increased unemployment benefits, aggregate demand increases. Also the other components of the fiscal stimulus package ($100 billion to $200 billion were the numbers considered) increase aggregate demand. The *AD* curve shifts rightward from $AD_0$ to $AD_1$.
- The demand-side effects are (most likely) more powerful than the supply-side effects, so real GDP increases (and the price level rises).
- But the change in real GDP that results from the two policy actions is small compared to the size of the output gap, so a large output gap remains through 2009.
- Either a larger fiscal stimulus package or an expansionary monetary policy (see Chapter 14) would be needed to eliminate a recessionary gap of the size emerging in 2009.
- Greater fiscal stimulus (or monetary stimulus) risks putting upward pressure on the price level, so the inflation rate would likely rise.

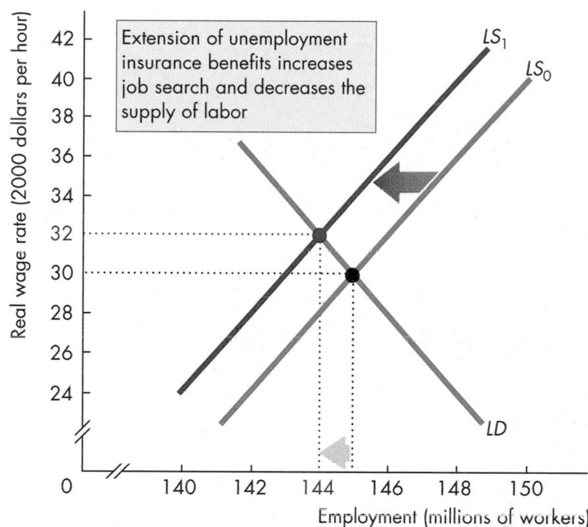


**Figure 1 The labor market and unemployment insurance benefits**

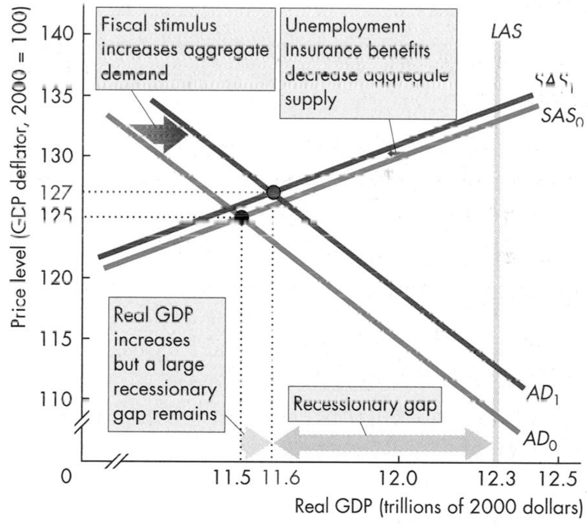


**Figure 2 Aggregate supply and aggregate demand in 2009**

## SUMMARY

### Key Points

**The Federal Budget** (pp. 326–331)

- The federal budget is used to achieve macroeconomic objectives.
- Tax revenues can exceed, equal, or fall short of outlays—the budget can be in surplus, balanced, or in deficit.
- Budget deficits create government debt.

**Supply-Side Effects of Fiscal Policy** (pp. 332–335)

- Fiscal policy has supply-side effects because taxes weaken the incentive to work and decrease employment and potential GDP.
- The U.S. labor market tax wedge is large but it is small compared to those of other industrial countries.
- Fiscal policy has supply-side effects because taxes weaken the incentive to save and invest, which lowers the growth rate of real GDP.
- The Laffer curve shows the relationship between the tax rate and the amount of tax revenue collected.

**Generational Effects of Fiscal Policy** (pp. 336–338)

- Generational accounting measures the lifetime tax burden and benefits of each generation.
- A major 2003 study estimated the U.S. fiscal imbalance to be $45 trillion—4 times the value of one year's production.
- Future generations will pay for 57 percent of the benefits of the current generation.
- About half of U.S. government debt is held by the rest of the world.

**Stabilizing the Business Cycle** (pp. 338–343)

- Fiscal stabilization can be discretionary or automatic.
- Discretionary changes in government expenditure or taxes can change aggregate demand but are hampered by law-making lags and the difficulty of correctly diagnosing and forecasting the state of the economy.
- Automatic changes in fiscal policy moderate the business cycle.

### Key Figures



### Key Terms

## PROBLEMS and APPLICATIONS

Work problems 1–10 in Chapter 13 Study Plan and get instant feedback.
Work problems 11–20 as Homework, a Quiz, or a Test if assigned by your instructor.

1. The government is proposing to increase the tax rate on labor income and asks you to report on the supply-side effects of such an action. Answer the following questions using appropriate diagrams. You are being asked about directions of change, not exact magnitudes.
   a. What will happen to the supply of labor and why?
   b. What will happen to the demand for labor and why?
   c. How will the equilibrium level of employment change and why?
   d. How will the equilibrium before-tax wage rate change and why?
   e. How will the equilibrium after-tax wage rate change and why?
   f. What will happen to potential GDP?
   g. How would your answers to the above questions change if at the same time as raising the tax rate on labor income, the government cut the rate of sales tax to keep the amount of tax collected constant?
   h. What evidence would you present to the government to support the view that a lower tax on labor income will increase employment, potential GDP, and aggregate supply?
2. Suppose that in China, investment is $400 billion, saving is $400 billion, tax revenues are $500 billion, exports are $300 billion, and imports are $200 billion.
   a. Calculate government expenditure.
   b. What is the government budget balance?
   c. Is the government exerting a positive or negative impact on investment?
   d. What fiscal policy action might increase investment and speed economic growth? Explain how the policy action would work.
3. Suppose that instead of taxing nominal capital income, the government changed the tax code so that the inflation rate is subtracted from the interest rate before the taxable income from capital is calculated. Use appropriate diagrams to explain and illustrate the effect that this change would have on
   a. The tax rate on capital income.
   b. The supply of loanable funds.
   c. The demand for loanable funds.
   d. Investment and the real interest rate.
4. The economy is in a recession, and the recessionary gap is large.
   a. Describe the discretionary and automatic fiscal policy actions that might occur.
   b. Describe a discretionary fiscal stimulation package that could be used that would *not* bring a budget deficit.
   c. Explain the risks of discretionary fiscal policy in this situation.
5. The economy is in a recession, the recessionary gap is large, and there is a budget deficit.
   a. Do we know whether the budget deficit is structural or cyclical? Explain your answer.
   b. Do we know whether automatic stabilizers are increasing or decreasing aggregate demand? Explain your answer.
   c. If a discretionary increase in government expenditure occurs, what happens to the structural deficit or surplus? Explain.
6. **Comprehensive Tax Code Overhaul Is Overdue**

   Some right-wingers in Congress claim that … tax cuts pay for themselves. Despite their insistence, there is ample evidence and general expert agreement that they do not. …

   *Washington Post*, April 24, 2006

   a. Explain what is meant by tax cuts paying for themselves. What does this statement imply about the tax multiplier?
   b. Why would tax cuts not pay for themselves?
7. **How the Next President Should Fix the Economy**

   The message many Republicans took from Reagan's successes of the early 1980s, and still preach today, is that tax cuts pay for themselves. That's nonsense—Reagan's rate cuts for the rich may have paid for themselves, but the 1981 tax package as a whole (which included cuts for the poor, the middle class and corporations) clearly did not. The real lesson of the 1980s was that the U.S. can get away with running far bigger deficits than anyone thought possible while still enjoying strong growth and low inflation … but it can't go on forever. There comes a point at which government debts grow so large that they start to weigh down on the economy, through higher interest rates, bigger debt payments, a weaker currency, etc.

*Time*, May 26, 2008

a. Explain under what circumstances it is possible that "tax cuts pay for themselves" and draw a Laffer curve to illustrate this outcome.
b. Explain why Reagan's tax rate cuts for high-income taxpayers may have paid for themselves, but cuts for lower-income and middle-income taxpayers did not.
c. Explain the negative consequences of running persistently large budget deficits.

8. **Stimulus Debate Turns on Rebates**

As pressure builds on Washington to juice the economy, a one-time consumer rebate has emerged as the likely centerpiece of a $150 billion stimulus program. … But … Democrats and Republicans still disagree on who should actually get rebates. Bush has said he wants rebates for those who pay income taxes. … Democrats contend such an approach would mean tens of millions of households would get only a partial rebate or none at all. … Proponents of the rebate-for-all assert that more of lower- and middle-income households should be included in any rebate plan because they are more likely to spend a bigger chunk of their rebate than are higher-income households … and targeted to people most likely to spend it quickly, every dollar spent on stimulus could generate a dollar in gross domestic product.

*CNN*, January 22, 2008

a. Explain the intended effect of the $150 billion fiscal stimulus package and draw a graph to illustrate the effect.
b. Explain why the effect of this fiscal policy depends on who receives the tax rebates.
c. What would have a larger effect on aggregate demand: $150 billion worth of tax rebates or $150 billion worth of government spending?
d. Explain whether a stimulus package centered around a one-time consumer tax rebate is likely to have a small or a large supply-side effect.

9. **What Obama Means for Business**

The core of Obama's economic plan is (a) more government spending: $65 billion a year for universal health insurance, $15 billion a year on alternative energy, $20 billion to help homeowners avoid default, $60 billion to bolster the nation's infrastructure, $10 billion annually to give students college tuition in exchange for public service, and on and on; and (b) shifting the tax burden upward: ending the Bush tax cuts on families making more than $250,000 and raising payroll taxes on those same higher-income earners. … Middle-class earners would receive tax cuts, and low-income seniors would pay no income tax. … Obama also wants to raise a range of other taxes on business and investment. He would increase the 15 percent capital gains tax rate—probably to 25 percent, according to advisors. … He would raise the dividends tax, reinstate a 45 percent tax on estates worth more than $3.5 million, and close $1.3 trillion in "corporate tax loopholes."

*Fortune*, June 23, 2008

a. Explain the potential supply-side effects of the various components of Obama's economic plan. How might these policies change potential GDP and its growth rate?
b. What would be the impact on aggregate demand of a same-sized increase in taxes and government expenditure?

10. **2008 U.S. Budget Deficit Bleeding Red Ink**

The Bush administration sent its final budget request to Congress last week, projecting that the deficit for all of 2008 will total $410 billion. … For 2007, the budget deficit totaled $162 billion. … [T]he slowing economy is expected to stunt the growth of tax revenues while the $168 billion economic stimulus plan passed by Congress last week will swell the deficit. It is hoped the stimulus plan will keep the economy out of a recession or at least make the downturn milder and shorter than it otherwise would have been. …

*CBS News*, February 12, 2008

a. Explain why the business cycle increased the federal budget deficit in 2008.
b. Explain how the fiscal stimulus package might lead to a smaller budget deficit.

11. Suppose that in the United States, investment is $1,600 billion, saving is $1,400 billion, government expenditure on goods and services is $1,500 billion, exports are $2,000 billion, and imports are $2,500 billion.
    a. What is the amount of tax revenue?
    b. What is the government budget balance?
    c. Is the government exerting a positive or negative impact on investment?
    d. What fiscal policy action might increase investment and speed economic growth? Explain how the policy action would work.
12. Suppose that capital income taxes are based (as they are in the United States and most countries) on nominal interest rates. And suppose that the inflation rate increases by 5 percent. Use appropriate diagrams to explain and illustrate the effect that this change would have on
    a. The tax rate on capital income.
    b. The supply of loanable funds.
    c. The demand for loanable funds.
    d. Equilibrium investment.
    e. The equilibrium real interest rate.
13. The economy is in a boom and the inflationary gap is large.
    a. Describe the discretionary and automatic fiscal policy actions that might occur.
    b. Describe a discretionary fiscal restraint package that could be used that would not produce serious negative supply-side effects.
    c. Explain the risks of discretionary fiscal policy in this situation.
14. The economy is in a boom, the inflationary gap is large, and there is a budget deficit.
    a. Do we know whether the budget deficit is structural or cyclical? Explain your answer.
    b. Do we know whether automatic stabilizers are increasing or decreasing aggregate demand? Explain your answer.
    c. If a discretionary decrease in government expenditure occurs, what happens to the structural balance? Explain your answer.
15. **Juicing the Economy Will Come at a Cost**

    Within weeks, lawmakers hope to pass a package of measures intended to minimize the effects of a recession. … President Bush and leading Democrats have indicated they envisioned stimulus measures—cash rebates, business breaks and other proposals—worth roughly $150 billion. … Even if the stimulus package proves wildly successful, however, it won't pay for itself in full, at least not in the near term. The Congressional Budget Office estimated Wednesday that the federal budget deficit this year will increase to $219 billion or 1.5 percent of gross domestic product. … And that doesn't count the cost of a stimulus plan. Stimulus will bump that deficit up, but not necessarily dollar for dollar. Here's why: If the stimulus effort works, the increased economic activity will generate federal tax revenue. … Some lawmakers want the cost of any stimulus measures to be offset by other revenue-raising steps, such as raising taxes. But proponents of the stimulus package note that it would defeat the purpose to spend money to stimulate the economy and at the same time replace it. … Of course, there's another way to view cost in the stimulus debate: How much will it cost the country if the economy continues to slide and Congress takes no action? … What's not clear is the cost to the economy if a stimulus package comes too late—a real concern since legislation could get bogged down by politics.

    *CNN*, January 23, 2008

    a. Explain the intended effect of this fiscal stimulus package and draw a graph to illustrate it.
    b. Why might the stimulus package come "too late?" What are the potential consequences of the stimulus package coming "too late?"
    c. Explain why $150 billion of tax cuts won't increase the budget deficit by $150 billion.
    d. Explain why the government doesn't just raise taxes to cover the cost of the stimulus package so that it does not add to the budget deficit.
    e. Will the total budget deficit for 2008 be only the result of a structural deficit, a cyclical deficit, or a combination of the two? Explain.
16. **Hair of the Dog**

    Here we are, plunging into a recession. The proximate cause is irresponsible mortgage loans made to people who can't pay the money back. The deeper cause is, at least in part, years of too much borrowing and spending by Americans, both as individuals and collectively through the government. … Although quibbling over the details, everyone—Republicans and Democrats, the White House and Congress, all the presidential candidates—agrees that what we need is a "fiscal stimulus." In other words, the government should go out and borrow even more money and pass it around for us to spend. The experts caution that for maximum stimulus effect, we must be sure to spend it immediately. No squirreling it away for a rainy day. In drinking circles, they call this hair of the dog: to cure a hangover, you have another drink. … My gripe is that telling Americans they need to borrow and spend just a little bit more to get us past this recession—and then reform their ways—is like telling an alcoholic he needs one more drink before sobering up. I think we should sober up first. …

*Time*, January 24, 2008

a. Explain the argument made that "too much borrowing" by individuals and the federal government can contribute to a recession.
b. Why does effective fiscal stimulus require less saving (or even dissaving) by both the government and households?
c. How does fiscal stimulus reflect the "hair of the dog" mentality?

17. **Obama: Give Economy $50 Billion Boost**

Barack Obama said Monday that lawmakers should inject another $50 billion immediately into the sluggish U.S. economy. … "Such relief can't wait until the next president takes office." … He said that he supports the expansion and extension of unemployment benefits. … One bill, expected to go to the House floor for consideration this week, calls for an additional 13 weeks of benefits to be added to what is typically a 26-week cap on federal payments. In addition, it calls for 13 weeks on top of that for workers in states with very high unemployment rates. … Obama in his speech criticized his Republican rival, John McCain, for proposing to extend all of President Bush's 2001 and 2003 tax cuts. …

*CNN*, June 9, 2008

a. Explain the potential demand-side effect of extending unemployment benefits.
b. Explain the potential supply-side effect of extending unemployment benefits.
c. Draw a graph to illustrate the combined demand-side and supply-side effect of extending unemployment benefits.
d. Compare the supply-side effect of Obama's proposal to extend unemployment benefits with McCain's policy to extend Bush's 2001 and 2003 tax cuts.

18. **The Evolution of John McCain**

McCain wants to make the Bush tax cuts permanent; then he wants to keep going. He would repeal the alternative minimum tax, slash the corporate tax, double the child-care tax credit, and … allow businesses to write off the full cost of capital investments in one year. It'll be expensive … but McCain insists that he can balance the budget in four years with promised savings from running a tighter ship and increased tax revenues as the economy expands. … [H]e's in favor of tax cuts … because he'll insist on linking them to spending cuts.

*Fortune*, July 7, 2008

a. Explain the potential supply-side effects of the various components of McCain's economic plan.
b. Explain McCain's argument that a balanced budget is possible within four years, even with tax cuts.

19. **U.S. Budget Deficit Will Climb to $250 Billion as Economy Weakens**

The U.S. deficit for the current budget year will jump to about $250 billion … as a weaker economy and lower corporate profits weigh on the government's fiscal ledger.

*International Herald Tribune*, January 23, 2008

a. How did the business cycle influence the U.S. federal budget in 2008?
b. Explain why the federal budget deficit was larger in 2008 than in 2007.
c. How did automatic stabilizers influence the budget deficit in 2008? Did they change the structural deficit?

20. Study *Reading Between the Lines* on pp. 344–345.

a. Describe the key proposals to help middle income families and boost the economy outlined by president-elect Obama in November 2008.
b. Explain why extending unemployment insurance benefits has both a supply-side and demand-side effect on real GDP and the price level.
c. Going forward in 2009 and 2010, do you think the federal budget should be brought back into balance or do you think a large and perhaps even larger deficit should be maintained? Explain and illustrate your answer.

# 14 Monetary Policy

**After studying this chapter, you will be able to:**

- Describe the objectives of U.S. monetary policy and the framework for setting and achieving them
- Explain how the Federal Reserve makes its interest rate decision and achieves its interest rate target
- Explain the transmission channels through which the Federal Reserve influences the inflation rate
- Explain and compare alternative monetary policy strategies

**At eight regularly scheduled meetings a year, and** in an emergency between regular meetings, the Federal Reserve decides whether to change its interest rate target. And every business day, the Federal Reserve Bank of New York operates in financial markets to implement the Fed's decision and ensure that its target interest rate is achieved. Financial market traders, economic journalists, and pundits watch the economy for clues about what the Fed will decide at its next meeting.

How does the Fed make its interest rate decision? What exactly does the New York Fed do every day to keep the interest rate where it wants it? And how do the Fed's interest rate changes influence the economy? Can the Fed speed up economic growth and lower unemployment by lowering the interest rate and keep inflation in check by raising the interest rate?

The Fed's monetary policy strategy isn't the only one that might be used. Is the Fed's current monetary policy strategy the best one? What are the benefits and what are the risks associated with the alternative monetary policy strategies?

What special measures can the Fed take in a financial crisis like the one that engulfed the U.S. and global economies in 2008?

You learned about the functions of the Fed and its long-run effects on the price level and inflation rate in Chapter 8. In this chapter, you will learn about the Fed's monetary policy in both the long run and the short run. You will learn how the Fed influences the interest rate and how the interest rate influences the economy. You will also review the alternative ways in which monetary policy might be conducted. In *Reading Between the Lines* at the end of the chapter, you will see the Fed in an aggressive move against recession and deflation in 2008 and 2009.

# Monetary Policy Objectives and Framework

A nation's monetary policy objectives and the framework for setting and achieving those objectives stem from the relationship between the central bank and the government.

We'll describe the objectives of U.S. monetary policy and the framework and assignment of responsibility for achieving those objectives.

## Monetary Policy Objectives

The objectives of monetary policy are ultimately political. The objectives of U.S. monetary policy are set out in the mandate of the Board of Governors of the Federal Reserve System, which is defined by the Federal Reserve Act of 1913 and its subsequent amendments.

**Federal Reserve Act** The Fed's mandate was most recently clarified in amendments to the Federal Reserve Act passed by Congress in 2000. The 2000 law states that mandate in the following words:

> The Board of Governors of the Federal Reserve System and the Federal Open Market Committee shall maintain long-run growth of the monetary and credit aggregates commensurate with the economy's long-run potential to increase production, so as to promote effectively the goals of maximum employment, stable prices, and moderate long-term interest rates.

**Goals and Means** This description of the Fed's monetary policy objectives has two distinct parts: a statement of the goals, or ultimate objectives, and a prescription of the means by which the Fed should pursue its goals.

**Goals of Monetary Policy** The goals are "maximum employment, stable prices, and moderate long-term interest rates." In the long run, these goals are in harmony and reinforce each other. But in the short run, these goals might come into conflict. Let's examine these goals a bit more closely.

Achieving the goal of "maximum employment" means attaining the maximum sustainable growth rate of potential GDP and keeping real GDP close to potential GDP. It also means keeping the unemployment rate close to the natural unemployment rate.

Achieving the goal of "stable prices" means keeping the inflation rate low (and perhaps close to zero).

Achieving the goal of "moderate long-term interest rates" means keeping long-term *nominal* interest rates close to (or even equal to) long-term *real* interest rates.

Price stability is the key goal. It is the source of maximum employment and moderate long-term interest rates. Price stability provides the best available environment for households and firms to make the saving and investment decisions that bring economic growth. So price stability encourages the maximum sustainable growth rate of potential GDP.

Price stability delivers moderate long-term interest rates because the nominal interest rate reflects the inflation rate. The nominal interest rate equals the real interest rate plus the inflation rate. With stable prices, the nominal interest rate is close to the real interest rate, and most of the time, this rate is likely to be moderate.

In the short run, the Fed faces a tradeoff between inflation and interest rates and between inflation and real GDP, employment, and unemployment. Taking an action that is designed to lower the inflation rate and achieve stable prices might mean raising interest rates, which lowers employment and real GDP and increases the unemployment rate in the short run.

**Means for Achieving the Goals** The 2000 law instructs the Fed to pursue its goals by "maintain[ing] long-run growth of the monetary and credit aggregates commensurate with the economy's long-run potential to increase production." You can perhaps recognize this statement as being consistent with the quantity theory of money that you studied in Chapter 8 (see pp. 202–203). The "economy's long-run potential to increase production" is the growth rate of potential GDP. The "monetary and credit aggregates" are the quantities of money and loans. By keeping the growth rate of the quantity of money in line with the growth rate of potential GDP, the Fed is expected to be able to maintain full employment and keep the price level stable.

To pursue the goals of monetary policy, the Fed must make the general concepts of price stability and maximum employment precise and operational.

## Operational "Stable Prices" Goal

The Fed pays attention to two measures of inflation: the Consumer Price Index (CPI) and the personal consumption expenditure (PCE) deflator. But the *core PCE deflator,* which excludes food and fuel prices, is the Fed's operational guide and the Fed defines the rate of increase in the core PCE deflator as the **core inflation rate.**

The Fed focuses on the core inflation rate because it is less volatile than the total CPI inflation rate and the Fed believes that it provides a better indication of whether price stability is being achieved.

Figure 14.1 shows the core inflation rate alongside the total CPI inflation rate since 1992. You can see why the Fed says that the core rate is a better indicator. Its fluctuations are smoother and represent a sort of trend through the wider fluctuations in total CPI inflation.

The Fed has not defined price stability, but the Fed almost certainly doesn't regard price stability as meaning a core inflation rate equal to zero. Former Fed Chairman Alan Greenspan suggests that "price stability is best thought of as an environment in which inflation is so low and stable over time that it does not materially enter into the decisions of households and firms." He also believes that a "specific numerical inflation target would represent an unhelpful and false precision."[1]

Ben Bernanke, Alan Greenspan's successor, has been more precise and suggested that a core inflation rate of between 1 and 2 percent a year is the equivalent of price stability. This inflation range might be thought of as the Fed's comfort zone for the inflation rate.

**FIGURE 14.1** Operational Price Stability Goal: Core Inflation

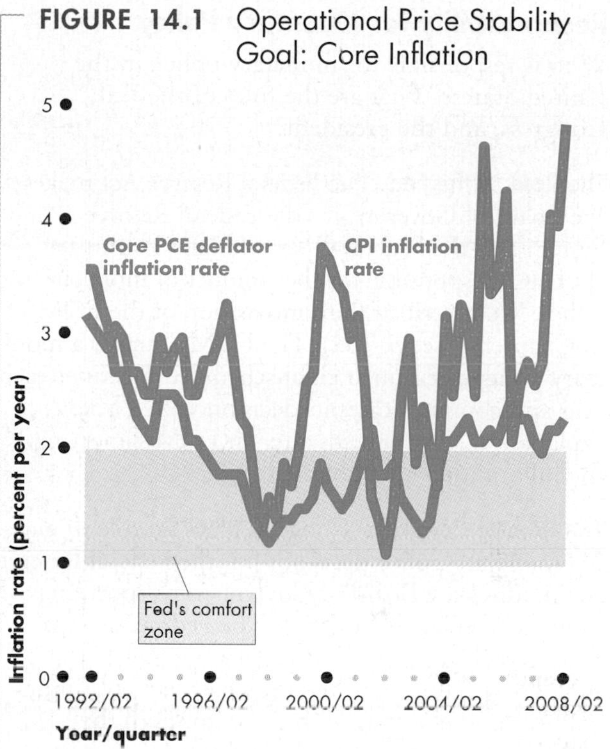


The CPI inflation rate fluctuates more than the core inflation rate. If a 1 to 2 percent core inflation rate is price stability, then the Fed achieved stable prices between 1996 and 2004. In all the other years, the inflation rate was above the level consistent with price stability.

*Source of data:* Bureau of Labor Statistics.

myeconlab animation

## Operational "Maximum Employment" Goal

The Fed regards stable prices (a core inflation rate of 1 to 2 percent a year) as the primary goal of monetary policy and as a means to achieving the other two goals. But the Fed also pays attention to the business cycle and tries to steer a steady course between inflation and recession. To gauge the state of output and employment relative to full employment, the Fed looks at a large number of indicators that include the labor force participation rate, the unemployment rate, measures of capacity utilization, activity in the housing market, the stock market, and regional information gathered by the regional Federal Reserve Banks. All these data are summarized in the Fed's *Beige Book.*

While the Fed considers a vast range of data, one number stands out as a summary of the overall state of aggregate demand relative to potential GDP. That number is the *output gap*—the percentage deviation of real GDP from potential GDP.

When the output gap is positive, it is an inflationary gap that brings an increase in the inflation rate. And when the output gap is negative, it is a recessionary gap that results in lost output and in employment being below its full-employment equilibrium level. So the Fed tries to minimize the output gap.

[1] Alan Greenspan, "Transparency in Monetary Policy," *Federal Reserve of St. Louis Review,* 84(4), 5–6, July/August 2002.

### Responsibility for Monetary Policy

Who is responsible for monetary policy in the United States? What are the roles of the Fed, Congress, and the president?

**The Role of the Fed** The Federal Reserve Act makes the Board of Governors of the Federal Reserve System and the Federal Open Market Committee (FOMC) responsible for the conduct of monetary policy. We described the composition of the FOMC in Chapter 8 (see p. 192). The FOMC makes a monetary policy decision at eight scheduled meetings each year and communicates its decision with a brief explanation. Three weeks after an FOMC meeting, the full minutes are published.

**The Role of Congress** Congress plays no role in making monetary policy decisions but the Federal Reserve Act requires the Board of Governors to report on monetary policy to Congress. The Fed makes two reports each year, one in February and another in July. These reports and the Fed chairman's testimony before Congress along with the minutes of the FOMC communicate the Fed's thinking on monetary policy to lawmakers and the public.

**The Role of the President** The formal role of the president of the United States is limited to appointing the members and the chairman of the Board of Governors. But some presidents—Richard Nixon was one—have tried to influence Fed decisions.

You now know the objectives of monetary policy and can describe the framework and assignment of responsibility for achieving those objectives. Your next task is to see how the Federal Reserve conducts its monetary policy.

### Review Quiz

1 What are the objectives of monetary policy?
2 Are the goals of monetary policy in harmony or in conflict (a) in the long run and (b) in the short run?
3 What is the core inflation rate and how does it differ from the overall CPI inflation rate?
4 Who is responsible for U.S. monetary policy?

Work Study Plan 14.1 and get instant feedback.

## The Conduct of Monetary Policy

In this section, we describe the way in which the Federal Reserve conducts its monetary policy and we explain the Fed's monetary policy strategy. We evaluate the Fed's strategy in the final section of this chapter, where we describe and compare alternative monetary policy strategies.

### Choosing a Policy Instrument

A **monetary policy instrument** is a variable that the Fed can directly control or closely target. As the sole issuer of the monetary base, the Fed is a monopoly. Like all monopolies, it can fix the quantity of its product and leave the market to determine the price; or it can fix the price of its product and leave the market to choose the quantity.

The first decision is whether to fix the price of U.S. money on the foreign exchange market—the exchange rate. A country that operates a fixed exchange rate cannot pursue an independent monetary policy. The United States has a flexible exchange rate and pursues an independent monetary policy. (Chapter 9 explains the foreign exchange market and the factors that influence the exchange rate.)

Even with a flexible exchange rate, the Fed still has a choice of policy instrument. It can decide to target the monetary base or a short-term interest rate. While the Fed can set either of these two variables, it cannot set both. The value of one is the consequence of the other. If the Fed decided to decrease the monetary base, the interest rate would rise. If the Fed decided to raise the interest rate, the monetary base would decrease. So the Fed must decide which of these two variables to target.

### The Federal Funds Rate

The Fed's choice of monetary policy instrument, which is the same choice as that made by most other major central banks, is a short-term interest rate. Given this choice, the Fed permits the exchange rate and the quantity of money to find their own equilibrium values and has no preset views about what those values should be.

The interest rate that the Fed targets is the **federal funds rate**, which is the interest rate on overnight loans that banks make to each other.

Figure 14.2 shows the federal funds rate since 1992. You can see that the federal funds rate ranges between a high of 6.5 percent and a low of 1 percent. In 1992 and again in 2000, when the federal funds rate was high (6.5 percent), the Fed's actions were aimed at lowering the inflation rate.

Between 2002 and 2004 the federal funds rate was set at historically low levels. During these years, inflation was well anchored at close to 2 percent a year, and the Fed was less concerned about inflation than it was about recession. So the Fed set a low interest rate to limit the risk of recession.

Although the Fed can change the federal funds rate by any (reasonable) amount that it chooses, it normally changes the federal funds rate by only a quarter of a percentage point.[2]

**FIGURE 14.2** The Federal Funds Rate

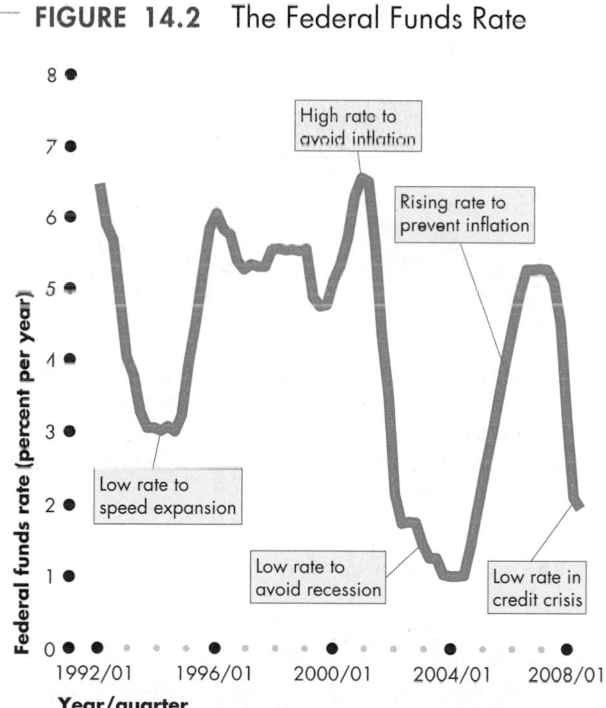


The Fed sets a target for the federal funds rate and then takes actions to keep the rate close to its target. When the Fed wants to slow inflation, it takes actions that raise the federal funds rate. When inflation is low and the Fed wants to avoid recession, it takes actions that lower the federal funds rate.

*Source of data:* Board of Governors of the Federal Reserve System.

myeconlab animation

How does the Fed decide the appropriate level for the federal funds rate? And how, having made that decision, does the Fed move the federal funds rate to its target level? We'll now answer these two questions.

## The Fed's Decision-Making Strategy

Two alternative decision-making strategies might be used. They are summarized by the terms:

- Instrument rule
- Targeting rule

**Instrument Rule** An **instrument rule** is a decision rule for monetary policy that sets the policy instrument at a level that is based on the current state of the economy. The best-known instrument rule is the **Taylor rule**, in which the instrument is the federal funds rate and the rule is to make the federal funds rate respond by formula to the inflation rate and the output gap. (We compare the Fed's decisions with the Taylor rule on the next page.)

To implement the Taylor instrument rule, the FOMC would simply get the best estimates available of the current inflation rate and output gap and then mechanically calculate the level at which to set the federal funds rate.

**Targeting Rule** A **targeting rule** is a decision rule for monetary policy that sets the policy instrument at a level that makes the forecast of the ultimate policy goal equal to its target. If the ultimate policy goal is a 2 percent inflation rate and the instrument is the federal funds rate, the targeting rule sets the federal funds rate at a level that makes the forecast of the inflation rate equal to 2 percent.

To implement such a targeting rule, the FOMC must gather and process a large amount of information about the economy, the way it responds to shocks, and the way it responds to policy. The FOMC must then process all these data and come to a judgment about the best level for the policy instrument.

The FOMC minutes suggest that the Fed follows a targeting rule strategy. But some economists think the interest rate settings decided by the FOMC are too responsive to the output gap and outlook for the real economy.

[2] A quarter of a percentage point is also called 25 *basis points*. A basis point is one hundredth of one percentage point.

## Influences on the Federal Funds Rate

### Does the Fed Overreact to Output Fluctuations?

Stanford economist John B. Taylor has suggested a rule for the federal funds that he says would perform better than the FOMC's historical performance.

The *Taylor rule* sets the federal funds rate (*FFR*) at the equilibrium real interest rate (which Taylor says is 2 percent a year) plus amounts based on the inflation rate (*INF*), and the output gap (*GAP*) according to the following formula (all the values are percentages):

$$FFR = 2 + INF + 0.5(INF - 2) + 0.5GAP$$

In words, the Taylor rule sets the federal funds rate at 2 percent plus the inflation rate plus one half of the deviation of inflation from its implicit target of 2 percent, plus one half of the output gap.

The figure shows how the Fed has deviated from the Taylor rule. Part (a) shows the extent to which the inflation rate has exceeded 2 percent a year—the extent to which the Fed has missed the goal of price stability. This variable had a downward trend through mid-1998 and then an upward trend.

Part (b) shows the output gap—the extent to which the Fed missed its maximum employment goal. This variable cycles.

Part (c) shows the federal funds rate (the green line labeled FOMC decision) alongside the federal funds rate that would have been set based on parts (a) and (b) if the Taylor rule had been followed (the blue line labeled Taylor rule).

You can see that the Fed moves the federal funds rate in the same general directions as the Taylor rule, but in swings that have much greater amplitude.

Between 1992 and 1994 and again between 2002 and 2006, the Fed set the federal funds rate at a lower level than what the Taylor rule would have achieved. Between 1994 and 2001 and again between 2007 and 2008, the Fed set the interest rate higher than what the Taylor rule would have set.

One reason for the Fed's deviation from the Taylor rule is that the Fed places a greater weight on achieving the goal of "maximum employment" and a lower weight on the inflation rate than the Taylor rule's equal weights. Notice the similarity in the cycles of the output gap in part (b) and the federal funds rate in part (c).

Another reason for the deviation is that the Fed uses more information than just the output gap and inflation rate. For example, after 9/11, the Fed lowered the federal funds rate to ensure that financial markets did not collapse during a period of increased political uncertainty and pessimism. But interestingly, the Taylor rule and the Fed's decision delivered the same level of the federal funds rate during the sub-prime credit crisis of 2008.

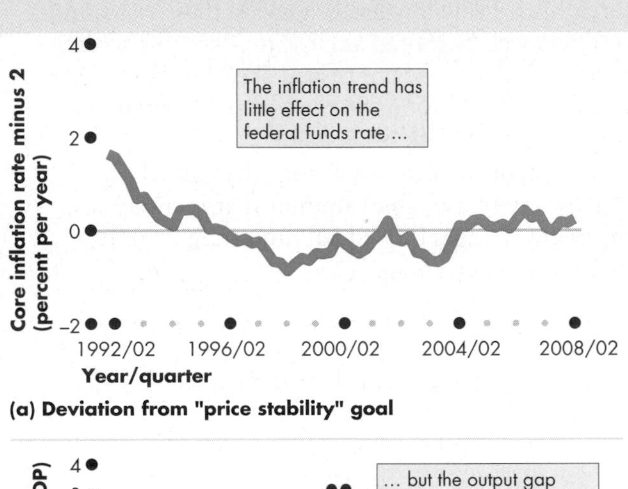


(a) Deviation from "price stability" goal

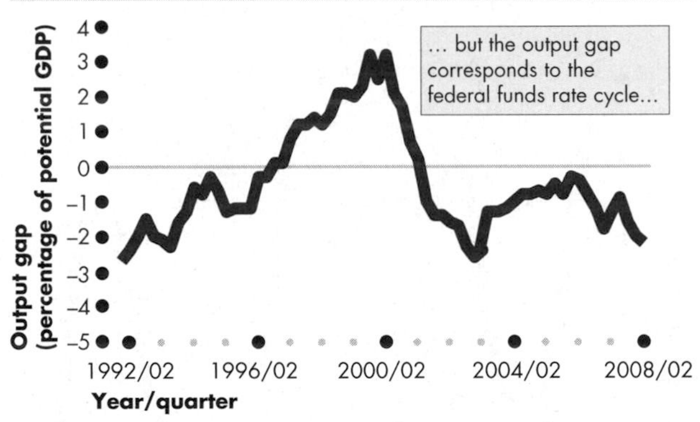


(b) Deviation from "maximum employment" goal

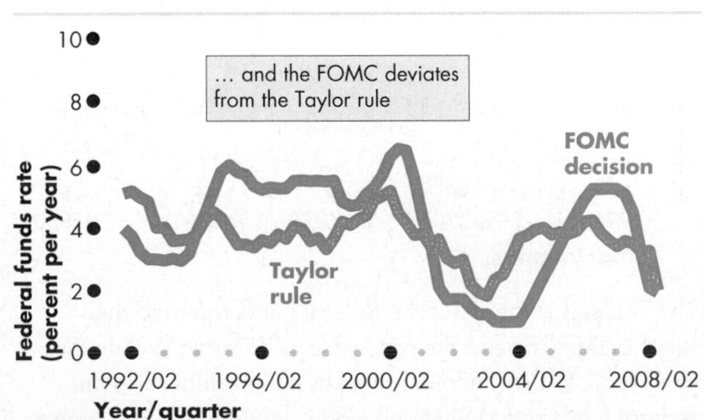


(c) FOMC decisions and the Taylor rule

**Influences on the Federal Funds Rate**

*Sources of data*: Board of Governors of the Federal Reserve System, Congressional Budget Office, and Bureau of Labor Statistics.

## Hitting the Federal Funds Rate Target: Open Market Operations

Once an interest rate decision has been made, the Fed achieves its target by instructing the New York Fed to make *open market operations*—to purchase or sell government securities from or to a commercial bank or the public. When the Fed buys securities, it pays for them with newly created reserves held by banks. When the Fed sells securities, it is paid for them with reserves held by banks. So open market operations directly influence the reserves of banks.

**An Open Market Purchase** To see how an open market operation changes bank reserves, suppose the Fed buys $100 million of government securities from the Bank of America. When the Fed makes this transaction, two things happen:

1. The Bank of America has $100 million less securities, and the Fed has $100 million more securities.
2. The Fed pays for the securities by placing $100 million in the Bank of America's deposit account at the Fed.

Figure 14.3 shows the effects of these actions on the balance sheets of the Fed and the Bank of America. Ownership of the securities passes from the Bank of America to the Fed, so the Bank of America's assets decrease by $100 million and the Fed's assets increase by $100 million, as shown by the blue arrow running from the Bank of America to the Fed.

The Fed pays for the securities by placing $100 million in the Bank of America's reserve account at the Fed, as shown by the green arrow running from the Fed to the Bank of America.

The Fed's assets and liabilities increase by $100 million. The Bank of America's total assets are unchanged: It sold securities to increase its reserves.

**An Open Market Sale** If the Fed *sells* $100 million of government securities in the open market:

1. The Bank of America has $100 million more securities, and the Fed has $100 million less securities.
2. The Bank of America pays for the securities by using $100 million of its reserves deposit account at the Fed.

Figure 14.4 shows the effects of these actions on the balance sheets of the Fed and the Bank of America.

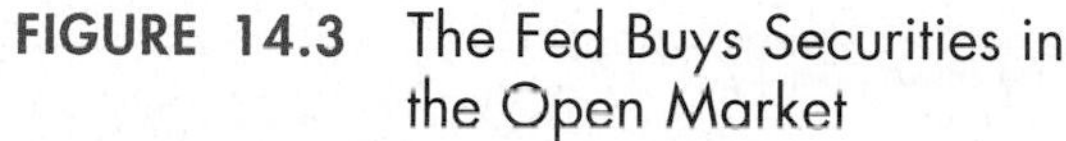

**FIGURE 14.3** The Fed Buys Securities in the Open Market

**Federal Reserve Bank of New York**

| Assets (millions) | | Liabilities (millions) | |
|---|---|---|---|
| Securities | +$100 | Reserves of Bank of America | +$100 |

The Federal Reserve Bank of New York buys securities from a bank ...

... and pays for the securities by increasing the reserves of the bank

**Bank of America**

| Assets (millions) | | Liabilities (millions) |
|---|---|---|
| Securities | –$100 | |
| Reserves | +$100 | |

When the Fed buys securities in the open market, it creates bank reserves. Fed assets and liabilities increase, and the selling bank exchanges securities for reserves.

myeconlab animation

**FIGURE 14.4** The Fed Sells Securities in the Open Market

**Federal Reserve Bank of New York**

| Assets (millions) | | Liabilities (millions) | |
|---|---|---|---|
| Securities | –$100 | Reserves of Bank of America | –$100 |

The Federal Reserve Bank of New York sells securities to a bank ...

... and the bank uses its reserves to pay for the securities

**Bank of America**

| Assets (millions) | | Liabilities (millions) |
|---|---|---|
| Securities | +$100 | |
| Reserves | –$100 | |

When the Fed sells securities in the open market, it reduces bank reserves. Fed assets and liabilities decrease, and the buying bank exchanges reserves for securities.

America. Ownership of the securities passes from the Fed to the Bank of America, so the Fed's assets decrease by $100 million and the Bank of America's assets increase by $100 million, as shown by the blue arrow running from the Fed to the Bank of America.

The Bank of America uses $100 million of its reserves to pay for the securities, as the green arrow running from the Bank of America to the Fed shows.

Both the Fed's assets and liabilities decrease by $100 million. The Bank of America's total assets are unchanged: It has used reserves to buy securities.

## Equilibrium in the Market for Reserves

To see how an open market operation changes the federal funds rate, we must see what happens in the federal funds market—the market in which banks lend to and borrow from each other overnight—and in the market for bank reserves.

The higher the federal funds rate, the greater is the quantity of overnight loans supplied and the smaller is the quantity of overnight loans demanded in the federal funds market. The equilibrium federal funds rate balances the quantities demanded and supplied.

An equivalent way of looking at the forces that determine the federal funds rate is to consider the demand for and supply of bank reserves. Banks hold reserves to meet the required reserve ratio and so that they can make payments. But reserves are costly to hold. The alternative to holding reserves is to lend them in the federal funds market and earn the federal funds rate. The higher the federal funds rate, the higher is the opportunity cost of holding reserves and the greater is the incentive to economize on the quantity of reserves held.

So the quantity of reserves demanded by banks depends on the federal funds rate. The higher the federal funds rate, other things remaining the same, the smaller is the quantity of reserves demanded.

Figure 14.5 illustrates the market for bank reserves. The $x$-axis measures the quantity of reserves on deposit at the Fed, and the $y$-axis measures the federal funds rate. The demand for reserves is the curve labeled *RD*.

The Fed's open market operations determine the supply of reserves, which is shown by the supply curve *RS*. To decrease reserves, the Fed conducts an open market sale. To increase reserves, the Fed conducts an open market purchase.

**FIGURE 14.5** The Market for Reserves

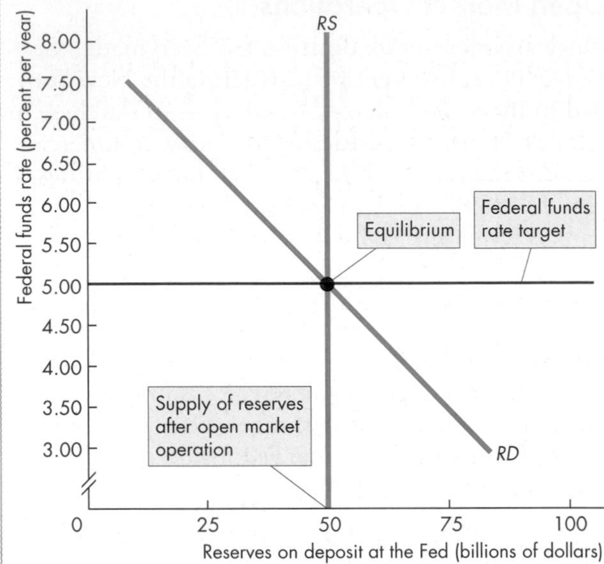


The demand curve for reserves is *RD*. The quantity of reserves demanded decreases as the federal funds rate rises because the federal funds rate is the opportunity cost of holding reserves. The supply curve of reserves is *RS*. The Fed uses open market operations to make the quantity of reserves supplied equal the quantity of reserves demanded ($50 billion in this case) at the federal funds rate target (5 percent a year in this case).

animation

Equilibrium in the market for bank reserves determines the federal funds rate where the quantity of reserves demanded by the banks equals the quantity of reserves supplied by the Fed. By using open market operations, the Fed adjusts the supply of reserves to keep the federal funds rate on target.

## Review Quiz

1. What is the Fed's monetary policy instrument?
2. What are the main influences on the FOMC federal funds rate decision?
3. What happens when the Fed buys or sells securities in the open market?
4. How is the federal funds rate determined in the market for reserves?

Work Study Plan 14.2 and get instant feedback.

## Monetary Policy Transmission

You've seen that the Fed's goal is to keep the price level stable (keep the inflation rate around 2 percent a year) and to achieve maximum employment (keep the output gap close to zero). And you've seen how the Fed can use its power to set the federal funds rate at its desired level. We're now going to trace the events that follow a change in the federal funds rate and see how those events lead to the ultimate policy goal. We'll begin with a quick overview of the transmission process and then look at each step a bit more closely.

### Quick Overview

When the Fed lowers the federal funds rate, other short-term interest rates and the exchange rate also fall. The quantity of money and the supply of loanable funds increase. The long-term real interest rate falls. The lower real interest rate increases consumption expenditure and investment. And the lower exchange rate makes U.S. exports cheaper and imports more costly, so net exports increase. Easier bank loans reinforce the effect of lower interest rates on aggregate expenditure. Aggregate demand increases, which increases real GDP and the price level relative to what they would have been. Real GDP growth and inflation speed up.

When the Fed raises the federal funds rate, as the sequence of events that we've just reviewed plays out, the effects are in the opposite directions.

Figure 14.6 provides a schematic summary of these ripple effects for both a cut and a rise in the federal funds rate.

These ripple effects stretch out over a period of between one and two years. The interest rate and exchange rate effects are immediate. The effects on money and bank loans follow in a few weeks and run for a few months. Real long-term interest rates change quickly and often in anticipation of the short-term interest rate changes. Spending plans change and real GDP growth changes after about one year. The inflation rate changes between one year and two years after the change in the federal funds rate. But these time lags are not entirely predictable and can be longer or shorter.

We're going to look at each stage in the transmission process, starting with the interest rate effects.

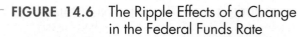

**FIGURE 14.6** The Ripple Effects of a Change in the Federal Funds Rate

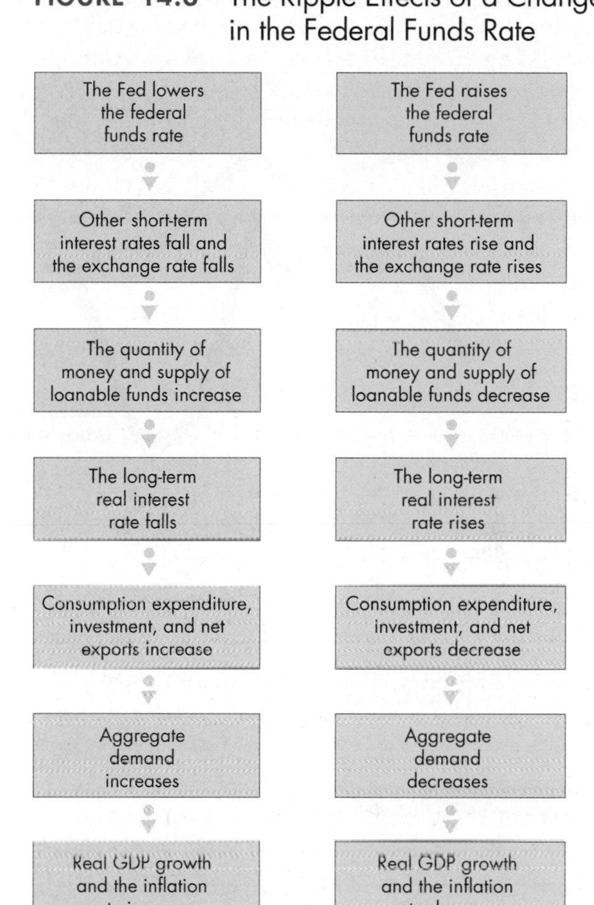


### Interest Rate Changes

The first effect of a monetary policy decision by the FOMC is a change in the federal funds rate. Other interest rates then change. These interest rate effects occur quickly and relatively predictably.

Figure 14.7 shows the fluctuations in three interest rates: the federal funds rate, the short-term bill rate, and the long-term bond rate.

**Federal Funds Rate** As soon as the FOMC announces a new setting for the federal funds rate, the New York Fed undertakes the necessary open market operations to hit the target. There is no doubt about where the interest rate changes shown in Fig. 14.7 are generated. They are driven by the Fed's monetary policy.

**FIGURE 14.7** Three Interest Rates

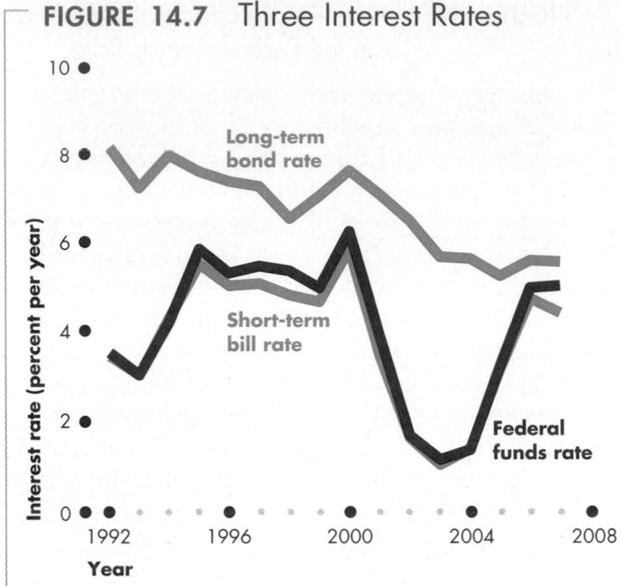


The short-term interest rates—the federal funds rate and the short-term bill rate—move closely together. The long-term bond rate is higher than the short-term rates, and it fluctuates less than the short-term rates.

*Source of data*: Board of Governors of the Federal Reserve System.

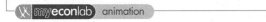

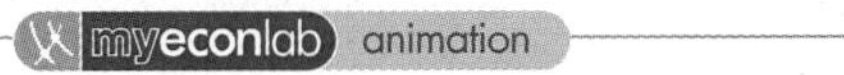


**Short-Term Bill Rate** The short-term bill rate is the interest rate paid by the U.S. government on 3-month Treasury bills. It is similar to the interest rate paid by U.S. businesses on short-term loans. Notice how closely the short-term bill rate follows the federal funds rate. The two rates are almost identical.

A powerful substitution effect keeps these two interest rates close. Commercial banks have a choice about how to hold their short-term liquid assets, and an overnight loan to another bank is a close substitute for short-term securities such as Treasury bills. If the interest rate on Treasury bills is higher than the federal funds rate, the quantity of overnight loans supplied decreases and the demand for Treasury bills increases. The price of Treasury bills rises and the interest rate falls.

Similarly, if the interest rate on Treasury bills is lower than the federal funds rate, the quantity of overnight loans supplied increases and the demand for Treasury bills decreases. The price of Treasury bills falls, and the interest rate rises.

When the interest rate on Treasury bills is close to the federal funds rate, there is no incentive for a bank to switch between making an overnight loan and buying Treasury bills. Both the Treasury bill market and the federal funds market are in equilibrium.

**The Long-Term Bond Rate** The long-term bond rate is the interest rate paid on bonds issued by large corporations. It is this interest rate that businesses pay on the loans that finance their purchase of new capital and that influences their investment decisions.

Two features of the long-term bond rate stand out: It is higher than the short-term rates, and it fluctuates less than the short-term rates.

The long-term interest rate is higher than the two short-term rates because long-term loans are riskier than short-term loans. To provide the incentive that brings forth a supply of long-term loans, lenders must be compensated for the additional risk. Without compensation for the additional risk, only short-term loans would be supplied.

The long-term interest rate fluctuates less than the short-term rates because it is influenced by expectations about future short-term interest rates as well as current short-term interest rates. The alternative to borrowing or lending long term is to borrow or lend using a sequence of short-term securities. If the long-term interest rate exceeds the expected average of future short-term interest rates, people will lend long term and borrow short term. The long-term interest rate will fall. And if the long-term interest rate is below the expected average of future short-term interest rates, people will borrow long term and lend short term. The long-term interest rate will rise.

These market forces keep the long-term interest rate close to the expected average of future short-term interest rates (plus a premium for the extra risk associated with long-term loans). The expected average future short-term interest rate fluctuates less than the current short-term interest rate.

## Exchange Rate Fluctuations

The exchange rate responds to changes in the interest rate in the United States relative to the interest rates in other countries—*the U.S. interest rate differential.* We explain this influence in Chapter 9 (see p. 221).

When the Fed raises the federal funds rate, the U.S. interest rate differential rises and, other things remaining the same, the U.S. dollar appreciates, and when the Fed lowers the federal funds rate, the U.S. interest rate differential falls and, other things remaining the same, the U.S. dollar depreciates.

Many factors other than the U.S. interest rate differential influence the exchange rate, so when the Fed changes the federal funds rate, the exchange rate does not usually change in exactly the way it would with other things remaining the same. So while monetary policy influences the exchange rate, many other factors also make the exchange rate change.

### Money and Bank Loans

The quantity of money and bank loans change when the Fed changes the federal funds rate target. A rise in the federal funds rate decreases the quantity of money and bank loans, and a fall in the federal funds rate increases the quantity of money and bank loans. These changes occur for two reasons: The quantity of deposits and loans created by the banking system changes and the quantity of money demanded changes.

You've seen that to change the federal funds rate, the Fed must change the quantity of bank reserves. A change in the quantity of bank reserves changes the monetary base, which in turn changes the quantity of deposits and loans that the banking system can create. A rise in the federal funds rate decreases reserves and decreases the quantity of deposits and bank loans created; and a fall in the federal funds rate increases reserves and increases the quantity of deposits and bank loans created.

The quantity of money created by the banking system must be held by households and firms. The change in the interest rate changes the quantity of money demanded. A fall in the interest rate increases the quantity of money demanded, and a rise in the interest rate decreases the quantity of money demanded.

A change in the quantity of money and the supply of bank loans directly affects consumption and investment plans. With more money and easier access to loans, consumers and firms spend more. With less money and loans harder to get, consumers and firms spend less.

### The Long-Term Real Interest Rate

Demand and supply in the market for loanable funds determine the long-term *real interest rate*, which equals the long-term *nominal* interest rate minus the expected inflation rate. The long-term real interest rate influences expenditure decisions.

In the long run, demand and supply in the loanable funds market depend only on real forces—on saving and investment decisions. But in the short run, when the price level is not fully flexible, the supply of loanable funds is influenced by the supply of bank loans. Changes in the federal funds rate change the supply of bank loans, which changes the supply of loanable funds and changes the interest rate in the loanable funds market.

A fall in the federal funds rate that increases the supply of bank loans increases the supply of loanable funds and lowers the equilibrium real interest rate. A rise in the federal funds rate that decreases the supply of bank loans decreases the supply of loanable funds and raises the equilibrium real interest rate.

These changes in the real interest rate, along with the other factors we've just described, change expenditure plans.

### Expenditure Plans

The ripple effects that follow a change in the federal funds rate change three components of aggregate expenditure:

- Consumption expenditure
- Investment
- Net exports

**Consumption Expenditure** Other things remaining the same, the lower the real interest rate, the greater is the amount of consumption expenditure and the smaller is the amount of saving.

**Investment** Other things remaining the same, the lower the real interest rate, the greater is the amount of investment.

**Net Exports** Other things remaining the same, the lower the interest rate, the lower is the exchange rate and the greater are exports and the smaller are imports.

So eventually, a cut in the federal funds rate increases aggregate expenditure and a rise in the federal funds rate curtails aggregate expenditure. These changes in aggregate expenditure plans change aggregate demand, real GDP, and the price level.

## The Change in Aggregate Demand, Real GDP, and the Price Level

The final link in the transmission chain is a change in aggregate demand and a resulting change in real GDP and the price level. By changing real GDP and the price level relative to what they would have been without a change in the federal funds rate, the Fed influences its ultimate goals: the inflation rate and the output gap.

## The Fed Fights Recession

If inflation is low and real GDP is below potential GDP, the Fed takes actions that are designed to restore full employment. Figure 14.8 shows the effects of the Fed's actions, starting in the market for bank reserves and ending in the market for real GDP.

**Market for Bank Reserves** In Fig. 14.8(a), which shows the market for bank reserves, the FOMC lowers the target federal funds rate from 5 percent to 4 percent a year. To achieve the new target, the New York Fed buys securities and increases the supply of reserves of the banking system from $RS_0$ to $RS_1$.

**Money Market** With increased reserves, the banks create deposits by making loans and the supply of money increases. The short-term interest rate falls and the quantity of money demanded increases. In Fig. 14.8(b), the supply of money increases from $MS_0$ to $MS_1$, the interest rate falls from 5 percent to 4 percent a year and the quantity of money increases from \$3 trillion to \$3.1 trillion. The interest rate in the money market and the federal funds rate are kept close to each other by the powerful substitution effect described on p. 762.

**Loanable Funds Market** Banks create money by making loans. In the long run, an increase in the supply of bank loans is matched by a rise in the price level and the quantity of *real* loans is unchanged. But in the short run, with a sticky price level, an increase in the supply of bank loans increases the supply of (real) loanable funds.

**FIGURE 14.8** The Fed Fights Recession

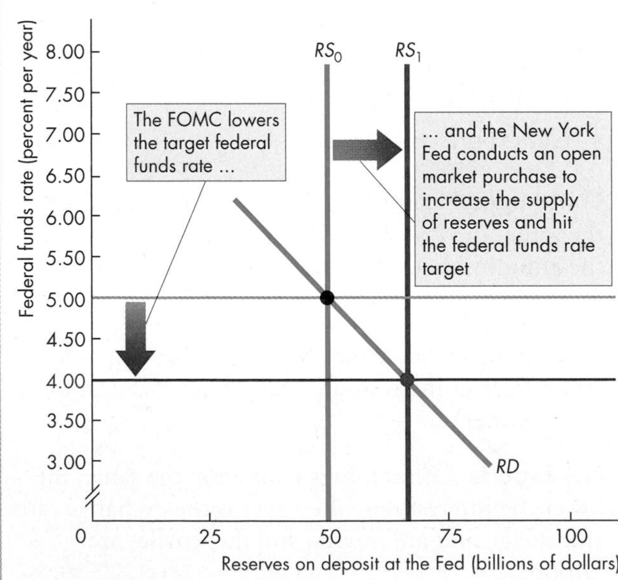


**(a) The market for bank reserves**

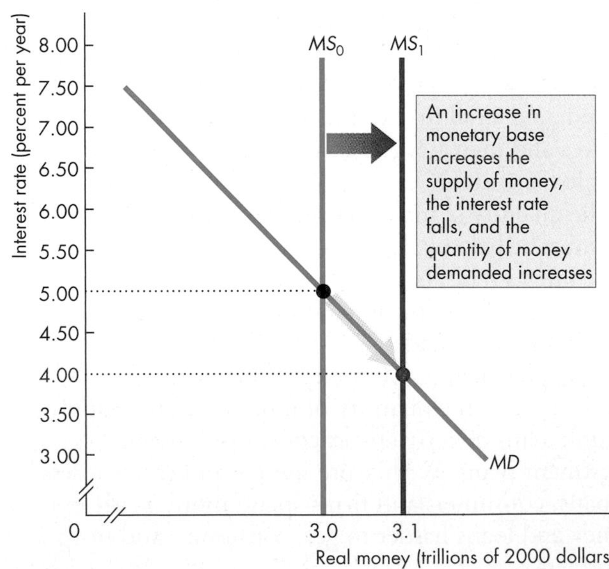


**(b) Money market**

In part (a), the FOMC lowers the federal funds rate target from 5 percent to 4 percent. The New York Fed buys securities in an open market operation and increases the supply of reserves from $RS_0$ to $RS_1$ to hit the new federal funds rate target.

In part (b), the supply of money increases from $MS_0$ to $MS_1$, the short-term interest rate falls, and the quantity of money demanded increases. The short-term interest rate and the federal funds rate change by similar amounts.

myeconlab animation

In Fig. 14.8(c), the supply of loanable funds curve shifts rightward from $SLF_0$ to $SLF_1$. With the demand for loanable funds at *DLF*, the real interest rate falls from 6 percent to 5.5 percent a year. (We're assuming a zero inflation rate so that the real interest rate equals the nominal interest rate.) The long-term interest rate changes by a smaller amount than the change in the short-term interest rate for the reason explained on p. 762.

**The Market for Real GDP** Figure 14.8(d) shows aggregate demand and aggregate supply—the demand for and supply of real GDP. Potential GDP is $12 trillion, where *LAS* is located. The short-run aggregate supply curve is *SAS*, and initially, the aggregate demand curve is $AD_0$. Real GDP is $11.8 trillion, which is less than potential GDP, so there is a recessionary gap. The Fed is reacting to this recessionary gap.

The increase in the supply of loans and the decrease in the real interest rate increase aggregate planned expenditure. (Not shown in the figure, a fall in the interest rate lowers the exchange rate, which increases net exports and aggregate planned expenditure.) The increase in aggregate expenditure, $\Delta E$, increases aggregate demand and shifts the aggregate demand curve rightward to $AD_0 + \Delta E$. A multiplier process begins. The increase in expenditure increases income, which induces an increase in consumption expenditure. Aggregate demand increases further, and the aggregate demand curve eventually shifts rightward to $AD_1$.

The new equilibrium is at full employment. Real GDP is equal to potential GDP. The price level rises to 120 and then becomes stable at that level. So after a one-time adjustment, there is price stability.

In this example, we have given the Fed a perfect hit at achieving full employment and keeping the price level stable. It is unlikely that the Fed would be able to achieve the precision of this example. If the Fed stimulated demand by too little and too late, the economy would experience a recession. And if the Fed hit the gas pedal too hard, it would push the economy from recession to inflation.

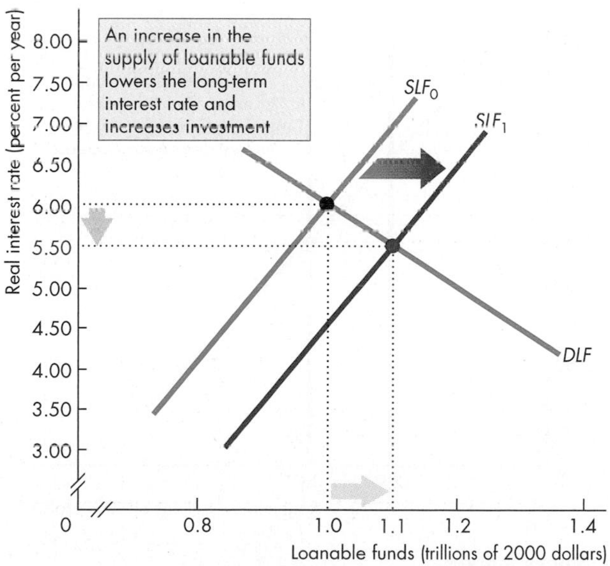


**(c) The market for loanable funds**

In part (c), an increase in the supply of bank loans increases the supply of loanable funds from $SLF_0$ to $SLF_1$ and the real interest rate falls. Investment increases.

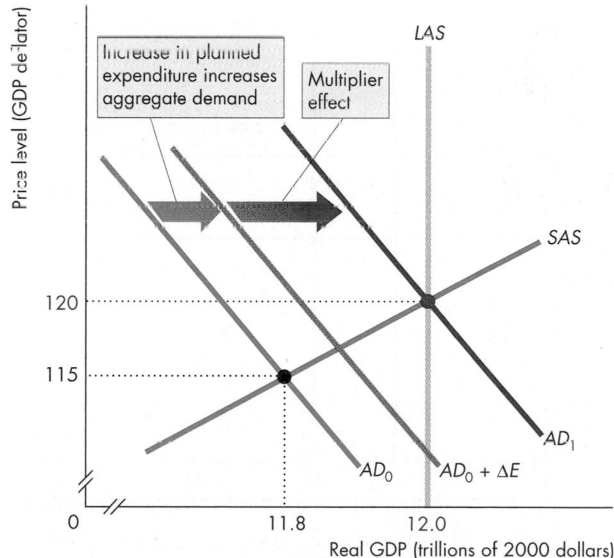


**(d) Real GDP and the price level**

In part (d), aggregate planned expenditure increases. The aggregate demand curve shifts to $AD_0 + \Delta E$ and eventually it shifts rightward to $AD_1$. Real GDP increases to potential GDP, and the price level rises.

## The Fed Fights Inflation

If the inflation rate is too high and real GDP is above potential GDP, the Fed takes actions that are designed to lower the inflation rate and restore price stability. Figure 14.9 shows the effects of the Fed's actions starting in the market for reserves and ending in the market for real GDP.

**Market for Bank Reserves** In Fig. 14.9(a), which shows the market for bank reserves, the FOMC raises the target federal funds rate from 5 percent to 6 percent a year. To achieve the new target, the New York Fed sells securities and decreases the supply of reserves of the banking system from $RS_0$ to $RS_1$.

**Money Market** With decreased reserves, the banks shrink deposits by decreasing loans and the supply of money decreases. The short-term interest rate rises and the quantity of money demanded decreases. In Fig. 14.9(b), the supply of money decreases from $MS_0$ to $MS_1$, the interest rate rises from 5 percent to 6 percent a year and the quantity of money decreases from \$3 trillion to \$2.9 trillion.

**Loanable Funds Market** With a decrease in reserves, banks must decrease the supply of loans. The supply of (real) loanable funds decreases, and the supply of loanable funds curve shifts leftward in Fig. 14.9(c) from $SLF_0$ to $SLF_1$. With the demand for loanable funds at *DLF*, the real interest rate rises from 6 percent to 6.5 percent a year. (Again, we're assuming a zero inflation rate so that the real interest rate equals the nominal interest rate.)

**The Market for Real GDP** Figure 14.9(d) shows aggregate demand and aggregate supply in the market for real GDP. Potential GDP is \$12 trillion where *LAS* is located. The short-run aggregate supply curve is *SAS* and initially the aggregate demand is $AD_0$. Now, real GDP is \$12.2 trillion, which is greater than potential GDP, so there is an inflationary gap. The Fed is reacting to this inflationary gap.

**FIGURE 14.9** The Fed Fights Inflation

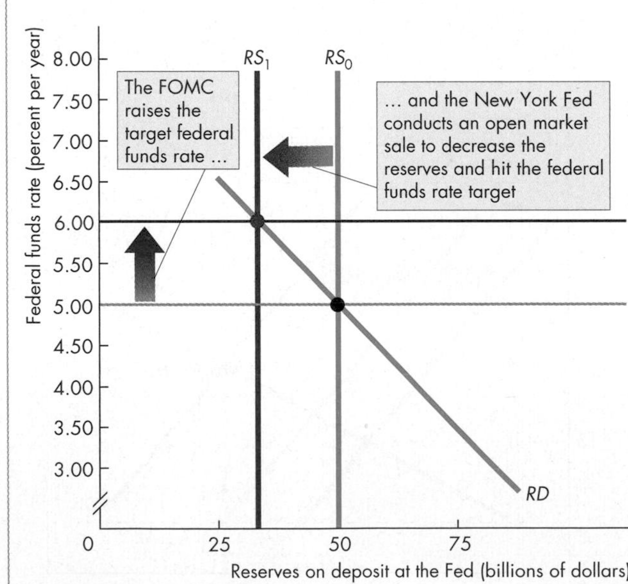


**(a) The market for bank reserves**

In part (a), the FOMC raises the federal funds rate from 5 percent to 6 percent. The New York Fed sells securities in an open market operation to decrease the supply of reserves from $RS_0$ to $RS_1$ and hit the new federal funds rate target.

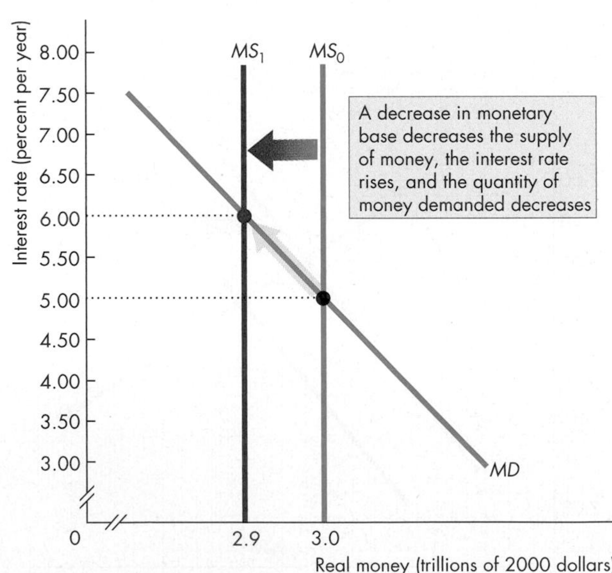


**(b) Money market**

In part (b), the supply of money decreases from $MS_0$ to $MS_1$, the short-term interest rate rises, and the quantity of money demanded decreases. The short-term interest rate and the federal funds rate change by similar amounts.

The increase in the short-term interest rate, the decrease in the supply of bank loans, and the increase in the real interest rate decrease aggregate planned expenditure. (Not shown in the figures, a rise in the interest rate raises the exchange rate, which decreases net exports and aggregate planned expenditure.)

The decrease in aggregate expenditure, $\Delta E$, decreases aggregate demand and shifts the aggregate demand curve to $AD_0 - \Delta E$. A multiplier process begins. The decrease in expenditure decreases income, which induces a decrease in consumption expenditure. Aggregate demand decreases further, and the aggregate demand curve eventually shifts leftward to $AD_1$.

The economy returns to full employment. Real GDP is equal to potential GDP. The price level falls to 120 and then becomes stable at that level. So after a one-time adjustment, there is price stability.

Again, in this example, we have given the Fed a perfect hit at achieving full employment and keeping the price level stable. If the Fed decreased aggregate demand by too little and too late, the economy would have remained with an inflationary gap and the inflation rate would have moved above the rate that is consistent with price stability. And if the Fed hit the brakes too hard, it would push the economy from inflation to recession.

## Loose Links and Long and Variable Lags

The ripple effects of monetary policy that we've just analyzed with the precision of an economic model are, in reality, very hard to predict and anticipate.

To achieve price stability and full employment, the Fed needs a combination of good judgment and good luck. Too large an interest rate cut in an underemployed economy can bring inflation, as it did during the 1970s. And too large an interest rate rise in an inflationary economy can create unemployment, as it did in 1981 and 1991. Loose links between the federal funds rate and the ultimate policy goals make unwanted outcomes inevitable and long and variable time lags add to the Fed's challenges.

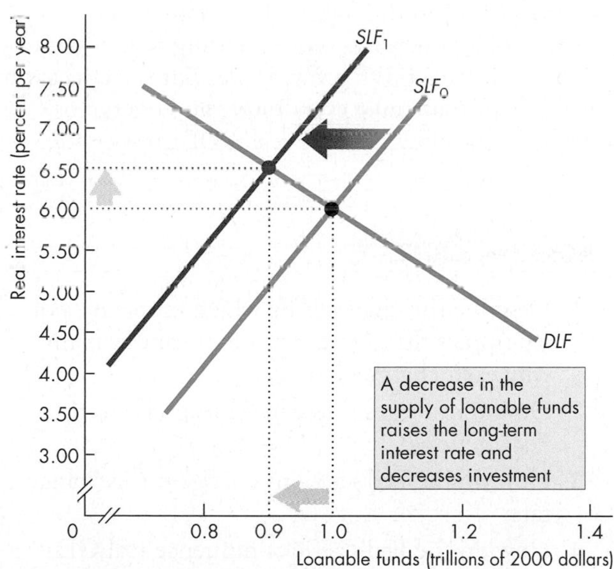


**(c) The market for loanable funds**

In part (c), a decrease in the supply of bank loans decreases the supply of loanable funds from $SLF_0$ to $SLF_1$ and the real interest rate rises. Investment decreases.

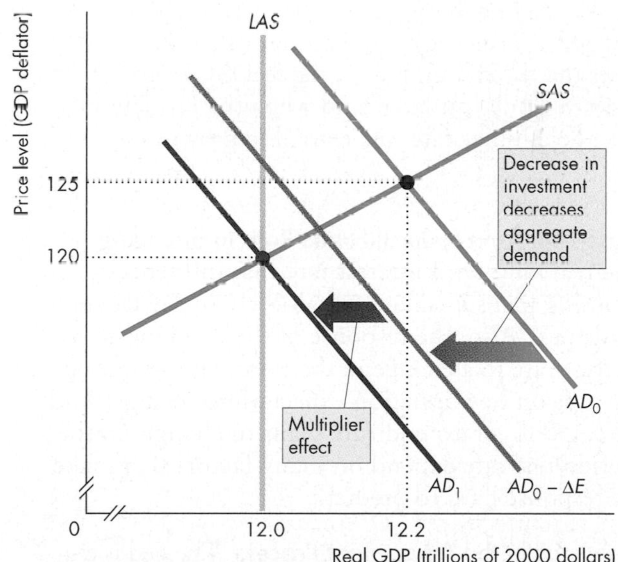


**(d) Real GDP and the price level**

In part (d), aggregate planned expenditure decreases. Aggregate demand decreases and the $AD$ curve shifts leftward from $AD_0$ to $AD_1$. Real GDP decreases to potential GDP, and the price level falls.

## A Reality Check

### A View of the Long and Variable Lag

You've studied the theory of monetary policy. Does it really work in the way we've described? It does, and the figure opposite provides some evidence to support this claim.

The blue line in the figure is the federal funds rate that the Fed targets *minus* the long-term bond rate. (When the long-term bond rate exceeds the federal funds rate, this gap is negative.)

We can view the gap between the federal funds rate and the long-term bond rate as a measure of how hard the Fed is trying to steer a change in course.

When the Fed is more concerned about recession than inflation and is trying to stimulate real GDP growth, it cuts the federal funds rate target and the gap between the long-term bond rate and the federal funds rate widens.

When the Fed is more concerned about inflation than recession and is trying to restrain real GDP growth, it raises the federal funds rate target and the gap between the long-term bond rate and the federal funds rate narrows.

The red line in the figure is the real GDP growth rate *one year later*. You can see that when the FOMC raises the federal funds rate, the real GDP growth rate slows one year later. And when the Fed lowers the federal funds rate, the real GDP growth rate speeds up one year later.

Not shown in the figure, the inflation rate increases and decreases corresponding to the fluctuations in the real GDP growth rate. But the effects on the inflation rate take even longer and are not as strong as the effects on the real GDP growth rate.

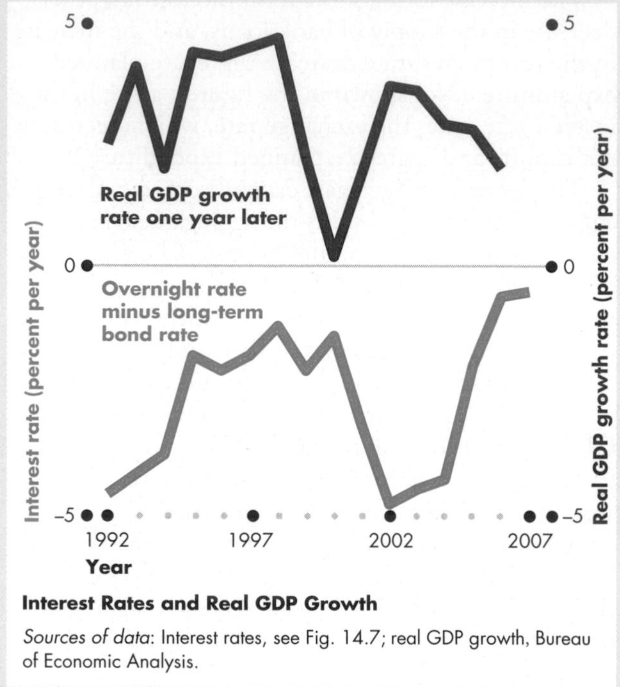


**Interest Rates and Real GDP Growth**

*Sources of data*: Interest rates, see Fig. 14.7; real GDP growth, Bureau of Economic Analysis.

**Loose Link from Federal Funds Rate to Spending** The real long-term interest rate that influences spending plans is linked only loosely to the federal funds rate. Also, the response of the *real* long-term interest rate to a change in the nominal interest rate depends on how inflation expectations change. And the response of expenditure plans to changes in the real interest rate depend on many factors that make the response hard to predict.

**Time Lags in the Adjustment Process** The Fed is especially handicapped by the fact that the monetary policy transmission process is long and drawn out. Also, the economy does not always respond in exactly the same way to a policy change. Further, many factors other than policy are constantly changing and bringing new situations to which policy must respond.

## Review Quiz

1. Describe the channels by which monetary policy ripples through the economy and explain why each channel operates.
2. Do interest rates fluctuate in response to the Fed's actions?
3. How do the Fed's actions change the exchange rate?
4. How do the Fed's actions influence real GDP and how long does it take for real GDP to respond to the Fed's policy changes?
5. How do the Fed's actions influence the inflation rate and how long does it take for inflation to respond to the Fed's policy changes?

Work Study Plan 14.3 and get instant feedback.

## Alternative Monetary Policy Strategies

So far in this chapter, we've described and analyzed the Fed's method of conducting monetary policy. But the Fed does have choices among alternative monetary policy strategies. We're going to end our discussion of monetary policy by examining the alternatives and explaining why the Fed has rejected them in favor of the interest rate strategy that we've described.

You've seen that we can summarize monetary policy strategies in two broad categories: *instrument rules* and *targeting rules.* And you've seen that the Fed uses a *targeting rule* strategy but one that comes close to being the same as the Taylor rule, an instrument rule for the federal funds rate. So the Fed has rejected a pure or simple instrument rule. It has also rejected some other possible instrument and targeting rules.

The Fed might have chosen any of four alternative monetary policy strategies: One of them is an instrument rule, and three are alternative targeting rules. The four alternatives are

- Monetary base instrument rule
- Money targeting rule
- Exchange rate targeting rule
- Inflation rate targeting rule

### Monetary Base Instrument Rule

Although the Fed uses open market operations to hit its federal funds rate target, it could instead shoot for a target level of the monetary base.

The idea of using a rule to set the monetary base has been suggested by Carnegie-Mellon University economist Bennet T. McCallum, and a monetary base rule bears his name.

The **McCallum rule** makes the growth rate of the monetary base respond to the long-term average growth rate of real GDP and medium-term changes in the velocity of circulation of the monetary base.

The rule is based on the *quantity theory of money* (see Chapter 8, p. 202). McCallum's idea is to make the monetary base grow at a rate equal to the target inflation rate plus the long-term real GDP growth rate minus the medium-term growth rate of the velocity of circulation of the monetary base. This rule for the monetary base growth rate keeps the inflation rate close to target and the economy close to full employment.

The McCallum rule has some advantages over the Taylor rule. To target the interest rate using the Taylor rule, the Fed must estimate the long-run equilibrium real interest rate and the output gap.

In the Taylor rule, which we described on p. 356, the long-run equilibrium real interest rate is 2 percent a year. The federal funds rate is set at this level if the inflation rate and output gap are zero. But if the long-run equilibrium real interest rate is not 2 percent a year, the Taylor rule would set the interest rate either too high on the average and bring persistent recession or too low on the average and bring persistent and accelerating inflation.

Similarly, if the Fed overestimated the output gap, it would set the federal funds rate too high on the average and bring persistent recession. And if the Fed underestimated the output gap, it would set the federal funds rate too low on the average and bring persistent inflation.

Because the McCallum rule doesn't react to either the real interest rate or the output gap, the McCallum rule doesn't suffer from the problems of the Taylor rule.

A disadvantage of the McCallum rule compared to the Taylor rule is that it relies on the demand for money and demand for monetary base being reasonably stable.

The Fed believes that shifts in the demand for money and the demand for monetary base would bring large fluctuations in the interest rate, which in turn would bring large fluctuations in aggregate demand.

### Money Targeting Rule

As long ago as 1948, Nobel Laureate Milton Friedman proposed a targeting rule for the quantity of money. Friedman's ***k*-percent rule** makes the quantity of money grow at a rate of $k$ percent a year, where $k$ equals the growth rate of potential GDP.

Like the McCallum rule, Friedman's $k$-percent rule relies on a stable demand for money, which translates to a stable velocity of circulation. Friedman had examined data on money and nominal GDP and argued that the velocity of circulation of money was one of the most stable macroeconomic variables and that it could be exploited to deliver a stable price level and small business cycle fluctuations.

Friedman's idea remained just that until the 1970s, when inflation increased to more than 10 percent a year in the United States and to much higher rates in some other major countries.

During the mid-1970s, in a bid to end the inflation, the central banks of most major countries adopted the *k*-percent rule for the growth rate of the quantity of money. The Fed, too, began to pay close attention to the growth rates of money aggregates, including M1 and M2.

Inflation rates fell during the early 1980s in the countries that had adopted a *k*-percent rule. But one by one, these countries abandoned the *k*-percent rule.

Money targeting works when the demand for money is stable and predictable—when the velocity of circulation is stable. But in the world of the 1980s, and possibly in the world of today, technological change in the banking system leads to large and unpredictable fluctuations in the demand for money, which make the use of monetary targeting unreliable. With monetary targeting, aggregate demand fluctuates because the demand for money fluctuates. With interest rate targeting, aggregate demand is insulated from fluctuations in the demand for money (and the velocity of circulation).

## Exchange Rate Targeting Rule

The Fed could, if it wished to do so, intervene in the foreign exchange market to target the exchange rate. A fixed exchange rate is one possible exchange rate target. The Fed could fix the value of the U.S. dollar against a basket of other currencies such as the *trade-weighted index* (see Chapter 9, p. 204).

But with a fixed exchange rate, a country has no control over its inflation rate. The reason is that for internationally traded goods, *purchasing power parity* (see p. 224) moves domestic prices in line with foreign prices. If a computer chip costs $100 in Los Angeles and if the exchange rate is 120 yen per $1.00, then the computer chip will sell for 12,000 yen (ignoring local tax differences) in Tokyo. If this purchasing power parity didn't prevail, it would be possible to earn a profit by buying at the lower price and selling at the higher price. This trading would compete away the profit and price difference.

So prices of traded goods (and in the long run the prices of all goods and services) must rise at the same rate in the United States as they do on the average in the other countries against which the value of the U.S. dollar is fixed.

The Fed could avoid a direct inflation link by using a *crawling peg exchange rate* (see Chapter 9, p. 232) as a means of achieving an inflation target. To do so, the Fed would make the exchange rate change at a rate equal to the U.S. inflation rate minus the target inflation rate. If other countries have an average inflation rate of 3 percent a year and the United States wants an inflation rate of 2 percent a year, the Fed would make the U.S. dollar appreciate at a rate of 1 percent a year against the trade-weighted index of other currencies.

Some developing countries that have an inflation problem use this monetary policy strategy to lower the inflation rate. The main reason for choosing this method is that these countries don't have well-functioning markets for bonds and overnight loans, so they cannot use the policy approach that relies on these features of a banking system.

A major disadvantage of a crawling peg to target the inflation rate is that the real exchange rate often changes in unpredictable ways. The **real exchange rate** between the United States and its trading partners is the relative price of the GDP basket of goods and services in the United States with respect to that in other countries. U.S. GDP contains a larger proportion of high-technology products and services than GDP in other countries contain. So when the relative prices of these items change, our real exchange rate changes. With a crawling peg targeting the inflation rate, we would need to be able to identify changes in the real exchange rate and offset them. This task is difficult to accomplish.

## Inflation Rate Targeting Rule

**Inflation rate targeting** is a monetary policy strategy in which the central bank makes a public commitment

1. To achieve an explicit inflation target
2. To explain how its policy actions will achieve that target

Of the alternatives to the Fed's current strategy, inflation targeting is the most likely to be considered. In fact, some economists see it as a small step from what the Fed currently does. For these reasons, we'll explain this policy strategy in a bit of detail. Which countries practice inflation targeting, how do they do it, and what does it achieve?

**Inflation Targeters** Several major central banks practice inflation targeting and have done so since the mid-1990s. The best examples of central banks that use inflation targeting are the Bank of England, Bank of Canada, the Reserve Bank of New Zealand, and the Swedish Riksbank. The European Central Bank also practices inflation targeting. Japan and the United States are the most prominent major industrial economies that do not use this monetary policy strategy. But it is interesting to note that when the chairman of the Board of Governors of the Federal Reserve System, Ben Bernanke, and a member of the Board of Governors, Frederic S. Mishkin, were economics professors (at Princeton University and Columbia University, respectively), they did research together and wrote important articles and books on this topic. And their general conclusion was that inflation targeting is a sensible way in which to conduct monetary policy.

**How Inflation Targeting is Conducted** Inflation targets are specified in terms of a range for the CPI inflation rate. This range is typically between 1 percent and 3 percent a year, with an aim to achieve an average inflation rate of 2 percent per year. Because the lags in the operation of monetary policy are long, if the inflation rate falls outside the target range, the expectation is that the central bank will move the inflation rate back on target over the next two years.

All the inflation-targeting central banks use an overnight interest rate (the equivalent of the federal funds rate) as the policy instrument. And they use open market operations as the tool for achieving the desired overnight rate.

To explain their policy actions, inflation targeters publish an inflation report that describes the current state of the economy and its expected evolution over the next two years. The report also explains the central bank's current policy and how and why the central bank expects that its policy will achieve the inflation target.

**What Does Inflation Targeting Achieve?** The goals of inflation targeting are to state clearly and publicly the goals of monetary policy, to establish a framework of accountability, and to keep the inflation rate low and stable while maintaining a high and stable level of employment.

There is wide agreement that inflation targeting achieves its first two goals. And the inflation reports of inflation targeters have raised the level of discussion and understanding of the monetary policy process.

It is less clear whether inflation targeting does better than the implicit targeting that the Fed currently pursues in achieving low and stable inflation. The Fed's own record, without a formal inflation target, has been impressive over the past several years.

But monetary policy is about managing inflation expectations. And it seems clear that an explicit inflation target that is taken seriously and toward which policy actions are aimed and explained is a sensible way to manage expectations.

It is when the going gets tough that inflation targeting has the greatest attraction. It is difficult to imagine a serious inflation-targeting central bank permitting inflation to take off in the way that it did during the 1970s. And it is difficult to imagine deflation and ongoing recession such as Japan has endured for the past 10 years if monetary policy is guided by an explicit inflation target.

The debate on inflation targeting will continue!

## Why Rules?

You might be wondering why all monetary policy strategies involve rules. Why doesn't the Fed just do what seems best every day, month, and year, at its discretion? The answer lies in what you've just read. Monetary policy is about managing inflation expectations. In both financial markets and labor markets, people must make long-term commitments. So these markets work best when plans are based on correctly anticipated inflation outcomes. A well-understood monetary policy rule helps to create an environment in which inflation is easier to forecast and manage.

### Review Quiz

1 What are the four main alternative strategies for conducting monetary policy (other than the one used by the Fed)?

2 Briefly, why does the Fed reject each of these alternatives?

Work Study Plan 14.4 and get instant feedback.

The next two pages provide a quick guide to the extraordinary financial crisis policy actions of the past two years and *Reading Between the Lines* on pages 372–373 examine the Fed's aggressive interest rate cuts in 2008.

# Extraordinary Policies for Extraordinary Times

## The Fed Acts in Concert with the U.S. Treasury

A financial crisis began in the United States in August 2007 and quickly spread though the global economy. You are now well-equipped to understand the key elements in this crisis and its spread to the broader economy.

You studied the market for loanable funds in Chapter 7, the U.S. money market in Chapter 8, and the foreign exchange market in Chapter 9. All of these markets interacted in the financial crisis. And the crisis quickly became a broader economic crisis through its influence on aggregate demand and aggregate supply, which you studied in Chapter 10.

### The Key Elements of the Crisis

We can describe the key elements of the crisis by thinking about the events that changed the values of the assets and liabilities of banks and other financial institutions.

Figure 1 shows the stylized balance sheet of a bank: deposits plus equity equals reserves plus loans and securities (see p. 592). Deposits and equity are the bank's sources of funds (other borrowing by banks is ignored here). Deposits are the funds loaned to the bank by households and firms, and equity is the capital provided by the bank's stockholders. Equity includes the bank's undistributed profits (and losses). The bank's reserves are currency and its deposit at the Fed. The bank's loans and securities are the loans made by the bank and government bonds, private bonds, asset-backed bonds, and other securities that the bank holds.

Three main events can put a bank under stress:

1. Widespread fall in asset prices
2. A significant currency drain
3. A run on the bank

Figure 1 summarizes the problems that each event presents to a bank. A widespread fall in asset prices means that the bank suffers a *capital loss*. It must write down the value of its assets and the value of the bank's equity decreases by the same amount as the fall in the value of its securities. If the fall in asset prices is large enough, the bank's equity might fall to zero, in which case the bank is insolvent. It fails.

A significant currency drain means that depositors withdraw funds and the bank loses reserves. This event puts the bank in a liquidity crisis. It is short of cash reserves.

A run on the bank occurs when depositors lose confidence in the bank and massive withdrawals of deposits occur. The bank loses reserves and must call in loans and sell off securities at unfavorable prices. Its equity shrinks.

The red arrows in Fig. 1 summarize the effects of these events and the problems they brought in the 2007–2008 financial crisis. A widespread fall in asset prices was triggered by the bursting of a house-price bubble that saw house prices switch from rapidly rising to falling. With falling house prices, sub-prime mortgage defaults occurred and the prices of mortgage-backed securities and derivatives whose values are based on these securities began to fall.

People with money market mutual fund deposits began to withdraw them, which created a fear of a massive withdrawal of these funds analagous to a run on a bank. In the United Kingdom, one bank, Northern Rock, experienced a bank run.

With low reserves and even lower equity, banks turned their attention to securing their balance sheets and called in loans. The loanable funds market and money market dried up.

Because the loanable funds market is global, the same problems quickly spread to other economies, and foreign exchange markets became highly volatile.

Hard-to-get loans, market volatility, and increased uncertainty transmitted the financial and monetary crisis to real expenditure decisions.

| Event | Deposits | + Equity | = Reserves | + Loans and securities | Problem |
|---|---|---|---|---|---|
| Widespread fall in asset prices | | ▼ | | ▼ | Solvency |
| Currency drain | ▼ | | ▼ | | Liquidity |
| Run on bank | ▼ | ▼ | ▼ | ▼ | Liquidity and solvency |

**Figure 1 The Ingredients of a Financial and Banking Crisis**

### The Policy Actions

Policy actions in response to the financial crisis dribbled out over a period of more than a year. But by November 2008, eight groups of policies designed to contain the crisis and minimize its impact on the real economy were in place. They are

1. Open market operation
2. Extension of deposit insurance
3. Term auction credit
4. Primary dealer and other broker credit
5. Asset-backed commercial paper money market mutual fund liquidity facility
6. Troubled Asset Relief Program (TARP 1)
7. Troubled Asset Relief Program (TARP 2)
8. Fair value accounting

Figure 2 summarizes these actions, their effects on a bank's balance sheet (red and blue arrows), and the problem that each action sought to address.

An open market operation is the classic policy (described on pp. 759–760) for providing liquidity and enabling the Fed to hit its interest rate target. With substantial interest rate cuts, heavy open market operations were used to keep the banks well supplied with reserves. This action lowered bank holdings of securities and increased their reserves.

By extending deposit insurance (see p. 592) people with bank and money market mutual fund deposits became more secure and had less incentive to withdraw deposits. This action increased both deposits and reserves.

Three actions by the Fed supplemented open market operations to provide additional liquidity in exchange for troubled assets. Term auction credit, primary dealer and broker credit, and the asset-backed commercial paper money market mutual fund liquidity facility enabled institutions to swap troubled assets for reserves or safer assets. All of these actions decreased bank holdings of securities and increased reserves.

The Troubled Asset Relief Program (TARP) was an action by the U.S. Treasury, so technically it isn't a monetary policy action, but it has a direct impact on banks and other financial institutions. The program is funded by $700 billion of national debt.

The original intent, (we'll call it TARP 1) was for the U.S. Treasury to buy troubled assets from banks and other holders and replace them with U.S. government securities. Implementing this program proved more difficult than initially anticipated and the benefits of the action came to be questioned.

So instead of buying troubled assets (we'll call it TARP 2), the Treasury decided to buy equity stakes in troubled institutions. This action directly increased the institutions reserves and equity.

The final action was neither monetary policy nor fiscal policy but a change in accounting standards. It relaxed the requirement for institutions to value their assets at current market value—called "mark-to-market"—and permitted them, in rare conditions, to use a model to assess "fair market value."

Taken as a whole, a huge amount of relief was thrown at this financial crisis. Events through 2009 will show whether enough was done.

| *Action* | Deposits + | Equity = | Reserves + | Loans and securities | *Problem addressed* |
|---|---|---|---|---|---|
| Open market operation | | | ▲ | ▼ | Liquidity |
| Extension of deposit insurance | ▲ | | ▲ | | Liquidity |
| Term auction credit | | | ▲ | ▼ | Liquidity |
| Primary dealer and other broker credit | | | ▲ | ▼ | Liquidity |
| Asset-backed commercial paper money market mutual fund liquidity facility | | | ▲ | ▼ | Liquidity |
| Troubled Asset Relief Program (TARP 1) | | | ▲ | ▼ | Liquidity |
| Troubled Asset Relief Program (TARP 2) | | ▲ | ▲ | | Solvency |
| Fair value accounting | | ▲ | | ▲ | Solvency |

**Figure 2 Policy Actions in a Financial and Banking Crisis**

# Monetary Policy in Action

## Concerned Fed Trims Key Rate by a Half Point

http://www.nytimes.com
October 30, 2008

The Federal Reserve lowered its benchmark interest rate by half a percentage point on Wednesday, its second big rate cut this month, as policy makers tried to fend off what could be the worst economic downturn in decades.

The move brought the target rate for federal funds … to 1 percent, down to the near-record lows reached in 2003 and 2004, when the Fed was trying to encourage an economic recovery after the bursting of the Internet bubble. The central bank left open the possibility of going still lower, warning "downside risks to growth remain." …

In a statement, the Fed acknowledged that the economy had lost steam on almost every front—consumer spending, business investment, financial markets and even exports, which had been the one bright spot recently. For the time being, inflation is of little concern.

"The pace of economic activity appears to have slowed markedly, owing importantly to a decline in consumer expenditures," the central bank said. Industrial production and investment in new equipment have also slowed, it said, and slumping growth around the world has reduced demand for American exports. …

But analysts said lower interest rates were not likely to accomplish much at this point, because the economy's biggest problem is the fear among banks and financial institutions about lending money.

"The difference between 1.5 percent and 1 percent is really pretty insignificant, particularly when the banking system is as weak as it is," said Ethan Harris, a senior economist at Barclay's Capital. "You have a big uncertainty shock. It's not just that the markets have declined. People are uncertain about where the world is going." …



## Essence of the Story

- The Federal Reserve lowered the federal funds rate target to 1 percent on October 29, 2008 in a bid to avoid a deep and long recession.
- The Fed warned that "downside risks to growth remain," a hint that the interest rate might go even lower.
- The Fed said that consumer spending, business investment, and even exports were all down.
- Analysts said lower interest rates would have a small effect because banks and financial institutions were not lending.

## Economic Analysis

- The first estimate of GDP for the third quarter of 2008 suggested that real GDP was falling slightly (at an annualized rate of 0.25 percent) and the price level was rising sharply (at an annualized rate of 4.1 percent).
- Despite these numbers, the Fed believed recession was a more serious risk than inflation.
- The Fed's goal in cutting the federal funds rate was to help stimulate aggregate demand and boost real GDP in the following quarters.
- But in 2008, credit markets were not working normally. The perception of risk was unusually high, and institutions normally willing to lend to each other were reluctant to do so. Without an increase in lending, the interest rate cut would not have its desired effect.
- The figures illustrate the economy in late 2008.
- In Fig. 1, the Fed cuts the federal funds rate target and hits its new target by increasing the supply of reserves from $RS_0$ to $RS_1$.
- In Fig. 2, the economy average real interest rate is 3 percent at the intersection of the supply of loanable funds curve $SLF_0$ and the demand for loanable funds curve *DLF*.
- Normally, when the Fed cuts the federal funds rate, the supply of loanable funds increases and the supply curve shifts rightward, like the shift to $SLF_1$.
- In Fig. 3, real GDP is $11.7 trillion and the price level is 123 at the intersection of $AD_0$ and *SAS*. Potential GDP is $12 trillion, so there is a recessionary gap.
- Normally, when the Fed cuts the federal funds rate, aggregate demand increases and the *AD* curve shifts rightward, like the shift to $AD_1$.
- At the time when the Fed took its actions, it was not clear whether these normal responses to an interest rate cut would occur. That is probably why the Fed cut by such a large amount and to such a low level.

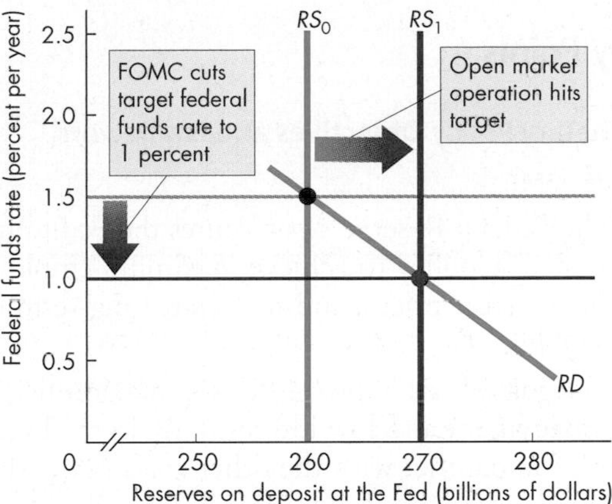


**Figure 1 The market for bank reserves**

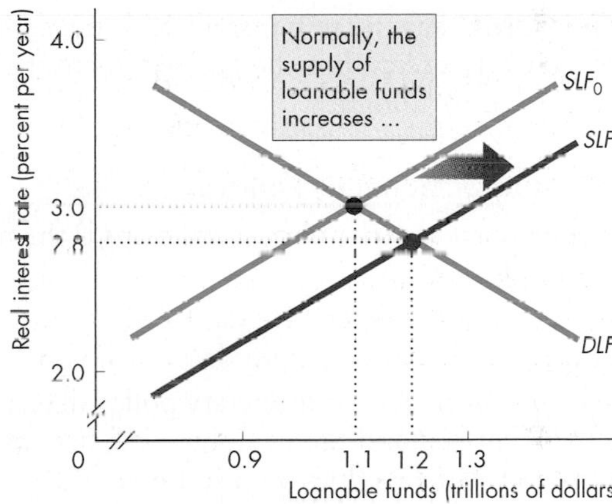


**Figure 2 The market for loanable funds**

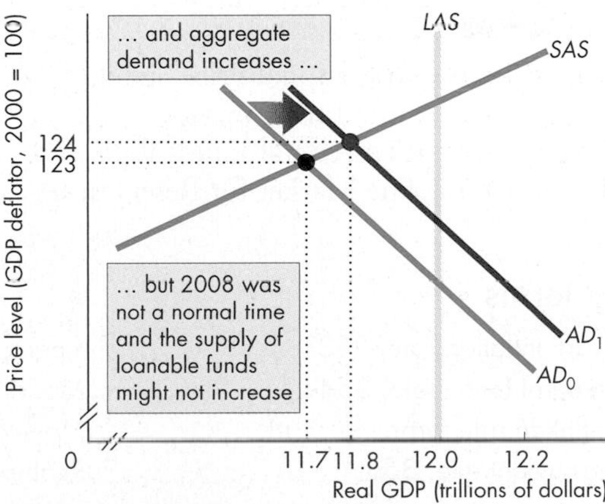


**Figure 3 Real GDP and the price level**

## SUMMARY

### Key Points

**Monetary Policy Objectives and Framework** (pp. 352–354)

- The Federal Reserve Act requires the Fed to use monetary policy to achieve maximum employment, stable prices, and moderate long-term interest rates.
- The goal of stable prices delivers maximum employment and low interest rates in the long run but can conflict with the other goals in the short run.
- The Fed translates the goal of stable prices as an inflation rate of between 1 and 2 percent per year.
- The FOMC has the responsibility for the conduct of monetary policy, but the Fed reports to the public and to Congress.

**The Conduct of Monetary Policy** (pp. 354–358)

- The Fed's monetary policy instrument is the federal funds rate.
- The Fed sets the federal funds rate target and announces changes on eight dates each year.
- An *instrument rule* for monetary policy makes the instrument respond predictably to the state of the economy. The Fed does *not* use a mechanical instrument rule.
- A *targeting rule* for monetary policy sets the instrument to make the forecast of the inflation rate equal to the target inflation rate. The Fed *does* use such a rule, but its actions are similar to an instrument rule.
- The Fed hits its federal funds rate target by using open market operations.
- By buying or selling government securities in the open market, the Fed is able to change bank reserves and change the federal funds rate.

**Monetary Policy Transmission** (pp. 359–366)

- A change in the federal funds rate changes other interest rates, the exchange rate, the quantity of money and loans, aggregate demand, and eventually real GDP and the price level.
- Changes in the federal funds rate change real GDP about one year later and change the inflation rate with an even longer time lag.

**Alternative Monetary Policy Strategies** (pp. 367–371)

- The main alternatives to setting the federal funds rate are a monetary base instrument rule, a money targeting rule, an exchange rate targeting rule, or an inflation rate targeting rule.
- Rules trump discretion in monetary policy because they better enable the central bank to manage inflation expectations.

### Key Figures



### Key Terms

## PROBLEMS and APPLICATIONS

Work problems 1–8 in Chapter 14 Study Plan and get instant feedback.
Work problems 9–17 as Homework, a Quiz, or a Test if assigned by your instructor.

1. Suppose that the Fed is required to keep the inflation rate between 1 percent and 2 percent a year but with no requirement to keep trend inflation at the midpoint of this range. The Fed achieves its target.
   a. If initially the price level is 100,
      i. Calculate the highest price level that might occur after 10 years.
      ii. Calculate the lowest price level that might occur after 10 years.
      iii. What is the range of uncertainty about the price level after 10 years?
   b. Would this type of inflation goal serve the financial markets well and provide an anchor for inflation expectations?
2. Suppose that the Bank of England decides to follow the Taylor rule. In 2005, the United Kingdom has an inflation rate of 2.1 percent a year and its output gap is –0.3 percent. At what level does the Bank of England set the repo rate (the U.K. equivalent of the federal funds rate)?
3. Suppose that the Bank of Canada is following the McCallum rule. The Bank of Canada has an inflation target range of between 1 percent a year and 3 percent a year. The long-term real GDP growth rate in Canada is 2.4 percent a year. If the velocity of circulation of the monetary base is 2, what is the
   a. Highest growth rate of monetary base that will occur?
   b. Lowest growth rate of monetary base that will occur?
4. In Freezone, shown in the figure at the top of the next column, the aggregate demand curve is *AD*, potential GDP is $300 billion, and the short-run aggregate supply curve is $SAS_B$.
   a. What are the price level and real GDP?
   b. Does Freezone have an unemployment problem or an inflation problem? Why?
   c. What will happen in Freezone if the central bank takes no monetary policy actions?
   d. What monetary policy action would you advise the central bank to take and what do you predict will be the effect of that action?

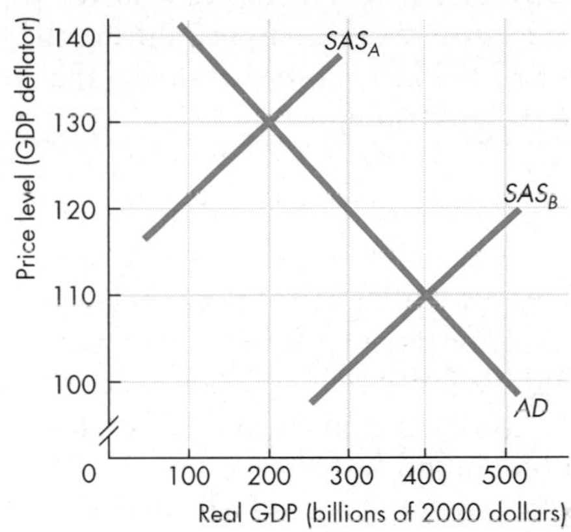


5. Suppose that in Freezone, shown in problem 4, the short-run aggregate supply curve is $SAS_A$ and a drought decreases potential GDP to $250 billion.
   a. What happens in Freezone if the central bank lowers the federal funds rate and buys securities on the open market?
   b. What happens in Freezone if the central bank raises the federal funds rate and sells securities on the open market?
   c. Do you recommend that the central bank lower or raise the federal funds rate? Why?
6. **Fed Sees Both Unemployment, Prices on Rise**
   The Federal Reserve sees worse economic problems ahead. ... But even so, the Fed may be reluctant to cut interest rates any further than it already has. ... The Fed lowered its economic growth forecast for the year. At the same time, it raised its projections for inflation and unemployment. ... The Fed raised its unemployment forecast ... to between 5.5 percent and 5.7 percent ... [and] now expects personal consumption expenditures to rise between 3.1 percent and 3.4 percent in 2008 ... [and] expects steeper "core" inflation. ... In an effort to keep the country from falling into recession and to deal with the credit crisis, the Fed has cut its key federal funds rate seven times since September. This short-term interest rate is now 2 percent, down from 5.25 percent at the start of the Fed's easing campaign.

... Some believe the Fed cuts since last September helped fuel inflation, especially the sharp run-up in oil prices, because the rate cuts have led to a weakening of the dollar. Along those lines, the two Fed members who voted against the last rate cut ... argued during the meeting that the Fed cuts were hurting the economy more than helping it.

*CNN*, May 21, 2008

a. Explain the intended effect of the Fed cutting the target federal funds rate from 5.25 percent to 2 percent and illustrate your explanation with an appropriate graphical analysis.
b. Explain how this monetary policy may have "helped fuel inflation, especially the sharp run-up in oil prices."
c. What is core inflation and why does the Fed tend to focus on that measurement of inflation more heavily than overall inflation?
d. Explain the dilemma that the Fed is facing when making decisions in the face of rising unemployment and rising inflation.

7. **Are Bernanke's Hands Tied on Inflation?**

Inflation has replaced the subprime meltdown and the possibility of recession as the hot-button economic issue. Bernanke's remarks in Spain signal that the central bank aims to keep the dollar ... from sliding anew and further eroding consumers' purchasing power. ... But with the U.S. economy slowing and the financial markets showing renewed signs of unrest, will the Fed actually follow through? That's another question altogether. ... Indeed, the Fed has spent the past nine months cutting interest rates and lending freely to financial firms in a bid to prevent the financial system from seizing up. Those unusual actions have succeeded in staving off a calamity, but the economy remains weak. ... So for now, the Fed simply wants to keep rates steady. ... Doing so could maintain stability in the dollar and help arrest the rise in food and energy prices that have punished U.S. consumers. ... Tough anti-inflation talk elsewhere in the world could also complicate the Fed's job. Jean-Claude Trichet, head of the European Central Bank, said Thursday the ECB hasn't ruled out raising interest rates next month. Many observers suspect the ECB is, like the Fed, trying to beat down inflation expectations by signaling that it is ready to take action—while hoping it doesn't need to do so. But the mere suggestion the ECB could soon raise rates sent the dollar lower against the euro again Thursday.

*Fortune*, June 5, 2008

a. Explain how the Fed raising interest rates would "defend" the U.S. dollar. Is the Fed's stance reflecting an exchange rate targeting rule monetary policy strategy?
b. What adverse consequences might result if the Fed does actually increase rates?
c. Explain the argument made that the Fed is "trying to beat down inflation expectations by signaling that it is ready to take action—while hoping it doesn't need to do so."
d. Why do the monetary policy decisions of other central banks (such as the ECB) "complicate" the Fed's job?

8. **Politicians Urged to Leave the Economy to the Fed**

The U.S. economy is teetering on the edge. Many economists... put the risk of recession next year at about 50 percent. ... The question on the minds of many in Congress and in the White House is this: What should they be doing now to keep the economy on track? The right answer: absolutely nothing. This advice isn't easy for politicians to follow. Because economic downturns mean fewer jobs and falling incomes, they are painful for many families. Voters can confuse inaction with nonchalance and send incumbents packing. ... Congress made its most important contribution to taming the business cycle in 1913, when it created the Federal Reserve System. The Fed remains the first line of defense against recession. ... Admittedly, monetary policy can sometimes use an assist from fiscal policy. If an economic downturn is deep, if a recovery is anemic or if the Fed is running out of ammunition, Congress can help raise aggregate demand for goods and services. ...

*International Herald Tribune*, December 23, 2007

a. Explain and evaluate the rationale for using monetary policy as a "first line of defense" and reserving fiscal policy for "deep" downturns and when monetary policy has already been exhausted.
b. Why is this a difficult guideline for the president and Congress to follow?

9. Suppose the Fed is required to keep the inflation rate between 0 and 3 percent a year and is also required to keep trend inflation at the midpoint of the range. The Fed achieves its target.
   a. If initially the price level is 100, what is the likely price level after 10 years?
   b. Compare this economy with the economy in problem 1. Which economy has the greater certainty about inflation over the longer term? Which has the greater short-term certainty?
10. Suppose that the Reserve Bank of New Zealand is following the Taylor rule. In 2009, it sets the official cash rate (the N.Z. equivalent of the federal funds rate) at 4 percent a year. If the inflation rate in New Zealand is 2.0 percent a year, what is its output gap?
11. The figure shows the economy of Freezone. The aggregate demand curve is *AD*, and the short-run aggregate supply curve is $SAS_A$. Potential GDP is $300 billion.

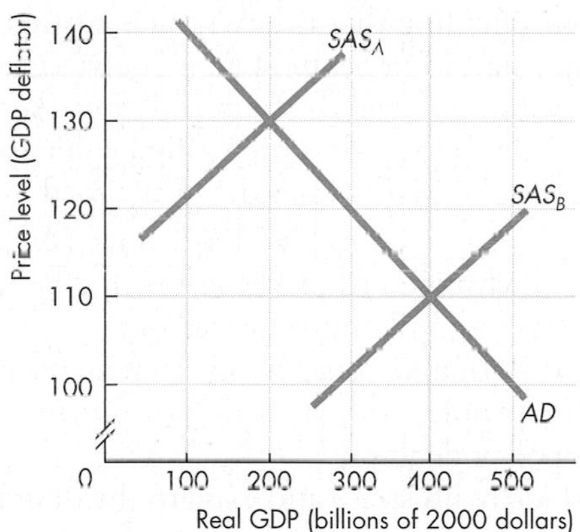


   a. What are the price level and real GDP?
   b. Does Freezone have an unemployment problem or an inflation problem? Why?
   c. What do you predict will happen in Freezone if the central bank takes no monetary policy actions?
   d. What monetary policy action would you advise the central bank to take and what do you predict will be the effect of that action?
12. Suppose that in Freezone, shown in problem 11, the short-run aggregate supply curve is $SAS_B$ and potential GDP increases to $350 billion.
   a. What happens in Freezone if the central bank lowers the federal funds rate and buys securities on the open market?
   b. What happens in Freezone if the central bank raises the federal funds rate and sells securities on the open market?
   c. Do you recommend that the central bank lower or raise the federal funds rate? Why?
13. **The Fed Finds its Missing Link**

   Elizabeth "Betsy" Duke, the newest addition to the Federal Reserve's chief policy making group, is a lifelong commercial banker who many Fed watchers hope can balance out a board riven by inflation pressures, a weakened Wall Street, and a slowing economy. …

   Duke is also the only member of the Federal Reserve Board with commercial-banking experience. … Duke, a graduate of the University of North Carolina who majored in theater, has spent 32 years as a banker. … Fed watchers expect her to play a key role in the Fed's ongoing examination of mortgage lending standards and bank regulations. As one of seven Fed board members, Duke will help set the country's monetary policy, which includes interest rates and banking standards. "The Federal Reserve's job is not only to tend to macroeconomic conditions, it must also ensure the integrity of borrowing and lending," said Lacy Hunt, a former Fed economist. … "The regulatory process obviously broke down in a massive way; and one can't help but wonder whether we should have had more actual bankers on the board."

   *CNN*, July 8, 2008

   a. What are the primary functions of the Federal Reserve System?
   b. How is a member of the Board of Governors of the Federal Reserve System appointed?
   c. Explain the potential advantages and disadvantages of adding Duke, a theater major with 32 years of commercial banking experience, to the Board of Governors.
   d. Explain how, even if no members of the Board were bankers, monetary policy debates and decisions would still be influenced by individuals with banking experience.
14. **Fed Prepares to Hit Pause**

   Federal Reserve chairman Ben Bernanke all but closed the door on the chances of any more rate cuts during the next few months. … Bernanke said that "for now, policy seems well positioned to promote moderate growth and price stability over time." Translation: Interest rates are going to remain at 2 percent for a while. Get used to it. … The Fed cut its key federal funds rate to 1 percent following the 2001 recession and some market observers say that these low rates created the easy money environment that got banks and borrowers into the subprime mess that the Fed now has to clean up. It would appear that Bernanke would not want to make the same mistake. … What's more, Bernanke also seems to have gotten the message that more rate cuts may cause irreparable harm to the value of the dollar. The moribund greenback has been blamed by some economists for helping to lead to the surge in oil prices and other commodities, which in turn have led to rising prices of food and gas.

*CNN*, June 3, 2008

a. What are the potential consequences of the Fed cutting rates too much in the face of a recession?
b. Explain how rate cuts may have contributed to the "surge" in oil prices.

15. **Fed Rate Cuts and Your Wallet**

We've already had five interest rate cuts since September of last year. And we may be on the verge of yet another one. … It's hard to see the connection between what the Fed does and what the economy does. To some economists, the Fed has done its job. "The Fed has tried to stimulate bank lending. And to some extent, they've been successful," says Hugh Johnson of Illington Advisors. The bottom line here is that the Fed is fighting an uphill battle. There are serious drags on the economy, from housing and oil to unemployment and bad credit markets. … Keep in mind there is a limit to how much the Fed can cut rates before inflation becomes a real problem. … And it may be some time until we see exactly what the rate cuts do for the economy. "Rate cuts by the Fed are only effective with a lag," says Greg McBride of Bankrate.com. "That lag can be anywhere from 9–18 months. The five rate cuts so far … represent a lot of juice for the economy that's in the pipeline." … Fed rate cuts are not likely to help mortgage rates, because investors don't want to get locked into long-term investments with low interest rates in a high inflation rate environment. … Even if the Fed cuts rates, credit cards don't have to pass that reduced rate onto you. This is a turbulent time in the credit card industry.

*CNN*, March 17, 2008

a. Explain the intended effect of the Fed cutting the target for the federal funds rate and illustrate your explanation with an appropriate graphical analysis.
b. Explain what will limit the effectiveness of this monetary stimulus.

16. **Bernanke's Inflation Focus Boosts Rate Hike Odds**

Bernanke sent a fresh warning that the Fed will be on heightened alert against inflation dangers, especially any signs that investors, consumers and businesses think prices will keep going up and change their behavior in ways that will aggravate inflation. The Fed "will strongly resist an erosion of longer-term inflation expectations, as an unanchoring of those expectations would be destabilizing for growth as well as for inflation," Bernanke said. The Fed chief and his colleagues have been signaling that the Fed's rate-cutting campaign, started in September, is probably over given mounting concerns about inflation. And, little by little, Bernanke is preparing people for the prospects of higher rates down the road.

*MSNBC*, June 10, 2008

a. Explain why the Fed places so much emphasis on managing inflation expectations.
b. Why is Bernanke using public statements to prepare people "little by little" for future monetary policy decisions?
c. Graphically illustrate and explain the desired effect of the Fed raising the target for the federal funds rate.

17. Study *Reading Between the Lines* on pp. 372–373 and then answer the following questions.
a. How did the Fed's expectation about future real GDP growth and inflation differ from most recent actual changes in real GDP and the price level?
b. How would the market for loanable funds and aggregate demand normally respond to a large cut in the federal funds rate?
c. What made 2008 unusual and how would you analyze the special features of 2008 in the market for loanable funds?
d. If the Fed had not cut the federal funds rate, what might the consequences have been?

# 15 International Trade Policy

After studying this chapter, you will be able to:

- Explain how markets work with international trade and identify its winners and losers.
- Explain the effects of international trade barriers.
- Explain and evaluate arguments used to justify restricting international trade.

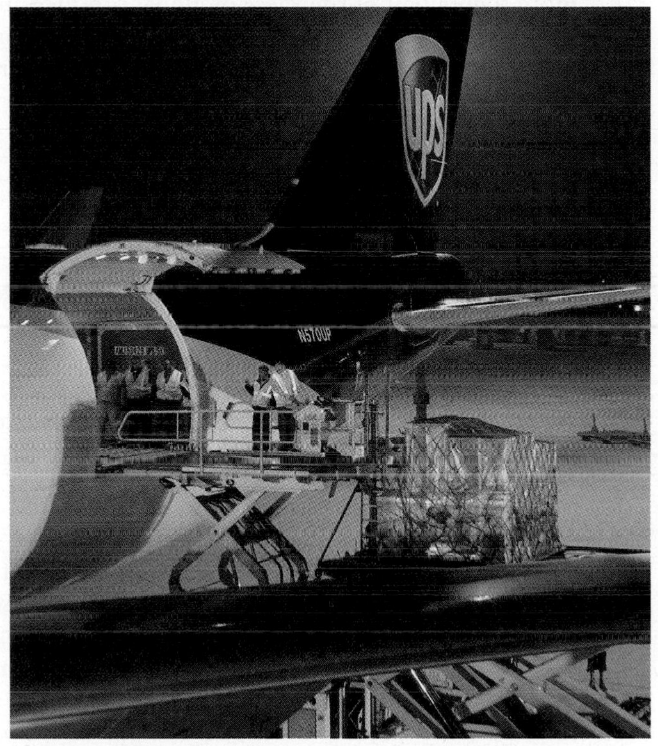


**iPods, Wii games, and Nike shoes are just three of** the items you might buy that are not produced in the United States. In fact, most of the goods that you buy are produced abroad, often in Asia, and transported here in container ships or cargo jets. And it's not just goods produced abroad that you buy—it is services too. When you make a technical support call, most likely you'll be talking with someone in India, or to a voice recognition system that was programmed in India. Satellites or fiber cables will carry your conversation along with huge amounts of other voice messages, video images, and data.

All these activities are part of the globalization process that is having a profound effect on our lives. Globalization is controversial and generates heated debate. Many Americans want to know how we can compete with people whose wages are a fraction of our own.

Why do we go to such lengths to trade and communicate with others in faraway places? You will find some answers in this chapter. And in *Reading Between the Lines* at the end of the chapter, you can apply what you've learned and examine the claims of developing countries about so-called "fair trade" policies.

## How Global Markets Work

Because we trade with people in other countries, the goods and services that we can buy and consume are not limited by what we can produce. The goods and services that we buy from other countries are our **imports**; and the goods and services that we sell to people in other countries are our **exports**.

### International Trade Today

Global trade today is enormous. In 2008, global exports and imports were $35 trillion, which is more than a half of the value of global production. The United States is the world's largest international trader and accounts for 10 percent of world exports and 15 percent of world imports. Germany and China, which rank 2 and 3 behind the United States, lag by a large margin.

In 2008, total U.S. exports were $1.8 trillion, which is about 13 percent of the value of U.S. production. Total U.S. imports were $25 trillion, which is about 18 percent of the value of total expenditure in the United States.

We trade both goods and services. In 2008, exports of services were about 30 percent of total exports and imports of services were about 16 percent of total imports.

## Items Most Traded by the United States

### Trading Services for Oil

The figure shows the five largest exports and imports for the United States. Services top the list of exports and oil is the largest import by a large margin.

The services that we export are banking, insurance, business consulting, and other private services. Airplanes are the largest category of goods that we export.

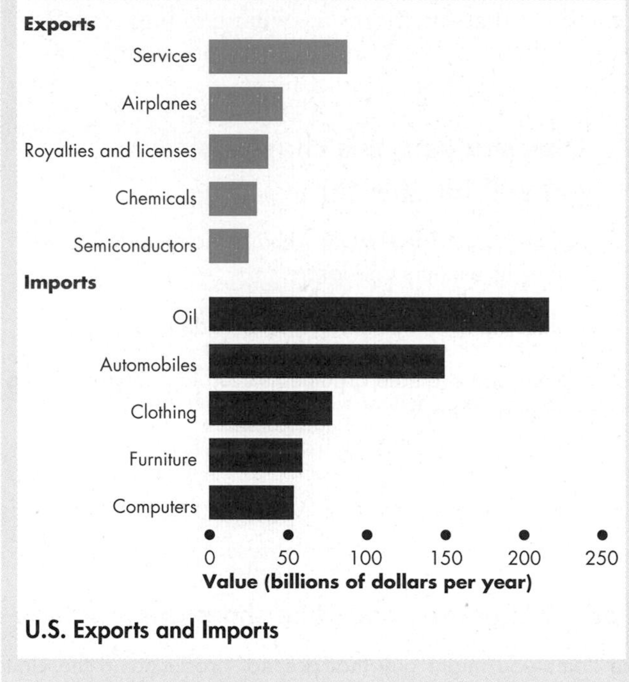


U.S. Exports and Imports

### What Drives International Trade?

*Comparative advantage* is the fundamental force that drives international trade. Comparative advantage (see Chapter 2, p. 40) is a situation in which a person can perform an activity or produce a good or service at a lower opportunity cost than anyone else. This same idea applies to nations. We can define *national comparative advantage* as a situation in which a nation can perform an activity or produce a good or service at a lower opportunity cost than any other nation.

The opportunity cost of producing a T-shirt is lower in China than in the United States, so China has a comparative advantage in producing T-shirts. The opportunity cost of producing an airplane is lower in the United States than in China, so the United States has a comparative advantage in producing airplanes.s.

You saw in Chapter 2 how Liz and Joe reap gains from trade by specializing in the production of the good at which they have a comparative advantage and trading. Both are better off.

This same principle applies to trade among nations. Because China has a comparative advantage at producing T-shirts and the United States has a comparative advantage at producing airplanes, the people of both countries can gain from specialization and trade. China can buy airplanes from the United States at a lower opportunity cost than that at which Chinese firms can produce them. And Americans can buy T-shirts from China for a lower opportunity cost than that at which U.S. firms can produce them. Also, through international trade, Chinese producers can get higher prices for their T-shirts and Boeing can sell airplanes for a higher price. Both countries gain from international trade.

Let's now illustrate the gains from trade that we've just described by studying demand and supply in the global markets for T-shirts and airplanes.

## Why the United States Imports T-Shirts

The United States imports T-shirts because the rest of the world has a comparative advantage in producing T-shirts. Figure 15.1 illustrates how this comparative advantage generates international trade and how trade affects the price of a T-shirt and the quantities produced and bought.

The demand curve $D_{US}$ and the supply curve $S_{US}$ show the demand and supply in the U.S. domestic market only. The demand curve tells us the quantity of T-shirts that Americans are willing to buy at various prices. The supply curve tells us the quantity of T-shirts that U.S. garment makers are willing to sell at various prices. This supply curve tells us the quantity supplied at each price when all T-shirts sold in the United States are produced in the United States.

Figure 15.1(a) shows what the U.S. T-shirt market would be like with no international trade. The price of a shirt would be $8 and 40 million shirts a year would be produced by U.S. garment makers and bought by U.S. consumers.

Figure 15.1(b) shows the market for T-shirts with international trade. Now the price of a T-shirt is determined in the world market, not the U.S. domestic market. The world price is less than $8 a T-shirt, which means that the rest of the world has a comparative advantage in producing T-shirts. The world price line shows the world price at $5 a shirt.

The U.S demand curve, $D_{US}$, tells us that at $5 a shirt, Americans buy 60 million shirts a year. The U.S. supply curve, $S_{US}$, tells us that at $5 a shirt, U.S. garment makers produce 20 million T-shirts a year. To buy 60 million T-shirts when only 20 million are produced in the United States, we must import T-shirts from the rest of the world. The quantity of T-shirts imported is 40 million a year.

**FIGURE 15.1** A Market With Imports

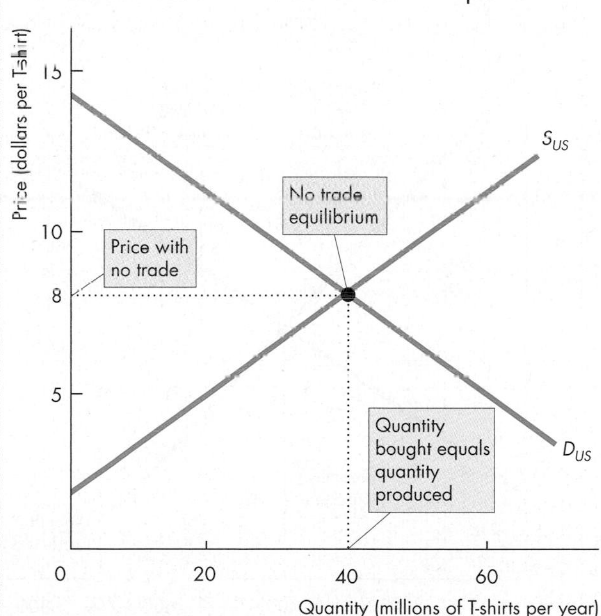


**(a) Equilibrium with no international trade**

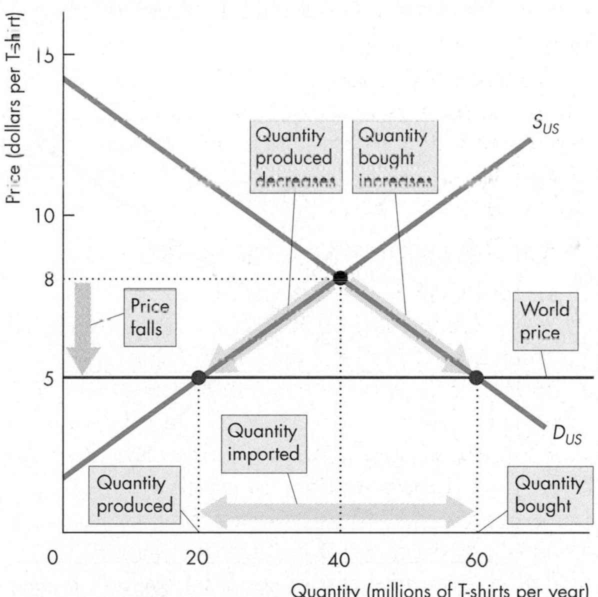


**(b) Equilibrium in a market with imports**

Part (a) shows the U.S. market for T-shirts with no international trade. The U.S. domestic demand curve $D_{US}$ and U.S. domestic supply curve $S_{US}$ determine the price of a T-shirt at $8 and the quantity of T- shirts produced and bought in the United States at 40 million a year.

Part (b) shows the U.S. market for T-shirts with international trade. World demand and world supply determine the world price, which is $5 per T-shirt. The price in the U.S. market falls to $5 a shirt. U.S. purchases of T-shirts increases to 60 million a year, and U.S. production of T-shirts decreases to 20 million a year. The United States imports 40 million T-shirts a year.

myeconlab animation

## Why the United States Exports Airplanes

The United States exports airplanes because it has a comparative advantage in producing them. Figure 15.2 illustrates how this comparative advantage generates international trade in airplanes and how this trade affects the price of an airplane and the quantities produced and bought.

The demand curve $D_{US}$ and the supply curve $S_{US}$ show the demand and supply in the U.S. domestic market only. The demand curve tells us the quantity of airplanes that U.S. airlines are willing to buy at various prices. This demand curve tells us the quantity demanded at each price when all airplanes produced in the United States are bought in the United States. The supply curve tells us the quantity of airplanes that U.S. aircraft makers are willing to sell at various prices.

Figure 15.2(a) shows what the U.S. airplane market would be like with no international trade. The price of an airplane would be $100 million and 400 airplanes a year would be produced by U.S. aircraft makers and bought by U.S. airlines.

Figure 15.2(b) shows the U.S. airplane market with international trade. Now the price of an airplane is determined in the world market and the world price is higher than $100 million. Because the world price exceeds the U.S. price with no international trade, the United States has a comparative advantage in producing airplanes. The world price line shows the world price at $150 million.

The U.S. demand curve, $D_{US}$, tells us that at $150 million an airplane, U.S. airlines buy 200 airplanes a year. The U.S. supply curve, $S_{US}$, tells us that at $150 million an airplane, U.S. aircraft makers produce 700 airplanes a year. The quantity produced in the United States (700 a year) minus the quantity purchased by U.S. airlines (200 a year) is the quantity of airplanes exported, which is 500 airplanes a year.

**FIGURE 15.2** A Market With Exports

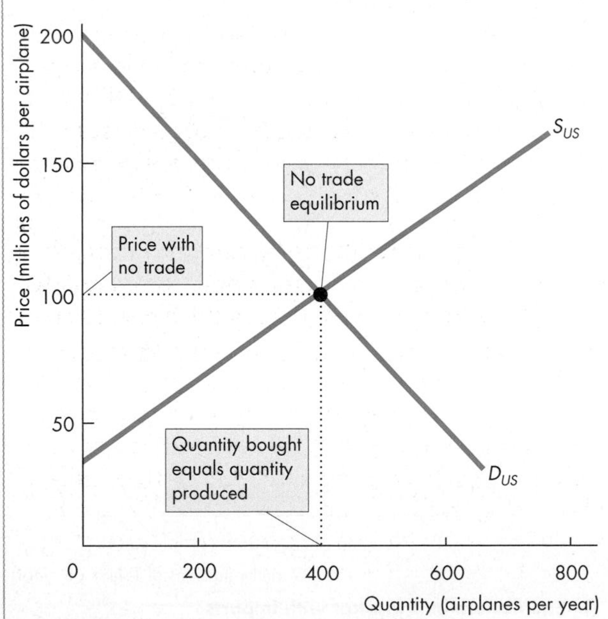


**(a) Equilibrium without international trade**

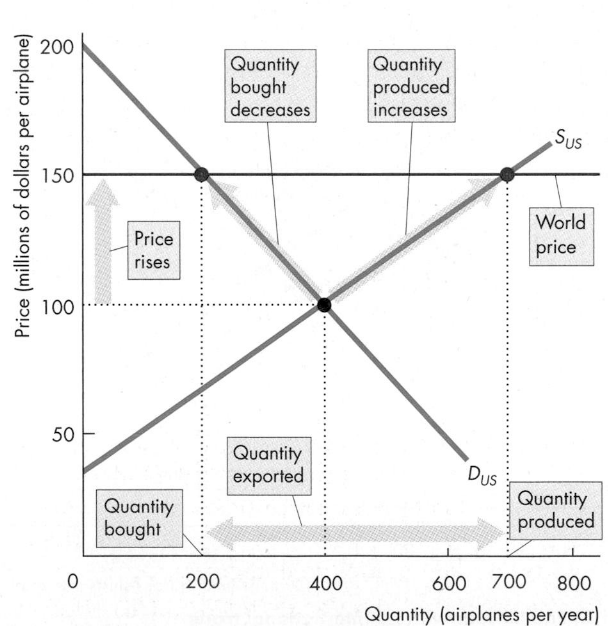


**(b) Equilibrium in a market with exports**

In part (a), the U.S. market with no international trade, the U.S. domestic demand curve $D_{US}$ and the U.S. domestic supply curve $S_{US}$ determine the price of an airplane at $100 million and 400 airplanes are produced and bought each year.

In part (b), the U.S. market with international trade, world demand and world supply determine the world price, which is $150 million per airplane. The price in the U.S. market rises. U.S. airplane production increases to 700 a year, and U.S. purchases of airplanes decrease to 200 a year. The United States exports 500 airplanes a year.

myeconlab animation

## Winners and Losers from International Trade

International trade has winners and it has losers. It is because some people lose that we often hear complaints about international competition. We're now going to see who wins and who loses from international trade. You will then be able to understand who complains about international competition and why. You will learn why we hear producers complaining about cheap foreign imports. You will also see why we never hear consumers of imported goods and services complaining and why we never hear exporters complaining except when they want greater access to foreign markets.

**Gains and Losses from Imports** We can measure the gains and losses from imports by examining their effect on the price paid and quantity consumed by domestic consumers and their effect on the price received and quantity sold by domestic producers.

***Consumers Gain from Imports*** When a country freely imports something from the rest of the world, it is because the rest of the world has a comparative advantage at producing that item. Compared to a situation with no international trade, the price paid by the consumer falls and the quantity consumed increases. It is clear that the consumer gains. The greater the fall in price and increase in quantity consumed, the greater is the gain to the consumer.

***Domestic Producers Lose from Imports*** Compared to a situation with no international trade, the price received by a domestic producer of an item that is imported falls. Also, the quantity sold by the domestic producer of a good or service that is also imported decreases. Because the domestic producer of an item that is imported sells a smaller quantity and for a lower price, this producer loses from international trade. Import-competing industries shrink in the face of competition from cheaper foreign produced imports.

The profits of firms that produce import-competing goods and services fall, these firms cut their workforce, unemployment in these industries increases and wages fall. When these industries have a geographical concentration, such as steel production around Gary, Indiana, an entire region can suffer economic decline.

**Gains and Losses from Exports** Just as we did for imports, we can measure the gains and losses from exports by looking at their effect on the price paid and quantity consumed by domestic consumers and their effect on the price received and quantity sold by domestic producers.

***Domestic Consumers Lose from Exports*** When a country exports something to the rest of the world, it is because the country has a comparative advantage at producing that item. Compared to a situation with no international trade, the price paid by the consumer rises and the quantity consumed in the domestic economy decreases. The domestic consumer loses. The greater the rise in price and decrease in quantity consumed, the greater is the loss to the consumer.

***Domestic Producers Gain from Exports*** Compared to a situation with no international trade, the price received by a domestic producer of an item that is imported rises. Also, the quantity sold by the domestic producer of a good or service that is also exported increases. Because the domestic producer of an item that is exported sells a larger quantity and for a higher price, this producer gains from international trade. Export industries expand in the face of global demand for their product.

The profits of firms that produce exports rise, these firms expand their workforce, unemployment in these industries decreases and wages rise. When these industries have a geographical concentration, such as software production in Silicon Valley, an entire region can boom.

**Net Gain** Export producers and import consumers gain and export consumers and import producers lose. But the gains are greater than the losses. In the case of imports, the consumer gains what the producer loses and then gains even more on the cheaper imports. In the case of exports, the producer gains what the consumer loses and then gains even more on the items it exports. So international trade provides a net gain for a country.

### Review Quiz

1. Explain the effects of imports on the domestic price and quantity, and the gains and losses of consumers and producers.
2. Explain the effects of exports on the domestic price and quantity, and the gains and losses of consumers and producers.

myeconlab Work Study Plan 15.1 and get instant feedback.

## International Trade Restrictions

Governments use four sets of tools to influence international trade and protect domestic industries from foreign competition. They are

- Tariffs
- Import quotas
- Other import barriers
- Export subsidies

### Tariffs

A **tariff** is a tax on a good that is imposed by the importing country when an imported good crosses its international boundary. For example, the government of India imposes a 100 percent tariff on wine imported from California. So when an Indian imports a $10 bottle of Californian wine, he pays the Indian government a $10 import duty.

The temptation for governments to impose tariffs is a strong one. First, they provide revenue to the government. Second, they enable the government to satisfy the self-interest of the people who earn their incomes in the import-competing industries. But as you will see, tariffs and other restrictions on free international trade decrease the gains from trade and are not in the social interest. Let's see why.

**The Effects of a Tariff** To see the effects of a tariff, let's return to the example in which the United States imports T-shirts. With free trade, the T-shirts are imported and sold at the world price. Then, under pressure from U.S. garment makers, the U.S. government imposes a tariff on imported T-shirts. Buyers of T-shirts must now pay the world price plus the tariff. Several consequences follow and Fig. 15.3 illustrates them.

Figure 15.3(a) shows the situation with free international trade. The United States produces 20 million T-shirts a year and imports 40 million a year at

FIGURE 15.3 The Effects of a Tariff

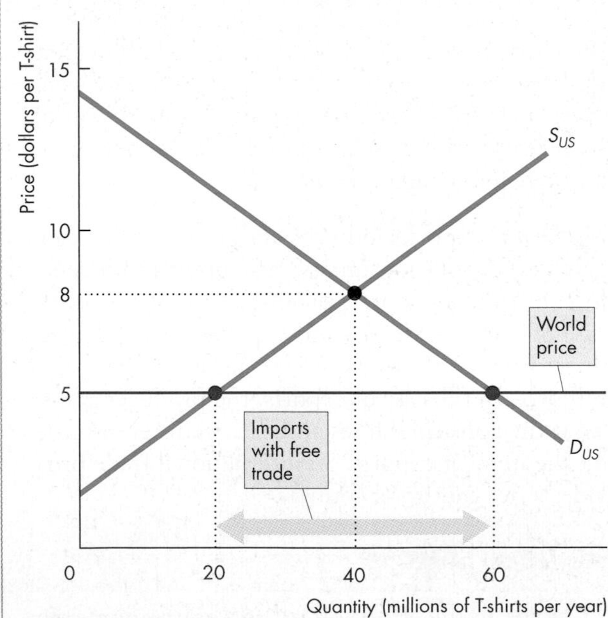


**(a) Free trade**

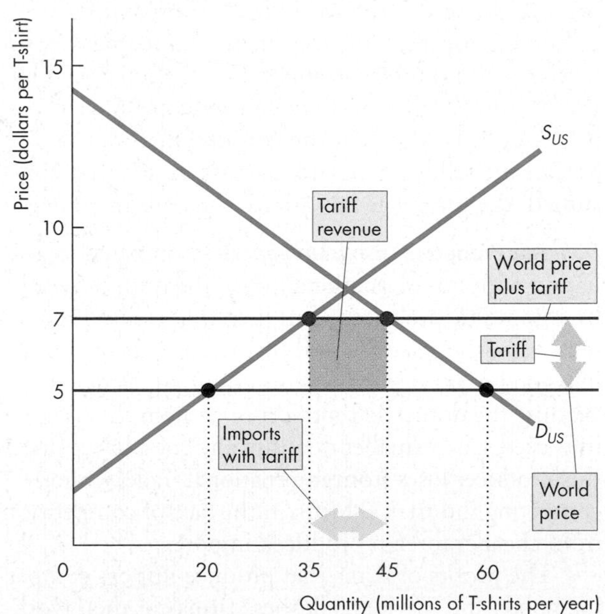


**(b) Market with tariff**

The world price of a T-shirt is $5. With free trade in part (a), Americans buy 60 million T-shirts a year. U.S. garment makers produce 20 million T-shirts a year and the United States imports 40 million a year.

With a tariff of $2 per T-shirt in part (b), the price in the U.S. market rises to $7 a T-shirt. U.S. production increases, U.S. purchases decrease, and the quantity imported decreases. The U.S. government collects a tariff revenue of $2 on each T-shirt imported, which is shown by the purple rectangle.

myeconlab animation

the world price of $5 a shirt. Figure 15.3(b) shows what happens with a tariff set at $2 per T-shirt. The following changes occur in the market for T-shirts:

- The price of a T-shirt in the United States rises by $2.
- The quantity of T-shirts bought in the United States decreases.
- The quantity of T-shirts produced in the United States increases.
- The quantity of T-shirts imported into the United States decreases.
- The U.S. government collects a tariff revenue.

***Rise in Price of a T-Shirt*** To buy a T-shirt, Americans must pay the world price plus the tariff, so the price of a T-shirt rises by $2 to $7. Figure 15.3(b) shows the new domestic price line, which lies $2 above the world price line.

***Decrease in Purchases*** The higher price of a T-shirt brings a decrease in the quantity demanded along the demand curve. Figure 15.3(b) shows the decrease from 60 million T-shirts a year at $5 a shirt to 45 million a year at $7 a shirt.

***Increase in Domestic Production*** The higher price of a T-shirt stimulates domestic production and U.S. garment makers increase the quantity supplied along the supply curve. Figure 15.3(b) shows the increase from 20 million T-shirts at $5 a shirt to 35 million a year at $7 a shirt.

***Decrease in Imports*** T-shirt imports decrease by 30 million, from 40 million to 10 million a year. Both the decrease in purchases and the increase in domestic production contribute to this decrease in imports.

***Tariff Revenue*** The government's tariff revenue is $20 million—$2 per shirt on 10 million imported shirts—shown by the purple rectangle.

**Winners, Losers, and the Social Loss from a Tariff** A tariff on an imported good creates winners and losers and we're now going to identify the winners and losers. When the U.S. government imposes a tariff on an imported good,

- U.S. consumers of the good lose.
- U.S. producers of the good gain.
- U.S. consumers lose more than U.S.producers gain: society loses.

***U.S. Consumers of the Good Lose*** Because the price of a T-shirt in the United States rises, the quantity of T-shirts demanded decreases. The combination of a higher price and smaller quantity bought makes the consumer worse off when a tariff is imposed.

## U.S. Tariffs
### Almost Gone

The Smoot-Hawley Act, which was passed in 1930, took U.S. tariffs to a peak average rate of 20 percent in 1933. (One third of imports was subject to a 60 percent tariff.) The **General Agreement on Tariffs and Trade (GATT)**, was established in 1947. Since then tariffs have fallen in a series of negotiating rounds, the most significant of which are identified in the figure. Tariffs are now as low as they have ever been but import quotas and other trade barriers persist.

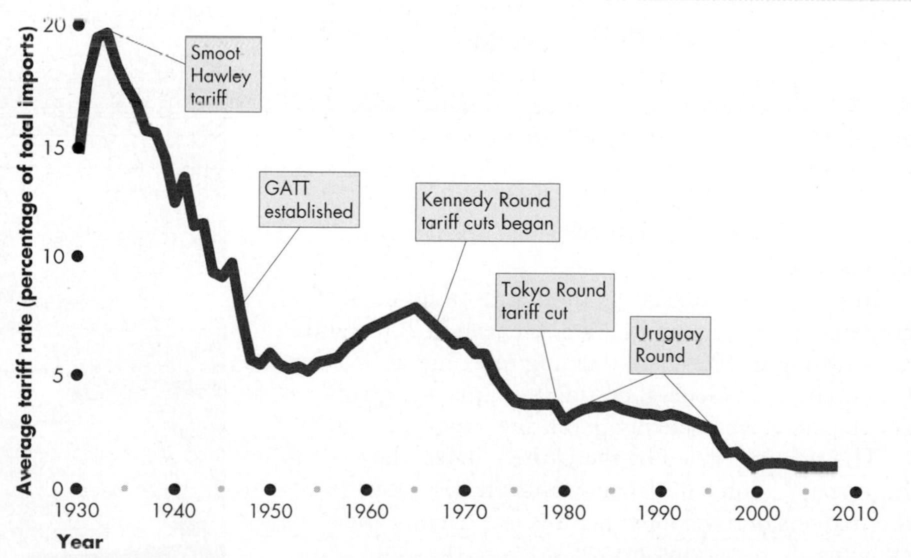


**Tariffs: 1930–2008**

*Sources of data:* U.S. Bureau of the Census, *Historical Statistics of the United States, Colonial Times to 1970*, Bicentennial Edition, Part 1 (Washington, D.C., 1975); Series U-212: updated from *Statistical Abstract of the United States:* various editions.

***U.S. Producers of the Good Gain*** Because the price of an imported T-shirt rises by the amount of the tariff, U.S. T-shirt producers are now able to sell their T-shirts for the world price plus the tariff. At the higher price, the quantity of T-shirts supplied by U.S. producers increases. The combination of a higher price and larger quantity produced increases producers' profits. So the U.S. producers gain from the tariff.

***U.S. Consumers Lose More Than U.S. Producers Gain: Society Loses*** Consumers lose from a tariff for three reasons:

1. They pay a higher price to domestic producers
2. They consume a smaller quantity of the good
3. They pay tariff revenue to the government

The tariff revenue is a loss to consumers but is not a social loss. The government can use the tax revenue to buy public services that consumers value. But the other two sources of consumer loss include some social losses.

There is a social loss because part of the higher price paid to domestic producers pays the higher cost of domestic production. The increased domestic production could have been obtained at lower cost as an import. There is also a social loss from the decreased quantity of the good consumed at the higher price.

## Import Quotas

We now look at the second tool for restricting trade: import quotas. An **import quota** is a restriction that limits the maximum quantity of a good that may be imported in a given period. Most countries impose import quotas on a wide range of items. The United States imposes them on sugar and bananas and manufactured goods such as textiles and paper.

Import quotas enable the government to satisfy the self-interest of the people who earn their incomes in the import-competing industries. But you will discover that like a tariff, an import quota decreases the gains from trade and is not in the social interest.

## Failure in Doha

### Self-Interest Beats the Social Interest

The **World Trade Organization (WTO)** is an international body established by the world's major trading nations for the purpose of supervising international trade and lowering the barriers to trade.

In 2001, at a meeting of trade ministers from all the WTO member-countries held in Doha, Qatar, an agreement was made to begin negotiations to lower tariff barriers and quotas that restrict international trade in farm products and services. These negotiations are called the **Doha Development Agenda** or the **Doha Round**.

In the period since 2001, thousands of hours of conferences in Cancún in 2003, Geneva in 2004, and Hong Kong in 2005, and ongoing meetings at WTO headquarters in Geneva, costing millions of taxpayers' dollars, have made disappointing progress.

The rich world, led by the United States, the European Union, and Japan, wants greater access to the markets of developing nations in exchange for allowing those nations greater access to the rich world's markets, especially for farm products.

The developing world, led by Brazil, China, India, and South Africa, wants access to the farm product markets of the rich world, but they also wants to protect their infant industries.

With two incompatible positions, these negotiations are stalled and show no signs of a breakthrough. The self-interest of rich and developing nations is preventing the achievement of the social interest.

**The Effects of an Import Quota** The effects of an import quota are similar to those of a tariff. The price rises, the quantity bought decreases, and the quantity produced in the United States increases. Figure 15.4 illustrates the effects.

Figure 15.4(a) shows the situation with free international trade. Figure 15.4(b) shows what happens with an import quota of 10 million T-shirts a year. The U.S. supply curve of T-shirts becomes the domestic supply curve, $S_{US}$, plus the quantity that the import quota permits. So the supply curve becomes $S_{US}$ + *quota*. The price of T-shirts rises to \$7, the quantity of T-shirts bought in the United States decreases to 45 million a year, the quantity of T-shirts produced in the United States increases to 35 million a year, and the quantity of T-shirts imported into the United States decreases to the quota quantity of 10 million a year. All these effects of a quota are identical to the effects of a \$2 per shirt tariff, as you can check in Figure 15.3(b).

**Winners, Losers, and the Social Loss from an Import Quota** An import quota creates winners and losers that are similar to those of a tariff but with an interesting difference.

When the government imposes an import quota,

- U.S. consumers of the good lose.
- U.S. producers of the good gain.
- Importers of the good gain.
- Society loses.

***U.S. Consumers of the Good Lose*** Because the price of a T-shirt in the United States rises, the quantity of T-shirts demanded decreases. The combination of a higher price and smaller quantity bought makes the consumer worse off. So the U.S. consumers lose when a quota is imposed.

***U.S. Producers of the Good Gain*** Because the price of a T-shirt rises, U.S. T-shirt producers increase production. The combination of a higher price and larger

**FIGURE 15.4** The Effects of an Import Quota

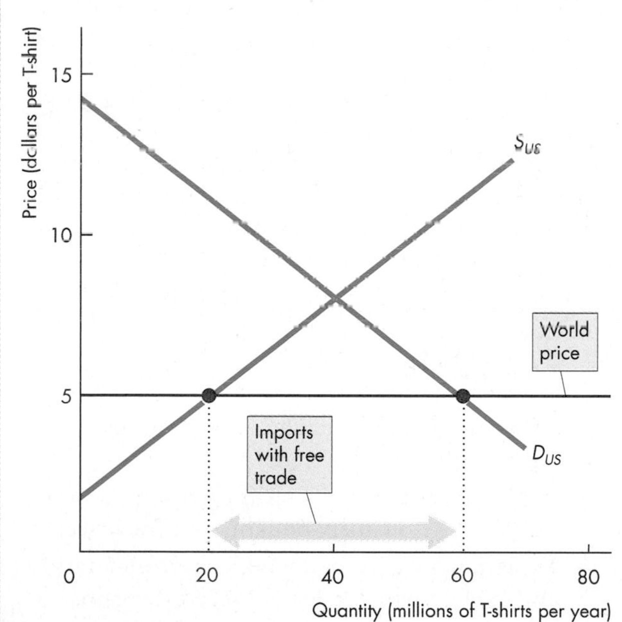


**(a) Free trade**

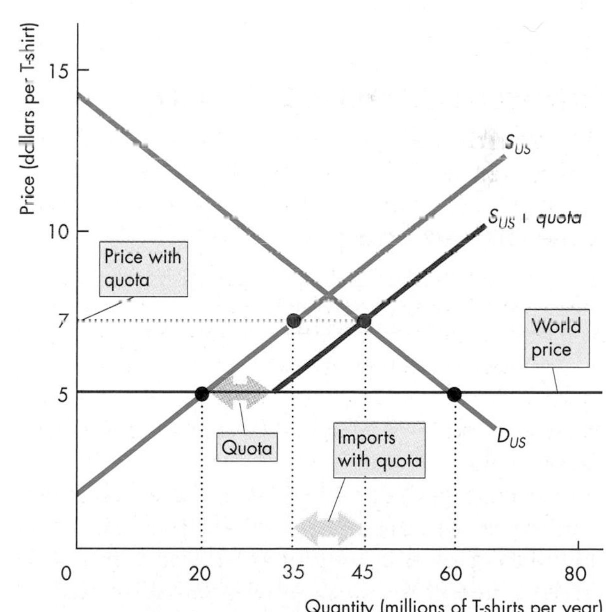


**(b) Market with import quota**

With free international trade, in part (a), Americans buy 60 million T-shirts at the world price. The United States produces 20 million T-shirts and imports 40 million a year. With an import quota of 10 million T-shirts a year, in part (b), the supply of T-shirts in the United States is shown by the curve $S_{US}$ + *quota*. The price in the United States rises to \$7 a T-shirt. U.S. production increases, U.S. purchases decrease, and the quantity of T-shirts imported decreases.

myeconlab animation

quantity produced increases producers' profits. So the U.S. producers gain from the quota.

***Importers of the Good Gain*** The importer is able to buy the good on the world market at the world market price, and sell the good in the domestic market at the domestic price. Because the domestic price exceeds the world price, the importer gains.

***Society Loses*** Society loses because the loss to consumers exceeds the gains of domestic producers and importers. Just like the social losses from a tariff, there is a social loss from the quota because part of the higher price paid to domestic producers pays the higher cost of domestic production. There is a social loss from the decreased quantity of the good consumed at the higher price.

**Tariff and Quota Compared** You've looked at the effects of a tariff and a quota and can now see the essential differences between them. A tariff brings in revenue for the government while a quota brings a profit for the importers. All the other effects of a quota are the same as the effects of a tariff, provided the quota is set at the same quantity of imports that results from the tariff.

Tariffs and quotas are equivalent ways of restricting imports, benefiting domestic producers, and harming domestic consumers.

Let's now look at some other import barriers.

## Other Import Barriers

Two sets of policies that influence imports are

- Health, safety, and regulation barriers
- Voluntary export restraints

**Health, Safety, and Regulation Barriers** Thousands of detailed health, safety, and other regulations restrict international trade. For example, U.S. food imports are examined by the Food and Drug Administration to determine whether the food is "pure, wholesome, safe to eat, and produced under sanitary conditions." The discovery of BSE (mad cow disease) in just one U.S. cow in 2003 was enough to close down international trade in U.S. beef. The European Union bans imports of most genetically modified foods, such as U.S.-produced soybeans. Although regulations of the type we've just described are not designed to limit international trade, they have that effect.

**Voluntary Export Restraints** A *voluntary export restraint* is like a quota allocated to a foreign exporter of the good. This type of trade barrier isn't common. It was initially used during the 1980s when Japan voluntarily limited its exports of car parts to the United States.

## Export Subsidies

A *subsidy* is a payment by the government to a producer. When the government pays a subsidy, the cost of production falls by the amount of the subsidy so supply increases. An **export subsidy** is a payment by the government to the producer of an exported good so it increases the supply of exports. Export subsidies are illegal under a number of international agreements including the North American Free Trade Agreement (NAFTA) and the rules of the World Trade Organization (WTO).

Although export subsidies are illegal, the subsidies that the U.S. and European Union governments pay to farmers end up increasing domestic production, some of which gets exported. These exports of subsidized farm products make it harder for producers in other countries, notably in Africa and Central and South America, to compete in global markets.

Export subsidies bring gains to domestic producers, but they result in inefficient overproduction of some food products in the rich industrial countries, underproduction in the rest of the world, and create a social loss for the world as a whole.

### Review Quiz

1. What are the tools that a country can use to restrict international trade?
2. Explain the effects of a tariff on domestic production, the quantity bought, and the price.
3. Explain who gains and who loses from a tariff and explain why the losses exceed the gains.
4. Explain the effects of an import quota on domestic production, consumption, and price.
5. Explain who gains and who loses from an import quota and explain why the losses exceed the gains.

Work Study Plan 15.2 and get instant feedback.

## The Case Against Protection

For as long as nations and international trade have existed, people have debated whether a country is better off with free international trade or with protection from foreign competition. The debate continues, but for most economists, a verdict has been delivered and is the one you have just seen. Free trade promotes prosperity for all countries; protection is inefficient. We've seen the most powerful case for free trade—it brings gains for consumers that exceed any losses incurred by producers, so there is a net gain for society.

But there is a broader range of issues in the free trade versus protection debate. Let's review these issues.

Two classical arguments for restricting international trade are

- The infant-industry argument
- The dumping argument

### The Infant-Industry Argument

The **infant-industry argument** for protection is that it is necessary to protect a new industry to enable it to grow into a mature industry that can compete in world markets. The argument is based on the idea of *dynamic comparative advantage*, which can arise from *learning-by-doing* (see Chapter 2, p. 43).

Learning-by-doing is a powerful engine of productivity growth, and comparative advantage does evolve and change because of on-the-job experience. But these facts do not justify protection.

First, the infant-industry argument is valid only if the benefits of learning-by-doing *not only* accrue to the owners and workers of the firms in the infant industry but also *spill over* to other industries and parts of the economy. For example, there are huge productivity gains from learning-by-doing in the manufacture of aircraft.

But almost all of these gains benefit the stockholders and workers of Boeing and other aircraft producers. Because the people making the decisions, bearing the risk, and doing the work are the ones who benefit, they take the dynamic gains into account when they decide on the scale of their activities. In this case, almost no benefits spill over to other parts of the economy, so there is no need for government assistance to achieve an efficient outcome.

Second, even if the case is made for protecting an infant industry, it is more efficient to do so by giving the firms in the industry a subsidy, which is financed out of taxes. Such a subsidy would encourage the industry to mature and to compete with efficient world producers and keep the price faced by consumers at the world price.

### The Dumping Argument

**Dumping** occurs when a foreign firm sells its exports at a lower price than its cost of production. Dumping might be used by a firm that wants to gain a global monopoly. In this case, the foreign firm sells its output at a price below its cost to drive domestic firms out of business. When the domestic firms have gone, the foreign firm takes advantage of its monopoly position and charges a higher price for its product. Dumping is illegal under the rules of the WTO and is usually regarded as a justification for temporary tariffs, which are called *countervailing duties*.

But there are powerful reasons to resist the dumping argument for protection. First, it is virtually impossible to detect dumping because it is hard to determine a firm's costs. As a result, the test for dumping is whether a firm's export price is below its domestic price. But this test is a weak one because it can be rational for a firm to charge a low price in a market in which the quantity demanded is highly sensitive to price and a higher price in a market in which demand is less price-sensitive.

Second, it is hard to think of a good that is produced by a *global* monopoly. So even if all the domestic firms in some industry were driven out of business, it would always be possible to find alternative foreign sources of supply and to buy the good at a price determined in a competitive market.

Third, if a good or service were a truly global monopoly, the best way of dealing with it would be by regulation—just as in the case of domestic monopolies. Such regulation would require international cooperation.

The two arguments for protection that we've just examined have an element of credibility. The counterarguments are in general stronger, however, so these arguments do not make the case for protection. But they are not the only arguments that you might encounter. There are many other new arguments against globalization and for protection. The most common ones are that protection

- Saves jobs
- Allows us to compete with cheap foreign labor
- Penalizes lax environmental standards
- Prevents rich countries from exploiting developing countries

## Saves Jobs

First, free trade does cost some jobs, but it also creates other jobs. It brings about a global rationalization of labor and allocates labor resources to their highest-valued activities. International trade in textiles has cost tens of thousands of jobs in the United States as textile mills and other factories closed. But tens of thousands of jobs have been created in other countries as textile mills opened. And tens of thousands of U.S. workers got better-paying jobs than as textile workers because U.S. export industries expanded and created new jobs. More jobs have been created than destroyed.

Although protection does save particular jobs, it does so at a high cost. For example, until 2005, U.S. textile jobs were protected by an international agreement called the Multifiber Arrangement. The U.S. International Trade Commission (ITC) has estimated that because of import quotas, 72,000 jobs existed in the textile industry that would otherwise have disappeared and that the annual clothing expenditure in the United States was $15.9 billion ($160 per family), higher than it would have been with free trade. Equivalently, the ITC estimated that each textile job saved cost $221,000 a year.

Imports don't only destroy jobs. They create jobs for retailers that sell imported goods and for firms that service those goods. Imports also create jobs by creating incomes in the rest of the world, some of which are spent on U.S.-made goods and services.

## Allows Us to Compete with Cheap Foreign Labor

With the removal of tariffs on trade between the United States and Mexico, people said we would hear a "giant sucking sound" as jobs rushed to Mexico. Let's see what's wrong with this view.

The labor cost of a unit of output equals the wage rate divided by labor productivity. For example, if a U.S. autoworker earns $30 an hour and produces 15 units of output an hour, the average labor cost of a unit of output is $2. If a Mexican auto assembly worker earns $3 an hour and produces 1 unit of output an hour, the average labor cost of a unit of output is $3. Other things remaining the same, the higher a worker's productivity, the higher is the worker's wage rate. High-wage workers have high productivity; low-wage workers have low productivity.

Although high-wage U.S. workers are more productive, on average, than low-wage Mexican workers, there are differences across industries. U.S. labor is relatively more productive in some activities than in others. For example, the productivity of U.S. workers in producing movies, financial services, and customized computer chips is relatively higher than their productivity in the production of metals and some standardized machine parts. The activities in which U.S. workers are relatively more productive than their Mexican counterparts are those in which the United States has a *comparative advantage*. By engaging in free trade, increasing our production and exports of the goods and services in which we have a comparative advantage and decreasing our production and increasing our imports of the goods and services in which our trading partners have a comparative advantage, we can make ourselves and the citizens of other countries better off.

## Penalizes Lax Environmental Standards

Another argument for protection is that many poorer countries, such as China and Mexico, do not have the same environmental policies that we have and, because they are willing to pollute and we are not, we cannot compete with them without tariffs. So if poorer countries want free trade with the richer and "greener" countries, they must clean up their environments to our standards.

This argument for protection is weak. First, a poor country cannot afford to be as concerned about its environment as a rich country can. Today, some of the worst pollution of air and water is found in China, Mexico, and the former communist countries of Eastern Europe. But only a few decades ago, London and Los Angeles led the pollution league table. The best hope for cleaner air in Beijing and Mexico City is rapid income growth and free trade contributes to that growth. As incomes in developing countries grow, they will have the *means* to match their desires to improve their environment. Second, a poor country may have a comparative advantage at doing "dirty" work, which helps it to raise its income and at the same time, enables the global economy to achieve higher environmental standards than would otherwise be possible.

## Prevents Rich Countries from Exploiting Developing Countries

Another argument for protection is that international trade must be restricted to prevent the people of the rich industrial world from exploiting the poorer people of the developing countries and forcing them to work for slave wages.

Child labor and near-slave labor are serious problems that are rightly condemned. But by trading with poor countries, we increase the demand for the goods that these countries produce and, more significantly, we increase the demand for their labor. When the demand for labor in developing countries increases, the wage rate also increases. So, rather than exploiting people in developing countries, trade can improve their opportunities and increase their incomes.

The arguments for protection that we've reviewed leave free-trade unscathed. But a new phenomenon is at work in our economy: *offshore outsourcing*. Surely we need protection from this new source of foreign competition. Let's investigate.

## Offshore Outsourcing

Citibank, the Bank of America, Apple Computer, Nike, Wal-Mart: What do these U.S. icons have in common? They all send jobs that could be done in America to China, India, Thailand, or even Canada—they are offshoring. What exactly is offshoring?

**What Is Offshoring?** A firm in the United States can obtain the things that it sells in any of four ways:

1. Hire American labor and produce in America.
2. Hire foreign labor and produce in other countries.
3. Buy finished goods, components, or services from other firms in the United States.
4. Buy finished goods, components, or services from other firms in other countries.

Activities 3 and 4 are **outsourcing**, and activities 2 and 4 are **offshoring**. Activity 4 is **offshore outsourcing**. Notice that offshoring includes activities that take place inside U.S. firms. If an U.S. firm opens its own facilities in another country, then it is offshoring.

Offshoring has been going on for hundreds of years, but it expanded rapidly and became a source of concern during the 1990s as many U.S. firms moved information technology services and general office services such as finance, accounting, and human resources management overseas.

**Why Did Offshoring of Services Boom During the 1990s?** The gains from specialization and trade that you saw in the previous section must be large enough to make it worth incurring the costs of communication and transportation. If the cost of producing a T-shirt in China isn't lower than the cost of producing the T-shirt in the United States by more than the cost of transporting the shirt from China to America, then it is more efficient to produce shirts in the United States and avoid the transport costs.

The same considerations apply to trade in services. If services are to be produced offshore, then the cost of delivering those services must be low enough to leave the buyer with an overall lower cost. Before the 1990s, the cost of communicating across large distances was too high to make the offshoring of business services efficient. But during the 1990s, when satellites, fiber-optic cables, and computers cut the cost of a phone call between America and India to less than a dollar an hour, a huge base of offshore resources became competitive with similar resources in the United States.

**What Are the Benefits of Offshoring?** Offshoring brings gains from trade identical to those of any other type of trade. We could easily change the names of the items traded from T-shirts and airplanes (the examples in the previous sections of this chapter) to banking services and call center services (or any other pair of services). An American bank might export banking services to Indian firms, and Indians might provide call center services to U.S. firms. This type of trade would benefit both Americans and Indians provided the United States has a comparative advantage in banking services and India has a comparative advantage in call center services.

Comparative advantages like these emerged during the 1990s. India has the world's largest educated English-speaking population and it is located at a time zone a half a day ahead of the U.S. east coast and midway between Asia and Europe, which facilitates 24/7 operations. When the cost of communicating with a worker in India was several dollars a minute, as it was before the 1990s, tapping these vast resources was just too costly. But at today's cost of a long-distance telephone call or Internet connection, resources in India can be used to produce services in the United States at a lower cost than those services can be produced by using resources located in the United States. And with the incomes that Indians earn from exporting services, some of the services (and goods) that Indians buy are produced in the United States.

**Why Is Offshoring a Concern?** Despite the gains from specialization and trade that offshoring brings, many people believe that it also brings costs that eat up the gains. Why?

A major reason is that offshoring is taking jobs in services. The loss of manufacturing jobs to other countries has been going on for decades, but the U.S. service sector has always expanded by enough to create new jobs to replace the lost manufacturing jobs. Now that service jobs are also going overseas, the fear is that there will not be enough jobs for Americans. This fear is misplaced.

Some service jobs are going overseas, while others are expanding at home. The United States imports call center services, but it exports education, health care, legal, financial, and a host of other types of services. Jobs in these sectors are expanding and will continue to expand.

The exact number of jobs that have moved to lower-cost offshore locations is not known, and estimates vary. But even the highest estimate is a tiny number compared to the normal rate of job creation.

**Winners and Losers** Gains from trade do not bring gains for every single person. Americans, on average, gain from offshore outsourcing. But some people lose. The losers are those who have invested in the human capital to do a specific job that has now gone offshore.

Unemployment benefits provide short-term temporary relief for these displaced workers. But the long-term solution requires retraining and the acquisition of new skills.

Beyond providing short-term relief through unemployment benefits, there is a large role for government in the provision of education and training to enable the labor force of the twenty-first century to be capable of ongoing learning and rapid retooling to take on new jobs that today we can't foresee.

Schools, colleges, and universities will expand and get better at doing their jobs of producing a highly educated and flexible labor force.

### Avoiding Trade Wars

We have reviewed the arguments commonly heard in favor of protection and the counterarguments against them. There is one counterargument to protection that is general and quite overwhelming: Protection invites retaliation and can trigger a trade war.

The best example of a trade war occurred during the Great Depression of the 1930s when the United States introduced the Smoot-Hawley tariff. Country after country retaliated with its own tariff, and in a short period, world trade had almost disappeared. The costs to all countries were large and led to a renewed international resolve to avoid such self-defeating moves in the future. The costs also led to the creation of GATT and are the impetus behind current attempts to liberalize trade.

## Why Is International Trade Restricted?

Why, despite all the arguments against protection, is trade restricted? There are two key reasons:

- Tariff revenue
- Rent seeking

**Tariff Revenue** Government revenue is costly to collect. In the developed countries such as the United States, a well-organized tax collection system is in place that can generate billions of dollars of income tax and sales tax revenues. This tax collection system is made possible by the fact that most economic transactions are done by firms that must keep properly audited financial records. Without such records, the revenue collection agencies (the Internal Revenue Service in the United States) would be severely hampered in the work. Even with audited financial accounts, some potential tax revenue is lost. Nonetheless, for the industrialized countries, the income tax and sales taxes are the major sources of revenue and the tariff plays a very small role.

But governments in developing countries have a difficult time collecting taxes from their citizens. Much economic activity takes place in an informal economy with few financial records, so only a small amount of revenue is collected from income taxes and sales taxes. The one area in which economic transactions are well recorded and audited is international trade. So this activity is an attractive base for tax collection in these countries and is used much more extensively than it is in the developed countries.

**Rent Seeking** Rent seeking is the major reason why international trade is restricted. **Rent seeking** is lobbying for special treatment by the government to create economic profit or to divert the gains from trade away from others. Free trade increases consumption possibilities *on average*, but not everyone shares in the gain and some people even lose. Free trade brings benefits to some and imposes costs on others, with total benefits exceeding total costs. The uneven distribution of costs and benefits is the principal obstacle to achieving more liberal international trade.

Returning to the example of trade in T-shirts and airplanes, the benefits from free trade accrue to all the producers of airplanes and to those producers of T-shirts who do not bear the costs of adjusting to a smaller garment industry. These costs are transition costs, not permanent costs. The costs of moving to free trade are borne by the garment producers and their employees who must become producers of other goods and services in which the United States has a comparative advantage.

The number of winners from free trade is large. But because the gains are spread thinly over a large number of people, the gain per person is small. The winners could organize and become a political force lobbying for free trade. But political activity is costly. It uses time and other scarce resources and the gains per person are too small to make the cost of political activity worth bearing.

In contrast, the number of losers from free trade is small, but the loss per person is large. Because the loss per person is large, the people who lose *are* willing to incur considerable expense to lobby against free trade.

Both the winners and losers weigh benefits and costs. Those who gain from free trade weigh the benefits it brings against the cost of achieving it. Those who lose from free trade and gain from protection weigh the benefit of protection against the cost of maintaining it. The protectionists undertake a larger quantity of political lobbying than the free traders.

## Compensating Losers

If, in total, the gains from free international trade exceed the losses, why don't those who gain compensate those who lose so that everyone is in favor of free trade?

Some compensation does take place. When Congress approved the North American Free Trade Agreement, (NAFTA), with Canada and Mexico, it set up a $56 million fund to support and retrain workers who lost their jobs as a result of the new trade agreement. During NAFTA's first six months, only 5,000 workers applied for benefits under this scheme. The losers from international trade are also compensated indirectly through the normal unemployment compensation arrangements. But only limited attempts are made to compensate those who lose.

The main reason why full compensation is not attempted is that the costs of identifying all the losers and estimating the value of their losses would be enormous. Also, it would never be clear whether a person who has fallen on hard times is suffering because of free trade or for other reasons that might be largely under her or his control. Furthermore, some people who look like losers at one point in time might, in fact, end up gaining. The young auto-worker who loses his job in Michigan and becomes a computer assembly worker in Minneapolis resents the loss of work and the need to move. But a year later, looking back on events, he counts himself fortunate.

Because we do not, in general, compensate the losers from free international trade, protectionism is a popular and permanent feature of our national economic and political life.

### Review Quiz

1. What are the infant industry and dumping arguments for protection? Are they correct?
2. Can protection save jobs and the environment and prevent workers in developing countries from being exploited?
3. What is offshore outsourcing? Who benefits from it and who loses from it?
4. What are the main reasons for imposing a tariff?
5. Why don't the winners from free trade win the political argument?

myeconlab Work Study Plan 15.3 and get instant feedback.

We end this chapter on international trade policy with *Reading Between the Lines* on pp. 394–395. It applies what you've learned in both this chapter and earlier chapters about the source of an international trade deficit and the effect of protectionism.

READING BETWEEN THE LINES 

# Protectionism in Disquise?

## US May Seek to Narrow Trade Deficit With Asia

http://www.koreatimes.co.kr
November21, 2008

U.S. President-elect Barack Obama will likely encourage South Korea and other Asian countries to play a supporting role in narrowing the growing U.S. trade deficit, observed a U.S. economist. ...

"Korea, China and others cannot continue to run large trade surpluses vis a vis the United States indefinitely, and the imbalances should be brought down by expansionary monetary and fiscal policies that raise domestic consumption in Asian countries." ...

Obama and Vice President-elect Joseph Biden made it clear that they would fight for fair trade in the Obama-Biden Plan, which was unveiled this week.

They vowed to pursue a trade policy that "helps open foreign markets to support good American jobs," saying they will stand firm against agreements that undermine America's economic security. ...

The Obama-Biden team "will use trade agreements to spread good labor and environmental standards around the world and stand firm against agreements like the Central American Free Trade Agreement that fail to live up to those important benchmarks."

Their commitment rekindles the debate on so-called social dumping and the "race to the bottom" of wages and benefits of U.S. workers caused by cheap products made in developing countries under relatively inexpensive labor and poor working conditions.

Developing countries opposed the move, calling it disguised protectionism. ...

*The Korea Times*

## Essence of the Story

- Barack Obama will want Asian countries to help narrow the U.S. trade deficit.
- Asian surpluses should be lowered by expansionary monetary and fiscal policies that increase domestic consumption in Asian countries.
- Obama and Biden want fair trade that opens foreign markets to expand good American jobs.
- Obama and Biden will seek good labor and environmental standards in countries with which they do trade deals.
- Developing countries are calling this approach disguised protectionism.

## Economic Analysis

- In 2008, the United States had an international trade deficit of $700 billion.
- Much of this deficit was in trade with China, Korea, and other Asian economies.
- The U.S. international trade deficit results from the sum of consumption expenditure, investment, and government expenditure exceeding GDP (see Chapter 9, pp. 229–230).
- The Asian international trade surpluses result from real GDP exceeding the sum of consumption expenditure, investment, and government expenditure in those economies.
- If the Asian economies pursue expansionary fiscal and monetary policies, their international surpluses will shrink, U.S. real GDP will increase, and the U.S. international deficit will decrease.
- International trade policy influences the *volume* of exports and imports, not the *balance* of trade.
- Trade policies that seek "fair trade" by ensuring "high labor and environmental standards" are, as the developing economies claim, protectionism in disguise. The figures show why.
- Figure 1 illustrates the effects of "fair trade" policies that insist on high labor and environmental standards.
- The market is for a good or service that the United States imports. $D_{US}$ is the U.S. domestic demand curve and $S_{US}$ is the U.S. domestic supply curve.
- If other countries are left to pursue their own goals, the world price is $5 per unit and the United States imports 40 million units (60 million units bought by Americans minus 20 million units produced in the United States).
- Imposing the cost of "high labor and environmental standards" on countries with which the United States trades raises the world price and cuts U.S. imports to 10 million units (45 million units bought by Americans minus 35 million produced in the United States).
- Figure 2 shows how an identical outcome (except for tariff revenue) is achieved with a tariff.

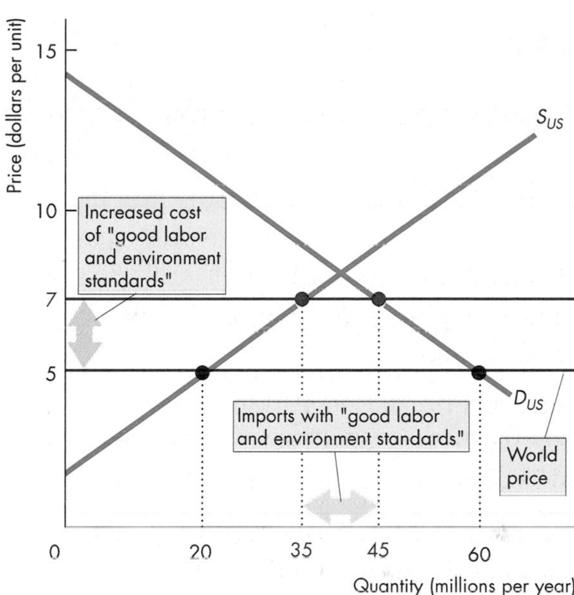


**Figure 1 Market with "fair trade" policies**

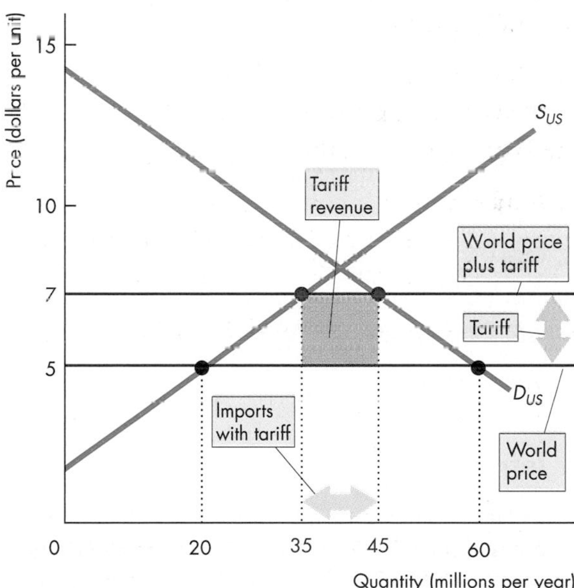


**Figure 2 Market with tariff**

## SUMMARY

### Key Points

**How Global Markets Work** (pp. 380–383)

- Comparative advantage drives international trade.
- If the world price of a good is lower than the domestic price, the rest of the world has a comparative advantage in producing that good and the domestic country gains by producing less, consuming more, and importing the good.
- If the world price of a good is higher than the domestic price, the domestic country has a comparative advantage in producing that good and gains by producing more, consuming less, and exporting the good.
- Compared to a no-trade situation, in a market with imports, consumers gain and producers lose but the gains are greater than the losses.
- Compared to a no-trade situation, in a market with exports, producers gain and consumers lose but the gains are greater than the losses.

**International Trade Restrictions** (pp. 384–388)

- Countries restrict international trade by imposing tariffs, import quotas, and other import barriers.
- Trade restrictions raise the domestic price of imported goods, lower the quantity imported, make consumers worse off, make producers better off, and damage the social interest.

**The Case Against Protection** (pp. 389–393)

- Arguments that protection is necessary for infant industries and to prevent dumping are weak.
- Arguments that protection saves jobs, allows us to compete with cheap foreign labor, is needed to penalize lax environmental standards, and prevents exploitation of developing countries are flawed.
- Offshore outsourcing is just a new way of reaping gains from trade and does not justify protection.
- Trade restrictions are popular because protection brings a small loss per person to a large number of people and a large gain per person to a small number of people. Those who gain have a stronger political voice than those who lose and it is too costly to identify and compensate losers.

### Key Figures



### Key Terms

## PROBLEMS and APPLICATIONS

Work problems 1–10 in Chapter 15 Study Plan and get instant feedback.
Work problems 11–21 as Homework, a Quiz, or a Test if assigned by your instructor.

1. Wholesalers of roses (the firms that supply your local flower shop with roses for Valentine's Day) buy and sell roses in containers that hold 120 stems. The table provides information about the wholesale market for roses in the United States. The demand schedule is the wholesaler's demand and the supply schedule is the U.S. rose growers' supply.

| Price (dollars per container) | Quantity demanded | Quantity supplied |
|---|---|---|
| | (millions of containers per year) | |
| 100 | 15 | 0 |
| 125 | 12 | 2 |
| 150 | 9 | 4 |
| 175 | 6 | 6 |
| 200 | 3 | 8 |
| 225 | 0 | 10 |

Wholesalers can buy roses at auction in Aalsmeer, Holland, for $125 per container.

a. Without international trade, what would be the price of a container of roses and how many containers of roses a year would be bought and sold in the United States?
b. At the price in your answer to a, does the United States or the rest of the world have a comparative advantage in producing roses?
c. If U.S. wholesalers buy roses at the lowest possible price, how many do they buy from U.S. growers and how many do they import?
d. Draw a graph to illustrate the U.S. wholesale market for roses. Show on the graph the equilibrium in that market with no international trade and the equilibrium with free trade. Mark on the graph the quantity of roses produced in the United States, the quantity imported, and the total quantity bought.

2. **Underwater Oil Discovery to Transform Brazil into a Major Exporter**

A huge underwater oil field discovered late last year has the potential to transform South America's largest country into a sizable exporter ... Just a decade ago the notion that Brazil would become self-sufficient in energy, let alone emerge as an exporter, seemed far-fetched. ... Petrobras was formed five decades ago largely as a trading company to import oil to support Brazil's growing economy. ... Yet two years ago ... Brazil reached its long-sought goal of energy self-sufficiency. ...

*International Herald Tribune*, January 11, 2008

a. Describe Brazil's comparative advantage in producing oil and explain why its comparative advantage has changed.
b. Draw a graph to illustrate the Brazilian market for oil and explain why Brazil was an importer of oil until a few years ago.
c. Draw a graph to illustrate the Brazilian market for oil and explain why Brazil may become an exporter of oil in the near future.

3. Use the information on the U.S. wholesale market for roses in problem 1 to
a. Explain who gains and who loses from free international trade in roses compared to a situation in which Americans buy only roses grown in the United States.
b. Draw a graph to illustrate the gains and losses from free trade.

4. **Postcard: Bangalore. Hearts set on joining the global economy, Indian IT workers are brushing up on their interpersonal skills**

The huge number of Indian workers staffing the world's tech firms and call centers ... possess cutting-edge technical knowledge, [but] their interpersonal and communication skills lag far behind. ... Enter Bangalore's finishing schools.

*Time*, May 5, 2008

a. What comparative advantages does this news clip identify?
b. Using the information in this news clip, what services do you predict Bangalore (India) exports and what services do you predict it imports?
c. Who will gain and who will lose from the international trade that you described in your answer to b?

5. **Steel Tariffs Appear to Have Backfired on Bush**

President Bush set aside his free-trade principles last year and imposed heavy tariffs on imported steel to help out struggling mills in Pennsylvania and West Virginia, two states crucial for his reelection. … Some economists say the tariffs may have cost more jobs than they saved, by driving up costs for automakers and other steel users. …

*The Washington Post*, September 19, 2003

a. Explain how a high tariff on steel imports can help domestic steel producers.
b. Explain how a high tariff on steel imports can harm steel users.
c. Draw a graph of the U.S. market for steel to show how a high tariff on steel imports
    i. Helps U.S. steel producers.
    ii. Harms U.S. steel users.
    iii. Creates a social loss.

6. Use the information on the U.S. wholesale market for roses in problem 1.
    a. If the United States puts a tariff of $25 per container on imports of roses, what happens to the U.S. price of roses, the quantity of roses bought, the quantity produced in the United States, and the quantity imported?
    b. Who gains and who loses from this tariff?
    c. Draw a graph to illustrate the effects of the tariff on production, consumption, and imports and on prices.
7. Use the information on the U.S. wholesale market for roses in problem 1.
    a. If the United States puts an import quota on roses of 5 million containers, what happens to the U.S. price of roses, the quantity of roses bought, the quantity produced in the United States, and the quantity imported?
    b. Who gains and who loses from this quota?
    c. Draw a graph to illustrate the effects of the import quota on production, consumption, imports and the prices paid by consumers and received by producers.
8. **Car Sales Go Up as Prices Tumble**

    Car affordability [in Australia] is now at its best in 20 years, fueling a surge in sales as prices tumble. … [In 2000, Australia cut the tariff to 15 percent and] on January 1, 2005, the tariff on imported vehicles fell from 15 percent to 10 percent.

    *Courier Mail*, February 26, 2005

    a. Explain who gains and who loses from the lower tariff on imported cars.
    b. Draw a graph to show how the price of a car, the quantity bought, the quantity produced in Australia, and imports of cars changed.
9. **Chinese tire maker rejects U.S. charge of defects**

    … regulators in the United States ordered the recall of more than 450,000 faulty tires. … The Chinese company that produced the tires … disputed the allegations Tuesday and hinted that the recall might be an effort by foreign competitors to hamper the company's exports to the United States. … Mounting scrutiny of Chinese-made goods has become a source of new trade frictions between the United States and China and fueled worries among regulators, corporations and consumers about the risks associated with many products imported from China. …

    *International Herald Tribune*, June 26, 2007

    a. What does the information in the news clip imply about the comparative advantage of producing tires in the United States and China?
    b. Could product quality be a valid argument against free trade?
    c. How would the product-quality argument against free trade be open to abuse by domestic producers of the imported good?
10. **Why the World Can't Afford Food**

    As [food] stocks dwindled, some countries placed export restrictions on food to protect their own supplies. This in turn drove up prices, punishing countries—especially poor ones—that depend on imports for much of their food.

    *Time*, May 19, 2008

    a. What are the benefits to a country from importing food?
    b. What costs might arise from relying on imported food?
    c. If a country restricts food exports, what effect does this restriction have in that country on
        i. The price of food?
        ii. The quantity of food produced?
        iii. The quantity of food consumed?
        iv. The quantity of food exported?
    d. Draw a graph of the market for food in a country that exports food. On the graph show how the price of food, the quantities of food consumed, produced, and exported change when food exports are restricted.

11. Suppose that the world price of sugar is 10 cents a pound, the United States does not trade internationally, and the equilibrium price of sugar in the United States is 20 cents a pound. The United States then begins to trade internationally.
    a. How does the price of sugar in the United States change?
    b. Do U.S. consumers buy more or less sugar?
    c. Do U.S. sugar growers produce more or less sugar?
    d. Does the United States export or import sugar and why?
12. Suppose that the world price of steel is $100 a ton, India does not trade internationally, and the equilibrium price of steel in India is $60 a ton. India then begins to trade internationally.
    a. How does the price of steel in India change?
    b. How does the quantity of steel produced in India change?
    c. How does the quantity of steel bought by India change?
    d. Does India export or import steel and why?
13. A semiconductor is a key component in your laptop, cell phone, and iPod. The table provides information about the market for semiconductors in the United States.

| Price (dollars per unit) | Quantity demanded (billions of units per year) | Quantity supplied (billions of units per year) |
|---|---|---|
| 10 | 25 | 0 |
| 12 | 20 | 20 |
| 14 | 15 | 40 |
| 16 | 10 | 60 |
| 18 | 5 | 80 |
| 20 | 0 | 100 |

Producers of semiconductors can get $18 a unit on the world market.

    a. With no international trade, what would be the price of a semiconductor and how many semiconductors a year would be bought and sold in the United States?
    b. At the price in your answer to a, does the United States have a comparative advantage in producing semiconductors?
    c. If U.S. producers of semiconductors sell at the highest possible price, how many do they sell in the United States and how many do they export?
14. **South Korea to Resume U.S. Beef Imports**

    South Korea will open its market to most U.S. beef. … South Korea banned imports of U.S. beef in 2003 amid concerns over a case of mad cow disease in the United States. The ban closed what was then the third-largest market for U.S. beef exporters. …

    *CNN*, May 29, 2008

    a. Which country, South Korea or the United States, has a comparative advantage in producing beef? What fact in the news clip did you use to answer this question?
    b. Explain how South Korea's import ban on U.S. beef affected beef producers and consumers in South Korea.
    c. Draw a graph of the market for beef in South Korea to illustrate your answer to b. Identify the changes in consumption, production, international trade and price.
    d. Assuming that South Korea is the only importer of U.S. beef, explain how South Korea's import ban on U.S. beef affected beef producers and consumers in the United States.
    e. Draw a graph of the market for beef in the United States to illustrate your answer to d. Identify the changes in consumption, production, international trade, and price.
15. **Act Now, Eat Later**

    … [L]ooming hunger crisis in poor countries … has its roots in … misguided policy in the U.S. and Europe of subsidizing the diversion of food crops to produce biofuels like corn-based ethanol. … [That is,] doling out subsidies to put the world's dinner into the gas tank.

    *Time*, May 5, 2008

    a. What is the effect on the world price of corn of the increased use of corn to produce ethanol in the United States and Europe?
    b. For a poor developing country with a comparative advantage in producing corn, how does the change in the world price of corn affect the quantity of corn it produces, the quantity it consumes, and the quantity that it either exports or imports?
    c. Draw a graph of the market for corn in a poor developing country to illustrate your answer to b. Identify the changes in consumption, production, international trade, and the price that consumers pay.

16. Before 1995, trade between the United States and Mexico was subject to tariffs. In 1995, Mexico joined NAFTA and all U.S. and Mexican tariffs are gradually being removed.
    a. Explain how the price that U.S. consumers pay for goods from Mexico and the quantity of U.S. imports from Mexico have changed. Who are the winners and who are the losers from this free trade?
    b. Explain how the quantity of U.S. exports to Mexico and the U.S. government's tariff revenue from trade with Mexico have changed.
    c. Suppose that in 2008, tomato growers in Florida lobby the U.S. government to impose an import quota on Mexican tomatoes. Explain who in the United States would gain and who would lose from such a quota.
17. Suppose that in response to huge job losses in the U.S. textile industry, Congress imposes a 100 percent tariff on imports of textiles from China.
    a. Explain how the tariff on textiles will change the price that U.S. buyers pay for textiles, the quantity of textiles imported, and the quantity of textiles produced in the United States.
    b. Explain how the U.S. and Chinese gains from trade will change. Who in the United States will lose and who will gain?
18. With free trade between Australia and the United States, Australia would export beef to the United States. But the United States imposes an import quota on Australian beef.
    a. Explain how this quota influences the price that U.S. consumers pay for beef, the quantity of beef produced in the United States, and the U.S. and the Australian gains from trade.
    b. Explain who in the United States gains from the quota on beef imports and who loses.
19. **Aid May Grow for Laid-Off Workers**

    … [T]he expansion of the Trade Adjustment Assistance (TAA) program would begin to reweave the social safety net for the 21st century, as advances permit more industries to take advantage of cheap foreign labor—even for skilled, white-collar work. By providing special compensation to more of globalization's losers and retraining them for stable jobs at home, … an expanded program could begin to ease the resentment and insecurity arising from the new economy.

    *The Washington Post*, July 23, 2007

    a. Why does the United States engage in international trade if it causes U.S. workers to lose their jobs?
    b. Explain how an expansion of the Trade Adjustment Assistance Program will make it easier for the United States to move toward freer international trade.
20. Study *Reading Between the Lines* on pp. 394–395 and answer the following questions.
    a. What determines the U.S. *balance* of international trade?
    b. Why is "fair trade" policy really protectionism in disguise?
    c. Who benefits from "fair trade" policy and why do developing nations oppose it?
21. **Trading Up**

    … the cost of protecting jobs in uncompetitive sectors through tariffs is foolishly high, … The Federal Reserve Bank of Dallas reported in 2002 that saving a job in the sugar industry cost American consumers $826,000 in higher prices a year, saving a dairy industry job cost $685,000 per year, and saving a job in the manufacturing of women's handbags cost $263,000.

    *The New York Times*, June 26, 2006

    a. What are the arguments for saving the jobs mentioned in this news clip?
    b. Explain why these arguments are faulty.
    c. Is there any merit to saving these jobs?
22. **Vows of New Aid to the Poor Leave the Poor Unimpressed**

    … the United States, the European Union, and Japan [plan] to eliminate duties and [import] quotas on almost all goods from up to 50 of the world's poor nations, … The proposal for duty-free, quota-free treatment is so divisive among developing countries that even some negotiators … are saying that the plan must be broadened.

    *The New York Times*, December 15, 2005

    a. Why do the United States, the European Union, and Japan want to eliminate trade barriers on imports from only the poorest countries?
    b. Who will win from the elimination of these trade barriers? Who will lose?
    c. Why is the plan divisive among developing countries?

PART FIVE

# UNDERSTANDING MACROECONOMIC POLICY

## Tradeoffs and Free Lunches

A policy tradeoff arises if, in taking an action to achieve one goal, some other goal must be forgone. The Fed wants to avoid a rise in the inflation rate and a rise in the unemployment rate. But if the Fed raises the interest rate to curb inflation, it might lower expenditure and increase unemployment. The Fed faces a short-run tradeoff between inflation and unemployment.

A policy free lunch arises if in taking actions to pursue one goal, some other (intended or unintended) goal is also achieved. The Fed wants to keep inflation in check and, at the same time, to boost the economic growth rate. If lower inflation brings greater certainty about the future and stimulates saving and investment, the Fed gets both lower inflation and faster real GDP growth. It enjoys a free lunch.

The first two chapters in this part have described the institutional framework in which fiscal policy (Chapter 13) and monetary policy (Chapter 14) are made, described the instruments of policy, and analyzed the effects of policy. This exploration of economic policy draws on almost everything that you learned in previous chapters. The final chapter (Chapter 15) has explained international trade policy.

These policy chapters serve as a capstone on your knowledge of macroeconom ics and draw together all the strands in your study of the previous chapters.

Milton Friedman, whom you meet below, has profoundly influenced our understanding of macroeconomic policy, especially monetary policy.

**Milton Friedman** *was born into a poor immigrant family in New York City in 1912. He was an undergraduate at Rutgers and a graduate student at Columbia University during the Great Depression. From 1977 until his death in 2006, Professor Friedman was a Senior Fellow at the Hoover Institution at Stanford University. But his reputation was built between 1946 and 1983, when he was a leading member of the "Chicago School," an approach to economics developed at the University of Chicago and based on the views that free markets allocate resources efficiently and that stable and low money supply growth delivers macroeconomic stability.*

*Friedman has advanced our understanding of the forces that determine macroeconomic performance and clarified the effects of the quantity of money. For this work, he was awarded the 1977 Nobel Prize for Economic Science.*

*By reasoning from basic economic principles, Friedman (along with Edmund S. Phelps, the 2006 Economics Nobel Laureate) predicted that persistent demand stimulation would not increase output but would cause inflation.*

*When output growth slowed and inflation broke out in the 1970s, Friedman seemed like a prophet, and for a time, his policy prescription, known as* monetarism, *was embraced around the world.*

"Inflation is always and everywhere a monetary phenomenon."

**MILTON FRIEDMAN**
*The Counter-Revolution in Monetary Theory*

**TALKING**
WITH

# Stephanie Schmitt Grohé

**Stephanie Schmitt-Grohé** is Professor of Economics at Columbia University. Born in Germany, she received her first economics degree at Westfälische Wilhelms-Universität Münster in 1987, her M.B.A in Finance at Baruch College, City University of New York in 1989, and her Ph.D. in economics at the University of Chicago in 1994.

Professor Schmitt-Grohé's research covers a wide range of fiscal policy and monetary policy issues that are especially relevant in today's economy as the consequences of the 2007 mortgage crisis play out.

Working with her husband, Martin Uribe, also a Professor of Economics at Columbia University, she has published papers in leading economics journals on how best to conduct monetary policy and fiscal policy and how to avoid problems that might arise from the inappropriate use of a simple policy rule for setting the federal funds rate. She has also contributed to the debate on inflation targeting.

In 2004, Professor Schmitt-Grohé was awarded the Bernácer Prize, awarded annually to a European economist under the age of 40 who has made outstanding contributions in the fields of macroeconomics and finance.

Michael Parkin talked with Stephanie Schmitt-Grohé about her work and the challenges of conducting stabilization policy.

*What attracted you to economics?*

When I graduated from high school, I was interested in both chemistry and economics but I wasn't sure which I wanted to study, so I enrolled in both programs. Within the first year of study, I realized that I wanted to pursue a career in economics. I took a class in which we learned how fiat money can have value and how the central bank can control the inflation rate. This seemed very important to me at the time—and still does after so many years.

*What led you to focus your research on monetary and fiscal stabilization policy?*

I always was very interested in economic policy and both monetary and fiscal stabilization policy have large and clear effects on a society's well-being. The same is certainly true for other areas of economics, but the benefits of macroeconomic stabilization policy are particularly easy to see; and it isn't difficult to find historical examples where bad monetary and fiscal policies unnecessarily lowered the standard of living.

*What was your first job as a professional economist? How did you get started?*

My first job out of graduate school was at the Board of Governors of the Federal Reserve System in Washington. This was a fabulous experience. Watching the policy-making process, I became motivated to work on having a more consistent and compelling theoretical framework on which to base monetary policy advice, and in particular, learning to develop tools to perform evaluation of alternative monetary policy proposals.

*Only a few years out of graduate school, you and your economist husband Martin Uribe accepted a challenge to contribute to an assessment of "dollarization" for Mexico. First, would you explain what dollarization is?*

When a country dollarizes, the U.S. dollar becomes legal tender, replacing the domestic currency. Ecuador, for example, is dollarized. In the case of Mexico in 1999, there were proposals, mainly coming from the business community, to replace the peso with the U.S. dollar.

*Why might dollarization be a good idea?*

Such proposals are typically motivated by the desire to avoid excessive inflation and excessive exchange rate volatility. Dollarization also makes inflationary finance of the Treasury Department impossible.

*And what are the costs of dollarization?*

One cost is that the country loses the revenues it gains from issuing money. A second cost is that the country loses the ability to conduct monetary stabilization policy. In effect, the domestic central bank can no longer influence the business cycle through interest rate or exchange rate policy. The question that Martin and I wanted to answer was "how costly is it for a country to give up the ability to conduct monetary stabilization policy?" We quickly realized that we didn't have the tools to answer this question in a way that we regarded as satisfying.

*Briefly, what did you have to do to enable you to say whether dollarization is a good or bad idea?*

We wanted to be able to quantify the loss in economic welfare that comes from not being able to target monetary policy at stabilizing the domestic economy. To do this, we needed to compute two measures of economic welfare, one arising from Mexican monetary policy and another under dollarization. But we wanted our measures to be based on an empirically compelling and sufficiently detailed model of the Mexican business cycle. At that time there were no measurement techniques available that allowed us to perform this task. So over the course of the next five years we developed the tools that we needed. One tool is an algorithm that computes (approximately but with sufficient accuracy) economic welfare under any given monetary policy, including the two of interest to us: Mexican dollarization and actual Mexican monetary policy. A second tool that we developed is another algorithm to compute optimal monetary policy—the best available monetary policy.

Knowing the highest level of economic welfare that can be achieved allows us to judge how close practical policy proposals come to optimal policy.

*And what was your biggest surprise?*

I think our biggest surprise in this research program was how small the welfare costs of some very simple policy rules are vis-à-vis the optimal policy. Martin and I have shown in a number of papers that simple interest rate rules are very close to the best that can be achieved.

*How would you describe the best stabilization policy for smoothing the business cycle and keeping inflation in check?*

Good stabilization policy is not necessarily a policy that smoothes the business cycle, in the sense that it minimizes output fluctuations. On the contrary, it might be that trying to avoid cyclical fluctuations lowers economic welfare. Suppose, for example, that business-cycle fluctuations arise from fluctuations in the growth rate of productivity—as real business cycle theory suggests. Then economic welfare decreases if we limit the cyclical increase in output that comes from the increase in productivity.

Good stabilization policy is not necessarily a policy that smoothes the business cycle

The findings of my work with Martin suggest that a simple and highly effective monetary policy is one whereby the central bank raises the short-term interest rate by more than one-for-one when inflation exceeds the targeted level of inflation. Interest rate feedback rules of this type are similar to the Taylor rule, but contrary to Taylor's rule, our results suggest that the central bank should not respond to output variations in setting the short-term nominal interest rate. We find that if the central bank responds to the output gap, economic welfare suffers.

Regarding fiscal policies, the results of several of our papers strongly suggest smoothing out distortionary tax rates and using variations in the level of government debt to address cyclical budget shortfalls.

*You've written about avoiding liquidity traps. What is the liquidity trap that we must avoid and how do we do so?*

A liquidity trap is a situation in which the nominal interest rate is at zero. At this point the central bank cannot lower the nominal interest rate any further to stimulate the economy.

In joint work with Jess Benhabib of New York University, Martin and I show that a liquidity trap can be avoided through the coordination of monetary and fiscal policy. In particular, liquidity traps, that is, zero nominal interest rates, can be avoided as equilibrium outcomes if the public becomes convinced that the government follows a fiscal policy that is inconsistent with zero nominal rates.

*What is your assessment of the Taylor Rule?*

Taylor-type interest rate feedback rules stipulate that the short-term nominal interest rate should be set as an increasing function of deviations of inflation from the target rate and of deviations of output from trend. In particular, the inflation coefficient of such a feedback rule should exceed unity, the so-called Taylor criterion. As mentioned above, in my work with Martin, I have found that simple interest rate rules that respond only to price inflation tend to bring outcomes with welfare levels very close to the optimal policy. In this sense Taylor-type interest rate feedback rules represent good monetary policy. An important caveat relative to Taylor's original specification of interest rate feedback rules is that our research (and that of several others) assigns very little, if any, value to including deviations of output from trend in the interest rate feedback rule. Moreover, such policies of leaning against the wind can under certain circumstances be harmful.

**interest rate rules that respond only to price inflation ... [are] very close to the optimal policy**

*... and of inflation targeting?*

Different people have different definitions of inflation targeting. This makes answering this question not straightforward. If inflation targeting is interpreted as a monetary policy specification, by which the short-term nominal interest rate responds only (or mainly) to inflation (as opposed to the output gap or other macroeconomic indicators), then the results of our work strongly support an inflation targeting policy.

*What are the implications of your work for avoiding and living with the credit market conditions that emerged in August 2007 and dominated the economy through 2008?*

Over the past decade, financial institutions that act like banks have developed. They are not, however, required by law to be under the regulations and supervision of the government in the same way as regular banks are. Going forward, I believe that it is desirable to have an overhaul of the existing regulatory system in order to ensure equal regulation and supervision for all financial institutions.

*What advice do you have for a student who is just starting to study economics? Is it a good choice of major? What subjects go well with it?*

If you are just starting studying economics, be patient. Economics can be more formal than other social sciences, and because of this, it may take a little while before you can apply what you learn in your economics classes to enhance your understanding of the economy around you. Subjects that are nice complements with economics are statistics and applied math.

*Do you have any special advice for young women who might be contemplating a career in economics?*

About one third of newly minted economics Ph.Ds are women, but only about 8 percent of full professors in a Ph.D.-granting economics department are women. Looking at statistics like this can be discouraging. However, from my fifteen years of experience of working in this field, I don't see any reason why young women who are about to start a career in economics will not be able to change these statistics.

# GLOSSARY

**Above full-employment equilibrium** A macroeconomic equilibrium in which real GDP exceeds potential GDP. (p. 256)

**Absolute advantage** A person has an absolute advantage if that person is more productive than another person. (p. 40)

**Aggregate demand** The relationship between the quantity of real GDP demanded and the price level. (p. 250)

**Aggregate production function** The relationship between real GDP and the quantity of labor when all other influences on production remain the same. (p. 139)

**Aggregate planned expenditure** The sum of planned consumption expenditure, planned investment, planned government expenditure on goods and services, and planned exports minus planned imports. (p. 270)

**Allocative efficiency** A situation in which goods and services are produced at the lowest possible cost and in the quantities that provide the greatest possible benefit. (p. 35)

**Automatic fiscal policy** A fiscal policy action that is triggered by the state of the economy. (p. 338)

**Automatic stabilizers** Mechanisms that stabilize real GDP without explicit action by the government. (p. 340)

**Autonomous expenditure** The sum of those components of aggregate planned expenditure that are not influenced by real GDP. Autonomous expenditure equals the sum of investment, government expenditure, exports, and the autonomous parts of consumption expenditure and imports. (p. 274)

**Autonomous tax multiplier** The magnification effect of a change in taxes on aggregate demand. (pp. 292, 339)

**Balanced budget** A government budget in which tax revenues and outlays are equal. (p. 328)

**Balanced budget multiplier** The magnification effect on aggregate demand of a simultaneous change in government expenditure and taxes that leaves the budget balanced. (pp. 293, 339)

**Balance of payments accounts** A country's record of international trading, borrowing, and lending. (p. 226)

**Barter** The direct exchange of one good or service for other goods and services. (p. 186)

**Below full-employment equilibrium** A macroeconomic equilibrium in which potential GDP exceeds real GDP. (p. 257)

**Big tradeoff** The tradeoff between equality and efficiency. (p. 9)

**Bond** A promise to make specified payments on specified dates. (p. 163)

**Bond market** The market in which bonds issued by firms and governments are traded. (p. 163)

**Budget deficit** A government's budget balance that is negative—outlays exceed tax revenues. (p. 328)

**Budget surplus** A government's budget balance that is positive—tax revenues exceed outlays. (p. 328)

**Business cycle** The periodic but irregular up-and-down movement in production. (p. 93)

**Capital** The tools, equipment, buildings, and other constructions that businesses use to produce goods and services. (p. 4)

**Capital account** A record of foreign investment in a country minus its investment abroad. (p. 226)

**Capital accumulation** The growth of capital resources, including human capital. (p. 38)

**Central bank** A bank's bank and a public authority that regulates the nation's depository institutions and controls the quantity of money. (p. 192)

***Ceteris paribus*** Other things being equal—all other relevant things remaining the same. (p. 24)

**Chained-dollar real GDP** A measure of real GDP derived by valuing production at the prices of both the current year and previous year and linking (chaining) those prices back to the prices of the reference base year. (p. 100)

**Change in demand** A change in buyers' plans that occurs when some influence on those plans other than the price of the good changes. It is illustrated by a shift of the demand curve. (p. 56)

**Change in supply** A change in sellers' plans that occurs when some influence on those plans other than the price of the good changes. It is illustrated by a shift of the supply curve. (p. 61)

**Change in the quantity demanded** A change in buyers' plans that occurs when the price of a good changes but all other influences on buyers' plans remain unchanged. It is illustrated by a movement along the demand curve. (p. 59)

**Change in the quantity supplied** A change in sellers' plans that occurs when the price of a good changes but all other influences on sellers' plans remain unchanged. It is illustrated by a movement along the supply curve. (p. 62)

**Classical** A macroeconomist who believes that the economy is self-regulating and that it is always at full employment. (p. 260)

**Classical growth theory** A theory of economic growth based on the view that the growth of real GDP per person is temporary and that when it rises above subsistence level, a population explosion eventually brings it back to subsistence level. (p. 149)

**Comparative advantage** A person or country has a comparative advantage in an activity if that person or country can perform the activity at a lower opportunity cost than anyone else or any other country. (p. 40)

**Competitive market** A market that has many buyers and many sellers, so no single buyer or seller can influence the price. (p. 54)

**Complement** A good that is used in conjunction with another good. (p. 57)

**Consumer Price Index (CPI)** An index that measures the average of the prices paid by urban consumers for a fixed "basket" of the consumer goods and services. (p. 116)

**Consumption expenditure** The total payment for consumer goods and services. (p. 87)

**Consumption function** The relationship between consumption expenditure and disposable income, other things remaining the same. (p. 270)

**Core inflation rate** The Fed's operational guide is the rate of increase in the core PCE deflator, which is the PCE deflator excluding food and fuel prices. (p. 353)

**Core CPI inflation rate** A measure of inflation based on the core CPI—the CPI excluding food and fuel. (p. 121)

**Cost-push inflation** An inflation that results from an initial increase in costs. (p. 302)

**Council of Economic Advisers** The President's council whose main work is to monitor the economy and keep the President and the public well informed about the current state of the economy and the best available forecasts of where it is heading. (p. 327)

**Crawling peg** A policy regime that selects a target path for the exchange rate and uses intervention in the foreign exchange market to achieve that path. (p. 232)

**Creditor nation** A country that during its entire history has invested more in the rest of the world than other countries have invested in it. (p. 228)

**Cross-section graph** A graph that shows the values of an economic variable for different groups or categories at a point in time. (p. 16)

**Crowding-out effect** The tendency for a government budget deficit to decrease investment. (p. 174)

**Currency** The notes and coins held by individuals and businesses. (p. 187)

**Currency drain ratio** The ratio of currency to deposits. (p. 196)

**Current account** A record of receipts from exports of goods and services sold abroad, payments for imports of goods and services from abroad, net interest income paid abroad, and net transfers abroad. (p. 226)

**Cyclical surplus or deficit** The actual surplus or deficit minus the structural surplus or deficit. (p. 342)

**Cyclical unemployment** The fluctuating unemployment over the business cycle. (p. 114)

**Debtor nation** A country that during its entire history has borrowed more in the rest of the world than other countries have lent in it. (p. 228)

**Demand** The entire relationship between the price of the good and the quantity demanded of it when all other influences on buyers' plans remain the same. It is illustrated by a demand curve and described by a demand schedule. (p. 55)

**Demand curve** A curve that shows the relationship between the quantity demanded of a good and its price when all other influences on consumers' planned purchases remain the same. (p. 56)

**Demand for loanable funds** The relationship between the quantity of loanable funds demanded and the real interest rate when all other influences on borrowing plans remain the same. (p. 168)

**Demand for money** The relationship between the quantity of money demanded and the interest rate when all other influences on the amount of money that people wish to hold remain the same. (p. 199)

**Demand-pull inflation** An inflation that starts because aggregate demand increases. (p. 300)

**Depository institution** A firm that takes deposits from households and firms and makes loans to other households and firms. (p. 189)

**Depreciation** The decrease in the value of a firm's capital that results from wear and tear and obsolescence. (p. 88)

**Desired reserve ratio** The ratio of reserves to deposits that banks want to hold. (p. 196)

**Direct relationship** A relationship between two variables that move in the same direction. (p. 18)

**Discount rate** The interest rate at which the Fed stands ready to lend reserves to depository institutions. (p. 195)

**Discouraged worker** A marginally attached worker who has stopped looking for a job because of repeated failure to find one. (p. 112)

**Discretionary fiscal policy** A fiscal action that is initiated by an act of Congress. (p. 338)

**Disposable income** Aggregate income minus taxes plus transfer payments. (pp. 252, 270)

**Doha Developing Agenda (Doha Round)** Negotiations held in Doha, Qatar, to lower tariff barriers and quotas that restrict international trade in farm products and services. (p. 386)

**Dumping** The sale by a foreign firm of exports at a lower price than the cost of production. (p. 389)

**Dynamic comparative advantage** A comparative advantage that a person or country possesses as a result of having specialized in a particular activity and then, as a result of learning-by-doing, having become the producer with the lowest opportunity cost. (p. 43)

**Economic growth** The expansion of production possibilities that results from capital accumulation and technological change. (p. 38)

**Economic growth rate** The annual percentage change in real GDP. (p. 134)

**Economic model** A description of some aspect of the economic world that includes only those features of the world that are needed for the purpose at hand. (p. 11)

**Economics** The social science that studies the *choices* that individuals, businesses, governments, and entire societies make as they cope with *scarcity* and the *incentives* that influence and reconcile those choices. (p. 2)

**Efficiency wage** A real wage rate that is set above the equilibrium wage rate. (p. 114)

**Employment Act of 1946** A landmark Congressional act that recognizes a role for government actions to keep unemployment low, the economy expanding, and inflation in check. (p. 326)

**Entrepreneurship** The human resource that organizes the other three factors of production: labor, land, and capital. (p. 4)

**Employment-to-population ratio** The percentage of people of working age who have jobs. (p. 110)

**Equilibrium expenditure** The level of aggregate expenditure that occurs when aggregate planned expenditure equals real GDP. (p. 276)

**Equilibrium price** The price at which the quantity demanded equals the quantity supplied. (p. 64)

**Equilibrium quantity** The quantity bought and sold at the equilibrium price. (p. 64)

**Excess reserves** A bank's actual reserves minus its desired reserves. (p. 196)

**Exchange rate** The price at which one currency exchanges for another in the foreign exchange market. (p. 214)

**Expansion** A business cycle phase between a trough and a peak—a period in which real GDP increases. (p. 93)

**Exports** The goods and services that we sell to people in other countries. (pp. 88, 380)

**Export subsidy** A payment by the government to the producer of an exported good, so it increases the supply of exports. (p. 388)

**Factors of production** The productive resources used to produce goods and services. (p. 3)

**Federal budget** The annual statement of the outlays and tax revenues of the government of the United States, together with the laws and regulations that approve and support those outlays and taxes. (p. 326)

**Federal funds rate** The interest rate that the banks charge each other on overnight loans of reserves. (pp. 192, 354)

**Federal Open Market Committee** The main policy-making organ of the Federal Reserve System. (p. 192)

**Federal Reserve System (the Fed)** The central bank of the United States. (p. 192)

**Final good** An item that is bought by its final user during the specified time period. (p. 86)

**Financial capital** The funds that firms use to buy physical capital. (p. 162)

**Financial institution** A firm that operates on both sides of the market for financial capital. It borrows in one market and lends in another. (p. 164)

**Firm** An economic unit that hires factors of production and organizes those factors to produce and sell goods and services. (p. 43)

**Fiscal imbalance** The present value of the government's commitments to pay benefits minus the present value of its tax revenues. (p. 336)

**Fiscal policy** The government's attempt to achieve macroeconomic objectives such as full employment, sustained long-term economic growth, and price level stability by setting and changing tax rates, making transfer payments, and purchasing goods and services. (pp. 252, 326)

**Fixed exchange rate** An exchange rate pegged at a value decided by the government or central bank and that blocks the unregulated forces of demand and supply by direct intervention in the foreign exchange market. (p. 231)

**Flexible exchange rate** An exchange rate that is determined by demand and supply with no direct intervention in the foreign exchange market by the central bank. (p. 231)

**Foreign currency** The money of other countries regardless of whether that money is in the form of notes, coins, or bank deposits. (p. 214)

**Foreign exchange market** The market in which the currency of one country is exchanged for the currency of another. (p. 214)

**Frictional unemployment** The unemployment that arises from normal labor turnover—from people entering and leaving the labor force and from the ongoing creation and destruction of jobs. (p. 113)

**Full employment** A situation in which the the unemployment rate equals the natural unemployment rate. At full employment, there is no cyclical unemployment—all unemployment is frictional and structural. (p. 114)

**Full-employment equilibrium** A macroeconomic equilibrium in which real GDP equals potential GDP. (p. 257)

**General Agreement on Tariffs and Trade (GATT)** An international agreement signed in 1947 to reduce tariffs on international trade. (p. 387)

**Generational accounting** An accounting system that measures the lifetime tax burden and benefits of each generation. (p. 336)

**Generational imbalance** The division of the fiscal imbalance between the current and future generations, assuming that the current generation will enjoy the existing levels of taxes and benefits. (p. 337)

**Goods and services** All the objects that people value and produce to satisfy human wants. (p. 3)

**Government debt** The total amount that the government has borrowed. It equals the sum of past budget deficits minus the sum of past budget surpluses. (p. 330)

**Government expenditure** Goods and services bought by government. (p. 88)

**Government expenditure multiplier** The magnification effect of a change in government expenditure on goods and services on equilibrium expenditure and real GDP (pp. 292, 338)

**Government sector balance** An amount equal to net taxes minus government expenditure on goods and services. (p. 229)

**Gross domestic product (GDP)** The market value of all final goods and services produced within a country during a given time period. (p. 86)

**Gross investment** The total amount spent on purchases of new capital and on replacing depreciated capital. (pp. 88, 162)

**Growth accounting** A tool that calculates the contribution to labor productivity growth of each of its sources. (p. 146)

**Human capital** The knowledge and skill that people obtain from education, on-the-job training, and work experience. (p. 3)

**Hyperinflation** A rapid inflation that exceeds 50 percent a month. (p. 116)

**Import quota** A restriction that limits the maximum quantity of a good that may be imported in a given period. (p. 386)

**Imports** The goods and services that we buy from people in other countries. (pp. 88, 380)

**Incentive** A reward that encourages an action or a penalty that discourages one. (p. 2)

**Induced expenditure** The sum of the components of aggregate planned expenditure that vary with real GDP. Induced expenditure equals consumption expenditure minus imports. (p. 274)

**Induced taxes** Taxes that vary with real GDP. (p. 341)

**Infant-industry argument** The argument that it is necessary to protect a new industry to enable it to grow into a mature industry that can compete in world markets. (p. 389)

**Inferior good** A good for which demand decreases as income increases. (p. 58)

**Inflationary gap** The amount by which real GDP exceeds potential GDP. (p. 256)

**Inflation rate** The annual percentage change in the price level. (p. 116)

**Inflation rate targeting** A monetary policy strategy in which the central bank makes a public commitment to achieve an explicit inflation rate and to explain how its policy actions will achieve that target. (p. 368)

**Instrument rule** A decision rule for monetary policy that sets the policy instrument at a level that is based on the current state of the economy. (p. 355)

**Interest** The income that capital earns. (p. 4)

**Interest rate parity** A situation in which the rates of return on assets in different currencies are equal. (p. 224)

**Intermediate good** An item that is produced by one firm, bought by another firm, and used as a component of a final good or service. (p. 86)

**Inverse relationship** A relationship between variables that move in opposite directions. (p. 19)

**Investment** The purchase of new plant, equipment, and buildings, and additions to inventories. (p. 88)

**Keynesian** A macroeconomist who believes that left alone, the economy would rarely operate at full employment and that to achieve full employment, active help from fiscal policy and monetary policy is required. (p. 260)

**Keynesian cycle theory** A theory that fluctuations in investment driven by fluctuations in business confidence—summarized in the phase "animal spirits"—are the main source of fluctuations in aggregate demand. (p. 310)

***k*-percent rule** A rule that makes the quantity of money grow at a rate of *k* percent a year, where *k* equals the growth rate of potential GDP. (p. 367)

**Labor** The work time and work effort that people devote to producing goods and services. (p. 3)

**Labor force** The sum of the people who are employed and who are unemployed. (p. 109)

**Labor force participation rate** The percentage of the working-age population who are members of the labor force. (p. 111)

**Labor productivity** The quantity of real GDP produced by an hour of labor. (p. 143)

**Laffer curve** The relationship between the tax rate and the amount of tax revenue collected. (p. 335)

**Land** All the "gifts of nature" that we use to produce goods and services. (p. 3)

**Law of demand** Other things remaining the same, the higher the price of a good, the smaller is the quantity demanded of it; the lower the price of a good, the larger is the quantity demanded of it. (p. 55)

**Law of supply** Other things remaining the same, the higher the price of a good, the greater is the quantity supplied of it. (p. 60)

**Learning-by-doing** People become more productive in an activity (learn) just by repeatedly producing a particular good or service (doing). (p. 43)

**Lender of last resort** The Fed is the lender of last resort—depository institutions that are short of reserves can borrow from the Fed. (p. 195)

**Linear relationship** A relationship between two variables that is illustrated by a straight line. (p. 18)

**Long-run aggregate supply** The relationship between the quantity of real GDP supplied and the price level when the money wage rate changes in step with the price level to achieve full employment. (p. 246)

**Long-run macroeconomic equilibrium** A situation that occurs when real GDP equals potential GDP—the economy is on its long-run aggregate supply curve. (p. 255)

**Long-run Phillips curve** A curve that shows the relationship between inflation and unemployment when the actual inflation rate equals the expected inflation rate. (p. 307)

**Lucas wedge** The dollar value of the accumulated gap between what real GDP per person would have been if the 1960s growth rate has persisted and what real GDP per person turned out to be. (p. 92)

**M1** A measure of money that consists of currency and traveler's checks plus checking deposits owned by individuals and businesses. (p. 187)

**M2** A measure of money that consists of M1 plus time deposits, savings deposits, money market mutual funds, and other deposits. (p. 187)

**Macroeconomics** The study of the performance of the national economy and the global economy. (p. 2)

**Margin** When a choice is changed by a small amount or by a little at a time, the choice is made at the margin. (p. 10)

**Marginal benefit** The benefit that a person receives from consuming one more unit of a good or service. It is measured as the maximum amount that a person is willing to pay for one more unit of the good or service. (pp. 10, 36)

**Marginal benefit curve** A curve that shows the relationship between the marginal benefit of a good and the quantity of that good consumed. (p. 36)

**Marginal cost** The opportunity cost of producing one more unit of a good or service. It is the best alternative forgone. It is calculated as the increase in total cost divided by the increase in output. (pp. 10, 35)

**Marginally attached worker** A person who currently is neither working nor looking for work but has indicated that he or she wants and is available for a job and has looked for work sometime in the recent past. (p. 112)

**Marginal propensity to consume** The fraction of a change in disposable income that is consumed. It is calculated as the change in consumption expenditure divided by the change in disposable income. (p. 272)

**Marginal propensity to import** The fraction of an increase in real GDP that is spent on imports. (p. 273)

**Marginal propensity to save** The fraction of an increase in disposable income that is saved. It is calculated as the change in saving divided by the change in disposable income. (p. 272)

**Market** Any arrangement that enables buyers and sellers to get information and to do business with each other. (p. 44)

**Market for loanable funds** The aggregate of all the individual markets in which households, firms, governments, banks, and other financial institutions borrow and lend. (p. 166)

**McCallum rule** A rule that makes the growth rate of the monetary base respond to the long-term average growth rate of real GDP and medium-term changes in the velocity of circulation of the monetary base. (p. 367)

**Means of payment** A method of settling a debt. (p. 186)

**Microeconomics** The study of the choices that individuals and businesses make, the way these choices interact in markets, and the influence of governments. (p. 2)

**Minimum wage** A wage set by law above the equilibrium wage rate. (p. 114)

**Monetarist** A macroeconomist who believes that the economy is self-regulating and that it will normally operate at full employment, provided that monetary policy is not erratic and that the pace of money growth is kept steady. (p. 261)

**Monetarist cycle theory** A theory that fluctuations in both investment and consumption expenditure, driven by fluctuations in the growth rate of the quantity of money, are the main source of fluctuations in aggregate demand. (p. 310)

**Monetary base** The sum of Federal Reserve notes, coins and depository institution deposits at the Fed. (p. 194)

**Monetary policy** The Fed conducts the nation's monetary policy by changing interest rates and adjusting the quantity of money. (p. 252)

**Monetary policy instrument** A variable that the Fed can control directly or closely target. (p. 354)

**Money** Any commodity or token that is generally acceptable as the means of payment. (pp. 44, 186)

**Money multiplier** The ratio of the change in the quantity of money to the change in the monetary base. (p. 197)

**Money price** The number of dollars that must be given up in exchange for a good or service. (p. 54)

**Mortgage** A legal contract that gives ownership of a home to the lender in the event that the borrower fails to meet the agreed loan payments (repayments and interest). (p. 163)

**Mortgage-backed security** A type of bond that entitles its holder to the income from a package of mortgages. (p. 164)

**Multiplier** The amount by which a change in autonomous expenditure is magnified or multiplied to determine the change in equilibrium expenditure and real GDP. (p. 278)

**National saving** The sum of private saving (saving by households and businesses) and government saving. (p. 167)

**Natural unemployment rate** The unemployment rate when the economy is at full employment—natural unemployment as a percentage of the labor force. (p. 114)

**Needs-tested spending** Government spending on programs that pay benefits to suitably qualified people and businesses. (p. 341)

**Negative relationship** A relationship between variables that move in opposite directions. (p. 19)

**Neoclassical growth theory** A theory of economic growth that proposes that real GDP per person grows because technological change induces an amount of saving and investment that makes capital per hour of labor grow. (p. 149)

**Net borrower** A country that is borrowing more from the rest of the world than it is lending to it. (p. 228)

**Net exports** The value of exports of goods and services minus the value of imports of goods and services. (pp. 88, 229)

**Net investment** The amount by which the value of capital increases—gross investment minus depreciation. (pp. 88, 162)

**Net lender** A country that is lending more to the rest of the world than it is borrowing from it. (p. 228)

**Net taxes** Taxes paid to governments minus cash transfers received from governments. (p. 166)

**Net worth** The total value of what a financial institution has lent minus the market value of what it has borrowed. (p. 165)

**New classical** A macroeconomist who holds the view that business cycle fluctuations are the efficient responses of a well-functioning market economy bombarded by shocks that arise from the uneven pace of technological change. (p. 260)

**New classical cycle theory** A rational expectations theory of the business cycle that regards unexpected fluctuations in aggregate demand as the main source of fluctuations of real GDP around potential GDP. (p. 310)

**New growth theory** A theory of economic growth based on the idea that real GDP per person grows because of the choices that people make in the pursuit of profit and that growth will persist indefinitely. (p. 151)

**New Keynesian** A macroeconomist who holds the view that not only is the money wage rate sticky but also that the prices of goods and services are sticky. (p. 261)

**New Keynesian cycle theory** A rational expectations theory of the business cycle that regards unexpected and currently expected fluctuations in aggregate demand as the main source of fluctuations of real GDP around potential GDP. (p. 310)

**Nominal exchange rate** The value of the U.S. dollar expressed in units of foreign currency per U.S. dollar. (p. 214)

**Nominal GDP** The value of the final goods and services produced in a given year valued at the prices that prevailed in that same year. It is a more precise name for GDP. (p. 91)

**Nominal interest rate** The number of dollars that a borrower pays and a lender receives in a year expressed as a percentage of the number of dollars borrowed and lent. (p. 167)

**Normal good** A good for which demand increases as income increases. (p. 58)

**Official settlements account** A record of the change in official reserves, which are the government's holdings of foreign currency. (p. 226)

**Offshoring** A U.S. firm hires foreign labor and produced in a foreign country or a U.S. firm buys finished goods, components, or services from firms in other countries. (p. 391)

**Offshoring outsourcing** A U.S. firm buys finished goods, components, or services from other firms in other countries. (p. 391)

**One third rule** The rule that, on average, with no change in technology, a 1 percent increase in capital per hour of labor brings a 1/3 percent increase in labor productivity. (p. 146)

**Open market operation** The purchase or sale of government securities—U.S. Treasury bills and bonds—by the Federal Reserve in the open market. (p. 195)

**Opportunity cost** The highest-valued alternative that we give up to get something. (pp. 9, 33)

**Output gap** Real GDP minus potential GDP. (pp. 114, 256)

**Outsourcing** A U.S. firm buys finished goods, components, or services from other firms in the United States or from firms in other countries. (p. 391)

**Phillips curve** A curve that shows a relationship between inflation and unemployment. (p. 306)

**Positive relationship** A relationship between two variables that move in the same direction. (p. 18)

**Potential GDP** The value of production when all the economy's labor, capital, land, and entrepreneurial ability are fully employed; the quantity of real GDP at full employment. (p. 92)

**Preferences** A description of a person's likes and dislikes. (p. 36)

**Present value** The amount of money that, if invested today, will grow to be as large as a given future amount when the interest that it will earn is taken into account. (p. 336)

**Price level** The average level of prices as measured by a price index. (p. 116)

**Private sector balance** An amount equal to saving minus investment. (p. 229)

**Production efficiency** A situation in which goods and services are produced at the lowest possible cost. (p. 33)

**Production possibilities frontier** The boundary between the combinations of goods and services that can be produced and the combinations that cannot. (p. 32)

**Profit** The income earned by entrepreneurship. (p. 4)

**Property rights** Social arrangements that govern the ownership, use, and disposal of anything that people value that are enforceable in the courts. (p. 44)

**Purchasing power parity** A situation in which the prices in two countries are equal when converted at the exchange rate. (pp. 95, 224)

**Quantity demanded** The amount of a good or service that consumers plan to buy during a given time period at a particular price. (p. 55)

**Quantity supplied** The amount of a good or service that producers plan to sell during a given time period at a particular price. (p. 60)

**Quantity theory of money** The proposition that in the long run, an increase in the quantity of money brings an equal percentage increase in the price level. (p. 202)

**Rational expectation** The most accurate forecast possible, a forecast that uses all the available information, including knowledge of the relevant economic forces that influence the variable being forecasted. (p. 305)

**Real business cycle theory** A theory of the business cycle that regards random fluctuations in productivity as the main source of economic fluctuations. (p. 310)

**Real exchange rate** The relative price of U.S.-made goods and services to foreign-made goods and services. (pp. 214, 368)

**Real GDP** The value of final goods and services produced in a given year when valued at the prices of a reference base year. (p. 91)

**Real GDP per person** Real GDP divided by the population. (pp. 92, 134)

**Real interest rate** The nominal interest rate adjusted for inflation and is approximately equal to the nominal interest rate minus the inflation rate. (p. 167)

**Real wage rate** The money (or nominal) wage rate divided by the price level. The real wage rate is the quantity of goods and services that an hour of labor earns. (p. 140)

**Recession** A business cycle phase in which real GDP decreases for at least two successive quarters. (p. 93)

**Recessionary gap** The amount by which potential GDP exceeds real GDP. (p. 257)

**Reference base period** The period in which the CPI is defined to be 100. (p. 116)

**Relative price** The ratio of the price of one good or service to the price of another good or service. A relative price is an opportunity cost. (p. 54)

**Rent** The income that land earns. (p. 4)

**Rent seeking** The lobbying for special treatment by the government to create economic profit or to divert the gains from trade away from others. (p. 393)

**Required reserve ratio** The minimum percentage of deposits that depository institutions are required to hold as reserves. (p. 195)

**Reserve ratio** The fraction of a bank's total deposits that are held in reserves. (p. 196)

**Reserves** A bank's reserves consist of notes and coins in its vaults plus its deposit at the Federal Reserve. (p. 196)

**Rule of 70** A rule that states that the number of years it takes for the level of a variable to double is approximately 70 divided by the annual percentage growth rate of the variable. (p. 134)

**Saving** The amount of income that households have left after they have paid their taxes and bought their consumption goods and services. (p. 162)

**Saving function** The relationship between saving and disposable income, other things remaining the same. (p. 270)

**Scarcity** Our inability to satisfy all our wants. (p. 2)

**Scatter diagram** A diagram that plots the value of one variable against the value of another. (p. 17)

**Self-interest** The choices that you think are the best ones available for you are choices made in your self-interest. (p. 5)

**Short-run aggregate supply** The relationship between the quantity of real GDP supplied and the price level when the money wage rate, the prices of other resources, and potential GDP remain constant. (p. 247)

**Short-run macroeconomic equilibrium** A situation that occurs when the quantity of real GDP demanded equals the quantity of real GDP supplied—at the point of intersection of the *AD* curve and the *SAS* curve. (p. 254)

**Short-run Phillips curve** A curve that shows the tradeoff between inflation and unemployment, when the expected inflation rate and the natural unemployment rate remain the same. (p. 306)

**Slope** The change in the value of the variable measured on the y-axis divided by the change in the value of the variable measured on the x-axis. (p. 22)

**Social interest** Choices that are the best ones for society as a whole. (p. 5)

**Speculative bubble** A process in which the price is rising because expectations that it will rise bring a rising actual price. (p.68)

**Stagflation** The combination of inflation and recession. (pp. 259, 303)

**Statistical discrepancy** The gap between GDP measured by total expenditure and GDP measured by total income. (p. 90)

**Stock** A certificate of ownership and claim to the firm's profits. (p. 164)

**Stock market** A financial market in which shares of stocks of corporations are traded. (p. 164)

**Structural surplus or deficit** The budget balance that would occur if the economy were at full employment and real GDP were equal to potential GDP. (p. 342)

**Structural unemployment** The unemployment that arises when changes in technology or international competition change the skills needed to perform jobs or change the locations of jobs. (p. 113)

**Subsistence real wage rate** The minimum real wage rate needed to maintain life. (p. 149)

**Substitute** A good that can be used in place of another good. (p. 57)

**Supply** The entire relationship between the price of a good and the quantity supplied of it when all other influences on producers' planned sales remain the same. It is described by a supply schedule and illustrated by a supply curve. (p. 60)

**Supply curve** A curve that shows the relationship between the quantity supplied of a good and its price when all other influences on producers' planned sales remain the same. (p. 60)

**Supply of loanable funds** The relationship between the quantity of loanable funds supplied and the real interest rate when all other influences on lending plans remain the same. (p. 169)

**Supply-side effects** The effects of fiscal policy on employment, potential GDP, and aggregate supply. (p. 332)

**Targeting rule** A decision rule for monetary policy that sets the policy instrument at a level that makes the forecast of the ultimate policy target equal to the target. (p. 355)

**Tariff** A tax that is imposed by the importing country when an imported good crosses its international boundary. (p. 384)

**Tax wedge** The gap between the before-tax and after-tax wage rates. (p. 333)

**Taylor rule** A rule that sets the federal funds rate at the equilibrium real interest rate (which Taylor says is 2 percent a year) plus amounts based on the inflation rate and the output gap. (p. 355)

**Technological change** The development of new goods and of better ways of producing goods and services. (p. 38)

**Time-series graph** A graph that measures time (for example, months or years) on the *x*-axis and the variable or variables in which we are interested on the *y*-axis. (p. 16)

**Tradeoff** A constraint that involves giving up one thing to get something else. (p. 8)

**Trade-weighted index** The average exchange rate, with individual currencies weighted by their importance in U.S. international trade. (p. 216)

**Trend** The general tendency for a variable to move in one direction. (p. 16)

**Unemployment rate** The percentage of the people in the labor force who are unemployed. (p. 110)

**U.S. interest rate differential** The U.S. interest rate minus the foreign interest rate. (p. 221)

**U.S. official reserves** The government's holding of foreign currency. (p. 226)

**Velocity of circulation** The average number of times a dollar of money is used annually to buy the goods and services that make up GDP. (p. 202)

**Wages** The income that labor earns. (p. 4)

**Wealth** The value of all the things that people own—the market value of their assets—at a point in time. (p. 162)

**Working-age population** The total number of people aged 16 years and over who are not in jail, hospital, or some other form of institutional care. (p. 109)

**World Trade Organization (WTO)** An international organization that places greater obligations on its member countries to observe the GATT rules. (p. 386)

# INDEX

Key terms and pages on which they are defined appear in **boldface.**

# PHOTO CREDITS

College campus (p. 1) Image Source/Getty Images Inc-Image Source Royalty Free.

Ethenol plant (p. 31) Jim Parkin/Shutterstock.

Gas station price sign (p. 53) Anthony Berenyi/ Shutterstock.

Adam Smith (p. 81) Corbis-Bettmann.

Man at computer (p. 85) Getty Images, Inc.-Blend Images.

Job interview (p. 107) OJO Images/Getty Images Royalty Free.

Great Depression (p. 108) Library of Congress.

David Hume (p. 129) Library of Congress.

Shanghai skyline (p. 133) Claudio Zaccherini/ Shutterstock.

Outdoor market (p. 147) Jose Silva Pinto/ AP Wide World Photos.

Wall Street (p. 161) Don Emmert/AFP/ Getty Images.

Fannie Mae (p. 165) Karen Bleier/AFP/Getty Images.

Freddie Mac (p. 165) Paul J. Richards/AFP/ Getty Images.

Alan Greenspan (p. 177) Scott J. Ferrell/Congressional Quarterly/Getty Image, Inc.

Smart card (p. 185) B2M Productions/Getty Images/ Digital Vision.

Zimbabwe currency (p. 205) Alexander Joe/AFP/Getty Images.

Exchange rates (p. 213) Steve Cole/Getty Images Inc.-Photographer's Choice Royalty Free.

Foreign exchange dealers (p. 217) KATSUMI KASAHARA/AP Wide World Photos.

Joseph Schumpeter (p. 241) Corbis-Bettmann.

Recession (p. 245) William Casey/Shutterstock.

Harry Reid and Mitch McConnell (p. 252) Evan Vucci/Associated Press.

Ben Bernanke (p. 252) Susan Walsh/AP Wide World Photos.

Jean-Claude Trichet ECB (p. 252) Bernd Kammerer/AP Wide World Photos.

Marvyn King, Bank of England (p. 252) Martin Rickett/AP Wide World Photos.

Mark Carrey Bank of Canada (p. 252) Adrian Wyld/The Canadian Press/AP Wide World Photos.

Container ship in port (p. 269) ©Nasser Younes/AFP/Getty Images.

Couple paying bills (p. 299) Jose Luis Pelaez Inc/ Getty Images.

John Maynard Keynes (p. 321) Stock Montage.

U.S. Capitol (p. 325) Doug Litchfield/Shutterstock.

Barack Obama (p. 344) Evan Vucci/AP Wide World Photos.

Federal Reserve (p. 351) Jonathan Larsen/ Shutterstock.

# The Addison-Wesley Series in Economics

**Abel/Bernanke/Croushore**
*Macroeconomics**

**Bade/Parkin**
*Foundations of Economics**

**Bierman/Fernandez**
*Game Theory with Economic Applications*

**Binger/Hoffman**
*Microeconomics with Calculus*

**Boyer**
*Principles of Transportation Economics*

**Branson**
*Macroeconomic Theory and Policy*

**Bruce**
*Public Finance and the American Economy*

**Byrns/Stone**
*Economics*

**Carlton/Perloff**
*Modern Industrial Organization*

**Caves/Frankel/Jones**
*World Trade and Payments: An Introduction*

**Chapman**
*Environmental Economics: Theory, Application, and Policy*

**Cooter/Ulen**
*Law & Economics*

**Downs**
*An Economic Theory of Democracy*

**Ehrenberg/Smith**
*Modern Labor Economics*

**Ekelund/Ressler/Tollison**
*Economics**

**Fusfeld**
*The Age of the Economist*

**Gerber**
*International Economics*

**Ghiara**
*Learning Economics*

**Gordon**
*Macroeconomics*

**Gregory**
*Essentials of Economics*

**Gregory/Stuart**
*Russian and Soviet Economic Performance and Structure*

**Hartwick/Olewiler**
*The Economics of Natural Resource Use*

**Hoffman/Averett**
*Women and the Economy: Family, Work, and Pay*

**Holt**
*Markets, Games and Strategic Behavior*

**Hubbard**
*Money, the Financial System, and the Economy*

**Hughes/Cain**
*American Economic History*

**Husted/Melvin**
*International Economics*

**Jehle/Reny**
*Advanced Microeconomic Theory*

**Johnson-Lans**
*A Health Economics Primer*

**Klein**
*Mathematical Methods for Economics*

**Krugman/Obstfeld**
*International Economics: Theory and Policy**

**Laidler**
*The Demand for Money*

**Leeds/von Allmen**
*The Economics of Sports*

**Leeds/von Allmen/Schiming**
*Economics**

**Lipsey/Ragan/Storer**
*Economics**

**Melvin**
*International Money and Finance*

**Miller**
*Economics Today**

**Miller**
*Understanding Modern Economics*

**Miller/Benjamin**
*The Economics of Macro Issues*

**Miller/Benjamin/North**
*The Economics of Public Issues*

**Mills/Hamilton**
*Urban Economics*

**Mishkin**
*The Economics of Money, Banking, and Financial Markets**

**Mishkin**
*The Economics of Money, Banking, and Financial Markets, Alternate Edition**

**Murray**
*Econometrics: A Modern Introduction*

**Parkin**
*Economics**

**Perloff**
*Microeconomics**

**Perloff**
*Microeconomics: Theory and Applications with Calculus*

**Perman/Common/McGilvray/Ma**
*Natural Resources and Environmental Economics*

**Phelps**
*Health Economics*

**Riddell/Shackelford/Stamos/Schneider**
*Economics: A Tool for Critically Understanding Society*

**Ritter/Silber/Udell**
*Principles of Money, Banking, and Financial Markets*

**Rohlf**
*Introduction to Economic Reasoning*

**Ruffin/Gregory**
*Principles of Economics*

**Sargent**
*Rational Expectations and Inflation*

**Scherer**
*Industry Structure, Strategy, and Public Policy*

**Sherman**
*Market Regulation*

**Stock/Watson**
*Introduction to Econometrics*

**Stock/Watson**
*Introduction to Econometrics, Brief Edition*

**Studenmund**
*Using Econometrics: A Practical Guide*

**Tietenberg**
*Environmental Economics and Policy*

**Tietenberg/Lewis**
*Environmental and Natural Resource Economics*

**Todaro/Smith**
*Economic Development*

**Waldman**
*Microeconomics*

**Waldman/Jensen**
*Industrial Organization: Theory and Practice*

**Weil**
*Economic Growth*

**Williamson**
*Macroeconomics*

*denotes  titles

Log onto www.myeconlab.com to learn more

# READING BETWEEN THE LINES

# Macroeconomic Data

These macroeconomic data series show some of the trends in GDP and its components, the price level, and other variables that provide information about changes in the standard of living and the cost of living—the central questions of macroeconomics. You will find these data in a spreadsheet that you can download from your MyEconLab Web site.

| | NATIONAL INCOME AND PRODUCT ACCOUNTS | 1962 | 1963 | 1964 | 1965 | 1966 | 1967 | 1968 | 1969 | 1970 | 1971 |
|---|---|---|---|---|---|---|---|---|---|---|---|
| | **EXPENDITURES APPROACH** | | | | | | | | | | |
| the sum of | 1 Personal consumption expenditures | 363.3 | 382.7 | 411.4 | 443.8 | 480.9 | 507.8 | 558.0 | 605.2 | 648.5 | 701.9 |
| | 2 Gross private domestic investment | 88.1 | 93.8 | 102.1 | 118.2 | 131.3 | 128.6 | 141.2 | 156.4 | 152.4 | 178.2 |
| | 3 Government expenditures | 130.1 | 136.4 | 143.2 | 151.5 | 171.8 | 192.7 | 209.4 | 221.5 | 233.8 | 246.5 |
| | 4 Exports | 29.1 | 31.1 | 35.0 | 37.1 | 40.9 | 43.5 | 47.9 | 51.9 | 59.7 | 63.0 |
| less | 5 Imports | 25.0 | 26.1 | 28.1 | 31.5 | 37.1 | 39.9 | 46.6 | 50.5 | 55.8 | 62.3 |
| equals | 6 Gross domestic product | 585.6 | 617.7 | 663.6 | 719.1 | 787.8 | 832.6 | 910.0 | 984.6 | 1,038.5 | 1,127.1 |
| | **INCOMES APPROACH** | | | | | | | | | | |
| | 7 Compensation of employees | 327.2 | 345.3 | 370.7 | 399.5 | 442.6 | 475.1 | 524.3 | 577.6 | 617.2 | 658.9 |
| plus | 8 Net operating surplus | 150.6 | 159.6 | 172.4 | 190.9 | 204.0 | 207.2 | 220.5 | 226.5 | 220.6 | 245.7 |
| equals | 9 Net domestic product at factor cost | 477.8 | 504.9 | 543.1 | 590.4 | 646.6 | 682.3 | 744.8 | 804.1 | 837.8 | 904.6 |
| | 10 Indirect taxes less subsidies | 48.1 | 51.2 | 54.6 | 57.8 | 59.4 | 64.2 | 72.3 | 79.5 | 86.7 | 95.9 |
| plus | 11 Depreciation (capital consumption) | 59.3 | 62.4 | 65.0 | 69.4 | 75.6 | 81.5 | 88.4 | 97.9 | 106.7 | 115.0 |
| | 12 GDP (income approach) | 585.2 | 618.5 | 662.7 | 717.6 | 781.6 | 828.0 | 905.5 | 981.5 | 1,031.2 | 1,115.5 |
| | 13 Statistical discrepancy | 0.4 | –0.8 | 0.9 | 1.5 | 6.2 | 4.6 | 4.5 | 3.1 | 7.3 | 11.6 |
| equals | 14 GDP (expenditure approach) | 585.6 | 617.7 | 663.6 | 719.1 | 787.8 | 832.6 | 910.0 | 984.6 | 1,038.5 | 1,127.1 |
| | 15 Real GDP (billions of 2000 dollars) | 2,715.2 | 2,834.0 | 2,998.6 | 3,191.1 | 3,399.1 | 3,484.6 | 3,652.7 | 3,765.4 | 3,771.9 | 3,898.6 |
| | 16 Real GDP growth rate (percent per year) | 6.1 | 4.4 | 5.8 | 6.4 | 6.5 | 2.5 | 4.8 | 3.1 | 0.2 | 3.4 |
| | **OTHER DATA** | | | | | | | | | | |
| | 17 Population (millions) | 186.5 | 189.2 | 191.9 | 194.3 | 196.6 | 198.7 | 200.7 | 202.7 | 205.1 | 207.7 |
| | 18 Labor force (millions) | 70.6 | 71.8 | 73.1 | 74.5 | 75.8 | 77.3 | 78.7 | 80.7 | 82.8 | 84.4 |
| | 19 Employment (millions) | 66.7 | 67.8 | 69.3 | 71.1 | 72.9 | 74.4 | 75.9 | 77.9 | 78.7 | 79.4 |
| | 20 Unemployment (millions) | 3.9 | 4.1 | 3.8 | 3.4 | 2.9 | 3.0 | 2.8 | 2.8 | 4.1 | 5.0 |
| | 21 Labor force participation rate (percent of working-age population) | 58.8 | 58.7 | 58.7 | 58.9 | 59.2 | 59.6 | 59.6 | 60.1 | 60.4 | 60.2 |
| | 22 Unemployment rate (percent of labor force) | 5.5 | 5.7 | 5.2 | 4.5 | 3.8 | 3.8 | 3.6 | 3.5 | 4.9 | 5.9 |
| | 23 Real GDP per person (2000 dollars per year) | 14,556 | 14,976 | 15,627 | 16,423 | 17,293 | 17,536 | 18,199 | 18,578 | 18,395 | 18,774 |
| | 24 Growth rate of real GDP per person (percent per year) | 4.4 | 2.9 | 4.3 | 5.1 | 5.3 | 1.4 | 3.8 | 2.1 | –1.0 | 2.1 |
| | 25 Quantity of money (M2, billions of dollars) | 362.7 | 393.2 | 424.7 | 459.2 | 480.2 | 524.8 | 566.8 | 587.9 | 626.5 | 710.3 |
| | 26 GDP deflator (2000 = 100) | 21.6 | 21.8 | 22.1 | 22.5 | 23.2 | 23.9 | 24.9 | 26.1 | 27.5 | 28.9 |
| | 27 GDP deflator inflation rate (percent per year) | 1.4 | 1.1 | 1.5 | 1.8 | 2.8 | 3.1 | 4.3 | 5.0 | 5.3 | 5.0 |
| | 28 Consumer price index (1982–1984 = 100) | 30.2 | 30.6 | 31.0 | 31.5 | 32.4 | 33.4 | 34.8 | 36.7 | 38.8 | 40.5 |
| | 29 CPI inflation rate (percent per year) | 1.0 | 1.3 | 1.3 | 1.6 | 2.9 | 3.1 | 4.2 | 5.5 | 5.7 | 4.4 |
| | 30 Current account balance (billions of dollars) | 3.4 | 4.4 | 6.8 | 5.4 | 3.0 | 2.6 | 0.6 | 0.4 | 2.3 | –1.4 |

| 1972 | 1973 | 1974 | 1975 | 1976 | 1977 | 1978 | 1979 | 1980 | 1981 | 1982 | 1983 | 1984 |
|---|---|---|---|---|---|---|---|---|---|---|---|---|
| | | | | | | | | | | | | |
| 770.6 | 852.4 | 933.4 | 1,034.4 | 1,151.9 | 1,278.6 | 1,428.5 | 1,592.2 | 1,757.1 | 1,941.1 | 2,077.3 | 2,290.6 | 2,503.3 |
| 207.6 | 244.5 | 249.4 | 230.2 | 292.0 | 361.3 | 438.0 | 492.9 | 479.3 | 572.4 | 517.2 | 564.3 | 735.6 |
| 263.5 | 281.7 | 317.9 | 357.7 | 383.0 | 414.1 | 453.6 | 500.8 | 566.2 | 627.5 | 680.5 | 733.5 | 797.0 |
| 70.8 | 95.3 | 126.7 | 138.7 | 149.5 | 159.4 | 186.9 | 230.1 | 280.8 | 305.2 | 283.2 | 277.0 | 302.4 |
| 74.2 | 91.2 | 127.5 | 122.7 | 151.1 | 182.4 | 212.3 | 252.7 | 293.8 | 317.8 | 303.2 | 328.6 | 405.1 |
| 1,238.3 | 1,382.7 | 1,500.0 | 1,638.3 | 1,825.3 | 2,030.9 | 2,294.7 | 2,563.3 | 2,789.5 | 3,128.4 | 3,255.0 | 3,536.7 | 3,933.2 |
| | | | | | | | | | | | | |
| 725.1 | 811.2 | 890.3 | 949.2 | 1,059.4 | 1,180.6 | 1,336.2 | 1,500.8 | 1,651.9 | 1,826.0 | 1,926.0 | 2,042.8 | 2,255.8 |
| 276.1 | 311.4 | 314.6 | 352.7 | 394.1 | 445.3 | 507.4 | 544.4 | 562.3 | 658.9 | 675.4 | 761.9 | 920.9 |
| 1,001.2 | 1,122.6 | 1,204.9 | 1,301.9 | 1,453.5 | 1,625.9 | 1,843.6 | 2,045.2 | 2,214.2 | 2,484.9 | 2,601.4 | 2,804.7 | 3,176.7 |
| 101.5 | 112.1 | 121.7 | 131.0 | 141.5 | 152.8 | 162.3 | 171.9 | 190.9 | 224.5 | 226.3 | 242.5 | 269.2 |
| 126.5 | 139.3 | 162.5 | 187.7 | 205.2 | 230.0 | 262.3 | 300.1 | 343.0 | 388.1 | 426.9 | 443.8 | 472.6 |
| 1,229.2 | 1,374.0 | 1,489.1 | 1,620.6 | 1,800.2 | 2,008.7 | 2,268.2 | 2,517.2 | 2,748.1 | 3,097.5 | 3,254.6 | 3,491.0 | 3,918.5 |
| 9.1 | 8.7 | 10.9 | 17.7 | 25.1 | 22.2 | 26.5 | 46.1 | 41.4 | 30.9 | 0.4 | 45.7 | 14.7 |
| 1,238.3 | 1,382.7 | 1,500.0 | 1,638.3 | 1,825.3 | 2,030.9 | 2,294.7 | 2,563.3 | 2,789.5 | 3,128.4 | 3,255.0 | 3,536.7 | 3,933.2 |
| 4,105.0 | 4,341.5 | 4,319.6 | 4,311.2 | 4,540.9 | 4,750.5 | 5,015.0 | 5,173.4 | 5,161.7 | 5,291.7 | 5,189.3 | 5,423.8 | 5,813.6 |
| 5.3 | 5.8 | –0.5 | –0.2 | 5.3 | 4.6 | 5.6 | 3.2 | –0.2 | 2.5 | –1.9 | 4.5 | 7.2 |
| | | | | | | | | | | | | |
| 209.9 | 211.9 | 213.9 | 216.0 | 218.0 | 220.2 | 222.6 | 225.1 | 227.7 | 230.0 | 232.2 | 234.3 | 236.3 |
| 87.0 | 89.4 | 91.9 | 93.8 | 96.2 | 99.0 | 102.3 | 105.0 | 106.9 | 108.7 | 110.2 | 111.6 | 113.5 |
| 82.2 | 85.1 | 86.8 | 85.8 | 88.8 | 92.0 | 96.0 | 98.8 | 99.3 | 100.4 | 99.5 | 100.8 | 105.0 |
| 4.9 | 4.4 | 5.2 | 7.9 | 7.4 | 7.0 | 6.2 | 6.1 | 7.6 | 8.3 | 10.7 | 10.7 | 8.5 |
| 60.4 | 60.8 | 61.3 | 61.2 | 61.6 | 62.3 | 63.2 | 63.7 | 63.8 | 63.9 | 64.0 | 64.0 | 64.4 |
| 5.6 | 4.9 | 5.6 | 8.5 | 7.7 | 7.1 | 6.1 | 5.8 | 7.1 | 7.6 | 9.7 | 9.6 | 7.5 |
| 19,557 | 20,488 | 20,199 | 19,962 | 20,826 | 21,570 | 22,531 | 22,987 | 22,666 | 23,011 | 22,350 | 23,148 | 24,598 |
| 4.2 | 4.8 | –1.4 | –1.2 | 4.3 | 3.6 | 4.5 | 2.0 | –1.4 | 1.5 | –2.9 | 3.6 | 6.3 |
| 802.3 | 855.5 | 902.1 | 1,016.2 | 1,152.0 | 1,270.3 | 1,366.0 | 1,473.7 | 1,599.8 | 1,755.4 | 1,910.3 | 2126.5 | 2309.9 |
| 30.2 | 31.8 | 34.7 | 38.0 | 40.2 | 42.8 | 45.8 | 49.5 | 54.0 | 59.1 | 62.7 | 65.2 | 67.7 |
| 4.3 | 5.6 | 9.0 | 9.4 | 5.8 | 6.4 | 7.0 | 8.3 | 9.1 | 9.4 | 6.1 | 4.0 | 3.8 |
| 41.8 | 44.4 | 49.3 | 53.8 | 56.9 | 60.6 | 65.2 | 72.6 | 82.4 | 90.9 | 96.5 | 99.6 | 103.9 |
| 3.2 | 6.2 | 11.0 | 9.1 | 5.8 | 6.5 | 7.6 | 11.3 | 13.5 | 10.3 | 6.2 | 3.2 | 4.3 |
| –5.8 | 7.1 | 2.0 | 18.1 | 4.3 | –14.3 | –15.1 | –0.3 | 2.3 | 5.0 | –5.5 | –38.7 | –94.3 |